American Slavers

American Slavers

Merchants, Mariners, and the
Transatlantic Commerce in Captives,
1644–1865

SEAN M. KELLEY

Yale UNIVERSITY PRESS/NEW HAVEN & LONDON

Published with assistance from the foundation established in
memory of Calvin Chapin of the Class of 1788, Yale College.

Yale University Press books may be purchased in quantity for
educational, business, or promotional use. For information,
please e-mail sales.press@yale.edu (U.S. office) or
sales@yaleup.co.uk (U.K. office).

Set in Minion type by Newgen North America
Printed in the United States of America.

ISBN 978-0-300-26359-6 (hardcover : alk. paper)
Library of Congress Control Number: 2022944880
A catalogue record for this book is available from the
British Library.

This paper meets the requirements of ANSI/NISO Z39.48-1992
(Permanence of Paper).

10 9 8 7 6 5 4 3 2 1

To Vicki and Kathleen

Contents

Maps ix

Introduction: Ships Coming In, Ships Going Out 1

Part 1. SLAVERS AS SETTLERS, 1644–1700	17
ONE Puritan Slavers, 1644–1700	23
TWO The Madagascar Moment, 1680–1700	48
Part 2. SLAVERS AS BRITONS, 1700–1775	73
THREE Newport and the Rise of the Rum Men, 1700–1750	77
FOUR Knowledge and Networks, 1751–1775	108
Part 3. SLAVERS AS AMERICANS, 1775–1807	147
FIVE Revolution and Reorientation, 1775–1803	151
SIX Crescendo, 1804–1807	185

Part 4. LIFE AND DEATH IN THE SLAVE TRADE,
1700–1807   211
SEVEN Captivity   215
EIGHT Slave-Trading Communities   255

Part 5. SLAVERS AS OUTLAWS, 1808–1865   303
NINE Evasion, 1808–1835   309
TEN Shills, Hirelings, and True Believers, 1835–1865 338

Conclusion A Reckoning of Accounts   387

Chronology 397
List of Abbreviations 401
Notes 403
Acknowledgments 461
Index 463

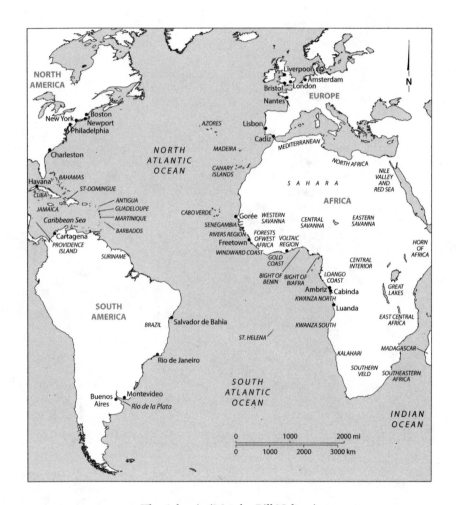

The Atlantic (Map by Bill Nelson)

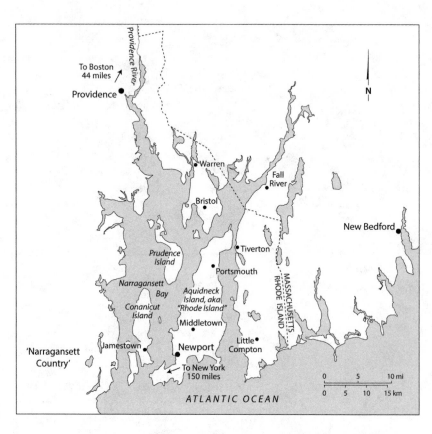

Maritime Rhode Island (Map by Bill Nelson)

WAALO

FUTA
TORO

KAYOR

Rufisque

Portudal BAOL

Senegal River

SIIN-SALOUM

NIUMI   NIANI-MARU

Barokunda

Gambia River

KAABU

Bijagos
Islands

Futa Jallon
Highlands

Rio Grande

Rio Nunez

Rio Pongo

Isles de Los

Scarcies River

SULIMA

Bance Island
Freetown

Sierra Leone River

Banana Islands

Plantain Islands

Sherbro

GALLINAS

ATLANTIC
OCEAN

Cape Mount

Cape Mesurado

N

0   100   200 mi
0   100   200   300 km

Upper Guinea (Map by Bill Nelson)

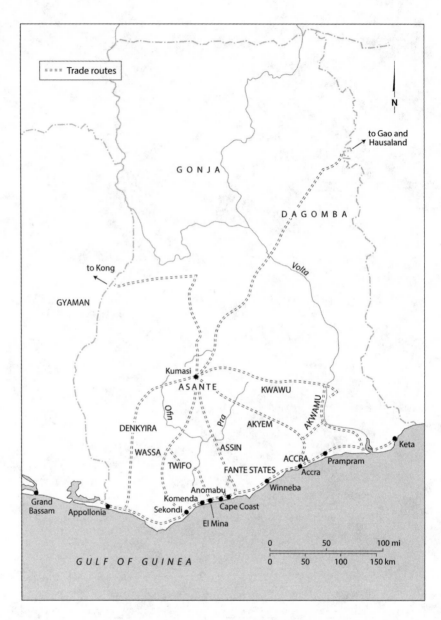

The Gold Coast (Map by Bill Nelson)

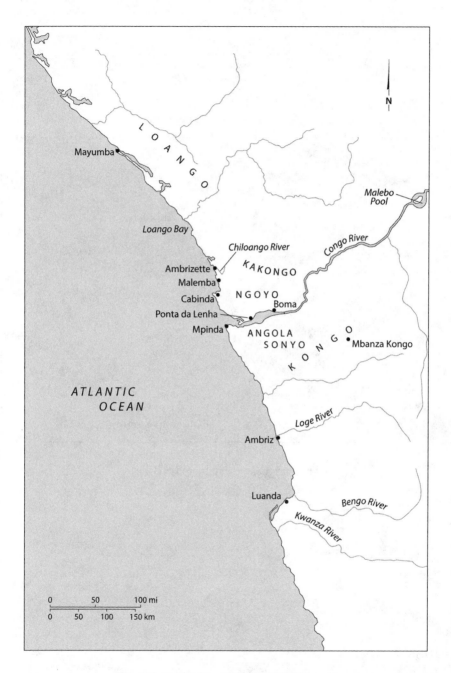

West Central Africa (Map by Bill Nelson)

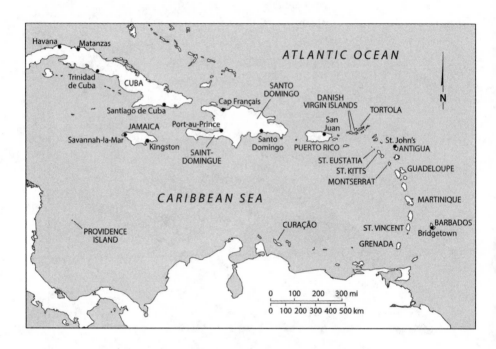

The Caribbean (Map by Bill Nelson)

American Slavers

Introduction
Ships Coming In, Ships Going Out

Decades after the fact, the man recalled the moment when he knew his enslavement was permanent. Born in the Kissi-speaking region that straddles modern-day Sierra Leone, Liberia, and Guinea, he was an adolescent in 1797 when several raiders from the Vai ethnic group grabbed him as he gathered fruit with his aunt. The youth's captors marched him to Cape Mount, fifty miles northwest of today's Monrovia, where he was eventually sold to Captain Edward Boss of Newport, Rhode Island. The youth had never seen a white man before, so he quickly deduced that Boss was "the devil," something he continued to believe even when later informed that Boss was a mere mortal. Though a captive, for a time he held out hope that his condition was not permanent. Even after his arrival in Savannah, the reality of his enslavement had not sunk in. Emaciated from his journey, the youth went unsold, so the factor fed him rice and hominy and even let him out to "plunder" for food. Eventually, some people arrived to examine and poke at him, after which a "jabbering" man with a mallet auctioned him off. The buyer was Oliver Bowen of Savannah, whom the young captive later described as "more a father than a master," and it was probably Bowen who gave the youth his new name: Robert. Soon after, Bowen sent Robert to a farm outside of Savannah for seasoning, where the man in charge whipped him—

severely. Robert returned to Bowen, who promised to free him in his will, but on Bowen's death soon afterward, his brother, Jabez, refused to honor the promise. As Robert later said, this was the point when he knew "I was in slavery."[1]

The life of Captain Edward Boss, who commanded the vessel that carried the youth across the sea, was shaped by slavery just as surely as Robert's was, though in radically different ways. He was almost certainly born in and lived most of his life in Newport, the capital of the American slave trade. He likely shipped aboard his first slaver as an adolescent, either as a cabin boy or as an apprentice to the captain, and by 1793 he was sailing to Africa as a mate. Boss ultimately skippered at least four slave ships, or "Guineamen," delivering between six hundred and seven hundred people into New World captivity, and when he was not slaving, he was transporting slave-grown plantation produce. So although Edward Boss was not a full-time slave-ship captain (few were), his life and career were enmeshed in Atlantic slavery. He even extended this enmeshment into a second generation through his son, Edward Jr., who at the age of sixteen was in Cuba, likely apprenticed to a shipmaster or merchant. Edward Jr., however, never went into the family business; he died of yellow fever in Havana in 1800. Edward the elder died within the next dozen or so years, thus bringing an end to the Boss family slaving dynasty.[2]

Although Robert and Boss sailed aboard the same vessel, they represent two distinct iterations of the American transatlantic slave trade. Robert was a coerced participant in what might be termed the "ships coming in" slave trade, or the process by which some 389,000 Africans were delivered into North American captivity from the seventeenth to the nineteenth centuries by vessels of all nations, particularly Britain. Boss, in contrast, was a very willing participant in what might be called the "ships going out" slave trade, or the process by which American-based merchants and mariners undertook nearly twenty-three hundred voyages to transport 305,000 Africans into captivity throughout the hemisphere over roughly the same period of time (chart 1).

Although it is natural to assume that North American slave ships delivered captives to North American plantation colonies, for two

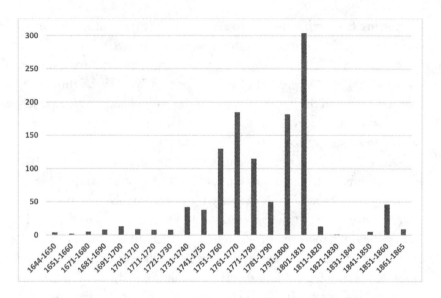

Chart 1. Voyages originating in North America, 1644–1865.
(Data from *Slave Voyages*, www.slavevoyages.org/voyages/20PsAGSP)

centuries these two trades—ships coming in, ships going out—were
for the most part quite separate. Overall, nearly seven in ten Africans arrived in North America aboard British vessels. Conversely, about 56 percent of all captives carried aboard American vessels wound up in the Caribbean. The latter percentage would have been higher but for the years
1804–1807, when slavers rushed to feed the slave market of Charleston,
South Carolina, before the federal ban took effect. American slavers
transported more than 40,000 people in just those four years, one of
the few periods when the mainland market outstripped the Caribbean
in importance.[3]

    The distinction between "ships coming in" and "ships going out"
has caused much confusion. American politicians have long exploited
this confusion to advance their particular agendas. The most famous
effort was by Thomas Jefferson, whose initial draft of the Declaration
of Independence excoriated King George III for "wag[ing] cruel war
against human nature itself, violating it's [*sic*] most sacred rights of life
& liberty in the persons of a distant people who never offended him,

captivating & carrying them into slavery in another hemisphere, or to incur miserable death in their transportation thither." Jefferson was, of course, referring to ships coming in, which in his time were indeed overwhelmingly (84 percent) of British origin. Hypocritical though he may have been on the larger question of slavery, in a technical sense Jefferson was mostly correct on the question of who delivered captives to the North American colonies.[4]

In this case, though, Jefferson's hypocrisy is less interesting than his deception, which comes in the form of an omission: at the time he wrote, North American merchants were deeply involved in the transatlantic slave trade but transported most of their captives to the Caribbean rather than to the mainland colonies. Jefferson knew this very well. In the same private journal where he recorded the Lower South's opposition to his original slave-trade clause, he also noted that "our Northern brethren . . . felt a little tender" about his criticism of the trade, for although they owned relatively few enslaved people themselves, "they had been pretty considerable carriers of them to others." In fact, it is likely that at least two signers of the Declaration of Independence, Philip Livingston of New York and William Ellery of Rhode Island, were the sons of slave traders. Jefferson was also not the first politician to deceive his audience by focusing on the transportation of captives from Africa to the colonies while omitting mention of American participation in what Ronald Bailey has aptly called "the slave-carrying trade." Benjamin Franklin did exactly that in an essay published more than six years earlier. The notion that the British were to blame for bringing captives to the North American colonies was a rhetorically attractive one during the Imperial Crisis, when tensions between the colonies and the mother country were high.[5]

The confusion over ships coming in and ships going out has outlived Jefferson. Many Americans, perhaps thinking of Jefferson, continue to believe their own country to be innocent in one of history's most heinous injustices. As a high school student in California in the early 1980s, I was explicitly taught that the British were to blame for the slave trade to North America. But this idea of British responsibility had also been popular among southern pro-slavery politicians in the antebellum period. It was most famously propounded on the Senate floor by William Loughton Smith of South Carolina during the Missouri debates. Paradoxically, this notion of British culpability sits in the popular imagination alongside a very different narrative, one that envisions American merchants as the principal suppliers of enslaved Africans to their own plantations. In the same speech in which he charged the British with supplying the South with captives, Smith made a special point of calling out Rhode Island (accurately) for its role in the slave trade. But perhaps the most famous example of confusing ships going out with ships coming in comes from *Roots,* the popular and influential television miniseries in 1977 based on Alex Haley's work of "faction." In the first episode, the ship *Lord Ligonier* sails from Annapolis in Maryland to London, to the Gambia, and back to Maryland. The actual *Lord Ligonier,* like most of the vessels that delivered captives to the Chesapeake, was based in Britain.[6]

Even professional historians have confused the various American slave trades. For much of the twentieth century, academic discussions of the "triangular trade" between Rhode Island, Africa, and the Caribbean often assumed that the Africans transported to North America must have arrived aboard American vessels (which, as we will see, can be defined in multiple ways). Even historians who knew better contributed to the confusion. Elizabeth Donnan was the mid-twentieth century's pre-eminent historian of the U.S. slave trade and the compiler of *Documents Illustrative of the History of the Slave Trade to America,* a four-volume collection that is still indispensable to anyone working in the field. But contrary to what her title suggests, Donnan's collection mingles ships-coming-in documents with ships-going-out documents. Donnan understood the difference, but casual readers of the collection and her articles on the subject could easily conclude that American slave markets were served primarily by American ships.[7] This tendency to conflate ships going out with ships coming in abated somewhat among professional historians during the 1970s, as a revisionist consensus emerged that the "triangular trade" was actually a "legend." Many works during these years grossly underestimated the number of American vessels involved in the transatlantic slave trade, especially during the colonial period, with a few going so far as to deny the existence of an American slave trade. Confusion reigned.[8]

A major corrective arrived in 1981 with the publication of Jay Coughtry's monograph on the Rhode Island slave trade of what historians now call the "long eighteenth century," the first modern scholarly book on the topic. Coughtry's exhaustive research addressed all phases of the trade, from its organization to its operation on the African coast to its legal restriction after the American Revolution. Like Donnan, Coughtry understood the difference between ships going out and ships coming in. The work cleared up numerous long-standing misconceptions and is still essential reading more than forty years after publication. So comprehensive and definitive was the book that for a long time it actually deterred further research.[9]

That situation changed with the publication of the *Transatlantic Slave Trade Database* on CD-ROM in 1999 (and now online as *Slave Voyages*). Although "The Database" (as specialists in the field call it) further clarified the distinction between ships going out and ships coming in and confirmed many of Coughtry's arguments, it also highlighted some blind spots. It made clear, for example, that the notion that the Rhode Island trade was essentially synonymous with the American slave trade was mistaken. Towns as diverse as New York, Boston, Philadelphia, Portsmouth, Newburyport, Charleston, and Perth Amboy dispatched slave ships, although Rhode Island was still responsible for just more than half of all voyages. The new data also called into question Coughtry's vision of the eighteenth-century trade as embodying certain essential characteristics, rather than as a single period in a long and varied history. Since the publication of *Slave Voyages,* the illegal trade of the nineteenth century has attracted the most attention, with Leonardo Marques, Sharla Fett, and John Harris all publishing valuable works. By pushing beyond the spatial and temporal boundaries of Coughtry's study, these historians have done much to demystify the post-1808 slave trade.[10]

In contrast, work on the seventeenth and eighteenth centuries has been uneven. The New England trade of the seventeenth century, tiny though it was, remains poorly understood, treated only in passing in works focused on other topics.[11] The New York–Madagascar trade of the 1690s has attracted more attention, but from historians of piracy more than from historians of the slave trade.[12] And the trade of the long eighteenth century, which accounts for 87 percent of all American slaving voyages, has not been the subject of a major study since Coughtry's in 1981.[13] Works on the American slave trade in historical memory by public historians and nonspecialists have partially filled the gap, but few are based on original research, and most are marred by a lack of engagement with the history of Africa and the larger transatlantic slave trade.[14]

One consequence of this long-standing confusion has been the omission of the transatlantic slave trade from the larger story of American slavery. No major synthesis of American slavery devotes significant attention to the ships-going-out slave trade, probably because most of it unfolded elsewhere, a case of "out of sight, out of mind." Yet if we consider the American slave trade in the larger context of American slavery, many aspects of the narrative need to be recalibrated. For example, historians have recently (and rightly) focused much attention on the domestic maritime (coastwise) slave trade of the nineteenth century. But going solely by the numbers, this trade was about one-third the size of the transatlantic trade.[15] Or consider the topic of slave sales. Several works have drawn much needed attention to the sales process during the antebellum period, including one study of the largest sale in American history, in which more than four hundred men, women, and children were auctioned off. But that is "only" about one-third of the approximately twelve hundred people from the ship *Memphis* who were sold in Cuba in 1859, one of the highest totals ever for an American slaver. In fact, at least forty-eight American slave ships transported more than four hundred captives.[16]

Or consider the question of slave rebellion. Every U.S. historian knows that the nation's bloodiest slave revolt was Nat Turner's, which resulted in the deaths of approximately 60 whites and 56 Blacks (not counting reprisals). But if we consider slave-ship uprisings as slave rebellions, the bloodiest in American history actually occurred aboard the Charleston-based slaver *Independence* in 1807. Rebels detonated the ship's powder stores, killing the crew and all 240 captives. If current estimates that one in ten voyages experienced some form of uprising are correct, it would put the total number of rebellions aboard American slave ships at nearly 200, a figure that rivals Herbert Aptheker's (much criticized) estimate of 250 American slave rebellions. Simply put, the story of American slavery becomes even more monstrous with the transatlantic slave trade included.[17]

This book examines the ships-going-out phase of the American slave trade, by which I mean the involvement of American merchants and mariners in the transportation of enslaved Africans across the Atlantic Ocean, over a two-hundred-year period, from around 1644 to around 1865. It builds on pioneering works like W. E. B. Du Bois's monograph from 1896 and Coughtry's work on the Rhode Island trade of the long eighteenth century, as well as the recent studies of the nineteenth-century trade by Marques, Fett, and Harris. Examining the American slave trade over the centuries reveals the many transformations it underwent in terms of its organization, its connections with Africa, its political valence and legality, and its social history. Far from constituting a single, static pursuit, the North American slave trade was punctuated by discontinuities, by fits and starts, and by a series of reconfigurations, with its volume and significance to local and regional economies fluctuating greatly. In some eras, politicians proudly served the interests of slave traders but at other times legislated against them. In some periods, slave trading was a major part of local and regional economies, but in others it was marginal. Sometimes, American slave traders were drawn from the political and social elite, whereas at other times they were ostracized as criminals. The only constants were misery, disease, and death.

To capture this uneven history, this book is organized chronologically, offering a periodization for two centuries of American slaving in Africa. The framework borrows from Jack P. Greene and J. R. Pole's synthesis of early American history. Arguing against the notion of "declension," Greene and Pole contended that the British colonies in North America developed along a trajectory in which the simplified, stripped-down, dependent settlements of the seventeenth century underwent a process of social elaboration as they became more complex, variegated, and self-sufficient replicas of British provinces over the eighteenth century. Greene and Pole's framework, advanced during the 1980s but rooted in the social history of the 1970s, has been overtaken by the discipline's recent suspicion of sweeping master narratives of national history and by newer paradigms, such as Atlantic history, the latter obviously being particularly applicable to the present topic. My interest here, however, is pragmatic, since such a framework, in combination with an Atlantic perspective, offers a useful way to make sense of a "national" slave trade that touched four continents, connected two oceans, and spanned ten generations.[18]

Examining the slave trade of a single nation over the *longue durée* can yield valuable insights. Knowing that 87 percent of all Africans carried aboard American slavers traveled within a seventy-seven-year period between 1730 and 1807 not only underscores the importance of those years, it places into perspective the pre-1730 slave trade (7.9 percent of the total) as well as the post-1807 trade (4.3 percent of the total). This is emphatically not to say that these eras matter any less than the peak period of 1730–1807. Human suffering cannot be quantified, and all eras will receive ample discussion in the succeeding chapters. But approaching the topic in this way provides a much needed sense of proportion (or disproportion, as the case may be), which is essential to any final reckoning of the trade's historical significance.[19]

Charting change over time can further reveal the economic, political, and ideological forces that shaped the American slave trade. For example, readers accustomed to viewing 1808 as the beginning of the American slave trade's illegal period may be surprised to learn that for most of its two-century existence, the trade contravened imperial, state, or national restrictions. Early slavers had to evade the agents of the Royal African Company (RAC), and many of those operating in the post-revolutionary era had to take measures to prevent the confiscation of their ships on evidence supplied by informers. The only period in which the trade was unambiguously legal was the sixty-two-year span between 1712 and 1774, when anyone with a ship could become a slaver. In all, only about two-fifths of American slaving was undertaken in this era of unquestioned legality. As the succeeding chapters detail, the presence or absence of legal restriction shaped the trade in many ways.

Economic changes arguably played an even more important role in shaping the American slave trade. Recent literature on slavery and capitalism in the nineteenth century has tended to emphasize American planters' economic strength.[20] However, most transatlantic slavers of the seventeenth and eighteenth centuries, though wealthy by the standards of the era, operated from a position of economic disadvantage. Competing with European slavers, colonists found it unprofitable to acquire and re-export sufficient quantities of the manufactures that drove the transatlantic slave trade. At the same time, all of the major North American exports—tobacco, grain, fish, and, later, cotton—were produced in Africa and were therefore not in demand. It took American slavers almost a century to find a trade good (rum) that enjoyed consistent demand in Africa, but even then the appeal was limited to two African regions. American slavers could therefore never be much more than poachers on the much larger trade of the Europeans. This peripheral, parasitic quality characterized the American slave trade through most of its existence. This situation changed temporarily with the re-export boom during the French Revolution, but by the time America industrialized in the mid-nineteenth century, slave trading was illegal. Illicit activity continued, but it is ironic that American slave trading declined sharply at the very moment that it might have soared. Legal abolition, although undoubtedly imperfect, was no dead letter.

Borrowing Greene and Pole's formulation, the American slave trade can be divided into four periods, which correspond to the major sections of this book. Part 1 examines the initial phase, which began in 1644 with the departure of the first "American" slaver from Boston for modern-day Senegal. For the remainder of the seventeenth century, Americans traded as settlers, as residents of underdeveloped, undercapitalized English outposts. They lived in small towns that were economically, militarily, and politically dependent on the mother country, with few residents at the outset possessing even basic maritime skills. Through a process of social elaboration, these outposts developed within a generation or two into maritime communities, engaged in various interstitial trades throughout the Atlantic. Dispatching voyages only sporadically, the slavers of the seventeenth century were inexperienced and lacked networks. Their voyages were almost always one-off, opportunistic ventures, and most of them violated mercantilist and other legal restrictions. Many were probably financial failures.

Part 2 examines the years 1700–1775, when slave trading became an established branch of the northern and especially the New England

economy. This was a largely "free trade," with no political or moral sanction to inhibit it. Eighteenth-century slavers were respected members
of their communities and were politically active. They manufactured
their own trade goods and knew much more about Africa than their
seventeenth-century forebears. Their operations grew increasingly sophisticated. Most significantly, they were wholly integrated into British
commercial networks, at home, in Africa, and in the Caribbean. They
operated, in other words, as Britons.

Part 3 tracks the Americanization of the American slave trade after
1776. Shut out of British markets (though still in debt to British merchants), slavers soon built new networks and explored new markets in
both Africa and the Americas. The political environment changed, as
the trade was now regulated by an increasingly hostile Congress, which
finally outlawed it altogether as of 1808. Legal abolition ushered in the
final period, in which slave traders were quite simply criminals. Slaving
continued (as part 5 details), but it was no longer organized by respectable members of the business community. Nineteenth-century slavers
operated in shadowy networks and hid behind a bewildering screen of
vessel transfers, "flags of convenience," false captains, and silent partners. In this era, American slavers were hired hands working for an international confederation of outlaws that was led by Cuban and Portuguese slavers. This group carried on the American slave trade until the
Civil War finally ended it.

Two very important aspects of the American slave trade do not
lend themselves well to this sort of chronological treatment and will be
discussed in part 4. The first of these is the experience of the captives
who traveled in the holds of American slavers. Although this did vary
somewhat over time, as routes, distances, and African regions fluctuated, the experience of being transported in chains was fairly unchang-
ing. For that reason, rather than exploring that experience in each of
the chronological chapters, an entire chapter is devoted to it. American
slave-trading communities are the subject of the second chapter in this
section. As with the experience of enslavement and transportation, conditions in these maritime communities were fairly constant in many
(though not all) aspects. The focus of this chapter will be on the legal
period, before 1808, when two American towns, Newport and Bristol,

Rhode Island, can be said to have been true slave-trading communities, where the trade put its imprint on the local economy, society, and culture.

Although the perspective here is Atlantic and the organizational scheme is chronological, an important theme runs through all of the chapters: the importance of Africa in any analysis of the slave trade. Discussing Africa in this context is always a complex and fraught prospect. For some, to draw attention to the role of African states and merchants is to imply that Africans were somehow responsible for their own enslavement in the Americas. The situation is not helped when the idea is disingenuously invoked by those who assert—much like Jefferson—that the United States was somehow an innocent bystander to the transatlantic slave trade. For those on the political right, especially, it is rhetorically convenient to argue that Africans "sold their own people" into slavery. Of course, nothing can be further from the truth. Slavery, wherever it was practiced, was almost always reserved for outsiders, as defined in political, religious, ethnic, and social terms, in addition to the more commonly understood racial terms. Africans, then, almost never sold "their own people" into captivity; for the most part, they sold their enemies or those who, according to prevailing rules, forfeited their freedom. Needless to say, the definitions of "enemies" and "prevailing rules" tended to become more expansive as European demand for captive labor grew, which only underscores the importance of contextualizing the slave trade within specific African regional histories. Finally, we should not forget the obvious: African merchants may have sold outsiders to the Europeans and Americans, but those groups very willingly bought and transported the captives to the colonies. In fact, economic historians have argued for decades that the growth of the slave trade was driven primarily by European and American demand for captives (or that the supply of captives was elastic) and not by an innate African compulsion to enslave.[21]

At the other end of the political spectrum, the notion that some Africans delivered others into slavery is sometimes too painful to contemplate. A few, mostly nonacademics, even reject the notion altogether, dismissing a mountain of evidence to argue that Europeans somehow forcibly abducted millions of people over nearly four centuries without any response or resistance.[22] Although slavers, including Americans, did occasionally abduct people, arguments that this accounted for anything more than a miniscule proportion of the slave trade as a whole can be dismissed out of hand. More credibly, some historians have proposed that the European demand for captives was responsible for introducing slavery to Africa, where it had not existed before. Although there is little doubt that the external demand for captives spurred enslavement and greatly increased the number of people held captive in Africa, the notion that there were no "slaves" prior to European contact is only true in an overly narrow, semantic sense, if even that.[23]

A central contention of this book is that there can be no understanding the transatlantic slave trade, or indeed American slavery, without deep engagement with African history. For a long time, even the best histories of the American slave trade paid little attention to Africa. The outfitting of vessels and the trade's political and legal status have been the traditional focus for studies of the American trade, with perhaps some attention paid to operations "on the African coast," but few works have attempted to situate slavers' activities within specific African historical contexts. The result, whether intentional or not, has been a distorted picture of how the slave trade actually operated, a picture rooted in the misconception that African societies were only too happy to supply a virtually unlimited number of captives to any white person with a ship and a few trinkets. In reality, as has been demonstrated through several decades of Africanist history, no society delivered captives on demand. Different African regions became involved at different times, entering and withdrawing from the slave trade for reasons that included dynastic and imperial politics, economic shifts, and climate change and were often only partly related to an external demand for captives. These developments articulated in complex ways with external factors, which included not just the transatlantic demand for captives, but also the trans-Saharan and Indian Ocean trades.

The goods accepted by Africans in exchange for captives exerted a great influence on the trade. Consumers in Africa, as elsewhere in the world, desired certain items, and coastal middlemen knew what their African customers wanted. Although many of the goods that Europeans provided were, by their own estimation, of poor quality, it is not the case that human beings were sold into slavery for mere "gewgaws." After all, any item can acquire exchange value, and African consumers often used trade goods in ways that Europeans never contemplated or fully understood. The famously coarse "Guinea cloth" carried by many slavers might be worn as a wrapper or might be unraveled and rewoven into local textiles. Shoddily constructed trade guns could be used to equip armies but could also become objects of ritual and status. Alcohol could fuel bacchanals or could be integrated into ceremonies and rites of passage. Work on the consumption of European trade goods in pre-colonial Africa is just getting started, but it is already quite clear that tastes shifted constantly, that goods were used in multiple and nonintuitive ways, and that slavers worked hard to understand these trends. Failure to read African demand could make it difficult or even impossible to profit in the trade.[24]

For all of these reasons, this book places much emphasis on the activities of American slavers on the African coast and on the related questions of consumption and trade goods. I realize that some Americanist readers may find these sections to be something of a digression. But the exchanges that took place on the African coast were the most crucial of the entire process. The other aspects of the slave trade, such as connections with American captive markets in the Caribbean, although obviously essential, were much simpler, involving the creation of links among merchants who subscribed to the same conventions. In Africa, however, slavers often found procuring captives quite difficult, since it required nothing less than the forging of transoceanic commercial relationships with distant merchants who subscribed to very different cultural values. To even begin this process, American slavers needed a basic knowledge of African markets and geography to know where to send their vessels and which goods were in demand. Dispatching vessels without this information—as several slavers discovered—was a recipe for financial failure. Experienced captains, familiar with regional geography, trading conventions, and even specific merchants, were prized because they increased the odds of a successful voyage. These aspects, neglected in earlier histories, receive careful attention here, whereas topics that have traditionally garnered more attention, such as the Caribbean networks, are treated but with slightly less emphasis.[25]

Geographically, this book divides the arena of American activity in Africa into two main regions. The first, "upper Guinea," is used in contradistinction to lower Guinea and refers to a large part of West Africa running on the coast from the Senegal River to modern-day Côte d'Ivoire. However, in the context of the American slave trade, it usually encompassed a smaller stretch between Senegal and Cape Mount, in modern Liberia. For those familiar with the regionalization devised by Philip Curtin and used in the *Slave Voyages* database, "upper Guinea," as used here, is equivalent to Senegambia, Sierra Leone, and the Windward Coast. The second major zone of American activity was the Gold Coast, or the area between Assini and the Volta River. American slavers did visit other parts of Africa, of course, and these will be defined in the text, but these two regions, upper Guinea and the Gold Coast, accounted for the vast majority of American activity in Africa.[26]

Inevitably over the course of a project like this one, topics emerge that deserve more attention but for reasons of space and time cannot be fully addressed. The symbiosis between the transatlantic slave trade and the intra-American (intercolonial) trade, in which Africans landed in the Caribbean and were carried to North America, and to other New World destinations, is well worth further investigation. The legal history of the American slave trade, intricate and virtually unexplored, also deserves much more attention than it receives here. Finally, over the course of researching this book, it became obvious that a great amount of material on the American slave trade rests in difficult-to-access Cuban archives. For a variety of reasons, I was only able to sample a modest amount of this material, through works published by Cuban scholars and via the British Library's Endangered Archives Programme, but I have little doubt that future studies will be able to take full advantage.[27]

In a popular and influential series of articles, later published in book form, a team of journalists characterized northern involvement in the slave trade as part of a larger pattern of "complicity" in American slavery, with the choice of word implying a crime. If anything, the term "complicity" understates the relationship that these communities had to American and, even more so, to Atlantic slavery. To charge a person with "complicity" implies that someone else is the main perpetrator, which in the case of American slavery almost always means the South. But when it comes to the slave trade, Americans from all regions were not so much complicit in someone else's slavery as they were the perpetrators of a largely independent, circum-Atlantic commerce in human beings. The Americans may have operated on a smaller scale than metropolitan slavers, but there can be no doubt that they were slavers in full.[28]

Part One

SLAVERS AS SETTLERS

1644–1700

Portudal, Senegambia, the Dry Season, 1645.

IN THE PRE-DAWN darkness, the alcaide—the local official in charge of Atlantic trade for the Wolof kingdom of Baol—discerned three ships' boats fighting through the surf toward the beach. For the alcaide, the sight of white men in boats was nothing new. He dealt with them regularly, collecting the king's customs and ensuring that the rules were enforced. In decades past, most of the foreigners arriving on his shores were Portuguese, but in recent years they had been pushed aside by increasing numbers of French, Dutch, and English traders. And that was good, from his perspective: the rival nations bid against each other, all to Baol's benefit. Since Atlantic trade was the economic lifeblood of coastal towns like Portudal, the alcaide saw to it that language constituted no significant barrier, maintaining a corps of "linguisters" proficient in Portuguese, Dutch, French, and English, and who also expected "gifts" for their service.[1]

Usually the traders followed the rules, behaving respectfully, paying the correct customs, and giving gifts to the officials in charge of fresh water and wood. The pre-dawn landing, however, aroused the alcaide's suspicions, so he quickly alerted his forces, which consisted of dozens, perhaps even hundreds, of archers, foot soldiers, and horsemen. As the boats approached, he saw that the intruders were heavily armed, a clear sign of malice. On this occasion, however, there was not much of

---

Previous page: The Boston waterfront, the point of embarkation for the first American slave ships. Most early voyages were one-time exploratory ventures organized by merchants with no slave-trading experience. Boston dispatched slave ships for over two hundred years, but at no point did it ever become a major slave-trading center. (J. Carwitham, Engraver, "A South East View of the Great Town of Boston in New England in America / I. Carwitham sculp," possibly between 1730 and 1760, www.loc.gov/item/2004671510)

a battle. When the boats were a few dozen yards from the shore, the archers let loose a few volleys. Several arrows found their marks. Hastily, the boats turned around and returned to the ships.

The alcaide could hardly have known it, but one of the three vessels would go down in history as the first American-based ship to undertake a transatlantic slaving voyage. The ship was called the *Rainbow,* and it had sailed from Boston in November 1644. It is not certain that the original intent was to seize captives in Africa. The *Rainbow,* skippered by James Smith, sailed first to Madeira, probably for wine, a profitable commodity in Puritan Massachusetts. There, Smith signed a consortship agreement with two London captains, Miles Cawson of the *Blossom* and Robert Shapton of the *Seaflower.* The three captains pledged to sail to the African coast and, while there, to "assist each other to the utmost of their power in all extremeties, or convenances whether by casualties of the sea, or force of enemy," and that should any of their number be captured, the others would "indeavor . . . to redeeme them." For Cawson, the main instigator, this was a voyage of revenge as well as profit. On a previous voyage in 1642, he had sailed from London to Portudal and made a deal with the alcaide to leave some trade goods ashore in a warehouse with a few of his men. Something had gone wrong, and the goods were confiscated and the men were attacked, possibly even killed. Cawson returned to England vowing vengeance. It is not certain that the rendezvous at Madeira and consortship agreement were initially part of his plan, but Cawson, Shapton, and Smith clearly anticipated that there would be violence at Portudal.[2]

The rest of the voyage was a continuation of the confrontation on the beach. Later the same day, having been repulsed by the alcaide's archers, Smith, Cawson, and Shapton sent word that they were interested in trading and invited him out to their ships. The alcaide agreed, a surprising decision from a twenty-first-century perspective. However, these kinds of violent exchanges between buyers and sellers, known as "palavers," were quite common in the slave trade and were often settled through payments or by simply talking things out. In this light, the alcaide's decision to come out to the ships is not so strange. He sent a half dozen or so men aboard each of the three vessels, boarding the lead vessel, the *Blossom,* himself.

But it did turn out to be a bad decision. The crew of the *Blossom* immediately seized the alcaide, along with his aides and linguisters, and the men he sent aboard the *Seaflower* and the *Rainbow* were likewise captured. The alcaide's subordinates were shackled in the hold of the *Blossom*, but in apparent recognition of his high standing, the alcaide was locked in the captain's cabin. This was an outrage, to be sure, but it was neither unprecedented nor an insoluble problem. In fact, there were procedures to be followed when a person was seized. Relatives of the captives had the right to redeem them in exchange for paying a ransom, which was often done by providing enslaved outsiders to take the hostages' place. The higher the captive's rank, the more slaves the captors could demand "in his room," as the English said. Several of the alcaide's men were quickly redeemed, but his own confinement dragged on. After a week, the English removed him from the cabin and placed him in the hold. This did not augur well, but soon afterward the alcaide was relieved to learn that he too had been ransomed and could return to Portudal. He left the vessel, and shortly afterward the three ships set sail, carrying away about seventeen substituted captives, including the alcaide's own linguister.

So went the voyage of the *Rainbow*, the first "American" transatlantic slave ship. In one sense, the *Rainbow* was atypical—few voyages ended in such a grand-scale fiasco.[3] At the same time, however, the *Rainbow* exemplifies many of the challenges faced by the first generation of American slave traders. Slave trading was a complicated process, and seventeenth-century American settlers sorely lacked knowledge of Africa, let alone the complex conventions and rules that governed coastal trade. Captain Smith's attempt to abduct, rather than purchase, captives at Portudal underscores this lack of experience, as well as his lack of networks. Smith's violent gambit highlights a second problem, which was that New England produced virtually nothing that African traders wanted. These two problems—inexperience and the lack of a suitable trade good—created a vicious circle. Without financing and a trade good, a sustained trade was impossible; and without sustained activity, New Englanders could not hope to gain the necessary experience to run a profitable trade.

The first six decades of the American slave trade were therefore marked by amateurism and improvisation. The colonists' problems were aggravated by the fact that they were barred from trading in Africa by the charters of a succession of African companies and later enjoined from trading with imperial rivals by the Navigation Acts. Criminality was rife, with slavers resorting at turns to smash-and-grab raids, trading with rival powers, and colluding with pirates. From the captives' perspective, general conditions were probably worse in this era than in others, the voyages nasty, brutish, and long. Viewed in the context of two centuries of American slave trading, the first six decades consisted of a series of unconnected ventures, blind alleys leading nowhere.

Puritan Slavers, 1644–1700

T he American slave trade began in John Winthrop's "City upon a Hill," but before turning to why New Englanders delved into the transatlantic slave trade, it is worth pondering the question from a slightly different angle: Was it ever likely that they should *not* have become slave traders? To start, there were few serious cultural or moral impediments to participation. The English held complicated and often contradictory views on the subject of slavery, but the general tendency was to criticize it in the abstract (especially when it was "free-born Englishmen" who were being enslaved) while endorsing it either implicitly or explicitly for certain "others." As of 1644, the year the *Rainbow* made its voyage, the English slave trade was in its infancy. English ships had only transported about 0.5 percent of their eventual total number of captive Africans across the Atlantic, and the vast majority of these had been transported only in the preceding five years. English interest in African trade, however, which included commodities other than human beings, was relatively long-standing. Starting in the 1550s, an irregular trickle of vessels left England for Africa, at least two dozen but possibly as many as fifty, if Cabo Verde is included. Most of these voyages appear to have focused on gold but also sought out dyewoods (valuable to England's woolen textile industry), ivory, wax, and ambergris. The English carried captives as well, most famously on

John Hawkins's three voyages in the 1560s, but most of the early ventures focused more on gold than human beings. Saying so implies no moral superiority on the part of the English. As Hawkins's disastrous third voyage demonstrates, it was one thing to seize and transport captives, but quite another to find good, safe markets for them. Regardless, English trade with Africa, whether for captives, gold, or dyewood, was well established when New England was settled, to the extent that it is difficult to imagine circumstances in which the settlers would not have become involved. It is hardly surprising that less than fifteen years elapsed between the arrival of John Winthrop's Massachusetts Bay Company's flagship, the *Arabella*, and the voyage of the *Rainbow*.[1]

New England entered the slave trade at a moment of economic transition. The so-called Great Migration of 1630–1642, which saw some twenty thousand English people move across the Atlantic, drove the embryonic regional economy. During those years, the New England economy revolved around selling goods to newcomers. Established residents sold their farm surpluses, and merchants, many with prior experience and contacts in London, did a brisk business importing manufactured goods and selling them to newer arrivals. New England soon racked up a large trade deficit with old England, but for the moment that was not a problem. In addition to being a movement of people, the Great Migration was also a great transfer of capital, much of which soon found its way back to England to pay for the imports. As long as the migrants kept arriving with their capital and credit, the system could sustain itself.[2]

But that was not to be. In 1642, the onset of the English Civil War brought a halt to the migration, as many would-be settlers decided to remain home. The result was a sharp recession, part of a global economic downturn, and it forced New Englanders to explore alternate pursuits. Some of the activities they pursued had been going on since the establishment of the colony. Farming, of course, was the main economic activity throughout the region. But New England's rocky soil and short growing season produced only modest surpluses, nothing that would enable colonists to pay their debts to London merchant houses. The earliest investors in both Plymouth Colony and the Massachusetts Bay Colony believed that the trade in beaver pelts might bring a healthy return, but most of the region's rivers did not reach very far inland

and the local beaver population was quickly trapped out. Never a real moneymaker, the fur trade was in steep decline by 1660 and by 1675 it was finished. Another strategy for dealing with the trade deficit was to reduce imports by producing more manufactures at home. John Winthrop Jr. established an ironworks in 1645, but this and similar schemes proved to be failures.[3]

The New England slave trade can be traced, indirectly, to two other strategies of the economic recalibration of the 1640s. The first of these was fishing. Commercial fishing in New England pre-dated the establishment of both Massachusetts Bay and Plymouth. However, in these early years, fishing was financed and organized not by New Englanders, who had no experience with it, but by fishing companies in the English West Country. These companies manned their vessels with servants recruited in England and shipped the catch back across the Atlantic. New England settlers were only minimally involved, partly because few had maritime experience, but also because in an environment of abundant land, most young men preferred to acquire farms and work for themselves rather than labor for someone else in a squalid fishing camp. With the coming of the English Civil War, the West Country investors drastically curtailed their activities. New Englanders stepped into the gap and over time developed a fishing industry. Of particular importance was cod, which bred prodigiously in the cold waters off the North American coast. Packed with protein, cod was easily preserved for transportation over long distances. American cod of varying grades and preparations found markets in Europe, especially in Catholic Iberia and, in due time, in the Caribbean, where it was fed to enslaved plantation laborers. Cod fishing would become an essential pillar of the regional economy. It became the region's greatest export, by far, and gave rise to an economic elite eventually known as the "codfish aristocracy."[4]

Cod fishing allowed New England merchants to accumulate credits and capital, which in turn allowed them to diversify their activities. So although the link between cod fishing and slave trading is hardly a direct one (there appear to be no major fish merchants among the earliest slave traders), fishing was nonetheless the midwife to the New England "carrying trade," or shipping, of which slave trading was but a small part. Fishing not only furnished monetary capital for other pursuits, it fostered the development of what is sometimes called "human capital," or the reservoir of knowledge, skills, and institutions that allows a particular economic activity to flourish. Cod fishing nudged settlers, most of whom had been landsmen before migrating, to acquire maritime skills. It also encouraged them to build long-distance trade networks and learn to finance voyages and manage the risks of ocean-going trade. In addition to profiting from the simple process of buying low and selling high, these ancillary skills allowed New Englanders to accumulate considerable credits from shipping, what economists call "invisible earnings." Cod, in short, induced coastal New Englanders to become a maritime trading people.[5]

New England ships soon fanned out over the North Atlantic. Spain, through the port of Bilbao, was one of the prime destinations for New England's cod exports, but the Atlantic "wine islands," Madeira in particular, were important as well. Many colonists had personal experience with these islands, since the vessels that carried them to North America often called at one of them.[6] A Boston–Madeira trading axis emerged in the 1630s and grew over the course of the seventeenth century because it helped merchants in scattered locations solve a set of problems. For Boston's cod merchants, who could not sell their product in England, Madeira supplemented the Iberian market. At Madeira, New Englanders exchanged their cod for wine, a trade that over the next few decades would come increasingly under the control of English merchants and which facilitated the balancing of accounts in London. From the perspective of Madeira's merchants, whether English or Portuguese, New England's taste for wine solved the parallel problem of paying for their own English imports. And from the perspective of London's shippers, a stop at Madeira for wine helped to ensure that the extra space in the holds of their ships did not go unused.[7]

The Madeira trade brought New Englanders ever closer to Africa. Straddling one of the main shipping routes in the North Atlantic, which ran from Europe to Africa to the Caribbean and up the coast of North America, Madeira was something of a crossroads. The Canary Islands, also wine producers, were even closer to Africa. In fact, the *Rainbow* apparently cleared customs initially for the Canaries with barrel staves intended for the wine industry. These routes eventually brought New

Englanders to Cabo Verde, which was within easy sailing distance of the African mainland. Notarial documents from the 1640s reveal a sustained link between Boston and Cabo Verde, sometimes in conjunction with the Madeira trade. Cabo Verde was a provisioning hub for European-based vessels bound for the African mainland, but also an important slave-trading entrepôt in its own right. Calling regularly at Madeira, the Canaries, and Cabo Verde, New Englanders would have picked up intelligence about the slave trade. Captain James Smith of the *Rainbow* visited Cabo Verde at least once on a previous voyage and may have called there on the homeward-bound voyage from Portudal.[8]

New Englanders, then, were trading off the coast of Africa by the 1640s, but they could never have developed a transatlantic slave trade without a market for enslaved labor. Prior to 1644, those markets were remarkably few. Although slavery existed in all corners of the Atlantic World, its gravitational center was in northeastern Brazil, which was very far away and, in any case, was well served by the Portuguese and the Dutch. There was substantial demand in mainland Spanish America, but that trade was illegal, first under Spanish law and soon under the Navigation Acts. English vessels trading there risked confiscation and worse. More realistically, Santa Catalina, or Providence Island, as the English called it, might have furnished a market. In 1630, the very same year the Winthrop fleet arrived in Massachusetts, a related group of Puritan investors founded their colony on an island off the coast of modern-day Nicaragua, one claimed by Spain. In short order Providence Island imported several hundred African captives, becoming the first English colony to base its economy primarily on enslaved labor. In 1638, however, an abortive slave rebellion—also a first for an English colony—rattled the white settler population and raised doubts about relying so heavily on enslaved labor. The question was never resolved, because three years later, Spain captured the island and expelled the English. Had it survived, the Providence Island colony would surely have become a steady market for New England's slave ships.[9]

Virginia had enslaved laborers, but as yet very few, since planters could still rely on a steady supply of English servants. New Netherland was another potential market, but it was also very small and amply supplied by the Dutch. These markets were much too limited to sustain a regular slave trade, but a far better market was emerging: the Caribbean island of Barbados. It was here that the *Rainbow* had carried its captives, and it would soon become the prime market for the captives carried aboard New England's slavers. In fact, without Barbados as a market, it is difficult to imagine New Englanders getting involved in the slave trade at all, at least during the seventeenth century. Before 1700, almost three-quarters of all New England slave ships carried their human cargoes there, with Jamaica coming in at a distant second. There was really no other possibility. Settled in 1627, Barbados was a plantation colony from the start. Tobacco was the early crop, worked largely by English indentured servants. Their labor was soon supplemented by the importation of enslaved laborers from Africa, and by the 1640s, Barbados was shifting from indentured to enslaved labor. Approximately twenty-six thousand Africans were carried to Barbados during the 1640s, mostly aboard English ships. Even so, by the end of the decade, English indentured laborers still outnumbered enslaved Africans by more than two to one. Enslaved Africans would not constitute a majority of the population until about 1660. As sugar planting spread to Saint Kitts, Nevis, Antigua, and Montserrat, and after 1655 to Jamaica, competing colonies inevitably ate into Barbados's share of the English slave trade, but even at the end of the century, the island consumed almost half of all captives carried by British ships, including those carried to the Spanish, Dutch, and French colonies.[10]

Although the Puritans viewed the settlement of New England as a sacred moral errand, their vision presented no serious impediment to the commerce in human beings. Their thinking on the topic was far from systematic or coherent, but most Puritans saw few problems with slavery or the slave trade, as the Providence Island episode clearly demonstrates. Early modern Englishmen were familiar with the concept of slavery well before the founding of New England. They possessed an abstract understanding of slavery as a result of its prominence in the Bible, from their studies of Ancient Greece and Rome, and from travel narratives of the kind collected and published by Richard Hakluyt and Samuel Purchas. Slavery, for early modern Englishmen, existed in multiple forms. It might be political in nature, as in the tyranny of a king, or

it might refer to institutions like servitude or convict labor. But the English were also quite familiar with the notion of chattel slavery as practiced in Iberia and the Atlantic World, and they understood that slavery
of that kind was reserved for Africans and Native Americans, though
there was some doubt regarding the latter.[11]

What made Africans enslaveable in English eyes was the notion
that they were essentially different from Europeans. As many scholars
have pointed out, slavery, although common in human history, has
been almost universally regarded as an aberrant or exceptional status
requiring positive justification to exist. With the exception of criminal
conviction, which implies its own justification, enslavement has historically been reserved for outsiders or "others." The nature of outsiderness
has taken many forms. Political outsiderness has been one of the more
frequent justifications, as seen most commonly in the case of war captives. Religious outsiderness has been another marker of enslaveability, accommodated in both Christianity and Islam. In addition to these
justifications, the English also began to invoke phenotypical variations
between Africans and Europeans as markers of difference connoting enslaveability, the forerunner to the more scientistic racial justification of
later centuries.[12]

As the English became increasingly involved in slavery and enslavement, they invoked all of these justifications in different measures,
adopting and adapting the ideas of their colonizing predecessors, the
Portuguese and the Spanish. The result was an inconsistent blend of
religious, political, and racial justifications, one peculiar to the seventeenth century. Englishmen of the era often used the words "slave" and
"Negro" interchangeably, and in contradistinction to terms like "English" and "Christians." Any of these terms or the larger ideas they
signified could be activated to justify slavery. Thus, the Massachusetts
Body of Liberties, passed just three years before the voyage of the Rainbow, confirmed the legality of slavery under certain circumstances, including war captivity and sale. Invoking the authority of "the law God
established in Israel," the code made no explicit reference to race or
color. This was partly because the clause was intended to apply to Native
Americans as well as Africans, but also because it was simply not necessary to invoke what we would call race as a justification; there are, after

all, many historical examples of slavery without race and vice versa. But that was changing quickly. Elsewhere, Englishmen had begun drawing on a discourse of bodily difference to justify slavery, often intermingled with the age-old justification of religious-political difference. A Virginia statute of 1660 punished "Christian servants" who ran away with "negroes," and another of 1680 prescribed thirty lashes for any "Negro" who attacked a "Christian." By the end of the century, Christianity had been dropped from the equation, and the terms "Negro" and "slave" were used interchangeably.[13]

Given the low volume of the early New England trade, there are few sources that might tell us how the Puritans viewed their tentative foray into the slave trade. Two incidents, however, allow us to take soundings. The first of these is the bizarre epilogue to the story of the *Rainbow*. Having abducted the alcaide, his translator, and a dozen or two others, the *Rainbow* and its consorts made for Barbados. Most of the captives were sold there, at which point the *Blossom* and *Seaflower* sailed home to London, their crews depleted from illness. Captain Smith and his mate, John Keyssar, however, got into a disagreement over the *Rainbow*'s cargo, with the end result that Keyssar took the *Rainbow* to Boston. Once the ship was there, rumors began to circulate of a massacre perpetrated by the crew while in Africa, a mass killing involving a cannon and up to one hundred dead.[14]

That story was inaccurate, but some Bostonians were quite alarmed by what they heard. Samuel Saltonstall soon lodged a complaint against Smith and Keyssar before the General Court, charging Smith with murder, manstealing, and (because the incident took place on a Sunday) Sabbath-breaking. In the course of his trial, Smith was found guilty of Sabbath-breaking but cleared of the other charges. The murder charge was dropped because the court doubted its jurisdiction in Africa, although this reasoning did not apply to the Sabbath-breaking charge. And although Smith was not convicted of manstealing, the court nonetheless recognized that a wrong had been committed. To right the wrong, the General Court ordered two men, including the alcaide's interpreter, to be returned to Africa at public expense. The men were taken from their erstwhile enslavers in frigid Portsmouth, New Hampshire, and sent back to Africa with a letter of explanation and apology. The alcaide's reaction in Baol has gone unrecorded.[15]

Nineteenth-century historians liked to point to the story of the *Rainbow*'s "negro interpreter" as an example of New England's long-standing hostility to slavery. Modern historians have not been as generous, pointing out that Smith was convicted of Sabbath-breaking, not enslaving a free fellow human being. If Smith had the foresight to seize his captives between Monday and Saturday, presumably all would have been well. The incident shows that the Puritans had no serious problems with slavery as an institution. They only became squeamish when slavers transgressed certain parts of God's law.

Our second sounding on New Englanders' attitudes toward the slave trade comes from one of the more famous episodes in the history of early American slavery. John Saffin was a Boston merchant who had lived in Virginia in the 1650s. In 1680, he, along with four partners, dispatched the slaver *Elizabeth* on an African voyage in violation of the RAC monopoly. The *Elizabeth*'s principal New World destination is not known (Barbados would seem the most likely possibility), but the ship was carrying at least one captive African when it returned to New England the following year. Having heard that the vessel would be seized in Rhode Island if it attempted to land there (whether for violating the RAC monopoly or for some other reason is unknown), Saffin sent new instructions via another ship, ordering the *Elizabeth* to make for Nantasket, south of Boston, where the captives could be landed under cover of darkness. The outcome is unknown, but presumably Saffin succeeded in landing the captives.[16]

Nearly twenty years later, Saffin found himself at the center of a major controversy over the nature of slavery in New England. Saffin owned a man named Adam, with whom he had concluded a compact granting him freedom for seven years of faithful service. Adam, however, consistently resisted Saffin's authority, and when Saffin decided to hire Adam out to a third party rather than free him, Adam challenged the transfer. Adam told his story to Samuel Sewall, a judge on the Supreme Court of Judicature. Sewall was sympathetic, and Adam's situation inspired him to write a landmark anti-slavery tract titled *The Selling of Joseph* (1700), a reference to the biblical tale of a man unjustly delivered into bondage by his brothers. Sewall began by asserting that no man had a right to sell another, which meant that, "Originally, and Naturally, there is no such thing as Slavery." He then proceeded to interrogate the moral validity of slavery. Could slavery be justified as a result of the curse of Ham? No: the Bible mentioned the curse of Canaan, not Ham. Was enslavement permissible in order to redeem Africans from "paganism"? No: conversion to Christianity did not justify the evil of enslavement. Could slavery be justified by the notion that enslaved Africans were captives taken in just wars? No: there was no way to know whether these wars were just. Did the fact that Abraham and other Old Testament figures bought slaves imply divine sanction? No: it had not been proven that Abraham purchased slaves. And finally, could the blackness of the "Ethiopians" justify their enslavement? No: though Black, Africans were the sons and daughters of Adam, "offspring of GOD," and "ought to be treated with a Respect agreeable."[17]

Incensed at Sewall's charge that he was in the wrong, Saffin published a sharp response. He began by asserting that God had "ordained different degrees and orders of men, some to be high and honorable, some to be low and despicable." This was in effect a statement of Puritan common sense, an idea sanctioned in such texts as John Winthrop's sermon, "A Model of Christian Charity." The Bible, Saffin argued, endorsed the enslavement of "heathens," and he denied any parallel with the story of Joseph. Saffin then proceeded to refute all of Sewall's propositions: whether it was Ham or Canaan who had been cursed was irrelevant, since it was permissible to enslave heathens; the good of Christian conversion did indeed outweigh any evil connected with enslavement; neither Sewall nor any other New Englander could say with certainty whether African wars were just or unjust; and Abraham's ownership of slaves was both "lawful and good."[18]

But Saffin saved his strongest argument for Sewall's final proposition, that Africans as descendants of Adam were entitled to "Respect." True, argued Saffin, Africans were "creatures of God," but this did not obligate him (or by implication any other white Christian) to "make them equal with ourselves," nor did it mean he had to "love" his servants as much as his own kin. To crown his argument, Saffin, who was given to writing poetry, concluded with a bit of verse he titled "The Negroes Character":

> Cowardly and cruel are those *Blacks* Innate,
> Prone to Revenge, Imp of inveterate hate,
> He that exasperates them, soon espies
> Mischief and Murder in their very eyes.
> Libidinous, Deceitful, False and Rude,
> The spume Issue of Ingratitude.
> The Premises consider'd, all may tell,
> How near good *Joseph* they are parallel.

Though Saffin wrote that in the first year of the eighteenth century, his words would hardly have been out of place in the writings of later generations of pro-slavery polemecists.[19]

Saffin's screed, though written at the end of the period under discussion here, is the most complete statement we have of the views of a seventeenth-century New England slave trader on matters of race and servitude. We cannot know for certain whether his thoughts were typical; strands of anti-slavery sentiment wound through the thinking of the radical Protestant sects, as Sewall demonstrates. However, it is very likely that Saffin's views on the morality of slavery and Black inferiority were shared widely throughout the region, especially among slaveholders and slave traders. Saffin, after all, was hardly an original thinker. The ideas he expressed circulated throughout the English Atlantic, allowing him, as a slaveholder and trader, to reconcile his economic pursuits with his professed faith. Saffin's response to Sewall serves as a reminder that Puritan New Englanders saw no categorical problem with slavery. They sometimes disagreed over the rules that should govern slavery and enslavement, as the experiences of both the *Rainbow*'s "negro interpreter" and Adam Saffin demonstrate, but these disagreements in no way constituted a barrier to involvement in the transatlantic slave trade.[20]

The number of New England voyages in the seventeenth century was very small, apparently no more than a half dozen in the 1640s–1650s, followed by a long period of inactivity that coincided with the Second

Anglo-Dutch War. Another half dozen vessels embarked in the 1670s, followed by another decade of very low activity, before a late-century revival. This later burst, beginning in the 1690s, though still irregular and small in scale, did represent a transition of sorts from the poorly organized, sporadic trade of the seventeenth century to the more mature, sophisticated trade of the eighteenth century.

There have long been intimations that the New England slave trade of the seventeenth century was significantly larger than surviving documents suggest. Yet although the documentary record is incomplete, extremely so for some periods, and although slave traders often had cause to hide what they were doing from colonial officials, there is little reason to believe that the volume of the seventeenth-century New England–based trade was anything but miniscule, certainly in comparison with later eras. Some studies conflate the disembarkation of captive Africans with outward-bound vessels that carried them to other colonies. Others fail to differentiate between the transatlantic trade and the intra-American slave trade. But though it is virtually certain that some voyages have gone unrecorded, to argue that this was a significantly higher number ignores the great amount of contrary evidence contained in numerous statements from colonial officials, travelers, and other observers. These sources are unanimous in suggesting that transatlantic slaving voyages were rare. More importantly, however, to suggest that the number of voyages was significantly greater is to underestimate the many difficulties of organizing such voyages, including high capital requirements, access to trade goods and merchant networks, and knowledge of African markets and trading practices, and to overestimate the ability of New Englanders to procure captives in Africa.[21]

For most of the seventeenth century, Englishmen were barred from trading in Africa between Cape Blanco (in modern-day Mauritania) and the Cape of Good Hope. This massive stretch of coastline was the exclusive preserve of the various chartered trading companies. The earliest of these was the Senegal Adventurers in 1588, though little is known of their activities (if any). More important was the Company of Adventurers Trading into the Parts of Africa, chartered in 1618, which received monopoly rights to the trade of "Guinea and Binny [Benin]," which is to say West Africa. Sir Ferdinando Gorges, a member of the

Plymouth Company and sponsor of many early New England ventures, was on the board of the Guinea Company, as it was usually called,
though there is no evidence that he attempted to merge his New England and African interests. The Guinea Company's ventures centered
on the trade in gold, dyewoods, and other nonhuman commodities, and
mostly ended in failure. During the English Civil War, the company's
close association with the Stuarts forced a reorganization. In 1660 it was
rechartered as the Royal Adventurers into Africa and began slave trading in earnest. But like all such companies, it faced financial problems
stemming from the cost of maintaining forts on the African coast while
simultaneously fending off "interlopers," or independent traders. To
cope with these difficulties, the Royal Adventurers sold licenses to private traders in the 1660s, which in theory would have offered a path to
legitimacy for American-based traders, but there is no evidence that any
of them actually purchased licenses. With the start of the Second Anglo-
Dutch War in 1664, these compounding financial challenges finished
the Royal Adventurers for good.[22]

The African trade monopoly was transferred to the newly chartered Royal African Company (RAC) in 1672. As before, colonial merchants were excluded, and governors were instructed to prevent ships
from leaving the Americas for Africa. More successful than its predecessors, the RAC lasted until 1752. But its close association with the Catholic Duke of York, later King James II, caused it political problems after
the Glorious Revolution of 1688. Political weakness made the company
vulnerable to pressure from merchants who resented its monopoly, and
from colonial planters, especially those in the Caribbean, who complained that it could not deliver sufficient numbers of laborers. Inad-
equate as the RAC may have been in the eyes of the planters, colonial
interlopers had to be aware that it could create costly legal difficulties for
them should one of their vessels be libeled.[23]

John Willoughby, master of the Boston-based *Rose,* was one of the
unlucky ones who ran afoul of the RAC's monopoly. The *Rose* set out
in February 1684 under the command of John Dowers. It sailed first
to Faial in the Azores, where it took on a cargo of wine and brandy.
It then set sail for Cabo Verde, where it took on salt. There, according
to Willoughby, who was at the time still the first mate, the Portuguese

governor commandeered his vessel to ferry soldiers to Cacheu, a trading town on the upper Guinea coast. While at Cacheu, Captain Dowers
died and Willoughby assumed command of the *Rose*. Willoughby then
took on fifty-five captives, apparently on the initiative of the Portuguese
commandant at Cacheu, and set sail for Santiago, the administrative
center of Cabo Verde. Contrary winds forced him to put in at Fogo, the
archipelago's volcanic island, where the governor promptly seized most,
but not all, of the captives. The *Rose* then departed for Santiago, but after battling foul weather for five days, Willoughby crossed the Atlantic,
touching first at French Guadeloupe. From there the *Rose* sailed to Saint
Kitts (the English half—it was divided with the French), where it was
promptly seized for violating the RAC's monopoly.[24]

In the libel (accusation) filed against him by the RAC agent in
Saint Kitts, Willoughby was also accused of placing African goods
(though apparently not captives) aboard another vessel, the *Lawrell* of
New Haven. In his defense, Willoughby told the court that he had intended to trade in Cabo Verde, which was not covered by the RAC's
monopoly. He also claimed that he placed goods aboard the *Lawrell* because his own vessel was "ready to sink." The local court, perhaps out
of a lingering resentment toward the company's monopoly, accepted
Willoughby's story and acquitted him. Whether he was telling the truth
about how he wound up with African captives and ivory aboard his
ketch, likely no one will ever know. But in addition to highlighting the
symbiosis between the wine and slave trades, the *Rose*'s voyage serves
as a reminder that the RAC was capable of causing trouble for colonial merchants who violated its monopoly. Although enforcement was
often toothless, anyone contemplating an illicit African voyage would
have to reckon with the possibility of confiscation.[25]

Information on voyage organization, which is the term for financing
and planning, is scant for New England's seventeenth-century slave
trade, a result of both the time elapsed and the very small number of
actual voyages. There is, however, enough information to suggest some
of the basic contours of ownership, financing, and networks. Overall,
the evidence confirms the sporadic, improvisational character of these

early voyages. The seventeenth-century slave trade was not so much organized as disorganized.

In the British slave trade, including trade conducted from the
American colonies, voyage organizers and vessel owners were generally
one and the same. This was a departure from the general pattern in
British shipping, in which sole ownership of a vessel was rare, or, in the
words of historian Ralph Davis, "shipowning was no man's trade." Merchants instead purchased shares in vessels, delineated in sixteenths and
thirty-seconds, so that at any given moment a single investor might own
pieces of multiple ships. One of the partners would serve as a managing
owner who took the initiative in organizing the voyage. Captains would
invest if they could, which was seen as both a path to merchant status
and a way to ensure that they acted in the investors' best interests.[26]

New England replicated the general pattern of metropolitan shipowning. Bernard and Lotte Bailyn's analysis of the Massachusetts merchant fleet at the turn of the seventeenth century reveals that it too was
characterized by plural ownership. Most Massachusetts vessels were locally owned, but some Bostonians invested in West Indian and British-
based vessels. The roster of shareholders was fluid but broadly distributed, with a surprising three in ten adult male (along with nine female)
Boston residents having a concern in a vessel. Within this structure were
several larger investors, who owned shares in ten or more vessels, led by
two who owned parts of more than twenty ships.[27]

Slave ships are almost entirely absent from the shipping register of
1697–1714 that the Bailyns analyzed, but other information suggests slavers of the mid-seventeenth century had a similarly diffuse ownership
structure. The *Rainbow,* for example, had at least three owners. Captain James Smith owned one-quarter, a common arrangement, with the
other shares owned by David Selleck, a Boston soap boiler, and Isaac
Grosse, a local brewer. These occupations might imply that the early
slave trade was a relatively democratic pursuit, but looks can be deceiving. Selleck, at the very least, was no ordinary soap maker. A native of
Somerset, England, he arrived in Massachusetts sometime after 1635, apparently driven by declining opportunities in the soap trade. Although
he never apprenticed, he practiced the trade for several years in Boston.

By the mid-1640s, however, he had turned his sights to commerce, with the *Rainbow* constituting one of his earliest ventures. Perhaps as a result of the voyage's failure, he never invested in another African voyage, instead devoting his time and money to the Virginia tobacco trade and transporting Irish indentured servants to Barbados. His partner, Isaac Grosse, appears not to have been as ambitious, running the *Three Mariners* tavern in Boston around the same time as the *Rainbow*'s voyage. In his will he left personal property worth £587.[28]

Another sign that the owners and organizers of these early New England voyages were not the same people is the survival of several "charter party" documents. In fact, much of what we know about this trade is derived from these sources. A charter party is a maritime rental agreement, a contract between the owner(s) of a vessel and a group of merchants who would like to use it to transport goods. A typical charter party outlines the proposed itinerary and specifies a time frame for its completion. It also stipulates the penalties for failure to fulfill any of the terms. The frequency of charter parties in this era points to a very occasional participation in the slave trade. Chartering a vessel was a cheap way of experimenting with the slave trade. When the New England slave trade matured in the mid-eighteenth century, charter parties all but disappeared as owner-organizers became the norm.[29]

The activities of John Parris, uncle of Salem's famous witch hunter, exemplify the early separation of voyage organization and vessel ownership. As the organizer of two transatlantic voyages, Parris, along with Thomas Windsor, was New England's leading slave trader of the seventeenth century. He arrived in Massachusetts before 1642 and began trading with Madeira and Barbados. He bought land in Barbados in 1646, which became his main base, though he maintained strong ties to Boston. In 1649 he concluded an agreement with Captain Thomas Willoughby of the ship *Fortune* for a voyage to "the coast of Ginney, thence to Barbados & so for New England" and signed a more detailed charter party to that effect in April 1650. Two months later, in May 1650, Parris chartered the London-based *Gift of God*. Another early enterprise was structured in the same way, splitting vessel ownership and voyage organization. Rhode Islander William Withington was a part owner of the *Beginning*, which in 1649 became the first Rhode Island–connected ship to undertake a transatlantic slave voyage. He hired the other half of the vessel from Henry Parkes of Boston.[30]

The financing of these early voyages is obscure, but surviving evidence suggests a combination of local and metropolitan backing. Parris, for example, operated within a network linking Boston with Barbados, England, and Madeira. Notarial records from 1649 include a letter of credit by Aaron Williams of Deal, Kent, to Captain Henry Gay and Richard Spanswick "for the getting out of yor vessel for Guiney." This was likely one of Parris's voyages, since he, Williams, Gay, and Spanswick all were involved in a venture that brought fifteen pounds sterling in ivory and forty-two pounds sterling in gold back to Boston. (The account makes no mention of captives, however.) In other instances, as with Selleck and Grosse's backing of the *Rainbow,* the interests appear to have been, if perhaps not local (given Selleck's Virginia involvement), at least cisatlantic.[31]

We know still less about the vessels' crews. The earliest crews were all surely born and raised in England's maritime communities; New England was a new settlement and as yet had not developed a reservoir of deepwater maritime knowledge. James Smith of the *Rainbow* and John Thompson of the *Gift of God* both appear to have been natives of Greater London, but little is known about the other masters of the 1640s and 1650s. The origins of the later generation of captains are likewise obscure, though it is far more likely that they were New England natives. Thomas Windsor, who skippered two vessels at the end of the century and a third at the start of the next, seems to have been a Boston native, but most others are untraceable. The charter parties further reveal that the ship captains of the seventeenth century were often part owners of their vessels, more so, it appears, than in the eighteenth century. This was a probable outgrowth of the separation between vessel ownership and voyage organization. John Thompson, for example received ninety-five pounds per month for eight to twelve months for skippering the *Gift of God,* and John Peters received thirty pounds per month for eight to sixteen months for commanding the *Fortune.* William Withington and John Smith also received monthly payments for the charter of their vessels, though the rates are unknown. In addition to payments for the charter of their vessels, ship captains probably received additional income in the form of commissions and free freight on captives of their own purchase, known as "privilege slaves." John Thompson, as a quarter owner of the *Gift of God,* owned one-quarter of the captives. He was also allowed to transport four captives of his own free of charge, though he was responsible for their provisioning.[32]

Like all merchants, the early New England traders would have preferred to operate within networks. Their networks, however, were quite primitive: these were largely improvisational, speculative ventures. Connections with London and Barbados were strong in some cases, as Parris's operations testify, but links with merchants on the African coast were nonexistent. It is possible that some of the merchants had connections in the Atlantic islands, which they used as jumping-off points, but there is no evidence for it. There are also some hints at connections for future development, though these seem to have been unrealized. The charter party for the *Gift of God* refers to the unlading of the vessel at Cape Lopez, in modern-day Gabon, which would suggest the existence of a contact there. But the reference is couched in legalism and highly contingent, so it more likely envisions the speculative advancement of goods to a locally based factor who was as yet unknown to the organizers.[33]

But perhaps the most important obstacle to a regular, profitable slave trade—and one more reason to believe the total volume remained very small through the seventeenth century—was the lack of suitable trade goods. It is no coincidence that Captain Smith and his mate Keyssar of the *Rainbow* resorted to violence and trickery: trading for captives was time-consuming and required both experience and the right wares. The old notion that Africans were easily duped by "trinkets"—what historian Philip D. Curtin called the "gewgaws myth"—was put to rest long ago. Recent research has emphasized African merchants' savvy and African consumers' discriminating tastes. The problem was that little of what New Englanders produced was in demand in Africa. Africans had plenty of fish, lumber, and foodstuffs, and by the later seventeenth century even tobacco was spreading quickly.[34]

As a result, the early slavers had little choice but to engage in a series of preliminary exchanges in order to procure the optimal "assortment" of trade goods. One way to do this was to sail to Barbados before crossing the Atlantic. Parris's *Gift of God* and Withington's *Be-*

ginning both pursued this strategy. The latter carried cattle, in an effort to convert the agricultural surplus of New England into trade goods. The charter party for the *Gift of God* did not specify what goods it carried to Barbados, but it expressly allowed the vessel to sail to another port in the event that a suitable cargo was unavailable at Bridgetown. Exactly what trade goods these vessels took on at Barbados is not clear. The most likely candidate would be some form of sugarcane-derived alcohol. Barbadians had begun distilling rum (or something resembling it, called "kill-devil") in the 1640s, with the first unambiguous evidence dating to 1647. It is therefore possible, even probable, that these early Yankee slavers carried at least some. But even if rum was not available, they could have taken on a variety of fermented (as opposed to distilled) cane beverages. A stop at the Azores, Madeira, or the Canaries for wine could serve the same purpose. But although alcohol certainly made it easier to procure captives, not all varieties were equally popular in Africa. So even though Barbadian rum allowed North Americans to enter the slave trade, it still had to win over consumers and their preferred other varieties of alcohol.[35]

Cabo Verde was another place where American ships could solve the problem of trade goods by "re-sorting" their cargoes. There is abundant evidence to suggest they did so in the eighteenth and nineteenth centuries, and given the strength of the connection between New England and Cabo Verde, they likely did so in the seventeenth as well. In fact, Cabo Verde was at its height as a slave-trading center in the seventeenth century, so it would be surprising if the New Englanders did not visit both to take on captives and trade goods. The most valuable good would not have been alcohol but textiles, or *panos.* Over the preceding century, Cabo Verde had developed a vibrant textile industry, which ran, at least initially, on the labor of enslaved Senegambians. Cabo Verdean colonists actually sought out weavers from regions known for their cotton textiles. The textiles they produced, a fine melding of African and European styles, were in great demand along the coast and would have furnished an excellent opportunity for the New Englanders to enhance the value of the provisions and other goods they carried.[36]

The occasional nature of the early New England slave trade meant that voyage organization was always experimental. Of those merchants who sent vessels to Africa in the seventeenth century, only John Parris and Thomas Windsor did so more than once. As a result, there was no accumulation of knowledge, no building of networks, no learning from trial and error. Undercapitalized, these colonials could not sustain losses from unsuccessful voyages. Parris's slaving expenses were so great—he paid several thousand pounds in shipping alone—that he was forced to liquidate some of his Barbados holdings in order to pay his debts. He was fortunate that his brother purchased them for what we must assume was a better-than-fair price. Parris never went bankrupt, but he also never organized another slave-trading venture.[37]

The New England traders of the seventeenth century purchased most of their captives in a single region of Africa, Senegambia, although later in the century some also visited Madagascar. (This trade is discussed along with New York's in chapter 2.) At least four New England vessels appeared on the Gold Coast in the 1680s and 1690s with foodstuffs, but it is not clear that these were slavers, and if they were, their trade was not successful enough to prompt regular voyages. The New Englanders' focus on a single region, Senegambia, is unexpected, given the improvisational nature of their enterprise. After all, it was the experienced traders who tended to focus their efforts on one or two African ports where they had contacts and understood the markets, operating whenever possible within well-established networks. But the early New Englanders were just as single-minded in their choice of destination as their more experienced rivals and descendants. The reason had less to do with networks on the African coast (which they did not have) and probably more to do with the Madeira, Canary Islands, and Cabo Verde trades, which had inspired their efforts in the first place. Not only could a vessel take on provisions and re-sort its cargo at these islands, but they served as jumping-off points for the mainland. Wind patterns, which played an important role in all maritime trade, were another factor. For New Englanders, Senegambia was the closest part of Africa, despite the fact that winds and currents were not favorable on the outbound passage. And the return journey from Senegambia to Barbados was short by slave-trading standards, averaging about forty-four days. Finally, unlike some other regions of Africa, such as Portuguese Angola, the Senegambian slave trade was not dominated by a rival European power, though this did mean that New Englanders had to compete with English, French, and Dutch ships.[38]

The exact African destinations are known for only two of the New England vessels that traded during the seventeenth century. The *Rainbow*, as previously mentioned, visited Portudal, just south of Cap Vert on the mainland, and the *Rose* called at Cacheu, though it may have stopped at other places as well. But, for a variety of reasons, it is likely that New Englanders purchased most of their captives at different ports in the region. By the mid-seventeenth century, the Petite Côte, where Portudal is located, had lost most or all of its *lançados,* or Luso-African middlemen. Important trade brokers, lançados resided in coastal polities under the terms of the landlord-stranger convention, a reciprocal arrangement in which the owners of the land allowed outsiders to conduct trade in exchange for the payment of a ground rent and the right to charge customs. Lançados elsewhere in upper Guinea married local women and became integrated into local lineages, but this was much harder in the hierarchical, patrilineal societies in and around Cap Vert. In addition, several of these states—specifically, Waalo, Kayor, and Baol—had begun to confiscate the traders' property on the death of the lançado. In response, lançados abandoned the Petite Côte for friendlier polities to the south. New Englanders could still trade in the area, but they would have to deal directly with the Wolof alcaides, as Smith had with the *Rainbow*. Inexperienced in the trade, most New Englanders would have found it easier and safer to deal with lançado middlemen. Cacheu, where the *Rose* traded, had a town and plenty of middlemen, but Portuguese officials were hostile to English competition. The commandeering of the *Rose* (if the captain's story is true) by Portuguese officials speaks to the problems posed by trading there.[39]

For those reasons, New England traders very likely focused their efforts on the Gambia River, to the immediate south. The Gambia possessed several advantages over the Petite Côte. To start, the river itself was wide and navigable for three hundred miles inland to Baro Kunda, which meant English ships could trade with any of the dozen or so states along the banks. Some of the states, such as Niumi (known to the English as "Barra") at the entrance to the river, specialized more in providing services to slave traders than in trading captives. In 1661, the Merchant Adventurers struck a deal with Niumi for permission to take control of a small island in the Gambia River from a group of Baltic investors and build a trading fort on it. Niumi became the landlord to the English strangers. The installation, which tended to fall in and out of repair, at times approaching dereliction, eventually became known as James Fort. In addition to possessing an English fort, the Gambia had its own Luso-African lançado population, which tended to enjoy better landlord relations than along the Petite Côte.[40]

The Gambia would, over time, prove to be a more prolific supplier of captives for the Atlantic slave trade than the Petite Côte. Most of the states along the Gambia River were ruled by Mandinka speakers, and several were clients or tributaries of the slave-raiding Kaabu Empire. Like most Mandinka polities, Kaabu was hierarchical, with a king, known as the *mansa,* whose office rotated among three elite families. Below them were the numerous provincial rulers (also known as mansas), followed by a military aristocracy known as the Nyaanco, then the free commoners, the occupational castes, and finally an enslaved population. The geographic center of Kaabu was to the southeast of the Gambia River, but it exerted great influence all along the river through its client states, the most notable of which were Kantor and the Sereer state of Siin-Saloum, which at times asserted tributary authority over Niumi. The Nyaanco military aristocracy had a reputation for spartanness, which depressed its demand for luxury trade goods, but it craved horses for its cavalry and paid for them in captives. At various times young male members of Nyaanco families who lacked tributaries of their own simply conquered new areas, all of which generated captives. The Kaabu elite exalted martial values and denigrated commerce, so they allowed a diasporic network of Muslim merchants, known as Jahanke or Juula, to handle trade on their behalf.[41]

Without specific information on trade goods, it is impossible to say with certainty how the New England economy managed to articulate itself with those of upper Guinea. In the seventeenth century, European trade was a proportionately small part of the larger regional economic picture. The area north of the Casamance exported cloth, salt, and gold, while importing iron, kola nuts, and horses. Iron, gold, and cloth were also major imports south of the Casamance, where salt and kola nuts were transported from the area between the Nunez River and Scarcies estuary. The region as a whole had strong ties to the Western Sudan, the Sahel, and the trans-Saharan trade. It was not feasible for the New Englanders to export iron, let alone gold, on a scale sufficient to carry on a regular slave trade, and while horses were an option, they were expensive to transport and their value was declining. It is hardly surprising, then, that Captain Smith, of the *Rainbow*, never actually traded for captives. Forcible abduction, his method, requires expenditures on vessels, men, and weapons, but it does not establish an economic link and contributes nothing to the building of networks. On the contrary, abduction makes it more difficult to procure captives later on, since the target societies soon take defensive action. The *Rose* did apparently trade for some captives, since the Portuguese who commandeered the vessel allowed it to retain some of them. Although the captives were taken on at Cacheu, it seems more likely that they were purchased from the Cabo Verdeans who took over the vessel, in which case the usual New England produce—cod, staves, foodstuffs—would have sufficed.[42]

Exactly what the other dozen or so seventeenth-century vessels carried is impossible to know for certain, which makes it difficult to determine the nature of the economic link between New England and Africa. Most likely, New England vessels exchanged their produce for panos and other goods at Cabo Verde. They also likely carried alcohol, perhaps Barbadian kill-devil (or New England rum in later decades), but also wine. Finally, it is conceivable that they may have carried horses or cattle. Horses were in demand throughout the region, both for military uses and as status items, though their value had fallen since the previous century. William Withington's *Beginning* carried cattle, but these were probably exchanged at Barbados for more suitable and less perishable goods. A variation on this strategy would have been to procure horses in the Atlantic islands and carry them to the African mainland, as one Boston vessel did as late as the 1730s.[43]

Who were the men, women, and children who were transported to the New World in New England's first slave ships? The best clues as to their cultural and linguistic origins come from Spanish America, which imported many captives from these same areas in the years just prior to the arrival of the New Englanders, when the crowns of Spain and Portugal were united and merchants from the latter enjoyed a monopoly on the slave trade to Iberian America. Unlike the English, the Spanish often recorded the "nation" of the Africans residing in their colonies in church and court records. From these it is quite clear that the vast majority of captives came from coastal communities not too far from where they embarked. They were speakers of the coastal Atlantic languages, with Brame and Biafada as the most prominent, together accounting for almost 60 percent in one survey. However, because the Spanish colonies in this era (up to 1640) were supplied by the Portuguese, they drew disproportionately on the Rivers of Guinea, where these groups resided in large numbers. Most English vessels took on captives farther north along the Gambia. Here Kaabu and its client states were the prime suppliers. Kaabu's wars and raids on their neighbors likely resulted in a similar ethnolinguistic breakdown aboard English slave ships, though perhaps with more Serer- and Mandinka-speaking captives.[44]

As the slave trade grew, several Senegambian states, such as Waalo, Kayor, Baol, and Kaabu, became increasingly militarized, the so-called *ceddo* states, after the Wolof word for "soldier." As growing numbers of Senegambians were caught up in the slave trade, a movement began to take shape. In 1673, a Berber marabout, or religious teacher, named Nasir al-Din led a rebellion that at the core was a critique of the slave trade. Din charged that the Wolof and Serer states, along with others, such as the Denyanke dynasty of the Fulbe and the Mandinka states of the Gambia, most of them at least nominally Muslim, violated Islamic strictures on the enslavement of Muslims and their sale to non-Muslims. The "War of the Marabouts," as it is known, ended in the capture and execution of Nasir al-Din, but it proved a harbinger of things to come.[45]

For most of the seventeenth century the New England slave trade had been undertaken experimentally and likely unprofitably, at least judging by the dearth of repeat voyages. Whatever knowledge merchants may have gained from these voyages was never redeployed, each successive merchant starting from scratch. With no lasting connections in Africa, each voyage ran considerable risks. Captains learned to operate on the African coast only through trial and error. Trade goods had to be advanced to people of uncertain trustworthiness. Information on African markets reached North America only in the most haphazard channels, if at all. Mechanisms for storing trade goods or for carrying over debts and credits from successive voyages did not exist. In combination with other obstacles, such as the vulnerability of colonial vessels to seizure for violating the RAC monopoly and the lack of a valuable trade good, it is hardly surprising that the New England trade was so sporadic. However, as later developments suggest, the problems would all find solutions.

The Madagascar Moment, 1680–1700

Under close questioning aboard an East Indiaman off the Cape of Good Hope, Francisco Domingo turned informer. Enslaved to Jacobus Cortlandt of New York, he had embarked for Madagascar in 1698 aboard the slaver *Margaret*, which was laden with wine, rum, sugar, and European manufactures. "Franck," as Domingo was known in New York, was a cooper, a valuable trade in the maritime world, and was apparently promised a wage for his work. After an Atlantic crossing of some months, the *Margaret* had rounded the Cape of Good Hope and made for Saint Mary's (now known as Nosy Boraha), a small forested island just off the northeastern coast of Madagascar, which at the time was the world's most famous pirate's nest. There, Domingo told his inquisitors, the *Margaret* encountered two pirate vessels prepared for a fight, their broadsides commanding the entrance of the harbor. The pirates had vowed to sink any English naval vessel that might appear, but on discovering that the *Margaret* was a merchantman, they held fire. The *Margaret*, they realized, was useful. Loaded down with plunder, the pirates wanted passage to New York and were willing to pay. Twenty of them would become passengers aboard the *Margaret*.[1]

Domingo gave his questioners what they wanted, which was information on pirates. In helping to bring about the condemnation and confiscation of the *Margaret* and the trial of its captain, Samuel Burgess, Domingo became free. He said nothing, however, about slave trading, probably because his questioners were more interested in eradicating pirates' nests than in hampering honorable commercial pursuits like slave trading. And the *Margaret* was, unquestionably, a slave ship; Captain Burgess's instructions make clear that slave trading was his main mission, and he ultimately took on about 115 captives. But the *Margaret* was simultaneously a pirate tender, with secret instructions on dealing with pirates and how to land booty in New York, all of which points to the strange fusion of piracy and slaving that defined this particular moment.[2]

On the surface, the New York–Madagascar chapter in the history of the American slave trade could hardly be more different from the one that preceded it. Unlike the New England–based trade of the mid- and late seventeenth century, which focused on upper Guinea, the New York–based trade was not limited to the Atlantic, but rather spilled into the Indian Ocean and linked the Asian textile and bullion trades with the Americas. Although piracy and slave trading often intersected, the New York–Madagascar slave trade was wholly entwined with piracy, to the point where it is impossible to separate one from the other. For the present discussion, however, the New York trade is interesting because it represented a significant advance in sophistication compared with the New England trade of the mid-seventeenth century. The New York merchants who organized the Madagascar trade actually managed to establish strong networks, far beyond anything the New Englanders ever put together for their West African ventures. To an extent, the New Yorkers' success belies the portrait of the seventeenth-century North American slave trade as a chaotic, improvised affair. But the New Yorkers' networks were not sustainable. Piracy, the very thing that enabled this trade, was also a tremendous liability. European states, England in particular, were shifting away from a policy of tolerance and toward one of hostility to piracy. Moreover, pirates hardly embodied the sort of manageable risk and predictability favored by merchants. In addition to their occasional predations toward slaving vessels, Madagascar's pirate-slave dealers failed to establish stable ties with Malagasy leaders, and as a result they saw their settlements repeatedly attacked. The New York traders' networks, such as they were, lasted only a few years, disappearing entirely by about 1702.

The New York–based trade differed from the New England–based trade in that it was often bilateral. Unlike New England, New Netherland—as the original Dutch colony was called—had a non-negligible demand for enslaved labor. Since the founding of New Netherland by the Dutch West India Company (WIC) in the 1620s, enslaved Africans had been integral to the colony, if relatively few in number. During the Dutch period before 1664, most of the Africans in New Netherland had been transported by the WIC, and indeed, many were owned by it. Settlers, however, wanted more laborers and petitioned the company in 1652 for the right to purchase them either in the Caribbean at Curaçao or in Africa. Although the WIC normally guarded its monopoly privileges, it acceded to the request and granted permission for New Netherlanders to trade for captives on the African coast east of Popo, on the Bight of Benin. This boundary was not chosen arbitrarily. In 1637, the WIC had seized the Portuguese Gold Coast fort of Elmina and was now locked in an escalating competition with the English for the region's trade, primarily for gold, but secondarily for captives. The WIC forbade New Netherland vessels to compete with them on the Gold Coast but permitted them trade farther down the coast, toward Ouidah, where the Dutch were not well established. And, having lost control of Portuguese Angola in 1648, the WIC probably hoped the interlopers would trade in territory claimed by the Portuguese on the "Loango Coast," to the north of the Congo River. In the end, however, New Amsterdam never sent any vessels to Africa. The reasons are unclear. Permission to trade in Africa arrived just in time for the start of the First Anglo-Dutch War, so merchants may have been loath to organize a potentially risky and expensive voyage. They would also have faced the same problem of trade-good assortment that confronted all colonial traders, as African demand for beaver pelts was surely quite small.[3]

The first documented transatlantic slaving voyage from what was now New York sailed in 1682 and established a template for the next twenty years. Organized by Frederick Philipse, the colony's wealthiest merchant, the voyage took on captives at Madagascar. Between 1682 and 1698, New Yorkers dispatched no fewer than sixteen vessels to Madagascar, transporting some fifteen hundred Malagasy into captivity, mostly in New York and Barbados. At least four additional slavers sailed to Madagascar from Boston, beginning with a voyage in 1679. As with New York, this number represents a minimum, and there were likely more. Whereas the New Yorkers usually made bilateral voyages, supplying their own market for enslaved labor, the Boston slavers tended to follow a triangular route, carrying captives to the Caribbean. Altogether, North American vessels accounted for between 35 and 40 percent of the trade at Madagascar in the late seventeenth century, with the remainder consisting of English vessels. Madagascar, then, was the first place where colonial traders actually provided any real competition for metropolitan merchants.[4]

The original inspiration for the Madagascar trade is not recorded, but it was very likely an outgrowth of the East India trade. Dutch East India Company vessels normally steered well south of Madagascar but did occasionally land for provisions and repairs. The first recorded slaving voyages to Madagascar involved Dutch vessels, at least eight of which visited Madagascar during the 1640s and 1650s. The first documented English slaving voyage to Madagascar occurred in 1663, but London merchants were quite familiar with Madagascar before that as a result of their Asian trade. North Americans sailed aboard both English and Dutch East India Company vessels, which may explain how information about Madagascar reached the colonies. But Madagascar was already well established in the English consciousness as a result of a colonization scheme promoted by Sir William Courteen in the 1630s. Courteen argued that England's East India Company (EIC) had not taken full advantage of its privileges and was granted a charter in order to inspire competition. No settlement resulted, but Madagascar continued to garner interest in English mercantile circles. Finally, in 1644, a settlement was launched by one of Courteen's partners, with slaving as one of their stated aims. Conflict with the local Malagasy, however, forced the abandonment of the camp, by which time only a dozen out of the initial 143 settlers remained; the rest had died or scattered. The English mercantile community, however, was now familiar with Madagascar.[5]

Several mostly political factors contributed to the rise of New York's (and to a lesser extent, New England's) trade with Madagascar. The first had to do with the monopoly trading companies: though the RAC charter barred colonial interlopers from trading in West Africa (up to 1698), its monopoly ended at the Cape of Good Hope, at which point the EIC monopoly came into effect. Technically, English vessels were forbidden to trade in the Indian Ocean without a license from the EIC. However, because the EIC was only minimally interested in the slave trade, it did little to combat the slave-trading interlopers and even ignored the RAC's request that it enforce its monopoly at Madagascar. The Indian Ocean, then, constituted a gray zone that allowed colonial interlopers to enter the slave trade with minimal risk of seeing their vessels libeled by the RAC in New World ports. This is not to suggest that the EIC turned a complete blind eye to slave trading. In 1688, it brought proceedings in New York against a vessel that had traded for captives in Madagascar. The outcome is unknown, but given the general hostility of colonial courts to the chartered monopolies, the EIC probably lost.[6]

The Madagascar trade increased after 1688 with the outbreak of the War of the League of Augsburg, in which England fought as part of a coalition against France. Colonial officials commissioned privateers, many of which made their way to the Indian Ocean. The privateers' primary goal was plunder, directed not so much at French vessels but toward vessels plying routes between India and the Arabian Peninsula. Ships carrying pilgrims for the hajj were especially attractive targets, since passengers often traveled with much wealth. Many Christians, moreover, considered it a sacred right and duty to raid Muslim shipping. As we shall see, once the war ended, those wishing to continue raiding found slave trading to be a convenient cover story for their Indian Ocean thievery.[7]

Local politics also fueled the Madagascar trade. Although a few vessels sailed from New York to Madagascar in the 1680s, Leisler's Rebellion, as the New York chapter of the Glorious Revolution is known, helped to smooth the way in the next decade. Jacob Leisler was a German merchant who, in the wake of the English seizure of New Netherland in 1664, had aligned himself with the older Dutch mercantile community.

When news of an uprising against the Jacobite governor of the Dominion of New England reached New York, Leisler initiated his own rebellion against the Jacobite lieutenant governor. Although he and his faction controlled New York for two years, he was eventually deposed and executed in 1691. In 1692 King William appointed Benjamin Fletcher to govern the colony. New York was still deeply divided by recent events, so Fletcher soon forged a cordial relationship with the colony's mercantile elite, lubricated by his willingness to issue privateering commissions to shipowners. Fletcher and the merchants understood that the war had provided an ideal opportunity to plunder for specie and valuable India goods, which were normally scarce in the North American colonies. The governor received a fee for issuing the commissions, and he and the merchants all took cuts from the sale of the fenced goods. New England joined the game as well, with Rhode Island's governor John Easton furnishing the commissions.[8]

The stream of colonial vessels departing for the Indian Ocean prompted the authorities to take countermeasures, which, in the history of English piracy, amount to something of a turning point. Up to this time, England had maintained a studied ambivalence toward piracy. After all, men like John Hawkins, Francis Drake, and Henry Morgan had proven of great use to the Crown in its long struggle with Spain and had been at the center of many local economies, from Jamaica to Devon. Westminster, however, was changing its views. As its own empire grew and matured, England saw piracy as a hindrance rather than a handmaiden to commerce and empire. The effort to rid Jamaica of the buccaneers in order to make the island safe for plantation slavery was but one manifestation of this new attitude. As the War of the League of Augsburg drew to a close, policy makers began to worry about the consequences of allowing pirates to construct bases in places like Madagascar. As a result, Parliament adopted a new strategy to end piracy. Rather than focus on capturing pirates on the high seas, they would deny them haven on shore. In 1696 a new Navigation Act was passed, which allowed the Crown to establish vice-admiralty courts in the colonies. Departing from previous practice, the running of these courts would be by judges appointed by the king, and the courts would have no juries, the better to insulate them from interference by colonial governments, which had proved all too willing to wink at piracy as long as their local economies were enriched with plunder.[9]

The second phase in the crackdown on piracy in New York involved replacing the manifestly corrupt governor, Fletcher, with someone more willing to stand up to the local merchants. That person was Richard Coot, the Earl of Bellamont (also Bellomont), a well-connected Whig who, along with Robert Livingston and several other powerful Whigs, was behind the pirate-hunting mission of William Kidd to the Indian Ocean in 1695. Bellamont's appointment covered Massachusetts, New Hampshire, and Rhode Island in addition to New York. On his arrival in the colonies in 1698, he launched an investigation into his predecessor's connection with the pirates and sent a steady stream of reports and recommendations back to London. His first dispatch charged that local customs officers were wholly corrupt, that piracy was flourishing, and that there was a "great trade" between New York and Madagascar in which "great quantities of India goods are brought." Reports like these, along with the seizure of suspect vessels, made Bellamont instantly unpopular with the merchants throughout the northern colonies. Massachusetts punished him by reducing his salary to penurious levels.[10]

A third measure, the reorganization of the EIC in 1698, left the New York–Madagascar trade outside of the law. As a result of a political rivalry between Tory and Whig politicians, Parliament had opened Asian trade to all British subjects in 1694. The EIC lobbied fiercely to have this rescinded, citing the spread of piracy. Parliament responded by restructuring the EIC and restoring its monopoly, although independent merchants could now purchase trading licenses. The catch was that all goods obtained east of the Cape of Good Hope had to be taken to London, where duties would be paid before re-export. The legal status of the New York–Madagascar slave trade had altered three times over the course of the decade. Before 1694 it was of questionable legality under the RAC and EIC charters. Between 1694 and 1698 it was legal, and starting in 1696 it served as an honorable cover for trading with pirates. And finally, the New York–Madagascar trade became clearly illegal after 1698 (in the absence of a license and commitment to re-export from London). The restoration of the EIC monopoly, coupled with the strengthened vice-admiralty courts, went a long way toward ending the New York–

Madagascar slave trade but did not kill it off entirely. At least three additional New York vessels are documented as having visited Madagascar after 1700, possibly as late as 1703. There are no additional documented voyages after that date, however. The outbreak of the War of the Spanish Succession in 1701 encouraged merchants to shift away from their usual shipping businesses to pursue government contracts and privateering. That same year, the leading New York trader, Frederick Philipse, died, and with him, it appears, the Madagascar slave trade.[11]

New York in the late seventeenth century was a very different place from Boston. Founded six years before its neighbor and competitor up the coast, it began as an isolated trading post of the WIC. In contrast to Boston, which received a spectacular surge of settlers during the Great Migration of 1630–1642, New Amsterdam (New York) grew more slowly, with a population of just twenty-five hundred when the English took over in 1664, and about five thousand at the close of the century. A company town throughout the Dutch period, the economy revolved around the exportation of beaver pelts, which were supplied by Iroquois traders, with diplomatic relations absorbing a great deal of the leadership's attention. The city's merchant fleet grew rapidly from a few "small shipps and a ketch" in the 1670s, to 32 oceangoing craft in 1684, to 102 deepwater vessels in 1694, 20 of which were classified as "ships."[12]

By the 1690s, New York's merchants had come a long way from the company-dominated pelt-trading economy of the Dutch period. Most of the city's merchants were engaged in local and regional trade, but a small, well-capitalized elite had successfully entered the long-distance transatlantic trade. Many of the merchants were of Dutch origin, having stayed on in the colony when offered the chance to become English subjects. Their links were primarily with the Netherlands, which caused some problems under the Navigation Acts. The English merchants brought strong London ties, which year upon year tended to overshadow the Amsterdam connections. The two cohorts merged to some extent, sharing concerns and connections, although ethnic rivalry faded slowly. Dutch merchants maintained their links to the United Provinces and traded a great deal with Portugal and the wine islands, even as they developed ties with London. The English merchants dominated the market in manufactures, fueled by London credit. Both groups faced the same challenge of paying for these goods in Europe. They solved this in part by plunging into the intra-American carrying trade, exporting grain and taking in Virginia tobacco for re-export. Voyage itineraries were often extremely complicated, involving various combinations of ports in England, the Netherlands, the Chesapeake, and the West Indies.[13]

When word of a pirate base off Madagascar reached New York in about 1690, the city's merchants immediately grasped its commercial potential. Like all American colonies, New York craved manufactured goods, most of which had to be imported from Europe. Direct importations from places other than England were outlawed under the Navigation Acts and, in any case, needed to be paid for. Moreover, in the case of Asian goods, the most coveted, New York would not have been able to pay for them since this required access to large amounts of specie. New York, therefore, like New England, ran trade imbalances with European merchants, which needed to be financed. Normally, this involved exporting surplus produce to other colonies to purchase goods, such as sugar and wine, which could be sold in Europe. Pirates, too, were a source of specie, both in the earlier buccaneer phase of Caribbean piracy and in the later Indian Ocean phase. The latter region, in fact, offered the chance to obtain not just bullion, but the very same "India goods" that were in such demand. Merchants could tap this stream in two ways. One was to secure privateering commissions from the governor and raid Muslim shipping. The other was by trading for the goods with the pirates at Saint Mary's. The latter activity could easily be combined with slaving, with each pursuit offering a hedge against the other.[14]

At its peak, it seems most of the city's transatlantic merchants entered the Madagascar trade, either as slave traders, suppliers of pirates, or both. The list of names reads like a seventeenth-century social register: Jacobus and Stephanus van Cortlandt, Rip Van Dam, Nicholas Bayard, John Cruger, Stephen De Lancey, Peter and Brant Schuyler, and Thomas Wenham, among others. But the New York–Madagascar trade was dominated by one man: Frederick Philipse. Born Frederick Flypsen in the Netherlands in 1626, he came to New Amsterdam in the late 1640s or early 1650s as a carpenter in the employ of the WIC. By 1660 he had

moved into commerce, trading in *sewant,* the shell currency of the Iroquois fur trade, along with West Indian sugar and Virginia tobacco. His
commercial fortunes took a great leap forward in 1662, when he married Margaret Hardenbroeck de Vries, the widow of a rich trader, after
which he became the city's wealthiest merchant. In politics, Philipse was
firmly aligned with the anti-Leislerians, having been part of the Jacobite
governing faction at the time of the rebellion. With the appointment of
Benjamin Fletcher as governor, Philipse returned to the inner circle and
made the most of his connection.[15]

Philipse's first known involvement in the slave trade occurred in
1684 with a vessel called the *Charles.* The *Charles* sailed first to the Isle of
Wight, then to Amsterdam to pick up trade goods. From there it sailed
to Cabo Verde, probably for water and provisions, before making its way
to Angola. After stopping at the Portuguese port of Luanda in Angola,
the *Charles* made its way up the coast of Africa to Sonyo, at the mouth
of the Congo River, where it took on 140 captives. Although the English
traded here and to the north, in the area called the "Loango Coast,"
the region was much more important to the Dutch. For that reason,
along with the fact that the *Charles* went to Amsterdam for trade goods,
this was probably a voyage undertaken on Dutch more than English
networks. The nature and extent of Philipse's involvement is not clear,
but he seems to have partnered with Dutch and English investors. The
Charles sold most of its captives in Barbados but carried a handful to
New York. The fact that the *Charles* sailed to England and the fact that it
relied on largely Dutch trade goods and networks underscore the challenges faced by colonial merchants in organizing their own slave trade.[16]

The organization of the New York–Madagascar trade is difficult
to address due to its dual nature. The pirate and slave trades overlapped
so much that it can be difficult to say whether a given merchant was a
slave-trading pirate or a pirate who dabbled in slave-trading. In addition, given the nature of long-distance maritime trade, in which ship
captains often had to respond to unforeseen events and market conditions, the purpose of a voyage could easily change. Philipse, at least, was
fairly clear about his intentions. In a letter to his primary connection in
the pirate trade, he stated quite clearly that he considered the slave trade
to be his "chiefest Profett" and "chief design." That said, Philipse was

clearly open to additional pursuits. His instructions unrelated to the slave trade, to Samuel Burgess of the *Margaret,* touched on the prices he should charge for alcohol sold to the pirates; his preferred varieties of silver coins; the need to hide all "contraband," including textiles, ivory, and indigo; and the amount to charge pirates seeking passage back to North America. The partnership of Thomas Wenham, Brant Schuyler, and Rip Van Dam was less specific in its instructions to Jonathan Rensselaer, first mate and supercargo (the merchant's representative in charge of all trade) of the slave ship *Peter,* but explicitly endorsed the possibility of carrying "calicoes" obtained from the pirates back to New York.[17]

Philipse began building his Madagascar network in the early 1690s, when he established contact with a former pirate, Adam Baldridge, in Madagascar. Baldridge had deserted a ship called the *Fortune* at Madagascar in January 1691, "being minded to settle among the Negros" on the island of Saint Mary's, off the northeast shore of the main island. According to his testimony, he aided a group of Malagasy in war, and for this was rewarded with seventy head of cattle and some slaves. The nature of his aid is not clear but likely involved providing firearms and gunpowder, which were major trade goods. It is even possible that he took part in local fighting, as other Europeans did. Baldridge married a Malagasy woman, which allied him with a prominent lineage. For the next several years, Baldridge and another ex-pirate, Lawrence Johnston, did a brisk business supplying pirates, including many from North America, with liquor, arms, powder, and everyday goods. In return, he received Indian textiles and bullion from plundered Muslim shipping. He also supplied captives, mostly to the New Yorkers, by staging raids with his Malagasy allies and through simple abduction. In one instance, he reportedly "inveigled" some local Malagasy aboard his ship, imprisoned them, and carried them to the Mascarene Islands for sale.[18]

The Philipse-Baldridge axis prospered for about six years over the course of at least five voyages, but the relationship was never free of difficulty. In 1694, after doing business with Baldridge for a couple of years, Philipse wrote the ex-pirate a long letter detailing several complaints, all of which highlight the imperfect nature of their network. Philipse had dispatched the *Charles* in the previous year, laden with a cargo of diverse origin, including European re-exports like shoes, stockings, shirts, and gunpowder; colonial produce in the form of rum; and Iberian goods, including wine and oil. In return, Baldridge sent Philipse eleven hundred pieces of eight, some iron, cattle, and thirty-four captives. This, however, was not what Philipse had asked for. Captives, Philipse reiterated, were his "chiefest Profett." The merchant then instructed the pirate in the economics of the shipping business. The fixed costs associated with the *Charles,* including the wages of the crew and depreciation of the vessel, Philipse explained, were about £1,000. Captives, he reckoned, would fetch £30 each, possibly more. Had Baldridge provided him with the two hundred captives he requested, Philipse calculated that he would have cleared £4,000 more than he did from the cargo that had been dispatched (exactly how he received the cattle is not recorded). That Philipse did not end the relationship over the affair suggests both the lack of alternatives and how much he valued having a Madagascar connection. The next year he dispatched a vessel under Captain Samuel Burgess expecting an adjustment of accounts. If that were done to his satisfaction, Philipse said, he would "not be unwilling of a good Correspondence . . . provided it was wth. equall profit and danger on both sides." The matter was presumably resolved, because Philipse continued to do business with Baldridge for two more years.[19]

Philipse's connection with Baldridge and his successors at Saint Mary's provided him with a simple but valuable network, making it much easier to run his operation. The ideal correspondent was trustworthy, someone to whom advances could be made, a form of credit and the lifeblood of the slave trade. Correspondents also sent information on prices and political conditions through the network. Intelligence could only travel as fast as a sailing ship, of course, which between Madagascar and New York amounted to several months, so it was far from perfect. Even so, it was far better to have old intelligence than not to have it at all. Finally, networks allowed merchants like Philipse to carry over accounts. Trade goods and credits could be stored and put toward future voyages. And the more trade there was, the stronger the bond of trust between merchants.[20]

The relationship, however, was not sustainable. In 1697, Baldridge handled a Boston brig called the *Swift.* While the vessel was at Saint Mary's, Baldridge purchased an interest in it and embarked on a trading

voyage. During his absence, Malagasy soldiers attacked Baldridge's settlement, killing about thirty whites and plundering his stores. Three
ships were present at Saint Mary's during the attack, and when one
of them informed Baldridge that his trading post had been destroyed,
he decided to abandon Madagascar for New York. At the root of Baldridge's problems was his business model for procuring captives, which
relied heavily on raiding. As others had learned, seizing captives by force
initially paid because it eliminated the need to procure trade goods, but
it quickly became dangerous and was hardly a route to long-term profitability. Baldridge's role as Philipse's correspondent was soon filled by
a New Englander, Edward Welch, under whose stewardship the pirate/
slave trade of Saint Mary's reached its peak. Welch also seems to have
relied on violence to procure captives, and in 1699 was reported to have
been "dangerously wounded" in a war, although he appears to have survived, prospered, and later died of natural causes in 1708.[21]

Because the New York–Madagascar trade is better documented than
the earlier New England–upper Guinea trade, more is known about its
organization. Although the New York trade was tightly connected with
piracy and the pirate trade, it was far more sophisticated than the haphazard, improvised New England trade of the mid-seventeenth century.
New York's merchants, and Philipse in particular, approached it as they
did other branches of trade, that is, with an understanding that long-
range planning and the construction of networks paved the way toward
serial voyages and resulted in efficiencies of other kinds, all of which
would increase profits.

One area New Yorkers seem to have invested some thought in was
the size of the ships they employed. The New York vessels tended to be
large by colonial standards, full-rigged ships and brigs of up to 160 tons,
capable of carrying 250 or more captives. The New England vessels at
Madagascar seem to have consisted mostly of smaller sloops and brigs,
some as small as 30 tons. These variations may reflect the traders' differing goals. New Yorkers, led by Philipse, were more interested in the slave
trade than in dealing with the pirates and therefore sought larger vessels
to carry more captives, whereas New Englanders, lacking a domestic
market for captives, were more interested in piracy and the pirate trade,

which could be best carried by small, fast vessels. There were exceptions, of course—Philipse's ship *Margaret* was only 50 tons, and the brig *Peter* was only 30 tons—but overall the choice of vessel seems to have reflected the owners' goals and priorities.[22]

The ownership structure for these vessels is much less certain. New England traders replicated the plural ownership structure of the mother country, as surviving charter parties suggest. Comparable information on New York is not available, but the historian Cathy Matson has suggested that plural ownership of vessels was the norm. The *Peter*, which sailed in 1698, had at least three managing partners. Philipse's involvement in 1684 in the *Charles*, which sailed to England and the Netherlands for trade goods, suggests that he partnered with merchants in those locales, but his later correspondence contains no mention of partners. They may have been "silent," or it may be that Philipse preferred sole ownership.[23]

Networks were also important to the New Yorkers, especially Philipse. The existence of a New York–Madagascar network, however unstable, was visible in the choice of ship captains and contrasted sharply with the earlier New England–upper Guinea trade. The New England trade of the mid-seventeenth century had been carried on without any African connections whatsoever. One of the consequences was a total discontinuity in the use of ship captains: not a single one made more than one voyage. As a result, any knowledge gained was lost rather than banked. Philipse's serial voyages over a period of years, made possible by his connections with Baldridge and Welch, meant that he and his shipmasters could learn from their errors and successes. Samuel Burgess, Thomas Mostyn, John Thurber, and Cornelius Jacobs all made at least two voyages for Philipse. As they gained experience, Philipse felt confident enough to grant them wider latitude in their decision-making. His instructions to Samuel Burgess on his second voyage allowed him to trade in the Dutch Mascarenes, an emerging market for captives in the Indian Ocean, if in his judgment it would be profitable. Philipse also compensated his captains well, paying them (in addition to a wage) a 2.5 percent commission on all captives.[24]

As Philipse and the other New Yorkers gained experience in the Madagascar trade, they were able to plan voyages with great precision.

All shipowners instructed their captains. Instructions were functional documents, telling a captain where to go, whom to contact, and what prices to seek. They were also legal documents, coming into play in barratry (maritime fraud) cases and other types of litigation. The level of detail varied. Some instructions were quite brief, allowing the captain great discretion, but others were quite detailed. This sometimes indicated a lack of trust between shipowner and captain, perhaps stemming from a lack of experience on the latter's part. In other cases, it likely reflected the complexity of a voyage carried out over long spans of time and distance. Two sets of instructions from the era have survived, one from Philipse to Samuel Burgess for his voyage of 1698 aboard the *Margaret,* the other from Wenham, Schuyler, and Van Dam to Jonathan Rensselaer, the supercargo of the *Peter* in the same year.[25]

Both sets of instructions highlight the importance of networks. This comes through both in the fact that the instructions name a specific person to contact in Madagascar (Edward Welch, in both cases) and in their familiarity with the geography, winds, and general hazards of the trade. Philipse's instructions were particularly detailed, reflective of his decade of involvement in the Madagascar trade. His instructions to Samuel Burgess in 1698 detailed the route he should take to Saint Mary's and instructed him on precisely which ports he should visit on Madagascar and which he should avoid. Having gained knowledge of the monsoon winds of the Indian Ocean, Philipse advised him to leave Madagascar before mid-September, but also instructed him on what to do if that was not possible. Practical advice followed concerning provisions (purchase before obtaining captives or else local merchants will raise prices) and on dealing with "privateers" (avoid at all costs). He provided further instructions for the ivory trade on the coast of Mozambique, on carrying captives to the Mascarenes, and on the need to guard against attacks by the "Natives." Finally, he reminded Burgess to return to New York before May 1, "Least the cold should injure the Negoros."[26] Wenham, Schuyler, and Van Dam's instructions to Jonathan Rensselaer, supercargo of the *Peter,* were much shorter and less specific than Philipse's but still substantial. They too named Edward Welch as the factor to contact at Saint Mary's, an indication that Welch handled New York cargoes in general and not just Philipse's. They were also more intent on trading with the Mascarenes, informing Rensselaer that he was allowed to shuttle back and forth as he saw fit.[27]

An important part of the organization of the Madagascar trade involved evading customs officials, and this was another topic that received extensive coverage in the instructions. The Madagascar trade was at best semi-legal, one in which vessels tended to take on, in addition to captives, stolen and contraband goods. The owners of the *Peter* gave detailed instructions on exactly where to land in the event that dry goods were part of the cargo. Philipse's instructions on that subject were even more extensive. Burgess was to try to obtain a certificate at Saint Helena, an EIC-controlled island in the South Atlantic, for the India goods he carried, but not at the risk of drawing too much attention to himself. If he had dry goods, he was told to go to South Hampton or East Hampton on Long Island and send a letter to Philipse. The crew was to be put ashore and Burgess was to pretend to have arrived from the West Indies, bound for New England. He would then rendezvous with another Philipse vessel at Barnegat Bay Island off New Jersey. If no vessel met him there in twelve days, he was to go to Cape Henlopen at the entrance to Delaware Bay and await further instructions.[28]

Like all traders, the New Yorkers needed to solve the problem of trade goods, to find the optimal assortment. They succeeded remarkably well, especially when compared with other North American examples. The New Englanders of the mid-seventeenth century, as mentioned earlier, probably relied on a haphazard combination of Barbados rum, Portuguese wine, a few re-exported manufactures, and livestock. Even the more sophisticated New England trade of the eighteenth century was predicated almost entirely on rum exports. The New Yorkers in the Madagascar trade, on the other hand, laded both local produce and European re-exports. Customs declarations filed in New York for four ships show them carrying beer, wine, rum, flour, small arms, and gunpowder. The rest of the cargo, in an apparent effort not to draw attention, was listed as "sundry merchandise." Burgess's declaration for the *Margaret* was slightly more specific, listing Hamburg linens, osnaburg (a coarse linen), hats, and cotton textiles, along with guns, knives, flints, looking glasses, and sewing utensils. Communications not intended for official scrutiny are more revealing. The merchant Barthelmy

Jordan shipped textiles and hatbands "Allamode" aboard the *Margaret,* hoping to receive India goods in exchange. But these outbound cargoes were not necessarily exchanged directly for captives. Rather, they were calculated to appeal to the pirates of Saint Mary's, to be traded for an assortment better suited to the slave trade. Baldridge apparently kept quite detailed records for some of the ships he handled. Liquor, firearms, gunpowder, and luxuries from home (which surprisingly included Bibles) were what the pirates wanted. They also wanted tools and equipment for maintaining their settlements, such as saws and grindstones. For this the New Yorkers received a few captives from Baldridge and Welch, but, more significantly, they received plunder, including India goods, which could be brought to other points on the island, where more captives were available, or which could be carried back to New York to be put aboard future slaving vessels.[29]

Although trading with pirates gave the New Yorkers and smaller numbers of New Englanders access to a much better than usual assortment of trade goods, it could never support a long-term trade. Pirates made unreliable business partners, and even though merchants like Philipse were happy to trade with settled traders like Baldridge and Welch, they understood that havens like Saint Mary's attracted more transient characters who were not interested in developing long-term networks. Philipse, as mentioned, instructed his captains to leave port on the appearance of any "privateer." And the threat was real, as the crew of the *Peter* discovered. On July 13, 1699, a French pirate ship captured the *Peter* while it was slaving off the northern tip of Madagascar. The pirates rifled the vessel and detained the crew for five weeks before releasing them. Then, while taking on stores for the voyage home, more pirates under the command of Evan Jones arrived, seized the *Peter,* and burned their own ship. The trading settlements were not safe, either. Raiding by Baldridge and Welch made their situation untenable, and Saint Mary's was targeted at least twice by local Malagasy. Finally, the illegality of their trade made the vessels and cargoes subject to seizure by authorities, especially once England began its crackdown on piracy and pirate havens. Philipse lost the *Margaret* when it called at the Cape of Good Hope on the return voyage and was seized. Captain

Burgess was even sent to London for trial, although he was ultimately acquitted.[30]

The manning of the vessels in the Madagascar trade also stands apart from the norms of the slave trade at large. The reason for this has everything to do with the close relationship with piracy. Most merchant seamen in this era were paid a daily or monthly wage for their labor. Vessels employed on longer voyages invariably paid monthly wages. The *Margaret* was typical in this respect, paying most of its seamen between 25 and 38 shillings per month, which was actually slightly high by the standard of the era. The ship's officers received more. The second mate and boatswain each received 48 shillings. First mate Weybrand Lazinbey received 3 pounds 10 shillings, along with the right to transport one "privilege Negroe" freight free, as did Benjamin Herring, the ship's carpenter, a reflection of his skill and importance to the voyage. The *Margaret* carried a "doctor," who earned a wage of 30 shillings but also was allowed one privilege slave and 12 pence "head money" for every live captive delivered.[31] This may have stemmed from an awareness of the danger to the captives, and hence to profits, posed by such a long voyage, but it may also reflect the higher degree of organization in the New York trade as compared with the earlier New England trade. But working in the New York–Madagascar trade offered more than a wage. The less adventurous could acquire valuable India goods and silver through side trading, a time-honored (if frowned-upon) perquisite of sailors in all time periods. For the more daring, service aboard a slaver could be free transportation to Saint Mary's and a chance to join the pirates. Some of these eventually took up permanent residence on Madagascar, marrying into local families and contributing to the making of a new hybrid identity known as Betsimisaraka.[32]

Another notable difference between the crews of the New York trade and the crews of the New England trade was the presence of slaves in the former. Although enslaved seamen occasionally did sail aboard New England vessels in the eighteenth century, the New Yorkers apparently used them in greater numbers. Francisco Domingo, whose story began the chapter, was one of two enslaved crew members aboard the *Margaret*. The other, a man named Maramitta, of probable Malagasy origin, belonged to the captain. He may have served as a translator and may have been paid a wage. The presence of men like Maramitta reflected the relative importance of African labor in New York City, where between 10 and 17 percent of the population was enslaved.[33]

Most of the captives that the Americans took on at Madagascar had been enslaved during the formation of the Sakalava Empire, which dominated the western part of the island. At the start of the seventeenth century, Madagascar had no large states; smaller regional polities were the rule. In the late sixteenth or early seventeenth century, a group of elite families, known as the Maroserana, in the southeastern part of the island conquered an area to the west, near the Onilahy River. This kingdom became known as Menabe and was one of two major provinces in what would eventually be known as the Sakalava Empire. A succession struggle in about 1685 led the brother of the ruler of Menabe to conquer lands in the northwestern part of the island. This resulted in the creation of the Boina kingdom, the second major province of the Sakalava Empire. Consolidation of the empire took time, however, and it was still in process during the 1690s, when most of the New York vessels arrived. One of Boina's prizes was the Muslim trading town of Massaliege, which the Sakalava initially sacked but later allowed to continue its activities. The Sakalava built their regional capital near the site of Massaliege in an upland location that protected them from seaborne raids while allowing them to control maritime commerce.[34]

Many of those who wound up in the holds of New York slave ships in 1695–1696 were Vazimba people, the original inhabitants of Menabe, who had been enslaved during Sakalava's northwestern conquests. Sakalava expansion continued to generate captives through the 1690s. The constant strife resulted in the death or enslavement of many of the region's agriculturalists. To replace them, Sakalava raided the interior for captives, some of which were retained for labor and others were sold to Europeans. By 1700, interior peoples had managed to fortify themselves against these raids, forcing the Sakalava to look to the Comoro Islands for captives. Although the New Yorkers disappeared from Madagascar shortly after 1700, the slave trade itself would continue in this manner for some time.[35]

Sakalava was successful at least in part because it had access to European firearms and powder, which it paid for with captives. For a long time, conventional historical wisdom held that African polities were trapped in a "gun-slave cycle," selling captives for firearms, which were then used to wage war to procure more captives. More recently, historians have questioned the concept's blanket application. They note, for example, that the slave trade was well established before guns were widely traded in Africa. They also note the limited utility of guns in certain theaters of warfare, though this certainly varied across the regions.[36] Sakalava exemplifies some of these ambiguities. On one hand, although the expansion began before the widespread availability of firearms, the New Yorkers and others exchanged large numbers of firearms for captives. The coincidence with Sakalava's northwestern campaigns of the 1680s and 1690s suggests that its armies relied heavily on firearms. On the other hand, the historian Jane Hooper cites evidence suggesting that Sakalava's troops were armed primarily with spears, at least before 1700. That date, of course, raises the possibility that Sakalava forces were transitioning toward firearms and that the New Yorkers were part of that. Whatever their military significance, Hooper argues that guns had a ceremonial function for the rulers of Sakalava, who for centuries afterward kept two muskets from the era as ritual objects. In the final analysis, although guns may have been a factor in the Sakalava conquests at the end of the seventeenth century, weighing their military value against their psychological and ritual values is difficult to do with confidence.[37]

To Hooper's point, it is clear that even though New York vessels carried guns, most of their cargoes consisted of different types of goods. The accounts of Philipse's *Margaret,* the only detailed document on the question, reveal that he shipped three chests, containing a total of 106 firearms of all descriptions, including "gunns," pistols, blunderbusses, and "privateer gunns" (likely a cousin to the small muskets known as "buccaneer guns"), along with flints and powder. But these were outstripped by other goods: three chests of cloth, thread, and hats; eight casks of beads and personal ornaments, hatchets, and tobacco; eleven hogsheads of rum and twenty-three barrels of wine; and eleven half barrels of sugar. Philipse did not list the values, so it is impossible to say how much the guns were worth in New York, much less what they sold for in Madagascar, but by volume they took only a fraction of the cargo space. The cargo of the *Margaret* was, by the standards of the American slave trade, remarkably "well-sorted."[38]

To procure captives, the New Yorkers dealt both with the pirates and with Sakalava. Saint Mary's played an important role, less as a place to embark captives and more as a place to exchange rum for India goods and silver, both of which could be used to purchase captives. In fact, fame notwithstanding, Saint Mary's seems to have failed as a slave-trading station. Philipse's complaint that Baldridge had embarked only thirty-four of a desired two hundred captives was probably symptomatic of an inability to establish strong ties with the Malagasy in general and Sakalava in particular. Consonant with that idea is the fact that both Baldridge and Welch appear to have had to raid for captives, though presumably with the help of Malagasy allies. Their experience contrasts to some extent with that of Abraham Samuel, the Martinican pirate of mixed ancestry who became famous as the "king" of Madagascar's Fort Dauphin. Samuel was incorporated into the local Malagasy lineage by virtue of being the "lost" son of a local elite family (or so everyone was content to agree). He used these ties to ascend to power and wage war to procure captives, which he sold to visiting slavers. Despite his integration into the local society, Samuel's continuing ties to pirates apparently caused him problems with some Malagasy, and he was forced to live in a veritable fortress. He died in about 1705 after a military expedition.[39]

Although Saint Mary's furnished some captives, New Yorkers could not rely solely on them and therefore regularly visited other ports on Madagascar. Most of these were on the western coast of the island, in areas controlled by Sakalava. Firearms would of course have been in demand in these places, but personal items such as beads and bracelets were also popular. Philipse, demonstrating familiarity with both the geography and the dynamics of slave supply, instructed Burgess to go to "Port Dauphin" if no captives were available at Saint Mary's. "Mattatanna" (Matitanana, on the southeast coast) was another place Philipse sent his vessels, and at least three are documented as having called there. Saint Augustine, on the southwestern coast, was yet another place mentioned by Philipse and several other American traders as well positioned to tap the flow of captives from Sakalava. Indeed, Burgess was aboard the *Margaret* at Saint Augustine when Wenham, Schuyler, and Van Dam's *Peter* was seized by pirates. With the exception of Samuel at Fort Dauphin, trade at these and other locations would have been negotiated directly with the Malagasy. Given the comparative remoteness of Saint Mary's, along with the pirates' failure to establish trust and stable ties with the local population, it appears that the New Yorkers used the island primarily as a point of initial exchange, a place to careen and provision, while procuring most of their captives from ports on the other side of the island.[40]

European and American traders also raided for captives, usually in cooperation with the Malagasy. Baldridge and Welch both did so, and sailor Henry Watson reported that the Malagasy allowed their pirate allies at Saint Mary's half of any captives they took in a raid. Two of Philipse's vessels were reported to have allied with Sakalava in an attack for the purpose of gaining captives. One of Philipse's vessels, trading up the coast toward Massaliege, spotted a column of smoke, the universal invitation to trade. The men came ashore and soon allied with Tsimanato, the Sakalava conqueror of Boina. The deal was simple: Tsimanato furnished provisions, and the vessels sent twenty of their men to help seize a "great city," for which they received a large number of captives (reportedly six thousand, but that is surely a great exaggeration). With too many captives to carry, the vessels left twenty men with Tsimanato, who promised to furnish more captives whenever the vessels returned. The ships reportedly did return, providing passage home for those of the twenty who wanted to go. Their efforts helped to extend Tsimanato's conquests while generating captives for the New York trade.[41]

The Navigation Act of 1696, the reaffirmation of the EIC monopoly, and the anti-piracy legislation of 1698 effectively outlawed the New York–Madagascar slave trade. Illegality was never an obstacle in itself, as Philipse's voyages of around 1700–1703 suggest. The crackdown did, however, raise the level of risk associated with this trade, which was already considerable given the enormous distances involved, to say nothing of the unpredictability inherent to consorting with pirates. The outbreak of the War of the Spanish Succession in 1701 combined with these factors to end the trade. War brought opportunities in the form of privateering commissions, which in the past had fueled the Madagascar trade, but with new regulations in place, merchants were more likely to use them as intended. After all, raiding enemy shipping closer to home was still quite profitable. The partial lifting of the RAC's monopoly in 1698 was another, perhaps unexpected, nail in the coffin of the New York–Madagascar trade. For a 10 percent fee on exported goods, it gave American slave traders a chance to trade legitimately in West Africa, which was much nearer than Madagascar. Finally, the New York trade had been spurred in part by its own domestic demand for captives. But that market was not infinite, and the dozen or so Madagascar voyages likely satisfied local demand for some time.

The death of Frederick Philipse in 1702 was another factor in bringing about an end to the trade. It is rare for a single individual to have such an impact on a branch of commerce; structural and economic factors are almost always more influential. But Philipse so utterly dominated the New York–Madagascar trade—he was responsible for about 60 percent of known voyages—that his death was nearly sufficient to bring it to an end. At least one historian has speculated that Philipse abandoned the slave trade with the seizure of the *Margaret* and the arrest of the captain, Samuel Burgess, in 1699 at the Cape of Good Hope. The *Margaret* was condemned, the captives sold on the spot, and the vessel and remaining cargo, valued at £20,000, were sold in Bombay. Hoping to make an example of Burgess, the EIC took him to London for trial before the High Court of Admiralty. Because he had sailed before the crackdown on trading with pirates, and with clearance from Bellamont, Burgess was charged with having engaged in piracy in the early 1690s. Philipse, sensing danger, dispatched his son, Adolph Philipse, to help defend Burgess. As a member of the anti-Leislerian faction, Philipse also used his political influence with the Tory Party. Burgess was convicted, but the lobbying apparently worked, and he was eventually pardoned. Still, the notion that Philipse quit the slave trade as a result of the loss of the *Margaret* seems to be untrue. At the same time that Burgess was in London, two of his vessels were helping Tsimanato raid for captives. Only death seems to have stopped Philipse's slaving.[42]

The New York–Madagascar slave trade was inevitably short-lived. It emerged in the legal seam between the RAC and EIC, and it depended on pirates who, in addition to becoming targets for metropolitan authorities, procured their captives through violence. Pirate attacks on slave ships, the Malagasy attacks on Saint Mary's, the seizure of vessels and cargoes by the EIC, and the need to have crew members join in local wars all made for an unsustainable trade. Merchants tend to prefer calm pursuits, with low risk, predictability, and steady profits, all of which require networks. The New York–Madagascar trade, although more sophisticated than the New England–upper Guinea trade, was only marginally less ephemeral. To enjoy a consistent and profitable slave trade, American merchants would need to solve the problems of trade goods and networks.

Part Two

SLAVERS AS BRITONS

1700–1775

Newport, Rhode Island, December 5, 1752.

ON A LATE fall evening, with the smell of tar and molasses hanging in the air, a group of men met at the residence of Captain John Lawton. After some discussion, they agreed on articles for a "Fellowship-Club," whose membership would consist of two-thirds "Commanders of vessels" and one-third from the "other Professions." James Cahoone, who had skippered at least three Guineamen, was there, along with John Easton, who had completed his second of an eventual six African voyages just a few years earlier. John Duncan was there, although he did not skipper his first slaver for another five years, as was the young Peter Dordin, who was still ten years from commanding his first Guineaman. Several more captains who were at sea when the meeting was held joined in the coming months, men such as Benjamin Hicks, who took six ships to Africa and whose son would captain one, and Caleb Godfrey, a veteran of the trade since at least the 1730s, perhaps even before that. Over the years, most of Newport's slave-ship captains (along with others who shipped aboard slavers as ordinary seamen and mates but never captained one) joined the Fellowship Club, which was eventually rechristened the Marine Society and lasted well into the nineteenth century.[1]

The purpose of the club was to provide members with rudimentary insurance against death and disability, as well as a small subsidy in old age. Members pledged to attend each other's funerals or face a

---

Previous page: Cape Coast Castle, a British slave-trading fort on the Gold Coast. In the decades before 1775, American slavers operated almost entirely on British networks, with the Gold Coast as the most frequent destination for their vessels. (Captain John Matthews, "Colonial Fort in West Africa, circa 1797 March," Captain John Matthews Papers, Courtesy of Princeton University Library)

four-shilling fine and could be expelled for drunkenness, although we can probably assume they defined intoxication in generous terms. The twelfth article, however, was ultimately no less important: members pledged to share intelligence on navigation and geography, which was to be recorded in the club's books. None of this information survives, but we can be certain that plenty was shared, for if there is any one historical constant across maritime societies, it is that sailors tell sea stories. They tell them largely for entertainment's sake, but these stories also serve a secondary function, which is to convey information and advice about the maritime world. Newport's Fellowship Club was not the only place to exchange information—taverns and coffeehouses in port towns everywhere functioned similarly—but it helped to make Newport into the continent's premier slaving port. No town in North America possessed a comparable reservoir of knowledge about the transatlantic slave trade. The Fellowship Club, then, did more than signal Newport's dominance in the slave trade: it helped to perpetuate it.[2]

The existence of the Fellowship Club was emblematic of a fundamental change in the nature of the American slave trade. If seventeenth-century American slavers traded as residents of isolated, underdeveloped colonial outposts, their eighteenth-century descendants traded as inhabitants of more populous, more economically varied settlements that aspired—successfully, for the most part—to become British provincial towns. Regarding the slave trade in particular, several developments stand out. The first of these was the rise of Newport, Rhode Island, as the undisputed center of the North American slave trade. Like their counterparts in Bristol and Liverpool, Newport's merchants developed specialized knowledge and expertise, which they used to dominate slave trading for the rest of the century. A second emblem of their status as provincials was their embeddedness in British commercial networks. London was the center of their financial universe, and almost all of their trade was conducted within the framework of British mercantilism, with captives purchased from British factors in Africa and sold in British colonies. In contrast to the amateurs and pirates of the previous century, slavers in this era were regarded by metropolitan merchants as valuable, if perhaps somewhat provincial, commercial partners, which is to say as fellow Britons. Finally, whereas traders of the previous period had to gather trade goods from the metropole, from the Caribbean, and from the pirate trade, traders in this era manufactured their own trade good. Dependable access to a trade good was one of the most important factors that allowed the American slavers to go from transporting just more than 4,000 captives in the seventeenth century to embarking 121,000 between 1700 and 1775, a thirtyfold increase. The discovery of a trade good was so important that it inspired a nickname that applied to both the traders and the vessels: rum men.

Newport and the Rise of the Rum Men, 1700–1750

I n the late seventeenth and early eighteenth centuries, American interest in slave trading was slowly rising. Merchants in several ports sent out exploratory voyages. Boston and New York both continued their activities of the previous century. But perhaps the most notable efforts involved several ventures organized in the plantation colonies. Their trade differed from New England's in that it was designed not to earn credits in London but to supply a domestic slave market. However, as peripheral markets for captive labor, these colonies were perpetually underserved by the RAC, whose vessels arrived at unpredictable intervals and often only when the larger Caribbean markets were saturated. The Chesapeake colonies of Virginia and Maryland, for example, together received a grand total of only twenty-five RAC shipments before 1712, which accounted for less than one-quarter of the total number of captives imported. Virginia and Maryland had hitherto relied very heavily on the intra-American and interloper trades, but these lay beyond local control, so they dispatched several experimental ventures to Africa. These turn-of-the-century Chesapeake expeditions were an effort to supplement the other sources and to ensure a more steady supply of captives.[1]

Chesapeake residents organized a handful of voyages in the 1680s and 1690s, in violation of the RAC monopoly. In 1694, for example,

Maryland's Richard Hill attempted to get clearance for the *Hope* to sail to Africa. The local customs collector denied his request, as did the colonial governor, citing his instructions to enforce the company monopoly. Hill ignored the injunction and sent the *Hope* to the Bight of Biafra, one of the few American vessels ever to trade in that part of Africa, and the vessel delivered captives to the Patuxent River in Maryland the following year. More colonials became involved after 1698, when the trade was opened to anyone willing to pay the 10 percent surcharge on goods exported to Africa. William Byrd I, one of the richest planters in Virginia, attempted to get into the action, though apparently while he was based in England. He partnered with several London factors, including the Huguenot refugee and glass-bead wholesaler Daniel Jamineau and the tobacco merchant Micaiah Perry, a native of New Haven, Connecticut, whose family had returned to England at the onset of the Civil War. All but Byrd had been or would be involved in additional slave-trading voyages. The partners' *William and Jane* sailed from London to Senegambia in 1698–1699, and even paid the RAC's 10 percent duty. While trading off Portudal, the vessel was seized by the French for violating the monopoly of the Senegal Company. After a diplomatic protest, the French responded by acknowledging an English right to trade in Senegambia and suggested uniting to exclude the Dutch. The outcome for Byrd and his partners, however, is uncertain, but we do know that Virginians organized few voyages after that.[2]

Carolinians were more persistent in their efforts, but Charles Town (as Charleston was called at the time) never became a major embarkation port for slave-trading vessels during the colonial era. It had every reason to, since in that era, like Virginia, Carolina was a second-rank plantation colony that was underserved by the RAC. For a moment at the start of the eighteenth century, it appeared that Charles Town might actually become a major dispatch point for African voyages. William Rhett, a mariner and sometime privateer, had a hand in at least seven voyages between 1700 and 1705, mostly to Senegambia. But his list of exported wares suggests one reason why so few voyages originated in Charles Town: Carolinians struggled, as most Americans did, to assemble a suitable assortment of trade goods. Some of the exported goods, such as tar and pitch, were clearly of local origin, surely intended for the fleet of vessels maintained by the RAC forts. The agricultural goods, like beef, were likely destined for the same market. Rum, of probable Barbadian origin, also featured prominently in most of these cargoes. Seemingly aware that these goods could not support a profitable African trade on their own, the Carolinians supplemented their cargoes with large quantities of re-exported European manufactures, including guns, swords, stockings, and woolens. They also carried Asian textiles, which, given Carolina's status as a haven for pirates, probably originated as plunder in the Indian Ocean. Although Carolina would continue to send out slaving vessels throughout the colonial period, a steady inflow of imported (and probably illicit) trade goods was required to sustain it at a high level. Given the expense and difficulty of securing these goods, this was unlikely ever to be the case.[3]

Lack of a trade good certainly played a role in Charles Town's failure to become a major dispatcher of slaving vessels, but so did its status as a plantation colony. On one hand, Carolina possessed a true seaport in Charles Town, and one that would eventually become North America's leading disembarkation point for African captives. But although importing captives and dispatching vessels were both considered "the slave trade," they were in reality completely different pursuits. One was primarily a maritime enterprise, involving the organization of voyages and predicated on access to ships and skilled mariners, or ships going out. The other was principally a commission merchant or factorage business and focused on serving the plantations, or ships coming in. Both pursuits required great amounts of capital and credit, the former for outfitting vessels and hiring crews, and the latter for covering the debts of the planters, who usually purchased on credit. Bilateral trading by plantation colonies was far from unknown, but combining and financing all of these activities was very difficult. The Brazilian slave trade, the largest and most successful of all bilateral trades, flourished because it was organized on a very different basis from the North Atlantic trades, in ways that made it easier for merchants to address questions of finance and trade goods.[4]

But the most important reason for Carolina's failure to develop a strong bilateral trade was simply that it had other ways of securing laborers, all of which were easier and cheaper than organizing its own transatlantic trade. Early settlers enslaved Indians, who of course did not need to be transported across the ocean (unless to be sold elsewhere). They also imported African laborers via the intra-American trade. Unlike transatlantic vessels, which needed to carry large numbers of people aboard a dedicated vessel in order to be profitable, the intra-American trade could be conducted on a small scale by any vessel on a routine voyage to the Caribbean. Finally, the number of captives supplied by metropolitan carriers, who possessed the necessary capital and experience, grew steadily, obviating the need for Carolinians to organize a trade themselves. The repeal of the RAC's vestigial monopoly in 1712 and a lengthy peace (on the high seas if not on the North American continent) between 1714 and 1739 helped the situation. In the long run, then, the failure of the Charles Town merchants to become major players in the slave trade stemmed from the fact that their interest was primarily in importing captives. As long their needs were met, they had little incentive to organize their own voyages.[5]

The northern colonies had different, but for them more compelling, reasons to engage in the transatlantic slave trade. Unlike Carolina, they did not seek primarily to supply their own markets, although New York stands as a partial exception to the rule. Between 1700 and 1776, about 45 percent of all voyages organized in New York were bilateral, against about 9 percent for New England, concentrated in the first half of the century. The northerners' main purpose was to pay their transatlantic debts by earning credits in the form of bills of exchange on British mercantile houses—that is to say, the very same reason the Bostonians entered the business in the 1650s. By the eighteenth century, however, their trade imbalance had grown in tandem with colonial consumer culture. New Englanders consumed increasing quantities of cloth, hardware, and luxuries, some originating in British workshops, others representing Indian re-exports, but almost all of them arriving courtesy of metropolitan ships and merchants. As historians have long known, the colonies financed their purchases not by exporting goods to Britain, but through the "carrying trade," which generated "invisible earnings," or credits not represented in import-export figures, consisting of shipping charges and commissions, as well as simple profits from buying low and selling high. Quantifying these earnings has proven difficult, but there can be no doubt that their value was very significant, likely exceeding the value of all colonial exports except tobacco. The North American transatlantic slave trade before 1776 was, in essence, merely another branch of this carrying trade. It also more or less tracked the rise and fall of the colonial current account deficit, suggesting once again that its economic function was, in a large part, to finance consumption.[6]

Over the first quarter of the eighteenth century, Massachusetts, Rhode Island, and New York dispatched vessels in roughly equal numbers. In the 1720s, however, Rhode Island began to increase its share. Then suddenly, during the 1730s, the number of voyages departing from Rhode Island increased almost ninefold, from nine to seventy-nine. Massachusetts and New York increased their participation as well, but much more modestly. Rhode Island's surge bears a strong relationship to the emergence of the Gold Coast as an important source of captives. Before about 1725, most captives carried aboard American vessels probably came from Senegambia. After 1730, most came from the Gold Coast (the wartime decade of the 1740s notwithstanding), with a more pronounced surge after 1750. The 1730s, then, saw a transformation of the American slave trade. Rhode Island (meaning Newport, in this context) emerged as the clear center of a trade that now focused on the Gold Coast. What changed? The answer to that question is complex. Conditions in Africa played an important role and will be explored shortly. In North America, at least two factors seem to have played a role early on: competition with Boston and New York, and Rhode Island's monetary policy. These two factors allowed Newport merchants to establish a small advantage over other colonial merchants at a crucial moment in the 1730s. Newporters were then able to increase their advantage by building networks and accumulating experience on the African coast, which compounded over time and allowed the town to dominate through the colonial era (charts 2 and 3).

Rhode Island's trade at the beginning of the eighteenth century fell squarely within the economic shadow of Massachusetts. The Bay Colony's population of about 55,900 in 1700 was almost exactly ten times Rhode Island's. But perhaps a better measure of Massachusetts's economic dominance can be found in the size of its merchant fleet,

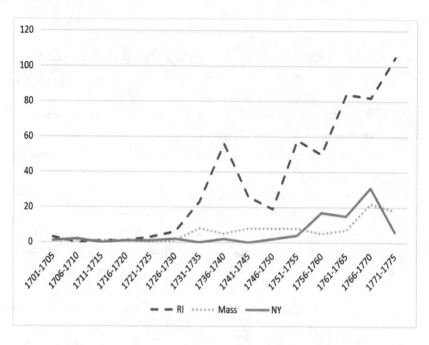

Chart 2. Number of voyages organized in Rhode Island, Massachusetts, and New York, 1701–1775. (Data from *Slave Voyages,* www.slavevoyages.org/voyages/epTDFEqh)

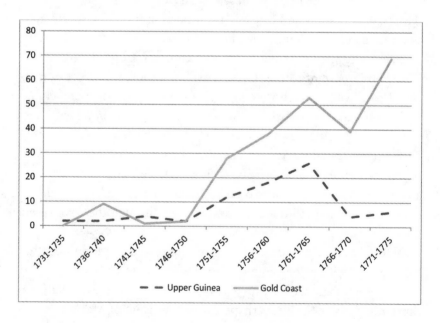

Chart 3. Destinations of Rhode Island, Massachusetts, and New York slave vessels, 1731–1775. (Data from *Slave Voyages,* www.slavevoyages.org/voyages/uJneTNa1)

which numbered 171 oceangoing vessels (8,500 tons) in 1698, comparable to the British ports of Liverpool, Whitby, and Yarmouth. Rhode Island punched above its weight, boasting a fleet of 29 vessels in 1708 (all but 2 of which were smaller, single-masted sloops) and a population of 140 "seafaring men," but it hardly presented a serious challenge to Massachusetts. With this fleet, Rhode Island exported lumber, staves, pork, foodstuffs, and horses in exchange for West Indian sugar and molasses, Carolina rice, pitch, and deerskins, Pennsylvania flour, and Madeira wine.[7]

Newport's merchants undoubtedly profited from these trades, but they failed to break into the most lucrative and prestigious trade of all—direct commerce with Britain. The importation of luxuries and manufactures was almost entirely in the hands of Boston merchants, with Rhode Island as part of their economic hinterland. Newport merchants chafed at their dependence on Boston and on the higher prices that entailed. Rhode Islanders circumvented Boston when they could, purchasing luxuries and manufactures in the Caribbean and the Chesapeake, but these carried similar, if not higher, costs. Direct trade with Britain became a paramount goal. Thomas Richardson, a Boston merchant who came to Newport in 1712, devoted much energy to establishing a direct trade with Britain but met with little success. Newport merchants, then, needed to find ways to pay the Bostonians who acted as regional middlemen.[8]

Transatlantic slave trading was one of many ways to earn the bills of exchange needed to pay the merchants in Boston and elsewhere. Bills could be obtained through any of the carrying trades in which Rhode Islanders were engaged, but the transatlantic slave trade was a particularly effective way to get them. Commodified human beings are among the least bulky cargoes, second only to specie. Captives were usually worth more than any return cargo of sugar or molasses, so vessels returning home to Newport after carrying captives to the Caribbean often made up the difference by carrying bills. These bills, drawn on mercantile firms in Britain (with London being the preferred location), were essentially instructions for the merchant to transfer credits from one person's account to another's, much like checks drawn on a modern bank. Bills drawn on reliable sources (and there was an element of caveat emptor to the system) were in great demand and could be bought, sold, and circulated. Newport merchants used them to finance their European imports, but since Rhode Island never established a robust direct trade, many of these bills found their way to Boston.

Newport's rise as a slave-trading center was not inevitable and it did not follow a straight path. In 1700, nobody would have foreseen that the small town on the southern tip of Aquidneck Island would be the center of the American slave trade for most of the century. Other colonies and ports showed interest in the transatlantic slave trade, and some of these were larger and could muster greater resources. Newport began the century as one of several towns making forays into the slave trade and only separated itself from the others in the 1730s. This raises two related questions: Why Newport, and why the 1730s?

To begin with, it is helpful to think of Newport not just as a port town, but as what social scientists call a commercial "cluster" or "agglomeration." These two terms, largely interchangeable, have been used to explore why cities often specialize in a particular trade, or conversely, why some trades become concentrated in certain locales. In this instance, the concept of a commercial cluster helps to explain why Newport, with a small population and limited hinterland, came to dominate the North American slave trade over larger cities like Boston and New York. The economic literature on clusters emphasizes three main factors to explain why the domination of certain trades tends to be not distributed randomly throughout a geographic area but rather concentrated in certain spots. The first of these is that geographic concentration and the resulting proximity of related businesses creates economic efficiencies. In the example of Newport, it was less costly and more profitable for rum distillers to locate themselves close to their supply of molasses and to the buyers who exported their finished product. Second, agglomeration theorists argue that competing businesses often locate near each other because they hire from the same labor market. Merchants who need to hire ship captains, riggers, and other laborers situate themselves in places where these are abundant, and Newport, as the fifth-largest port in North America, had plenty of these. Finally, and perhaps most relevant for this discussion, clustering creates a pool of specialized skill and knowledge, which confers economic benefits. Newport's accrued knowledge of Africa and slave trading was in this way comparable to Silicon Valley's know-how in chip manufacturing and software coding.[9]

Newport's plunge into the slave trade during the 1730s gave it an advantage in experience that became self-perpetuating. This was true not only of the merchants and shipowners, who through trial and error grew increasingly familiar with African geography and markets, but also among mariners. Shipmasters acted as the agents for the merchants who sent them. Communications being what they were, captains were called on to make vital decisions as circumstances changed. In the 1730s a cohort emerged of "Guinea captains," or skippers who were experienced in slave trading and who accumulated knowledge over serial voyages: George Scott, Pollipus Hammond, Caleb Godfrey, John Godfrey, Thomas Teakle Taylor, and others. Meanwhile, a second generation was apprenticed to the trade, serving ships' officers. As early as 1740 there was a sense in Newport's maritime community that expertise mattered in the slave trade. John Gunthorp, a factor in Antigua, told Abraham Redwood that Captain Francis Pope "has not the qualifications necessary to carry on that trade to advantage," and urged that he be limited to Caribbean trade. Pope, who had actually commanded a vessel on a previous African voyage, never skippered another slaver. As will be shown in chapter 4, Newport's accumulated expertise in slave trading meant that when merchants elsewhere organized voyages, they often turned to Newport for their captains. Slave-trading experience thus remained concentrated in Newport.[10]

The second answer to the questions "Why Newport?" and "Why the 1730s?" has to do with political developments in Rhode Island. Although the documents do not allow for the establishment of a strong causal connection, it seems that Newport's entry into the African trade in the 1730s was eased by the colony's monetary policy. Rhode Island, like all of the colonies, had a chronic problem with its circulating medium of exchange. Specie, particularly silver, was valued the most, but it was also quite scarce and often went to pay debts incurred in Boston and London. Bills of exchange circulated as well, but good bills were often scarce and available only at a premium. During the War of the Spanish Succession (1701–1714), the New England colonies began experimenting with another system: paper money. In principle, a colonial legislature could authorize a loan in the form of a currency emission. Farmers and merchants could then borrow the currency, putting up land as collateral, and use it for their activities. After a set period of time, the loan would come due and the borrowers would have to repay the legislature, which would then retire the notes. In practice, however, it was politically difficult to demand full repayment, so legislatures had a tendency to extend forbearance. And despite opposition from the mercantile elite, who could not use colonial currency to pay their British debts, it proved politically expedient to authorize additional emissions. The literal printing of money led inevitably to inflation, but since it was in essence a loan, it also boosted the regional economy, as borrowers invested the funds in all manner of enterprises, from land speculation to commerce.[11]

Colonial currency emissions helped to finance Newport's rise to dominance in the slave trade. When the emissions began in the 1710s, Rhode Island was effectively part of a wider New England currency union. All of the region's colonies had the ability to issue paper money, and they adhered to the exchange rate of £133.33 New England currency to £100 sterling, as set out in Stuart-era decrees and legislation. This "New England currency," or "Old Tenor," circulated widely throughout the region in the early eighteenth century. Massachusetts, as the largest and most economically powerful of the colonies, led the way, with the smaller colonies usually following in its wake. Rhode Island authorized nine currency emissions totaling £820,000 between 1715 and 1751, repeatedly postponing the repayment dates. There was some opposition among elite merchants in Newport, since they could not use the currency to pay obligations outside of New England. Even so, because Rhode Island was an economic appendage of Boston, opposition was not as strong as it might have been. Beginning in 1730, the Board of Trade in London, alarmed at the proliferation of inflated currency, issued instructions forbidding the postponement of loan repayment. Massachusetts, as a royal colony, had to comply, which meant the notes needed to be redeemed by taxation and removed from circulation. Rhode Island, as a charter colony, considered itself not subject to Board of Trade authority and so continued to issue notes without redeeming them. Massachusetts residents, desperate for a circulating medium as their own notes were retired, began using Rhode Island currency.[12]

Whether Rhode Islanders saw currency games as a deliberate strategy to break Boston's hold over them or whether they simply saw them as a general economic boon is not certain. Bostonians certainly perceived Rhode Island's shenanigans as a revolt against their hegemony, and there can be little doubt that Newport gained from the policy. As one Bostonian pamphleteer complained in 1731, "With this Money [Rhode Island merchants] fitted out at least Thirty Sail of Vessels for Martineco, Surranam, Jamaica, & our Leeward Islands, [and] bring their Molasses, Sugar, & other Goods from those Places direct hither.... This keeps their trade going to the best advantages." The writer omitted mention of the slave trade, likely since it had yet to surge, but the emissions surely helped to fund the seventy-eight African voyages launched in the colony between 1731 and 1740. Moreover, currency emissions advantaged Newporters specifically, for although the notes circulated throughout New England, the system used to place them in circulation, in which borrowers applied for loans to a board appointed by the governor, meant that Rhode Islanders with political connections received them first. In sum, even though a direct causal relationship cannot be established, circumstances strongly suggest that Rhode Island's decision to continue printing money without redeeming it, at a time when Massachusetts was forced to impose taxes and repay its loans, gave Newport merchants an advantage at a pivotal moment. With the passage of the Currency Act of 1751, Parliament forced the colonies to back their paper with silver and thus ended Rhode Island's currency hijinks. By this time, Newporters had parlayed a momentary advantage in the African trade into lasting dominance.[13]

Without goods that appealed to African consumers, there could have been no slave trade. The major colonial exports—fish, lumber, rice, and tobacco—were all produced in Africa. Of these, only tobacco found any demand at all. In the previous century, organizers wrestled with the problem of trade goods. Since American produce had little value in Africa (outside of the European forts), trade goods would have to come from elsewhere, via the carrying trade. Wine, via Madeira and the Canaries, and livestock appear to have been the solution for the earliest voyages, but they did not solve the problem. India goods via the Madagascar pirate trade of the 1690s furnished a temporary solution. However, the supply route could not survive the crackdown on Indian Ocean piracy.[14]

A lasting solution appeared toward the end of the seventeenth century in the form of rum. Cane spirits first appeared in the Anglo-American colonies in the middle of the seventeenth century. The industry was centered in the Caribbean, Barbados initially. The precise date when Barbadians began making rum is uncertain. The earliest reference to distilling in Barbados dates to 1631, only four years after English settlement began. However, Frederick H. Smith, the foremost historian of Caribbean rum, has registered doubt about whether it was rum that was being distilled, since cane was not yet grown on the island. Whatever the case, the first clear reference to rum distillation on Barbados dates to 1647, and it seems to have been solidly established shortly thereafter. The North American colonies were an important market from the start, importing most of the island's considerable output.[15]

Within a few decades—the precise timing is obscure—New Englanders began to produce their own rum from Caribbean molasses. Puritan settlers were distilling alcohol from grain as early as the 1640s, but high grain prices drove them to explore alternatives. Rum distilling appears to have been well established in Massachusetts by the 1660s, enough to arouse official concern. Much of this product was channeled into the Newfoundland fisheries trade, but it was also consumed locally. Rhode Island's first recorded distillery was running by 1684 in Providence, although it is hard to imagine Newport without one before that time. By the eve of the American Revolution, Newport had surpassed New York and Philadelphia and rivaled Boston in output. New England rum was crude, lacking in color and harsh to the taste. Most colonists preferred the West Indian variety but made do with the local distillation as needed. It was also high-proof, which meant that small amounts could be shipped and then watered at the point of sale.[16]

Barbadian merchants likely pioneered the rum-for-captives trade, but the North Americans were not far behind. Early traders like John

Parris had strong ties to Barbados, and we know that Frederick Philipse's vessels carried rum to Madagascar in the 1690s. William Rhett's Carolina vessels of the 1700s also carried spirits. The origin of the rum on these voyages, however, is an open question. No doubt American vessels at times carried both the domestic and the West Indian product, but the overwhelming dominance of Barbados in distilling implies that most of the rum carried in the early eighteenth century came from there. Further support can be found in the rum-for-captives trade between Barbados and Africa, which began toward the end of the seventeenth century but really flourished in the first two decades of the eighteenth century. It is usually thought of as a bilateral trade, but about one in ten vessels clearing for Africa from Barbados was actually based in North America. Merchants in New England, New York, and Pennsylvania likely partnered with their Barbadian correspondents to organize voyages. They sent their vessels on complex, multilateral itineraries, from North America to Barbados for rum, to Africa for captives, back to Barbados for sugar and molasses, and finally home to the mainland. The *Mary*, which sailed in 1701 and whose owners included Andrew Belcher from one of Boston's great merchant clans, came to Barbados by way of Madeira before sailing on to Africa.[17]

The voyage of the *Hawke* is a good example of this New England–Barbados–Africa trade. Built in Bristol, Massachusetts, in 1706, it was owned by Jonathan Belcher and William Foye of Boston, in partnership with John Harbin of Barbados. The captain, Richard Thomas, made his career sailing out of Boston and was regularly employed by the Belcher clan. In 1707, the *Hawke* sailed for Barbados. Its cargo is unrecorded but likely included the usual fish, lumber, and foodstuffs. At Barbados, the *Hawke* took on 4,089 gallons of rum, along with 116 pewter basins and 650 perpets (or perpetuans, an English woolen). This combination of rum with manufactures was in fact typical of the cargoes carried from Barbados to Africa. The *Hawke* paid its 10 percent duty to the RAC and ultimately carried 131 captives back to Barbados.[18]

Whether from Barbados or New England, rum was not without its drawbacks. Leakage, intrinsic to the commodity itself, would trouble slavers for as long as the rum trade was carried on. Jay Coughtry has suggested that leakage of 5 to 10 percent was "considered standard," but sometimes ran as high as 20 percent and in extreme cases to 50 percent. John McCusker estimates a slightly higher average leakage of 15 percent. Whatever the case, rum and other liquids required "tight," as opposed to "slack," casks. Tight casks were made of special woods and were always stowed on their sides, bunghole up, never on end. Whether as a result of ignorance or shoddy workmanship, complaints about leaky casks and poor stowage were perennial. A Boston lawsuit in 1738 hinged on the quality of the casks carried aboard a slave ship. According to a British sailor who claimed to have observed rum stowage aboard several American slavers, the tuns aboard this particular ship "Suffered a great Deal of Leakage for want of [iron] bound Casks," and implied that they were also larger than the optimum size. Leaked rum could also spoil other goods in the hold. One captain discovered, just was he was about to make payment, that a rum spill had ruined his tobacco.[19]

Two other problems with rum will receive full discussion shortly but are worth mentioning briefly here. One was rum's tendency to glut African markets, and the other was that it drew the Americans into over-reliance on a single trade good. These two factors frequently worked in tandem to undercut profitability. Merchants seem to have understood this from the start and did what they could to diversify their cargoes, or, in the language of the slave trade, to improve their "assortments." That was sooner said than done, however. In 1740 a Newport merchant apparently imported some dry goods that he hoped to sell to the town's slave traders. The goods, however, were "not a proper Sortment," meaning that they were not of the type preferred by African consumers, and some of the goods were apparently in poor condition from having made the trip there once already. Other merchants tried to sell locally made pewterware in Africa. New York actually experienced a pewter shortage in 1748 when Guineamen bought up all available supplies. Pewter worked as a supplemental trade good in small quantities, especially in upper Guinea, but it was similarly prone to gluts. Three years after New York shipped all of its extra pewter to Africa, an official from the Company of Merchants Trading to Africa (CMTA, successor to the RAC) on the Gambia River informed the Board of Trade that "Pewter will not sell here."[20]

Foodstuffs were another minor good carried aboard American slavers. These were produced both in New England and in the other continental colonies and included pork, beef, flour, and vegetables. Onions, of all things, were among the most common food items. Africans produced foodstuffs, of course, and were not generally in the market for American produce. In fact, the reverse was true: American slavers depended on Africans for food. But there was a market for produce at the European forts and on the ships. American produce not only allowed the forts' personnel to consume familiar fare, it helped feed the castle and shipping slaves, offsetting the traders' dependence on African sources. And, as one of the governors in Senegambia noted, in addition to food for cooking, American produce could be used to "cook the books." Responding to complaints that he overspent on African foodstuffs, John Barnes told the CMTA that some governors profited by paying their garrisons in cheap imported produce instead of the more expensive local goods and then pocketing the difference.[21]

Nonfood items of American origin frequently appeared in the holds of American slavers. Spermaceti candles, the prime market for which was fort and ship personnel, were common wares. But by far the most important American product—second only to rum—was tobacco, mostly obtained from the Chesapeake. Tobacco, however, could never be more than a small supplement to American rum cargoes, for the simple reason that by the eighteenth century it was grown in much of coastal Africa. Imported varieties were popular, but in several important slaving regions the preference was for Brazilian rolled tobacco, which was specially cured in molasses. Rolled tobacco was most popular on the Bight of Benin, but it was also the favored variety on the nearby Gold Coast, the Americans' most important source for captives. The market for American tobacco on the Gold Coast was very limited, but it was slightly better in Senegambia. Robert Heatley, a longtime Gambia trader, noted that as long as the tobacco had "long leaves" and was packed in half barrels, it "ought to be very Good."[22]

In the end, however, provisions, candles, and tobacco did not permit American slavers to "assort" their rum cargoes properly. This led several merchants and captains to compensate for the shortcomings of rum through fraud and trickery. In 1736 Captain Thomas Silk of Boston stopped in Cabo Verde to purchase horses, which he then carried to the Gambia. The move showed some awareness of African markets, although purchasing power of horses in Senegambia had fallen over the centuries. Silk's venture, in any event, was apparently unsuccessful. In an incident reminiscent of James Smith's voyage aboard the *Rainbow* almost a century earlier, Silk lured nine Luso-African traders aboard his ship and imprisoned them. His actions produced an outcry from metropolitan traders who feared the abduction would prompt retaliation against all British vessels. In 1733, Captain Samuel Moore attempted to pass phony Spanish silver dollars on the Gambia River. When his African trading partners discovered the coins were made of pewter, they made several attempts on his life. These events, both of which occurred just as the American slave trade was taking off, should be seen as efforts to deal with the persistent problem of trade goods. By the 1730s, rum was established as the staple of the American slave trade, but traders consistently looked to supplement it with additional goods, whether in horses or (counterfeit) silver. These incidents underscore the economic weakness of the American traders. European captains with well-assorted cargoes did not need to resort to such dangerous ruses as these. For the Americans, the problem of trade goods never entirely disappeared.[23]

Rum was not immediately or universally accepted as a trade good in Africa in the early eighteenth century. For the American slave trade to succeed, consumers somewhere in Africa would have to embrace rum. The problem was, other varieties of imported alcohol had already established themselves in the various slave-trading regions. Africans had long produced fermented beverages from local products. Palm wine, made by tapping trees, was widely consumed up and down the coast. Elsewhere, people fermented beerlike drinks from grains such as millet and sorghum. When the Portuguese arrived in the fifteenth century, they introduced wine, which served as a trade good for many years. Knowledge of distilling was widespread in Europe as of the sixteenth century, and by the seventeenth century, if not earlier, various spirits began to find their way to Africa. Brandy was very popular, and Dutch gin appeared from time to time. Around the middle of the century, planters in the sugar-producing colonies began distilling beverages from molasses and cane juice. These spirits went by various names: rum and kill-devil in the English Caribbean, *tafia* in the French colonies, *aguardiente* in the Spanish colonies, and *cachaça* or *gerebita* in Brazil.[24]

Although any liquor will do for the purpose of getting drunk, one of the more perplexing questions in the history of alcohol consumption is why certain drinks become popular in particular places and times but others do not. Of course, as intoxicants, the high-proof distilled spirits sold by slavers were qualitatively superior to local fermented beverages. That might explain why some Africans preferred rum and brandy to palm wine, but it does not tell us why some preferred rum over brandy and vice versa. Availability played a role but similarly cannot explain why certain beverages were favored over others. Taste, or the sensual reception of a drink, was surely the most important factor, but its dynamics are elusive. Food historians offer two basic explanations for how and why some things catch on but others do not. One emphasizes the increased availability of a food or beverage, which entails a drop in price. In other words, some things catch on because they become easy to obtain. The other interpretation holds that certain consumer goods become popular because they serve as markers of social distinction or because they allow for the performance of national, ethnic, class, and other types of identity. This explanation stands in tension with the first, since the goods that are most likely to confer distinction are also likely to be the scarcest. Whatever the dynamic at the start, once a particular food or drink becomes popular, it tends to continue so to the detriment of other products, all other things being equal. Because food and drink are embedded in ritual and spiritual life, cultural attachments to particular items can grow quite strong. This was certainly the case in Africa, where competing spirits had already established themselves in some regions before the American rum men began their activities. European brandy, for example, ruled the market at Ouidah, but Brazilian cachaça was preferred in Portuguese Angola, having superseded wine throughout the seventeenth century. The Bight of Biafra, a major source of captives for the British trade of the eighteenth century, imported almost no alcohol, its residents seemingly preferring locally made fermented beverages. None of these regions furnished a market for New England rum, so none became important sources for American slavers.[25]

One market that was not dominated by any single spirit, and was therefore open to American rum, was upper Guinea, or the stretch encompassing Senegambia, Sierra Leone, and the Windward Coast. This area was the earliest source of captives for the European slave trade, and it was where the New Englanders had sent most of their vessels in the seventeenth century. British slave traders, including the North Americans, focused most of their activities on the Gambia River. In the early eighteenth century, the Gambia region was divided into a dozen or so predominantly Mandinka, Sereer, and Fulbe polities. Several of these were ceddo military states, or as they were known on the Gambia River, *soninke,* the name for the ruling elite, which developed along with the slave trade. These states sustained themselves by waging war and seizing captives for sale to the Europeans and Americans. Alcohol was valued quite widely by these states. In fact, according to Mungo Park, one of the meanings of the word "soninke" was "people who drink strong liquors."[26]

The values of these ceddo-type regimes were, above all, martial. These were cultures that honored warriors, looked askance at manual labor, and eschewed material comfort. For the Nyaanco military aristocracy of Kaabu, for example, it was considered dishonorable to die rich; material wealth was equated with corruption, and honor could be found only on the field of battle. To the extent that such anti-consumerist values prevailed, the ceddo states might appear to constitute a poor market for European goods, but that was, of course, not the case. Weapons and the iron to make them were in demand. And alcohol, of course, did not conflict with the martial values of the ceddo states; in fact, in the time-honored way of soldiers everywhere, it complemented those values and became integral to the culture.[27]

The military regimes along the Gambia River formed the principal African market for American rum before the mid-1730s and continued as a secondary market into the nineteenth century. However, it is far from clear that rum was the favored spirit in the region. In the 1720s the Royal African Company, locked in a competition with the French for the Gambia trade, resolved to ship large quantities of rum there for the express purpose of changing the local preference from brandy to rum. Francis Moore, a British employee of the RAC who lived on the Gambia in the 1730s, just as the American rum trade was on the upswing, provides a unique portrait of alcohol consumption in the region, with an emphasis on complexity and diversity. Locally produced fermented beverages, such as the ever-present palm wine, were popular, but so was "Honey-Wine," which Moore likened to mead. Brandy and rum, however, were in the process of superseding indigenous concoctions in popularity. Whenever distilled spirts were available, Moore noted, "they drink but a small Quantity of the others."[28]

Moore's Gambia travelogue is filled with anecdotes on alcohol consumption. Many of these concern the ruler of the Sereer state of Saloum ("Barsally"), a classic ceddo-type predator with whom Moore had many dealings. Brandy was the king's passion. According to Moore, whenever the king wanted brandy, he would summon a sloop from the RAC's James Fort. To pay for the brandy and other goods, he "ransacks some of his Enemies Towns, seizing the People, and selling them." When war against an enemy was not possible, he "falls upon his own Towns." Another of Moore's vignettes has the king visiting the RAC outpost at the town of Joar and forcing the factor to let him sleep in his bed, consuming brandy almost continuously. The consumption of one man, however prodigious, was not sufficient to sustain an entire branch of trade. As part of the region's military culture, distilled spirits cemented the bonds between superiors and subordinates. The king of Saloum traveled with a military guard of between one and three hundred, which shared in the spoils. Later in the century, one of the factors of James Fort in the Gambia River complained of having to dispense twenty gallons of rum per day to a visiting ruler's "numerous Retinue."[29]

Warlords and ceddos did not make up the only market for rum. Over time, spirits, rum among them, became essential to a variety of rituals throughout the region. Several of these were life-stage or coming-of-age rituals, which were particularly important in many of the region's cultures. Many important aspects of life were governed by age grades, with a formal ceremony marking the progression from one to the next. Because Europeans were generally not able to observe these ceremonies, it is impossible to say which, if any, involved rum, but some surely did. Descriptions of other rituals do survive, and rum appears integral to several of them. An entire hogshead of rum—worth one prime male captive—was consumed at a week-long funeral in Kajaaga on the upper Senegal River. On the Rio Pongo, which lay between the Gambia and Sierra Leone, wedding protocol required five gallons of rum for the father of the groom and ten gallons as a gift to the residents of the town.[30]

Despite the inroads made by rum into the palate and culture of upper Guinea, countervailing forces limited the size of the market. The most powerful of these was the simple fact that consumer demand for European and Asian goods was much greater. Iron, textiles, and personal items such as beads were all more important in the region's trade. One way to gauge the relative importance of alcohol is by examining the functioning of the region's unit of account, the iron bar. Originally, the bars were physical pieces of iron, but by the eighteenth century the bar had long since become an abstract unit that denoted the prices of all types of goods. Dealers in upper Guinea preferred to receive an "assortment" of multiple goods, and they prioritized five "heads of goods" that they wanted to see in any assortment. The "heads of goods" on the Gambia River in the 1730s were iron bars, crystal beads, brass pans, arrangoes (carnelian beads), and Spanish "Spread Eagle" silver dollars. The bar prices for these goods were negotiated before all others, and traders who lacked them would find their merchandise devalued. This suggests that although rum enjoyed some demand in upper Guinea, it was not among the more valued trade goods.[31]

Islam was another obstacle to the popularity of American rum in upper Guinea. In the early eighteenth century, when the rum men were establishing their product, Islamic reform was barely getting started. But the signs of change were visible, and reformers became increasingly influential as the century progressed. Islam had come to upper Guinea several hundred years earlier as part of the long-distance trade networks that connected the coast with the interior. Muslims tended to live in enclaves, known as Moricunda (Muslim towns) or Fulacunda (Fulbe towns), and often served as administrators for local rulers. Senegambian Muslims were strict abstainers, "chusing rather to die than drink strong Liquors," as Francis Moore put it. Rulers of ceddo-type states

often professed Islam but were not strictly observant. The king of Saloum, for example, considered himself a Muslim and prayed, again in
Moore's words, "when he is sober, or not quite fuddled." To reformers,
the ceddo regimes were libertine and corrupt. This applied not only to
their drinking but, much more importantly, to their willingness to enslave free Muslims and sell them to Christians, which was strictly forbidden. Anger over the practice had simmered among the region's Muslims over the seventeenth century with the growth of the slave trade and
the predatory practices of the ceddo states. Nasir al-Din's uprising in
1673 against the ceddo regimes in Senegambia had been motivated both
by the ceddos' violation of slave-trading strictures and a general sense
of moral decline, of which alcohol consumption was one part. In 1725–
1726 another Muslim rebellion broke out in the Futa Jallon, a highland
district southeast of the Gambia and northeast of Sierra Leone. As yet,
however, the conflict in the Futa Jallon produced only a modest stream
of captives. So although rum allowed the Americans to purchase captives in upper Guinea, their activities helped to set off an Islamic reform
movement that limited the market for alcohol even as it produced captives for sale. Upper Guinea could never serve as a prime market for the
rum men.[32]

The rum men who traded in upper Guinea in the 1730s had to
contend with this situation, and as they did, they picked up techniques.
Stopping at Cabo Verde remained a common practice. One vessel called
there to trade 983 gallons of rum for some horses, but obtaining cloth
was almost certainly the more common tactic. Another trader augmented his rum cargo with silver of probable Spanish American origin, and gunpowder. Whereas most of the voyages were relatively un-
eventful, a seemingly significant proportion of them ran into the kind
of retaliatory violence that was so common on this stretch of the African coast. One cause for this was Yankee slavers' tendency to engage
in *panyarring*, or abduction of captives, and fraud in order to procure
captives when rum was not enough. The other was simple ignorance of
coastal trading conventions, which had been the undoing of so many
voyages going all the way back to the *Rainbow* in 1644. A large percentage of those incidents seem to have involved vessels and captains from
ports other than Newport. This would tend to confirm the notion that

inexperience was a factor, since Newporters had by this time begun to accumulate expertise.[33]

Captain John Major of the New Hampshire schooner *Gambia* ran into trouble due to both inexperience and problems with trade goods. In 1731, Major arrived on the Gambia River with a cargo of rum and salt, the latter likely obtained in Cabo Verde. He quickly sold some pork and venison to the garrison at James Fort, then headed upriver to Kassan in Niani Maru. There, he got into a dispute with Antonio Voss, a Luso-African trader who was known for his ability to drive a hard bargain. As far as Major knew, Voss had tried to renege on a deal he had made for a captive and was now demanding that the captive be returned. But there was much more to the conflict than that. We can get a view from the other side from an oration by a *silatigi,* or caravan leader, at Kassan. The silatigi's words were taken down by an RAC employee who was investigating the *Gambia*'s seizure.[34]

The silatigi's perspective went far beyond a dispute over a single transaction to encompass a pattern of wrongdoing. In his telling, trade relations had recently broken down because ship captains persisted in "carrying away several of our Friends and Relations by Force, without any Provocation." Recently, he said, a ship had departed with his own nephew, who had been given in pawn, simply because the promised captives had not been delivered on time. But the cause of the latest difficulties stemmed from Major's actions. The mansa of Lower Niani had sent the silatigi a captive to sell, whom he promptly brought to the American vessel. The silatigi, however, was not impressed with the American trade goods offered in exchange. He consulted with the mansa, who agreed and instructed the silatigi not to sell. When the silatigi delivered the news, Major fell into a "great Passion" and refused to return the captive. The silatigi returned to Kassan and reviewed the situation, placing Captain Major's actions squarely within the context of the recent surge in panyarring. "At last we resolved to take the schooner," explained the silatigi, which resulted in the death of Captain Major. He was "very sorry" for the captain's death, but not for the seizure, which he viewed as justified. The silatigi gave the crew a boat and provisions and allowed them to leave. Realizing that they did not have the power to do much to the silatigi, the RAC investigators simply left.[35]

Major's death, however, was not the final act in the drama. He had sailed in consort with Samuel Moore of Boston, who continued to trade on the Gambia River. Several attempts were made on Moore's life, but he survived thanks to the protection of the RAC, which also conducted trade negotiations for him. But when Moore passed off several fake silver dollars, his enemies redoubled their efforts, attacking his vessel one night as it passed one of the narrower parts of the river. The sloop ran aground; Moore managed to get away, but his supercargo was killed. The RAC factors, whose job it was to protect British traders, did little at that point. This was partly due to a sense that Major and Moore had brought their troubles on themselves, but it also showed an acceptance that this was how business was done. Incidents like these underscore just how important it was to understand local trading conventions.[36]

More than anything else, it was the demand for rum on the Gold Coast that fueled Newport's rise to prominence in the slave trade during the 1730s. It was in that decade, and in trade with that market, that the Newporters accumulated their experience and connections. From 1730 to 1775, the Gold Coast supplied approximately seven out of ten captives carried aboard American vessels, reaching a peak of 87 percent during the early 1770s (chart 4). Without the Gold Coast rum market, it is difficult to imagine the American slave trade as anything more than a sporadic, if tragic and cruel, endeavor.[37]

The distance between the Gold Coast and Senegambia is about fifteen hundred miles by sea. It was a very different place from upper Guinea, environmentally, culturally, and economically. Whereas Senegambia was closely linked to the Western Savanna region, the Gold Coast and much of its hinterland lay within the forest belt of the Voltaic region. Most of the population spoke dialects of the Akan (Twi) language, although this changed the farther east and north one traveled. When New England traders first visited the Gold Coast at the end of the seventeenth century, few realized that they were encountering a region in the midst of a profound economic and political transformation. In economic terms, this involved a change in orientation from the Muslim trade networks of the central savanna toward the European Atlantic networks, a development that had been under way since the sixteenth

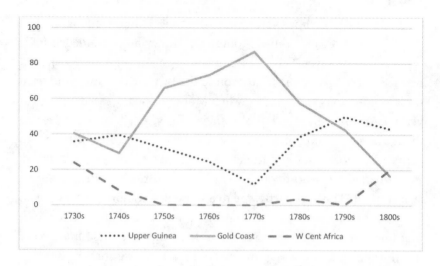

Chart 4. African destinations of American slave ships, by percentage, 1730–1807. (Data from *Slave Voyages,* www.slavevoyages.org/assessment/estimates)

century and was now more or less complete. Gold, produced in the Akan forestlands, had long been the staple of this trade, exchanged for iron and other wares. With the arrival of the Portuguese in the fifteenth century, the flow of gold was bent southward toward the Atlantic. In the sixteenth century, Akan merchants sometimes purchased captives from the Portuguese to work the goldfields. In the seventeenth century, rival European traders negotiated tenancies with coastal politics and built impressive castles to protect their gold stores, chiefly from each other, as evidenced by the fact that the forts' guns faced the sea. A new elite merchant class emerged, known as the *abirempon,* which, in collaboration with a tributary elite, the *afahene,* increased the region's commercial gold production. Although production eventually declined, gold would remain the chief export into the early eighteenth century.[38]

In addition to these economic changes, the seventeenth century saw remarkable political changes. Here the trend was toward consolidation, as several dozen smaller Akan states conquered, negotiated alliances with, and imposed suzerainty on their neighbors. The principal cause of this consolidation has been the subject of much debate, but there is little question that it was related at least in part to the rising

European demand for gold and captives. A recurring theme in these conflicts was a desire on the part of inland polities to gain access to the coast, including the guns that were essential to military dominance, whether by controlling the roads that connected the coast and interior or by conquering or otherwise dominating coastal polities.[39]

Gold Coast geopolitics is famously complex, but for the purpose of understanding the American slave trade, two Akan polities are of central concern: Asante and Fante. Asante was the dominant regional power, although that had only been the case since the first decade of the eighteenth century, when it displaced its former overlord, Denkyira. During the late seventeenth century, Denkyira's military force, strengthened by imported firearms, had controlled much of the trade in both gold and slaves, but its excessive tributary demands had led several subordinate provinces to challenge its rule. Led by the dynamic Osei Tutu, these provinces became the Asante state and defeated Denkyira in a climactic battle in 1701. Enstooled (analogous to being crowned) as the *asantehene* (ruler of Asante), Osei Tutu spent most of the next two decades consolidating his rule and expanding his dominions. Although some modern historians hesitate to apply the term "empire," there is no doubt that Asante exercised its hegemony throughout the region in a variety of forms, ranging from direct rule to the extraction of tribute, which was rendered in captives or gold. In Akan-speaking, gold-producing provinces, Asante generally levied a tribute in gold, though it did also accept captives. More distant, non-Akan-speaking areas were more likely to pay tribute in captives, who would be transported to the coast for sale. Efficient transport to the coast was therefore essential to Asante, and it maintained a well-designed system of roads, which radiated from the capital of Kumasi and linked it with both coastal and inland markets. One of these paths linked Kumasi with the western Gold Coast, the location of the key British forts of Cape Coast and Anomabu (also called Anomabo or Annamaboe). Conflicts over this path would figure prominently in the American slave trade for the next several decades.[40]

When American slavers began frequenting the Gold Coast in the 1730s and 1740s, Asante was conducting several military campaigns that would furnish captives. In the 1720s it had succeeded (temporarily) in subduing its closest neighbors to the south, the states of Twifo, Wassa, and Aowin. Osei Tutu's successor as asantehene, the fearsome Opoku Ware, focused his attention on the area to the north of Asante, a Muslim region that sat astride the long-distance trade routes of the central savanna. In 1730, Opoku Ware's forces, armed with European rifles, attacked Banda on the Black Volta. In 1740–1741, he attacked Gyaman, in the northwest, which lay between Asante and the vital trading center of Kong. In 1745–1748 he devastated Dagomba, to the northeast, on the other side of the Black Volta. Muslim chroniclers in Gonja, another of his northern targets, left a terse but poignant record of Opoku Ware's predations. In 1722–1723, his army "came to Ntakima and plundered it." In 1732–1733, seeking control of lucrative kola-nut trade routes, he "came and ruined" western Gonja. Opoku Ware was infamous in the region, so when word of his death reached Gonja, a chronicler recorded, "may Allah curse him and put his soul to hell. It was he who harmed the people of Ghanja [Gonja] to incorporate it into their kingdom. He reigned violently as a tyrant, enjoying his authority. Peoples of the horizons feared him much."[41]

Opoku Ware's attention was not solely focused on the north; he also led a number of major campaigns against other Akan states in the forest region. The most important of these was Akyem, which sat on Asante's eastern frontier. In Gold Coast geopolitics, Akyem had aligned itself with Denkyira and was therefore a threat to Asante. To counter the danger posed by Akyem, Asante quite naturally had allied with Akwamu, which sat on Akyem's eastern flank. Akwamu had extended its power eastward during the late seventeenth century, gaining control over Accra in 1681, over the Ewe regions on the Bight of Benin in the succeeding years, and over the slaving port of Ouidah in 1702, which remained a tributary until 1727. These conquests had given Akwamu control over the major trading paths of the eastern Gold Coast; in fact, the ability to sell gold and captives for guns and powder played a great role in its success. Tensions and intrigue with Asante and Akyem, which resented Akwamu's control over the eastern trade routes, mounted through the 1720s. The situation finally broke in 1730, precipitated by a succession dispute in Akwamu. Asante and Akyem, though normally rivals, supported the pretender in hopes of securing improved access to Accra. Akyem achieved total victory over Akwamu, devastating the population and producing many captives for the North Americans and others.[42]

Akyem's conquest and growing power, however, threatened Asante's dominance and ability to control coastal trade. Tensions ran high through the 1730s, as Akyem faced hostility on two fronts, from Opoku Ware to the west, acting in concert with remnants of Akwamu to the east. The final clash came early in 1742, with Opoku Ware emerging as the victor. Asante promptly subordinated Akyem and the port of Accra to its rule, which furnished an all-important outlet to the Atlantic. Akyem was now a tributary of Asante, with Akwamu submitting two years later. Like the Akwamu defeat of the previous decade, the defeat of Akyem produced additional captives for sale on the coast. Opoku Ware had done well for American slavers.[43]

The expansion of Asante was a necessary condition for the growth of the American slave trade, but Yankee slavers did not generally deal directly with it. For all of its power, Asante was unable to extend its control to the coastal areas directly to the south. The conquest of Akyem and the subordination of Akwamu did give Asante an outlet at Accra, but the link to Kumasi, the economic and political center of Asante, was rather roundabout. The more direct roads to the seaports all ran through Fante, a strategic rival of Asante and the strongest power on the coast. Unlike Asante and many other more centralized Akan states, Fante was a looser coalition. The timing and reasons for Fante's consolidation have been the subject of historical debate, but it appears that it came together in the final decades of the seventeenth century. It had its origins in a polity known as Borbor Fante, which was in existence at least since the early seventeenth century. Over the course of the seventeenth century, Fante engaged in a series of conflicts, emerged as the major coastal power, and by 1726 controlled most Atlantic trade between the Pra River and Accra, an area that encompassed the slave-trading forts of Elmina, Cape Coast Castle, Kormantin, and Anomabu.[44]

The Fante town of Anomabu was the principal port of call for American slavers on the Gold Coast. It is mentioned by name in the records of about 40 percent of all voyages from 1730 to 1776, but that record almost certainly understates Anomabu's significance. Almost all American vessels on the Gold Coast at least tried to trade at Anomabu;

it is difficult to imagine an American ship in this era calling on the Gold Coast and *not* calling there. American vessels did trade elsewhere on the Gold Coast, but no other African location had stronger ties to North America than Anomabu. (This relationship is explored in detail in chapter 4.)[45]

If it was Opoku Ware's wars of expansion that produced so many captives for sale on the Gold Coast, it was the demand for rum that made it possible for Americans to buy them. Demand for alcohol on the Gold Coast was much greater than in Senegambia or anywhere else in Africa. Even so, it took several decades for Gold Coast residents to develop a taste for rum. A German observer in the mid-seventeenth century described the highly ritualized drinking culture based on palm wine. After a dinner, he recalled, the men gathered and took turns decanting palm wine into calabashes, repeating ritual phrases, reciting names, and pouring libations on the ground. According to the observer, the men often finished the evening in a state of inebriation, but that implies that this was not always the case.[46]

French brandy appeared on the Gold Coast by the 1610s, when Samuel Brun noted its popularity among Akani traders.[47] Brandy was still the spirit of choice fifty years later, which is when another traveler noted (with more than a hint of racial and cultural condescension) that the residents of Fetu "lay into it as if it were water." The same traveler noted that Barbadian rum (kill-devil) was test-marketed at Fetu in the 1660s, but residents "were not willing to take this drink in their mouths," nor would they accept distilled grain spirits (likely Dutch gin), which they "greatly despised" and referred to as "stink jar." By 1700, however, tastes had changed. Requests for rum shipments by fort personnel began appearing in RAC correspondence, a clear indication of its popularity. In fact, in the years around 1700, before the 1730s surge in American slave trading, the RAC actually employed vessels in a shuttle trade with Barbados to maintain rum stores.[48]

Even after rum was established on the Gold Coast, it is not clear that it was the dominant spirit. American rum competed with European brandy for regional favor, just as it did in Senegambia. Danish traders, for example, reported that consumers in their vicinity "would rather have Danish brandy than any other kind." While negotiating a treaty, authorities at Keta told the Danes that "our [Danish] goods were better than others, our flintlocks did not explode, [and] our [Danish] brandy did not give them headaches when they drank too much." This may have been diplomatic flattery on the part of the merchants of Keta, but there is every reason to believe that consumers there really preferred the Danish product. Even in the British-dominated stretches of the Gold Coast, European brandy continued to find a strong market. RAC personnel seem to have considered rum and brandy to be interchangeable. "Rum is as acceptable as English brandy or Spirritts," wrote one factor in 1706, adding however that "this trade does not take much of Liquors." Nearly fifty years later, at a time when rum had long since been accepted, an official wrote that "a Fort here may as well be without Guns as without Rum or Brandy." So even though rum was certainly preferred in some locations, it is clear that European brandy was an acceptable substitute.[49]

As the preceding quotation suggests, the trading forts of the Gold Coast themselves provided a major market for spirits. Personnel not only drank liquor, but many of the soldiers and tradesmen were paid with liquor. The same writer lamented, "I find myself greatly distress for Liquor to defray the necessary Expences of the Castle." The castles also used alcohol in their interactions with the Fante. Because the British presence at Anomabu was entirely contingent on Fante goodwill, fort personnel had to engage with the local alcohol culture. Spirits were used as "dashes," or small payments, for an infinite array of services. Presents of rum or brandy were required for all negotiations and palavers. Bottles of spirits had to accompany every message sent from the forts to their landlords. In finding an enduring market for their wares, the rum men had succeeded where the Bostonians and New Yorkers of the seventeenth century had failed.[50]

The rum men who began frequenting the Gold Coast in the 1730s were only bit players in the larger history of the region and, for that matter, in the slave trade. Spirits of all types only accounted for only 8 percent of the total value of all goods shipped by the RAC to the Gold Coast in the late seventeenth and early eighteenth centuries. Three-quarters of a century later, the percentage had barely changed. Based on

the records of the Gold Coast slave trader Richard Miles, only 9.2 percent of the goods he exchanged for captives consisted of liquors, which
probably included brandy and gin in addition to rum. Textiles, on the
other hand, were the cornerstone of his trade, accounting for just more
than half of the total value of the goods he exchanged for captives. The
rum men's share of captives was proportionate to the share of rum in regional trade. North American vessels were responsible for 10 percent of
all captives embarked on the Gold Coast, rising to 15 percent during the
period of peak activity between 1730 and 1807. As historians continue to
debate the degree to which slave trading drove events in West Africa, it
seems fairly clear that the North American impact was proportionately
small. But it is nevertheless true that the histories of Senegambia, the
Gold Coast, and North America became entwined starting in the 1730s
and would remain so for more than three-quarters of a century.[51]

From a macro perspective, the slave trade can be explained with reference to global structures and systems. But to explain why Newport,
specifically, and not Boston, New York, or another port, became a slave-
trading center, it is necessary to look carefully at historical circumstance.
Newport became the capital of the North American slave trade as a result of several factors, all of them necessary pieces of the larger puzzle,
but none of them sufficient to "cause" a slave trade. The first piece had
to do with local conditions. Needing to finance their debts owed to British merchants, Newporters entered the trade in order to procure good
bills of exchange. Rhode Island's policy of currency emissions through
the 1730s and 1740s allowed merchants to finance their ventures on easy
terms. In doing so, the colony actually subsidized slave trading (among
other pursuits). Rum was the second piece. For the first time, American
slavers had a product that could be exchanged profitably for captives.
Newport was neither the first nor the only North American town to dis-
till rum, but once committed, it embraced the slave trade like no other.
But an African rum trade was neither easy nor inevitable. American
traders had to confine their activities to Senegambia and the Gold Coast,
the only two African regions that were receptive to the spirit. Knowledge
of these regions, their markets, and their trading practices accrued in
Newport's maritime community and was passed on, both casually and

formally, though institutions like the Fellowship Club. Opoku Ware's conquests were the missing piece for the rum men. He led a major political expansion in a region that was open to American trade goods at the very moment Newporters were looking to enter the slave trade. To be sure, not all of the captives who embarked on the Gold Coast were enslaved as a result of Asante's expansion, but it was the main driver for enslavement, generating captives both directly, through seizures and tribute, and indirectly, by destabilizing the region as a whole.

It is no wonder that Opoku Ware's name lived on in the Americas. In the early 1790s, when the Jamaican planter Bryan Edwards took it upon himself to interview some of his slaves, a man named Cudjoe, who was born in Asante, recalled Opoku Ware's death in 1750. According to Cudjoe, the asantehene had "the power of life and death, and that executions are very frequent." When Opoku Ware died, Cudjoe recalled, at least a hundred slaves were sacrificed. Another man from Asante who was enslaved in the Danish West Indies, where most of the captives came from the Gold Coast, also recalled the asantehene's death. Interviewed by the Moravian missionary C. G. A. Oldendorp in the 1760s, he told a story in which Opoku Ware, dying from illness by the bank of a river, offered a water spirit a great amount of gold to allow him to continue living. The water spirit answered that "his time had come, as others' would. Nothing could be saved from death." That Opoku Ware figured prominently in the minds of Gold Coast exiles would hardly come as a surprise to him, but he surely never realized how much he did for the merchants of Newport, Rhode Island.[52]

Knowledge and Networks, 1751–1775

I n the years after 1750, the American slave trade reached unprecedented heights. Average annual departures trended steadily
upward from about twenty for the decade of the 1750s to about
thirty-five during the early 1770s.[1] In many respects, this period
resembled the previous one. This was still a rum trade, Newport continued to dominate, the Gold Coast was the primary destination for
most vessels, upper Guinea continued as the secondary destination,
and most captives were sold in the British Caribbean. These broad continuities, however, masked important changes. The general theme of
these changes was a greater familiarity with African regions, markets,
and customs. The years of trial and error, of searching for the optimal
assortment of trade goods, of one-off voyages, and of vague instructions
to captains to make trade "on the coast of Guinea" were over. Voyages
organized after 1750 were much more likely to be based on a fine-tuned
sense of captive markets in Africa. On the Gold Coast, this meant that
American merchants and mariners cultivated ties with factors on the
Gold Coast. In upper Guinea, slavers mastered the regional geography
and trading conventions. These advances enabled the major traders to
dispatch multiple, coordinated voyages to specific African ports and
to run ongoing accounts with trusted correspondents. By the end of
the period, some Americans were even partnering with metropolitan

merchants, organizing complex, multilateral voyages. Of course, not all merchants traded on the same scale or operated at the same level of sophistication. This was also an era in which anyone with a ship might try his luck by organizing a slaving voyage.

Intelligent voyage planning could only go so far, however. The success of an individual voyage, or even an entire trade, was not determined solely by the merchants, regardless of how knowledgeable or well-connected they were, because the supply of captives lay outside their control. Of course, the presence of slavers on the African coast could and did stimulate enslavement. European demand for captives was a major driver of the transatlantic slave trade, with price increases consistently outstripping the increase in the numbers delivered to the coast. But the rum men played a role, albeit a secondary one, in stimulating the slave trade. On the Gold Coast from 1751 to 1775, their share reached 24 percent of all captives embarked, but even at that level all the Americans could really do was divert a portion of the larger European trade. Unable to generate much of a trade on their own, the rum men, therefore, could do little more than act on the best available information and hope that the vessels they dispatched would meet with an ample supply of captives. Ultimately, that supply was determined by the politics and economics of the Gold Coast.[2]

Despite the steadily rising level of participation, there was considerable year-to-year fluctuation in the number of departures. Global politics was one reason for the variability. For most of the 1740s, Britain and its North American colonies had been at war, and American shipowners outfitted more privateers than slavers. In 1748, the return of peace prompted American merchants to re-enter the slave trade. Clearances for Africa rose through the early 1750s but then declined sharply during the Seven Years' War, as enemy warships and privateers patrolled the waters off Africa and the Americas and pushed insurance rates upward. After some early losses, Britain asserted naval supremacy, which led to a resurgence of the trade even as the war continued. Europe (and therefore the Americas) waged no global wars after 1763, so slave trading continued fairly steadily, with a temporary dip in 1768 as a result of colonial protest against the Townshend Duties. In the 1770s, however, the number of African clearances almost doubled, with some merchants dispatching multiple vessels and engaging in complex exchanges with African factors, before declining sharply as the Imperial Crisis reached a critical stage. American slave trading came to a virtual halt after 1775.

Economic factors were even more important than the political factors. Many considerations influenced merchant decision-making, but for simplicity's sake it is useful to focus on what contemporaries and historians alike call "prime cost," or the cost in trade goods paid for each captive. Actual transactions for a single adult ("prime") male captive can be extracted from trading records. To calculate prime cost, we need to know two things: the price paid for the trade goods and the price paid for a captive in Africa. A third piece of information would have been vital to merchants' decisions, and that was the price received for captives in the Caribbean. Using the price at Jamaica is useful for the sake of comparison, although not all vessels carried their captives there. The three key factors in merchant decision-making therefore were: the purchase price of rum, the purchase price of captives in Africa, and the sales price for captives in Jamaica, as the ratio of cost of a captive to the sale price. It should be emphasized that these figures do not represent an actual accounting of the trade; many other significant expenses, such as crew wages and vessel costs, are not included here. But focusing on prime costs for captives in Africa and sales prices in the Americas offers a simplified model for how slavers decided whether, when, and where to send their vessels.

Before 1750 the amount received for one human being in Jamaica was almost four times the initial investment at Anomabu (table 1). In the 1750s, this ratio climbed above four, and merchants responded by dispatching more vessels (although they had to contend with wartime conditions). In the 1760s, the price of rum declined slightly, which lowered the slavers' prime costs, even as prices for captives at Anomabu gradually rose. A continuous rise in prices for captives in the Caribbean helped the slavers' bottom line, so that by 1769 the money invested in rum for Africa yielded almost eight times its value in captives on the Jamaica market. That situation reversed suddenly in the 1770s. Although rum prices were low, the amount of rum demanded for captives on the Gold Coast soared, doubling by 1774. Prices for captives in Jamaica rose as well, though not as quickly. On the eve of the American

Table 1. Ratio of Prime Costs for Adult Males at Anomabu, Gold Coast, to Captive Prices in Jamaica, 1736–1774

Captive Cost in Gals. Rum	Rum Cost (shillings/ gallon, stg.)	Captive Prime Cost (stg.)	Captive Price @ Jamaica, currency	Captive Price @ Jamaica (stg.)	Cost: Price (stg.)	Notes
Unknown vessel, Anomabu, 1736						
112	1.31	7.3		28.1	3.8	Price at Jamaica is 1730–1739 average from *Slave Voyages* database.
Venus, Anomabu, 1756						
100	1.54	7.7	50	35.7	4.6	Sales price given in Jamaica currency in original.
Royal Charlotte, Anomabu, 1762						
106	1.38	7.3		35.9	4.9	Price at Jamaica is 1760–1764 average from *Voyages*.
Sally, Gold Coast, 1767 (two captives)						
108	1.08	5.8		39.3	6.7	Price at Jamaica is 1765–1769 average from *Voyages*.
120	1.08	6.5		39.3	6.1	
Othello, Anomabu, 1769						
98	1.14	5.6		43	7.7	Price at Jamaica is 1769–1771 average from *Voyages*.

(*continued*)

Table 1. (*continued*)

Captive Cost in Gals. Rum	Rum Cost (shillings/ gallon, stg.)	Captive Prime Cost (stg.)	Captive Price @ Jamaica, currency	Captive Price @ Jamaica (stg.)	Cost: Price (stg.)	Notes
Othello, Anomabu, 1770 (two captives)						
113	1.13	6.4		43.8	6.9	Price at Jamaica is 1769–1771 average from *Voyages*.
180	1.13	10.2		43.8	4.3	
Adventure, Anomabu, 1774						
225	1.08	12.2		47.5	3.9	Price at Jamaica taken from Eltis and Richardson, "Prices," 198.

Note: stg. = sterling.

Sources: *Slave Voyages* database, www.slavevoyages.org. For captive prices in Africa, see the relevant trade books for each voyage. For rum prices, see John J. McCusker, "Rum and the American Revolution: The Rum Trade and the Balance of Payments of the Thirteen Continental Colonies, 1650–1775" (Ph.D. diss., University of Pittsburgh, 1970), 1134–1135. For captive prices in Jamaica, see notes column and David Eltis and David Richardson, "Prices of African Slaves Newly Arrived in the Americas, 1673–1865: New Evidence on Long-Run Trends and Regional Differentials," in *Slavery in the Development of the Americas*, ed. David Eltis, Frank D. Lewis, and Kenneth L. Sokoloff (Cambridge: Cambridge University Press, 2004), 181–218.

Revolution, each captive purchased on the Gold Coast cost about four times what had been paid in rum. This was likely still an acceptable level of profit, in fact about the same as in the 1730s. But the situation would have troubled the rum men on the Gold Coast if the revolution had not suspended virtually all American slave trading.

American fortunes in upper Guinea followed a slightly different trajectory (table 2). Here, it is more difficult to calculate prime costs. Upper Guinea received less than one-quarter of all American slavers in the era, so the record is thinner. Moreover, North American vessels could never off-load as much rum here as on the Gold Coast and often

Table 2. Ratio of Prime Costs for Adult Males in Upper Guinea
to Captive Prices in Jamaica, 1749–1774

Captive Cost in Gals. Rum or N.E. Currency	Rum Cost (shillings/ gallon, stg.)	Captive Prime Cost (stg.)	Captive Price @ Jamaica, currency	Captive Price @ Jamaica (stg.)	Cost: Price (stg.)	Notes
Rhode Island, Banana Islands, 1749						
60 gals.	1.51	4.5		31.5	**7.0**	Jamaica price is average of 1747–1751 from *Voyages*.
Sally, Gambia River, 1766						
£14 currency		10.5		39.4	**3.7**	Assumed £14 N.E. currency @ 1.33 to stg.
Sally, Isles de Los, Sierra Leone, 1767						
90 bars = 120 gals.	1.08	6.5		39.4	**6.1**	1 bar = 1.33 gals. rum, conversion taken from *Othello* ("Unknown Trade Book") for 1774.
Othello ("Unknown Trade Book," NYHS), Gambia River, 1774						
£20 currency		14.8	70	50	**3.4**	Purchase price taken from trade book. Assumed N.E. currency @ 1.35 to stg. Jamaica price, taken from trade book, @ 1.4 to stg.
Othello ("Unknown Trade Book," NYHS), Isles de Los, 1774						
150 bars = 200 gals.	1.08	10.8	70	50	**4.6**	1 bar = 1.33 gals. rum, taken from trade book.

Note: stg. = sterling.

Sources: For captive prices in Africa, see the relevant trade books for each voyage. For rum prices, see John J. McCusker, "Rum and the American Revolution: The Rum Trade and the Balance of Payments of the Thirteen Continental Colonies, 1650–1775" (Ph.D. diss., University of Pittsburgh, 1970), 1134–1135. For captive prices in Jamaica, see notes column. "Unknown Trade Book" is from Slavery Collection, New-York Historical Society (NYHS).

had to acquire other kinds of trade goods before purchasing captives, all of which complicates the task of calculating prime cost. But select examples of adult men sold to American slavers in upper Guinea tell a similar story, in which falling rum prices at home coupled with rising captive prices in Jamaica allowed the slavers to earn more for their initial rum outlays through the 1760s, followed by a decline to previous levels on the eve of the American Revolution. However, one contrast with the Gold Coast stands out: the pronounced intraregional differential between Senegambia and Sierra Leone, with prime costs being consistently greater in the former than in the latter. This stemmed from the fact that captive prices were simply higher in Senegambia, and from the fact that rum was valued less than in Sierra Leone. Sierra Leone had not been a major destination for the Americans before 1750. Its emergence was the result of many factors, some of which are in the discussion to come, but clearly one reason for its post-1750 popularity had to do with its lower captive prices. The rising and falling prices for captives on both the Gold Coast and the upper Guinea coast serve as a reminder that the fortunes of American slavers depended at least in part on the supply of captives. The reasons for these fluctuations in both regions will also be discussed shortly.

American slavers, then, dispatched a rising number of vessels in the years after 1750. Political factors, such as global warfare and the Imperial Crisis, certainly influenced their decision-making. This is most evident in the brief, sharp declines during the Seven Years' War in the late 1750s and during the crises arising out of the Stamp Act and the Townshend Duties in the late 1760s. Equally important, however, were the microeconomics of the trade, which hinged on the price of rum, the price for captives in Africa, and the price of captives in the Americas. The changing relationship of these three factors, which surely figured prominently in the minds of slave traders, prompted merchants to organize more voyages. The peak years of 1772–1773 were no doubt inspired by the favorable returns of the late 1760s and early 1770s. Merchants in those years did not yet realize it as they planned these voyages, but the boom times were actually over; they would learn as much when dispatches from their captains began to roll in.

There is something of a paradox in all of this: at a time when slave trading reached new heights in terms of voyages organized, there were almost no North American slave traders, if by "slave trader" we mean a merchant whose principal business was procuring captives in Africa and selling them in the Americas. Slave trading might constitute an important part of a merchant's wider enterprise and at times even a significant share of his earnings, but it was never the whole of the enterprise. This was the case even for the most prolific traders of the era, such as Newport's Samuel and William Vernon. They began their slave-trading career in 1753 on a joint venture with Jacob Rivera. From this date until 1775, the Vernons organized or invested in twenty-eight slaving voyages, but they dispatched many more non-slaving vessels to an array of destinations, including the Caribbean, Britain, and Scandinavia.[3] Over the years 1769–1774 (a period for which the best records survive), the Vernons dispatched seven slavers and at least sixteen non-slavers.[4]

This raises the question of the profitability of slave trading versus more conventional trading voyages. It is very difficult to calculate the profitability of most voyages with any precision. The documentary record rarely allows for it. However, given the consistent participation over the years, it was unquestionably profitable, with anecdotal evidence suggesting that profits of 10–20 percent were not unknown. But there is also enough anecdotal evidence to suggest that some voyages lost money for their organizers, reducing overall profitability. Moreover, when considering the profitability of slaving voyages, it is important to consider the profitability of other branches of commerce. If slave trading was significantly more profitable than other trades, then we would expect merchants to pursue slave trading almost exclusively. Of course, not anyone could raise the funds to finance a slaving voyage, so some never had the option. But it is significant that all of the major traders of the era did pursue other branches of commerce. This suggests that the profits from slave trading were not radically greater than those of the West Indian and other trades. Jay Coughtry has estimated that Rhode Island's non-slave trades consistently earned between 2 and 8 percent. This was lower than the slave trade both as a rate of return and in absolute terms, since African voyages were more capital intensive. But if we assume a 10 percent rate of return on slaving voyages, the disparity is not too great. Moreover, the non-slave trades distributed the risk over the many smaller voyages, but slave-trading voyages risked large amounts on a single venture. In sum, though slavers reaped significant profits from their African voyages, they all continued their non-slave-trading activities both as a hedge against losses in the slave trade and because those activities were lucrative in their own right.[5]

Whether the late-colonial-era slave trade was concentrated in a few hands or spread among many is difficult to know. In all, there is some record for six hundred voyages undertaken between 1751 and 1775, but information on ownership exists for only about one-third of these. Only eleven merchants or partnerships are on record as having organized more than five voyages during the period, and only four firms dispatched more than ten (table 3). These eleven merchants accounted for about one-fifth of all vessels sent to Africa during the period. This

Table 3. Merchants Dispatching Five or More Voyages, 1751–1775

Name	Residence	Voyages	Captives (est.)
Samuel and/or William Vernon	Newport, R.I.	28	3,444
Aaron Lopez and/or Jacob Rivera	Newport, R.I.	23	2,500
Timothy Fitch	Boston/Medford, Mass.	13	1,105
Joseph and/or William Wanton	Newport, R.I.	12	1,521
Peleg Clarke	Newport, R.I.	6	1,121
Thomas Teakle Taylor	Newport, R.I.	6	463
Christopher and/or George Champlin	Newport, R.I.	6	514
Benjamin Mason	Newport, R.I.	6	636
Caleb Gardner	Newport, R.I.	5	552
Simon Pease	Newport, R.I.	5	295
Simeon Potter	Bristol, R.I.	5	700

Source: *Slave Voyages*, www.slavevoyages.org. To account for voyages missing captive totals, the mean voyage total for the firm was used.

figure suggests that slave trading was not dominated by a small number of traders. The incomplete nature of the data, however, means that any conclusion must be qualified. Because ownership records for two-thirds of the era's voyages are lacking, we can only represent the lowest possible level of concentration. But if we assume that the same proportion applies to the missing data, then thirty-three firms organized five or more voyages. Under those assumptions, about 6 percent of slave-ship owners were responsible for about half of all voyages. This suggests that the level of concentration was very high, with a few firms responsible for most voyages. The truth probably lies somewhere between these two poles. It is reasonable to assume that a relatively small group of Newport merchants accounted for between 25 and 40 percent of all voyages. Existing alongside this cohort was a much larger group that dispatched a small number of vessels, many in Newport but also scattered throughout the colonies. For these merchants, slave trading was an opportunistic venture or perhaps an experiment. Of the voyages for which we have ownership information, 18 percent were one-off ventures, and many probably lost money.[6]

One outgrowth of the increased activity and the greater number of large traders was a rise in the frequency of two or more vessels sailing in consort. There is some evidence of this practice dating back to the earliest years of the American trade in the activities of John Parris. The advantages are apparent: by working together, vessels can purchase captives faster than if alone and can better coordinate their dispatch to the Americas. Often, this was done in the hope that one of the vessels might be sold to a factor on the African coast after having made its purchases, transferring its captives to the second ship. Timothy Fitch used the tactic on several occasions, making sure that the lines of authority were as clear as possible by giving one captain command over the others and consigning the cargo to him. In 1759, he sent William Ellery to Senegal with instructions to rendezvous with the *Bacchus* and the *Peggy*, both of which were under orders to dispose of the vessel if possible and transfer all captives to Ellery. One year later, Fitch instructed Peter Gwinn to meet his schooner *Pompey* in Senegal, where the latter was to serve as a tender. If Ellery should succeed in selling the *Pompey*, all captives would be transferred to his vessel. The Vernons pursued a similar strategy in

1756 with the *Casada Garden* and the *Titt Bitt.* Lopez and Rivera also favored the strategy, allowing one vessel to deposit captives or trade goods
with one of the forts, to be redeemed later by the second.[7]

About 64 percent of all voyages for which a record of ownership
survives list two or more partners. Most of these partnerships concerned just two individuals, but in a few cases up to six investors were
involved. Here again, there is a possibility that the available information, which was gathered from customs records, newspapers, and other
diverse sources, understates the true degree of collaboration. Many of
the single-owner ventures in the data set probably had additional back-
ers who simply never made it into the record. To complicate the picture, different partners played different roles. Sometimes two or more
merchants pooled resources and risks, with one of them taking the lead
while the others simply collected a share of the profits. In other cases,
the ties between the individuals listed as owners were much stronger,
often members of the same family, to the point where they are more
properly regarded as a single firm. The Vernon brothers exemplify both
of these tendencies. Although William dealt with most of the correspondence, they worked as one. Even when the record lists only one brother
(often William) as the owner of a vessel, they functioned as a single firm.
Aaron Lopez and his cousin Jacob Rivera also worked closely together,
although they did operate on separate accounts. Members of the Champlin and Wanton families also frequently partnered, though seemingly
not with the same closeness as the Vernons.[8]

It also appears that traders of the eighteenth century, in contrast
to those of the previous century, owned their own vessels. One sign of
this change is the simple fact that although charter parties are very important documents for the reconstruction of the seventeenth-century
trade, none appear to have survived for the eighteenth century. The
reasons for the shift toward ownership and away from charters are not
clear. The move did bring the Americans in line with practices in the
British slave trade. It also speaks to the fact that, as a group, merchants
of the eighteenth century were financially stronger than those of the
seventeenth century and more committed to the slave trade. New England, moreover, became a major shipbuilding center, which it had not
been in the mid-seventeenth century, and even British merchants some-

times commissioned new ships there. Finally, American slavers in this era realized that owning the ship gave them the option of selling the vessel on the African coast and forgoing the slave trade altogether.[9]

Cross-referencing ownership data with tax lists shows that most slave-ship owners were quite wealthy. Rhode Island taxed personal property, but the tax rolls record only the amount owed, not the amount of property owned. This makes it possible to gain a relative sense of a person's ranking among taxpayers, but not to measure their actual wealth. Not surprisingly, Newport's elite accounted for the lion's share of voyages, with Aaron Lopez, the Wantons, the Vernons, and other familiar names in the top echelon. Some of the owners at the lower end, such as William Redwood Jr. and Joseph Wanton Jr., were the younger sons of wealthy merchants and had yet to inherit, so in reality they were members of the elite. Another category included distillers, such as Jonathan Thurston and Joseph Tillinghast, who likely cut deals to supply rum in exchange for the occasional share in a voyage. But a few, such as Robert Crooke, who was involved in three voyages, including two as sole owner, were among the lowest rate payers but with no obvious explanation for their involvement in such a capital-intensive business. Exactly how Crooke managed to invest is a mystery. Because the tax record was compiled fifteen years after his involvement (no records survive for the 1750s or 1760s), it is possible that he lost his fortune in the interceding years. But owners like Crooke notwithstanding, investment in slavers was very much an elite pursuit.[10]

Another facet of the mid-century surge in slave trading was the involvement of seaports beyond Newport, Boston, and New York. Slave trading in this era was well established enough, probably even prestigious enough, to attract merchants up and down the eastern seaboard: from Portsmouth, New Hampshire; Marblehead, Newburyport, and Salem, Massachusetts; Providence, Rhode Island; New London, Connecticut; Perth Amboy, New Jersey; Philadelphia, Pennsylvania; Annapolis, Maryland; Williamsburg (or lower James River), Virginia; Charles Town, South Carolina; and Savannah, Georgia. For some merchants, it was a one-time effort to reap a windfall, but for others it was a hedge against their usual risks, a way to diversify their investments. Even as participation widened, Newport, Boston, and New York together still accounted for almost nine out of ten voyages. Newport alone was responsible for approximately 62 percent of the total, dispatching more than 350 vessels between 1750 and 1775. Newport also exported its accumulated expertise to the other ports in the form of its ship captains, who could be found commanding vessels from Massachusetts, New York, and beyond.[11]

Slave traders of the post-1750 era conducted most of their business through the larger British imperial and economic networks, purchasing captives in areas of Africa dominated by British merchants and selling the captives in British American colonies (chart 5). However, their most important connections were with London, the financial center of the empire. Merchants in the capital not only supplied the manufactures and textiles that colonial consumers craved, they furnished essential credit to colonial merchants. And it was the need to repay metropolitan lenders that was the raison d'être for the American slave trade. Virtually all colonial transatlantic merchants maintained relationships with one or more British mercantile houses. These houses fulfilled a variety of

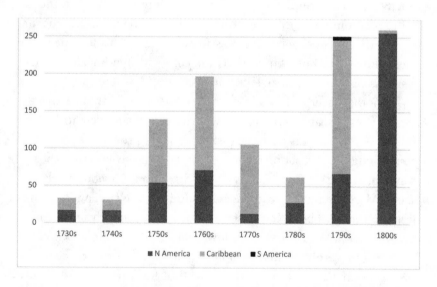

Chart 5. New World destinations of American slave ships, 1730–1807.
(Data from *Slave Voyages,* www.slavevoyages.org/voyages/ifIPYLlE)

necessary functions. They handled the sale of colonial commodities and arranged return cargoes of European and Asian goods. They also served as financial brokers, managing the accounts of colonial clients and accepting and issuing bills of exchange.

A simplified model of the relationship might look as follows: A London merchant dispatches European and Asian goods to his New England correspondent on credit in one or more of his own vessels. With little to export in return, the New England merchant would outfit a ship of his own to carry captives from Africa to Jamaica. The captain of the New England ship would sell the captives in Jamaica for bills of exchange that had been issued on the Jamaican merchant's account in London and carry the bills back to New England. The New England merchant would forward these bills to his London correspondent, who would then present the bills for payment to the Jamaica merchant's correspondent. The Jamaican's correspondent would pay the New Englander's correspondent, and the amount would be credited to the North American's account. His account now in balance, the New Englander would then be able to receive additional shipments on credit. Of course, few transactions actually unfolded in this rather schematic way. In reality, numerous additional actors and transactions intervened, and each cycle blurred into several others. But in the abstract, it illustrates the degree to which eighteenth-century American slave traders were embedded in British financial networks.

Insurance was another innovation of the period and a further example of the slavers' enmeshment within the larger imperial financial system. The British system of private marine insurance was pioneered by Lloyds, which began as a coffeehouse serving London's merchant community. Under the system, shipowners could outline the planned voyage and request that a certain amount of the voyage be insured. In 1772, for example, Peleg Clarke requested insurance for £400, a fairly typical amount for slave ships. The shipowner needed to pay a percentage of that amount as a premium, often around 10 percent but higher in wartime. In fact, one function of a London correspondent was to keep colonial merchants apprised of insurance rates and anything that might influence them. In the early years, when Lloyds was still a coffeehouse, the basic information about the voyage was written down and literally

placed on a table where patrons could opt to finance a specified proportion of the total by signing their names to the policy along with the
amount they were willing to cover, a process known as "underwriting."
In later years, of course, insuring and underwriting moved out of the
coffeehouses, but the terminology and basic structure lasted.[12]

Marine insurance was issued only on a very small scale in North
America. In the 1720s, merchants in Philadelphia and Boston replicated
a Lloyds-style system in miniature, and by the 1750s even Rhode Islanders were insuring small voyages. The Vernons, for example, insured several West Indian cargoes during the 1750s and 1760s. But as this example
shows, colonial insurers focused on the coastwise and Caribbean trades,
not on the transatlantic slave trade, which required much more capital. Colonial underwriters were not sufficiently capitalized to support
a business as costly as the slave trade. American slavers were therefore
compelled to buy insurance in the metropole, via their correspondents.[13]

Although the documentary record is filled with examples of North
American merchants requesting coverage, few sources outline the specific terms. The reason for this is straightforward: Americans were insured under the terms of the standard British marine policy, and no
written policy was necessary. The guiding principle in British marine
insurance was that damage to or loss of cargo due to a "hazard of the
sea," which included storms and seizure by naval vessels, privateers, and
pirates, would be covered. Slave ships, which carried living people as
cargo, required additional provisions. The average mortality rate for
eighteenth-century slave ships was about 15 percent. The standard marine insurance policy, therefore, did not cover what was referred to as
"natural deaths," which included death from illness or beatings. A second question had to do with the human agency of slave cargoes. Unlike conventional cargoes, people could damage themselves, whether
directly via suicide or indirectly, as in being cut down while in rebellion.
Under the standard policy, suicide was categorized as a "natural death"
and was not covered, but death brought about in the suppression of a
shipboard rebellion would be compensated out of the "general average,"
an insurance term that referred to a proportion of the value of the entire
cargo. A rare document confirms that these same terms applied in the
American slave trade. It was, in effect, a policy quote, relayed by one

merchant to another, offering to insure a voyage to Africa and Barbados, Antigua, or Saint Kitts at 12 percent and, in the event of an insurrection, to "Pay for Such Slaves as are Kill [sic] in Subdoing them."[14]

In addition to enjoying strong connections to the British mercantile community, North American slave traders used connections in Africa and the Caribbean to facilitate their enterprises. Like their connections to London, these links were superimposed on British imperial networks. One way to grasp these networks is through the analysis of voyage instructions. Some instructions were quite vague, simply ordering a captain to go to the "Coast of Guinea" and then to the West Indies, perhaps to a specific island. Vague instructions imply a high degree of improvisation and a lack of established connections. Other instructions were more explicit, specifying not only which regions to visit in Africa and the Americas, but which merchants to contact. Instructions like these suggest a much higher degree of networking. The naming of specific merchants implies pre-established connections, but the naming of specific regions indicates a rudimentary level of information.

An analysis of thirty-two captains' instructions from the years 1751–1775 suggests that merchants were well networked and possessed at least a basic knowledge of African geography and markets. More than 80 percent of merchants in this sample directed their captains to specific regions of Africa, most often to the Gold Coast, in contrast to the more vague instructions of earlier eras. More surprising and more significant is the finding that more than one-quarter of all voyage instructions directed vessels to specific British dealers in Africa, which speaks to the existence of actual relationships. One-quarter is a minority, of course; clearly, not all traders had trusted contacts in Africa. But this does suggest that the American slave trade had reached a new level of sophistication. It is important to note, however, that all Africa-based merchants named in the instructions were stationed on the Gold Coast. The region was not only the most frequented, but also the best connected part of Africa to colonial America. No merchants from upper Guinea appear by name in captains' instructions, which suggests weaker mercantile connections. That does not mean there were no links; rather, these were less consistent and less formal. Caleb Godfrey, for example, visited the same small trader in Sherbro on consecutive voyages in 1754 and 1755 because he knew the place and the person. Formal ties, in the form of balances and credits carried over from one year to the next, and regular transatlantic correspondence, which existed for the Gold Coast, were absent in the upper Guinea trade.[15]

Because the Gold Coast was the destination for about three-quarters of all American slavers in this period, it comes as no surprise that it was the focus of their African networks. The Gold Coast emerged as the most important region for the American rum trade in the 1730s, but there is little sign that the rum men of that era built networks. Serial voyages by individual merchants, which are essential to these kinds of relationships, were comparatively few, and the onset of the War of Jenkins' Ear in 1739, followed by the War of Austrian Succession in 1740, interrupted any connections that might have existed. When the rum men returned to the Gold Coast after 1748, there was little to build on other than the decade-old memory of the trade. One change probably stood out immediately: the construction of a major slave-trading installation at Anomabu. Americans had traded at Anomabu in the 1730s, but there was no fort; it had been abandoned and demolished in 1731, and trade revolved around the "floating factory," or ship with trade goods that anchored permanently off the coast. In the early 1750s the British received permission to build a new fort from the *abirempon* (elite merchant and local ruler) Eno Baisee Kurentsi, known to them as John Corrantee, which was operational by the end of the decade. Anomabu became the leading embarkation point for captives on the Gold Coast and the focal point for the North American slave trade.[16]

Anomabu and the other Gold Coast castles, such as Cape Coast and Tantumkwerry, along with the Dutch installations at Elmina and Kormantin, enabled what contemporaries referred to as the "fort trade." These forts fulfilled several functions. Some of these were purely ceremonial. Vessels were expected to acknowledge the fort's authority by a salute of the ships' guns, and in return the captain was entertained at the "public table" kept by the governor. But the chief function of the forts from the rum men's perspective was to serve as what historians call "bulking centers," or places where large numbers of captives were collected before embarkation. This in theory allowed vessels to purchase captives more quickly, which translated into lower provisioning costs, lower crew wages, and lower mortality rates for both captives and mariners. In practice, vessels rarely left the coast as quickly as planned, since the supply of captives was not something fort personnel could control. The forts provided numerous other services, such as arranging for boatmen, who were needed because vessels had to anchor well beyond the surf, and providing laborers for other chores. Forts were also information centers where skippers could learn the latest economic and political news. But the forts cost money, and ship captains paid a premium whenever they purchased captives from them. In times of high prices, such as the 1770s, American slavers might eschew the fort trade for direct trade with the Fante, which they called the "black trade." But the rum men preferred the fort trade and invariably tried it before trading directly with the Fante.[17]

The Gold Coast forts were the focus for American networks in Africa. Through serial voyages, merchants and mariners established ties with fort personnel that allowed for increasingly complex transactions. One benefit of these networks was to allow slavers to carry accounts over time from one voyage to the next. Running accounts across multiple voyages promised faster loading times and greater profits. In 1772, for example, Aaron Lopez and Jacob Rivera instructed Captain William English to redeem forty captives who had been left with David Mill, governor of Cape Coast Castle, by Captain Nathaniel Briggs on a previous voyage. This would have given English a significant head start had it worked. In this transaction, English was not actually embarking the same men and women that Briggs had left; imprisoning those captives at Cape Coast for months on end would have killed most of them and cost a great deal of money. The captives Briggs originally left were surely sold off as quickly as possible, but the captives English received were different people, newer arrivals, which is why Mill could only deliver thirty of them. This and similar transactions represented a new departure for the American slave trade. The people carried aboard American slavers had now become fungible, abstract values entered into the ledgers. And by contracting to receive forty captives several months to a year in advance, the Americans had entered into a crude futures market in human lives.[18]

In addition to purchasing captives there, American merchants viewed the Gold Coast as a potential market for their ships. For many American captains of the period one of the distinctive features in their instructions was an order to sell the vessel for bills of exchange if possible. Forts needed craft of all descriptions, and some of the personnel needed vessels for their private deals. In many cases, American merchants preferred ship sales over slave trading; after all, why take the time and assume the risks of carrying captives to the Caribbean when you can get bills of exchange immediately by selling the vessel? As it happened, Guinea captains rarely succeeded in selling their ships, although they occasionally pulled it off. In 1770, for example, David Mill and his counterpart at Anomabu purchased a Rhode Island vessel to use for their own trade. The crew members probably sailed the vessel for Mill to the West Indies and were then discharged, forced to make their own way home. Gold Coast factors even occasionally sent their vessels to New England for repairs, since in sailing terms it was closer than Britain and could be done for less money.[19]

One figure stands out as the Americans' most important contact on the Gold Coast: Richard Brew, the *enfant terrible* of the British slave trade. Brew's career coincided almost perfectly with the peak decades of the North American trade, and he dealt regularly with most of the prominent Newport traders. Born in Ireland around 1725, Brew came from a family of Protestant wine merchants. He arrived in Africa in 1745, probably as an employee of the RAC. By 1750 he was a clerk at Cape Coast Castle and later served as factor at several smaller forts before coming to Anomabu, where he settled and married into the ruling Fante family. His marriage gave him a strong connection to the local elite, which he used to build his fortune and to found a lineage.[20]

A continuing theme of Brew's career was his willingness to breach RAC and CMTA rules against using his position for private gain. All company officials did so, but Brew was notably brazen. He left the CMTA in 1764, built a "castle" a few yards from the fort at Anomabu, and set up as a private trader, partnering with Steven Smith of London. Ambitious and audacious, Brew aspired to create a private trading empire across the Gold Coast and into the Bight of Benin, in pursuit of which he frequently inserted himself into major regional conflicts. In

the mid-1760s, for example, he offered to broker a peace between Fante
and Asante. His position was strengthened when the Fante asked him
to house several elite Asante prisoners, including a cousin of the asantehene, at Castle Brew. British and Dutch company officials, who hoped
to broker a settlement themselves, were outraged by Brew's maneuvering. No final resolution of the Fante-Asante conflict resulted, but Brew's
intervention, which involved the eventual release of the hostages, did
bring about a détente and confirmed his position as a force to be reckoned with on the Gold Coast.[21]

Brew's connection with the New Englanders was strong. The Vernons, Redwoods, Champlins, Gardners, and undoubtedly many others
did regular business with him. Brew's marriage had positioned him perfectly to tap into regional trade networks. With capital and credit from
his London partners, Brew cultivated relationships with Fante traders
and eventually, via his role as mediator with Asante, traders from there
as well. By allying with Brew, American merchants became connected
to those same networks. This was not a one-sided relationship, however. Brew cultivated his North American clients, which says something
about the importance of American traders on the Gold Coast in this era.
An early gesture by Brew probably helped to cement ties. In 1758, during
the Seven Years' War, a French privateer cruised down the African coast,
capturing four North American vessels. Their crews, numbering forty-
five in all, were put ashore in Africa. Brew offered to lend the stranded
captains £1,000 to ransom their vessels back from the privateer. Newporters Joseph G. Wanton of the *King of Prussia* and Walter Buffum
of the *Annamaboo* both accepted Brew's offer and were soon headed
home. William Taylor of the Connecticut ship *Fox* was not empowered to ransom his vessel, so he reluctantly declined. When the French
threatened to burn the *Fox,* Brew purchased it and sent the crew back
to Connecticut in it. The CMTA criticized Brew for trading with the
enemy, but the North American press praised his generosity and hos-
pitality, the first of several instances over the years in which he received
favorable coverage.[22]

Brew provided a number of additional services for the North
Americans. The most fundamental of these was to supply captives. Brew
rarely furnished an entire cargo, although he sometimes provided very

large numbers of captives, eighty on one occasion. For the most part, he seems to have supplied in the dozens, sometimes fewer.[23] His ability to house captives at Castle Brew allowed American captains to carry accounts over multiple voyages. If prices were good, a captain might opt to purchase extra captives and leave them with Brew for future transportation. In 1776, for example, Caleb Gardner and Robert Johnson empowered Peleg Clarke to collect thirty-eight captives from Brew, left from a previous voyage. In such cases, Brew almost certainly sold the deposited captives as soon as he could and supplied the subsequent voyage with captives taken later. A variation on the scheme was for the captain to deposit a certain amount of rum to be redeemed in captives at a later date. These kinds of arrangements, similar to the one Lopez and Rivera had with David Mill at Cape Coast, represented a significant advance over earlier ways of doing business. They allowed American merchants to establish what were in effect credit relationships with dealers on the African coast, which reduced friction and allowed for greater flexibility.[24]

Brew's services were not limited to selling captives and storing goods. He was an important source of information, as his letters to Newport merchants occasionally made the rounds through the colonial press. In 1766, his letter to a Newport correspondent warning of pirates off the coast of Africa was reprinted in Charleston and Philadelphia. For the many captains who had been instructed to try to sell their vessels, Brew, as a private trader who was trying to build his own trading empire across lower Guinea, was often the first person they contacted. In most instances he declined to buy, but he did do it at least once, in 1763, when he purchased the Vernons' *Renard* and its rum cargo for £3,300 in bills of exchange. Another sale in 1769 appears to have fallen through when, due to the insolvency of his London partner Steven Smith, Brew was unable to offer good bills of exchange.[25]

Brew was a perpetual thorn in the side of the CMTA, competing with it and using his relationship with the Fante elite to influence regional politics in his favor. The Americans' close relationship with Brew seems to have tainted them in the company's eyes. Fort officials viewed the rum men as somewhat lawless and disorderly. An incident in 1769 demonstrated that skippers valued their relationship with Brew over their relationship with the CMTA. John Grossle, governor at Cape Coast, had set up several small trading posts, in violation of company rules. A group of seven British captains, including Newport's Caleb Gardner and Boston's Hector McNeal, wrote an official letter of complaint, charging that the factories were driving up prices in markets where they had previously purchased directly and more cheaply from African traders. The captains explained that they thought "such Proceedings illegal and not in the least Convenant [*sic*] to the Institution of the British Forts."[26]

John Grossle, the governor at Cape Coast, sensed the hidden hand of Richard Brew at work. Grossle had heard rumors that Brew had come aboard one of the American vessels beforehand and that the signing of the letter was saluted by the ships' great guns. Brew, he charged, was using the captains to stir up trouble in London so he could take control of the forts and trade freely with "Foreigners." Grossle rebutted the captains' charges by claiming that he performed an "infinite service" to British traders by selling captives "at a very moderate profit." The alternative, should the Board of Trade side with the captains, was nothing less than a breakdown of all order on the Gold Coast. The Dutch would engross their share of the trade by buying from renegade factors. Worse, argued Grossle, the Fante "gold-takers," or brokers, who were essential to the trade, would be given the honor of admittance to the captains' tables "and made companions of" in "riotous Assembly." The authority of the CMTA would diminish, and the "Negroes" would grow more licentious. In going down this path, Grossle clearly hoped that by raising the specter of racial disorder he could induce the CMTA to support his position. He was wrong. The following year, the CMTA instructed employees to evacuate all private installations. The order made explicit reference to the captains' petition. Brew's patronage of the rum men had paid dividends.[27]

As strong as Brew's relationship with the Americans was, it is important to remember that Brew was a hardheaded businessman who put profit before all else, including his friendship with the rum men. He continually schemed to drive up prices by monopolizing the trade in captives (though in this he probably was not successful). And much as he cultivated a relationship with the Americans, he valued the assortment of manufactures and textiles carried by British ships over the rum carried by the New Englanders. When, in 1759, Brew was dealing with a Liverpool ship and a Rhode Islander, he let the Liverpool captain choose the best twenty-one captives and sold the remaining captives to the rum man, noting that "I wanted none of that commodity." Brew was even successfully sued in a Rhode Island court for a debt owed to Sion Martindale. At this point in his career he was close to bankruptcy, which explains why he failed to pay, but the existence of the debt underscores the depth of his connection to Rhode Island. Connections with people like Brew and Mill had not existed in the earlier years. They were both a cause and a consequence of the fast-growing American slave trade, as the rum men went from being an occasional curiosity along the African coast to becoming a fixture in regional trade.[28]

Dealing with Brew or the CMTA forts, or even with the Dutch and Danish installations, as the rum men were known to do, was as a rule more expensive than the "black trade." Fort personnel were middlemen who took the requisite markup. In exchange, they promised speed, although they often failed to deliver on that point. They also served as a cultural buffer between the Americans and African suppliers. Ship captains always preferred to do business with Europeans, rather than with Africans, whose customs they did not understand and whose power they feared. However, when captive prices at the forts were too high or when the supply of captives was too low, ship captains dealt directly with Africans.

Dealing directly with Africans did not mean the captains dealt directly with the suppliers of captives. In almost all cases on the Gold Coast, business was conducted through a broker known as a gold-taker. These were Africans, or Fante in most of the places where the Americans traded, and virtually all slavers hired them. The job of a gold-taker was to serve as a translator and to assay any gold paid or taken in payment, services for which they received a commission. As well-connected members of their communities, gold-takers were the main links between the economic worlds of the Atlantic and the African interior. Descriptions of the relationship between gold-takers and American captains are rare, but payments to them appear frequently in trade books. One captain noted a payment of twenty gallons of neat rum to the "Gold taker for Buying 27 slaves." Another recorded several payments, including a dash (small payment, analogous to a gratuity) of rum, some calico as a customary retainer, known as "sea cloth," and a payment for six boat trips by the gold-taker out to the ship.[29]

One of the main functions of the gold-taker was to connect ship captains with "bush sellers," or African slave dealers. Some of these were quite wealthy, but others were small-scale, occasional sellers. The process of exchange usually involved advancing trade goods, in effect an extension of credit. These advances were secured by pawns in the form of people or gold. Failure to repay an advance resulted in the forfeiture of the pawns. That seems to have happened rarely, but it did occur. According to custom, ship captains were not allowed to leave with unredeemed pawns. Peleg Clarke took this obligation seriously enough to abduct a woman so that he could release a boy who had been given to him in pawn. At another point, three of Clarke's pawns were killed in a major shipboard insurrection off Cape Coast. He would have had to make good on the loss in order to settle the ensuing "palaver."[30]

Gold-takers had a mixed reputation among ship captains, but slavers had little choice but to hire them. One CMTA official referred to them as a "set of men generally very poor and who get their livelihood by being Interpreters between the Ships and the Traders, and by cheating both." William Chancellor, a surgeon on his first voyage and so hardly an expert, offered a more charitable assessment. According to him, gold-takers operated on a kind of honor system in which those who were caught defrauding a client were banished from the trade. Even so, Chancellor noted that "they are very little trusted here." But some level of trust seems to have existed, because when the captains at Anomabu petitioned against John Grossle, they apparently did so with the support of the local gold-takers. Gold-takers, then, were well known to the Americans and served as their principal connection to the African traders, translating, handling business, and channeling credit. The Gold Coast trade demanded a great deal of experience on the part of captains, and the existence of the gold-takers allowed it to run more smoothly than in other regions, as we will soon see.[31]

The death of the asantehene Opoku Ware in about 1750 brought changes to both the volume and mechanism of captive supply on the Gold Coast.

His death coincided with the post-1748 revival of the newly sophisticated North American slave trade. American traders were never directly connected to Asante; their links were with British coastal traders, like Richard Brew and David Mill, who in turn were connected to Fante sellers. But in so many ways, American fortunes were shaped by events in Asante and even points beyond. Although Asante could not dictate events—Fante was a formidable power in its own right, and other states proved able to cause Asante significant problems—it was the single most important determinant in the Gold Coast slave trade. American traders, though focused more on the forts and on the Fante, were aware of Asante's importance, gleaned in conversations with fort personnel. Theirs was a rudimentary, practical understanding, usually in relation to warfare and the opening and closing of the paths that were used to deliver captives to the coast. On a 1772 voyage, for example, Peleg Clarke noted that trade at Anomabu was slow, "Occasioned by a Disturbance that broke out between the Fantines [Fantes] and Shantines [Asantes] which has stop't the slaves, as that Trade comes chiefly threw [through] their hands."[32]

Opoku Ware's military conquests in the 1730s had helped to establish the American slave trade on the Gold Coast, but his final years were marked by instability and weakness. From the rum men's perspective, the main result of this weakness was an erratic supply of captives on the coast. In 1746, an ill-advised effort by Opoku Ware to centralize power at the expense of local leaders led to a rebellion in Kumasi, Asante's political heart. As this happened, several of the conquered states to the south—Denkyira, Twifo, Wasa, and Akyem—took advantage of the chaos at the center to rebel. These four states soon allied with Fante, that perpetual thorn in Asante's side, all of which posed a serious threat to Asante's dominance. After Opoku Ware's death in 1750, the new asantehene, Kusi Obodum, took control, but these were difficult times, and his reign was marked by efforts to reassert Asante's power. The four rebel states cooperated with Fante to block the paths between Asante and the coast, a situation that would persist for the next fifteen years. Asante was forced to conduct its Atlantic trade over the roads to the eastern Gold Coast, through Akyem, Akwamu, to Accra, a much less direct (and therefore more costly) option than sending them straight south to Anomabu or Cape Coast. Captives did continue to embark at Anomabu, however. A few small Asante caravans ran the blockade, "in a very difficult and dangerous way," but most of the captives sold at Anomabu in these years had probably been seized locally for debts and crimes. Still others were captured in the periodic skirmishes that flared up, and no doubt some, especially in the borderlands between the rebel states and Asante, were simply abducted. Given these conditions, it is little wonder that so many rum men reported long waits on the coast and an unpredictable supply of captives. Although the number of captives embarked on the Gold Coast surged briefly in the 1750s before falling sharply, the number embarked on American vessels on the Gold Coast dropped below one thousand per year in 1751 and stayed below that level for the entire decade, with the exception of the year 1757.[33]

The situation changed in the mid-1760s. Frustrated by the allies' road closures and fearful that Asante would invade and overrun Fante, the British and Dutch tried to mediate the conflict. These efforts were slow to bear fruit, owing not only to mistrust between the allies and Asante, but to divergent interests among the Europeans, with the Dutch favoring Asante and the British siding with Fante. By the late 1750s, however, Fante, which suffered from its own policy of road closure, signaled a willingness to reopen them. In 1760, rumors of Fante's volte-face prompted a retaliatory attack by Wassa, one of its erstwhile allies, accompanied by a threat to kill some high-ranking Asante hostages who had been kept there for some time. As Asante prepared to invade, the allies enlisted the aid of Oyo, the powerful Yoruba state that controlled much of the interior of the Bight of Benin, to the east. Oyo inflicted a devastating defeat on Asante, which led to Kusi Obodum's downfall and replacement in 1764 by the youthful and dynamic Osei Kwadwo. The era of road closures was about to end. Asante would soon re-emerge as the major supplier of captives to American vessels.[34]

In the early years of his reign, in the mid-late 1760s, Osei Kwadwo faced two main challenges. The one that most affected the Americans was the persistent tension between Asante and the polities between it and the coast. The other challenge was the newly resistant Akyem, which Asante had conquered in 1742 but which was now rising in rebellion. Of the two threats, Osei Kwadwo believed the Akyem revolt to be the more serious and moved to crush it. Although relations between Asante and its southern neighbors—Wassa, Twifo, and Fante—were tense and war a perpetual possibility, the paths remained open for most of the time, though they were subject to intermittent closure in times of crisis. It may be that Asante, having prioritized the pacification of Akyem, tolerated a certain level of conflict on its southern flank because it depended on a steady supply of guns and powder. As a result of these developments the number of captives embarked on the Gold Coast, which dipped in the mid-1750s to mid-1760s to an annual average of about 5,900 per year, began an unsteady climb to 7,700 per year into the mid-1770s. The American share of this trade fluctuated from year to year, but it saw an annual increase of about one-third through the late 1760s and early 1770s.[35]

To a great extent, then, the success of the American slave trade lay beyond the traders' control. Metropolitan merchants could react to the drops in the supply of captives by shifting their trade to other parts of the African coast, since they could draw on a large array of trade goods. Indeed, the Gold Coast accounted for only 17 percent of the British slave trade between 1751 and 1775. But the Americans, limited to trading in those parts of Africa where rum was valued as a trade good, were almost totally dependent on the Gold Coast trade, purchasing more than three-quarters of their captives there. For this reason, the political turmoil in Asante had a measurable, though only dimly understood, effect on American slave traders.[36]

Upper Guinea continued as a secondary source of captives for American slavers, accounting for slightly less than one-quarter of the American slave trade. From the merchants' perspective, the region served two functions. First, it gave them a market to offset their heavy reliance on the Gold Coast. Major traders sometimes sent out multiple vessels at once, directing one to upper Guinea and another to the Gold Coast to avoid placing them in competition with each other.[37] Vessels en route to the Gold Coast often touched in upper Guinea for water and repairs or to purchase rice before continuing on.[38] Some Gold Coast–bound vessels also purchased captives in upper Guinea. This was usually done to get a head start on completing the cargo and to reduce the time spent on the Gold Coast. Some older historical treatments of the slave trade referred to this practice as "coasting" and argued that it was a common practice. In reality, most of the purchases made en route down the coast were quite small, and the captives were likely resold to outbound slavers upon reaching the Gold Coast. Some merchants even instructed captains not to purchase captives in upper Guinea, since keeping them aboard the vessel for that long increased the risk of monetary losses through mortality. As Aaron Lopez told Captain William English, "as we have no opinion of the windward Coast [that is, upper Guinea] trade, we think it advisable, That as Soon as you procure the necessary rice that you proceed without delay to Anamaboe."[39]

Upper Guinea could only be a secondary market for the North Americans for the simple reason that it could not absorb large quantities of rum. As we saw in chapter 3, there was steady, low-level demand for rum from the ceddo-type regimes and from the forts, but it was limited. American merchants like the Vernons were aware of this fact, though they seem not to have known why it was the case. After sending some vessels to upper Guinea early in their career, they focused almost exclusively on the Gold Coast trade. In 1774, while contemplating a return to the upper Guinea trade, the Vernons proposed a joint venture to Robert Heatley of London. Heatley had traded for years along the Gambia River and knew the market well. His reply was discouraging: "A large Cargo from North Am.," he informed them, "is no way fit for Gambia. The Consumption of Rum is so small there to any other part of the Coast." American vessels, he offered (though the Vernons already knew), were better off "Down the Coast[,] which is the Way that most Vessels does wth Am[e]r. Cargo." For these reasons, American vessels intent on trading in upper Guinea still found it necessary to offset their reliance on rum by acquiring additional trade goods. This could be done by purchasing textiles at Cabo Verde, by trading with the forts for textiles and other goods, or by dealing with other ships for some of their trade goods. Upper Guinea cargoes were consequently more mixed than Gold Coast cargoes. Whereas rum financed anywhere from 50 to 90 percent of the captives purchased on the Gold Coast (with gold usually accounting for the remainder), it accounted for only 30 to 80 percent of purchases on the upper Guinea coast (with tobacco, textiles, provisions, and assorted goods comprising the remainder).[40]

By the mid-eighteenth century, upper Guinea had reached a turning point in its history, with great implications for the slave trade. Three centuries of Atlantic trade had fostered the development of the ceddo-type regimes, the centralized and often predatory states that generated most of the captives for sale. Decentralized polities engaged in smaller-scale raids in order to procure iron to make farming implements, along with other goods. Toward the end of the seventeenth century, however, dissent stirred. Muslim clerics, incensed by a general sense of moral decay, targeted the ceddo regimes for reform. Although these clerics did not object to slavery per se, they did object to the enslavement of Muslims by the ceddo regimes. Moreover, because Islam justified enslavement in part as a way to bring non-Muslims to the true faith, the marabouts (as Muslim teachers were called) objected to the sale of captives to non-Muslim purchasers. Although the reformers did not focus specifically on alcohol consumption, they condemned it as a matter of course, viewing it as a sign of the general moral degradation in the ceddo regimes.[41]

The earliest Muslim revolts were crushed in fairly short order, but that changed with events in the Futa Jallon, the highland area northeast of Sierra Leone. The original inhabitants of the region were farmers who spoke Jalonke, a Mande language. Beginning in the fifteenth century, Fulbe cattle herders, who spoke an Atlantic language close to Wolof, arrived in search of pasture. As firstcomers, or landlords, the Jalonke reserved the right to tax the Fulbe herders, but over time Jalonke demands increased and caused great tension between the two groups. Many Fulbe were also Muslims who had been influenced by earlier reformist ideas, so as tensions came to a head, their frustrations found expression in the language of religion. The Futa Jallon jihad erupted in 1725–1726, led by Karamoko Alfa, whose name signified his status as a respected religious leader. With a committee of twenty-two, Karamoko Alfa founded a theocratic state aimed at purifying the region of the influence of those regimes they perceived as corrupt. And because the Futa Jallon was the source for the Senegal, Gambia, and Niger Rivers, along with the Rivers of Guinea, its influence spread rapidly.[42]

The Futa Jallon jihad had a complex and contradictory effect on the transatlantic slave trade. The new regime opposed the enslavement of Muslims and the sale of captives to non-Muslims, and because it exercised a theoretical monopoly over the sale of captives, it was in a position to limit the flow to Christian traders on the coast. But establishing the new state entailed warfare, which generated captives, and while many were sold on the intra-African market, others inevitably ended up in caravans headed to the European forts. The leadership attempted to screen out Muslims, but a combination of unauthorized activity and a willingness to sell some non-Muslims to the Christians—rationalized by the need to procure weapons and other goods—meant that plenty of people still made it to the coast. In the first half of the 1720s, upper Guinea exported about twenty-one thousand captives. In the first five years following the start of the jihad, some twenty-eight thousand captives were embarked. The increasing number of captives embarked at Senegambia and Sierra Leone suggests that the clerics' opposition to the sale of captives to non-Muslims was empty rhetoric, and many historians have agreed. However, recent work has offered a more nuanced picture, arguing that whereas the creation of Futa Jallon did indeed lead to a surge in captives sent across the Atlantic, the number actually dispatched was not as great as it might have been had Islam not discouraged the practice. Many of those enslaved by Futa Jallon were retained to work on its own plantations, which grew considerably over the eighteenth century. From the perspective of American slavers, events in the Futa Jallon resulted in more captives for sale in the Gambia and Sierra Leone. However, the growing influence of religious reform, coupled with the growth of slavery in Futa Jallon itself, meant that demand for rum would not grow apace.[43]

In 1751, at the very moment that North Americans were reviving their slave trade, Futa Jallon embarked on a new series of conquests. The new departure came about with the death of Karamoko Alfa, the founder of the state. More a religious than a military leader, he had steered Futa Jallon through its early years and defended it against its enemies. His successor, Sori Mawdo, or "Sori the Great," came from a martial faction. With Futa Jallon now securely established, he inaugurated a series of campaigns aimed at conquering and converting neighboring polities. Sori's initial target was Sankaran, a wealthy agricultural and stock-raising region situated on a tributary of the Niger to the southwest of Kankan, a major kola-nut trading center. His army seized large amounts of cattle (an important form of wealth and status) and captives. Over the next few years Sori undertook annual campaigns, ravaging the areas north of Labe and near Futa Bundu. By the mid-1750s, the regional polities had begun to mount an effective resistance to Sori. The ruler of Koranko, inland from Sierra Leone, who had at one time accepted Islam, renounced the faith and fought back. Sori crushed the rebellion and laid waste to the region, generating additional captives. Sori's string of victories was halted, however, in 1762, when he attacked Wassoulou, to the east of Futa Jallon. The rains came early that year, and his army was forced to retire. Konta Brinah, the leader of Wassoulou, harassed Sori's army as it retreated, and eventually routed it. The defeat prompted the defection of Futa Jallon's ally, Sulimana, which resulted in the burning of Sori's capital town of Timbo in 1764. Through the 1760s, Sulimana, allied with Wassoulou, attacked and destroyed several more towns in Futa Jallon. Warfare between Futa Jallon and Sulimana continued into the 1770s.[44]

Religious conflict in Futa Jallon resulted in a shift in the geography of the American slave trade. For a century, American slavers coming to upper Guinea had focused their activities on the Gambia, and they continued to trade there during in this period, tapping the ongoing ceddo trade and the trade from Segu to the upper river. After 1750, however, the area to the south, the coastline from the modern-day Republic of Guinea to Sierra Leone, emerged as a destination of equal importance. These areas had long been strictly second- or even third-tier embarkation points for the slave trade. The area soon became quite well known to them, although the detailed knowledge seems to have resided primarily with the skippers rather than with the merchants. Few geographically explicit references to Sierra Leone or the Rio Pongo appear in ships' instructions. Timothy Fitch, who was the only major slaver to specialize in the upper Guinea trade, was an exception, issuing specific instructions at various times to make for Senegal and the Isles de Los. The Vernon brothers were another firm that instructed their skippers to specific locations on the upper Guinea coast.[45]

Captives from upper Guinea reached the holds of American slavers in two basic stages. The first was via the Muslim merchant networks or trade diasporas, collectively known as the Juula, which handled almost all long-distance trade in the interior. The Juula networks predated the arrival of the Portuguese and focused on gold, textiles, kola nuts, iron, and salt. Their diasporic nature, in which scattered members spoke a distinctive language and adhered to Islam, implied not only a shared faith but a shared commercial code, which allowed for the establishment of trust and the movement of goods over long distances. With the arrival of the Europeans, these networks became the principal mechanism of slave supply to the coast. Caravans ranging from a few dozen to several hundred people traveled to the coastal factories during the dry season.[46]

Juula caravans were vulnerable to disruption. Polities large and small attempted to tax them and sometimes blocked their passage altogether. This was often the case in the mid-eighteenth century, as warfare rocked the region and Futa Jallon tried to use its location as a crossroads to isolate its rivals. When the political situation stabilized, the rulers of the Futa Jallon decided that taxing caravans was a better policy than blocking them. Caravan routes changed little over the years, but leaders had the ability to alter course as needed. Juula networks were very good at channeling information, and often the decision to alter course came as a result of new intelligence. Mungo Park tells of a caravan leader on the Gambia River who received word of low captive prices and decided to halt where he was, rent land, use the captives to grow rice, and see if the market improved after the harvest. All of this meant that the supply of captives on the coast fluctuated in response to factors beyond the slavers' control. When the supply of captives on the coast was down, American rum vessels, with their limited assortments of goods, were at a particular disadvantage.[47]

For the Americans, trade in upper Guinea was what contemporaries called a "ship trade" rather than a "fort trade." There were forts at

Saint-Louis, at the mouth of the Senegal River (under British control from 1758 to 1783), on Gorée Island (under British control from 1758 to 1763 and from 1779 to 1783), at James Fort in the Gambia River, in the Portuguese towns of Cacheu and Bissau, and at Bance Island in the Sierra Leone River, but Americans did relatively little business with them and never developed long-term relationships with the factors as they had on the Gold Coast. American vessels did peddle rum and produce to the garrisons, but more to improve their assortment of trade goods than to acquire captives.[48] Captive prices at the forts were high and supplies were irregular. On the Gambia, the Americans were particularly unhappy with the customs charges imposed by Niumi for wood and water and often avoided payment. Their actions caused problems for the British at James Fort, since Niumi, as landlords, held the CMTA responsible for American avoidance. In one incident, the fort's governor fired warning shots at a Boston vessel that had refused to identify itself and pay customs.[49]

On the Gambia, the Americans usually traded a hundred or more miles up the river, at towns such as Joal and Niani Maru (rendered "Yanamarow" in American correspondence). To the south, they favored the so-called Rivers of Guinea and the Sierra Leone River, where several of the trading routes from Futa Jallon terminated. The Isles de Los, a small archipelago and bulking center opposite the River Dembia, was an important destination in the region. American skippers preferred the islands' safe and comparatively healthy location to the mangrove swamps on the mainland. That did not stop them from doing quite a bit of business in the coastal estuaries, which were dotted with clusters of small-scale European and Eurafrican traders, at places such as the Rio Pongo, Wonkafong, and the Scarcies. The rum men began frequenting these settlements after 1750, as the flow of captives from the interior highlands increased. Ships went as far up these rivers as they could and then dispatched boats. The boats then wandered through the mangroves, purchasing captives in ones, twos, and threes. It was time-consuming, but for the Americans it was the best way to ensure value for money. Farther south still, slavers traded at the Banana and Plantain Islands and at Sherbro, but these destinations were not as significant as the rivers to the north of Sierra Leone.[50]

Avoiding the big forts may have lowered costs, but it also placed American seamen into direct contact with African and Luso-African dealers and forced them to trade very much on their terms. This was a far more complicated task than bargaining with the factors at the forts, and it was the main reason why experience was so valuable. Thomas Eldrid of Rhode Island, who made several trips in the 1760s, spent almost a year going up and down the estuaries opposite the Isles de Los in a boat, lodging with the small traders for three or four nights at a time. During the months he spent on the upper Guinea coast, he acquired a working knowledge of Susu, the lingua franca of regional trade (one suspects through a relationship with a local woman). Eldrid is the only American slaver known to speak an African language, but given the nature of the upper Guinea trade, he is unlikely to have been the only one.[51]

Trading was highly ritualized. Although some deals were done aboard the ship, most important negotiations were done on shore, according to local custom. When the *Sally* came to the region in 1764, negotiations were conducted underneath a "palaver tree." Elsewhere in upper Guinea, negotiations were conducted in palaver houses, or multipurpose civic structures at the center of many towns. On the Gambia River, deals were concluded on the *bentang*, an elevated platform. By agreeing to do business in these spaces, slave traders signaled their acceptance of local norms.[52] Gifts were another important feature of local trade. Failure to supply the right gifts in the right quantities could poison a negotiation and was yet another reason why experience mattered. To open trade, one captain supplied, in addition to seventy-five gallons of rum in customs, five kegs and fourteen flasks of rum, receiving a cow in return. When negotiating with non-alcohol-consuming Muslims, trade was opened with a gift of kola nuts or tobacco. Traders committed themselves to negotiations by biting into a kola nut, after which orations were given recounting the difficulties and hazards of the journey from the interior. Negotiations over lesser goods like salt ensued, with captives coming last.[53]

Close contact of this kind often led to palavers, a regional term that denoted both a dispute and a process of conflict resolution. One of the most common causes of palavers was abduction by the Americans, which the locals called "panyarring." The term was adapted from the

Portuguese word *penhorar*, meaning "to seize something for a debt."
Many panyarrings grew out of wider disputes about trade and payment,
and some of these were resolved via palaver, which is to say, according
to local rules. But some panyarrings were due to simple opportunism,
as when a Boston skipper lured nine Luso-Africans on board his vessel
and carried them away. Palavers could easily spiral out of control, as
each side panyarred and retaliated for wrongs, both real and perceived.
One of the worst examples took place in 1761 at Niani Maru, when some
British and American captains accused local traders of conspiring to
raise prices. Acting in concert, the ships bombarded the port with heavy
shot, killing seven or eight and leveling trees and houses.[54]

Clashes like this point to a rather paradoxical situation among
American slavers. On one hand, in this and other incidents, the ship
captains cast themselves as upholding "the Laws of the said River &
Country," implying an awareness that the trade was governed by rules
and norms. At the same time, it was their repeated violation of the rules
that caused problems. Were the Americans playing by the rules, or were
they flouting them? The answer to that question lies, in part at least, in
the origins of the captains and vessels. In most recorded incidents, the
captains and vessels came from places other than Rhode Island. Inexperience, in other words, lay at the root of many of these conflicts. Many
non–Rhode Island vessels were commanded by skippers making their
first and only slaving voyage. Those on one-off voyages were not only
less experienced, but felt freer to violate whatever rules they understood,
since they did not have to worry about future relationships. Rhode Islanders, by contrast, rarely appear in the record as being involved in
tit-for-tat violence. They really did know the rules.

A final anecdote involving a veteran Newport slaver is the exception that proves the rule. In 1754, Caleb Godfrey took the sloop *Hare* to
Sierra Leone. Several months before his arrival, a Bullom force from the
northern shore of the Sierra Leone estuary had attacked a British vessel,
killing the captain. A few months later, as Godfrey was purchasing captives to the north of Sierra Leone, local white traders captured the man
they believed responsible. Worried that an execution might alienate
their landlords, the traders quietly handed the man to over to Godfrey

with instructions to "make an Example" of him. Godfrey scheduled a public execution, but the man died before he could carry it out. Determined to fulfil his mission, Godfrey cut off the man's head and hands and displayed them aboard the *Hare* for "Several Days."[55]

This chilling incident reveals quite a bit about the conduct of American mariners in upper Guinea. It highlights not only the ruthlessness that was a virtual job requirement for any slaver, but also the importance of local and regional experience in the conduct of the slave trade. Godfrey's shocking display was qualitatively different from the fumbling, bumbling actions of the Boston and New York skippers. He had no quarrel with his own trading partners. He became involved because he believed an "Example" needed to be set in order to bring proper order to the trade and because the resident traders were not in a position to do it themselves. In other words, he knew the rules.

In the final few years before the American Revolution, British slave merchants awakened to the possibility that the Americans could be something more than irritating, rule-flouting poachers: they could be partners in profitable ventures. Of course, British merchants had been partners of sorts from the beginning. American slavers relied on British credit and insured their voyages with British underwriters, and a few British merchants had invested in American ventures over the decades. Still, the vast majority of American voyages had always been organized by merchants based in the colonies and without significant metropolitan involvement. Now, however, some British merchants realized that the Americans could bring certain advantages into a partnership. One advantage was access to ships. As we have seen, British merchants occasionally relied on Americans for ships, and slavers often sought to sell their vessels in Africa. The leap from purchasing vessels to partnering in voyages took little imagination. Access to rum was another possible attraction, although probably not as important. The Gold Coast forts, especially, liked to keep a supply on hand. In the early eighteenth century, before the rum men began trading regularly, the RAC actually explored establishing a shuttle trade with the West Indies. Indeed, several vessels in the Barbados–Africa trade seem to have been doing exactly that.

Partnerships with the North Americans could accomplish the same end. Combining American rum with British trade goods could make a good assortment, indeed.

One of the more ambitious British American ventures involved John Grossle, the CMTA governor at Cape Coast. Like so many company employees, Grossle engaged in illegal private dealings. In the late 1760s, he struck a deal with David Dunn. Grossle had established an illicit trading post a few miles east of Tantumquery, another CMTA fort on the Gold Coast. Grossle's London contacts forwarded letters of credit to Boston, which Dunn used to procure a vessel, with Grossle as one-third owner. Dunn then carried rum from Boston to Cape Coast. There, Grossle combined the rum with a shipment of high-quality textiles to create an optimal assortment. The rum and textiles were used to purchase captives, who were then carried to Barbados. The partners' *Beggar's Benison* seems to have undertaken two such voyages, landing captives in Barbados in 1771 and South Carolina in 1772. However, as we saw earlier, Grossle's illegal forts attracted the attention of Richard Brew, who, with the aid of Caleb Gardner and his fellow petitioners, managed to put an end to his enterprise.[56]

Peleg Clarke's ventures with John Fletcher in the 1770s were even more elaborate. Clarke was the son of a prominent Newport mariner with ties on his mother's side to the Gardner family. He captained his first slaver in 1767, and at some point in the next few years made the acquaintance of John Fletcher, a merchant based in London but with possible origins in Hull and strong ties to Jamaica. Fletcher had additional connections in Liverpool and some experience in the slave trade. He also spent time in Newport and Boston, perhaps on a return trip from the Caribbean. Beginning in 1771, the two men joined forces on several complex, multilateral ventures, which ran over the next several years. The itineraries are difficult to reconstruct with precision, but the basic arrangement involved Fletcher taking a half share and providing financing and trade goods while arranging for sale through his Jamaican connections. Meanwhile, for a quarter share, Clarke obtained and skippered the vessel. The final share was owned by Peatt and Westmoreland, Fletcher's Jamaica correspondents.[57]

For their first venture, Clarke purchased rum and a brig, chris-tened the *Fletcher*, and Fletcher supplied a "Liverpool Guine furnace." Clarke then sailed to the Gold Coast, where, despite some delay due to the closure of the paths, he managed to procure close to one hundred captives. While on the Gold Coast, Clarke made several "Advantageous Ingagements," by which he almost certainly meant depositing trade goods or captives for a future voyage. Clarke then delivered the captives to Fletcher's contacts in Jamaica for bills of exchange. The partners ap-pear to have organized another voyage shortly afterward, but details are few and the vessel never completed its voyage.[58]

Their next venture was more convoluted and took quite a while to come together. Clarke had taken the *Thames* from Boston to En-gland in 1773. The plan was to load the vessel with manufactures, then return to Boston and Newport. Once there, Clarke would dispatch the *Thames* to the Caribbean for rum (it seems to have been in short supply in Rhode Island) and purchase a larger vessel in Boston. In addition, Clarke was to arrange for the purchase of a smaller vessel of forty to fifty tons, which the partners planned to use as a tender on the African coast, which says something of their ambition for this voyage. This venture was plagued by various delays but was successful enough to inspire several more joint ventures, with Fletcher at times assembling trade goods in England and forwarding them to Clarke. The two even organized voy-ages after the passage of the Prohibitory Act in late 1775, which barred the colonies from overseas trade. Clarke's partnership with Fletcher was far from the norm, but it did exemplify the new sophistication of the American slave trade.[59]

Although the American slave trade did not reach its zenith in terms of captives transported until after the American Revolution, the years 1751–1775 represented the high-water mark of its political and economic importance in North America. Slave trading was entirely legal and car-ried no moral stigma outside of Quaker circles, and even within them the condemnation was not unequivocal. The fact that the trade's capital-intensive nature restricted it primarily to wealthy merchants gave it an aura of prestige. Slavers were elected to colonial legislatures and governor's chairs, and filled an endless variety of lesser positions. By the late colonial period, metropolitan traders were partnering with them on joint ventures, and CMTA officials viewed them as a significant, if perhaps lawless, presence on the African coast.

The prominence of the slave trade in this era is evident in a "Remonstrance" sent by the Rhode Island legislature to Parliament in 1764 in response to the Sugar Act. The petitioners' central argument was that the Sugar Act would make it impossible for Rhode Island to pay for its British imports, which it estimated at £120,000 per year. In support, the Remonstrance offered a mini-history of the colony's slave trade, stressing its importance as a source of bills of exchange to repay metropolitan merchants. For good measure, petitioners also mentioned the gold and ivory from the trade, which was shipped to England for the same purpose. Altogether, they argued, the Guinea trade generated £40,000 in remittances each year. Hoping to play on mercantilist anxieties, the petitioners also asserted that the loss of the American rum trade in Africa would provide an opening for French brandy, which would in turn lead to a reduction in Britain's share of the slave trade.[60]

The Remonstrance is significant in two respects. First, it offers the most complete contemporary statement on the economic importance of the slave trade to colonial society. The authors, of course, had an incentive to maximize its importance, and historians have rightly treated the £40,000 figure with skepticism. A crude calculation based on modern slave-trade estimates and price data suggests that the true value was probably closer to £30,000, which means the Remonstrance exaggerated the slave trade's importance to the Rhode Island economy, but not wildly. Put differently, the slave trade probably financed between a quarter and a third of Rhode Island's mercantile debt to Britain. Outside of Rhode Island, of course, the proportion was far smaller. The Remonstrance was also a major political statement, an unembarrassed, full-throated, public exaltation of the trade in human beings, unique to the historical moment. Within a decade, a statement of this kind would have invited major condemnation. If ever there was a heyday for American slavers, this was it.[61]

Part Three

SLAVERS AS AMERICANS

1775–1807

Pointe-à-Pitre, Guadeloupe, September 19, 1775.

WHEN CAPTAIN STANTON Hazard cleared Newport customs for the French colony of Guadeloupe, he planned to sail from there to Africa. On arrival in Guadeloupe, however, a group of ten New England sea captains asked to meet with him. The captains accused Hazard of violating Article 2 of the Continental Association, in which the colonies pledged to "wholly discontinue the Slave Trade" as of December 1, 1774. Hazard protested that the article did not apply to slaving voyages embarking for Africa from the French Caribbean, adding that this interpretation came directly from one of Rhode Island's delegates to the Continental Congress. "Several" Rhode Island vessels, claimed Hazard, had sailed to Africa from the French islands. He further claimed that in Newport "the Community looked upon every Man at liberty to use his pleasure in this Matter" and that his voyage had been "publickly known, & universally approv'd of." The captains informed Hazard that his interpretation of Article 2 was mistaken and that the ban on slave trading was total. Hazard responded that he could furnish a "certificate" prov-

---

Previous page: Portrait of James D'Wolf, ca. 1820s. D'Wolf family members, of Bristol, Rhode Island, were the most prolific slave traders in American history. James D'Wolf, the wealthiest and most active slaver in the family, was indicted for murdering a captive woman at sea but escaped punishment. Almost all of his slave trading took place after the American Revolution and was therefore in violation of state or federal laws, or both. D'Wolf held political office for many years, culminating in his selection in 1820 as a U.S. senator. (Ann Hall, *James De Wolf* (1764–1837), ca. 1825–1830, watercolor on ivory, Museum Collection: 1953.6.2, RHi X4 246, Courtesy the Rhode Island Historical Society)

ing that he was correct, but after several days of avoiding the captains he slipped away to Africa. The captains formally resolved to treat Hazard with "that Contempt & Detestation which every Traitor to the rights of his Country deserves," but that did not stop Hazard from making a successful voyage.[1]

Hazard's experience encapsulates many features of the post-1775 American slave trade. Most significantly, it captures changes in both the moral and political valence of the slave trade. The pro-slave-trade boosterism of the Rhode Island Remonstrance of 1764 belonged to a seemingly distant pre-revolutionary era in which such activities carried no moral or political stigma. Now they did, but as the captains' report on Hazard's activities reveals, the political and moral status was ambiguous. The Continental Congress, the body that passed the ban, was not a sovereign government; Article 2 was, in essence, an exhortation, not a law, prescribing no remedy or penalty for slave trading. Moreover, the captains' objection was rooted not in a sense that slave trading was an absolute moral evil, but rather that it was contrary to the public good, a violation of the Continental Association. This ambivalence, this impulse to restrict slave trading without applying the full force of the law to its eradication, set the tone for the next three decades. And just as Captain Hazard completed his voyage in the face of moral condemnation, many post-revolutionary slavers traded quite profitably. In fact, despite the legal restrictions and moral condemnation, American slavers transported more captives in this period than in any other.

Hazard's voyage also pointed to a reorientation of the American slave trade in the wake of political independence. The strategy of sailing to a French colony foretold a slave trade that would no longer center on British networks or work in harmony with British mercantilism. As it happened, France and its colonies would not play a significant role in the post-1775 American slave trade, so Hazard's voyage was an aberration, but the Spanish colonies would. Also in this era, American slavers at last discovered the value of the United States as a captive market. It is in this period more than any other that American slave ships supplied American plantations, although the British were still responsible for about one-third of all ships coming in. On the African coast and in the Caribbean, the Americans increasingly moved out of the British orbit. By the end of the era, American slavers would establish their own slave-trading enclave on the African coast. In short, the post-1775 period saw the Americanization of the American slave trade.

Revolution and Reorientation,
1775–1803

The Imperial Crisis that led to American independence played out mostly in port cities, and Newport, the capital of colonial slave trade, was no exception. Heavily dependent on the molasses, rum, and slave trades, Newporters had more reason than most to fear the Sugar Act of 1764, as their Remonstrance expressed. As it happened, the various revenue acts and boycotts of the Imperial Crisis dented but did not destroy the American slave trade. Merchants in New York and Boston pulled back slightly in the late 1760s as nonimportation emerged as a response to parliamentary regulation, but they participated fully in the boom of the early 1770s. In Newport, the center of the trade, slavers largely ignored the revenue acts and continued to dispatch their vessels while waging a campaign of intimidation against the king's customs men. In 1767, a mob actually scuttled one of the king's ships. And most famously, a group of masked men, led by the Providence slaver John Brown, burned the customs schooner *Gaspee* on Narragansett Bay in 1772. At the same time, Rhode Island refused to cooperate in nonimportation, incurring the wrath of Whig politicians in Massachusetts and New York, who believed (correctly) that Newporters were trying to gain at their expense.[1]

After years of avoiding both colonial and British trade measures, Newporters were eventually forced to take sides. When, in 1774, the colonies passed the Continental Association, a pact that imposed severe restrictions on transatlantic trade, Newporters had to choose between compliance, which would destroy their overseas commerce, or ignoring the Association, which would isolate them from the other colonies. They chose to stand with the other colonies. In December 1775, amid worsening tensions, a British naval vessel bombarded Newport. Within weeks, the three-quarters of Newport's population that was of the Whig persuasion, a group that included most of the major slave traders, had abandoned the town. Notable exceptions included Francis Malbone and members of the Wanton clan. Joseph Wanton had been governor through much of the turmoil but ultimately remained loyal to the Crown. He would later go into exile, thus ending one of Newport's major slaving dynasties.[2]

Even at the height of the Imperial Crisis, slave ships continued to embark from American ports. No fewer than thirty-six vessels sailed for Africa in 1774, including at least five from Boston (or more likely, from nearby harbors) after the official closure of the port on June 15. But although slavers found it easy enough to ignore British restrictions, they were less inclined to flout those of the Continental Association, which enjoined colonists not only from being "concerned" in slaving voyages, but also from chartering vessels for or selling commodities and manufactures to slave traders starting December 1, 1774. Six vessels set sail in November, presumably to beat the deadline, and only four vessels, Hazard's among them, are known to have sailed from American ports after that date.[3]

Elsewhere, Peleg Clarke devised his own scheme to evade the scrutiny of both the Continentals and the British. Building on his strong relationship with John Fletcher, he organized a voyage in London and set sail for the Gold Coast in October 1775. True to the sophisticated nature of his trade, the plan involved redeeming several captives (or rather, the equivalent in value of several captives) from Richard Brew at Anomabu and carrying them to Jamaica. The voyage was disastrous. On arrival at Anomabu, Clarke discovered that Richard Brew had died owing captives to multiple vessels, including at least one fellow Newporter. Clarke was forced to purchase captives from the Danes at Accra, but they took so much time to deliver that he initiated a £3,000 claim against them for failure to fulfill their agreement. When he finally managed to get some captives, they rose in revolt. The uprising was suppressed, but Clarke lost thirty-six captives, mostly men who jumped overboard when it became clear that the slavers had gained the upper hand. When he finally reached Jamaica, nineteen months after setting out, he found the market "very Disadvantagus." The affair reached its denouement when a Continental privateer seized the vessel. Although Clarke contemplated outfitting a voyage from Jamaica to Africa the next year, this was his last venture until after the American Revolution.[4]

Those slavers who did venture out during the war faced the threat of seizure by the British. Under the terms of the Prohibitory Act of 1775, all American vessels were to be treated as enemy ships, and the CMTA forts were ordered to refrain from any dealings with them. After 1775, however, the main British concern was not that Americans might ignore the rules on slave trading, but that their privateers might raid the lightly defended British installations in Africa to procure gunpowder to aid the war effort. To prevent this, the Royal Navy swept the seas of American ships, scooping up several slavers. In early 1776, the British captured a New Hampshire sloop off Cape Mesurado. The captors traded rum for slaves at Cape Coast and hired the vessel's captain to take them to the Caribbean. A short distance to leeward, a British naval vessel seized a New York sloop and a South Carolina schooner, and there were rumors that another New Yorker had been pursued up the Gabon River—an unusual destination for an American vessel, probably intended to evade British patrols—but it escaped.[5]

American privateers returned the favor by prowling the African coast for British vessels. In 1778, CMTA officials expressed concern for the "loss of so many ships" on the African coast and hoped the region was no longer "infested by such unwelcome visitors." They were probably referring to the recent capture of eight British slavers off the Gold Coast, which were brought to the French Caribbean to be sold. Another privateer, which had already taken three British prizes, tried to pick up a pilot in Niumi at the mouth of the Gambia River to guide him upriver and destroy James Fort. He failed, but the French succeeded in leveling James Fort once and for all in 1779. But the true significance of American privateering in Africa was that it allowed merchants and mariners from ports that had not been traditionally involved in the slave trade to gain familiarity with the region and its practices. In 1781, Joseph and Joshua Grafton, merchants of Salem, Massachusetts, sent a privateer skippered by Joseph Waters to the Gambia River. As soon as the war ended, the Graftons would send out at least six slavers, with at least three to the Gambia; Waters, as owner, would send out at least two.[6]

War interrupted slave trading for almost a decade, but the real impact of the revolution involved the rise of an anti-slavery movement, which posed a serious challenge to slavery's legality and legitimacy. Although the Guineamen of the pre-1775 period operated with no serious political impediments, a very small, limited abolitionist movement had been advancing a critique of slavery rooted in spiritual equality. A few individual Quaker activists had been working to get their fellow Friends to renounce slaveholding. The trade in captives, viewed as a product of war and therefore as a violation of the Quaker Peace Testimony, was integral to their critique. Rhode Island was home to many slave-trading Quakers, including members of the Wanton, Shearman, Thurston, Easton, Hicks, Redwood, and Stanton families, but they resisted all pressure. John Woolman, a Friend and pioneer abolitionist, visited Newport in 1747 and 1760, well aware of the town's status as a slave-trading hub. He managed to convince the Yearly Meeting to forbid the buying and selling of slaves, but clearly many ignored the resolution. The next generation of Quaker abolitionists, led by Anthony Benezet, had more success. In 1770, thanks in a large part to his activism, the Yearly Meeting prohibited the ownership (as opposed to simply the buying and selling) of slaves and succeeded in moving anti-slavery beyond Friends circles. Of course, these successes coincided with the peak years of the colonial-era slave trade, so the fact remains that the movement's impact was very limited.[7]

Another late-colonial anti-slave-trade campaign enjoyed greater political success, but it is hard to characterize it as anti-slavery. This was the movement to restrict the importation of Africans into North America, which found support in several legislatures. Fears of rebellion and simple anti-Black racism accompanied many of these efforts. Sporadic efforts to reduce or eliminate captive importations dated to the seventeenth century and usually involved prohibitive import duties, but sometimes outright moratoriums were declared. South Carolina's restriction of 1740–1744, passed in response to the Stono Rebellion of 1739 and accomplished via taxation, was one of the more successful and consequential efforts. Other campaigns (Rhode Island, 1770; Massachusetts, 1774) died in colonial legislatures. Still others (Pennsylvania, 1712; New Jersey, 1763; Virginia, 1710, 1727, 1766; South Carolina, 1760) were either explicitly disallowed by the Crown or otherwise failed to gain royal assent as they were considered illegal efforts to restrain an important branch of British trade. Even Rhode Island passed a ban but made sure to specify that it did not apply to any Africans who were taken into the colony after a failed attempt to sell them in the Caribbean.[8]

Legislative battles over the importation of captive Africans resulted in a new and influential framing of the American slave trade as something that involved the importation of captives into North America, rather than the transportation of enslaved Africans by North Americans. For a disparate group of colonies searching for unity during an imperial crisis, "ships coming in" was a more politically convenient definition of the "slave trade," since it allowed blame to be placed squarely at the feet of the king and his ministers. Political figures actually began to frame the slave trade in this way as early as 1770, which is when Benjamin Franklin published an imaginary conversation between an Englishman, a Scot, and an American colonist in which the latter responds to accusations of hypocrisy regarding slavery by saying that England "began the Slave Trade" and that traders from London, Bristol, Liverpool, and Glasgow "tempt us to purchase them," before finally condemning the nullification of colonial restrictions. Six years later, when Thomas Jefferson charged in his original draft of the Declaration of Independence that the king had "prostituted his negative" by disallowing laws barring the landing of captives, he was not being particularly innovative. Even in the declaration's final, watered-down form, which said that the king had "refused his Assent to laws, the most wholesome and necessary for the public good," most readers probably knew that he was referring to the effort to restrict slave ships coming in. But even though the focus had shifted away from ships going out to ships coming in, these protests fed a growing sense that the slave trade was a bad thing.[9]

As slave trading reached new heights in the late colonial period, scattered incidents provided a foretaste of things to come. In 1773, sailor Charles Sorisco of the slave ship *York* filed a criminal complaint before the New York mayor, Whitehead Hicks, that the mate, John Lovell, had beaten the captives "in a cruel manner with ropes, staves, Hedding, & the handle of a broom." Lovell also tied a captive woman to the main shrouds and lashed her to death with a "Fishe's tail full of notches, in a very Inhuman manner." Sorisco's language reflected a new humanitarian sensibility and was probably not typical of most sailors. He had even learned the woman's name: Neura. The following year, New York's distillers resolved not to provide rum for use in the slave trade. Whether they did so as a result of Sorisco's complaint is not certain, but change was clearly in the air. Slavers now faced a general moral condemnation that had simply not existed through most of the colonial period.[10]

The American Revolution provided an opportunity for these sentiments to enter the public discourse, as notions of liberty and natural rights contributed to the emergence of what historians often call "revolutionary anti-slavery." Early iterations can be found in the anti-slavery petitions signed by African American residents of Massachusetts and in the writings of figures like James Otis. By the 1780s, slavery and slave trading were under attack throughout the northern states. Massachusetts abolished slavery by court decision in 1783. The following year, Rhode Island went the more typical route of gradual emancipation, in which children born after a certain date would be technically free, though they would still be required to serve their masters into their twenties. New York, the northern state with the largest enslaved population, did not pass its post-nati ("after birth") emancipation law until 1799. These laws seem very mild to modern sensibilities, but they were significant in their time and did bring about the end of slavery in half of the United States.[11]

Shortly after these laws were passed, several states passed laws aimed at ending not just slavery, but the transatlantic slave trade as well. The Continental Congress had adopted its resolution in 1774, but it lacked the force of law, so state statutes of the 1780s constitute the first binding prohibitions on slave trading in United States history. Ironically, the first state to prohibit the trade was Rhode Island, in 1787. Exactly how the undisputed capital of the American slave trade accomplished this—where slavers controlled all levers of government and just more than twenty years earlier had, without a hint of embarrassment, represented the slave trade as an economic necessity—is a remarkable story. At the center was an alliance between Black Rhode Islanders, some of whom had served in the military during the War for Independence, and Moses Brown, a former slaver, a "convinced" Quaker, and an anti-slavery dynamo. Brown had twice failed to persuade the legislature to ban slave trading, the most recent time in 1784, when the provision was cut from the gradual emancipation bill. At the time, Moses's brother John, a legislator and unrepentant slaver, had mounted a vigorous defense of the trade during debate, emphasizing its economic importance. Moses renewed his campaign in 1787, but this time John and his allies were curiously absent. John Brown was at the time pivoting (temporarily) to the Asian trade, which may account for his apathy. Moses ran a strikingly modern grassroots campaign and won the day by an astonishing margin: 44–4 in the lower house, and unanimous support in the upper chamber. The following year, Brown worked with allies in Massachusetts and Connecticut to pass similar measures, arguing that such laws were needed to prevent Rhode Islanders from crossing state lines to continue their business. To bring cases, Brown and his fellow Quakers formed the Providence Society for the Abolition of the Slave Trade in the following year.[12]

The Rhode Island, Massachusetts, and Connecticut laws were similar. All three barred citizens and residents from serving as master, factor, or owner of any vessel that transported, bought, or sold African captives. Violations were penalized by fines of between £100 per captive transported (£50 in Massachusetts and $167 in Connecticut) and £1,000 for each vessel employed (£200 in Massachusetts and $1,667 in Connecticut). Enforcement was by a writ of qui tam, which was to say that action was initiated by private citizens who furnished information on lawbreaking, with a guilty verdict entitling the informant to half of the fines. There was, however, one significant difference between the three New England state laws. Whereas Massachusetts and Connecticut both declared any insurance policy taken out on an illegal slave voyage to be null and void, the Rhode Island statute was silent on the matter. Given Moses Brown's dedication to the issue, this was surely an oversight rather than a deliberate attempt to create a loophole. But the omission became consequential in due time.[13]

All of the known actions that were brought under the state laws took place in Massachusetts, though often involving Rhode Island traders. The inaugural case was brought in 1789 but was not heard until 1791. In consultation with Moses Brown and the Abolition Society, Massachusetts resident William Gordon brought an action against Caleb Gardner and John Stanton of Newport, who had outfitted their brig *Hope* in Boston. Arguments at the trial hinged on whether the defendants could be sued under the Massachusetts law. The law barred any "citizen or resident" of the state from organizing voyages, but Gardner and Stanton were Rhode Islanders. The plaintiffs parsed the definition of "citizen or resident" and argued that even sojourners were still subject to state law. A verdict was rendered in favor of the plaintiffs, and Gardner and Stanton were fined £200. The verdict was upheld on appeal.[14]

The *Hope* action was not the only successful one. In 1792–1793, a Massachusetts court found two men guilty of "manning and fitting out a ship" and importing thirteen captives (which raises the question of whether it had gone to Africa or the Caribbean). The defendants were fined £200 for the ship and £850 for the captives, half of which went to the informant. In 1792, a Salem sailor-turned-shopkeeper brought an action against Joseph Waters and his skipper for outfitting a vessel that carried ninety captives from Africa to the Caribbean. The plaintiff asked for the maximum, or £200, for the vessel and £50 for each captive, for a total of £4,700. He won a judgment, although it appears to have been overturned two years later by a higher court.[15]

Despite some favorable judgments, historians have seen these state prohibitions as failures. After all, slave trading not only continued but increased after their passage.[16] The Rhode Island, Massachusetts, and Connecticut laws were full of loopholes, and the ratification of the United States Constitution in 1788 cast doubt over state efforts to regulate overseas commerce. But although slave trading continued and even increased, it is not correct to say that the state laws had no effect at all. For one thing, slavers had to factor illegality into their voyage planning. Samuel Brown of Boston touched on several concerns in a letter to the

Vernons. The New England laws led him to contemplate outfitting in
New York, but it was not certain that enough "merchandize," meaning rum, could be procured there. This would force the vessel to come
to Newport, where it was exposed to seizure. Brown was "at [a] loss"
for a solution. After losing a judgment against one of his vessels, Caleb
Gardner tried to hide his assets by transferring them to a relative, hoping then to take refuge in Rhode Island's debt-relief laws. In the end,
the laws did not stop Brown, Gardner, or others from continuing their
slaving activities, but the statutes did make it harder to conduct business
as usual.[17]

More consequentially, prosecutions under state law, whether successful or not, brought the issue of slave trading before the public, often
in the most graphic way, and gave a platform to anti-slavery activists.
The jury in the *Hope* case was treated to the harrowing story of one
of the captives, a woman who gave birth on the voyage. The case of
Captain William Sinclair roiled the townspeople of Salem, Massachusetts, for two years. In addition to slave trading, Sinclair faced criminal
charges for assaulting Thomas Groves, a mariner of Salem, allegedly
beating him about the head, seizing him by the collar, and shaking him
"with great violence" at a time when Groves was "very sick and weak."
Abolitionists held bonfire rallies, and friends of the accused threatened
the lives of informers. According to William Bentley, Salem residents
agreed that the prosecution was just but they were divided between
those who thought the focus should be on protecting sailors and those
interested in paying a "debt to humanity." Bentley seems to have been
in the former camp, noting the deaths of local mariners in his diary at
various times over the years. Legal action under state law therefore provided a focal point and forum for local communities to debate the slave
trade, which in Massachusetts was almost always bad for the slavers.
Finally these state laws, particularly the Massachusetts statute, had a
longer-term, delayed impact. Because Rhode Island and Massachusetts
accounted for about two-thirds of post-revolutionary voyages, these
laws effectively outlawed two-thirds of the American slave trade. From
then on, only bilateral voyages leaving from ports outside New England,
which in practice meant Charleston, South Carolina, would be legal.

Two decades after their passage, British vice-admiralty courts were still citing state prohibitions to justify the seizure of American slave ships and the liberation of their captives.[18]

The passage of the state prohibitions in New England coincided with calls to revise or replace the Articles of Confederation. At the Constitutional Convention in Philadelphia, most of the debate on the slave trade focused on ships coming in, resulting in the famous clause (Article I, Section 9) enjoining Congress from passing any sort of ban on the introduction of foreign captives before January 1, 1808. Little was said in regard to ships going out. But as merchants engaged in international and interstate commerce, most slavers favored the ratification of the Constitution of 1787. Although it was probably not the decisive factor, many slavers probably perceived the Constitution as a counterweight to the new state prohibitions; indeed, as we have seen, several of those accused under the state laws argued that the federal government had jurisdiction over all international commerce, including the slave trade. The Constitution's prohibition on state laws "impairing the Obligation of Contracts" (Article I, Section 10) also appealed to slavers. Of greatest concern was South Carolina's law shielding debtors. Charleston's resident slave merchants, known as Guinea factors, who often extended credit to buyers, found it impossible to collect for several years, and this in turn delayed remittances to New England (and British) slavers. Salem's Joseph Grafton cited the Constitution's new prohibition as a measure that would help slavers collect their debts. Although some abolitionists opposed the Constitution of 1787 because of the slave-trade clause (and petitioned to amend it), once it was ratified, they too saw possibilities in it. "The new proposed Constitution for the United States is incomparably preferable to the old one," argued a letter in the *Massachusetts Centinel*, "in which no provision is made either for the suppression or circumscription of this wicked trade." Rhode Island famously refused to send a delegation to the Philadelphia convention and only ratified the Constitution belatedly. This, however, had little to do with the slave trade and more to do with a generalized political conflict between indebted farmers and merchant creditors. What is interesting is that slavers and abolitionists alike saw great potential in the Constitution.[19]

Opponents of the slave trade were the first to take advantage of the new political configuration. In 1789, the first year of government under the new Constitution, several different groups of Quakers, including Moses Brown's Abolition Society, petitioned Congress to use federal power to end slavery and the slave trade. The episode represented the first discernibly modern pressure-group political movement in U.S. history, involving the gathering of evidence, efforts to educate the public, the recruitment of high-profile advocates (most notably, Benjamin Franklin), and the continuous lobbying of lawmakers. This and subsequent movements during the Second U.S. Congress failed, but the petitioners were able to extract a formal acknowledgment that Congress at least had the right to prohibit the carriage of captives to foreign countries. In 1793, Moses Brown and his allies sprang back into action. This time, several Quakers from Massachusetts managed to gain an audience with George Washington, who ignored the separation of powers to introduce the resolution in the Senate. To help, Moses Brown lobbied James Madison, then a member of Congress. With Madison's support, the bill passed unanimously, as opponents, hoping to avoid the embarrassment of a "no" vote, simply absented themselves. The measure was quickly passed by the Senate and signed by President Washington.[20]

The Slave Trade Act of 1794 barred American citizens or any person in the United States from owning, outfitting, or supplying a vessel intended to carry captives to any *foreign* destination (since, under the Constitution, no action against the importation of Africans into the United States could be taken before January 1, 1808). Violators could have their vessels seized and face fines of $2,000 plus $200 for every captive taken aboard. As with the state statutes, proceedings were to be qui tam, initiated by third parties, who would receive half of the fines. An additional provision required any vessel departing for Africa to post a bond to guarantee that it would not engage in slave trading. However, this provision was triggered only when a citizen declared a "suspicion" to a port official. The act was rife with loopholes. It did not, for example, prohibit Americans from investing in non-U.S. ships, or bar American seamen from serving on them. These issues were addressed in an updated law in 1800, though only after Congress turned back a threat by

pro-slavery legislators to repeal the act of 1794. An additional statute
in 1803 barred the importation of captives into states that prohibited
it. Unaddressed in all of these laws was the fate of the captives aboard
illegal slavers. This was probably because the slavers had to be libeled
in U.S. ports, which in practice meant either before their departure or
on their return at the end of a voyage, after having sold the captives
in the Caribbean (carrying captives to the United States was still legal
and therefore could not trigger the act). Navy captains, who were under orders to "annihilate" illegal slaving, did not know what to do with
captives removed from illicit slavers. One officer who inquired was told
by the secretary of the U.S. Navy that the law probably intended for the
captives to be sold in the Caribbean, and noted another case in which
the captives were taken to Philadelphia and bound out to masters for a
term of years. The failure to address the fate of captives carried aboard
illicit vessels would become a serious problem in the ensuing years and
result in the continued illegal enslavement of thousands.[21]

Like the state laws, the federal ban of 1794 has generally been regarded as a failure. Most important, the number of voyages leaving
from American ports continued more or less apace. And before 1804,
when Charleston suddenly became a major port of departure, almost
all of them were illegal. Those departing from New England (which was
most) violated state law regardless of where they carried the captives.
Transporting captives to Cuba and other foreign destinations contravened the federal acts of 1794 and 1800, and any voyage that landed captives in the United States but contrary to state law violated the act of
1803. The only state that permitted the disembarkation of captive Africans before the passage of the federal act of 1803 had been Georgia, but
it barred the practice in 1798. The records we have are incomplete, but it
appears that, at most, eight out of more than three hundred American
voyages undertaken during the 1790s actually met all of the conditions
to be considered legal. Merchants quickly devised ways to circumvent
the law. These included buying back confiscated vessels at auction by
applying political pressure to officials and, when necessary, threatening bodily harm to those entering honest bids. Another ruse was to engineer a transfer of the vessel's title to the captain, who would undertake the voyage. On return, a pre-planned suit for nonpayment of crew

wages would be filed and the vessel would be sold at auction back to the original owners. The tactic was predicated on having the "crew" sue for wages before the vessel could be libeled by activists. It worked but entailed more complication and risk than simply repurchasing vessels at auction, so it was not used often.[22]

But the act of 1794 was not entirely toothless. In Rhode Island alone between 1794 and 1803, twenty-two actions were brought in federal courts. In many cases, owners never bothered to contest the actions and the vessels were sold at auction, some to be bought back. The threat of federal action stopped at least one slaver. Cyprian Sterry was Providence's most prolific slave trader, with a stake in at least eighteen voyages since 1785. In 1797 the Abolition Society libeled one of Sterry's ships under the act of 1794. The society then pressured Sterry to renounce slave trading in writing in exchange for a promise to drop the case. Sterry agreed and appears to have kept his word. A simultaneous campaign against John Brown of Providence did not produce the same result. Moses's brother refused and actually became the foremost political defender of the slave trade. In the final analysis, erratic enforcement and concerted resistance on the part of the slavers rendered the federal acts of 1794, 1800, and 1803 ineffective.[23]

The men who restarted the slave trade after the American Revolution were largely a different set of people from those who had carried it out ten years before. Some pre-revolutionary traders, such as Aaron Lopez and Benjamin Mason, had died in the intervening years. Others left Newport or, in the case of the Tory members of the Wanton family, left the United States. And others still, such as Timothy Fitch, never reentered the trade. Of course, a critical mass of major Newport traders did continue trading after the war. These included the Vernon brothers, the Champlins, Caleb Gardner, and Peleg Clarke. Their activities belie the myth that British occupation and the abandonment of the town by most residents put an end to Newport's infamy as a slave-trading center.

But the real story was that post-war slave trading was no longer quite so concentrated in Newport. The town did persist as a cluster of know-how and continued to furnish captains, but other towns challenged Newport's dominance. The only significant colonial-era slaving port not to continue into the 1780s was New York. Providence, which surpassed Newport as the largest town in Rhode Island during the 1790s, picked up the slack. There, the activities of Cyprian Sterry and John Brown, who between them carried more than three thousand Africans into captivity, transformed that city from an occasional to a regular participant. Boston dispatched an average of three voyages every two years during the 1790s, before throttling back its participation after 1800. Charleston, which in the colonial era sent one ship to Africa every two years, continued at a slightly higher rate through the 1790s, but its day was yet to come. In Charleston, slave trading still meant ships coming in, despite the state ban. For the most part, these rising entrepôts relied on local merchants to organize voyages, which accounted for most of the new entrants in the 1780s and 1790s. Even then, Newporters continued to pop up in connection with ventures organized in the other ports, their expertise and connections clearly in demand.[24]

The post-revolutionary era saw smaller ports enter the slave trade as well. Salem, Massachusetts, which dispatched only two vessels before 1775, sent out fourteen in the 1780s and 1790s. Salem was a medium-sized port that had historically relied on fishing and the coastal and Caribbean trades. As elsewhere, Salem's merchants found themselves deeply in debt to British merchants after the revolution. Joseph Grafton, who had already sent out an exploratory African voyage and soon became the town's leading slaver, detailed his thinking in a remarkable battery of letters sent out to traders in upper Guinea, the Gold Coast, and London. They told essentially the same story: independence had shut American merchants out of their key markets in the British Caribbean. It had also placed the United States outside the system of protection payments that had shielded British shipping from the Barbary corsairs, which had the effect of shutting Yankee merchants out of their accustomed Mediterranean cod markets. Grafton, like others, needed bills of exchange on London to finance his debts. "Our Navigation," he told a London merchant house, was "confined principally to Africa." To the dealers on the African coast, he offered to establish a relationship in which he furnished rum, tobacco, and ships for bills of exchange on London. Saying nothing about the slave trade, he probably hoped that he could sell these goods for bills without actually having to purchase captives, though he surely knew that was unlikely.[25]

Joseph Grafton and his brother Joshua became Salem's leading slavers, inspired, it appears, by their privateering voyage to Africa in 1781. By the mid-1780s, they had begun organizing regular ventures. They focused their efforts on upper Guinea and established contacts on the Isles de Los and in the Kru trading town of Bassa. Their activities sparked great protests in Salem. William Pynchon followed the Graftons' activities closely though the 1780s, chronicling the "shocking account of the treatment of the negroes" and Africans being "starved to death" aboard the Graftons' ships. Reverend William Bentley referred to the brothers as "sons of Belial" and "of contemptible character" and devoted entire sermons to denouncing their activities. Moral condemnation, accompanied by prosecution under state law, seems to have played a role in driving the Graftons and other Salem merchants from the slave trade. Giving up on the African trade was made easier by the fact that Salem's shipowners at the very same moment found another source of income: Asia. Merchant families such as the Crowninshields and Derbys (both of which had experimented with slave trading) and the Peabodys would transform Salem into a major center in the China trade. Salem also developed a significant "legitimate" African trade, but its moment as a slave-trading port was largely over by the early nineteenth century.[26]

Bristol, Rhode Island, was another small port that experimented with slave trading after the revolution, as a solution to its economic woes, but the outcome could hardly have been more different from Salem's. Located on Narragansett Bay midway between Providence and Newport, Bristol had been part of Massachusetts until 1747, at which point it had a population of just more than 1,000, including 128 slaves. In the colonial period, the small mercantile community made its living in the usual coastal and Caribbean trades, augmented by privateering in times of war. One of the more flamboyant privateers, Simeon Potter, became the town's leading slaver, owning a share of at least five voyages in the 1760s and 1770s. On a voyage to Guadeloupe, Potter met the eighteen-year-old multilingual Mark Anthony D'Wolf, and hired him as his secretary. D'Wolf married Potter's sister, Abigail, who bore fifteen

children, five of whom—Charles, John, William, James, and Levi—
went on to make up the most prolific slave-trading dynasty in American
history.[27]

The D'Wolfs dispatched their first slave ship in August 1787, two
months before the passage of Rhode Island's state prohibition, making
it one of their few legal African ventures. For most of the 1790s, they
organized voyages at a rate of about five per year, often, but not always,
sharing the costs and profits four ways. Because Bristol was about one-
fifth the size of Newport and Providence, the D'Wolfs and several other
families—the Dimans, Ingrahams, Wardwells, and others, often related
by marriage—were able to dominate the local economy. Their closeness allowed them to pool risk in multiple ventures, producing almost
endless permutations of investors. This practice seems also to have inspired them to found their own insurance companies, since unlike the
Massachusetts and Connecticut laws, Rhode Island's slave-trade law of
1787 did not specifically bar issuing policies on slavers. Insurance eventually led the brothers to found their own bank. By 1816, James D'Wolf
was rumored to be New England's greatest stockholder in the Second
Bank of the United States, although exactly what his involvement was
in earlier years (the First Bank expired in 1811) is uncertain. Collectively,
the D'Wolfs and their allies employed large numbers of seamen, ware-
housemen, and clerks. Bristol was in effect a company town.[28]

The traders' economic domination translated easily into political
domination, which was essential since their activities were for the most
part illegal. William Bradford had been deputy governor of Rhode Island
and was later appointed to the U.S. Senate; Benjamin Bourne served in
the state legislature, the U.S. Congress, and on the federal bench; and
James D'Wolf served in the Rhode Island legislature and eventually the
U.S. Senate. Unlike most slavers, he was a Republican, and had gone so
far as to name one of his vessels after Thomas Jefferson. His political
affiliation turned out to be an asset. After 1800, D'Wolf's influence at
both the state and federal levels provided vital cover for his activities,
allowing him to influence judicial proceedings and the enforcement of
customs laws, and it sometimes even allowed him to send out thugs to
intimidate opponents with impunity. No incident dramatizes his pull
more vividly than the creation of a new customs district expressly for

Bristol. Through the 1790s, Rhode Island's slavers had faced opposition from Newport customs collector William Ellery, who had supported several of the federal prosecutions. In 1800, James D'Wolf used his influence with President-elect Jefferson to create the new jurisdiction. When the new collector proved too willing to enforce the law, D'Wolf orchestrated his replacement in 1804 with Charles Collins, his brother-in-law, who had skippered several of the family's slavers.[29]

Between 1787 and 1804, various combinations of D'Wolfs sent out sixty-two slavers, carrying about 5,700 people into captivity, but this was merely a warmup for what was to come in 1804–1807. No slaving concern in American history is comparable to that of the D'Wolfs. What set them apart from other major traders, such as the Vernons, the Wantons, and Caleb Gardner, was their complete devotion to Atlantic slavery. For other merchants, the transatlantic slave trade was one part of a portfolio of business activities, which included the European and coastal North American trades. Although a major part of their non-slave-trading activity involved the transportation of slave-produced goods, such as sugar and molasses, they were not plantation owners. The D'Wolfs were involved in diverse businesses as well, but central to their enterprise was a vertically integrated family empire based on slavery, and they eventually acquired three plantations in Cuba. Their ships supplied captives for their plantations (along with others'); their Cuban estates supplied coffee, sugar, and molasses, with the latter being distilled into rum and shipped to Africa to begin the cycle again. They dominated their company town economically and politically in a manner that resembled a twentieth-century political machine. In the annals of American slavery, the D'Wolfs were sui generis.[30]

Slavers in the early republic built on the sophistication of their late-colonial predecessors, taking full advantage of the era's many financial innovations. Some of the innovation was necessitated by American independence, which had disrupted mercantile relationships with Britain. Traders still did business with London, but since they could no longer earn credits by carrying cargoes to British colonies, ties were inevitably looser. Though indebted and suffering through a post-war recession, American merchants were developing more sophisticated financial institutions, which increased the distance from London. The Bank of North America was chartered in 1781, superseded by the Bank of the United States in 1791. One year later a group of New York merchants founded what eventually became the New York Stock Exchange. Although slavers supported and were involved in these enterprises, the most directly relevant financial innovation related to insurance. Colonial-era slavers were invariably insured through London, but only a few of their successors were. After the war, insurance on American slave voyages was almost always underwritten in the United States. In the 1780s and early 1790s, marine insurance was sold through brokers, who connected customers with underwriters. The Graftons' vessels, for example, were underwritten by Boston and Salem merchants.[31] Chartered insurance companies began to form in the early 1790s, able to raise more capital than private insurers by selling shares. Insurance on slaving vessels was illegal under Massachusetts (but not Rhode Island) law. Some companies, such as the Boston Marine Insurance Company, explicitly refused to insure slaving vessels.[32]

Even so, through much of the 1790s, slave traders continued to insure their vessels in Boston. The D'Wolfs, for example, bought policies from Peter Chardon Brooks, one of that city's leading brokers. Around 1800, however, Rhode Islanders began to form their own companies. They may have done so out of concern that the Massachusetts prohibition of 1788 on insuring slavers left their policies vulnerable to litigation, but there is no direct evidence to that effect. Some of the new Rhode Island–chartered companies, such as the Providence Washington Insurance Company, founded in 1799, and the Warren Insurance Company, founded in 1800, refused to write policies on slavers. Slavers therefore had to form their own. The Newport Insurance Company emerged out of an informal circle of slave-trading merchants, who had been insuring each other's vessels since 1784. It was incorporated in 1799 and over the next year wrote policies on thirty-three African voyages before suddenly cutting back. It seems that crypto-abolitionists on the board were giving information to the authorities. From mid-1800 until the 1807 federal ban, the company insured fewer than two slavers per year. The sudden reluctance to insure slavers led the Bristol traders to found their own companies. The D'Wolfs and their associates founded two companies, the Bristol Insurance Company (1800–1803) and the Mount Hope Insurance Company (around 1805), to insure their own and their friends' vessels. Surviving records suggest that each year during the first decade of the nineteenth century these companies insured African trade goods worth between $25,000 and $50,000.[33]

Exodus from the British Empire brought further changes to the way voyages were organized. For the first several years of independence, American slave traders continued to pursue the rum-for-captives formula that had dominated since about 1700. Rum remained a staple item in the holds of slavers well into the nineteenth century, but after 1793 slavers increasingly managed to "sort" their cargoes with textiles. What made it possible was the global war that broke out between revolutionary France and the rest of Europe. As a neutral nation with a large merchant marine, the United States soon became the preferred carrier for French and Dutch goods, including textiles from India, one of the staple items in the metropolitan slave trades. The Browns, among others, quickly saw the significance. Martin Benson, one of their associates, told his New York correspondent to send him blue and white *bafts, niconnees,* Guinea stuffs, romals, "& all kinds [of] coarse India Goods, the Coarser the better, if colours [are] suitable." Whereas rum had long constituted 85–90 percent of the value of cargoes bound for Africa, from 1794 to 1800 the spirit accounted for about 68 percent of the value of all goods carried aboard Newport slavers. For a small number of vessels, the rum quotient sank as low as 20 percent. After a century of trading in colonial produce, Americans were starting to trade more like the Europeans. Political independence made it possible.[34]

But perhaps the most significant post-revolutionary shift had to do with the New World markets for captives. Independence shut United States merchants out of the British Caribbean, which had been the destination for 56 percent of American captives before 1775, but Americans were excluded from trading there when the revolutionary war between the colonies and Britain disrupted their relations with the mother country. Even after the signing of the Jay Treaty of 1795, which partially opened up the British Caribbean to American trade, slavers were effectively excluded since captives were not the "growth, manufacture or produce of the said states" and most vessels were above the treaty's seventy-ton limit. For the Americans, the British Caribbean would never again be the market it was. Only 3 percent of the captives carried aboard American ships after 1775 wound up in the British Caribbean.[35]

The French colonies might have offered an alternative as a result of the Treaty of Amity and Commerce in 1778, but regulations proved a barrier, relations soured during the 1790s, and the Haitian Revolution eventually eliminated the biggest market (but that did not stop American merchants from trading in other commodities at Saint-Domingue). Ultimately, only about 4 percent of American captives were taken to the French Caribbean, most of them to Saint-Domingue. Suriname, a Dutch colony, was slightly more open to American slavers, receiving about 8 percent between 1783 and 1803. At the height of the Suriname trade in the 1790s, only a few American ships a year went there. After 1795, Suriname's plantations came under great stress due to the war and the alternating British and French blockades. Planters had trouble paying debts and marketing their produce, and some even abandoned their holdings. From 1799 to 1802, and then again from 1804 to 1816, the colony was under British control. The British briefly allowed limited commerce with the United States, but eventually shut down most American trading. Suriname could not pick up the slack.[36]

With these places either unwilling or unable to accept large numbers of captives, two major markets emerged. The first of these was the United States itself, chiefly South Carolina and Georgia, which together absorbed three in ten captives carried by American slavers before 1804. Both had seen their plantations destroyed by invasion, occupation, and guerrilla warfare. When the war was over, South Carolina had lost, by some estimates, twenty-five thousand, or about one-quarter of its plantation labor force, to flight and death. Perhaps because it was less densely populated and closer to Spanish Florida, Georgia lost two-thirds of its enslaved population. Desperate to revive their plantations, South Carolinians and Georgians turned heavily to the captive market, absorbing about one thousand per year in the decade immediately following the revolution. The appearance of the cotton gin in the 1790s launched another increase in captive importations. The major surge occurred in 1804, both for ships coming in to South Carolina and going out from American ports.[37]

From the 1780s until the surge of 1804–1807, the South Carolina and Georgia trade functioned along the same lines as in the colonial era. The trade was still mostly triangular, with New England (and British) slavers carrying captives from Africa to Charleston or Savannah. Many of the factors in these ports were British, which was an advantage because they were well-positioned to obtain bills of exchange on London. As in the colonial period, Carolina and Georgia merchants were essentially correspondents of the slave traders, handling sales and remittances for a commission. Yankee merchants preferred to work with trusted factors, which often led to enduring connections that smoothed the way for trade, so the tie was one of mutual convenience bolstered by a desire to maintain a good reputation. However, as South Carolina emerged as a major market for the Americans in the 1780s and 1790s, this long-standing configuration began to change. Gradually, New England slavers began sending their own people, often younger family members, to Charleston. Nathaniel Ingraham, one of the D'Wolfs' retainers, was active in Charleston in 1800 (and soon afterward was imprisoned for several months as skipper of the slaver *Fanny*, for failing to pay fines incurred by violating the statute of 1794). Although the agents for the New England slaving concerns operated on a commission basis and handled other cargoes, this represented a higher level of integration than previously. The reason for this change is not entirely certain, but it may well have been a reaction to the difficulties of the 1780s, when slavers had a hard time collecting debts for captives sold in South Carolina.[38]

The biggest change of all was the emergence of Cuba as a major destination for Africans transported in American vessels. For most of its history, Cuba had not been a major plantation colony. The enslaved population had always been a minority, employed in pursuits ranging from stock raising to agriculture, mining, and urban labor. Sugar planting began to take hold with the British occupation of 1762, intensifying greatly in the late 1790s with the sudden collapse of the sugar plantations in world-leading Saint-Domingue. The slave trade to Spanish America had long been contracted out to other nations, leaving Cuban merchants without the necessary contacts and experience to supply their own growing demand for enslaved labor. During the American Revolution, the Spanish government cautiously opened the Cuban produce market to American merchants, who responded by shipping the usual foodstuffs and lumber. This door slammed shut after the war ended, but Americans had seen Cuba's potential and by this time had contacts there. In 1789, Cuban planters, arguing that sugar planting held the key to the island's future prosperity, succeeded in liberalizing the slave trade. That year, royal decrees allowed foreign traders temporary access to the Cuban slave market. A 1791 order streamlined some of the bureaucracy and extended access for a period of five years. These orders were re-newed periodically, and the number of American transatlantic slavers visiting Cuba went from four in 1792 to thirty-one in 1799. Cuba was the solution to the loss of the British Caribbean captive market and was now the leading destination for American slavers.[39]

American slave traders were just part of a larger rush into the Cu-ban market that set off what can only be described as a trade diaspora. In 1797, eight years after liberalizing the slave trade and after several false starts, Spain opened Cuba to neutral trade in general, a policy that stood for five years. American merchants, many from New England but also from New York, Philadelphia, and Charleston, rushed in. Although the vast majority of vessels traded in goods other than captives (specie was the goal of many), slavers were well represented, and even some who had not previously been involved in slave trading had no scruples about diving into it. These included Nathaniel Fellowes Sr. and Jr. and Zacha-riah Atkins. Career slave traders who set up shop in Cuba included the Graftons, who established a house in Havana in 1782, even before their entry into the slave trade. Joseph Grafton died in Havana in 1794. The D'Wolfs first sent George and then John to handle their Havana busi-ness, charging them with selecting consignees to sell the captives and finding return cargoes for the produce. Adam Tunno, a Scot working out of Charleston, sent his relative Richard Tunno to handle the Havana end of the business. Other slave-trading clans dispatching members to Cuba included the Fales family of Bristol and the Jenkes family of Provi-dence. George Cushing, of Dorchester, Massachusetts, was one of the crowd that descended on Cuba in the 1790s. He took a dim view of his contemporaries and warned correspondents to avoid the "brokers, small dealers, secret speculators" who charged low commissions but made up for it by cheating their clients.[40]

The Americans soon extended their networks to link with the Cuban merchants and planters. Spanish law prohibited foreign merchants from operating independently, so each firm had a local partner. Through these partnerships, slavers connected themselves to the Cuban elite. A few merchant clans crop up repeatedly in the slavers' correspondence, suggesting a tendency toward specialization. Several, including William Vernon and the D'Wolfs, worked with David Nagle, who in turn was closely associated with the wealthy widow Poëy y Hernandez, the matriarch of one of Cuba's most prolific slave-trading clans. Another house, Santa Maria y Cuesta, handled business for the D'Wolfs along with Bristol traders, such as Fales and Ahearn, owners of the slaver *New Adventure*, and the firm of Bourne & Wardwell. Santa Maria y Cuesta ran into problems, however, and by 1801 its reputation in both Bristol and Charleston was tarnished.[41]

Remittances from these Cuban ventures are somewhat obscure. As always, slavers hoped to receive bills of exchange, preferably on London. Numerous bills of lading also suggest that American slave ships returned with a great deal of produce, sugar and molasses, of course, but also coffee. The trade to Cuba also opened up the possibility of gaining access to specie from the mines of mainland Spanish America. A great deal of gold and silver passed through Havana, and the trade was tightly controlled. American merchants gained a share of this treasure by using their agents to obtain forged documents and direct bribes to the appropriate authorities. Ironically, the only legal route for the exportation of specie by foreigners was as payment for captives. Slave trading, in other words, furnished a respectable cover for the smuggling of gold and silver. Non-Spanish vessels trading in the West Indies sometimes carried small numbers of captives to Cuba from the other islands just to take advantage of this loophole. Guineamen, of course, did not have to resort to the practice. So although it is likely that British bills of exchange were scarcer in Havana than in Kingston or Bridgetown, Cuba offered slavers something the old British West Indian markets could not.[42]

American slavers' connections with Africa underwent a corresponding reorientation in the post-revolutionary period, though perhaps not quite as radical as with their New World markets. The most important change was a steep decline in the importance of the Gold Coast as a source of captives. In the colonial era, between two-thirds and three-quarters of all captives carried aboard American slave ships were embarked on the Gold Coast. In the two decades from 1783 to 1803, the proportion fell to about 43 percent; the percentage purchased in upper Guinea rose to exactly the same level. Although politics in the form of a temporary exclusion from the British forts played a small role, by far the most important reason had to do with economic changes on the Gold Coast. Meanwhile, American slavers actually strengthened their connections to upper Guinea, particularly in the rivers to the north of Sierra Leone.[43]

When the Americans returned to the Gold Coast after an eight-year hiatus, they found conditions were very different. For one thing, the British policy barring the Gold Coast forts from trading with the Americans continued, since the latter were now outside of the British Empire. There was some illicit trade with them, but continuing it at pre-war levels was not possible. The loss of the British forts as a source of captives was compounded by the death of Richard Brew in 1776. The man who purchased his installation, Horatio Smith, lacked Brew's deep connections with Fante society. His ignorance of trading protocols (among other mistakes, he had failed to provide enough rum to some Fante visitors) led him into a major controversy that curtailed his effectiveness as a factor. The Americans found other sources of trade on the Gold Coast, with the Dutch, the Danes, and in direct exchanges with the Fante and the Ga, but their ties to coastal traders had atrophied since 1775.[44]

Of greater consequence were the economic changes that had taken place. One effect of the American Revolution had been to cut off the supply of rum. Rum had been the lubricant of trade, used to "dash" (tip or pay) canoemen, formalize agreements, and (as Horatio Smith learned) honor visitors. British factors substituted brandy for rum but found it second-best. When, in 1783, a Captain Saltonstall anchored off Anomabu, the fort's governor warned the captain to leave within the customary forty-eight hours allotted to foreign vessels. Saltonstall then began trading with the residents of the nearby town of Mouri, where the governor at Cape Coast accused him of trying to "inflame the minds of the Blacks, and instill into them that spirit of Republican freedom and independence, which they, through rebellion, have established for themselves." Saltonstall then began sailing up and down the western Gold Coast dispensing rum, prompting Britain to confirm its policy of exclusion. The governor's royalist hyperventilation aside, the policy of excluding American traders was doomed. There was simply no way to prevent them from selling rum, and even if the policy did succeed, it would force British fort officials, who needed it for their operations, to buy it from local traders at a markup. The British were forced to abandon the exclusion policy in 1789. None of this, however, altered the larger dynamic of the rum trade. Over the 1780s and 1790s, as the trade recovered, the old cycle of glut and scarcity reasserted itself. The re-export boom of the 1790s mitigated the problem by giving Americans access to cheap textiles, but the fact remained that rum was always a problematic trade good.[45]

More serious still, from the slavers' perspective, were economic changes on the Gold Coast and in Asante. From about 1700, slave trading had overshadowed gold trading, though the latter was still much sought after and served as a unit of account. Prices were customarily quoted in ounces of gold, but these were fictive "trade ounces," worth only half as much as specie. In the 1760s, European traders noted a new development: African merchants were now demanding gold in addition to trade goods in their negotiations, and they were demanding it in actual ounces, not the fictive trade ounces, a "pernicious practice," in the eyes of Richard Brew. In 1777, the Board of Trade looked into the issue and brought several traders in to explain the situation. David Dunn, the Boston merchant who had tried to establish his own trading posts in partnership with Grossle, testified that since 1762, nominal prices had nearly doubled, but the expense was compounded by the fact that gold had "become a necessary article in the purchase of slaves," and said he believed that "the chiefs in the interior amass it."[46]

This situation worsened during the 1780s. Americans visiting the Gold Coast in the post-revolutionary period complained endlessly about high prices and the need to supplement rum with gold. To get the gold, captains had to engage in preliminary trades. One common strategy was to stop at Cape Apollonia, which lay to windward of Cape Coast and Anomabu, to trade rum and whatever else was aboard for gold dust, which could then be expended on captives. In 1792, one of the Vernons' skippers told them that he had sold his rum to the forts at the price of twenty-eight gallons per ounce and was now "buying for gold every day." At Elmina, Captain John Sabens reported paying 125 gallons and "Soum in gold" for each captive. Sometimes skippers had the option of paying partly in gold to get a lower price or paying solely with rum for a higher price. In 1796, one of James D'Wolf's skippers informed him that he had the choice of paying 1 hogshead (about 100 gallons) and 30 gallons of rum (approximately 130 gallons total) or 1 hogshead plus 7 "Joes," which was the American name for a Portuguese gold coin that was most often obtained in Cuba.[47]

Historians have offered several explanations, by no means mutually exclusive, for the sudden reversal in the flow of gold from net export to net import. One explanation is that the transatlantic slave trade simply deprived gold producers of potential laborers, creating a shortage. Another explanation holds that tension between the Fante and Asante cut off gold shipments to the coast, driving up prices and leading Fante traders to demand it from slavers. A third explanation has to do with the growing monetization of the regional economy over the course of the eighteenth century. Gold, which had long been important as a commodity, was now the region's undisputed medium of exchange. This can be seen in the fact that although African traders were willing to give gold in pawn during the early part of the eighteenth century, as time passed they gave human beings instead. By the nineteenth century, gold was all-pervasive as a currency throughout Asante and the Gold Coast and retained its importance as a commodity, all of which militated in favor of scarcity. American slavers on the Gold Coast, then, found themselves squeezed between rising nominal prices and the need in many, if not most, cases to pay part of the amount in gold that was counted in actual ounces, not in fictive trade ounces.[48]

Political developments in the region created further problems for the Americans. The roads to the coast had been open since the mid-1760s (apart from a few crises), with the major exception of the one that ran from Kumasi, though Assin and Fante, to Anomabu, Kormantine, and Cape Coast. To defend their middleman position, the Fante had set up markets on its northern border. Asante traders were forced to sell their captives to Fante dealers, who then sold them on the coast. Asante could do little about the situation because the 1780s was a period of internal political turmoil. The new asantehene was a young boy, and his mother, who was very unpopular in political circles, acted as regent. The chaos furnished vassal states to the north and south with a chance to rebel. These uprisings were all crushed, resulting in more captives for sale, but the situation meant there was little Asante could do to open the road to the western forts.[49]

By 1790, the asantehene had come of age, and stability returned for a few years, but political dissent roiled the kingdom again after 1797. As the leader of Asante, Osei Kwame had shown some admiration for Muslims, and there was fear among the political elite that he might attempt to institute Sharia law and make Islam the state religion. Given the importance of Asante's own spiritual traditions in legitimating elite and state power, such a move had revolutionary potential. Political infighting at the highest levels prevented Asante from confronting the Fante over the issue of the road. Periodic closures forced Asante to direct its Atlantic trade over the much longer eastern and western roads, driving up costs in general but most crucially for guns and powder. Osei Kwame was deposed in 1803, and his successor, Osei Bonsu, eventually broke the deadlock, but for the time being the supply of captives was constricted. The number of captives embarked on the Gold Coast plummeted from a high of twenty-two thousand in 1790 to six thousand in 1794, and remained below ten thousand for much of the decade.[50]

Merchants back in the United States knew nothing of the inner workings of the asantehene's court, but they were well aware that the Gold Coast was not the same market for captives that it had been before the war. As early as the mid-1780s they were considering alternatives. In 1785, Samuel Brown, a major Boston merchant who partnered frequently with the Vernons, surveyed the disappointing returns of a recent voyage and, after concluding that the Gold Coast would soon be inundated with rum men, contemplated sending a vessel to the Gambia or to "Angola," by which he probably meant the region north of the Congo River. After trying the Gold Coast again, Brown and the Vernons decided to try Mozambique, on the Indian Ocean. The voyage was disastrous. The New Englanders had no understanding of the Indian Ocean monsoons, and their vessel arrived "intirely out of Season." Learning that a Baltimore-based vessel had completed a successful voyage in which it carried captives from Mozambique to the Île de France in the Indian Ocean, the partners decided to learn from their experience and dispatch a second vessel to Mozambique. "It's a Voy[age] of speculation on which we proceed blindfolded," said William Vernon. This time, the returns were apparently good; Brown and the Vernons dispatched at least two more vessels to Mozambique. As a group, American slavers sent a total of thirty-six ships there before the close of the legal slave trade.[51]

As the Gold Coast receded in importance, American slavers turned to upper Guinea to make up the difference. For fifty years the region had been an afterthought in their calculus, a hedge against poor conditions on the Gold Coast. For American slavers, the problem was most acute in Senegambia, which furnished fewer and fewer captives. The voyage of the *New Adventure* in 1798 was probably typical of many to the region. It sailed first to Gorée Island, but finding captives "rather difficult to purchase," it continued south to the Gambia, where it stayed for just one week before returning to Gorée. The slave trade in Senegambia had in fact begun to decline from its 1751–1775 peak. During those years, an average of nearly fifty-five hundred people were dispatched into transatlantic slavery every year. The number dropped to fifteen hundred in the 1780s, then even further to just more than eleven hundred during the 1790s, before recovering to fifteen hundred per year during the decade of the 1800s. American vessels in upper Guinea consequently purchased fewer and fewer captives from Senegambia.[52]

There were many causes for this, including the destruction of James Fort in 1779, as well as the wars of the French Revolution. The ongoing Islamic reform movement was another cause. The new states, such as Futa Jallon, had a contradictory impact on the slave trade, on one hand opposing the sale of captives to non-Muslims, and on the other hand destabilizing the region with their wars, which in turn fed the trade. In 1776, another Muslim state emerged, Futa Toro, on the middle Senegal River. Torodbe clerics of Fulbe background had begun a rebellion in 1776 against the Denyanke dynasty, which had a long history of warfare and slave trading. Their motives were similar to those of previous movements, with the enslavement of Muslims and their sale to non-Muslim Europeans high on the list of grievances. The new state enjoyed the support of Bundu and Futa Jallon and extended its influence toward the coast, all the way to the Wolof states of Waalo and Kayor. Although the rise of Futa Toro sparked warfare and generated captives, the flow across the Atlantic was reduced by the fact that the new regime instituted a strict ban on the enslavement and sale of Muslims. State authorities even forced the French to let them inspect any captives they purchased to ensure that no Muslims were among them. These policies induced large numbers of people from the coastal ceddo states to convert to Islam (if not already Muslim) and to seek haven in Futa Toro. True to its principles, Futa Toro refused to sell those captives it took to transatlantic slavers, retaining them or selling them to other Muslims in Africa.[53]

The supply of captives was further interrupted by parallel development even nearer the coast. Kayor had been one of the classic ceddo polities, participating in the slave trade both by seizing captives and by supplying slave ships. In 1790, Kayor was destabilized by the accession of a new *damel* (king), who resented the influence of Futa Toro, which had been exacting tribute from Kayor for several years. Tensions between the damel and the Muslim community rose through the early 1790s, culminating in the murder of many clerics. Supported by Futa Toro and other regional polities, the clerics gave the damel an ultimatum, which, among other things, included an order to stop selling slaves to Christians. The damel refused, and so in 1796 the *almami* (ruler) of Futa Toro invaded with an army of thirty thousand. The damel waged a scorched-earth defense, selling the prisoners he took into slavery. Kayor managed to defeat Futa Toro, which accelerated the latter's decline. The struggle had produced its share of captives, but on balance probably disrupted more than enabled the slave trade.[54]

Another reason for the drop in the number of captives embarked from Senegambia was a corresponding increase in the number retained to work in agriculture. Here, religious-ideological factors meshed with economic necessity. Senegal had experienced a series of droughts throughout the century, with the worst one coming in the

1750s, followed by lesser but serious recurrences in the 1770s, 1780s, and 1790s. Coastal polities, such as Kayor and Waalo, which had long functioned as middlemen in the slave trade and therefore had access to unfree labor, began using slaves to grow food, which could be consumed locally or sold to slave ships. Inland polities followed the same path. The Bamana state of Segu, one of the most important producers of captives in the region throughout the century, also turned to enslaved labor in agriculture. The transatlantic slave trade, which subtracted both labor and provisions from local societies, left residents more vulnerable than they might otherwise have been. Retaining captives to grow millet and other foodstuffs provided some states with a hedge against drought, but it limited the number of captives available for sale to slave ships.[55]

Although the jihads and the increasing use of slave labor reduced the flow of captives from Senegambia, the area to the south, including Sierra Leone and the Rivers of Guinea, continued to gain in importance for American slavers. Two recent changes contributed. The first of these was the emergence after 1787 of a British colony at Sierra Leone, the product of a unique confluence of circumstances. During the 1780s, a committee of white and Black activists proposed settling Britain's "black poor" on the shore of one of West Africa's best harbors, at the mouth of the Sierra Leone River. Organizers envisioned the outpost not only as a "Province of Freedom," but also as a commercial venture, a way to tap into the trade in Africa's (nonhuman) commodities. The initial settlement was a disaster. The death rate was appallingly high, and tensions with the Temne landlords ended in the burning of the initial settlement in 1789. The enterprise was soon reincorporated as the Sierra Leone Company, and with the arrival of a group of "Nova Scotians"—which is to say African Americans who had fled the United States during the American Revolution and had been temporarily settled in British territory—the colony slowly found its footing. They were later joined by former maroon rebels, expelled from Jamaica, in the new capital of Freetown.[56]

The Sierra Leone colony provided a focal point for American vessels in upper Guinea, all the more important since the destruction of James Fort. Ships coming to Sierra Leone could obtain the best fresh water in coastal West Africa and purchase provisions from the company or from a growing number of English-speaking small producers and marketers. In that sense, Sierra Leone had a great advantage over the other ports, where small garrisons manned the forts and where supplies had to be obtained from hard-bargaining African merchants who often enjoyed an effective local monopoly. American slavers pop up repeatedly in the correspondence and reports of the Sierra Leone Company, engaged in the usual activities, including ongoing rounds of retaliatory violence for various infractions.[57]

There was, of course, one drawback to Sierra Leone: it was an anti-slavery settlement. The rum men, however, soon learned that this was a minor obstacle. For one thing, the actual settlement was tiny, covering only a limited area on the northern tip of the Sierra Leone peninsula. Bance Island and the rest of the Sierra Leone estuary, along with the rivers to the north and Sherbro and Gallinas to the south, lay entirely outside British control and continued as major slaving entrepôts. It proved impossible to insulate the new settlement from slavery and slave trading. Settlers, who were initially forced into an exploitive tenant-type status, soon began exploring alternatives. Slavery was a major institution in the region, and it was almost impossible to avoid it. The company purchased supplies produced with slave labor, with some employees going further than that, and a few settlers began working for the slavers. All of this led one American slaver, blissfully unaware that slave trading was banned in the settlement, to walk straight up to the governor and tell him that "he hoped they would favour him with all the slaves he wanted in the course of a few days." The governing council was not amused. On paper at least, the colony was free of slavery, and blatant violations could not go unopposed. The council asked whether his state had a law against slave trading, and he replied that it did. Councillors informed him that they would be sending a report to the state, to which the slaver replied, "I hope, sir [that] you will not do so unfriendly a thing." He then pretended to have been joking, professed a great "abhorrence" for the slave trade, and sailed away. A letter to Boston followed, but to little effect.[58]

Freetown furnished a good outlet for American rum, but slavers really made up for the decline in captives from Senegambia by purchasing more in the rivers to the south, especially around the Rio Pongo. This represented the continuation of a trend that had accelerated after

1750, although now the region was more important to the Americans than ever before. One reason for this had to do with the extraordinarily strong networks that developed. Colonial-era merchants, especially the Newporters, had developed ties with some of the Gold Coast factors, such as Richard Brew and David Mill. But the connections that some merchants developed with Rio Pongo factors were different in that several of these were actually Americans by birth who had settled in Africa. In the 1790s, there were no fewer than five Americans operating factories in the greater Pongo area, and the names of their factories—"Boston," "Charleston," and "South Carolina"—provide an accurate indication of the extent of their networks. Others, such as the Holman family, moved in the other direction, from Africa to South Carolina. Samuel and John Holman were the sons of British trader John Holman, who settled in the Pongo after 1750. John Holman Sr. married into a powerful Baga clan, which allowed him privileged access to local trade networks. In 1787, the family purchased and moved to a plantation in South Carolina. John Holman Sr. died in 1791, and John Jr. returned to Africa, all the while continuing to trade in human beings. Paul Cross, whose origins are unknown, was another Pongo-area factor who moved to Charleston, although he did not maintain his slaving activities. This cluster of traders, along with several others from Britain, France, Germany, and the Netherlands, made the Rio Pongo into the leading destination for American slavers in upper Guinea.[59]

The Rio Pongo connection conferred several advantages to American slavers. Its most basic function was as a bulking center for the collection of captives. Resident traders used their connections, often via their wives' families, to attract caravans to their installations. From the American perspective, having a trusted correspondent was advantageous because it allowed slavers to carry over debts for later collection, as they once had with the Gold Coast factors. Fragments from their many transactions have been preserved in legal records in the United States, since these traders often used American courts for their business. A trader named Daniel McNeill, for example, sued the estate of another slaver for a debt contracted in the Rio Pongo in 1794. McNeill had advanced some goods to the other trader and went to Africa several years later to collect. His debtor had died, and because there were no courts in Africa where he could pursue his claim, he sued in Charleston. In 1802, a Charleston resident named Greenwood forwarded trade goods to Benjamin Curtis and was issued with a signed note. Curtis failed to furnish all of the captives, which, as we will see in chapter 9, led to a lawsuit of some importance.[60]

With strong ties to the Futa Jallon, the Rio Pongo received a steady supply of captives that compensated for the declining number of captives taken aboard in Senegambia. By now, Futa Jallon, which had been founded in the spirit of reform, had become much like the ceddo-type states it had once deplored. Although the expansionist Ibrahima Sori ("the Great") died in 1791, his passing brought about a succession crisis that weakened the central authority of the state, even after it was resolved. Meanwhile, Islamic reform increasingly gave way to the need for revenue. As a noble of the Futa Jallon state told the British traveler James Watt, "the sole object of their wars was to get slaves, as they could not get any European articles they were in want of without slaves and they could not get slaves without fighting for them." Another official told Watt that if Futa Jallon could get European goods by selling ivory and rice, "it would be much better never to sell a slave," but for the moment that was wishful thinking. Slaving continued apace, as Futa Jallon sent annual caravans down to the Rio Pongo and other centers.[61]

As Futa Jallon sank deeper into slave trading, the flame of reform burned elsewhere. In 1790, a Boston newspaper published an article about a "prophet" called the "Mahady" who was threatening to "drive the English [and Americans] off their coast" with an army of four hundred armed men, four hundred slaves, along with horses and dogs. The report was broadly accurate, if understated. The previous year, a man known only as Fatta announced the he was the Mahdi, a leader appointed by God to purify the world before the "Last Days." Fatta invaded the coastal state of Moria with an army of fifteen thousand, attracting large numbers of fugitive slaves from the plantations that supplied rice to the slavers. Fatta sent a force to the Pongo to demand tribute from the traders, who responded by fleeing, some permanently. The regional states soon killed the Mahdi, as well as a second charismatic leader named

Karimou, who proclaimed himself prophet and claimed Fatta's mantle. A larger, more generalized slave rebellion raged for several years afterward before it was crushed once and for all in 1796.[62]

Fatta's jihad and the concurrent slave rebellion illustrate once again the contradictory effect of these conflicts on the slave trade. On one hand, the Mahdi's rebellion disrupted the trade, forcing several factors in the region to flee. Also, the incident represents another chapter in the slow spread of Islam through the region, which undermined the market for rum. On the other hand, the number of captives embarked in upper Guinea actually hit an all-time peak during the rebellion, and it was not surpassed until 1807.

The years 1775–1803 were important ones for the American slave trade. Revolutionary anti-slavery and the laws it inspired, though insufficient to end or even stem the trade, permanently altered its political and moral standing. Increasing numbers of Americans viewed the slave trade as a moral evil, and association with it was something to be hidden, at least outside Rhode Island and South Carolina. Federal regulation and public opinion notwithstanding, American slavers faced the additional challenge of exclusion from their customary markets, both in Africa and in the Americas. As it happened, they more than met these challenges, turning away from the Gold Coast and the British Caribbean and toward the Rio Pongo, South Carolina, and Cuba. By 1803, the reorientation was complete, with the American slave trade operating at pre-revolutionary levels. Few probably realized that the peak lay just ahead.

Crescendo, 1804–1807

Nothing in the history of the American slave trade could have foretold the surge in voyages that departed between January 1, 1804, and December 31, 1807. In a trade that lasted more than two centuries, that four-year period accounted for nearly one-quarter of all American-based transatlantic slaving voyages, a rate of sixty-two departures per year. By comparison, the period 1751–1803 averaged about twenty-two sailings per year, excluding the eight-year revolutionary hiatus. But there was more to the era than increased volume. The period 1804–1807 also saw a fundamental shift in the itineraries of American slavers. After a century and a half of serving mostly West Indian markets, American slavers suddenly carried more captives to North America than to the Caribbean. The ships going out and the ships coming in overlapped more closely in this era than in any other in the history of the American slave trade. The economic impact of this burst of trading was significant, furnishing much of the labor force for the eventual "Cotton Kingdom." In fact, a stunning 17 percent of all of the enslaved people who arrived in North America directly from Africa came during this four-year period. The toll in human suffering was similarly unprecedented, probably unparalleled in American history, as approximately sixty-five thousand Africans landed. At the peak of the trade, South Carolina's Cooper River undulated with decomposing corpses thrown from quarantined ships to save burial costs. In April 1807, Charleston convened juries of inquest for at least seven bodies found floating near the East Bay waterfront and in the marshes off Hog's Island, opposite the town. The city responded by imposing a hundred-dollar fine on anyone caught throwing corpses from a ship.[1]

The catalyst for these changes was the decision by the South Carolina legislature in late 1803 to re-legalize the transatlantic slave trade for both outgoing and incoming ships. This reversal, though short-lived, not only brought a surge in the number of Africans entering the United States, it transformed Charleston into one of the North Atlantic's premier slaving hubs. The reopening of the trade in 1804 brought a sudden influx of merchants and mariners with specialist knowledge of Africa and the transatlantic trade, something Charleston had never had before. Many of the newcomers were already deeply involved in the Cuban trade and recognized its potential symbiosis with the Carolina trade. They exploited this symbiosis so successfully that the Cuba and Carolina trades effectively became two branches of a single trade. Virtually overnight, Charleston came to resemble such cities as Salvador de Bahia and Rio de Janeiro, which imported captives and dispatched slavers with equal intensity. Charleston, once the cultured, decadent town of rice planters and their retainers, had suddenly become a bustling, money-hunting international trading center. Charleston was in the throes of what can only be described as a slave rush.

A change in the law was the catalyst, but the Carolina slave rush was really the product of major structural changes to the institution of slavery in the United States. Most important was the sharp rise in demand for laborers to clear and work the new cotton fields of the Lower South. The "cotton boom" began in the mid-1790s, ushered in by the Whitney gin, which sped the removal of seeds from short-staple cotton. Cotton differed from crops like rice and sugar in that it required no major capital outlays and could be grown with any number of hands. Laborers need not be enslaved, but the more hands a farmer could put into the field, the more cotton he could grow. In the southern United States, acquiring additional hands meant acquiring enslaved laborers, so with prices for the staple soaring on international markets, yeomen soon became slaveholders, and lesser slaveholders became planters. In the South Carolina Middle Country and Upcountry, the influx of captives drove the proportion of slaveholding households from roughly one-quarter in 1790 to about four in ten by 1810. Slaveholdings also grew in size. In 1790, only one Middle Country and Upcountry slaveholder in ten kept more than four enslaved people. By 1810, that figure was one in five. The region's enslaved population grew by 69 percent from 1790 to 1800 and again by 75 percent between 1800 and 1810. The Georgia Upcountry along the Savannah River underwent a similar transformation. About 25 to 30 percent of this population growth was natural, and some of it was fueled by the intra- and interstate slave trades. Working with population data to track the diffusion of enslaved laborers throughout the region, the historian Michael Tadman has proposed that twenty-nine thousand newly arrived Africans settled in Georgia and South Carolina between 1800 and 1809. The vast majority would have settled in the Middle Country and Upcountry, which suggests the transatlantic slave trade was responsible for about 28 percent of the growth in the labor force during the first phase of the cotton boom.[2]

The South Carolina and Georgia Upcountry was only one market for enslaved labor. Louisiana, acquired by the United States in 1803, also attracted a sizable share. Lower Louisiana—the area surrounding New Orleans—had a nearly century-long connection with Africa. In the 1720s, a small but steady transatlantic trade supplied a cluster of tobacco and indigo planters with enslaved labor. A decline in slave trading after 1730 meant that Louisiana's Black population creolized over the course of the century, as the colony shifted from French to Spanish control. Both transatlantic and intra-American slave trading picked up again in the 1790s, stimulated by two developments. The first was the emergence of sugarcane as a crop in the Mississippi River parishes near New Orleans, fed by an exodus of sugar-making expertise from revolutionary Saint-Domingue. As former indigo planters converted their fields to cane, the number of sugar plantations rose from zero in 1790 to ninety-one in 1810. The demand for labor was great, and planters routinely ignored Spanish restrictions on landing foreign captives.[3]

The United States' acquisition of Louisiana in 1803 (itself a consequence of the revolution in Saint-Domingue) accelerated both the rise of plantation agriculture and the slave trade. Louisiana planters favored the transatlantic slave trade over the intra-American slave trade as a source of labor, believing Africans to be uninfected by revolutionary ideas. Prohibited by federal law from landing captives directly from Africa, Louisiana relied on South Carolina merchants to meet their demand. Tadman estimates that seven thousand Africans arrived in Louisiana between 1800 and 1809, most of them transshipped from Charleston. Baptismal, notarial, and other records from the time confirm the rapid Africanization of Louisiana's enslaved population. Because so many of the Africans in Louisiana arrived by way of Charleston, which in turn drew heavily on West Central Africa, and because the existing enslaved population was small, the years 1804–1807 left a distinctly Kongolese imprint on the regional culture.[4]

Labor-hungry planters in the Natchez District of Mississippi, part of the territory ceded by Britain in the Treaty of Paris in 1783, diverted a significant number of captives upriver to work their cotton fields. According to Tadman's calculations, some 9,000 Africans arrived in Natchez between 1800 and 1809, almost all of them transshipped from Charleston via New Orleans. Even Tennessee, where the economy was based more on small farming and stock raising than on cotton, brought in an estimated 2,250 captive Africans between 1800 and 1809, nearly all of them by way of Charleston. Following the closure of the transatlantic slave trade in 1808, an interregional slave trade would become the principal mechanism for supplying the market for enslaved labor in the Old Southwest. But in the first decade of the nineteenth century, that trade had yet to be organized. Many enslaved people also arrived via planter migrations, but by Tadman's calculations at least, more arrived from Africa via Charleston.[5]

The continuing demand for enslaved labor in Cuba, driven primarily by the expansion of sugar, augmented the demand for enslaved laborers in the Cotton Kingdom. American slavers supplied this market through the 1790s and into the nineteenth century, but by 1804 the overall trade to Cuba was falling. Having undergone a rapid expansion during the 1790s, a period known in Cuban history as the "First Dance of the Millions," prices began to falter in 1800, and by 1804 they had dropped by nearly a quarter and did not reach that level again until 1819,

as abolition loomed. By the latest figures, about fifty-four thousand enslaved Africans disembarked in Cuba over the first decade of the nineteenth century. This was low by later standards, though revolutionary in
its time. About eighteen thousand, or one in three of those arriving in
Cuba between 1801 and 1810, sailed aboard American slavers. Although
many of these captives probably wound up working on sugar *ingenios*
(mills), a disproportionate number likely worked on tobacco farms, as
American merchants established strong ties with Matanzas, an area east
of Havana, which had not yet transitioned to sugar.[6]

The emergence of cotton meant that for the first time in 150 years
of slave trading, Americans were the principal suppliers of enslaved
labor to mainland North American plantations. This does not mean
that the suppliers and consumers of enslaved labor had become one.
That was only true from a national perspective; in reality, the buyers
and sellers of captive Africans were almost never the same people (with
the partial exception of the D'Wolfs). In fact, many of the slavers of
1804 were not even Americans; they simply used Charleston as a base
of operations. But what mattered more than the personnel was the fact
that American slavers now had the option to carry enslaved cargoes to
the United States. The emergence of a home market, coupled with the
ongoing Cuban trade, gave slavers flexibility in their voyage planning,
allowing them to divert their vessels to the best possible markets in response to the latest intelligence. Triangular voyages could become bilateral voyages and vice versa. A vessel might sail with orders to carry
captives to Havana, only to switch to Charleston as news arrived or in
response to shipboard conditions. The two trades reinforced each other.

Although the underlying causes of the Carolina slave rush were economic, politics was the proximate cause, as the conflicting forces of
revolutionary anti-slavery and slavery-based expansionism combined
to create an unprecedented set of circumstances. Under the Constitution, Congress could not ban the introduction of captives (euphemized
as "such Persons as any of the states now existing shall think proper
to admit") before January 1, 1808. Despite the fact that they were allowed to receive captive Africans, as of 1803 all of the states had prohibited the practice (though these restrictions were widely flouted in

the Lower South).[7] In South Carolina, the nation's largest potential market for enslaved labor, the issue of captive importations had been a live one for many years. Having lost a large percentage of their laborers to the chaos of the American Revolution, Carolina planters spent the mid-1780s purchasing large numbers of enslaved Africans, almost invariably on credit extended by British merchants. Then in 1787, alarmed at the state's trade imbalance, the legislature passed a five-year ban on the transatlantic slave trade. The new injunction was supported by the wealthy but indebted Lowcountry planters. Having replaced the labor lost during the war, these planters now hoped to keep captive prices high in South Carolina by opposing both the transatlantic and interstate slave trades. The yeomen and lesser slaveholders of the Upcountry, on the other hand, advocated both trades in the hope that an increased supply would lower prices. However, Lowcountry control of the legislature, combined with fears that captives from Saint-Domingue and other foreign sources would import revolutionary ideas, led to repeated renewals of the transatlantic ban through 1803. In 1792, Lowcountry planters also succeeded in barring the introduction of enslaved laborers from outside the state. The biggest slave market in the United States now barred both the transatlantic and interstate trades.[8]

As the cotton boom progressed, South Carolina's prohibition on the introduction of captive Africans came under attack. As ever, the battle was between the wealthy Lowcountry planters and the lesser slaveholders of the Upcountry. In 1802, Lowcountry legislators won the first round, turning back an Upcountry bid to reopen the transatlantic trade, but Jefferson's acquisition of Louisiana in 1803 soon altered the political dynamic. Recognizing the potential of the Louisiana market and seeing themselves in a prime position to supply it, Lowcountry planters reconsidered their opposition to the foreign slave trade. Upcountry slaveholders, who, as a result of the ban on the interstate trade, had to purchase all of their labor from the Lowcountry planters in a protected market, pressed for the reopening of the overland trade. Here was grounds for compromise. Repealing the ban on the transatlantic trade would allow Lowcountry planters and merchants to supply the Carolina and Georgia Piedmont and the Mississippi and Louisiana Territories, and a repeal of the interstate ban would lower prices even further for Upcountry cotton planters. The legislature legalized both trades on December 17, 1803. Two large British slave ships that had been sitting offshore in anticipation of a lifting of the ban entered the port just hours after the news reached Charleston.[9]

The rush was on. Merchants scrambled to land as many captives as possible before the door closed. The general expectation was that Congress would ban the trade at the earliest permissible moment, as of January 1, 1808, and that President Jefferson would sign any such bill into law. Congress had already demonstrated its hostility to the trade, initially during the 1790s but more recently in the debate over the question of the slave trade to newly acquired Louisiana, which, as a territory and not a state, was under federal control. In 1804, anti-slavery legislators, led by James Hillhouse of Connecticut, succeeded in barring both the foreign and interstate slave trades to Louisiana (despite the efforts of James Ellery of Newport, who cast one of only six "no" votes in the Senate). The only enslaved people allowed into the territory were those who accompanied masters intending to settle there. Hillhouse's law would be difficult to enforce, but it served as a reminder that Congress would almost certainly end the transatlantic trade as soon as it could.[10] The federal government was not the only jurisdiction that seemed likely to end the slave trade, however. Rumors circulated in 1804 and again in 1805 that the South Carolina legislature would reimpose the ban, all of which fueled the slavers' sense of urgency.[11]

Charleston's native sons rarely sullied their hands in commerce, so nearly all merchants came from other places. The merchants who organized the Carolina slave rush consisted both of veterans who sensed opportunity in a reopened trade and newcomers, some with little experience. Greater precision regarding Charleston-based slavers is hampered by a lack of data, with only 15 percent of vessel owners identified. Much of the uncertainty regarding Charleston's slave trade can be traced to a list of merchants compiled by Senator William Loughton Smith during the Missouri debates of 1820, which has influenced many historical interpretations. To highlight northern and British hypocrisy on slavery, Smith presented a list of slavers extracted from customs records. The original records no longer exist, which means that Smith's excerpts are the closest we can get to them. Unfortunately, Smith did not specify whether it was a list of ships coming in or ships going out. It was almost certainly the former, although some information may have been taken from a register of clearances. Smith added to the confusion by applying the word "proprietor" to what were in most cases commission merchants, not shipowners. A few of Charleston's Guinea factors did make the jump into voyage organization, but most stuck to familiar territory by handling captive sales. Finally, Smith listed "what country" the "proprietors" came from, without differentiating longtime residents from new arrivals. The result has been long-standing confusion over whether this really was a Charleston trade, financed and organized primarily in the city, or whether it was organized from outside.[12]

It is unlikely that the original customs records will ever surface, but enough information survives in other sources to suggest the basic patterns of voyage organization in the Carolina trade of 1804–1807. As it happens, Smith's charge that the vast majority of this trade was orchestrated by northern and British merchants seems correct. More than that, British and American slavers operated on two distinct circuits, with relatively little overlap. Yankee merchants tended to organize voyages from New England, with some houses sending family members to Charleston to handle captive sales and remittances. Only seldom did the agents of New England firms organize voyages from Charleston. The house of Phillips and Gardner, among the more prominent Yankee slavers in Charleston, exemplifies the pattern. John Phillips and John Gardner, both in their early twenties and both from Newport slaving families, announced their presence in Charleston only four days after the legal reopening of the trade, on January 4, 1804. They handled their first of an eventual twenty-seven slavers the following year, dispatching nearly three thousand people into bondage. Although as commission merchants they handled other New Englanders' vessels, they are known to have organized one voyage from Charleston in 1807.[13] The D'Wolf family opened its Charleston branch around 1806 in the firm of Christian & D'Wolf. Charles Christian anchored the business in Charleston, and Henry D'Wolf appears to have operated mostly from Rhode Island. The activities of Phillips & Gardner and Christian & D'Wolf were more expansive and better integrated than most, but they probably typify

New England involvement in the Carolina trade, in that the voyages were organized in New England but handled by a Charleston-based agent. What changed was the tendency after 1804 to open branches of the firms' own mercantile houses rather than rely on local commission merchants.[14]

British and Irish merchants operated the second major circuit in the Carolina trade. To some extent, this was a continuation from the colonial period, when British vessels supplied the vast majority of South Carolina's coerced laborers and British factors handled the sales. After the revolution, a contingent of British merchants, Scots in particular, operated in Charleston. Indeed, it was the debt owed to them by local planters that helped to bring about the 1787 and subsequent state bans on slave trading. When the market opened back up in 1804, Charleston's British merchants were poised to become major players. Most, however, were really Guinea factors, organizing voyages only occasionally. For example, the firm of Gibson & Broadfoot, active in Charleston by 1801, operated primarily as commission merchants. William Gibson was based in Liverpool, and William Broadfoot, originally from Galloway, Scotland, was responsible for the American side of the business. Gibson & Broadfoot handled no fewer than a dozen slave-ship commissions, mostly for British correspondents. There is no evidence to suggest that Broadfoot actually organized voyages during the rush years, although he did own an illegal slaver a few years later. A probable kinsman, James Broadfoot, also operated mostly as a commission merchant but outfitted at least one vessel. He used his Liverpool contacts to import British trade goods, which he then re-exported to Africa.[15]

William Boyd was the major exception to the rule that most Charleston-based merchants were Guinea factors who did not organize voyages. The British-born Boyd, who had contacts in London and possibly Scotland, seems to have come to Charleston initially in the 1790s but left and returned around 1804. As a Guinea factor, Boyd handled twenty-six vessels, vending more than seven thousand people. He owned shares in at least sixteen ventures, often with partners in London, and specialized in the Loango and Kongo trades. Although he resided in Charleston for much of the period, he may have spent time in Britain as well. As a result of his sprawling connections, his voyages often traced complex routes. In 1806, for example, Boyd had a share in the *Port Mary*, whose itinerary stretched from London to the Congo River, to Charleston, and then to Rotterdam. When the congressional ban became effective on January 1, 1808, Boyd was caught with nine hundred captives that he was unable to land legally. He was forced to sell them "at a very reduced price," though whether that was in Carolina or elsewhere is unknown. Boyd, more than any other individual, was responsible for the tremendous influx of Central Africans into South Carolina and Louisiana.[16]

Unlike Boyd, most British slavers orchestrated their Charleston-based voyages through local agents and supercargoes. George Aylwin of London probably typifies British involvement, both in his reliance on Charleston-based agents and in the sophistication of his ventures. Beginning in December 1803, perhaps in anticipation of re-legalization, he organized the first in a series of voyages. He began by hiring John Campbell to be his main man in the Carolina trade. For the next five years, Campbell moved continuously between Charleston, Havana, Africa, and Río de la Plata. He served as supercargo on three slave ships, two to Africa and one from Havana to Charleston. By the time he died, en route from Río de la Plata, Campbell had been involved with at least six Aylwin vessels that made no fewer than twenty-five separate passages, touching at Charleston eight times, at London and Africa five times each, at Havana four times, and at Río de la Plata once.[17]

Whereas most of Charleston's outgoing slavers were probably owned and directed by nonresidents like Aylwin, some longtime Charlestonians did organize voyages. The number was inevitably small because few possessed the requisite knowledge of Africa. Some local commission merchants probably picked up enough information through conversations with captains. Wisely, most commission merchants hired supercargoes. Indeed, although supercargoes were rare in the earlier phases of the American slave trade, they were common during 1804–1807, as more and more amateurs clamored for a piece of the action. Experienced slavers even advertised their services in the local newspapers. Most of Charleston's supercargoes were British and directed vessels to the parts of Africa they knew best. The area between Loango and the Congo River was one many British supercargoes were familiar with, and it soon became a major destination for Charleston slavers. British supercargoes invariably operated on British networks, sometimes even sailing to Europe to pick up trade goods before continuing to Africa. James Broadfoot's *Washington* is a case in point. In 1806, Broadfoot hired David Adams of New York to skipper the vessel to the Congo River but also employed Duncan Stewart of Liverpool (via Scotland, one suspects) as supercargo. Stewart had "been in the habit of trading in Africa" and had made at least one voyage to West Central Africa, which we know because he took the opportunity to collect a debt from a previous trip. The *Washington* sailed from Charleston to Liverpool before making for Africa.[18] Most supercargoes were British, but not all. Swiss-born Fredrick Tavel hired Francis Roux of French Saint-Domingue to oversee the *Tartar*'s voyage to the Rio Pongo. The *Tartar* was making for Martinique when it was captured, which suggests Roux was working his own French Caribbean networks. The slavers of 1804 were nothing if not cosmopolitan.[19]

Complicating matters for British merchants was the progress of the abolitionist movement. In 1806, Parliament passed the Foreign Slave Trade Act, which prohibited British subjects from transporting captives to non-British possessions, effective January 1, 1807. This law was soon followed by the Slave Trade Abolition Act, passed in March 1807, which barred British subjects and residents from participating in the slave trade, effective May 1, 1807 (though it exempted voyages already in progress). To skirt the law, George Aylwin arranged a false conveyance of a vessel to one of his captains, and in 1808 a British vice-admiralty court condemned a vessel belonging to the Charlestonian Frederick Tavel, in part because it ruled that the ship had been sold to him in order to "cover" for a British owner or partner. Other British owners no doubt did the same, which has probably led historians to overestimate the level of local involvement in voyage organization. We may never know the precise number, but British merchants were deeply involved in this trade at all levels.[20]

Because the two major players, New England and Britain, operated within their respective networks, they made use of different trade goods. The New Englanders, led by the D'Wolf family, conducted a fairly standard rum trade. This was offset to some extent by an increased access to textiles and manufactures, courtesy of the Americans' role as a neutral carrier during the wars of the French Revolution. This trend continued during the slave rush, as Charleston's newspapers filled with advertisements for textiles, many targeted expressly at slavers. Advertised as "India goods," many textiles no doubt came to Charleston in the holds of British vessels, but a significant quantity was re-exported from northern ports, including Salem, Boston, New York, and even Baltimore. Many advertised the eligibility of the goods for a drawback on imports that were destined for re-export. One vendor offered pre-sorted packages tailored to the "leeward Coast" market. Textiles even made it to Charleston aboard slave ships returning from Africa, as leftover trade goods.[21]

Even so, traders based in New England and Charleston still relied heavily on rum. Given that most New England vessels in this trade embarked from New England, most of their rum was probably distilled locally. With the rise of the Charleston slave trade, advertisements for New England rum filled the columns of Charleston's newspapers. One such notice offered "5th proof RUM" to "African Traders" on six and nine months' credit. Another made a point of advertising New England rum that was "suitable for the African market."[22] But the slave trade was also a boon to Charleston's distillers, who had been active since the colonial era and over the years had been responsible for the small number of vessels to sail to Africa from that port. One of these, Christopher Fitzsimons, was probably one of the very few longtime Charlestonians to dispatch a slaver in the 1790s and during the rush of 1804–1807.[23]

The New Englanders and other northern traders focused their attention on upper Guinea and the Gold Coast in roughly equal proportions. They knew these regions well and saw little reason to change the way they operated. Traders' continued dependence on rum as a trade good, though offset to some extent by the re-export trade, made this the prudent course of action. In upper Guinea, the fundamentals of the slave trade changed little. American ships continued to sell food, lumber, and rum at Gorée Island and Saint-Louis for textiles and some captives, though usually not enough for a complete voyage.[24] New Englanders also frequented the Sierra Leone estuary and the area to the south, spots such as Gallinas, which is where Captain John Sabens went in 1804–1805 after failing to purchase enough captives at Gorée. The likely reason for this southward shift was the persistence of Islamic reform in Senegambia, which undermined the rum market and, through the prohibition on the enslavement and sale of Muslims, threatened at times to choke off the slave trade as a whole. Abdul Kader's Futa Toro state was weakening, but it was still strong enough to trade tit-for-tat raids with the French in 1805–1806, all of which impeded the flow of captives. Experienced skippers like Sabens surely noted the tight market and may even have understood the cause. Gallinas was not yet the major captive market that it became in later decades, but the smaller Muslim presence and the lack of turbulence may have well drawn Sabens there.[25]

The Rio Pongo continued as an important place for American slavers, although what had originated as a New England–Africa connection increasingly incorporated Charleston as one of its nodes. South Carolina's connection to the Rio Pongo pre-dated 1804, but it had mostly involved ships coming in, especially those of the New Englanders. As the slave rush inspired local commission merchants to organize their own African ventures, the Rio Pongo emerged as a natural source of captives. Intense involvement gave Charlestonians a stronger connection to the Rio Pongo than to any other region of Africa. These interactions were bolstered by the frequent consignment of Pongo traders' captives to Charleston merchants, as described in chapter 5. It was a small step from there to organizing voyages in partnership with Pongo traders. Thus, in 1806, Charlestonian Frederick Tavel outfitted the *Tartar* in partnership with John Holman, a major Rio Pongo slaver, and several others. The group shipped separate consignments of trade goods aboard the *Tartar,* which were used to procure separate consignments of captives. While on the Pongo, the captain picked up several additional consignments of captives from local traders, suggestive once more of the strong ties to Charleston. The skipper even hired three locally born men as sailors for the return voyage. Toward the end of 1807, with the cutoff date fast approaching, reports reached Charleston of a flotilla of American slavers on the Pongo frantically bidding on scarce rice stocks for the return voyage.[26]

Although the upper Guinea and Gold Coast trades represented continuity with the past, some Charleston-based merchants inaugurated a new route in the American trade: the Loango Coast of West Central Africa. Named for the state that dominated the region, and situated between Cape Lopez and the Congo River, Loango had emerged as a major player in the transatlantic slave trade during the late seventeenth and early eighteenth centuries. British slavers had carried large numbers of captives from Loango to Charleston since the 1730s, accounting for about 30 percent of those disembarked before 1804. When South Carolina reopened its slave trade, the British vessels continued in this traffic, clandestinely after the passage of the Foreign Slave Trade Act of 1806. The Charleston–Loango trade that emerged in 1804–1807 was a continuation of Britain's colonial-era trade, with commission merchants recruiting supercargoes from British vessels and London- and Liverpool-based traders like George Aylwin dispatching agents to South Carolina to be closer to the business. During the rush, at least thirty British vessels landed a combined eighty-five hundred West Central African captives in Charleston. Some of these vessels, such as William Boyd's *Africa*, originated as British vessels but then settled into the Charleston trade and officially became American ships, so that many of the ships that entered the record as locally based were still embedded in British networks.[27]

The Loango Coast slave trade was based on textiles. Weavers in the region had long produced a fine cloth from raffia palm fibers. Above all, textiles were used for clothing, but that was not their only function. In Vili society, cloth was central to many rituals. Newborn babies were placed on fine cloth; adolescents undergoing initiation wore special cloth skirts; male suitors presented cloth to their prospective bride's parents; the deceased were wrapped in cloth, and the wealthy were dispatched to the land of the dead with extra stores of "prestige" cloth. In addition to these uses, cloth served as the region's currency, a medium of exchange, store of value, and unit of account. With the rise of slave trading in the late seventeenth century, locally produced raffia cloth was gradually superseded by imported textiles. The influx diluted the value of cloth and caused inflation, but its ritual and economic significance remained.[28]

The centrality of cloth to Loango Coast society had historically excluded Americans from this trade, but Charleston's British merchants altered the situation. About one-quarter of all Charleston-based vessels undertook bilateral voyages to the Loango Coast and back. Others, such as James Broadfoot's *Washington,* sailed from Charleston to Britain for cloth before making for Loango and finally carrying captives back to Charleston—a quadrilateral voyage. A few northern merchants even got into the act, invariably with some kind of British connection. All of these seem to have been opportunists rather than career slavers; professionals like the D'Wolfs held to their own itineraries. The American vessels that sailed to the Loango Coast from ports other than Charleston were often in the Cuba trade. Thus, the *Mendon,* owned by John Mackey of Boston and skippered by a Nantucket-born British resident, sailed to London before continuing on to the Loango Coast, then to Cuba. The Philadelphia-based *Fame,* captained by a Scot, touched at Liverpool before proceeding down the African coast. Its destination was officially Charleston, but that seems to have been a cover story designed to hide the true (and illegal) destination, which was also Cuba.[29]

The decision to hire British supercargoes for the Loango Coast trade was a shrewd one. The trading system on the Loango Coast was not for beginners, no matter how well assorted the goods were, and inexperience could prove costly. Trade here was administered by politically appointed overseers known as *mafouks.* These officials enforced standards throughout the region based on "bundles" of trade goods. As elsewhere, negotiations occurred in stages, first fixing a price in cloth for each category of good, and only later agreeing on prices for captives. As with the "heads of goods" on the Gambia River, bundles on the Loango Coast needed to contain certain "large" goods, invariably fine cloth but also guns. Alcohol accounted for a scant 7 percent of the goods traded in the region.[30]

The instructions issued to the supercargo Charles Christie of the *Hindustan,* which sailed from Charleston to the Congo River in 1806, underscore the complexity of this trade. First, Christie was instructed to take stock of the competition, ascertaining which vessels were close to departure and what they were paying in cloth. Because vessels hoping to sail soon often paid higher prices for their final few captives, it was important to avoid getting into bidding wars with them. Next, Christie was to negotiate prices for his lesser trade goods: beads, knives, guns, crockery, and rum. Assuming the Vili traders agreed to prices for the lesser goods (which was hardly certain), Christie was to move on to the "long" goods, meaning the textiles. On this voyage, there was a problem with his chintz calicoes. These had been cut into nonstandard sizes and needed to be trimmed to meet the regional standard for trade. His most valuable good, the blue "Guinea" and bafts, should come out only at the final moment, as a way to seal the deal and get off the coast.[31]

Though brief, the Charleston trade was so intense that it altered the region's demography and culture. Historically, most of the Africans arriving in South Carolina came from two areas, from West Central Africa before 1750 and from upper Guinea after 1750. As the population became self-reproducing, a new creole culture emerged, which we know today as "Gullah." The rush of 1804–1807, massive though it was, did not result in an African-born majority—those days were past—but by drawing on the same two regions that had fed the colonial population, the slave rush of 1804 reinvigorated Gullah culture. Many of the Central African cultural features noted by later observers—Simbi spirits, ritual practices and objects—were strengthened and transformed in this period. The new wave of upper Guineans also reinvigorated the region's Muslim community, which needed literate, educated leaders to survive. Evidence of the region's revitalized Muslim community began to appear in scattered sources. In 1807, an article in a Charleston newspaper made oblique reference to the making of amulets, a common Muslim practice on both sides of the Atlantic. Nearby in Georgia, two Muslims who arrived during this period, Omar Ibn Said and Sitiki, left narratives. For once in its two-hundred-year history, the American slave trade had a significant and visible cultural impact on the mainland.[32]

The Carolina–Cuba trade accounted for most trading during these years, but another branch did emerge. Its focus was on the Río de la Plata in South America, and it dated back to the 1790s with voyages of "speculation" organized by William Vernon. Between 1797 and 1802, one or two American vessels per year carried captives to Montevideo or Buenos Aires. Those figures surged after 1804 and reached a peak in 1805–1806, when no fewer than thirty-six American slavers called at Buenos Aires and Montevideo. Although it was never a plantation society, the Río de la Plata area experienced chronic labor shortages in its urban centers and on its ranches and farms, all of which sustained a steady demand for enslaved labor. This trade proved contentious and unpredictable, with American vessels frequently detained by the British navy or by local officials. The Portuguese in Brazil supplied most of the captives in the Río de la Plata region, but the Americans began doing so on a small scale as Spain liberalized its colonial trade after 1789.

Most of the American vessels transporting captives to Río de la Plata were based in New England. A small number were owned by longtime slavers such as the D'Wolfs, but most were dispatched by newcomers to the trade, Bostonians such as George and Benjamin Joy, Amasa Davis, John Mackey, Francis Bradbury, George Cushing, and Daniel Edes.[33] A handful of Charleston-based merchants directed their vessels to Río de la Plata as well. Charleston's Margaret Schutt sent at least one and probably two ships to Montevideo, and Londoner George Aylwin used Charleston as a base for one of his Río de la Plata slavers. Others integrated Río de la Plata as a third option to the Charleston and Cuba markets. When first outfitted in December 1806, the *Hindustan*'s instructions were to carry captives from Kongo to Buenos Aires. The owner, Andrew Holmes, abandoned this plan on receiving late word that the British had captured the port, so he simply instructed the skipper to carry his captives to Charleston.[34]

The itineraries of these vessels were more complex than the triangular and bilateral voyages that were the norm in the American slave trade. One reason had to do with Spanish authorities in the Río de la Plata, who frequently seized American ships. Although Spain's South Atlantic ports opened to American and neutral shipping as part of the same imperial reform that allowed foreign vessels to bring captives to Cuba, in the Río de la Plata, opposition from local merchants and officials connected to the old mercantilist system, along with the standing rivalries between the ports of Montevideo and Buenos Aires, meant that the new rules were not always followed. Authorities also leveraged the rules limiting the amount of time a foreign vessel could remain in port to force captains to sell at low prices, probably at the behest of local merchants. The Americans' propensity to play fast and loose with Spanish restrictions also led to seizures. For many Americans, it appears, slave trading was really a convenient excuse to access the Spanish American market, with silver and gold as the real prizes. The boundary between sincerity and pretense is often difficult to discern, as American skippers "innocently" wandered into trouble in Spanish ports.[35]

The *Eliza* of Boston is one of the vessels that operated in this gray area. It did not start out as a slaver, or so it appears. The *Eliza* sailed first to the Netherlands, where it apparently picked up a cargo of Indian textiles, then made for Rio de Janeiro. While there, the supercargo received word that war had broken out between Portugal and Spain. According to the captain's story, several Spanish merchants in Rio engaged him to ferry them and their wares to Río de la Plata. Once in Spanish territory, authorities declared his voyage illegal and detained the *Eliza*. After months of wrangling and talk of selling the vessel, Spanish authorities permitted the *Eliza* to sail for Mozambique for captives and return with them to Buenos Aires. Supercargo Joseph Russell told owner Benjamin Joy that slave trading was "a business against which [I] am strongly prejudiced," but rationalized that "Negroes here . . . are extremely well treated, well fed, & worked but little, must, impartially viewed, be considered as an act of humanity." The *Eliza* carried captives from Mozambique to Buenos Aires under "special privilege," with local merchants apparently among the investors and with a Spanish captain and crew. On return, the ship was not allowed to take on a cargo, so Russell simply sold it. Another American vessel, the *Rising Sun,* was in port at the same time and undertook a similar voyage, rechristened as the *Angela*. The voyage was a financial failure, and the vessel was sold to local merchants on its return to Buenos Aires.[36]

Although many merchants used the slave trade to the Río de la Plata to pry open the Spanish American market, it was not insignificant to their businesses. Rather, it was understood to carry additional benefits. This helps to explain why so many New England shipowners who had never been deeply involved in slave trading suddenly took it up. Return cargoes from Montevideo generally included hides, horn, and Peruvian bark (the source of quinine). Some American slavers in Río de la Plata followed the "Tasajo Trail," named after a type of jerked beef. Produced on the ranches of the Río de la Plata, tasajo was shipped to Cuba, where it was a crucial source of animal protein for the enslaved population. The Charleston-based slaver Margaret Schutt gave explicit instructions to her captain to take payment for captives in tasajo and carry it to New Orleans, where it was also in demand. The D'Wolf's brig *Punch* also took on what was surely tasajo (listed as "beef"), which was hardly surprising given the family's presence in Cuba.[37] Given the Río de la Plata's status as the premier outlet for Andean silver (*plata* means "silver"), American merchants also used the slave trade to gain access to specie. John Sabens of the *Punch* did this openly, carrying gold for a local merchant who needed to pay off a debt in Philadelphia, and Aylwin's *Minerva* also took on specie. Margaret Schutt was more circumspect, instructing her captain to take on tasajo or "a more valuable article" if the opportunity presented itself.[38]

The Río de la Plata trade did not last. After soaring in 1806, it declined sharply. Slavers learned that Spanish authorities often detained vessels, and with the British invasion of the region in 1806 and again in 1807, American vessels were threatened with seizure for blockade-running and trading with the enemy. American shipowners undoubtedly concluded that the costs and risks were too great and directed their vessels elsewhere. The abolition of the U.S. slave trade in 1808 and Jefferson's embargo put an end to this route for slavers. However, later and throughout the nineteenth century, ordinary American merchant ships would rediscover the tasajo trade that had been pioneered by the slavers.

In December 1805, Senator Stephen Row Bradley, Republican of Vermont, introduced a bill to ban the transatlantic slave trade as of January 1, 1808, the earliest allowable date under the Constitution. The Senate postponed Bradley's motion for another year, due not so much to opposition as to a sense that, with two years to go, there was other business to transact. In February 1806, Congressman Barnabas Bidwell introduced a bill to levy a ten-dollar duty on captives brought in from outside the United States, with an additional provision for ending the slave trade on January 1, 1808. This time, John Randolph of Virginia, years ahead of his time as an ideological defender of slavery, argued that the Constitution precluded the passage (not merely the enactment) of a post-dated 1808 ban. Bidwell's bill was tabled.[39]

Thomas Jefferson restarted the drive in his annual message of December 1806 by calling for the immediate passage of a ban, to become effective on January 1, 1808. Framing the slave trade as a violation of the "human rights" of "the unoffending inhabitants of Africa," he urged Congress to salvage the "morality, the reputation, and the best interests of our country." Responding to Randolph's assertion that even debating such a measure before that date would be unconstitutional, Jefferson argued that slavers would need ample notice to complete voyages now under way. Sympathetic congressmen, dismissing Randolph's objections, soon drafted a bill to end the slave trade as of January 1, 1808. There was no serious opposition to the principle of barring the landing of captives, but several provisions proved contentious. Ardent foes of slavery argued that the language of the bill, in which ownership of the captives was "forfeited" on violation, unwittingly sanctioned the principle of property in humans and argued that Africans should be entered as free people. Southern congressmen, led by Peter Early of Georgia, insisted that doing so would inundate the slave states with free Blacks, and he raised the specter of revolutionary Haiti. When Early warned of a "civil war" over the issue, a compromise-minded bloc of representatives persuaded the anti-slavery faction to drop its objection to the notion of "forfeit." Penalties for violation were another issue. Initially set at death (proponents pointed out that the Bible prescribed that penalty for "man-stealing"), the punishment was reduced in the final bill to a fine of up to $10,000 and two to four years' imprisonment. Finally, because it was part of the same draft legislation, Congress also debated the regulation of the coastwise maritime slave trade, focusing on a clause prohibiting the use of vessels under forty tons, which would have excluded most of those involved. Despite Early's forecast of civil war and Randolph's threat that the provision would precipitate a secession movement, the bill with the forty-ton requirement passed. Two of the five "no" votes in the House came from northern New England, two from Virginia, and one from South Carolina. Randolph did not cast a vote.[40]

Although the passage of the bill garnered little attention in the press, voting alignments on several of the amendments prefigured those of the antebellum period, with pro- and anti-slavery representatives on opposing sides and a compromise-minded group in the center. Rhetorical themes of the 1807 debate included states' rights, natural rights, the biblical sanction of slavery, fear of Haitian-style rebellion, and secession and civil war. The most striking aspect of the congressional debate, however, was not the emergence of a pro-transatlantic-slave-trade political constituency, since no such thing existed. Rather, the debate exposed the incoherence of maintaining that slavery as an institution might be justified while simultaneously holding that the slave trade was wrong. The point came through clearly as the House debated the coastwise maritime slave trade. As always, it was John Randolph who furnished the sharpest critique, arguing that the forty-ton clause interfered with the property rights of slaveholders, which might eventually furnish a pretext for "universal emancipation." After the bill's passage, he introduced an "explanatory" resolution specifying that nothing in the act should be construed as abridging the "full, complete, and absolute right of property of the owner or master of any slave," and threatened secession if it were not adopted. Congress took no heed; Randolph's amendment was ahead of its time. But his argument that criticism of the slave trade implied a condemnation of slavery as an institution, and that one could not logically be abstracted from the other, would wind through future debates on enforcement and eventually prompt some politicians to seek a reopening of the trade. And although Randolph never said so, the converse also later proved true: a republic that countenanced slaveholding would find it difficult to isolate and suppress slave trading.[41]

The rumbling in Congress that began in 1805 made it obvious that the end would come at the earliest allowable moment. In 1807, the final year of the legal slave trade, no fewer than seventy-four ships embarked for Africa from American ports. Shipowners in Bristol, Boston, Newport, New York, and especially Charleston bought up trade goods, hired whatever crew they could, and turned their vessels around in a rush to beat the approaching deadline. It was in this final phase that a number of Charleston commission merchants seem to have made the decision to outfit vessels of their own. After all, they were in the best position to turn around recently arrived vessels and to rehire experienced crews. As the clock wound down, some merchants dispatched their vessels with "cash" (surely specie) in addition to the usual trade goods in hopes of speeding the acquisition of captives. At least sixteen vessels departed after July 1, with five sailing for Africa after September 1. One even sailed in December.[42]

Obviously, those slavers who dispatched vessels late in the year knew that they would likely miss the January 1 deadline. Phillips and Gardner acknowledged the possibility in their instructions to Josha Viall of the *Nancy.* "You will be particularly mindfull to leave the Coast timely (allowing double passage) to arrive at this Port previous to the 31st Decembr. Next," they wrote, adding that the insurance on the voyage expired on the same date. Some merchants reasoned that they could always land their captives in Cuba if they missed the deadline for landing in the United States. This violated the statutes of 1794, 1800, and 1807, but the chances of discovery were slim. Others simply landed captives in the United States after January 1. Charles Clarke sailed aboard a D'Wolf vessel that put into Georgetown, South Carolina, instead of Charleston. In a letter to his mother, he described a brisk clandestine trade, though one made less profitable by Jefferson's embargo, which prevented planters from exporting their produce and dampened the demand for enslaved labor. According to Clarke, five hundred captives had been landed since the ban took effect, equivalent to the amount that would fill two vessels. He believed two or three more vessels would be arriving soon from Africa and told of another ship that was allowed to land captives "in distress."[43]

Slavers regularly invoked distress as an explanation for their non-compliance with the law. In February 1808, the federal district court in Charleston invalidated the seizure of the schooner *Kitty* after the owners cited the death of several seamen, detention by the British, abandonment by the steward, and a scarcity of provisions as excuses for why the voyage ran long. An American merchant in Martinique reported that a Charleston vessel claimed distress in order to land captives there. Another slaver had the audacity to ask the federal government to pay him for missing the deadline. Captain James Frazer claimed that a leak forced him to land in Saint Kitts and that he was not able to get under way again before January 1. He "sold" most of his captives there, but officials would not allow him to land four captives who had leprosy. Frazer was forced to transport them to Charleston, where authorities required him to post a bond guaranteeing their return to Africa. Frazer asked for a return of his bond plus expenses.[44]

It was in this context that one American slave ship, the *Amedie*, wound up setting a major legal precedent in both slave trade and human rights jurisprudence. The *Amedie* had set sail from Charleston in September 1807, leaving it no realistic possibility of returning before January 1. Captain Martin Robin and his British supercargo purchased captives on the Bight of Biafra, but Robin died shortly after leaving Africa. The *Amedie*, now under James Johnson, was approaching the Caribbean on December 21, 1807, when it was taken by a British cruiser and brought before the vice-admiralty court at Tortola, in the British Virgin Islands. Under the terms of Britain's Slave Trade Abolition Act, any captives landed in British territory after May 1, 1807, would be confiscated and either "apprenticed" or, in the case of adult males, enlisted into the military.[45]

The *Amedie* was not the first American vessel captured by the British. Since the outbreak of war in 1793, the Royal Navy had intercepted hundreds of ships for trading with Britain's enemies, which at various times included not only France but Spain, the Netherlands, and Denmark. Though costly and politically controversial, for non-slavers these seizures were unremarkable. However, because the United States had barred the carriage of captives to foreign colonies in 1794, the legal implications for slavers were more complex. In 1800 the British seized the American slaver *Chance* for trading with the enemy while en route to Cuba and brought it before the vice-admiralty court at Jamaica. The court found no evidence of contraband but confiscated the captives on the grounds that the voyage was illegal under the federal statute of 1794. Because slave trading was still legal in the British Empire, the court auctioned off the captives to local planters with the proceeds going to the captors. With the *Chance* decision, the court had tentatively established a precedent that said one nation could enforce another's laws. But subsequent actions did not invoke this precedent. Just weeks before the capture of the *Amedie*, another American slaver, the *Nancy*, was seized and brought to the Tortola court. The court took note of the fact that the *Nancy*, which was headed for Saint Thomas, sailed in violation of the federal statute of 1794 but ultimately condemned it on the grounds that it was partly owned by a Frenchman (a spurious claim, it seems). Because the *Nancy* was taken after British abolition came into effect, the captives could not be auctioned off. Thirty-five of the men were placed aboard a Royal Navy vessel, and the rest were "indentured" and shipped to the Trinidad sugar estate of the commanding admiral.[46]

The court condemned the *Amedie* in February 1808, citing the *Chance* decision of 1800, which held that one nation could enforce another's slave-trading laws. This was a novel doctrine, and one that would have great implications for the slave trade as a whole. Upholding this doctrine on appeal, the High Court of Admiralty in London went even further, positing that the slave trade ran "contrary to the principles of justice and humanity" and could therefore have no "legitimate existence" unless explicitly sanctioned by "positive law." As Jenny S. Martinez has shown, the *Amedie* decision enshrined in law an embryonic notion of universal human rights. And for the better part of a decade, the doctrine that slaving vessels could be seized unless the nation of registry had expressly legalized the trade underpinned the Royal Navy's early interdiction efforts.[47]

British prize courts invoked the *Amedie* decision in two additional cases stemming from this final burst of American slaving, although the results were ambiguous. The *Ann* (*Anne*) was taken in the South Atlantic in 1807 while carrying captives from Cape Mount to Montevideo. The captors took it before the court at Cape Town, arguing that the voyage violated the federal act of 1794. The owners responded that the vessel should be restored because it made its voyage before January 1, 1808, the deadline set in the act of 1807. The Cape Town court condemned the *Anne*, asserting that Britain could enforce American slave-trading laws, and ordered the captives to be auctioned off (the vessel arrived before Britain's own abolition act had taken effect). Two years later, on appeal, the High Court of Admiralty in London cited *Amedie* in upholding the seizure, although this would have been of little consolation to the former *Anne* captives, who were now permanently enslaved. The case of the *Africa*, a Charleston vessel that took on captives on the Loango Coast in 1807, was even more problematic. Like the *Amedie*, the *Africa* had set sail too late to make the January 1 deadline for a legal voyage under U.S. law. William Boyd, the vessel's owner, understood this point, because he instructed his captain to land the captives at a U.S. port at the earliest possible date. The *Africa* missed that deadline and was making for Havana when taken. The skipper argued for special dispensation, claiming that an outbreak of smallpox had resulted in "unavoidable delays" and forced him to head for Cuba. The Tortola admiralty court accepted the captain's excuse and restored both the vessel and the captives to the owner. The captors appealed to the High Court in London and won a reversal, but the decision was based on evidence that the captain had intended all along to land in Cuba and not in Charleston. In other words, the case was decided not on the basis of *Amedie* but on a much narrower point of admiralty law. These decisions notwithstanding, the *Amedie* decision would prove very important to the American slave trade over the next decade.[48]

Although the American slave trade hit its statistical peak in the years 1804–1807 and vaulted the United States into the top tier of slaving powers, much of what happened in the period was aberrational. The volume of the trade, for one, was far above the historical norm, inflated by an awareness that Congress would close the door as soon as it was constitutionally allowed to, on January 1, 1808. The fact that the cotton boom began a dozen years before the magic date in the Constitution contributed greatly to the surge. Had those two dates not coincided, there might not have been a slave rush. The period 1804–1807 was also one of the few in which American slave ships primarily served an American captive market (the same was true of the late seventeenth and early eighteenth centuries, but the numbers were very small). Never again would the ships going out and the ships coming in coincide as they did in this era. The sudden emergence of Charleston as a major source of slaving voyages also ran counter to established norms. Long a port of disembarkation, Charleston had relatively little history as a dispatch point. Although some longtime commission merchants and distillers organized voyages, most relied on outside experience, from New England or Britain. These two outside groups operated on their own networks, one focused on upper Guinea and the other on the Loango Coast. The captives they delivered had a major impact on African American culture.

A few stragglers notwithstanding, after January 1, 1808, Charleston ceased to be a major point of dispatch or disembarkation for the transatlantic slave trade and became almost entirely a cotton port. Its brief career as a slaving port, however, had an unexpectedly long afterlife, as we will see in the coming sections.

Part Four

LIFE AND DEATH IN THE
SLAVE TRADE

1700–1807

Newport, Rhode Island, Present Day.

IN NEWPORT'S COMMON Burying Ground stands a slate-gray, cherub-topped tombstone marking the final resting place of Elizabeth Bush, who died in 1782 at the age of forty-one. Etched below her name is that of her husband, Captain John Bush, "who died at Senegal in Africa Augst 20th 1773, in the 33^d Year of his Age." In the same cemetery not too far away is the grave of Benjamin Searing, whose tombstone notes that he died "after the Death of his Brother Capt James Searing In Africa Jan^{ry} 15th 1762." Similar memorials can be found in cemeteries across Rhode Island. In North Kingstown stands a marker for Charles Congdon, "who died on the coast of Africa" in 1795. Those exact words adorn a marker in Warren for Benjamin Smith, who perished one year after Congdon.[1] There are more examples, but the number of markers does not even remotely represent the eleven hundred or so Rhode Islanders who died while working aboard slavers.[2] There are reasons why more markers do not exist. Cemeteries fall to developers, and acid rain erodes headstones. But the main reason is that the bodies of those sailors who died in the slave trade never made it home for burial. The memorials in Rhode Island cemeteries, in other words, are just that— memorials erected by grieving family members, not actual graves. The bones of many more surely lie in Black Dick's Nursery, which was the

---

Previous page: Slaveholding family in South Kingstown, Rhode Island, ca. 1740. The undisputed slave-trading capital of the United States during the eighteenth and early nineteenth centuries was Rhode Island, and the slave trade shaped society there more than anywhere else. Most notably, it was responsible for creating one of the largest Black communities in New England, which was dominated in the late colonial period by Akan speakers, many of whom arrived as "privilege slaves" from the Gold Coast. (53.3, "John Potter and Family," Collection of the Newport Historical Society)

name for the white graveyard at Cape Coast Castle, and in the small island in Havana Harbor, the burial ground for Protestant seamen—that
is, if they do not lie on the bottom of the ocean.

Also in Newport's Common Burying Ground but segregated from
the main section is the cemetery-within-a-cemetery known as "God's
Little Acre." It contains the graves of some three hundred Black Newporters, many of whom arrived as "privilege slaves." Most of the people
bearing African names (which is how we can identify them as African)
came from the Gold Coast, which is hardly surprising given its importance to the town's slave trade. For example, in that section of the cemetery lies Cuffe Gibbs, a probable Akan speaker, who died in 1768 and
whose brother and likely shipmate, Pompe Gibbs, carved his gravestone.
Pompe survived the American Revolution, became free, and eventually
changed his name to Zingo Gibbs. The gravestone he carved for his
brother is the first signed piece of African American art from North
America known to exist. Here also lies Violet Hammond, whose marker
memorializes her husband, Cape Coast James, who died in 1772. And
here lies Duchess Quamino, who took the Akan name of her husband
as a surname. Although those resting here lived very different lives from
those Newporters who transported them, they now spend eternity only
yards away from each other.[3]

The transatlantic slave trade was a way of life and a way of death
for Rhode Islanders of all backgrounds. Responsible for about half of
colonial New England's enslaved population, the transatlantic slave
trade gave Newport the region's largest Black community, for a time.
For those Africans who watched the rum men come and go year after
year, the ships were a symbol of how tantalizingly entwined their place
of exile and old homes were. Even if, as some believed, death reunited
them with their ancestors, their bones remained in Newport. For white
Rhode Islanders watching the ships come and go, the slave trade meant
something very different. It was a staple of the regional economy, en-
riching a select few while furnishing employment to hundreds more. But
many participants paid the ultimate price for this prosperity. So deadly
was the trade that over the years it had a measurable effect on Newport's
demographic structure, leaving it with the most female-skewed population of any New England maritime community.

This section examines the men, women, and children whose lives were shaped by the American slave trade. Chapter 7 explores the experiences of those African men, women, and children who experienced captivity and transportation in the holds of American Guineamen. Chapter 8 examines the impact of the slave trade over the long eighteenth century on two towns, Newport and Bristol, Rhode Island. While many American ports dispatched slave ships, only these two can be considered true slaving ports, where the trade accounted for a significant portion of the local economy. In both towns, slave trading influenced life—and death—in unexpected ways.

Captivity

It is a matter of record that American slavers sometimes produced their own captives by kidnapping people.[1] Abduction, however, accounted for a very small proportion of those taken aboard American slavers. The vast majority of those taken aboard American slave ships—probably more than 99 percent—were purchased, not abducted. On this, the record is unambiguous. The purchases are documented in hundreds of letters sent to merchants by captains from the African coast. Even more specific information can be found for thousands of individual exchanges as recorded in trade books and accounts. To believe that slavers filled their holds through abduction, as popular images often suggest, is to portray Africans as naive and completely powerless, which they were not. Not that slavers had qualms about kidnapping Africans. They certainly would have, but it was not possible, at least not on a scale sufficient to sustain a profitable trade in human beings. The slave ships of the long eighteenth century, then, were not in most cases the places where captives were transformed into commodities; the vast majority of the people in their holds had already been commodified when brought aboard ship. A more useful way to conceptualize the slave ship is as a means of connecting different systems of chattel slavery, one in which outsiderness was calculated in reference to multiple factors, and the other in which it was calculated primarily in reference to a discourse of race.[2]

To say so is to suggest that enslaved people in Africa were defined as property. Not everyone would agree. For Suzanne Miers and Igor Kopytoff, the authors of an influential essay published in 1977, Western concepts of property did not apply in pre-colonial Africa. Enslaved people in Africa, they argued, existed at one end of a continuum of "rights-in-persons" rooted in kinship. These rights, integral to "traditional" African societies, were transferrable, but that fact did not mean that enslaved people were chattels in the Western sense.[3] Historians applying this logic have argued that those entering the transatlantic slave trade underwent a subtle but significant change in status, from a captive, or a person over whom certain rights are exercised, to a person who has been commodified. For many historians of the transatlantic trade, the slave ship was more than a means of transportation: it was an engine of commodification.[4]

The problem with that interpretation is that it confuses the ideological justification for slavery—the notion that enslaved people were analogous to kin and not exploitable outsiders—with the institution's actual workings. This tendency was traceable in part to the fact that Miers and Kopytoff based much of their interpretation on fieldwork undertaken many decades, in some cases well over a century, after the abolition of the transatlantic trade removed American markets from the equation. They also focused more on the status of enslaved people within particular settings than on the violent process of enslavement and the trade in human beings. That enslaved people might be understood to exist on a continuum of kinship and belonging is, therefore, not wrong. It a reasonably good fit for a domestic (household) mode of slavery involving people of outsider descent who had been born into their communities and were now culturally assimilated. Even then, the dishonor of slave status persisted for generations.

But the kinship metaphor (for that is what it is) does not apply as well to the men, women, and children who were sent into the transatlantic slave trade via well-established African commercial networks. As Claude Meillasoux and others have argued, enslaved people, especially those sold to transatlantic slavers, were the opposite of kin: they were outsiders whose existence as commodities derived from and was shaped by external markets in human beings. By this line of thinking, the process of enslavement and the trade in people cannot be analyzed separately from the status of enslaved people in specific settings. Slavery as a system depended on externalizing the process of raising children (producing future slaves) to other societies. The outsider/insider distinction implies a dichotomy of status rather than a continuum of rights-in-persons: one either was or was not a slave, and enslaved people understood it in precisely those terms. This dichotomous outsider/insider distinction was moreover central to African slavery. While it was certainly possible for some of these outsiders to progress over time toward becoming insiders, especially for those born into the host society, the stigma of slave status endured as long as community memory of a person's enslaved parentage did. Enslaved people who managed to assimilate acquired special rights, the most important of which for this discussion was the right not to be sold to transatlantic traders.[5]

The applicability of the kinless-outsider model to West Africa in the era of the transatlantic slave trade is readily apparent in the many surviving narratives of enslavement from the era. It is often assumed that little autobiographical testimony survives from the eighteenth century, and interpretations that see the process of commodification as beginning aboard ship invariably rely much more on shipping records than on narratives from people who actually experienced enslavement. The 130 or so narratives from upper Guinea and the Voltaic region that form the basis for this chapter graphically underscore the outsiderness of the enslaved. Their status as political or religious "others" rendered them enslaveable, exploitable, and indeed saleable as commodities. To them, slavery was not an indistinct point on a hypothetical continuum; it was a real and immediate experience. And, contrary to suggestions that their ordeal "depersonalized" them (in anything more than an abstract sense), the testimonies demonstrate that nearly all captives carried with them memories of their lives and identities in Africa. Far from being discarded, these memories were the building blocks for who they would become in the Americas.[6]

Upper Guinea was a source of captives for American slavers for more than two hundred years. It was also a region with a long history of slavery. Ghana, Mali, and Songhai, the great medieval empires of the

Western Savanna region, all had slavery. These were hierarchical societies with nobilities and complex occupational caste systems. It is tempting to say that enslaved people occupied the bottom tier, but because enslaved soldiers and administrators often enjoyed better material conditions than free peasants did, it is probably more accurate to say that the enslaved were simply outsiders. Still, the existence of slavery does not mean that these societies were based primarily on it. Most historians believe that prior to European contact, slavery was a minor "social" rather than a major "economic" institution in Africa. In societies where control over people was more important than control over land, enslavement was a way for important individuals to acquire dependents. But, as Meillasoux has posited, in the absence of a major external demand for enslaved labor, there were material limits to the numbers of enslaved people that a given population could support, and these were difficult to transcend. Adding enslaved dependents meant increasing the demand on resources, so for a slave to contribute a net increase in production, a person needed to produce well above her (and most enslaved people were women) subsistence. This was possible, of course, but difficult given the technological constraints of the era. External demand could theoretically alter this situation, but before the arrival of the Europeans, this was limited (in West Africa) to the comparatively smaller trans-Saharan trade.[7]

The growth of an Atlantic market for captives resulted in the expansion of slavery in upper Guinea and its transformation from a social into an economic institution. Inland polities, such Kaabu and Segu, became major suppliers of captives, initiating wars for which the acquisition of captives was at least one goal. For these societies, people taken in battle and raids on enemy polities were enslaveable and saleable. But even the activities of these predatory states were not enough to make upper Guinea into a major supplier for the transatlantic trade. That changed in the middle of the eighteenth century with the rise of Futa Jallon, especially under Ibrahima Sori. Under his leadership, religion became an important category of outsiderness, delineating a boundary between free and enslaved status. The Futa Jallon state, which controlled most of the region's slave trade, attempted to screen out non-Muslim captives, in conformity with the prohibition on selling fellow Muslims to Christians. Even so, the need to procure arms and other goods meant that the caravans from Futa Jallon to the Rio Pongo and other nearby ports continued. Between 1751 and 1800, years that coincided with the maturation of the American slave trade, the number of captives embarking from ports in upper Guinea nearly tripled over the previous quarter century. Futa Jallon was directly or indirectly responsible for much of the increase, with non-Muslim religious outsiders constituting a majority of the enslaved.[8]

In Africa, the greater availability of captives led to more and larger slaveholdings and the spread of enslaved labor. As the transatlantic slave trade reached its peak in the eighteenth century, agricultural units that can only be described as plantations began to appear, with entire villages to house enslaved laborers. Even in the Futa Jallon almamate, founded as a protest against slave-trading regimes like Kaabu, a majority of the population was enslaved. As early as 1756 Futa Jallon had to suppress a major rebellion that had broken out in the special slave villages it maintained. Coastal polities also expanded their use of captive labor as they evolved into service centers for European and American slavers. Niumi, whose rulers were landlords to James Fort in the Gambia River, a frequent port of call for the Americans, used its growing access to enslaved labor to grow food and provide services. A similar situation pertained on the Senegal River near the slaving fort of Saint-Louis and at Gorée Island. Moria, a state in the Rivers of Guinea region and another haunt of the Americans, developed large rice plantations with an enslaved majority of between 70 and 80 percent, all to provision ships. In 1783, Moria's enslaved plantation laborers rebelled and eventually rallied to the standard of Fatta, the self-proclaimed Mahdi. Their rebellion was crushed in 1795, but the fact that it occurred illustrates the effect of an export market on the institution of slavery in some African polities.[9]

Slavery in upper Guinea was not confined to the larger hierarchical societies and centralized states like Futa Jallon and Segu. Many smaller polities practiced what is sometimes called "lineage slavery." Most of these societies were decentralized and egalitarian in their basic ethos. Slavery might at first appear to contradict the egalitarian nature of these societies, but that was not the case. In Balanta and many other societies of the rivers region, the enslavement of outsiders allowed elders a way to accumulate dependents and generate surpluses without endangering the social fabric through the exploitation of younger members. However, before the emergence of a European Atlantic market for captives, slavery in decentralized societies was a minor "social" institution whose growth was circumscribed by the limits suggested by Meillasoux. With the emergence of an Atlantic demand for captives after 1450, slavery grew more important to the decentralized polities. The Balanta and others responded to raids by centralized polities like Kaabu by moving from upland areas into less accessible mangrove areas. The move necessitated a shift from upland to paddy rice culture, which in turn required the use of iron tools to break through the tough mangrove roots. The easiest way to obtain iron was to trade captives for it. The Balanta and decentralized groups therefore began to raid for captives. Male captives generally went into the Atlantic market. As outsiders, female captives and their children were denied the rights and privileges of "insiders." This allowed "big men" to acquire and exploit dependents without violating the egalitarian ethos.[10]

Outsiders could be defined in political terms (prisoners of war), in religious terms (Muslim, non-Muslim), or in ethnic terms and were enslaveable under the correct circumstances. Certain ethnonyms, in the hands of outsiders, reflect the close association between enslaveability and outsider status. Among Juula traders, for example, the term "Bambara" came to denote an enslaveable non-Muslim. Insiders, in contrast, could only lose their freedom in certain circumstances, such as conviction of a crime or failure to pay a debt. Over time, however, enslaved outsiders could move closer to becoming insiders on Miers and Kopytoff's continuum of belonging. This usually took place over successive generations and involved an accumulation of rights, the most fundamental being the right not to be sold to outsiders. The distinction between those enslaved people who did and did not possess that right was reflected in many languages. In Wolof, a *jaam sayor* could be sold away, but a *jaam juddu* referred to an enslaved person who by virtue of birth into the local society had the right not to be sold. In Bamana, the language of Segu, *jonfin* referred to war captives who could be sold, whereas *jonba* designated those who were non-saleable.[11] The outsider/insider distinction was taken seriously but was not completely inviolable, especially as European demand for captives grew. An observer in the Rivers of Guinea region, to the north of Sierra Leone, noted that some dealers were getting around the stricture on selling locally born enslaved people by pawning and then not redeeming them. The practice is an excellent example of the changes that a soaring European demand for captives brought to Africa.[12]

Narratives from people enslaved in upper Guinea highlight the role of warfare in producing captives as well as their status as commodities. Upper Guinea generated more than one hundred enslavement narratives, a number unequaled by any other African region. The narratives, however, do not constitute an unbiased sample. Because they were taken down in almost all cases by whites, they reflect varying European interest in speaking with Africans. Some narratives were collected by missionaries for religious purposes, but others were taken in support of the abolitionist movement. A few interviews were even conducted by pro-slavery whites interested in countering abolitionist charges by suggesting that New World slavery was preferable to African "barbarism." For these reasons, the narratives are weighted toward the nineteenth century, although approximately one-third were generated by people who were enslaved before 1820, when the slave trade became widely illegal and practices changed.[13] The narratives also privilege the male experience, with only six generated by women. Interlocutors not only universalized the male experience of slavery, they favored those they found most impressive or most knowledgeable, invariably men. But perhaps the most surprising bias is the number of narratives generated by Muslims, which is far out of proportion to their probable representation in the enslaved population. The reason for this most likely has to do with the fact that many Europeans viewed Muslims as different from other Africans as a result of their literacy and easily identifiable piety. Muslims therefore attracted more attention, garnered more respect, and were more likely to be manumitted than other Africans, all of which provided more opportunity to tell their stories.[14]

The earliest narrative, which dates to about 1686, highlights the importance of the ceddo regimes in the process of enslavement and gives us a glimpse of the process that delivered captives to the earliest American slavers. A man we know only as Emanuel, who had been sold to the Dutch and taken to the Netherlands, managed to become free and make his way back to his native Kayor, in Senegambia. Emanuel was a cavalry leader who lost his freedom in a war with Baol. His account emphasized bravery and martial prowess: he was "surrounded by many men, who shot arrows at him like hail, he preserved himself by this dexterity in managing his shield . . . and that [his] troops were all armed with bows and arrows, and javelins, only twenty-five or thirty men having muskets." How much of this is attributable to his interlocutor is of course unknowable, but Emanuel's narrative vividly demonstrates the martial values of the ceddo regimes that likely supplied captives to the American slavers of the seventeenth century. A similar point can be made regarding captives taken by the martial states of Segu and Kaabu during the eighteenth century. Mungo Park spoke with a man who had been taken at Joka near the Middle Niger by the army of Segu in about 1796. Under established practice at Segu, two-thirds of those taken in a declared war were the property of the *faama,* or ruler, of the Segu state, and one-third belonged to his soldiers. In both cases, however, captives were usually sold as commodities to merchants. The man Park spoke with was taken to Segu immediately after his capture, where he was purchased by a merchant who then marched him to Kaarta for resale.[15]

But these stories aside, the picture that emerges from the upper Guinea narratives is the growing importance of jihad as a driver of enslavement in upper Guinea over the course of the eighteenth and into the early nineteenth centuries. Overall, about 65 percent of narrators enslaved in upper Guinea before 1820 were taken as a direct consequence of war. Determining whether the conflicts were jihad-related, however, is often difficult. The political circumstances behind individual enslavements are almost always obscure and can only be deduced. Another example from Mungo Park furnishes a rare exception. Taking a berth aboard a slave ship, he conversed in Mandinka with a number of the captives. Nine of them were Muslims who had been captured in the conflict between Kayor and the Futa Toro almamate.[16]

The fact that a disproportionate number of narratives were by Muslims reminds us that this was not merely a story of Muslims enslaving non-Muslims, but rather of a region convulsed in conflict. Sambo, or Abraham, who was probably enslaved in the 1750s, was undoubtedly a Muslim, since his biographer noted that he prayed "diligently" and had a "religious" outlook that was mixed "heathen superstition." When he returned home after receiving severe wounds in battle, his father, clearly an influential figure, dispatched a retaliatory raid. Sambo was taken in this second battle.[17] Abdul Rahman, another narrator, was very likely taken in a jihad-related conflict. The son of the almami of Futa Jallon and an experienced cavalry leader, he was captured on a campaign against a non-Muslim polity in 1788. Late in Sori's reign, Futa Jallon had become dependent on the sale of captives in order to support its armies. Abdul Rahman was taken in one of these raids, which, similar to Sambo, brought a scorched-earth retaliation from his father.[18]

As these narratives suggest, warfare had secondary effects, all of which resulted in a general destabilization that fed the cycle of warfare and enslavement. For many conflicts, then, the ultimate cause, whether religious or not, is impossible to know; the important thing was that conflict was rife. The narrative of Mohammedu Sisei provides more detail on the political background to his enslavement than almost any other, and yet it is difficult to say with certainty just what role religious conflict played. Born in about 1788 in Niani Maru, a Mandinka polity on the northern bank of the Gambia River, Mohammedu Sisei attended religious school and worked as a teacher. In about 1810, war broke out between Mansa Koi of the neighboring polity of Wuli, and Salam Mansa of Janjanbureh, an island in the Gambia. When Mansa Koi's army won, Salam Mansa called on the powerful slave-raiding state of Kaabu to come to its aid. Salam Mansa and Kaabu raided and took many captives in Niani Maru, Mohammedu Sisei among them. His captors marched him to Kaabu, where he almost certainly performed agricultural labor. After five months, his captors brought him back to the Gambia and sold him to a European slaver. Whether religion was the proximate cause of the conflict between Salam Mansa and Mansa Koi is unknown; it is certainly a possibility. But his story reveals the ways in which an external demand for slaves could cause and combine with political or religious conflict and warfare to set cycles of retaliation that could destabilize an entire region.[19]

Warfare, however, was a continuum rather than a thing in itself, and the distinction between all-out war and raiding is often unclear in the narratives. Battles between armies, such as the one that cost Abdul Rahman his freedom, were just one mode of warfare; smaller skirmishes and raids were another. The Segu state distinguished between three types of wars. The first was a large-scale, state-sponsored operation with a specific objective. Known as the *kèlè*, it could yield thousands of captives at one stroke. The second, or *soboli*, was smaller in scale, usually involving a few dozen horsemen, who raided border areas to enforce loyalty to the state. A third type, *jado*, was an unauthorized raid by small bands of ten to twenty soldiers. Such raids directed against insiders threatened the legitimacy and stability of the state and were therefore capital offenses. Many narratives capture this variation in their ambiguity on the nature of the conflicts that resulted in enslavement. Sitiki was a five-year-old boy who lived in the Western Savanna region. In about 1800, he recalled hearing "cries of war with the report of fire-arms" and was taken when soldiers burst into his house.[20] Salih Bilali was taken in about 1782 by a "predatory party" from Segu while traveling from Jenne to Kiannah.[21]

Even so, wars large and small were not the sole cause of enslavement. As long as an external market for human beings existed, some people would be tempted to simply abduct and sell others, regardless of rules and norms. Bandits kidnapped Muhammad Kaba Sagahanugu in 1777 as he was "walking some distance from his home" in the Western Savanna region.[22] Lamen Kebe of Futa Jallon was traveling to Timbuktu when he was "surrounded when asleep, and awoke to the act of his captors putting fetters upon him." Nearer to the coast, a ten-year-old Wolof boy was kidnapped by "Mandengas" in the 1760s or 1770s. As the latter example suggests, children were especially vulnerable to abduction because they were smaller and easier to whisk away. Evidence suggests that the percentage of children sold into Atlantic slavery jumped with the illegal trade of the nineteenth century, as children were easier to smuggle.[23]

Conviction for a crime or seizure for debt was another path to enslavement in upper Guinea. Both furnished a pretext for the enslavement of social insiders. In each case, the person was understood to have forfeited freedom either through his or her own actions or, in the case of debt, the actions of a kinsperson. Historians have long argued that the frequency of enslavement for crime and debt rose with Atlantic demand for enslaved labor, as rulers and societies progressively and opportunistically sought ways around existing strictures on the enslavement of one's own people. The charge was central to the abolitionist campaigns of the late eighteenth century. Although the claim is probably true, it has been difficult to document and quantify. About 3 percent of the pre-1820 enslavement narratives for upper Guinea indicate debt as the pretext, and another 3 percent involved sale by relatives, which was also debt-related in most circumstances. None of the pre-1820 narratives give criminality as the cause of enslavement. This is highly improbable given the number of observers who described enslavement for crimes and witchcraft, but it may be that narrators were reluctant to admit as much. Interestingly, among those enslaved after 1820, 14 percent admitted a criminal conviction, 13 percent were from sale by relatives (again, most often for debt), and 4 percent were for debt. The reason for the difference probably had more to do with the thorough and systematic questioning of enslaved people in the nineteenth century than with any significant changes in the nature of enslavement. What stands out is the comparative infrequency of conviction and debt as paths to enslavement. Both before and after 1820, most people lost their freedom in wars and raids.[24]

As the Atlantic market for captives grew, it combined with other factors to create a very dangerous environment, one in which the vicissitudes of life—of political turmoil and crop failures—all entailed the added possibility of losing one's freedom. One such event was the catastrophic drought that hit the Western Savanna in the 1750s, just as the Americans were reviving their slave trade after the War of the Austrian Succession (1740–1748). Because the Western Savanna lay near the Sahara, climate change had long influenced enslavement there. During the long-wave cycles of low rainfall, which prevailed between 1100 and 1500 and between 1630 and 1860, the southward retreat of the tsetse fly allowed the cavalry-dependent armies of the predatory states to extend their power, which aided enslavement. The fearsome drought of the 1750s aggravated matters even further, making agriculture unsustainable in places where it had only recently become viable. The resulting crop failures forced people to migrate in search of land, water, and food. Placing pressure on the carrying capacity of their "host" societies, the migrants were also outsiders vulnerable to enslavement. Some people enslaved themselves in exchange for food, and others were simply seized and sold.[25] The narrative of a Fulbe man who was enslaved in the 1750s illustrates the ways in which the Atlantic demand for enslaved labor combined with political destabilization and drought to create a lethal environment. Like many Fulbe, this narrator was a herder. When drought hit, his village was forced to migrate onto Wolof land to water their livestock. Wolof slavers attacked while the villagers slept. The herder and his companions were taken and sold to a French ship, probably at Saint-Louis or Gorée, while trying to escape to their original homeland.[26]

Gender is a major blind spot in the upper Guinea narratives. The whites who collected these narratives clearly viewed the male experience as the essential one. About 65 percent of those taken aboard slave ships during the long eighteenth century were male, and the ratio fluctuated by region. Upper Guinea was close to the average, although more male-heavy than several regions, including the Windward Coast, the Bight of Benin, and the Bight of Biafra. The reason had to do with the dynamics of enslavement in the region. Although the Europeans favored males for plantation labor, female captives were in demand in the trans-Saharan trade and in upper Guinea itself. Women did, of course, wind up in transatlantic slavery, just in smaller numbers. Only one eighteenth-century narrative by a woman survives from upper Guinea, and it does not provide much insight on these processes. The woman identified herself as "Mangree," a now-vanished ethnonym but one that from internal evidence appears to refer to a people living in inland regions of modern-day Côte d'Ivoire. She was taken in a war with an Akan-speaking polity from the Gold Coast and recalled that the leaders of her country had distributed muskets to soldiers and sent them to the border to repel the invasion. The rest of her experience is lost to time.[27]

Whereas upper Guinea was a source of captives for the Americas throughout the slave trade, the Voltaic region in the hinterland of the Gold Coast accounted for a plurality of the captives embarked by American slavers before 1808. Voltaic slavery shared many general characteristics with the upper Guinea versions. As in upper Guinea, slave status was reserved for outsiders, often war captives, but also for insiders convicted of crimes or unable to pay debts. And, as elsewhere, it was possible for enslaved outsiders to move toward insider status through the generations by the process of cultural assimilation.

Although Voltaic slavery exhibited many of the general features of African slavery, practices differed in some respects from those of upper Guinea. Most notably, Islam exerted much less influence on slavery in the Akan heartland. A second important feature, specifically among the Akan, was the relationship between slavery and the matrilineal kinship system. In matrilineal societies, belonging descends through the mother. Fathers in matrilineal societies do not have rights over their children. They do have some rights over their sisters' children but are not able to control how many they have. Any children born to a free woman, therefore, automatically became part of her kinship group. This made it difficult for an adult man to acquire dependents or pass on his accumulated property, so slavery furnished a way to do those things. Any children fathered with outsider women, who lacked kinship rights, "belonged" to their father. Outsider men could be deployed as laborers or sold to Europeans.[28]

The Asante state exerted strong control over the way captives were sold and distributed. Those taken in battle were placed into a common pool and channeled toward metropolitan Asante. There, authorities might use them as laborers or as soldiers in the asantehene's army or might send them into the Atlantic trade. Those taken in retreat following a military clash were considered to be the legitimate plunder of the captain who seized them and could be used or sold as he chose. The chance to raid for captives was one of the perquisites for army officers, and no doubt many people were enslaved via this route.[29]

As important as battlefield captures were for generating captives, more enslaved people in the region probably lost their freedom by being selected as tributary slaves. This was a related though distinct outgrowth of Asante military conquest, in which defeated powers were forced to pay tribute in fixed amounts of gold or captives or both. Most often, Asante demanded gold from Akan polities—partly because these groups had access to it—while demanding captives from more-distant non-Akan groups, a practice that once again highlights the connection between enslavement and outsider status. War debts or reparations were payable in captives. The Dagomba Drum History, a form of community memory, tells of the capture of Gariba, the ruler of Dagomba, by Opoku Ware's forces in the campaign of 1744–1745. When Dagomba ransomed Gariba, it incurred a "debt" to be repaid by furnishing Asante with an annual shipment of captives. In this case, the yearly quota was two thousand people, literally a king's ransom, but tribute obligations were more often set at one thousand. This was a significant number of people for any polity, but for smaller ones the tribute demand actually threatened depopulation. To meet their quotas, rulers occasionally offered up their own people, but this violated the general principle reserving enslavement for outsiders and therefore risked destabilization. More often, rulers met tributary demands by attacking neighboring polities for captives. On one occasion, Asante even supplied a conquered polity with the weapons to procure tributary captives. Thus, the consequence of military defeat—a tribute obligation—often perpetuated the cycle of warfare and raiding.[30]

This is, of course, a rather schematic representation of the paths to enslavement in the Voltaic region. As the enslavement narratives reveal, lived experience often defied easy categorization. That much is clear even though the corpus of testimony is much smaller than for upper Guinea. The smaller body of narratives owes much to the early and abrupt end of transatlantic slave trading on the Gold Coast after 1807.[31] So many narratives from elsewhere were generated as a result of the effort to suppress the slave trade, but the early decline of the trade on the Gold Coast meant that there were few liberated Africans in the region to give interviews. In contrast to upper Guinea, where the continuation of the trade generated more than one hundred narratives of enslavement, fewer than thirty survive for the Voltaic region. A few, such as the narratives of Venture Smith and Ottobah Cugoano, have entered the canon, but both were enslaved as children, which limits their usefulness. The narratives collected by the Moravian missionary C. G. A. Oldendorp in the Danish West Indies in the 1760s provide a much broader cross section of experience. Because American slavers concentrated on the same region as the Danes, Oldendorp's interviews provide a good sense of how the people carried aboard American ships lost their freedom. The Danish vessels would have transported proportionately more Ga speakers than American vessels, but the dynamic of enslavement was similar for the entire region, making Oldendorp's interviews a good proxy for the experiences of those transported aboard Yankee vessels. His interviews are supplemented here by others taken down in the British colonies.[32]

In comparison with upper Guinea, the paths to enslavement for narrators from the Voltaic region were more varied and less contingent upon war. Debt accounted for six enslavements (27 percent, as against about 3 percent), whereas enslavements via kidnapping equaled those done through war, with eight narratives giving warfare or military-style raiding as the cause of the enslavement. The dominant theme in these interviews, which all involve people taken in the eighteenth century, is the pervasive danger of enslavement that resulted when a region became a major supplier of captives. This same danger can be glimpsed in the narratives from upper Guinea, although the historical circumstances were different. In the Gold Coast hinterland, Asante, with its various wars of conquest and consolidation, was the driver of much enslavement. Asante's need to suppress rebellions in tributary states was another cause of military conflict. Here, no countervailing ideology analogous to the jihads emerged to check the flow of captives to the Atlantic ports. Of course, as with upper Guinea, it is important to remember that although the possibility of enslavement was ever present, only a small minority of the population actually lost its freedom.

War figured in the enslavement narratives of people who embarked from Gold Coast ports but at lower levels than for upper Guinea, with only eight of twenty-two (36 percent) of Oldendorp's narrators giving military conflict as their route to captivity. This is of interest because there has been some debate about the presence of former soldiers among Gold Coast captives (the so-called "Coromantees") and their prominence in New World slave rebellions. The Oldendorp interviews corroborate this military presence to a certain extent, but whether the narrators were soldiers or not is often unclear. One of Oldendorp's Asante informants was a high-ranking officer who commanded three thousand men, but he was not taken in battle. Another Asante man who claimed to be a brother of the "king" (whether he meant the asantehene or another leader is uncertain) reported that he "was taken away from his people in a native war and was taken to the fort," and yet another Asante informant "had the same thing happen." In neither case, however, is it obvious that the men were taken on the battlefield. Non-Akan narrators enslaved as a consequence of war were similarly ambivalent about exactly how they were taken. A Tchamba (Oldendorp's "Kassenti") man was simply "captured in a war," and a Mande speaker from the north ("Sokko") "was caught by the [Asante] in the war."[33]

The capture of soldiers on the battlefield, however, was only one of many ways in which warfare generated captives. A standard practice in Asante and likely other states was to allow military leaders to plunder enemy towns and villages. It was one of the rewards for military officers, and ordinary foot soldiers surely took the opportunity to enrich themselves as well. Several of Oldendorp's informants were enslaved as part of this process of plunder. A man who identified himself as of Tembu background told of fleeing to a cave in the nearby hills to escape a raid by troops that were likely an offshoot of the main Asante force. The attackers forced the fugitives out of the cave with pepper-infused smoke and seized them as they exited. In another case, a Tembu woman whose father was away fighting heard rumors that groups of Asante soldiers were ranging "far and wide seizing people, especially children. They put a gag in their mouths so that they could not scream, and put the children in sacks." She was seized before she could take evasive action. The raiders killed her brother and cut off her sister's hand to get her gold arm ring. The woman herself might have suffered the same fate had a previous bout of smallpox not reduced the size of her arm, making it easier to remove the band. A Tchamba man was discovered by "people catchers" while hiding in the forest. The fact that residents of the area heard rumors and knew enough to hide suggests that these "people catchers" may have been soldiers in search of loot. Another man, not one of Oldendorp's informants, told of his village being attacked at night by Fante soldiers seemingly bent on securing captives for sale. The raiders set fire to the houses and used muskets and cutlasses to slaughter the older residents while enslaving the young.[34]

As several testimonies suggest, many of those enslaved during warfare in the Voltaic region were not Akan. Instead, many came from regions to the west, north, and east of Asante. Though Oldendorp's narratives do not constitute anything like an unbiased sample, they do support recent work questioning the assumption that those who sailed from Gold Coast ports were uniformly of Akan background. The narratives are also consistent with the notion that ethnic and linguistic outsiders were more likely to be dispatched into the Atlantic trade, with enslaved Akan speakers more likely to remain in Asante to work in the gold fields. The "Kassenti," "Tembu," and "Sokko" informants were, in other words, what Fante and other Akan merchants sold as "Duncoes," a rendering of Odonko/Donkor, an Akan term for non-Akan people from the north, which implied outsiderness and enslaveability. Duncoes and other non-Akans were also more likely to be among the tribute slaves sent to Asante from outlying areas, since Akan tribute was often rendered in gold. In fact, the most famous person to travel aboard an American slaver, Venture Smith, was probably not Akan and was quite possibly sold as a Dunco.[35]

Several of Oldendorp's Voltaic-region informants gave reasons other than war for their enslavement. Travel emerges as particularly dangerous. A man from Accra took to the road to purchase corn at a time of famine and was seized by "by man-stealers who capture passing travelers on the road to the whites' fort." A boy who took to the road to escape his uncle's abuse was grabbed by Asantes, who kept him as a domestic slave for six years before selling him into transatlantic slavery. Yet another man was seized by "his own people" and sold away in what appears to have been a crime of opportunity.[36]

More striking still is the number of Oldendorp's informants who were enslaved for debt: eight of twenty-two, or 36 percent. The high rate is not surprising given the advanced level of monetization in the regional economy as a result of the gold trade. Some seizures seem to have been fairly straightforward, as in the case of a man seized and sold by his brother-in-law, presumably for a debt he incurred himself. Another, a young boy who was apprenticed to his uncle to learn the weaver's trade, was seized and sold to satisfy a claim against his father. Gambling, of all things, was the source of the debts that led to the enslavement of two of Oldendorp's Gold Coast informants. One, the son of a wealthy man, was apparently addicted to wagering *gagunga*, or "shell money," and had a habit of borrowing from his father to pay his debts. The father eventually tired of his son's "slovenly" ways and allowed his son's creditors to enslave him. Another informant, the Asante army officer who once commanded three thousand men, was enslaved as a consequence of his gambling debts, though via a more convoluted route. A man of wealth, he traveled to Fante territory with a small entourage bearing his money and weapons, possibly to purchase captives. He wound up incurring a gambling debt and soon saw two of his bearers taken from him and sold to one of the forts. The soldier's arms-bearer would also have been taken but managed to escape, so the soldier himself was enslaved in his place.[37]

In circumstances such as these, some people employed trickery to lure people into situations that let them be easily captured. A Tembu merchant who had once been a slave trader himself traveled to another country and was falsely accused (in his own telling) of carrying on an adulterous affair with the wife of a man who offered him food. The merchant was convicted and sold into slavery by the alleged cuckold. Ottobah Cugoano, not one of Oldendorp's informants, also told a story of deception. While playing with some other children, he was taken by some men who accused him of wronging a "great man." On the pretense that he would have to visit the great man to clear his name, he and his companions were lured farther and farther away from where they had been taken. Cugoano's captors were obviously taking advantage of his youthful credulity to secure a captive with minimal conflict. In the final stage of this complicated ruse, Cugoano found himself tricked into going all the way to the coast, where his fate was sealed.[38]

Women are slightly better represented in the Voltaic-region narratives than in those from upper Guinea, but only marginally so. Afiba, a fifteen-year-old girl who was interviewed by Edwards in Jamaica, told him she had already been enslaved to a presumably prominent man named Quamina Yati. This comports with the general point that most enslaved people in Africa itself were female. It also played to Edwards's desire to demonstrate that most of the Africans sold into Atlantic slavery had already been living as slaves, with the implication that it was better to be enslaved among Christians. The same point can be made in the case of Clara, another of Edwards's interviewees. From nearby Anomabu, her father was enslaved to a great man who died in debt. Although it is not clear that Clara herself was enslaved, since slave status descended through the mother, she nevertheless was seized for the debts of her father's master. Among the Voltaic narrators, only one woman linked her captivity with warfare. In keeping with the pattern, she was enslaved after an attack by Asante troops in which most prisoners were killed. She identified herself as Tembu from northeast of Asante, which underscores the connection between wars of expansion and enslavement.[39]

Throughout Africa, the value of an enslaved person rose the farther they traveled from home. The reasoning was simple: people who stayed near their home regions could escape, which made purchasers less willing to pay high prices. Still, as long as a person was reasonably close to home, there was another possibility: redemption by relatives through the payment of a ransom. It was a standard practice in both upper Guinea and the Voltaic region. In 1645, an unknown number of captives aboard the *Rainbow,* including the alcaide of Portudal, were redeemed. A century and a half later, Mungo Park reported the widespread practice of allowing for the redemption of one captive by the substitution of two. In such cases, social outsiders almost certainly took the place of insiders. Occasionally, European slavers allowed the redemption of a captive, especially if they wanted to maintain good relations with a trading partner. Muslims considered it a religious obligation to redeem any captives held by non-Muslims, and Islamic polities often went out of their way to do so. The distinction between a captive eligible for redemption and a permanent slave was a very blurry one. For the newly enslaved, redemption was often a very live possibility until distance extinguished all hope. This may well have been why Robert, whose narrative began the book, did not consider his enslavement permanent until well after his arrival in Savannah.[40]

Still, like Robert, most captives were not ransomed. The narratives from upper Guinea collected by Oldendorp and others illustrate this quite well, since interviewees in the New World obviously had not been redeemed. A Mandinka man, for example, told of his seizure by a creditor while traveling with his grandfather. Unable to pay the debt, the man was taken to some Europeans, likely in one of the forts. The grandfather paid the ransom, but the slavers refused to release their captive. As he was being rowed out to the ship, the captive jumped into the water and swam toward land. The slavers recaptured him and put him in irons. Similarly, in the 1770s, John Kizzell was seized on a visit to his uncle during a war in the Sherbro hinterland. His captors refused his father's offer of three slaves for his release, saying they would "not give him up for any price, and that they would rather put him to death." The captors sent Kizzell to the Gallinas, seventy-five miles away, where, as an outsider away from home, he would fetch a higher price.[41]

The possibility of redemption was also a feature of Voltaic slavery. Elites like the Asante military commander mentioned earlier probably expected to be redeemed, though obviously it did not always happen. In the commander's case, his brother offered the governor of the fort three captives and three sheep for his release, but the governor refused the offer and sold him to another fort. The commander's brother offered the governor at the next fort four captives and six sheep, which was also refused. The brother then sent word that he had tried and failed at redemption, at which point the commander surely realized his enslavement was permanent. Another failed redemption involved a man who was seized while traveling from Accra to Fante. His "friends" were prepared to give two slaves for his release but arrived too late. The fort's governor had already contracted with a captain to supply all the captives he had and refused to entertain the offer. The man's friends "raised the alarm and lamented all the way to the waterside" but to no avail.[42]

Those who were not redeemed locally were delivered to coastal dealers. Historians have long believed that most captives had to walk great distances, often hundreds of miles, from where they were enslaved to where they were ultimately put on board ship. Recent research has questioned just how widely applicable this generalization is, especially before the eighteenth century.[43] However, most of those who crossed the ocean on American ships probably did have to march some distance to the coast. Even some of those of Akan background, who lived close to the ports frequented by the Americans, seem to have spent much time traveling. The "great road" from the Asante capital of Kumasi to the British forts at Cape Coast and Anomabu ran 126 miles. Under ideal conditions it took ten seven-hour days to travel from end to end, but evidence from the narratives suggests that actual journeys were much longer. Enslaved people might additionally be forced to serve as porters, slowing them down and tiring them out. Salih Bilali of Massina was enslaved between Jenne and Kiana in the Western Savanna, carried to Segu, and then transferred multiple times before finally embarking on a slave ship at Anomabu, where he was probably sold as a Dunco. His precise route is not known but must have exceeded 700 miles.[44] Some captives were probably slowed by wounds sustained in their capture, and seasonal rains could halt caravans altogether. And sometimes the paths might simply be closed, as the main artery between Kumasi and Cape Coast was between 1748 and 1764. During these years, caravans traveling from Kumasi would have had to go more than 100 miles out of their way, southeastward toward Accra. Even in times of relative peace, Fante generally did not allow merchants from Asante to pass through directly to the coast. Fante maintained officially sanctioned markets on the border at Assin Manso, where Asante traders were forced to sell to Fante dealers, receiving gold in return. Sang, or "Oliver," who was interviewed in Jamaica by the planter Bryan Edwards, was from Asante. After being captured by Fante, he was sold six times before finally arriving at one of the forts, which suggests a very long journey broken up by periods of labor. Another of Edwards's Asante interviewees recounted that he and "many others" took two months to reach the coast.[45]

If travel from the Akan heartland was long and arduous, travel from northern regions, as many who embarked on the Gold Coast in the mid-eighteenth century had to, was worse. That many came from these areas is apparent in the ethnonyms reported by interviewees in the Americas. For example, among Oldendorp's Gold Coast informants, the Mande-speaking "Sokkos" from the Sudan, Gur-speaking "Tembus" and "Kassentis" from the northern borders of modern-day Ghana and Togo, and the Ga speakers from near the Volta all would have endured very long journeys through the forests to the coast. When Asante forces captured Abu Bakr al-Siddiq near Bouna, they "tore off my clothes, bound me with ropes, [and] gave me a heavy load to carry." He traveled hundreds of miles in this way, through Bonduku to Kumasi, and finally to the coastal town of Lago. His total journey was at least three hundred miles and by his own reckoning took about fifteen days. That works out to an improbable twenty miles per day, so the journey surely took longer than that.[46]

A similar situation pertained in upper Guinea, with the chief difference being that the networks that transported captives from the interior to the coast were almost entirely in Juula hands. A detailed description of a caravan and its workings comes from Mungo Park, who
traveled with one from Kamalia on the Middle Niger to the Gambia
River over about seven weeks in 1796. At several points in the journey,
the captives' status as commodities came into play. The coffle consisted
of five merchants who allied under the caravan leader. The merchants
spent some time acquiring captives at the nearby markets. When the
caravan was finally complete, it consisted of seventy-three people: the
five merchants, their thirty-five captives, several free people including
a teacher, the travelers' wives, their domestic slaves, and six *jeli* men,
or griots. The jeli men led the way, followed by the free travelers. The
captives marched in fours, secured with a rope around their necks and
shackled in twos at the ankles. The caravan marched several miles a day,
stopping in nearby towns for rest and food. On multiple occasions over
the course of the journey, captives grew ill and were unable to continue.
The silatigis simply exchanged them locally for other captives. They did
the same thing upon realizing that they would be passing near the Futa
Jallon, the home of one of the male captives. Fearing his escape, the silatigi exchanged him for another captive. The man tried to run but was
soon recaptured. Sometimes, however, it was not possible to exchange
an ill or recalcitrant captive. A woman named Nealee could not carry
on after being attacked by a swarm of bees, so the party simply left her
by the road to die. Security against bandits was always a concern. This
small caravan did not have a military escort, so when the silatigi learned
they were being stalked by robbers, he hired some armed men at a village. Finally, as the caravan neared the coast, the leaders learned that
there were no slave ships to buy their captives. The silatigi responded by
renting some land for the season and deploying the captives as agricultural laborers; they would be sold in the following year.[47]

Not all caravans were like Park's, however. The geographically central position of Futa Jallon—the source of the Senegal, Gambia, and
Niger Rivers—as well as its status as a major supplier of captives meant
that it was the point of origin for most of the Rio Pongo caravans. As
in the case of Asante, the paths were often blocked by coastal powers

hoping to protect their status as middlemen. For this reason, caravans coming from Futa Jallon often traveled with an armed guard, in case they needed to force their way to the coast. This made them much larger than the one that Park accompanied. One observer at Sierra Leone in the 1790s described a caravan that consisted of between one hundred and two hundred captives, with twice as many guards. The route from Futa Jallon involved a descent of more than two thousand feet, passing through boulder-strewn river gorges and finishing in mangrove swamps. Caravans traveled seven or eight hours per day, making regular stops at commercial towns every eight or ten miles. According to one African merchant, the journey from Timbo, the capital of Futa Jallon, to Freetown took fifteen days by one route and twenty via another. The roads themselves were extremely narrow in places, like "goat paths, just sufficient for the stepping of one man," as a slaver who made the journey in the nineteenth century put it.[48]

When the caravan reached the coastal zone, the member merchants usually sold their captives to resident dealers, who might be European, African, or Eurafrican. These merchants maintained holding facilities to imprison the captives until they could be sold to a ship captain. Installations varied greatly in size and design. Some, such as Anomabu, Cape Coast, Elmina, James Fort, and Bance Island, were literally castles. Others, such as Castle Brew at Anomabu, and Tantumquery, were smaller but still quite substantial forts. Here, captives were housed in dungeons and, when space was at a premium, outside in a walled yard. Many of the castles also maintained smaller posts, known as "out-forts." No descriptions of these survive, but they were almost certainly small, temporary buildings where captives were kept just after purchase while awaiting transfer to the main fort. Because American slavers were chronically undercapitalized compared with metropolitan traders, they purchased a disproportionate share of their captives in groups of fewer than ten from the small-scale dealers, who were especially numerous on the Gambia and in the Rivers of Guinea. A sketch of one such place survives in the journal of an Irish-born slaver who operated in Sherbro in the 1750s and who is known to have dealt with at least one Rhode Island skipper. It shows only a single-room house surrounded by a small fenced garden. Captives were probably kept outside under a crude shelter. Holding facilities changed in the nineteenth century, when the trade became illegal. Needing to conceal their activities from the Royal Navy, slavers moved out of the coastal castles and built less conspicuous facilities, often in a maze of smaller streams miles from the sea. These "barracoons," as the prisons were known, were little more than open-air sheds offering minimal shelter. An image of a Gallinas barracoon from the 1840s shows a building perhaps twenty-five feet long with a thatched roof and walls consisting solely of spaced timbers. Fifteen people are chained to each beam in a standing position, and another is shown being flogged just outside.[49]

Whatever their size, these prisons were usually the scene of the first encounter between the ships' crews and their captives. Captains, mates, and surgeons (rare for American vessels) would inspect each captive before negotiating a purchase. Few descriptions of this process survive for American slavers, but one observer did record the Providence skipper Isaac Carr performing an inspection at John Holman's installation in the Rio Pongo in the 1790s. Some seventy captives, including forty children, sat in the open air. Most were chained, but some pounded and winnowed rice. With the captives lined up, Carr and a British captain went "rank from rank and examining them from head to bottom often in a very indecent manner[,] particularly the women." As the captains inspected the captives, they evaluated each one as "picture" (meaning prime), "passable," or "bad." The slavers then negotiated prices, first for the assortment of trade goods and then for individual captives. American slavers kept track of these exchanges in their trade books, while African merchants used a sophisticated finger calculation system for smaller amounts, and gunflints or stones for larger amounts.[50]

Once aboard the vessels, captives passed from one system of captivity to another. Their status as human commodities was not what changed; slave ships did not transform people into property ab initio. In the vast majority of instances, that had already occurred, although it is certainly true that the process was extended aboard ship.[51] What changed, rather, was the racialized nature of captivity aboard European and American slave ships. Many African narrators immediately noted the whiteness of fort personnel and crews, and for many it marked the transition from one form of captivity to another. Children were especially struck by the whiteness of their new captors. Ten-year-old Gustavaus Vassa's first thought on boarding a slave ship was that he "had gotten into a world of bad spirits." Struck by the difference in skin color as well as the sailor's long hair and strange language, he was convinced his captors would soon kill him. Sitiki, later known as "Uncle Jack," recalled seeing a white person for the first time at a barracoon on the Rio Pongo. The man had come to inspect him. The young boy "scrutinized him closely to see what kind of being I could make out." Like Sitiki, the young Ofodo-bendo Wooma's first encounter with whites involved two men who inspected him before making a purchase. "We thought sure they were devils," he later recalled. Although many of the adults were similarly struck by the whiteness of their captors, they were less likely to dwell on it in their narratives. Those from the Western Savanna would have been quite familiar with lighter-skinned Berbers, and many, especially Muslims from urban areas, would have heard of Europeans through Juula traders, even if they had never seen one. It is perhaps for that reason that both Omar Ibn Said and Abu Bakr al-Siddiq processed the otherness of their ships' crews as "Christian" rather than "white."[52]

After initial impressions, the first impulse of some seems to have been to try to understand the sociology of the ship. Dhiagola Dha referred to the captain of the vessel that carried him to Maryland as the "king of the white people." Captives quickly learned to associate whiteness with power, since crews violently impressed that point upon them. The captain of George Dale's ship used a dog to intimidate the captives, as did Captain Caleb Godfrey of the Rhode Island sloop Hare. Crews punished resistance, or perceived resistance, brutally. A man aboard Boyrereau Brinch's vessel received eighty lashes for whispering about the possibility of rebellion. Dhiagola Dha related that whenever the "prisoners" aboard the vessel "talk for bread and water, and want to feel the wind, and to see the Great Spirit, to complain to him and tell him all," the captain ordered the crew to "kill many of the black prisoners, with whips, with ropes, knives, axes, and salt." Although it is hardly surprising that none of the female narrators mentioned sexual assault, given their probable reluctance to discuss it with male interlocutors, male narrators like Boyrereau Brinch did note the way crew members "made choice of such of the young women . . . to sleep with them in their hammocks." Further evidence of sexual assault can be found in the log of the *Mary*, a Rhode Island vessel, when Captain Nathan Sterry recorded that he "found our women Slave Appartments had been attempted to have been opened by some of the Ships crew, the locks being Spoild and sunderd."[53]

Before abolition, captives generally spent weeks or even months on board vessels right off the coast before crossing the ocean. The median time spent by American vessels on the Gold Coast was a bit more than one hundred days, but individual vessels might spend as few as thirty. A best-case scenario, then, would have had captives waiting on board for about two weeks before departure. The sloop *Rhode Island* was more typical, bringing on board its first captive at Sierra Leone on January 20 and its last on April 27 at Anomabu, which meant that captive "number one" (as he was logged in the trade book) was on board for 97 days before embarking on his Atlantic crossing. The *Rhode Island*'s passage took 107 days, just about the median for an American slaver. This means that if the man survived for the entire time, he spent almost seven months chained in the vessel's hold, with only brief periods of release for exercise. One woman recalled being kept for a "long time" in the "long house" as sailors brought new captives in by twos and threes. Waiting for weeks on end in the hold of a Guineaman on the coast of Africa must have been hellish. Disease would have threatened with each passing day, and the breeze that ventilated the hold while under way was often absent.[54]

Practices aboard American ships differed little from those of other slave-trading nations. Security was in the forefront of the slavers' minds and, more than any other factor, influenced the organization of space aboard ship. Men and women were kept apart, usually in separate "apartments," out of a belief that allowing them to communicate was more likely to result in an uprising. Below, slavers constructed platforms along the sides to allow for the layering of the captives, one row on top of another. Access was usually via a single hatchway, and when at sea the crew sometimes rigged a sail to funnel fresh air into the hold. While at sea, women might be allowed to spend some time on deck, but men were generally chained below. The only exception was a daily meal and exercise session. One man who sailed aboard a New York slaver recalled being fed horse beans and rice and being compelled to "jump for exercise, as high as their chains would permit," though doing this caused the shackles to rip their flesh. Those who refused were lashed with a cat-o'-nine-tails. Because slavers believed that melancholy caused death, they forced captives to sing. One slaver explicitly instructed the captain to force the captives to "clap their hands together with a song, whilst eating." But as a man named Primus recalled, "only lamentations were heard, or fragments of songs, broken with sobs."[55]

These sessions were attended by heightened security measures. We can get a detailed sense of the arrangements from the instructions that one slave-ship owner gave to her captain in 1805. Like all Guineamen, the vessel had a *barricado,* or wooden barrier, athwart the main deck. The barricado had a single door in it, which was to be opened only after peeping through a "loop hole." Crew members were to bring the captives on deck ten at a time for meals and exercise, but before doing so they needed to ensure that all handspikes and hatch bars were out of reach. They were then to fire a blunderbuss to alert the entire crew that the hatch was open, after which the carpenter inspected the captives' shackles. Once on deck, captives were secured by a deck chain that ran the length of the vessel, passed through the barricado, and looped through the eyelet in the ball attached to the captives' leg-irons.[56]

American practices were similar to those of other slaving powers, but there was one distinguishing feature: vessel size. Pre-1808 American vessels averaged 107 tons, compared with 212 tons for European vessels.[57] The problem with the small size of the American vessels, from the captives' point of view, was not that it led to more "tight packing." American vessels carried slightly less than 1 person per ton, compared with nearly 1.5 captives per ton aboard British ships. George Pinckard, who went aboard an American and a Liverpool slaver in Barbados, agreed that captives had more space aboard the American vessel, although he did note that the ship was crowded "in some degree" and that it was "scarcely possible to set a foot between their naked bodies" when they rested. The bigger problem was that traveling in the hold of a small vessel was torturous. Lack of space meant that captives were sometimes forced to lie (in chains, presumably) on top of casks and other containers. Crew members occasionally stuffed children into steerage, the small passageway outside the great cabin. Moreover, the undersized vessels favored by the Americans were often awash in seawater, adding to the misery. The captives aboard the sloop *Hare* endured a "Tumbleing passage" which left the decks "Continually Wet for Sixteen days." As a result they arrived in Barbados "Pintch[ed]" with cold, despite spending the entire voyage in the tropics. The decks of the sloop *Wolf* were similarly "overflown," with the captives' ankles "often in water" and leaving many to catch "Violent colds."[58]

American slavers' strategy of employing small vessels had additional implications for manning and security. The number of captives per ship increased steadily over time, from 89 in the years before 1750, to 115 after the American Revolution, but crew numbers stayed about the same, which meant that the ratio of captives to crew went from about 7:1 to more than 10:1 during that same period. To Mungo Park, small vessels and crews were the distinguishing feature of the American slave trade. Security aboard American ships was "abundantly more rigid and severe" than aboard British vessels due to the "weakness" of the crews, with correspondingly greater human suffering. Pinckard did not offer an opinion on the question but did note that the vessel he visited had experienced a rebellion while off the coast.[59]

Death stalked all slave ships. Brutal as crew members could be, most fatalities resulted from sickness. Guineamen were famous for their filth, and American ships were no exception. In fact, mortality aboard American slavers was significantly higher over the long eighteenth century than for the slave trade as a whole, averaging 16.4 percent against about 12.4 percent for British ships. Statistical analysis has concluded that "tight packing" did not affect mortality rates for the slave trade as a whole, but it seems very likely that the smaller American vessels and the more restrictive conditions described by Park were a factor, because vessel size was the only thing that distinguished American slavers from European ones. A small fraction of voyages—about 4 percent—apparently saw no captive deaths at all, although it is hard to know whether these records are accurate. Assuming the number is correct, it is worth noting that about the same number of voyages saw mortality rates of more than

50 percent, and about twice as many voyages tallied more than fifty individual deaths.[60]

Of the many maladies that plagued slave ships, none was feared more than smallpox. It was endemic to Africa, and ship captains did all they could to keep the disease off their vessels. Because very few American slavers carried surgeons, the responsibility for keeping the pox at bay fell to whomever inspected the captives, usually the captain, but when he fell ill (which was almost inevitable), the task fell to the mates. Inspection was hardly foolproof, and captives with smallpox frequently made it aboard ship. When John Duncan discovered that he had a woman aboard with the pox, his first impulse was to send her ashore. Fante authorities at Anomabu refused him permission, however, informing him that "the Laws of the Country are strict against it." He placed the woman in a boat, which floated at a safe distance from the ship. Duncan's solution was humane compared with James D'Wolf's. When a woman aboard one of his ships displayed symptoms of smallpox, he ordered her tied to a chair, which was then hoisted up one of the masts. As the woman's condition worsened, D'Wolf commanded members of his crew to kill her. They refused, so D'Wolf ordered that the woman be gagged and then personally threw her into the sea, later lamenting that he had lost a perfectly good chair.[61]

Though it was the most dreaded, smallpox was not the biggest killer. Diarrhea and dysentery, which contemporaries called "the flux," as well as pulmonary diseases such as pneumonia took many more lives. Because captive deaths constituted a financial loss, captains usually reported the total number of deaths in their correspondence and accounts. A few, however, went further and kept detailed logs. William Pinnegar of the *Venus* was one. On a voyage from Anomabu to Jamaica, he logged twenty-five deaths, each with a cause as he perceived it. According to him, thirteen people died of flux or flux in combination with another ailment, and one girl died of "bloody flux" and swelling. "Fever" and "consumption" (tuberculosis) claimed three lives each, while "dropsy," or edema, killed two. An ailment he diagnosed as "Quinsey sick," a tonsil infection, killed a teenaged boy, and a woman died of an unidentified malady listed only as "compleation," by which he may have meant consumption.[62]

William Chancellor kept a similar pestilence diary. As one of the few surgeons to sail aboard an American slaver, he examined and tended the captives regularly. He listed twenty-three deaths, but the causes were very different from those aboard the *Venus*. Measles was the biggest killer on this voyage, responsible for the deaths of five, all children. Four captives—again, all children—died of "worms," which could mean any number of parasites, and one man died of "obstructed lungs." Chancellor found the fact that so many of the dead were children— seventeen of twenty-three—to be troubling, most of all as he threw the body of a three-year-old girl over the side. Whatever remorse he may have felt was mixed with the feeling that the deaths reflected poorly on his professional reputation. He blamed the high mortality on not re- alizing in advance that the vessel would be taking on children, which prompted him to pack only "harsh" adult medicines. But disease was not the only killer on this voyage. Five more died as a result of a ship- board insurrection, four by jumping to their deaths in the sea; one was killed by crew members, and one girl was apparently killed by another captive in the hold.[63]

Accounts from the holds of American slavers are extremely rare, but the most detailed one we have highlights the issue of disease. The man later known as Primus recalled sailing from Senegambia to New York aboard a disease-stricken vessel, probably in the early eighteenth century. Illness came on suddenly and spread rapidly, as people were chained together. The ailing were removed from the hold and taken to a "hospital" area, seemingly in the cargo hold, where they were placed on top of some rough-hewn lumber, which tore the flesh from their limbs. Primus recalled the sound of bodies being thrown into the water and noted that nobody complained about the sickness, since it was widely assumed that the dead were returning to the land of their ancestors. His own father was among the dying, and Primus recalled his final words: "Come with me, my son! to the fields of pure light, where there are no white men, no slaves."[64]

Death also came through suicide. Records are incomplete and an- ecdotal, but all evidence suggests that suicide was very common aboard American slave ships. Often, as just seen in the case of the *Venus*, suicides were simply recorded as drownings. But in some cases suicides were recorded explicitly. Aboard the Philadelphia-based *Fame,* nine captives appear to have died by disease, one was "killed," and twenty-three, or more than one-tenth of the total, "jumped overboard." Although there is no evidence that it was a factor aboard the *Fame,* failed insurrection was often the inspiration for mass-suicide attempts. A rebellion aboard the *Othello,* for example, ended when thirteen men jumped to their deaths. After crushing an uprising aboard the *Thames,* the crew discovered that thirty-four men and boys had jumped overboard, along with two women.[65]

A final but hardly insignificant cause of death was the suppression of shipboard revolts. Plots and rebellions by captives were extremely common, though difficult to quantify because much of the surviving record consists of documents that are not concerned with revolt, such as customs and shipping returns. One study suggests quite credibly that 10 percent of all voyages saw some kind of conspiracy or rebellion. The American slave trade was hardly immune, with forty-eight documented instances of rebellion or conspiracy, a sure undercount. Rebellions are important not just because they were a reality of the trade—consider just how much money and effort went into preventing them—but because nothing refutes more strongly the notion that captives aboard slave ships underwent a process of depersonalization. They were very much people, and they fought back.

One of the more intriguing aspects of shipboard rebellion was the varied frequency across the different regions of Africa. The pattern is quite clear: vessels calling in upper Guinea, especially in Senegambia but also at Sierra Leone, saw significantly more insurrections on average than those going to other regions. American slavers were no exception to this rule. Although it was the main destination for less than a quarter of all American vessels, upper Guinea accounted for just under half of all rebellions. The Gold Coast, the destination for 41 percent of American voyages, accounted for less than 20 percent of insurrections, this despite the fierce reputation of the so-called Coromantees, which is what the British called Akan speakers. Historians have not yet produced a satisfactory explanation for the differing rates. Vessel and crew sizes, for example, were not significant factors, and neither was voyage length. One underexplored explanation has to do with the geography of upper

Guinea, which, unlike lower Guinea, features numerous navigable rivers. Vessels almost always sailed up the rivers, sometimes a hundred miles or more. The practice left them vulnerable to shore-based attacks, but these were almost always mounted by African traders and rulers and were not shipboard insurrections by captives. But by remaining so close to dry land for extended periods of time, it may be that people liked their chances of success better than when anchored a mile or more beyond the surf.[66]

Several detailed descriptions of revolts survive for American vessels. Each unfolded slightly differently, but most share basic characteristics. Every one of them was spectacularly violent, literally a fight to the death. Rebels shot, bludgeoned, drowned, and slit the throats of crew members. In one uprising, rebels tossed the skipper overboard and then harpooned him in the water. Sailors repaid the violence with interest, secure in the knowledge that they could act with unrestrained savagery, since the standard insurance contract compensated owners for captives killed in the process of suppressing a revolt.[67]

Rebellions usually began when someone managed to slip their shackles. Sailors often suspected women of providing the men with the spikes, knives, and other tools they could use to accomplish this, filched during exercise times and during forced sexual encounters with the crew. Whatever the method for getting free of their chains, captives then rushed the crew, up one of the companionways or through the barricado door, taking advantage of slack security or the illness of crew members. Rebels and crew then went at each other with whatever they could lay their hands on—guns, swords, axes, torches, gunpowder, handspikes, ropes, lumber—and when those could not be found, they simply fought with their fists. Crews raked the decks and scuttles with swivel guns and muskets. Sometimes the situation settled into a lengthy standoff. When the *Little George* erupted in rebellion one hundred miles off Sierra Leone, the crew barricaded itself in one of the cabins. And when the *Othello* captives broke loose, the crew hunkered down behind the barricado and entered into negotiations. The rebels "made slight" and "laughed" at every proposal and "made a great deal of noise in their savage manner." After two hours, the captain ordered the crew to open fire on the rebels, killing one, wounding three, and prompting another thirteen to jump overboard.[68]

The vast majority of rebellions ended in a like manner, but not all of them. Rebels occasionally managed to take the vessel and sometimes even make their way to land, but their subsequent fates were not always happy. After imprisoning the crew in the cabin for several days, the *Little George* rebels managed to run the vessel aground north of Sierra Leone and row ashore. What happened after that is not certain. As outsiders, they may have been re-enslaved, but at least for the moment they escaped captivity. In a similar occurrence, rebels ran a Boston vessel aground off the Rio Nuñez in 1794. This time, one of the local slave dealers, an American, mustered a small armed force that managed to retake the vessel and captives after more than six hours of fighting. The rebels were surely resold into slavery.[69]

Things worked out differently when rebels seized control mid-ocean. In 1808, a Charleston-bound brig encountered the American slaver *Leander* in the mid-Atlantic, "tight-rigged" but without sails. Thinking the vessel in distress, the brig's captain sent five men aboard with provisions. Through a translator, the rebels told the party that the entire crew had died. A torn page from the logbook told a different story: several crew members had been killed and the rest either driven or thrown overboard. It later emerged that no fewer than eight vessels had sighted the *Leander*. The captain of the brig retook the *Leander* and claimed both the vessel and the captives in salvage. Captives aboard the *Amelia,* an illegal slaver owned by Francis DePau of Charleston, rebelled three weeks after departing Cabinda for Havana in 1811. Seizing control of the ship, the rebels mercifully put most of the crew, which was predominantly Brazilian, into a boat. They retained the boatswain, who was Black, and three sailors (who may have been Black) to sail the vessel back to Africa. The rebels forced the men to sail the vessel for nearly four months up the African coast toward Cape Mount, where it was finally taken by a British privateer. By that time, provisions had given out, and most of those aboard had died of hunger. Those who were still alive could barely move, but some were eventually resettled in Sierra Leone, where they retained a strong sense of community. In contrast, the rebels aboard another American slaver, the *Independence,* were never recaptured. They detonated the ship's powder sometime after departing from Loango. More than two hundred erstwhile captives and the entire crew perished. It was the deadliest single event both in the history of American slave trading and in the history of American slavery as a whole.[70]

The vast majority of those who survived the Atlantic crossing aboard American slavers wound up working as agricultural laborers on the plantations of the New World. A bit fewer than six out of every ten transported before 1808 wound up in the Caribbean, in Jamaica and Barbados, before 1776 and in Cuba starting in the 1790s. The remaining four in ten wound up in North America, especially after the American Revolution, the period in which the ships going out and ships coming in were most likely to be the same. For historians working today, it is all but impossible to trace the people transported aboard American slave ships as individuals. We know them as statistics: 36 percent of all captives entering Cuba, 6 percent of all captives carried to Barbados, 1 percent of all captives arriving in Jamaica, all before 1808. Although the slave trade could never erase the humanity of living human beings, it could certainly render them into abstractions in the historical record.[71]

Occasionally, however, the historical sources allow us a glimpse of something more. Such is the case with the Newport sloop *Hare,* which purchased seventy-two people in upper Guinea in 1754. Uniquely for an American slaver, surviving documents allow us to pinpoint both the places where the captives were purchased in Africa and the planters who purchased them in the colonies. Four captives died and five were left in Barbados, but most—fifty-four to be exact—wound up in South Carolina. From their point of entry in Charles Town, they were dispersed in small numbers to twenty-four different white Carolinians. Most of the captives, therefore, left the sale with at least one other person from the vessel, a "shipmate" who shared the same experience. Thirteen of the *Hare* captives, however, did not find buyers at the main sale. These were what were known as "refuse slaves," rejected the first time around for appearing too old or ill. At this point, bargain hunters and speculators swooped in to pick up captives for less money, most for resale.[72]

Sixteen of fifty-four *Hare* captives wound up living in the fast-developing rice-planting area north of Charles Town, in St. James-Santee and St. Stephen's Parishes. Another thirteen wound up in the older inner ring of rice plantations nearer to Charles Town, while the same number ended up in the city itself to work as domestics, artisans, carters, and boatmen. The remainder were sent to outlying parishes, some quite remote, and to Georgia, which had legalized slavery only five years earlier. Death rates for newly arrived Africans were extremely high. Many were ill or weak from their journey, and South Carolina's rice swamps were extremely unhealthy. It is likely that one-third of the *Hare* captives died within a year. Even so, it is also probable that most of them found themselves on plantations with people who spoke their language and shared their cultural and religious beliefs. The structure of the slave trade, in which vessels tended to purchase most of their captives from one region, as well as the fact that warfare tended to result in large-scale enslavement in certain locales while not affecting others, made it all the more likely that people would be able to build on their African experiences in the Americas. The *Hare* captives are, of course, very rare in that they are traceable, but the experience would have been broadly similar had they been taken to Barbados, Jamaica, Cuba, or any of the other places served by American slavers.[73]

More specific information on post-voyage life survives for a tiny fraction of those who traveled aboard American slavers. These cases are extremely rare and, by their nature, unrepresentative, but they do allow us to speak of some of the victims of the American slave trade as individuals rather than as numbers. Many of the better known African narratives, including those by Ayuba Suleiman Diallo, Omar Ibn Said, Salih Bilali, and Bilali Muhammad, came from people who arrived aboard British ships. Other narrators, such as James Albert Ukawsaw Gronniosaw, Gustavus Vassa, Abdul Rahman, and all of the *Amistad* captives, arrived in North America aboard intra-American rather than transatlantic slavers. Venture Smith is one of the few who can be confirmed as arriving aboard an American vessel, having been purchased at Anomabu, as he later recounted, by a crew member for four gallons of rum and some calico cloth. After crossing the Atlantic and ending up in Rhode Island, he was taken to live on Fisher's Island in Long Island Sound, and later to Stonington, Connecticut. There he endured brutal beatings from several masters, but was finally purchased by a man who agreed to let him buy his freedom, which he did in about 1765. Venture Smith became an astute businessman who lived up to his name, earning money from various sources, and he eventually bought his family members' freedom and purchased a farmstead in Connecticut. He also bought slaves of his own. He returned one of them, at the man's request, to the previous owner, and two more ran away. Venture Smith died at Haddam Neck, Connecticut, in 1805, a propertied man and a very exceptional witness to the brutalities of the American slave trade.[74]

At least some of the life trajectory of the men and women who crossed the ocean aboard the American slavers *Nancy* and *Amedie* is traceable. Although their stories are very different from Smith's, they had one thing in common with him: they became free, which gave them an opportunity to tell their stories, a privilege almost never afforded to the enslaved. The *Nancy* and *Amedie* were the two American ships that were captured by the Royal Navy in late 1807 and condemned by the Tortola vice-admiralty court. Because Britain had abolished its slave trade, the *Nancy* and *Amedie* captives had to be freed. What actually constituted freedom, however, was for the moment undefined, apart from the fact that the Abolition Act outlawed the use of liberated Africans as plantation laborers. Convinced of the Africans' savagery and likely fearful of the influence of a free Black population on the enslaved population of Tortola, the vice-admiralty court delivered the captives from both vessels into various forms of unfreedom. The court was able to claim that it had followed the law because the institutions that the captives were delivered into—military service and indentured servitude, known as "apprenticeship"—were time-limited. And indeed, soon afterward, in March 1808, Britain issued Orders-in-Council prescribing those same options for what were now officially termed "captured Negroes."[75]

Of the seventy people who were taken off the *Nancy,* thirty-six, all male, were put aboard a British warship; twenty-four, consisting mostly of women and girls but also ten boys who were presumably too young to enter the navy, were sent as indentured laborers to the Trinidad estate of Admiral Sir Alexander Cochrane, the commander of the navy vessel, in apparent violation of the Abolition Act; and five died on Tortola before their fates could be determined. Of the seventy former *Nancy* captives, only five remained on Tortola, presumably because they were too young or too weak to be enlisted in the navy or to be shipped to Trinidad. The five were taken by the island's governor and given to his daughter, Eliza Turnbull. When Eliza moved to the United States around 1812, she gave the apprentices to her free Black servant, Kate Turnbull, who remained on Tortola. Their time with her, however, was not good. Kate Turnbull could not afford to maintain them and eventually gave them up, at which time they were described as "in a miserable condition." The five servants were then reassigned to different masters.[76]

Because they were at least nominally free, the five former *Nancy* captives who stayed on Tortola constitute one of the few American shipmate cohorts whose fate is known to us. Although the "freedom" they experienced did not live up to the name—as apprentices, the "captured Negroes" were subject to the full range of physical and sexual abuse—they were not enslaved. The difference lay in the fact that they had legal personhood and could at least occasionally call on the authority of the state to press for their rights, as they did before a Royal Commission in 1821. The five were not put to plantation labor, as British policy discouraged it, and Tortola's plantations were by that time in steep decline. Most of the population earned a living by farming, fishing, and maritime services. So although the experiences of these apprentices must not be taken as perfectly indicative of what their lives might have been like under slavery, the line between slavery and apprenticeship was blurry enough on Tortola to constitute what might be called a "natural experiment," which can be profitably compared with and offer insight into communities of Africans in the Americas, whose members are often historically invisible as a result of slavery.[77]

At the heart of the *Nancy* cohort was Sano, eventually known as John Sano or John Belisario, after the person to whom he was indentured. Sano married a woman named Mary, also an African apprentice. Because the *Nancy* shipmates were the only apprentices who had come from upper Guinea, it is all but certain that Mary was of a very different ethnolinguistic background from Sano. Their bond seems to have been strong, however. When offered the chance to migrate to Sierra Leone or Trinidad, or to enlist in the military, Sano declined, citing his marriage to Mary. As of 1821, when he was interviewed, the couple did not have any children, although they were still young and may have had children later. Sano was something of a model apprentice in the eyes of white Tortolans, described at one point as a "very good house servant." He became free in 1819 and worked as a sailor, plying the region's waters for eight dollars per month.[78]

Close to Sano was his half brother, Ali or William, who identified himself as a "Suriaga" (possibly Zenaga/Sanhaja, a Berber people) from the Senegal River region. Ali was sent to Eliza Turnbull's with his brother and the other three children and adolescents from the *Nancy*. He remained with her until her move to the United States, at which point he was transferred to James Grigg. This was not intended to be a permanent solution, however, so William was soon transferred to William Edney, a Black ship's carpenter who promised to teach William the trade. According to Edney, William was an indifferent student of the art and mystery of carpentry, though apparently he did become a skillful fisherman. After "quarreling" over an unspecified issue, Edney whipped William, for the first and only time, he claimed. William returned to Grigg, where he labored at a wide variety of tasks, including cooking, fishing, and growing yams on his provision ground. Trouble soon struck, however. Thieves raided his provision ground, which made William doubt whether growing yams had been worth his effort, and sometime afterward he broke his leg. Years later, the leg had healed but William could no longer stand for long periods of time, and he claimed to feel pain for a few days every year around the anniversary of the injury. He was still at Grigg's, sleeping aboard a shallop, cooking, fishing, and doing odd jobs.[79]

It is clear that Sano and Ali/William kept in touch. Sano, perceived as the more reliable of the two, was able to give detailed information about his half brother to the inquiry. Sano was also able to provide information on all of the other former *Nancy* captives, all of which suggests that the shipmates maintained contact after leaving Eliza Turnbull's and may well have had much more regular communication. According to Sano, Thomas, another male shipmate who spent time at Turnbull's, was illegally removed to Antigua, where he died, possibly as a slave. Sano did not reveal how he knew about Thomas's death, though as a sailor he was probably well aware of all of the latest gossip. Henry, also of the *Nancy*, was bound out to Kate Turnbull. According to Sano, he died in her care sometime before 1821. Angella was the only female shipmate to remain on Tortola. Like Henry, she was indentured at Kate Turnbull's, where she died sometime before 1821. Sano gave Angella's cause of death as a "venereal disease" but did not indicate how she had contracted it, whether by consensual sex or rape, or whether from a white or a Black man. Any of these is possible.[80]

The lives of the former captives of the *Amedie*, who were also liberated on Tortola, were broadly similar to those of the former *Nancy* captives. Eighty-two were sent to Cochrane's Trinidad estate, where they were eventually freed. Sixteen remained on Tortola, where they were apprenticed and eventually freed to eke out a life on the margins. Argus, or Hull, was apprenticed to a cooper, who taught him the trade. He never found employment as a cooper, but he did acquire a small plot of land and supported himself by cutting wood and fishing. The latter was apparently undertaken as a communal enterprise by a group of "free people" who invested in a seine. Like Sano, Argus/Hull declined an offer to go to Sierra Leone or Trinidad, citing his wife and children. And, like Sano, he was able to provide information on former *Amedie* captives who had died or been removed, suggesting once again the importance of the shipmate relationship.[81]

The experience of the *Amedie* captives differed from that of the *Nancy* captives in one important respect. Whereas the five *Nancy* shipmates who remained on Tortola were the only "captured Negroes" from upper Guinea, those from the *Amedie* had much better chances to form ties with people of similar ethnic and linguistic background. In the years following the seizure of the *Amedie*, five Spanish slavers were condemned at Tortola. Like the *Amedie*, all five ships had taken on captives on the Bight of Biafra. Many identified themselves as "Ebo" and "Mocco." These apprentices clearly formed a very tight community around shipmate and ethnolinguistic bonds. Harry Ecanyo, also known as Harry Belisario, who had arrived aboard one of the Spanish vessels, was the acknowledged "chief" or "head man" of Tortola's Ibo and Moko apprentices. The experiences of the former *Nancy* and *Amedie* captives, then, provide strong evidence that enslavement and the Atlantic crossing, as traumatic they undoubtedly were, could never permanently erase their sense of self or memories of Africa. To the contrary, these essentially human characteristics became the weapons they used to defeat the dehumanization of the slave trade.[82]

Slave-Trading Communities

hen Newport's Joseph Thurston was readying the sloop *Prudent Abigail* for a voyage in 1739, he employed two caulkers, two blacksmiths, three carpenters, three coopers, a rope maker, a painter, a sailmaker, a joiner, and a block maker, and worked with four ship's chandlers. From local artisans he purchased sails, nails, and two ship's boats. He bought ship's biscuits from a baker, pork from a butcher, and a host of other provisions, including cider, peas, flour, hogs' fat, cordwood, hoops, staves, swivel guns, gunpowder, lead balls, and cloth from unnamed suppliers. He paid eleven different people for unspecified services and hired two enslaved men from their owners for fifty days each. For just one voyage, then, he paid thirty-seven tradesmen, laborers, and merchants, none of whom would sail on the vessel, a total of £2,862 Old Tenor. And Thurston's account did not actually give a complete reckoning of all of the people involved. He paid an unknown number of distillers £2,522 for 8,409 gallons (approximately 84 hogsheads) of rum. His accounts do not name the many free and unfree laborers who worked for the tradesmen, and they do not mention the women and children who performed the domestic labor that made it possible for the artisans to ply their trades. The amount of local labor that made the *Prudent Abigail*'s voyage possible was typical for the era. A former clerk to one of Newport's slavers estimated that the major merchant houses employed as many as fifty people aboard their ships, in their counting houses, and on the docks. Multiplied over nearly two thousand voyages before 1808, it is clear that slaving involved not merely merchants and crew—it encompassed entire ports.[1]

Slaving ports were a very particular subspecies of maritime community. In those towns that participated heavily, slaving became a path to power and social mobility. It shaped the local demography by exaggerating the already high male death rate and increasing the enslaved population. Finally, slaving ports' direct connections with Africa produced unique cultural clusters and pockets of specialized knowledge that challenged (though never overcame) white racial assumptions.

Many ports dispatched Guineamen over the long history of American slaving, but in most cases the impact of the slave trade on the port itself was slight. Some ports, such as New London, Connecticut, and Perth Amboy, New Jersey, sent out too few slave ships to have much observable effect on the community at large. Other ports, such as Boston and New York, dispatched many vessels, but since their total shipping volume was so large, slave ships accounted for about six in every one thousand clearances. Of the many thousands of Bostonians and New Yorkers engaged in maritime pursuits in a given year, only a few would have touched a slave vessel. Charleston presents a different picture. Charleston was a major disembarkation point for ships coming in, but apart from the rush of 1804–1807, it was never a leading dispatch point. During those four years, maritime life in Charleston did revolve around slaving. Yet even then, the impact on the maritime community was diluted by the fact that so much of Charleston's know-how and personnel was imported from New England and Britain. Even the ordinary seamen who sailed aboard Charleston's slavers appear mostly to have been born elsewhere. In Charleston's case, then, the real impact was on the lives of those who arrived in the holds of the ships rather than those sailing before the mast.[2]

In the final analysis, only Newport and Bristol, Rhode Island, can be meaningfully considered as slave-trading communities, ports where the trade strongly influenced the local economy, culture, and community. There is a very important caveat to this point, which is that in many respects both of these ports broadly resembled other early American maritime communities in their cultures and economies. Even in Newport, the undisputed capital of the American slave trade, the vast majority of vessels—between 96 and 98 percent, depending on the year—cleared for North American and Caribbean ports. Bristol's run as a slave-trading port, shorter but more intense than Newport's, probably saw a higher percentage of clearances for Africa. In the very active years of 1804–1806, vessels bound for Africa accounted for about one-third of the insured value on local shipping, but that, of course, leaves two-thirds of the cargoes for other ports. Even considering the larger crews and outbound cargoes carried by slave ships, for Newport's and Bristol's sailors, artisans, and laborers, most employment still came in the conventional trades.[3]

But that minority of vessels that went to Africa made a difference. In Newport in most years the slave trade employed at least one hundred mariners of all ranks, reaching well over two hundred in peak periods, and after 1790 Newporters could find additional employment aboard Bristol slavers. In both towns, the influence of the slave trade spread beyond merchants and mariners to the wider community. If the *Prudent Abigail* is any indicator, about three hundred tradesmen per year found at least some employment in servicing or provisioning Newport's slavers. Women participated, occasionally, as active voyage organizers but more typically by performing the labor that allowed the trade to continue. The slave trade, which killed about one sailor out of every five who embarked, widowed a great many of these women. Indeed, about one in five Newport households was headed by a woman. Finally, the slave trade was responsible for making Newport (and on a smaller scale, Bristol) the most racially diverse communities in New England. Slave trading, then, left its distinct stamp on those communities that pursued it.[4]

As a maritime community, Newport was an in-between kind of place. It was larger than provincial ports like Salem, where family and neighborly connections structured maritime life, but smaller than Boston, where relations were much more likely to be mediated through the impersonal, circum-Atlantic labor market. As a result, maritime life in Newport had a hybrid quality that found expression in its social hierarchy. At the top end, merchants, captains, and ships' officers came mainly from local families. It was a tight circle, and most people knew each other well. For this group, kinship and neighborliness governed careers, much as they did in the smaller ports. Ordinary seamen, on the other hand, the main labor force, were more likely to be outsiders recruited from the wider labor market, as seen in the larger ports. There were exceptions on all sides, of course, but this divergence informed many aspects of maritime life in Newport. Bristol, with one-sixth of Newport's population, presented an exaggerated version of the same dualism. There, maritime life was very personal. Bristol was a company town, and the company was the D'Wolf family. The D'Wolfs so dominated slave trading that it was hard to separate the maritime community from their extended kin network, at least in the top echelons. This was much less true of Bristol's ordinary seamen. There were simply not enough young men in the town to crew the town's slavers at the peak of the trade, so the D'Wolfs and their allies were forced to turn outward for labor. Even so, a few Bristol men did find employment aboard their ships, so local ties operated at all levels.[5]

The duration of involvement in the slave trade was another thing that differentiated Newport from Bristol. In Newport, slave trading had been a major influence on maritime life for almost eighty years, approximately 1730–1807. By the end of the period, four generations in the trade had exacted a measurable demographic toll on Newport. Maritime communities often had slight female majorities as a result of high male death rates. Salem, for example, had a female majority of 53.6 percent in 1790, and New Bedford's was 51.7 percent. In that same year Newport had a female majority of 55.7 percent, more than 2 percent higher than Salem's. All three were maritime communities. The only significant difference was that Newport was about to enter its seventh decade as a slave-trading port. Newport's 2 percent difference with the other ports persisted through 1800 and only vanished in the 1810 census, a probable reflection of the overall decline in local slave trading and the shift toward Charleston in the years before 1808. Bristol's sex ratio, on the other hand, was in line with the rest of maritime New England's. In 1810, after fifteen years of intensive slave trading, Bristol had a female majority of 51 percent, which was actually slightly lower than Salem's.

Newport's skewed sex ratio appears therefore to have been the result of multiple decades of slave trading. Bristol was simply not involved long enough for that to happen. In addition, many of the men who sailed on Bristol vessels came from elsewhere and so were not counted in the town's census.[6]

In other respects, Newport and Bristol were similar. In both places, the slave trade was a mainstay of the local economy, furnishing employment for artisans and mariners and the funds to endow public institutions, including churches, libraries, and schools. Both towns drew on the local community to sustain the slave trade, and both sacrificed their young men to it. And, most enduringly, slave trading left both places with large Black communities, which signaled their involvement in the trade and also, through their coerced labor, perpetuated it.

A majority of the merchants who sat atop Newport's social pyramid during the long eighteenth century were slave traders. Most came from longtime resident families, although there were exceptions. Aaron Lopez, who arrived in 1752, was the most prominent outsider, and Caleb Gardner's family came originally from Massachusetts, but a list of leading slavers contains many of the same surnames as the list of seventeenth-century founders. By every measure, Newport's slave traders were significantly wealthier than the rest of the population. In 1772, the tax owed by the top tenth of Newport taxpayers, which included Aaron Lopez, Joseph and William Wanton, Simon Pease, Samuel and William Vernon, Benjamin Mason, Caleb Garner, and Christopher Champlin, was about fifteen times the median. Moreover, slave trading and wealth in Newport were linked, with the correlation strengthening the higher up the ladder one ascended. About one-quarter of taxpayers in the top decile were slave traders, including fourteen of the top slavers with two or more voyages to their names. Only five slave-ship captains made it into the top decile, and most of these were related to larger merchant families. The number of slave-ship owners drops sharply in the second and third deciles, and none appear below that. Among all taxpayers, the correlation between slave trading and wealth was weak, but it strengthened greatly in the top tiers and was very strong for the top 1 percent (table 4).[7]

Comparable tax rolls do not exist for Bristol, but estate inventories tell a similar story. Whereas tax rolls provide a snapshot of an

Table 4. Wealth and Slave Trading in Newport, Rhode Island, 1772

Decile (N = 1,112)	Median Tax (£, R.I. Currency)	Owners/ Captains (1+ Voyages)	Owners (2+ Voyages)	Captains (2+ Voyages)
1	5.10	28	14	5
2	1.35	15	6	6
3	.85	8	1	5
4	.50	4	0	2
5	.35	7	0	3
6–10	.10	14	0	8

Sources: Newport Tax List, 1772, Newport (R.I.) Historical Society. The names of slavers are taken from *Slave Voyages*, www.slavevoyages.org.

individual's tax obligation in a single year, inventories furnish an actual value for a person's property at the time of death. Many slavers died decades after their participation in the trade, so the relationship between the value of their estates and their slave-trading activity was often quite attenuated. Those who participated in the slave trade primarily as ship-owners had a mean wealth that was vastly greater than that of the average slave-ship captain, but this figure was inflated by a few extremely wealthy individuals. More meaningfully, median wealth among owners was $3,089, about 3.5 times greater than captains' wealth. A few of these ship owners even died in poverty, although often long after their stint as slavers, so they were presumably much wealthier at the time.[8]

Slave-trading merchants were not only far richer than average—as time passed, their wealth assumed different forms. In the colonial era, the wealth of Newport's slavers exceeded in degree but differed little in kind from that held by ship captains. Owners and captains who died before 1776 owned houses, vessels, enslaved people, and specie. After the American Revolution, and especially as banking, insurance, and other Federalist Era financial innovations took hold, merchants in both Newport and Bristol began to shift their profits into these more sophisticated holdings. Of the shipowners who made out wills or had estates inventoried after 1790, one-third mentioned bank stock (the Bank of the United States and the Bank of Newport most frequently), 12 percent

Table 5. Investments Reported in Slave Traders' Wills and Inventories,
1790–1841

Principal Role	Number	Percentage Mentioning Bank Stock	% Mentioning Insurance Co. Stock	% Mentioning Other Investments
Captains	34	17	6	3
Owners	49	33	12	18

Sources: Newport (R.I.) Probate Record, vols. 2–16; Bristol (R.I.) Probate Record, vols. 1–4.

owned insurance company stock (as distinct from insurance policies, which were more common), and 18 percent owned stock in another enterprise, such as a bridge company or a cotton factory (table 5). Several sat on corporate boards. Peleg Clarke, George Gibbs, George Champlin, Walter Channing, and Simeon Martin all sat on the board of the Bank of Rhode Island in the first decade of the nineteenth century, and Christopher Champlin and Caleb Gardner each served as chair. Similarly, the D'Wolfs and allied families, such as the Bournes and Bradfords, controlled the Mount Hope and Bristol Insurance Companies.[9]

Slave merchants in the post-revolutionary period, then, transitioned from being merchant capitalists who gained by arbitraging human and nonhuman commodities on a global scale, to being finance and industrial capitalists whose fortunes were increasingly abstract and divorced from the ebb and flow of the commodities trades. There can be little doubt that capital generated in the trade made its way into the financial system at large, where it was redeployed to finance ventures of all types. This, along with the fact that slave trading was always just one part of a wider enterprise, helps to explain merchants' acquiescence to the abolition of the slave trade. Of course, it must be kept in mind that although many slavers invested in the new ventures of the era, given their comparatively small numbers they contributed only a small fraction of the total capital that went into them. But they unquestionably participated, and eagerly so. Plantation agriculture, then, was not the only way in which slavery contributed to American capitalism; the transatlantic slave trade was also present at the creation.[10]

Wealth translated into political power. Slavers sat in the Rhode Island General Assembly, occupied the governor's chair, and served in both houses of Congress. This is not to say that they were able to impose their will on the populace. Slavers and merchants in general made up just one constituency in regional politics, albeit a very powerful one. Their power was never absolute, however; it was frequently offset by other considerations, such as the perpetual rivalry between Providence and Newport, or the clash with agrarian interests. Notably, the slavers were not strong enough to stave off the state's prohibition on the trade in 1787. By that time, slavers' political power had shifted from the state to the local level, where it was vital to the evasion of state and federal slave-trading laws. Bristol, more so than Newport, was small enough that the D'Wolf family could control the town in the manner of a political machine, which enabled their slave-trading empire.[11]

For all of their wealth, Newport's slave-ship owners tended toward aesthetic understatement. A few of them displayed their affluence in lavish showplaces. Godfrey Malbone, for example, owned a six-hundred-acre estate on the edge of town. The house was wooden but made to look like stone. The three-story Georgian townhouse of his son Francis was designed by the distinguished British-born and -trained architect Peter Harrison.[12] But most shipowners lived in substantial but hardly ostentatious clapboard houses, with perhaps a small Georgian pediment and fan window over the front door as the sole emblems of distinction. Many could have afforded more but chose to put their money into ships, goods, and later, financial instruments. Judging from estate inventories, merchants were equally modest in their personal possessions. Mahogany furniture, silver service, and china tea sets were almost universal, but only a few cocks of the walk, such as Simon Pease, gadded about in chaises. Bristol was different from Newport in that sense. Whereas some of the lesser traders built fine but understated homes in the Federal style, the D'Wolfs displayed their wealth by commissioning professionally designed showplaces. Perhaps because the family and the town's ruling class were nearly identical, they needed to send a clear message: the D'Wolfs ran Bristol.[13]

As the lack of ornament in their houses suggests, most slavers viewed themselves as living embodiments of a Protestant ethic, hard-working men who earned their fortunes through shrewd decision-making. For every slave-ship owner who referred to himself in his will as a "Gentleman" or "Esq." (or was referred to as such in an estate inventory), there were many more who designated themselves as "merchant," "shopkeeper," or most common of all, "mariner." Perhaps this is one reason behind suggestions that Rhode Island's slavers were mostly middling folk, but appearances can be deceiving.[14] James D'Wolf—a capitalist in every sense of the word and later a U.S. senator—was known around Bristol as "Captain Jim," although whether he approved of that appellation is unknown. This was not mere posturing. Many slave-ship owners had once been skippers, if only to gain experience in the family shipping business. In fact, the number of captains-turned-owners is almost certainly understated in the historical record because voyages to destinations other than Africa have not been compiled into a comparable database, and the names of those who sailed at ranks below captain were seldom recorded. Among Newport's top slave-ship owners, Caleb Gardner, Peleg Clarke, Nathaniel Briggs, Freeman Mayberry, and Joseph Wanton are all on record as having personally skippered a Guineaman. Bristol's leading slave-ship owners were even closer to the sea than Newport's. All of the D'Wolf brothers commanded slavers as they were getting started in the 1770s, 1780s, and 1790s, and James D'Wolf personally commanded a slave ship as late as 1803. Additional shipowners who are not on record as having skippered a slaver, such as Newport's Audley Clarke, were the sons of men who had, all of which probably tempered any tendency to view themselves as a class apart.[15]

Ship captains and, to a lesser extent, mates occupied an in-between position in slave-trading communities. On one hand, they were wage earners who sold their labor on the market and were in some sense part of the era's vast seagoing proletariat. And in contrast with the British slave trade, where captains' wages were about five times those of an ordinary seaman, American skippers' wages were rarely more than 1.5 times greater, and often they were lower than those of the first mate or the cooper.[16] There was, of course, more to the picture, for captains earned additional compensation in the form of a customary 4 percent "coast commission" on all captives purchased in Africa. They also were allowed to purchase a set number of "privilege slaves" on their own

Table 6. Hypothetical Earnings for Captain Nathaniel Briggs
of the *Hannah*, 1768–1769

Credits and Costs	Rate	£ R.I. Currency	£ Sterling
Wages	15 mos., 24 days @ £60 R.I. currency per month	948.00	27.09
Privilege	6 prime male captives @ £35 (minus one death)		175.00
Privilege Cost	6 prime male captives @ £6		–36.00
Privilege Net	5 prime male captives		139.00
Coast Commission	2.5% on 165 captives @ £6		24.75
Total			190.84

Sources: Based on the voyage of the *Hannah*, #36364. For wages, see Jay Coughtry, ed., *Papers of the American Slave Trade,* microfilm ed. (Bethesda, Md.: University Publications of America, 1998), ser. B, pt. 2, reel 28. The number of captives and the sale price at Jamaica are from *Slave Voyages,* www.slavevoyages.org; coast commission and mortality of 15 percent has been assumed. Currency conversions are Old Tenor to sterling at 35.6:1 and sterling to dollars at 1:4.44. See John J. McCusker, *Money and Exchange in Europe and America, 1600–1775* (Williamsburg, Va., and Chapel Hill: Institute of Early American History and Culture for the University of North Carolina Press, 1978), 136; John J. McCusker, *How Much Is That in Real Money?: A Historical Commodity Price Index for Use as a Deflator of Money Values in the Economy of the United States* (Worcester, Mass.: American Antiquarian Society, 2001), 33.

account, usually four to six but in rare instances as many as ten. These would be carried to the Americas freight free. Because some owners feared that captains might favor their own captives at the expense of the rest, there was a variation on the scheme in which the skipper would receive a share of the proceeds in the Americas, usually about 2 percent, in lieu of an actual privilege.[17] Based on the experience of Nathaniel Briggs, a hypothetical captain earning £60 per month Old Tenor, six privilege slaves, and a 2.5 percent coast commission for purchasing 165 captives could earn £190.84 sterling ($1,376 in 1800 dollars; table 6). In this grim accounting, wages constituted only a fraction of what a captain stood to earn by trading in human beings. The chance to buy and sell on privilege was clearly the most lucrative part of any voyage. Briggs probably earned five times more from his privilege than from his monthly wages, with his coast commission nearly equaling the wages. In the structure of their earnings, then, slave-ship captains were more like merchants than wage workers, although the fact that they had to risk their lives laboring aboard ships gave them something in common with their crews.[18]

The relationship of ship captains to shipowners was further complicated by the fact that many skippers *were* owners. According to existing data, captains had a stake in about 7 percent of all voyages, but the figure almost surely understates the level of ownership, since shipping notices in newspapers (an important voyage data source) did not state whether the captain owned a share or not. More captains than are shown in the data surely owned shares, though precisely how many and how much is impossible to say. Those captains who did have a share in a voyage usually owned one-eighth to one-quarter. For those who could, purchasing a share in a voyage represented a bid to make a significant amount of money that might allow them to retire from the sea and enter the merchant class. Thomas Teakle Taylor of Newport sailed as part owner for the first time in 1756, but was apparently not able to retire on the proceeds. He undertook another voyage without owning a share in 1757 and sailed again as part owner in 1760. That second voyage was apparently profitable, because after that, he owned fractions of four additional voyages, usually with the Vernons, and was sole owner for one, but never again sailed to Africa.[19]

Although Taylor and some others managed to transition from captain to merchant, moving from the quarterdeck to the countinghouse was not as easy as it seemed on paper, and as estate inventories suggest, most did not make it. The median estate value for slave-ship captains was $877, quite substantial but less than one-third of the median owner's wealth. Despite the chance to earn coast commission and "privilege," and to purchase voyage shares, the vast majority of captains did not die wealthy. It is not difficult to imagine the reasons. One was simply that purchasing voyage shares and privilege slaves, as potentially lucrative as these may have been, required significant outlays and costs. And once the investment was made, captains assumed all of the associated risks, so when a voyage in which a captain had a share lost money, he lost in proportion. Likewise, when a privilege slave died, the captain lost his investment. Coast commission would seem a rather reliable source of income since it was based solely on purchases, but sometimes the Guinea factors, who were responsible for paying it, flatly refused. And of course many slavers perished before they could accumulate significant sums. Even those who survived multiple voyages did not necessarily accumulate great wealth. David Lindsay, who skippered a remarkable twelve slavers over more than twenty years, left an estate worth £1,004 ($189 in 1800 dollars). Robert Elliott, who captained seven slavers, finished life with $371 in property; and Charles Moore, commander of six Guineamen, died with just $21 to his name. His belongings consisted of two pine chests of clothes, some buttons and buckles, money scales, an old silver watch, and a broken spyglass.[20]

Finally, we need to keep in mind that captains' estate values reflected the vicissitudes of other pursuits in addition to the slave trade. Only a small minority of captains spent their entire careers in the Guinea trade. Expertise did matter, so merchants tried to employ people they knew were experienced, but few could outfit enough Guineamen to employ captains in the slave trade on a full-time basis. Such people as David Lindsay, who must have been employed in the slave trade nearly continuously in order to fit twelve voyages into a twenty-one-year period, were rare. More typically, captains scattered a handful of African voyages in and among trips to the Caribbean, Europe, and other parts of North America, as their employers chased profit wherever it might lie. In times of war, shipowners often redeployed their slavers as privateers. The Vernons' accounts from the 1750s and 1760s show many of their slave-ship captains also making shorter voyages to American destinations, such as Barbados and Pennsylvania. Caleb Godfrey, who probably captained five or six slavers, interspersed many voyages to the Caribbean among his African voyages, but reconstructing individual careers is difficult because no American slave-ship captain left an autobiography. However, one skipper, Jonathan Fitch, did provide a career narrative of sorts when he was captured by the British, and it confirms the notion that skippers worked in multiple trades. Born in Nantucket in about 1782 and "brought up to the sea," Fitch began his career at a

young age, about twelve, if typical, but possibly younger. He sailed locally out of Nantucket until the age of nineteen, when he took a berth as
mate aboard a New York vessel bound for Ireland and London. He skippered a schooner on another European voyage before turning twenty
and spent several years in the Río de la Plata trade. His experience there
was his pathway into the slave trade. In 1806, a Boston-based merchant
hired Fitch to skipper the *Mendon* on a voyage to Loango and the Río de
la Plata, his only known slaving voyage.[21]

The tendency for captains to move in and out of the slave trade
notwithstanding, Guinea captains were wealthier on average than non-
slave-ship captains, and by a statistically significant margin. The mean
estate value for slave-ship captains was $1,572, but the mean estate value
for non-slavers was $699. The difference in wealth not only explains why
men entered into such a lethal trade, it reveals a key difference between
slave-trading and non-slave-trading maritime communities. Quite simply, slaving offered mariners the chance (if by no means the guarantee)
of greater wealth.[22] So although Newport slave-ship captains were not
as rich as the shipowners, they lived very respectably, in both material
and reputational terms. They almost always took the title "Captain,"
and were known around town. They were virtually all men of property
(even Charles Moore with his broken spyglass surely owned a house
at one time), residing in modest but respectable clapboard dwellings.
Their possessions tended toward the ordinary—linens, tea service, and
the obligatory mahogany furniture—but many accumulated substantial amounts of gold, almost surely from their African voyages, as well
as silver, probably from the Spanish Caribbean. For many, a significant
proportion of their wealth existed on paper in the form of notes (IOUs)
from their employers and bills of exchange, likely earned from the
sale of privilege slaves. After the American Revolution, some captains
bought life-insurance policies, which often made up a significant portion of their total worth, and a small segment (about one in six) emulated their employers by buying stock in banks and other corporations.[23]

There was one other very important but often overlooked form
of remuneration for slave-ship captains: human beings. Ownership of
enslaved people was nearly universal among colonial-era captains and
was undoubtedly another incentive to participate in the trade. Almost

certainly, most of the people enslaved to Guinea captains had been purchased on privilege, since the price of a person in Africa was anywhere from one-quarter to one-sixth what it was in the Americas. Some captains played the role of the sensible humanitarian by manumitting bondpeople in their wills (which of course allowed them to continue enjoying their services during their lifetimes). Lying near death off the Gold Coast in 1774, Thomas Rogers tried to square himself with his God by making out a will freeing "Negro George if it can be done with decency." After the passage of Rhode Island's gradual emancipation law in 1784, far fewer inventories listed enslaved people. But since the law only freed those born after 1784, a number of slavers retained bondpeople beyond that date. By 1791, however, enslaved people had completely disappeared from slavers' wills and inventories.[24]

Ship captains, slavers and non-slavers alike, seem to have been more attuned to their position as laborers with different interests from their employers than shipowners were, whose saltwater origins often obscured their own elite status. The clearest expression of this consciousness and craft solidarity was Newport's Fellowship Club (later renamed the Marine Society), the benevolent association whose membership consisted mostly of ship captains. The existence of a captains' fraternal order was undergirded (perhaps even inspired) by the constant tension and conflict between captains and owners. For all of their shared background and investments, the relationship between captains and owners was more oppositional than cooperative. Some of these disputes were trivial spats over who owned what. In 1757, for example, Caleb Godfrey sued the Vernons over a cake of beeswax and some ivory. Other disputes went straight to the heart of the complex relationship between captain and owner. The fundamental job of a captain was to serve the interests of the merchant. Much, therefore, rested on the skipper's judgment, but shipowners did not always approve of the on-the-fly decisions made on their behalf. Thomas Rogers got into a heated dispute with the Vernons over an unprofitable voyage. Rogers had taken the brig *Othello* to Africa in 1764 with instructions to carry his captives to Georgia or South Carolina, with an intermediate stop at Barbados. He sailed to Barbados and was en route to Saint Kitts when the captives rebelled. Rogers himself was injured, and the mate eventually died of a head wound. Rather than take the vessel to Carolina as instructed, Rogers sold the captives at Antigua. As it happened, prices at Antigua were very low, so the voyage proved a great loss to the owners. When Rogers returned to Newport, the Vernons sued him for ignoring orders, arguing that his decision to sell at Antigua "for a Trifling Sum" had cost them £1,300 sterling. The case's outcome is unknown, but the experience of being sued for not fulfilling instructions after a shipboard rebellion surely impressed upon Rogers the very different situations of captains and merchants.[25]

Like captains, mates were most often drawn from Newport's maritime community. In that sense, their relations with shipowners and captains ran through the matrix of kin and town. Young men generally received their berths through people they knew, and those who survived could expect to advance toward commanding their own vessels someday. Bristol differed from Newport in this respect. Relatively few natives or residents appear on crew lists for Bristol ships. Most of the mates listed for Bristol slavers came from Newport. Relatively few Bristol crew lists survive, however, and those that do, date to the 1790s when the town was just beginning to become heavily involved in slave trading. Later crews probably contained a higher ratio of native Bristolians, as local mariners acquired the necessary experience.[26]

Mates occupied a similar position to captains in the maritime hierarchy. Many had sailed as skippers in other trades at one time or another—upward career trajectories were hardly guaranteed—and they had to be able to command the vessel in the event of the captain's death. Monthly wages, which were often equal to or even higher than the captain's, reflected their professional status. In addition, first mates were allowed to purchase privilege slaves, usually two, with second mates often allowed one, much less than the four to six that was typical for captains. Finally, mates rarely if ever purchased shares in the voyages. These differences, along with the lack of a coast commission, meant that mates earned significantly less than skippers. On the same hypothetical voyage as mentioned earlier, a mate earning the same wage as the captain plus two privilege slaves would have netted about £85 sterling, a tidy sum but less than half what the skipper would have earned. Most of that consisted of privilege, so mates and their heirs fought hard to make sure they received what they saw as their due, as the widow of James Lewis of the *Othello* did. According to his wife, Lewis died at Sierra Leone after purchasing two captives, a man and a boy, as his privilege. Captain Rogers, however, presented a document saying that the man had jumped overboard during an uprising and that the boy had been sold at Antigua. Sarah Lewis discounted Rogers's story and charged that he was cheating her of her husband's privilege, leaving only his wages, which for her was a major loss.[27]

Mates are much more difficult to identify than captains. Their names entered the record only occasionally, so they tend to be invisible. But an examination of twenty-six surviving crew lists for Rhode Island vessels leaves the strong impression that serving as mate aboard a slaver frequently led to a captain's berth. From these twenty-four vessels, at least ten of the men listed as mates went on to command slavers themselves. Most of them were fairly straightforward advancements, as men moved from mate to captain within a few years (none of these examples involved a sudden promotion due to the death of a captain). James Searing was the mate aboard a slaver in 1759 and commanded his first in 1761. Gilbert Fuller sailed as mate in 1793 and went on to command his first slaver later that same year. Edward Boss moved from a mate's berth in 1793 to skipper his first of four Guineamen in the following year. Trajectories were not always upward, however. Thomas Underwood sailed as mate in 1756 and then skippered two slavers in 1758 and 1761. Five years later, he took a mate's berth under Esek Hopkins aboard the Brown brothers' *Sally*. The voyage was a disaster, partly because of Hopkins's lack of experience. Underwood presumably knew the trade well, which raises the question of why he let Hopkins make so many beginner's mistakes. It may be that Underwood's irregular career trajectory bespoke an underlying issue, such as alcoholism. Crooked career paths, however, like Underwood's, seem to have been the exception. More often than not, a mate's berth furnished mariners a ladder up the slave-trading hierarchy.[28]

Additional crew members can be classed among the officers. Most vessels carried a cooper, who sometimes doubled as a second mate. On some ships the cooper earned the highest monthly wage, though he was usually not allowed privilege. Ships' boys, though at the very bottom of the maritime hierarchy in terms of experience and authority, were often the sons of merchants and mariners. They were in the process of learning the trade, and at least some of them ascended to the top. In a remarkable coincidence, it is possible to trace the career trajectory of one of them through surviving crew lists. John Stanton was a member of a Newport maritime family and made his first appearance (and probably first voyage) aboard a slave ship as a ship's boy aboard the Vernons' *Marigold* in 1759. By 1770 he was sailing as mate aboard the Vernons' *Othello*. He took command of the *Othello* on the death of John Duncan and went on to captain at least two more slavers in the 1770s. Samuel D'Wolf was another member of a prominent family who was placed as a "cabin boy" aboard a D'Wolf-owned vessel. He seems never to have risen to captain and may have died in the trade.[29]

The ordinary seamen who sailed on Bristol's and Newport's slavers are far harder to trace than the officers. Few of them owned property, so they rarely appear among the "mariners" who left wills and inventories. Of colonial Newport's adult male population, 40 percent did not own enough property to vote.[30] For sailors, this lack of property meant that they did not appear on tax rolls or become admitted as freemen, and very few even appear in colonial-era censuses. Genealogical databases yield imperfect information but make fairly clear that most ordinary seamen came from Rhode Island, with smaller but significant numbers from elsewhere in New England. Even so, ships usually had a substantial minority from elsewhere. This is explained in part by the fact that the crew that returned to Rhode Island was often different from the one that left, as men died or deserted and others were hired to replace them. The new hires could come from virtually anywhere, but most seem to have come from Britain. On discharge, all seamen, local and foreign, entered Newport's maritime labor pool, which meant that it maintained a certain level of diversity. That was exactly how Nicholas Owen, author of the only existing autobiography by a colonial-era Newport slaver, wound up shipping out of the port. In 1751, he was among several seamen who deserted a Liverpool slave ship off the coast of Africa. After a very difficult experience, he sought shelter at Bance Island,

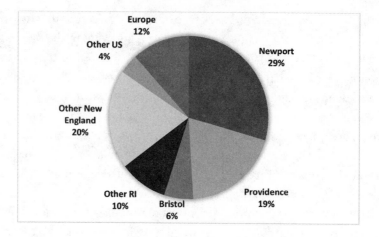

Chart 6. Reported birthplaces of seamen on Rhode Island slave
ships, 1793–1800. (National Archives and Records Administration
[NARA] RG 36, French Spoliation Claims, District of Providence,
Outward Manifests and Crew Lists; NARA RG 36, French Spoliation
Claims, District of Newport Outward Foreign Manifests, Entry 718;
British National Archives, Records of the High Court of Admiralty
and Colonial Vice-Admiralty Courts 42/303/1013)

where he signed on to a Rhode Island vessel and finished the voyage in
Newport. Over the next few years, he sailed twice more aboard Newport
slave ships.[31]

After independence, the United States government required all
outbound vessels to file crew lists, including places of birth and residence for each man, which makes it much easier to know their origins.
Lists from seven Rhode Island vessels that sailed between 1793 and 1800
suggest that about two-thirds of ordinary seamen were Rhode Island
natives, with almost half of those (or 29 percent of all seamen) coming
from Newport (chart 6). Interestingly, although Providence seems to
have been able to draw on its own growing population of propertyless
laborers to man its vessels, Bristol, because of its small size, relied heavily on Newport. The rest of the sailors on these crew lists came from
elsewhere in New England or the United States, and Europe, with most
of those from nations on the North and Baltic Seas. Jay Coughtry, examining a larger and more Newport-focused set of crew lists, found much

the same breakdown. Whatever their place of birth, most of the sailors claimed to reside in the ports from which they sailed. The exception again was Bristol, which depended on Newport and other towns for its crews.[32]

The question, then, is whether the post-revolutionary tendency to hire native-born Rhode Island crews also held for the colonial period, or whether independence brought a change in the recruitment of seamen. Definitive answers will likely remain elusive, but in all likelihood there truly was a shift in the composition of crews after 1776. Newport was a significant port in the colonial era, fully integrated into the British Atlantic economy and involved in several major long-distance trades, all of which would have enriched the local maritime labor force. The revolution and British occupation dealt Newport a heavy blow. By the 1780s the town had lost most of its population, and even though it eventually did recover, Newport never regained its status as a major port. Political independence also had an impact on crew composition. Shut out of British ports by the Navigation Acts, Newport's trade with the British Caribbean fell dramatically. These changes likely altered the composition of the maritime labor force, resulting in fewer outsiders, especially from Britain and its remaining colonies. Interestingly, none of the non-Americans in the post-revolutionary crew list sample were British; all came from other European countries.[33]

The size of Newport's maritime laboring population is difficult to measure. To bolster their claim that Rhode Island was a "nursery of seamen," the authors of the Remonstrance of 1764 boasted that the colony as a whole had twenty-four hundred mariners. The figure may have been exaggerated for rhetorical purposes, and of course not all Rhode Island seamen resided in Newport. But keeping in mind that about five hundred vessels sailed each year from Newport for all destinations, it seems reasonable to suppose that two thousand seamen sailed annually out of Newport, a number that may have risen to as high as twenty-eight hundred in the early 1770s. Making allowances for wartime fluctuation, a figure of roughly two thousand during most of the slave-trade era seems reasonable. If correct, it suggests that as a market for maritime labor, Newport was closer to the larger ports such as Boston than to smaller ones like Salem.[34]

A large proportion of Newport's ordinary seamen was therefore likely drawn in part from a sizable poor and often-transient population, especially during the colonial period. The poverty that plagued most of Newport's ordinary seamen can only be glimpsed around the edges. About one in four colonial-era seamen signed portledge bills and ships' articles with an "X," which points to a literacy rate about ten points below the average for New England males.[35] This suggests two things: first, that seamen were indeed drawn from society's bottom rungs, and, second, that many of the men who sailed out of Newport came from places with lower literacy rates. Additional indicators beyond literacy point to the same conclusion. Ruth Wallis Herndon has drawn attention to the prominence of seamen and their families among those who were "warned out" for having become public charges in the local towns. Newport saw fit to construct both an almshouse and a workhouse, and sailors (and their dependents) appear to have been well represented in both.[36]

Court records provide occasional glimpses of sailors' lives on the margins in Newport. Shopkeepers occasionally sued seamen for unpaid debts, although most probably avoided extending credit to them to begin with. Suits by innholders and boardinghouse landladies were more common, highlighting the sailors' transient, sometimes hand-to-mouth existence. As might be expected, "inns" with a seafaring clientele saw their share of brawling and rowdiness. In 1741, a shipboard dispute apparently carried over to Jonathan Nichols's inn. Edward Rouse and "divers other persons" were staying at Nichols's when Edward Barker stormed in and caned Rouse. Witnesses corroborated Rouse's complaint, and Barker was fined £5.16.4, plus costs. Other sailors boarded with townspeople. Schoolmaster John Chapman rented a room to sailor John Fling and quickly came to regret his decision. Fling racked up debts not only for his own room and board but for entertaining guests and even prevailed on Chapman to advance him money to pay various obligations across town. For some seamen, failure to pay debts resulted in incarceration.[37]

Many of those listed as "mariners" had other occupations. For Newport's poor, then, working aboard a ship was just one of several strategies for earning money. Court records often gave dual identifications to seamen. For example, John Clark was identified as a "mariner alias boatman"; Benjamin Burch was a "labourer alias mariner alias shoemaker"; and Robert Sisson Jr. was identified as a "mariner alias house carpenter." Some sailors tried to win extra money by buying lottery tickets. But perhaps the most common way to earn extra money was to carry goods to sell on their voyages. Known as "ventures" or "adventures," these small speculations were both fixtures and major perks of seafaring. Some sailors bought the goods themselves, but others agreed to sell on behalf of others, on commission, as it were. Rum and molasses were the most common goods, but items carried by Newport mariners ran the gamut from fish to mahogany desks. Some ventures were costly enough to warrant an insurance policy, although this was probably more common among officers than ordinary seamen.[38]

Newport's sailors frequently appeared in the town court to recover unpaid wages, though this was normally a preserve of admiralty courts. Exactly what conclusion can be drawn from this litigation, a commonplace throughout the Atlantic World, has been the subject of great debate among maritime historians. The fact that many sued for lost wages and other abuses has led some historians to interpret the relationship between sailors and skippers as essentially conflictual. Other historians point out that the vast majority of voyages never spawned litigation and conclude that relations were at least marked by consensus and sometimes by organic ties of family and community. The debate over the nature of maritime labor relations in general is complicated by the argument that slave ships were extraordinarily riven by conflict and violence. The slave trade, runs the argument, was implicitly violent to begin with, so the culture of violence perpetrated against captives carried over to relations between sailors and captain. As a result, most seamen chose to work in other trades, which forced slavers to rely more heavily on coercion to man the vessels, which of course only perpetuated the cycle of violence.[39]

There is, of course, no way to settle such a debate definitively. Newport's and Bristol's bifurcated labor force of locally born officers and poor and transient seamen raises the possibility that both perspectives have validity. Reports of abuse aboard slave ships, of beatings by officers and attacks on sailors by the captain's dog, of men being compelled to work while suffering from malaria and seamen being forced to get their drinking water out of a gun barrel placed high up one of the masts (a classic form of abuse aboard British slavers), are certainly plentiful. But whether conflict was significantly more frequent or more intense aboard slave ships is difficult to know for certain. If that was the case, it probably stemmed from the long, arduous voyages that tried the patience of both officers and men. It may also be that the threat of massacre by the captives caused stress that vented itself through violence. But these hypotheses are tempered by the fact that was no such thing as a "slave-ship sailor" in the American slave trade, apart from a few of the captains. That is, a slave-ship sailor was not a special category of seaman, just one who happened to sign on to a Guineaman. That said, slave ships do appear to have had higher desertion rates. The African trade had the highest desertion rate of all of the British trades. The same was probably true for the Americans, although desertion is difficult to measure. For the three Rhode Island slavers whose records did specify desertion, almost one of every five crew members "ran." The rate is quite remarkable, considering that men who jumped ship forfeited their wages, and points to the alienation of the ordinary seamen who sailed aboard American slavers.[40]

The general portrait of slave-ship-crew recruitment, based mostly on British practices, emphasizes its coercive nature. The use of "crimps," or procurers, who ensnared sailors in debt and forced them to work it off aboard Guineamen, was common in English ports like Liverpool and Bristol. No evidence of crimping has emerged for North America, although that does not mean that there was no coercion. Although the numbers were not large, it is clear that enslaved men and boys were occasionally conscripted to serve aboard Guineamen. This was a common practice aboard American vessels in all trades. In some cases it appears that the captain simply brought one of his own enslaved body servants, as Nathaniel Briggs did in 1768 when he forced Newport Briggs to serve as a ship's boy. Another enslaved man, Edward Abbie, appears on colonial-era portledge bills as a "negro boy," though whether he was enslaved to the captain or someone else is not known. Boston Coggeshall, an enslaved man, made at least two voyages to Africa, serving in 1768 as a cook and in 1774 as a "negro," which, despite the racialized terminology, probably constituted a promotion. Apart from Coggeshall's listing as a cook, the record tells us nothing of the enslaved men's actual duties, but given the small crews aboard American slavers, it is safe to assume that they performed all types of maritime labor plus personal service for the captain. Some of the men were surely African-born, so it is intriguing to contemplate their thoughts and feelings about returning to Africa, perhaps even to the very port where they first embarked.[41]

There is no evidence to suggest that any of the enslaved men served as interpreters, but it is certainly possible that some did. Slavers may even have seen language skills as a reason to bring them along. They may also have believed that Black men could better withstand the tropical diseases that killed so many whites.[42] For those reasons, it is possible to imagine colonial-era captains relying heavily on enslaved labor, but that was not the case. The modest resistance to malaria and yellow fever that many Africans had was not full immunity and provided no protection against the many other maladies and hazards of the slave trade. As Captain George Scott learned after the death of his "Negro Bonner" at Anomabu in 1740, the benefits of employing enslaved seamen had to be weighed against the costs of losing expensive human property on a dangerous voyage.[43]

From the slavers' perspective, indentured maritime labor might have offered advantages over enslaved labor. Because masters purchased only a few years' worth and not a lifetime of labor, servants were relatively cheap. Masters, moreover, had the right to all wages earned by indentured seamen, even if the servant died on the voyage. For this reason, masters sent servants to sea in various trades. However, there were two problems with servant labor in the maritime world. First, by law, all wages were forfeited if a seaman ran away. This mattered little to the servant, who had no right to his earnings, but for the master it meant that the loss of wages was compounded by the loss of the money paid for the servant. That is what happened to Nathan Bull and Joseph Scott when a "molatto" servant named James Dunbar jumped ship in Suriname. Their only recourse was to sue another captain for enticing Dunbar away, a case they actually won.[44] A second problem with indentured labor had to do with the lack of maritime skills on the part of most servants. Captains always hoped to minimize their reliance on "green" hands, and this was probably especially true of the slave trade, where the voyages were long and the loss of crew was a near certainty. A few servants do seem to have had maritime skills. Josiah Jones, a servant of John Scofield, served as "sailor" aboard the slaver *Ann* in 1772. Jones's wages of 1 pound, 17 shillings per month would of course belong to Scofield. But other indentured seamen worked in unskilled positions, such as the man listed as "Indian Jack," who served as a cook aboard the *Hannah* in 1768. However owners and captains weighed the advantages and disadvantages of using indentured and enslaved labor, from the servants' perspective being forced to sail aboard a slaver was a gamble with their lives for rewards they would never see.[45]

In the end, it simply was not necessary for slavers to turn to unfree labor. New England had a large enough population of men, many with maritime skills, for whom the opportunity to work aboard a slaver, even at the risk of their lives, was more attractive than the alternatives. This pool was supplemented by the large number of seamen from elsewhere who washed up in Newport. The vast majority of the men who sailed aboard Rhode Island's slavers chose to do so over working other jobs or in other trades (when available), being warned out of town, or entering the workhouse. Nicholas Owen, as we saw, signed on to two Newport slavers after arriving in the town, and Bristol's John Hoxse did the same four decades later because he did not enjoy his stint as a ship carpenter's apprentice. Samuel Patterson, the son of an impoverished seaman from Bristol, spent his youth working a series of jobs, including farm laborer, blacksmith's apprentice, ship's boy, and seaman aboard a naval vessel. He was working as a day laborer to prepare a Bristol slaver for sea when the captain of another Guineaman saw him toiling aloft and offered him a "healthy wage" to join his crew.[46]

The colonial-era recruitment process is obscure, but depositions from two separate legal actions against the D'Wolfs from 1801 to 1802 offer a window to its operation in the post-revolutionary period, a time when federal and state restrictions were mounting. In both cases, the D'Wolfs had to recruit actively, in one by sending the third mate to Providence, and in the other by James D'Wolf personally recruiting in Newport. Because slave trading was illegal in this era, in both instances it was necessary to deceive the men about the voyage's illegal nature by telling them that the vessel was making a "legitimate" voyage to Africa. In both cases, the recruiters offered generous wages and advances, which suggests a tight labor market. At that point, the two cases diverge. The Newport men boarded the vessel without further incident. In the other case, after traveling from Providence to Bristol at the D'Wolfs' expense, two of the men returned to Providence, having been advanced money to buy clothes. The D'Wolfs had the men arrested for desertion and marched them back to Bristol in leg-irons, where they were put aboard ship. The two cases illustrate several features of labor in the slave trade. First, they highlight its dualistic nature, at once "free" and voluntary but with strong undertones of coercion. They also underscore the difficulty of crewing vessels in Bristol and local slavers' continued reliance on the larger ports. Finally, the need to deceive the men highlights the changed moral and legal environment and possibly even an anti-slavery political consciousness among seamen.[47]

The thoughts of those who signed on to slavers as ordinary seamen have generally gone unrecorded, but there is reason to believe that many viewed it as a mistake. In contrast to ships' officers, who often made serial voyages, it appears that very few ordinary seamen did. Of 179 ordinary seamen, cooks, and ship's boys who appear on Rhode Island portledge bills, only three can be confirmed as having made more than one voyage, and one of those—Boston Coggeshall, mentioned earlier—was enslaved and so presumably did not do so voluntarily. Because portledge bills survive for only a fraction of the voyages made, the number is inevitably understated, but the contrast with ships' officers strongly suggests that serial voyages were rare for ordinary seamen. It is not hard to guess why so few made more than one trip. Somewhere between 15 and 20 percent of all seamen died on slaving voyages, and this certainly would have been on sailors' minds. The abuse by captains, even if no worse on slavers than on other vessels, still lasted much longer. Samuel Patterson had boiling water thrown at him, suffered a beating with a handspike, and was clapped in irons. He wrote his memoir in part so that "the reader may have some view of how sailors often fare." Then there was the outright fear that sailors had of their captive cargoes. John Hoxse recalled the captives "yelling, gnashing their teeth, and their glaring eyeballs, would strike terror into the evil one himself." Hoxse and his shipmates spent the crossing "hardly closing our eyes, night or day." Years later, he declared the slave trade "a wicked and most cruel business, and one what no *honest* man will ever attempt a second time," though whether he thought so at the time of his voyage is uncertain.[48]

As much of the scholarship on seamen has emphasized, the exploitation and abuse endemic to maritime life instilled in them an oppositional political consciousness. The slave trade accentuated this tendency. Hoxse, who served as a ship's carpenter before signing on to a D'Wolf slaver, saw the slave-ship sailor as part of a larger system of exploitation. "Thus these human beings [Africans] are brought from their native land," he noted, "to be sold into perpetual slavery, to enrich the pockets of some nabobs who have scraped together enough money to fit out a vessel with rum and tobacco, and hire men to do their dirty work for them." His words reflect the abolitionist sentiments that prevailed at the time he wrote, but his clear linkage of his own exploitation with that of the captives has a distinctly proletarian ring to it that went beyond the comfort zone of most middle-class abolitionists. One Bristol resident offered a rare glimpse of the class conflict that churned beneath the surface in a town that was so thoroughly dominated by the D'Wolfs. In his idiosyncratic collection of verses and anecdotes about the town, Joseph Wardwell offered a tart assessment of the town's ruling class. One item, a satirical town charter, was drafted by "Ephraim Wealthy, Timothy Overgrown, Jonas Iron-sides, Peter Money-catcher, Simon Leatherhead, Ben Thick-skull, and Moses Shallow-pate." Other items portrayed the town fathers as aristocrats, deplored the five-thousand-dollar property requirement for officeholders, and noted that the poor could only enter the homes of the wealthy in search of employment and through the back door. Although we do not know if Wardwell ever worked as a sailor, he was surely not the only Bristol resident to hold those views.[49]

The labor of women, of all colors, made the American slave trade possible. All societies have historically relied on women for social reproduction, which encompasses not merely the bearing and raising of children, but also the "various kinds of work—mental, manual, emotional—aimed at providing the socially, as well as biologically, defined care necessary to maintain existing life." Women sustained the slave trade—indeed, all maritime trade—in a host of ways, voluntarily and involuntarily, by boarding sailors (initially in private rooms, later in boardinghouses) and by serving as cooks, laundresses, provisioners, shopkeepers, tavern keepers, and caregivers. A few even spun thread and wove fabric to make trade goods, as the presence of spinning wheels and looms in slavers' estate inventories suggests. In American history, and certainly in Newport and Bristol, the responsibility for social reproduction was further refracted through the prism of race, initially as enslaved labor, then, as slavery withered, through other class-related mechanisms. Though necessary to all societies, social reproduction in maritime communities was a particularly complicated process. Maritime societies were structured according to patriarchal norms, but a large proportion of the male population was at sea at any given time. Women from seagoing households therefore had to labor in a world that did not acknowledge their legal agency. The slave trade, with its long voyages and high mortality rates, amplified all of these problems.[50]

Reproductive labor, in the most literal sense, was fundamental yet easy to overlook in slave-trading communities. The slave trade, as we have seen, was most profitable when undertaken by experienced merchants and mariners, and there was a tendency for that knowledge to pass through the generations. Merchants' and mariners' wives, though perhaps not central to this particular intergenerational knowledge transfer, were essential to everything else as they bore and nurtured the next generation of slavers. Slavers tacitly acknowledged this fact by naming vessels after their wives, mothers, and daughters, a veritable armada of ships called *Sally*, *Polly*, *Eliza*, and *Anne*. Although she never had a slave ship named after her, no woman deserved that dubious honor more than Abigail Potter, the sister of slaver Simeon Potter. She married the slaver Mark Anthony D'Wolf and gave birth to five sons, who collectively embarked more than eleven thousand people on to their ships, killing more than fifteen hundred of them.[51] There is no direct evidence that Abigail Potter or any other female member of a slave-trading clan actively encouraged their sons to enter the trade. In fact, the opposite was probably more common, since Abigail and other Rhode Island women understood the danger of the trade and may have been reluctant to sacrifice their sons to it.[52]

Whatever Abigail's thoughts and wishes, her labor (aided by two enslaved people) was essential to the D'Wolf slave-trading dynasty. Women's position in maritime society can be glimpsed in the hardship that resulted when they were not present. Bristol slave-ship captain John Sabens was a widower with children who made several voyages for the D'Wolfs. On one voyage, he placed his daughter Sally under the care of John D'Wolf, who in turn placed her in the care of a Miss (or Mrs.) Balch. D'Wolf reassured Sabens in at least two different letters that Sally was "contented" and that "nothing shall be wanted on my part to make her comfortable."[53]

But women's roles went well beyond rearing young slavers. Mariners' wives had to run the household during their husbands' absences. Although some women received advances on their husbands' pay, it was easy to run out of money, with voyages routinely lasting six months to a year and occasionally longer than that. As they did in maritime communities everywhere, seamen's wives relied on extensive kin and community networks for both money and muscle, borrowing, swapping, and calling in favors.[54] They also produced. Captains' wives in Salem distilled the molasses their husbands brought home into small batches of rum, which they then re-exported as an "adventure." It is possible that Newport women did so as well; although with a much larger distilling industry than Salem's, homemade rum surely amounted to a small portion of Newport's total production.[55] Whatever the case with rum, Newport women supported the maritime economy in other ways, such as by weaving the wicks for the spermaceti candles that helped to assort Africa-bound rum cargoes, and by sewing imported fabrics into finished goods on a piecework basis for re-export, among others.[56]

In a system governed by coverture, in which a married woman's legal personhood was subsumed under that of her husband, female-headed households combined with long absences by men to create very real difficulties. Maritime communities were patriarchies without men, where the simple conduct of household business could be problematic. Major public transactions, such as real estate sales, required special dispensation from the legislature, and even minor exchanges could be complicated by a married woman's inability to enter into contracts. New England's maritime communities solved these problems with a host of work-arounds that allowed things to get done without endangering the patriarchal social organization. The most common of these was to recast the dependent wife as a "deputy husband." This sufficed for many affairs, but for more technical matters or for business that required a more confrontational (hence, "masculine") stance, a husband might designate an attorney. In such cases, the boundary between the authority of the "deputy husband" and the agent was often unclear, which left an opening for women to extend their authority.[57]

Women almost never appear as slave-ship owners in the official record, but there are hints that some played an active role in the trade. Ann Dole of Boston conducted a series of complex transactions in relation to a slaving voyage undertaken by her husband, transferring credits for captives and gold between two different vessels. Philana Ward of Warren, Rhode Island, seems to have been familiar with the technical details of the slave trade. When her husband, Jonathan, wrote to her from the Rio Pongo, he offered brief pro forma wishes for everyone's health before launching into the details of his voyage, telling Philana exactly which factory he was visiting, which nation's vessels were there, and the price of captives in relation to "first [prime] cost." Philana's presumed knowledge of these matters suggests at the very least that she discussed them with her husband and may even have taken an active role in planning the voyage. Elizabeth Paeko[?] of Newport, wife to one of the Madagascar slaver/pirates of the 1690s, had her attorney send a letter to Saint Mary's Island to recover the treasure share of her husband, whom she presumed dead, again suggesting some knowledge of the business.[58]

Slavers' wills offer further glimpses of women's active participation in the trade. By their nature, wills address what will happen after a person's death, but that desire often reflects existing, pre-mortem reality. Sally Bradford, the wife of Leonard Bradford of Bristol, was probably running his "store" (which would have resembled a warehouse more than a modern shop) and wharf, since in his will he asked her to hand over control to his sons when they reached the age of twenty-one. Edward Wanton of Newport, believing his death imminent, ordered his estate to be liquidated with the exception of the sloop *Fanny*, which was about to clear for Africa. He left the final decision on whether to continue with the voyage to his wife, Frances (after whom the vessel was presumably named), and her father, Steven Ayrault, who jointly served as executors of his estate. And Sarah Champlin, the sister of the merchant and slaver George Gibbs, apparently shipped her own wares aboard her brother's vessels, since he stipulated that she should "have the Privilege of sending Adventures in the Vessels of my House as heretofore." And in 1799, as the widow and administratrix of Richard Woodman's estate, Elizabeth Woodman of Newport claimed to be the sole owner of her namesake vessel, the *Betsy,* although for legal reasons she had to deny that it was a slaver.[59]

None of this approaches the level of involvement of Charleston's Margaret Schutt, one of only two American women known to have taken the lead in organizing a slaving voyage in the era before 1808. Born in German-speaking Europe, probably Hamburg, she and her husband, the merchant Casper Schutt, were living in the United States before 1791. Casper Schutt died in 1803, less than a year before South Carolina re-legalized its slave trade, and he does not seem to have been involved in slave trading. Exactly how active Margaret was in Casper's business is not certain, but judging by her mastery of commercial protocol, she seems to have known quite a bit. In 1805 she organized a very compli-cated voyage for a ship called the *Margaret,* which Casper had presum-ably named after her. In fact, this may well have been her second slaving voyage, since her insurance request to Lloyds mentioned a previous trip from Mozambique to Cuba. Margaret Schutt was very much a hands-on manager, sending not one but three detailed letters of instruction to her captain: as a *femme sole* operating in a man's world, she may have felt the need to stress her authority and competence. Her initial plan was for the *Margaret* to purchase captives at Gorée, transport them to Buenos Aires, and then take on tasajo for the Bahamas and New Orleans. As the voyage unfolded, she managed affairs by corresponding with her agents in Buenos Aires, New York, and New Providence. Schutt's well-laid plans went awry, however, when the Royal Navy captured the *Mar-garet* after it left Montevideo in late 1806. The British released the ship in January 1807, and it sailed for Rio de Janeiro for provisions and repairs. The Royal Navy retook the *Margaret* after it left Rio, ending her slave-trading career.[60]

But not even Margaret Schutt could match the woman we know only as Mrs. Johnson for hands-on involvement. The wife of a Captain Johnson of Philadelphia, Mrs. Johnson accompanied her husband to Africa in 1802–1803. After Captain Johnson died at Gorée, Mrs. Johnson purchased a quarter share in the schooner *Charming Sally,* a former French vessel that apparently had been captured in Africa and sold to some Boston slavers who were in the area. She then transferred the captives from her original vessel to the *Charming Sally,* including one girl that she intended to keep for herself, and sailed under French colors for Saint Barthelemy. A Boston seaman later deposed that he had seen Mrs. Johnson kicking two naked, cuffed captives and ordering her sailors to place them in shackles, threatening that they "would not come out of Irons again very soon." As far as the witness knew, she "was the owner of the said vessel." Mrs. Johnson is the only white American woman known to have actually sailed aboard a slave ship.[61]

The wives and families of ordinary seamen suffered greatly in their absences. The families of captains and officers often received assistance from the shipowners, in the form of periodic advances on wages, but the wives of those who sailed "before the mast," many of whom did not belong to the town, rarely benefited from this sort of "maritime paternalism." Many seamen's wives had to scrap for a living, making it all but impossible for them to live up to the domestic ideals of the era. Much of their work was done for mariners and thus was directly responsible for sustaining the activity of the port. These tasks included taking in boarders (often sailors), working as laundresses, and preparing meals. A notable proportion of cases brought before the town court involved women recovering unpaid lodging debts from sailors. But not everyone managed to make ends meet. Town residents could wind up in the workhouse or boarding with a local family at public expense, but transient women were warned out. In both cases, the women had to face probing inquiries by the "Overseers of the Poor" and worry that their children would be removed from them and bound out as servants to local families.[62]

Mid-voyage letters from the wives of Rhode Island's ordinary seamen are almost nonexistent. However, several letters do survive from the families of pirate/slavers who went to Madagascar in the 1690s, and these offer rare glimpses into the hardships associated with long (in this case, extremely long) voyages. Sarah Horne wrote to her husband, Jacob, with news of their children and to report that they were now living with a cousin. Clearly, the couple had anticipated possible problems and planned accordingly. Ede Wilday wrote to her husband Richard to say that she and their two children "are alive and in good health" but that a cousin had died. She closed by promising to "wait in patience for the Shipps returne" and gave her "true Love to you with Dayly wishes for your Company." Robert Crosley had evidently made alternate living arrangements for his wife before departing, but his brother informed him in a letter that she "could nott Live any Longer whear you Left her, her father being dead." She stayed at Robert's for a time, then left for "friends" on Long Island. Robert's absence had "beene a great truble to her, she haveing two small Children to maintaine." Both his brother and wife seem to have feared that he had abandoned his family and implored him to return. These expressions of longing for the absent family member not only demonstrate the emotionally taxing nature of long voyages, they draw our attention to women's efforts to preserve their marriages over vast stretches of space and time, all while performing essential social reproductive labor. As the large number of widows, workhouse residents, and families on poor relief suggests, this was not an easy task.[63]

William Wardwell, author of the satirical city charter for Bristol, published an acrostic poem that expressed the anxiety of a local woman whose husband was "absent at Sea."

> P erplexing fear! how fruitless, and how vain!
> H ow little after all, by them we gain;
> E ver uneasy, and foreboding still,
> B eleiving [sic] not in GOD'S disposing will;
> E ver forgeting [sic] his *command;*—Be still.
>
> F irst seek an intrust in his pard'ning grace,
> A nd let all other *cares* to this give place.
> L ife is but short, at longest date,
> E ternal *joys* or *pains,* do us await;
> S urely our *time* is short, and *worth* is great.[64]

The woman whose name was spelled out in the acrostic, Phebe Fales, seems to have been Wardwell's sister. If so, then the poem may well come close to expressing her feelings at the probable loss of her husband.

By far the most important and enduring effect of the slave trade was the creation of one of New England's largest Black communities in Newport. This was not a new development. As early as 1680, about 6 percent of Rhode Island's population was enslaved, with most having arrived sporadically in small numbers from the Caribbean. Newport's plunge into the transatlantic slave trade during the 1730s fueled a surge, as Africans arrived both as "privilege" slaves and, during the 1750s and 1760s, aboard ships making the occasional bilateral African voyage. By 1750, 10 percent of Rhode Island's population was enslaved, compared with 2 percent in Massachusetts and 3 percent in Connecticut. For a time, Newport's Black community was larger than Boston's, and was concentrated in a much smaller compass. The town's enslaved population hit its peak in 1755 at 1,234, or nearly 1 in 5 residents. In 1774, 3 in 10 white Newport families owned slaves, a higher percentage than in the U.S. South in 1860. After the American Revolution the enslaved proportion of the population fell to 10 percent, driven both by outmigration and the growth of the white population, but Newport still had New England's second largest urban Black population, trailing only Boston.[65]

Enslaved Newporters lived scattered across the town in attics, cellars, and outbuildings. They performed all manner of work, most of it in support of the town's maritime economy, and they distilled a large portion of the spirit that gave the rum men their name. Enslaved women performed much of the labor that sustained the town's maritime workforce, lightening the burden for merchants' and captains' wives. Enslaved men crewed vessels in all trades, including the African trade. Around town, they worked as skilled artisans in the ship joineries, ropewalks, and workshops, and were hired out to merchants as longshoremen. Free Black men with a bit of property, though small in number, roamed the waterfront as carters and draymen. Across the bay in the Narragansett Country, enslaved people of all ages and sexes toiled on the farms that provisioned the town's fleet, with some of the produce destined to be traded for captives at the forts. It is difficult to imagine a colonial-era Guineaman that did not carry slave-produced produce or employ slave labor in the outfitting process. Newport's slave trade relied heavily on the labor of the very same people who were transported by its ships. Put differently, for the colonial-era slave trade to function, slavers needed to retain 1 or 2 percent of all of the captives they carried.[66]

    As a result of the slave trade, a very large percentage of eighteenth-century Newport's enslaved population was African-born. There are no statistics on the number of African-born versus American-born Black Newporters, but it is possible to gain some insight by analyzing the grave markers in the God's Little Acre section of Newport's Common Burying Ground. Only 4 percent of the names on the markers are identifiably African, but this greatly underrepresents the actual African-born population. First, slaveholders often forced their bondpeople to adopt the stereotypical "slave names" of the era: Cato, Prince, Scipio, Pompey, Samson. Undoubtedly, many of the stones bearing those names mark the graves of African-born people, but it is impossible to know which ones. Second, the graves span the eighteenth to the twentieth centuries, with the vast majority dating to the post-slave-trade era. Moreover, these markers do not represent the total number of people in the cemetery, let alone the entire African-born population. Many markers have deteriorated or vanished altogether, and the Common Burying Ground was not the only cemetery in the area. Finally, it cannot be assumed that every person with an identifiably African name was African-born, because American-born people occasionally adopted African names.[67]

    With those caveats in mind, the markers suggest the basic contours of Newport's African-born community (table 7). The fact that almost two-thirds of the markers bearing African names pre-date 1775 suggests an African-born population at its height during the colonial era, especially during the period 1751–1775. Newport continued as a slaving hub after that date, of course, but far fewer Africans arrived because it was illegal to bring enslaved people into the state. Most of the Africans buried during the post-revolutionary period therefore arrived before 1775. The markers further suggest that Newport's African-born population was predominantly male, which is hardly surprising given the gender dynamic of the transatlantic slave trade. Even so, the 3:1 ratio among

Table 7. African Names on Markers in God's Little Acre Cemetery

Burial Year	Number	Language			Gender		
		Akan	Non-Akan	Male		Female	Unknown
1729–1750	6	4	2	4		0	2
1751–1775	10	9	1	8		1	1
1776–1800	5	5	0	2		3	0
1801–1825	2	2	0	1		1	0
1826–1850	2	1	1	1		0	1
Totals	25	21	4	16		5	4

Source: God's Little Acre Stone Inventory, online at ripnewport.com/God's%20Little%20
Acre%20stone%20inventory%20a-z%20online.pdf.

the markers in God's Little Acre overstates the true imbalance, which was likely closer to 3:2. An unbalanced sex ratio would have exacerbated the difficulties that slavery posed to family formation, with a shortage of Black women that made the local Black population dependent on the arrival of more Africans just to sustain itself. Death rates for Black Newporters, moreover, were significantly higher than for white residents, indicative of material hardship and mistreatment. In its inability to reproduce itself naturally, the enslaved population of late-colonial Newport differed in degree but not in kind from those of the plantation colonies.[68]

The most intriguing information from the gravestones is the percentage of Akan names, which account for more than 80 percent of all African names in the cemetery. The obvious conclusion—that Akan speakers dominated Newport's African-born population—is surely the correct one. During the key years between 1730 and 1775, nearly nine in ten Rhode Island slavers went to the Gold Coast, as did three-quarters of the slavers that carried captives directly from Africa to Newport. Despite the general agreement of these figures, they probably overstate the cultural and linguistic homogeneity of Newport's African population. For one thing, it is possible that Newport slaveholders were more likely to let Akan speakers keep their names over other linguistic groups. Foreign though the names were, they were nonetheless familiar to whites and were thought of as suitable "slave names." It is reasonable to speculate that Africans with less familiar, more difficult to pronounce names may have been more likely to have a new one forced on them. Second, in Africa, a perfect correlation between an Akan name and Akan language or identity cannot be assumed. The eastward expansion of Akwamu and Asante in the seventeenth and eighteenth centuries set off a series of cultural encounters between Akan, Ga-Adangme, and Gbe speakers on the so-called "Slave Coast" (Bight of Benin). Refugees and migrants spread the Akan tongue along the coast, where it became a trade and second language for many non-Akan people. So although most of the stones with Akan names probably do mark the graves of Akan speakers from the Gold Coast, some may be for Ga-Adangme, Ewe, or Fon speakers.[69]

The matter is further complicated by the apparent use of Akan names among native-born or creole Newporters. One family in particular seems to have adopted the Akan name "Quamino" as a surname and passed it on to its American-born children. In Akan society, "Quamino" was a name given to male children born on a Saturday. In Newport, a free Black woman named Duchess Quamino (formerly Duchess Channing), well known throughout the town as an excellent baker, apparently adopted her husband's Akan day name as a surname. Whether Duchess Quamino was born in Africa or not, let alone whether she was of Akan background, is not known, but her gesture raises questions regarding Akan culture in Newport. Akan people reckoned kinship matrilineally. If Duchess Quamino was Akan, her decision to adopt her partner's name might be read as a deliberate strategy in her encounter with the Western patrilineal system. By this reading, taking a male day name as a surname was a way for her to assert a claim to her own children, which she apparently did for at least two of her daughters, both of whom carried the Quamino surname and are buried in the cemetery. Alternately, if she was not of Akan background, we might read her act as a gesture in honor of her children's father, a public affirmation not merely of their African but their Akan heritage. Her seemingly deliberate decision serves as a rare reminder of both the probable influence of Akan culture in Newport and its mutability in the American environment.[70]

With the preponderance of Akan speakers among the African-born (and at times perhaps among the Black populace as a whole), the

town's annual "Negro Election Day" festival takes on additional significance as a possible expression not merely of a Black consciousness,
but one influenced by specific African ideas. Most descriptions of these
celebrations were written by whites retrospectively, in the nineteenth
century, and as a result they lack the detail needed to assess the degree
of Akan influence. White reminiscences tended to emphasize the rau-
cousness, symbolic inversion, and outlandishness of Election Day ceremonies. One recollection, however, highlighted the "African" nature of
Newport's Election Day. Describing a celebration that took place in 1756,
at a moment when Newport's enslaved and Akan populations were both
at their height, the anonymous observer told of the usual parade and
election, after which the "Sons of Africa" "amused themselves with . . .
cudgeling, jumping, wrestling, playing at the various games, and on the
musical instruments of their native country." After the winner of the
election was announced, the crowd celebrated "in all the various languages of Africa . . . accompanied with the music of the fiddle, tambou-
rine, the banjo, drum, &c."[71]

Nothing in this rather vague account can be identified as distinctly
Akan. The most striking feature is the close resemblance between Newport's Election Day and similar festivals throughout the Black Atlantic,
such as Jonkonnu in the British Caribbean, Pinkster in the Dutch colonies, Carnaval in Brazil, Mardi Gras in the French Caribbean, and Three
Kings Day in Cuba. The broad similarity of these events speaks less to
any specific African cultural influence and more to their diasporic nature, as people from a wide variety of backgrounds discovered, explored,
and built upon whatever common cultural ground they could find. Yet
at the same time, the likely preponderance of Akan speakers in Newport
makes it very likely that Akan culture played a central role in the tradition. We know that many men from the Akan states had military train-
ing, if not as regular soldiers, then as members of Asafo companies, or
the local militia. It is very likely that some of the "cudgeling, jumping,
and wrestling" was performed by men with that background. And the
description, though similar to many diasporic festivals, resembles the
"Coromantee" and "Mina" festivals and "country plays" that took place
in other colonies where the probable proportion of Akan speakers was
lower than Newport's. Examining these festivals from the perspective of

the Gold Coast diaspora, Walter Rucker has cautioned against reading them as "restorationist" and proposed instead that they "simultaneously embodied cultural continuities and decisive sociopolitical breaks." In sum, although we would not want to essentialize Akan culture, it is probable, given the critical mass of Gold Coast natives, that Black culture in Newport was strongly influenced by Akan customs, at least in the mid-eighteenth century. This is not to deny creolized and other African influences. The use of Western musical instruments and the adoption of the language of local politics (electing a governor rather than crowning a king) provide just two glimpses of the kinds of dynamic adaptations that were probably taking place. But for seven decades, Akan people were at the center of this process.[72]

The American Revolution disrupted slavery in Newport. Occupation and military activity prompted the departure of much of the enslaved population, with some fleeing to the British. Revolutionary antislavery and Black military enlistment further weakened the institution of slavery to the point where it was unlikely ever to return to its former level of importance. Rhode Island's gradual emancipation law of 1784 technically freed nobody, forcing anyone born to an enslaved mother to serve as an "apprentice" for eighteen years (girls) or twenty-one years (boys). Some whites, including slavers, held people born before 1784 in slavery for years afterward. And local lore in Bristol holds that slavers there were still bringing in "privilege" slaves well after that date. Even so, the law made it clear that slavery was on its way out, and enslaved Newporters further undermined the institution through flight and other forms of resistance. By 1790, the proportion of free people in Rhode Island's Black community went from a tiny minority to 78 percent.[73]

Like many northern Black communities of the era, Newport's post-war free Black community proudly embraced its African roots—significantly, "African" and not "Akan" or another ethnic identity—both by celebrating its Africanness and by exploring the possibility of founding a colony in Africa. If Africa was an abstract symbol in many northern communities, in Newport, with its large African-born population and its continuing slave trade, it was a very real presence. In 1780 Newporters formed the Free African Union Society, the first known free Black association in the United States. Catering to the new and growing

Black property-owning class and preaching the doctrine of uplift, the society offered funeral and widows' benefits to members. As early as 1787 it was spearheading a colonization campaign, eventually establishing contact with the British abolitionist Thomas Clarkson and the promoters of the Sierra Leone colony. A perpetual lack of funds prevented the society from realizing its plans.[74]

The same lack of funds and the need to cultivate moneyed patronage may also be the reason for the society's surprising discretion on the issues of slavery and the slave trade. There are few hints of any serious anti-slavery campaigning in its correspondence or minutes. Some letters denounce slavery, though almost in passing. In a letter to the Providence Society for the Abolition of the Slave Trade, for example, members referred to themselves as "strangers and outcasts in a strange land" and noted the "wretched state" of "abject slavery" in which many "brethren" dwelt. Colonization, which absorbed a great deal of energy in the late 1780s and early 1790s, was implicitly anti-slavery, of course, but the society's public statements fell well short of strident denunciation. It may be that members felt the need to avoid alienating white merchants, many of whom still traded in captives. It is even possible that some members were connected to the slave trade, since the society felt the need to pass a resolution barring "those who are of the African race that do, or hereafter may be the Means of bringing, from their Native Country, the Males, Females, Boys & Girls from Africa into Bondage, to the hurt of themselves and the Inhabitants of the Country or Place where they may be bought and sold."[75]

Bristol, Rhode Island, did not emerge as a major slave-trading hub until after the gradual emancipation law of 1784 was passed. Although the raw numbers were lower than for Newport, enslaved people were proportionately significant, at about 12 percent of the total population in 1755. Since this was well before the town's plunge into the transatlantic slave trade, it seems likely that most had arrived via Newport or the town's small but thriving Caribbean trade. In 1790, as Bristol merchants ramped up their involvement in the slave trade, almost 8 percent of Bristol's population was Black, most still enslaved. Gradually, more people gained their freedom, but free Blacks continued to reside in the town. During the final decades of the legal slave trade, both Bristol and

Newport saw the percentage of Black residents fall, but as of 1808, both towns maintained Black populations of between 7 and 10 percent, the vast majority being free.[76]

Although by 1800 most Black Rhode Islanders were no longer enslaved, they now had to battle the twin scourges of racism and poverty. Gradual emancipation had released many people from slavery, but most exited their "apprenticeship" periods with little or no property and were thus forced to lead transient lives, selling their labor wherever they could. At the same time, the law's apprenticeship requirement perpetuated the notion that the proper condition for Black people was one of servitude. For many families, these two factors converged in Rhode Island's system of poor relief. A carryover from the colonial period, towns were responsible for the maintenance of legal residents who could not support themselves. Townspeople could denounce anyone they deemed likely to become a public charge. In such cases, the person or family would have to prove their right to live in the town. Local officials held regular hearings to screen applicants to ensure that they were indeed residents. Predictably, as Rhode Island's Black residents shed their formal bonds, increasing numbers found themselves warned out of the towns in which they resided.[77]

Tiverton, Rhode Island, located midway between Newport and Bristol and home to several slave-ship captains, had a long history of warning out Black residents. In 1786, the town fathers issued a blanket order to all Black inhabitants who could not prove legal residence to leave the town. Those who refused would be placed in the workhouse or be legally bound out to labor for local whites. In May 1804, Tiverton's "Receiver of the Poor" warned out six nonwhite men, including two families with children, and bound out a Black "boy," probably an adolescent, to a white family in Fall River, Massachusetts. Two of the men apparently refused to leave, because two months later the town had each one whipped "on his naked back" with twenty lashes. The following year, the town bound out yet another young Black male. There is no reason to suppose that Tiverton's practices differed from any other town's.[78]

As a consequence of these economic and political pressures, Black men continued to sail aboard slave ships in the 1790s and 1800s, possibly at higher rates than when forced to as slaves. Trapped by poverty and the threat of being warned out, and attracted by the wages and a shipboard culture in which an emphasis on color was partially offset by an emphasis on skill, Black men signed on to ships in great numbers. In the early nineteenth century, Black sailors made up almost one-fifth of American crews. Inevitably, some signed on to slavers, though at much lower rates than for the other trades, which suggests a conscious decision to avoid the slave trade. Emma Christopher has identified fifty Black seamen who sailed aboard Guineamen during the years 1803–1807, about one-third of whom were Rhode Island natives. More than half were employed in the customary posts of cook and steward, but the rest worked as seamen, a much higher percentage than in the colonial era. Propertyless and subject to the harsh poor laws of the era, these may have been the men that the Free African Union Society had in mind when it resolved not to admit those of the "African race" who were the "Means of bringing, from their Native Country, the Males, Females, Boys & Girls from Africa into Bondage."[79]

Slave traders were not a very reflective group. Their correspondence was businesslike and not given to philosophical musings of the sort that might offer clues as to how they understood their own actions. As a member of the Rhode Island General Assembly, John Brown defended the slave trade on several occasions when it was under direct attack. His public and private arguments emphasized the economic importance of the trade and the widespread idea that enslavement to whites rescued Africans from savagery. We can gain some sense of the Vernon brothers' thoughts from a 1784 clipping in their papers from a tract titled "The Origins of the Negroe Slave Trade" by the German geographer Matthias Christian Sprengel. A scholar with a special interest in the North American colonies, Sprengel lectured in opposition to the slave trade as early as 1779. The excerpt in the Vernon papers dwells on the early Portuguese trade, offering a dispassionate account of its rise and eventual displacement by Northern European slavers. The clipping, however, dwells on the economic value of the trade; issues of morality or human equality do not appear. If the decision by one of the brothers (most of the papers are by William Vernon) to cut out the article is at all indicative of slave traders' views, then the question of whether all men were indeed created equal and entitled to certain inalienable rights did not enter into their thinking. But that is surely not the end of the story. Race had occupied a central position in the minds of the New England traders since the seventeenth century. To get past the slavers' silence, it is necessary to understand the way that race was produced and lived in Newport and Bristol.[80]

Because Newport and Bristol were slave-trading societies (to adapt M. I. Finley's well-known formulation), social life in both was suffused by race.[81] That continued so even with the gradual decline of slavery after the American Revolution. We have seen how the power of the merchant elite was predicated in no small part on the traffic in Black captives, with totals for some individuals running into the thousands, and how social mobility, such as the progression of mariner to merchant, hinged on acquiring and selling Black privilege slaves. Race framed the use of enslaved and free Black laborers in the outfitting and crewing of vessels, and in the employment of Black men and women to sustain maritime households during sailors' absences. It defined social and political belonging through their exclusion from the electorate and other institutions, and even in death, as seen in the segregated section of Newport's ironically named Common Burying Ground.

Race was performed and remade in innumerable acts and utterances, most too ephemeral to enter the historical record. Humor—or mockery, really—was one site of racial formation and apparently began while still on the African coast. According to a local historian and member of the D'Wolf family, the town's slavers marked the captives' new racialized status by bestowing humiliating names on their "privilege" slaves: Cuffee Cockroach, Pea Soup, Flying Jib. Racialization continued in Bristol, where white children taunted an elderly Black couple with a ditty that ended with one of them falling down the cellar stairs while the other blew away in the wind. Bristol's local lore also includes a story about John Usher, the rector of St. Michael's Church, who, while drunk, shot a young Black boy in the leg for "tormenting" him. At his arraignment, Usher pleaded not guilty but jocularly confessed to shooting the boy, using a crude racial epithet. Both the event and the fact that the story was kept alive speak volumes about race in Bristol. Newport was little better. The same source relates the story of a church elder who, on the return of a slave ship, gave ironic thanks "that an over-ruling Providence had been pleased to bring to this land of freedom another cargo of benighted heathen, to enjoy the blessing of a Gospel dispensation."[82]

For white working-class Rhode Islanders, including most ordinary seamen, race soothed the scars and insults of marginal existence. Shipboard life was comparatively egalitarian, prizing skill over identity, but racial hierarchies were never absent. Before the American Revolution, many Black sailors—including all of those who sailed on Guineamen— were enslaved and ranked as ship's boys and cooks. After the 1780s, most were no longer enslaved, but many still occupied the lower rungs of the maritime social ladder. On shore, white seamen asserted and performed racial privilege in a range of settings. In 1764, the Newport town court heard a case that neatly summarized the interplay of class and race for white sailors. The case revolved around a mariner who had cut cordwood for a local farmer. The seaman refused to complete his contract with the farmer, and in his testimony the sailor's father cited his son's resentment at having to work alongside "a Negro." Cutting wood for another white man was apparently acceptable, but doing so alongside a Black man, presumably enslaved, was an insult. Four years later, Newport's artisans passed a resolution condemning the use of enslaved Black labor in the skilled trades. One group of seamen donned blackface to break into a house and forcibly escort a sailor's family to the workhouse. The details of the dispute are not known, but the use of blackface to enforce class and gender norms speaks to its valence in Newport maritime society.[83]

But although race resided on an ideological plane, an outgrowth of the slave system, its consequences were very real, as measured in birth rates, marriage rates, poverty rates, and death rates. To say so is to emphasize the structural position of race over individual attitudes. But attitudes and ideas were, predictably, consonant with slaveholding. These changed over time, slowly becoming more coherent over the course of the seventeenth and eighteenth centuries, acquiring new valences and articulations, with science, for example. One commonplace was the consensus that servility was the natural state for Black people in colonial society, with the concomitant notion that free Blacks and unsupervised slaves were by nature disorderly. This is easily visible in the efforts to control the behavior of enslaved people as their numbers grew. In 1728, for example, Rhode Island required slaveholders to post a one-hundred-pound bond to ensure that nobody manumitted from slavery became a public charge. The purpose was obviously to discourage manumissions and to keep the association between blackness and slavery as close as possible. The following year the legislature imposed a fine of three pounds on any ship captain who brought in a "negro" for permanent settlement. The fine functioned more like a tax, as the considerable sum collected was later directed toward street paving and bridge maintenance. The town of Newport, as the center of the colony's enslaved population, ordered its watch in 1733 to "take up all Negroes, Servants & Disorderly persons and Inform the Authority or Commit them to Gaol as the Circumstances may Require." The warning out and forced apprenticeship of Black transients during the years of gradual emancipation were additional ways to enforce the prevailing sense of order.[84]

In that sense, Newport and Bristol were of a piece with New England society in general. But as slave-trading societies, they were also different. Slave-ship sailors enacted the racial hierarchy of American society from the moment captives arrived aboard their vessels, initiating the work of associating Black bodies with servility. But unlike the white seamen who worked solely in the coastwise and Caribbean trades, for whom "negro" and "slave" were nearly synonymous, slavers were forced to deal with and acknowledge Africans in positions of power, political officers, military rulers, merchants, and brokers. Whatever thoughts they may have held, mariners in the slave trade had to reckon with the reality that the balance of power along the African coast (and even more so miles up the Gambia and Sierra Leone Rivers) tilted decidedly toward the people they referred to as "negroes." Thomas Eldrid spent significant amounts of time ashore, enough to observe several palavers and learn at least the rudiments of the Susu language. Did his experience, perhaps involving a long-term relationship with a woman, alter his views on Africans? One of the Vernons' captains apparently tried to transcribe some music he heard into notes on a staff. Did his music appreciation change his feelings about African cultural inferiority? And what of the IOU signed in Arabic that Captain John Sabens accepted from a man named Landemado on the upper Guinea coast? Did Sabens reconsider his views on African "savagery" as he watched the Muslim merchant sign his name in a hand far more elegant than his own uneducated scrawl? If so, then in none of these cases was it enough to prevent slavers from conducting their business.[85]

Dealing with powerful Africans more likely produced cognitive dissonance in slavers. That at least seems to have been the case with William Chancellor, whose journal is probably the most reflective document ever produced by an American slave trader. Chancellor was a Philadelphia native who sailed as surgeon aboard a New York sloop in a three-vessel flotilla commanded by Newport's David Lindsay. Chancellor's journal shows him continuously reconciling the reality of African power on the coast with his closely held belief in Black inferiority. In Chancellor's view, Africans were superstitious savages. He was convinced, for example, that the inhabitants of Lahou were cannibals, and he related tales of human sacrifice by Fante leaders. He also saw Africans as overawed by the slavers' "magic." "A Person of any sagacity," he wrote, "may easily penetrate [that is, fool or amaze] the negroes," and illustrated the point with an anecdote about a man who believed the ticking of his watch was "fetish." Chancellor's perceptions were strengthened by his personal encounter with the ruler of Anomabu, John Corrantee, whom he treated for a medical issue. Chancellor spent the night at Corrantee's residence and was amused to learn that the great man considered him his "son" as a result. For Chancellor, however, this was just another demonstration of the strange and savage ways of the Africans.[86]

On the other side of Chancellor's mental ledger was the reality that he and his compatriots were often "penetrated" by these same people. Chancellor himself seems to have accepted adulterated gold for one of his privilege trades, and on another occasion he narrates the failure of the Guinea captains to sustain a rum embargo against the Fante, who countered by withholding provisions. His diary also contains many examples of European deference to African practice in such areas as customs payment. Chancellor reconciled these contradictions by resorting to a view that, powerful and capable though the Fante may have been—

he estimated their military forces at 130,000—they were nevertheless "savage." Other slavers may have had their preconceptions challenged by reading the travel literature of the era. In 1808, the Mount Hope Library in Bristol reported that it owned a copy of Mungo Park's travel narrative, and after returning from the Gambia, Salem's George Ropes told associates that Park's narrative was "correct so far as his own knowledge went." Park presented the Gambia through the racialized lens of his era but at the same time offered a nuanced account that acknowledged and at times praised the intelligence of African people. Slavers like Chancellor and Ropes thus encountered a reality on the African coast that was dramatically at odds with the racial stereotyping that they brought with them from North America. That said, there is little evidence that their encounters ever broke down their beliefs. Motivated reasoning rooted in economic gain and an ability to accommodate contradictory ideas triumphed over experience. Race continued to frame and justify their actions, and no amount of contrary evidence would change their views.[87]

As slave-trading ports, Newport and Bristol possessed a distinct sociology. Although slave trading was never the sole or even the primary economic pursuit, and whereas Guineamen accounted for only a fraction of total clearances, slaving profits made the local elite and, through such mechanisms as privilege and coast commission, constituted the most reliable path to social advancement. Slavers dominated the politics of both ports. In Newport, slaver-politicians worked to keep criticism of the trade out of public discourse. In Bristol they went even further, operating as a political machine to shield operations from state and federal law, employing violence when necessary. Because the African trade gave residents easy access to captives at low prices, slaveholding was widespread in the colonial era, with most white, propertied households claiming at least one enslaved person. Slave trading left its cultural stamp on Newport's Black community, which at one time was likely dominated by people of Akan background. Bristol, which did not become a major slaving port until after the landing of captive Africans was banned, also had a disproportionately large Black population, although it was probably more heterogeneous than Newport's. As slave-owning societies, Newport and Bristol replicated the racial ideology of the era, but as members of slave-trading societies, many residents also had opportunities to observe powerful Black people in nonservile positions. To justify their continued engagement in the slave trade, they reconciled the contradictory racial ideas by dismissing African power and intelligence under the rubric of "savagery."

Part Five

SLAVERS AS OUTLAWS
1808–1865

Mediterranean Sea, 1830.

IT WAS THE highlight of Charles Tyng's young career. En route from Havana to Marseilles in his brig *Creole,* he met unexpectedly with his other vessel, the *Eight Sons,* skippered by his former mate, Clement Parsons. The two brigs "spoke" to each other for an hour, and Parsons transferred some much needed provisions to the *Creole.* The rendezvous between his two vessels filled Tyng with such pride that he commissioned a painting in commemoration. In a note on the back, he stipulated that the painting "should be kept by C Tyngs children . . . as a memento of their fathers perseverance, who from a sailor, without a dollar, by his own industry & perseverance, became a Captain and owner of these and other vessels—before he was 30 years old." Decades later, in the 1870s, Tyng sounded that theme in an autobiography detailing his path from seaman to merchant, a work very much in the Horatio Alger mode popular at the time. As often happened with self-made men, Tyng exaggerated his without-a-dollar roots. His father was a lawyer, his three brothers were Harvard graduates, and young Charles had once been a schoolmate of Ralph Waldo Emerson. Although Tyng did begin his maritime career as a ship's boy, he advanced quickly by exploiting his

---

Previous page: Liberated Africans aboard the Slave Bark *Wildfire,* 1860. This famous engraving, which appeared in *Harper's Weekly,* elicited sympathy for the plight of the captives of the slave trade while simultaneously playing on racialized notions of the "Other." The *Wildfire* exemplifies many of the features of the illegal trade of the 1850s. Although it sailed from New York, it was reportedly owned by Portuguese merchants and was en route to Cuba when captured by the U.S. Navy. After spending time in a camp on Key West, the former captives were deported to Liberia. ("The Africans of the Slave Bark 'Wildfire,'" Library of Congress)

kinship ties with the Perkins family, prominent Boston merchants. By 1830 he was more a shipowner than a skipper, and by 1837 he had settled in Havana, advertising himself as a ship broker and commission agent. Charles Tyng had become a respected man of commerce.[1]

And Charles Tyng was a slave trader. Of that there is no doubt, although his memoir ends in 1833, six years before his first known venture. His death in 1879, as he was still writing the memoir, was the probable reason for the abrupt ending, but it seems doubtful that Tyng would have disclosed his slaving career even if he had completed his life story; slave trading would have struck too discordant a tone for his type of ballad. Between 1839 and 1845, Tyng was involved in no fewer than fifteen probable slave ventures and was well known to American authorities, who prosecuted him in 1840; to British authorities, who tracked his activities extensively and seized four of his vessels; and even to authorities in Bremen and Hamburg, where he sent ships for trade goods and equipment. (It goes without saying that he was known to authorities in Cuba, but they never acted against him for slave trading.)[2]

Tyng exemplifies many of the changes that had come to the American slave trade after January 1, 1808. First, there is a distinctly modern cast to his activities. Tyng was not a merchant in the eighteenth-century mode of vessel owner and voyage organizer. He was a ship broker, a middleman who profited by assembling vessels, goods, and crews. Second, as a dual citizen, Tyng embodied the transnational quality of the slave trade. As Charles Tyng, American, he was valuable to his clients for his ability to procure U.S. vessels without forfeiting their American registry. As Don Carlos Tyng, Spanish subject, he retained the right to operate in Cuba and avoid prosecution under U.S. law, which, should he have been so unlucky as to have been convicted, equated slave trading with piracy and carried a penalty of death.

Last, Tyng illustrates the post-1808 American slave trade in his position as an important node in an illegal transnational network. As criminologists emphasize, most illegal enterprises bear little resemblance to the iconic image of the Italian American Cosa Nostra, with formal, elaborate hierarchies and hundreds of "soldiers." Instead, they consist of a small group of central organizers and an outer ring of occasional participants, often in legitimate businesses, who provide specialized services.

It was in the latter capacity that Tyng and other Americans participated in the illegal slave trade of the nineteenth century. As an American ship broker and commission merchant living in Havana, Tyng came into contact with many slavers, years before he entered the business himself. So although Tyng's memoir does not cover his slave-trading years, it details his growing connections with slave traders in the decade or so before he finally entered the trade, starting with his first trip to Cuba in 1819, when he met George Knight, a major trader. Tyng's Cuban visits became regular after 1826, and over the next six years he dealt at least seven times with Drake & Mitchell, another major Havana mercantile house and one involved in slave trading.[3]

As far as can be determined, none of these early deals had any connection with the slave trade, but when the opportunity eventually came, Tyng was positioned to act. Starting in about 1839, he became a small but key node in the major Cuban slave-trading network of the era, which centered on Pedro Martínez & Co. When Martínez needed ships, Tyng's role was to use his contacts in Baltimore and Boston to buy or charter them, and because he was a U.S. citizen, they flew the American flag. Tyng also procured outbound cargoes, signed bills of lading, and hired American skippers to serve as false "flag" captains. In short, he allowed a major Cuban slaving network to do business in the United States without attracting undue attention.

The final phase of the American slave trade in which Tyng was involved unfolded in two acts. In the first, Americans evaded the 1808 prohibition on slave trading by moving operations to Cuba. Merchant-shipowners continued to organize voyages and dispatch them to familiar African markets in upper Guinea. In 1820, that model became untenable. In May of that year, Congress made slave trading punishable by death, and in October an Anglo-Spanish treaty outlawed the slave trade in the Spanish Empire, depriving Americans of a flag of convenience. The two events largely drove Americans out of the trade as principal organizers of voyages, although individuals participated on the fringes by furnishing ships and occasionally by serving as mariners. Although the slave trade was illegal in Cuba, corruption and a lack of will to enforce the law meant that it could be carried on almost openly. This meant that slavers could avail themselves of the tools of legitimate business, securing bank loans and buying insurance policies, and had little need to adopt the strategies of criminal networks.[4]

All of that would change for the second act, after 1835, when an Anglo-Spanish treaty allowed the Royal Navy to seize all vessels carrying slave-trading equipment, rather than just those with captives aboard. The new standard led to a sharp increase in seizures and, in tandem with periodic crackdowns in Cuba, forced slavers to adopt clandestine measures that gave their networks an increasingly criminal look. In this environment, American ship brokers like Tyng became valuable to merchants in Havana, Rio, and other ports, because they could procure vessels for Cuban and Brazilian slave traders without surrendering their U.S. registration, which gave them protection from Royal Navy searches. For the same reason, American mariners were also in demand as "flag captains" on vessels carrying slaving equipment to the African coast. As Americans became role players in Cuban and Brazilian criminal organizations, their own connections to Africa withered. Upper Guinea receded and West Central Africa surged in importance. The Americans' adjunct status persisted even through the final phase in the late 1850s, when Portuguese slavers left Brazil to set up shop in New York.

Evasion, 1808–1835

T he vast majority of post-revolutionary slavers were criminals by the letter of the law, but through 1807 they had all the tools of legitimate business available to them. They could still insure their vessels and use the courts to enforce their contracts. In Rhode Island, at least, they made up an acknowledged (if embattled) political interest. Abolitionists denounced men like John Brown and the D'Wolfs, but they were elected to public office as active slavers. All of this was aided by the fact that although the importation of captives into the United States was regulated, it was still legal. Pre-1808 offenders faced fines, but they rarely lost their businesses, let alone their personal freedom (other than a luckless few who could not pay their fines). Slavers of the 1790s and 1800s were comparable to modern-day corporations that violate trade sanctions on rogue states: the activity itself was permissible, just not under all circumstances. It was hardly a strong moral stance.

All legal and moral ambiguity ended on January 1, 1808, as slave trading was prohibited both to and from the United States. Although imperfect, the Act to Prohibit the Importation of Slaves (1807) all but ended the practice of dispatching voyages from U.S. ports, and it seriously reduced the number of captives landed from overseas. It did not, however, end American involvement in the slave trade, as merchants

and mariners responded by moving their operations offshore, principally to Cuba, where they could operate openly until 1820. Even after
illegality, the toleration of the slave trade by Cuban officials meant that
slavers could still follow the practices of legitimate business. The move
offshore did come at a cost: by 1820, Cuban merchants, who had little
experience organizing slave voyages before 1808, gained the necessary
knowledge and contacts to run things for themselves. As a result, by
1820, Americans found themselves relegated to supplying ships and trade
goods; the initiative and the capital now came from Cuban firms. The
American slave-trading enclave on the Rio Pongo underwent a similar
transformation. The Americans remained active there, but they became
almost entirely dependent on the Cuban traders. Meanwhile, American
hirelings helped Cuban slavers establish a major center on the Gallinas.

Starting on January 1, 1808, U.S. slave trading plummeted. The precise
volume of the U.S. slave trade in the immediate aftermath of abolition
is uncertain, given both the imperative to hide criminal activity and the
difficulty of determining the true nationality of illegal vessels, but according to the *Voyages* database, the number of vessels embarking from
U.S. ports fell from an all-time high of 136 in 1807 to 16 in 1808, and to 1
in 1809. A look at the number of American-owned vessels sailing under
any flag and from any port suggests a higher rate of participation: 187
departures in 1807 (which would include American vessels sailing from
Cuba and other non-U.S. ports), 20 in 1808, and 4 in 1809. Even assuming that some voyages went undetected, the evidence points to a very
steep decline.[1]

Even though the act of 1807 was the main cause for the drop,
American policy in the lead-up to the War of 1812 also contributed.
Thomas Jefferson's Embargo Act became law on December 22, 1807,
nine days before the end of the legal slave trade. The embargo, which
barred Americans from trading internationally and entailed an uncom-
promising enforcement regime, was extremely unpopular in northern
seaports. Merchants exploited loopholes and found ways to evade the
law, but there is no question that the act devastated American overseas
commerce. Subsequent laws were less drastic but still damaged foreign trade. The Non-Intercourse Act (1809) prohibited commerce with

Britain and France, though it permitted Americans to trade with other jurisdictions, including Spanish Cuba. Macon's Bill Number 2 (1810) nominally reopened trade, but Napoleon used it to maneuver President James Madison into shutting down all commerce with Britain. Shipowners, including slavers, could not operate profitably in this environment. Some resorted to smuggling, mostly to Canada via Maine. Others redeployed their vessels into the coastal trade, and a few went into other businesses, such as manufacturing. The declaration of war against Britain that finally arrived on June 18, 1812, ended any chance that American merchants would continue slave trading on a pre-1808 scale. Quite a few outfitted their vessels as privateers. James D'Wolf, America's leading slaver, became one of its leading privateers, capturing eight British vessels worth a reported $300,000. A few privateers raided posts in Africa and sold the captives. But together, the slave-trading prohibition act of 1807, Republican trade policy, and two and a half years of naval warfare all but extinguished the practice of organizing voyages from United States ports.[2]

The slavers' response to abolition and other restrictions was predictable: led by the D'Wolfs, they moved offshore, dispatching their vessels from Cuba under the Spanish flag.[3] The shift happened almost immediately, as numerous cases reveal. The *Rapid,* for example, sailed from Bristol, Rhode Island, in early 1809, while the embargo was still in effect, clearing with false papers for Charleston. The *Rapid* then sailed to Havana and on to Africa before being captured by the Royal Navy.[4] The *Caroline* sailed to Charleston in 1810 and began fitting out for an African voyage. Local authorities, probably acting on a tip, seized the vessel for violating U.S. law. The owners then were apparently allowed to remove the fittings to convert it back to a non-slave vessel, at which point a court restored it to them. The *Caroline* cleared Charleston for Cuba on June 28, 1810, where it was "sold" to a Spanish subject who promptly re-equipped it for the slave trade.[5] On the other side of the Atlantic, the records of the British prize court at Sierra Leone tell the same story. Between 1809 and 1816, it found evidence of American ownership or involvement in a total of ten vessels, eight of which it condemned (the others were slavers but were restored because they had not taken on captives). Almost all had sailed under Spanish colors obtained in Cuba.[6]

The voyage of the *Numancia* offers a detailed portrait of just one of the American slavers that embarked from Cuba and probably typifies the strategies of the era. In early 1809, the brig's owners, Bristol's Charles D'Wolf and Boston's Isaac Packard and George Bayliss, hired Captain Azel Howard to sail the vessel to Cuba and act as supercargo, with instructions to call on Poëy y Hernandez, a firm with long-standing connections to American slavers. "You must be very carfull not to let any Person know the cituation of the Brig nor the real owners & not to let any of your men come home with you," warned Packard and Bayliss, adding, "NB at any rate don't bring the Brig to United States." The *Numancia* took on a cargo of rum, tobacco, and handkerchiefs in Havana, listing a Spanish captain on the bill of lading. The ruse was convincing enough to fool the brig's American surgeon into believing that Poëy y Hernandez actually owned the vessel, and only later did he realize that was not the case. The *Numancia* sailed to Africa, took on 264 captives, and delivered 237 of them to Havana in January 1810. By the owners' calculation, the voyage did extremely well, earning a "clear profit" of $19,032.[7]

Although voyages like the *Numancia*'s took place under the Spanish flag, they were essentially American ventures. Before the late 1810s, American slavers saw Cuba as both a staging ground for voyages and a final market for the captives. Cuban merchants were involved, but as junior partners. In these early years, most of the Americans' Cuban collaborators did little other than earn commissions on purchases and sales. The prevalence of American supercargoes was characteristic of U.S. dominance in the early years of the Cuba-based trade. Supercargoes were in charge of the commercial aspects of a voyage, responsible directly to the owners and empowered in most cases to direct the captain to specific ports. Ideally, they possessed a deep knowledge of the regional markets and networks of contacts. Supercargoes had been a rarity in the American slave trade for most of the long eighteenth century, but after 1808, American supercargoes began appearing regularly aboard vessels sailing from Cuba. Part of the reason may be that the Spanish maritime system separated nautical command (the pilot) from commercial responsibilities (the captain or shipmaster, who often owned a share of the vessel). Spanish vessels therefore always carried a "captain," who was analogous to an Anglo-American supercargo. But the main reason was that most of these were American-directed voyages operating on American networks and sailing under a Spanish flag of convenience.[8]

It is difficult to know for certain how many Cuban slavers carried American supercargoes, but the practice seems to have been quite prevalent during the 1810s. As a British report summarized in 1816, the typical ploy was for U.S. merchants to send their vessels to Cuba (Tenerife, another Spanish island, was also popular) and engineer a false transfer of the vessel to gain Spanish registry. The American captain and crew remained but were joined by a false Spanish captain and fake supercargo. The original American captain directed the voyage as a de facto supercargo, and the "nominal" captain was usually "some poor lad, who has never been to sea before, but whose services to carry the papers can be had cheap." Into the early 1820s, British cruisers frequently reported finding American supercargoes aboard Spanish-flagged vessels.[9]

The use of Cuba as a jumping-off point for African voyages strengthened the collaboration between American and Cuban merchants. Joaquín Madan (or "Madden") was one of those who made a career out of working with American slavers. A native of Ireland, Madan collaborated with Captain Edward Welsh of Charleston (and likely a few silent partners) on two voyages in 1811–1812, delivering captives from upper Guinea to Cuba and then returning immediately to upper Guinea. In 1815, Madan fronted for unnamed American owners, signing a false bill of sale that allowed the brig San Joaquín to fly the Spanish flag. Four years (and possibly additional undetected voyages) after that, on the voyage of the schooner Francisco, Madan teamed with Jacob (sometimes given as "Joseph") Bobbitt, a merchant and slaver from Bristol, Rhode Island; merchant Edward Spalding, formerly of Bristol and now resident in Trinidad de Cuba; and John Baker, who had married into a prominent trading family on the Rio Pongo. Spalding outfitted the vessel for Madan, advancing wages to the crew, overseeing the preparation of the vessel for sea, and purchasing aguardiente (a cane liquor similar to rum), guns, textiles, and iron to be used as trade goods, all for a 2.5 percent commission. With Spalding brokering between U.S. merchants such as the D'Wolfs, P. C. Greene of Rhode

Island, and James Dooley of Baltimore, and local merchants such as Madan and José García Álvarez, Trinidad de Cuba briefly became a minor hub for American slavers. The group organized at least four voyages, but the real total was surely higher.[10]

Illegality in 1808 ended the moral ambivalence that had prevailed under the law since 1794, and over the ensuing dozen or so years, public discourse increasingly associated slave trading with pure criminality. The embargo and the War of 1812 made the trade appear even more disreputable by forcing "respectable" slavers into other businesses. With the notable exception of the D'Wolfs and their satellites, very few pre-1808 slavers continued their activities after the restoration of peace in 1814. The departure of these "respectable" merchants left the field to a new generation of upstarts, which made it easier for the public and the politicians to view slavers as outlaws, pure and simple.

Two widely reported incidents helped to solidify the image of the slaver as criminal. The first was the invasion in 1817 of Amelia Island, located off Florida but close to Georgia, by a band of self-proclaimed anti-Spanish filibusters. For several months in 1817–1818, the area became the haunt of privateers bearing letters of marque from the new Latin American republics, who in just a few months brought in eight Spanish slave ships as prizes. Smugglers, led by a former Georgia governor who now served as the U.S. government's Muscogee (Creek) Indian agent, sold the captives to planters in nearby Georgia. In all, somewhere between one thousand and two thousand captives were landed in or near Amelia Island. There is no evidence to suggest that Americans played a significant role in organizing the original voyages; this was really a case of captured Spanish ships coming in rather than American vessels going out. But extensive press coverage alerted politicians and the public to the existence of corruption and slave smuggling, and the involvement of foreign privateers strengthened the perception that slave trading and piracy were linked.[11]

The second incident occurred in 1820 after President James Monroe approved the deployment of the USS *Cyane* and one escort vessel to upper Guinea to suppress the slave trade. The two vessels also carried ninety African American settlers, sponsored by the American Colonization Society (ACS), which hoped to establish a colony for former slaves and liberated Africans from U.S. slave ships. The cruise resulted in the capture of nine vessels, of which four were sent to back to the United States for adjudication, three broken up in Africa, and two released because of doubts regarding their U.S. nationality. The press covered the *Cyane*'s cruise from the start, and the arrival of the prize vessels and the trials of the crew elicited denunciations from across the country. One widely reprinted article characterized the defendants as "freebooters and pirates," and another reported with obvious satisfaction on their status as "prisoners" who were examined before a judge and taken into custody by federal marshals, indignities never suffered by Brown or the D'Wolfs. The aura of criminality only intensified when it turned out that one of the captured vessels had been condemned the previous year as a pirate ship. These stories circulated nationally, and some southern editors took notable pleasure in the fact that some of the vessels were owned by northerners. Coming just three years after the Amelia Island affair, the *Cyane*'s cruise helped to situate slave trading firmly in a discourse of criminality.[12]

With slave trading framed as a national problem, Congress passed three slave-trade-related laws in 1818, 1819, and 1820, each designed to remedy defects in the act of 1807. The laws passed easily, but congressional debate and votes on specific amendments exposed troubling sectional differences. The catalyst for the 1818 act was a petition from the Baltimore Society of Friends, which asked Congress to address the use of foreign flags by American slavers and, citing a clause from the Treaty of Ghent in 1814, to act in concert with Great Britain to end the slave trade. The resulting law revised the act of 1807 by lowering fines from $20,000 to $5,000, presumably to ease conviction, by prescribing prison terms of three to seven years for violators, and by shifting the burden of proof from prosecutors to slave owners, requiring anyone possessing an African-born slave to demonstrate that the person had not been disembarked within the previous five years. Crucially, the act of 1818 perpetuated one of the major deficiencies of the act of 1807, leaving the fate of recaptives up to the states where they landed. Slave states usually resold them, which not only violated the spirit of the law but encouraged corruption and threatened to increase smuggling. Apart from the fact that senators from the Lower South claimed a special interest in the question of whether Africans should be sold or liberated, the 1818 debate featured little overt sectionalism. Traces, however, are visible in the votes on specific amendments. A motion to strike the clause on international cooperation attracted southern support, particularly from the cotton states, but senators from the Upper South were divided. So whereas sectionalism had not been explicitly invoked during debate, the vote on the amendments suggested an incipient divide.[13]

The following year, 1819, Congress addressed the recaptives' fate. The new bill remedied the earlier defect by calling for captives to be liberated and resettled in Africa rather than handed over to authorities in the states where they landed. The law further authorized the U.S. Navy to patrol the African coast for slavers, established a system of prize money for captured vessels, and appropriated $100,000 for enforcement, all of which resulted in the cruise of the *Cyane*. Again, sectional animosities pulsed just below the surface in the efforts of southern politicians to tar their northern opponents as slave traders, much as William Loughton Smith had done in his exposure of British and Yankee participation in the Carolina trade during the Missouri debates. When Virginia's Charles F. Mercer, a champion of colonization, informed the House that twenty U.S. slave ships had been identified in recent months, his fellow Virginian George Strother, aware that these were mostly northern vessels, proposed an amendment to name and shame those involved and their home ports. Thomas Butler of Louisiana seems to have had the same aim when he proposed an amendment requiring that all slavers taken as prizes be adjudicated in the states from which they had sailed, knowing that northern states would most often have to bear the embarrassment. Forty-five congressmen voted against the final bill, but it passed.[14]

The climax of Congress's anti-slave-trade legislation came in 1820, just after the passage of the Missouri Compromise and as news of the *Cyane*'s cruise circulated in the press. Reporting on a petition from the ACS, a House committee recommended adding slave trading to a bill on piracy. Slavers would join pirates as *hostes humani generis*, "enemies of humankind," and, like pirates, face the death penalty. A group of southern representatives sought to kill the measure, but unlike the earlier acts, this one also attracted significant opposition from northern Republicans. Seven New Englanders and three Pennsylvanians voted to table the measure, presumably out of reluctance to subject their constituents to execution for serving on slavers. Class politics may also have attracted Republican opposition, since only ships' crews were subject to being labeled as pirates; shipowners did not face the same punishment. John Randolph, the villain of the 1807 debate, led the opposition, deriding the piracy measure as "hocus pocus" and "legerdemain" while professing personal hostility to the trade itself.[15]

The piracy law of 1820 was the high-water mark of the legislative assault on the slave trade. Although it is possible to think of additional ways in which slave-trading nations might have suppressed the trade—David Eltis has identified high taxes on plantation produce and suppression in Africa itself as roads not taken—none of these were politically feasible, and it is not certain that they would have worked. The slave trade was a transnational enterprise, and only international cooperation could defeat it. After 1820, the suppression effort moved into the realm of diplomacy. The problem there, however, was that there was no precedent or infrastructure for multilateral cooperation in peacetime; the world system of the nineteenth century revolved entirely around Great Britain. It helped that the dominant global power of the era was dedicated to destroying the slave trade, but that same dominance, which shaded too often into high-handedness, stoked Anglophobia and nationalism among the lesser powers and made cooperation by potential coalition partners politically difficult.[16]

For the United States, the diplomatic battle centered on the right of British naval vessels to search suspected slave ships. In the aftermath of the Napoleonic Wars, Britain renounced the *Amedie* precedent, which had been the legal basis for wartime seizures of slave ships. Britain turned instead to a series of bilateral treaties, most notably with Portugal (1815) and Spain (1817). Under these and subsequent treaties, Portugal and Spain agreed to outlaw the slave trade, allow a mutual right of search (which translated in practice into the Royal Navy stopping Portuguese and Spanish ships), and established a system of "Mixed Commission" courts in Freetown, Cape Town, Havana, and Rio de Janeiro to adjudicate prizes.[17]

British diplomats approached the United States for a similar agreement just as Congress was tightening the laws against slave trading. President Monroe was surprisingly sympathetic, but lingering resentment from the War of 1812, fought largely over the question of British naval stops, made such a treaty politically impossible. Congress and Monroe's cabinet debated the issue repeatedly during the years 1818–1822 but with no result. In 1823, however, after the House passed a resolution in favor of international cooperation, Monroe authorized the negotiation of a "convention" with Britain that was designed to institute a mutual right to search. To address the charge that naval searches violated American sovereignty, the United States called on Britain to define slave trading as piracy, as it had done in 1820, which would effectively denationalize slavers and allow the vessels of any nation to search them, thus clearing a path to Anglo-American cooperation. As Monroe explained to Secretary of State John Quincy Adams, "If the trade is made piratical, [navy ships] must enter the vessel, & search her for slaves."[18]

Britain passed its piracy law in 1824, but the Anglo-American convention of 1824 never became a reality. Monroe first struggled to get his own cabinet to support it. With the presidential election to come later in the year, no fewer than four cabinet members were hoping to succeed him. John Quincy Adams feared that his rival at the Treasury, William Crawford, was trying to lure him into conceding a British right to search in order to harm his presidential prospects. Once Adams endorsed the agreement, the Crawfordites denounced it. In the Senate, opponents loaded the treaty with poison-pill amendments. Most were motivated by a sincere reluctance to concede unlimited scope to the Royal Navy, still a very sensitive issue to the War of 1812 generation.[19]

But that likely does not describe the motivation of James D'Wolf, whose brief senatorial career happened to coincide with the vote on the convention. Stories that D'Wolf, a Crawfordite, led the opposition to the convention do not appear to be true. The spectacle of the old slaver killing the convention would have belied the opponents' high-minded national sovereignty arguments. The Rhode Island press noted the irony of D'Wolf's presence as the Senate voted on the matter, but he issued no public statements, which allowed allies to claim that he only wanted to protect American shipping from British abuses. D'Wolf did

try to sabotage the convention with his vote. He supplied just one of
two nays on an amendment that would allow signatories to withdraw
with six months' notice, presumably in hopes of making the agreement less palatable. He employed the same strategy on two additional
amendments barring searches in American and Caribbean waters, with
the former passing and the latter coming close. And when North Carolina's Nathaniel Macon proposed delaying consideration of the treaty
for six months, D'Wolf was one of sixteen Democratic-Republican senators, including several from northeastern states, to vote in favor. On
the final vote on the amended treaty (which passed), D'Wolf was one of
thirteen nays.[20]

Tales of Captain Jim single-handedly killing the convention are
apocryphal, but he won in the end. Although the heavily amended
convention passed the Senate, Britain, exasperated by American back-
sliding on the original agreement, never approved it. Charles Mercer
of Virginia kept the faith, declaring that he would "not regard a negotiation to be dissolved, which has approached so near consummation"
and introduced successive resolutions over the years urging Presidents
Adams and Jackson to reopen talks. Most of his resolutions did not get
very far thanks to southern and Democratic opposition. The exception
was Mercer's 1831 resolution urging the president to negotiate with the
"maritime Powers of Europe" to have the slave trade declared as piracy
in international law. But the resolution only passed on the final day of
the Congress, effectively ending its progress, and it is difficult to imagine
Andrew Jackson ever taking it up. Thirty-one of thirty-two votes against
came from slave-state congressmen, all of them Jacksonians.[21]

The failure of the 1824 convention ended any serious effort on the
part of the United States to curb the slave trade for almost two decades,
Mercer's lonely crusade notwithstanding. Between 1825 and 1839, no
major address by an American president mentioned the transatlantic
slave trade.[22] The failure of the convention and long fallow period raises
the question: Was this the work of a pro-slave-trade political constituency? W. E. B. Du Bois thought so, seeing a "systematic attack" by a
"proslavery party." Later historians have discerned a mixture of motives, acknowledging southern opposition but stressing hypersensitivity
to searches of American vessels by the Royal Navy—after all, Britain

repeatedly refused to renounce impressment—along with election-year political maneuvering.[23]

Du Bois's suggestion that a "proslavery party" sank the convention is close to the truth, although not in the way he imagined. Much of Du Bois's interpretation rested on the mistaken notion that southern cotton planters needed to import enslaved African labor. In other words, an economic need for imported labor gave rise to a political movement to undermine anti-slave-trade legislation. In reality, the Cotton Kingdom drew on the Upper South and eastern slave states for labor, not on Africa.[24] With no pro-slave-trade interest, there was no pro-slave-trade political constituency, and that continued to be the case until the 1850s. That said, southern politicians were very alert to attacks on slavery in the abstract. As shown in decades of work, during the 1820s, white southerners became hypersensitive to federal power, seeing potential threats to slavery in seemingly unrelated issues, such as the protective tariff. So although few southern politicians opposed the 1824 convention out of a desire to facilitate the entry of more captives into the United States, many wanted to hold the line on the power of the federal government to act against slavery. In that light, slave-trade suppression resonated with larger sectional tensions.[25]

Even so, opposition was hardly "systematic," with slave-state delegates never voting as a bloc. Lower South legislators tended to dominate in the opposition, but this was hardly universal. Cotton-state legislators were among those voting in favor of anti-slave-trade measures, up to and including the 1824 convention. But only five slave-state senators voted against the final version of the convention, with the other eight votes coming from free states. Moreover, many Upper South legislators favored stringent efforts to end the slave trade, often in tandem with support for the ACS. Meanwhile, some northern legislators opposed these efforts, especially the piracy amendment of 1820. Efforts to weaken the slave-trade acts were not particularly systematic, either. Although the votes on the various amendments revealed southern opposition, they involved an unstable, rotating cast of characters.[26]

In the final analysis, there was no political movement in favor of the slave trade in the 1810s and 1820s. Opposition to the slave-trade acts and the convention of 1824 stemmed from a developing ideological sensitivity to attacks on slavery in any form. Those occasions when the slave trade came before Congress became opportunities to check perceived attacks on the institution itself. This in many ways summed up the failure of the United States to curb the transatlantic slave trade: as long as slavery existed as an institution, slave-trade suppression would at best take second priority and at worst serve as a proxy for slaveholding.

Collaborations with the Americans during the 1810s gave Cuban merchants and shipmasters the experience needed to undertake their own ventures. This marked a turning point in a twenty-year quest by Cuban merchants and planters to supply their own market with captives. Since the 1790s, both the Spanish colonial authorities and the Cuban planters had been uneasy about the island's dependence on foreigners to supply their colonies with enslaved labor, and they looked for solutions. When the first Cuban-owned transatlantic slaver arrived in Havana in 1792, a year before Spain permitted its subjects to engage in direct trade with Africa, residents greeted it with civic fanfare. A few Cuban merchants followed up by accompanying U.S. vessels to Africa. In one instance, the house of Santa Maria & Cuesta of Havana sent an agent to Gorée aboard the *New Adventure* of Boston, indicative of a desire to move beyond earning commissions and toward organizing voyages. That same awareness of the need for experience can be seen in an 1803 petition by a group of Havana merchants asking the Crown to incorporate the Compañía Africana de la Havana. Modeled on the old chartered monopolies, the company proposed anchoring two or three floating factories (ships supplied with trade goods) off several places in Africa. These vessels would furnish goods for trading expeditions on the mainland and rivers and would be "the school where our youth will acquire a knowledge of the traffic." Little came from the proposal.[27]

These efforts gained traction as Cuban-American collaboration accelerated during the 1810s. Spanish-Cuban captains who on earlier voyages might have sailed under the direction of an American supercargo acquired the experience needed to command voyages on their own. And as merchants accumulated contacts and experience, they moved from being junior to senior partners in their joint ventures with the Americans. A symbolic threshold was crossed in 1816, when a group of Havana merchants collaborated to establish factories of their own in upper and lower Guinea. For the latter, they commissioned Andrés Pinto de Silveira, almost certainly a Portuguese or Brazilian, to set up one on the Bight of Benin at Onim (Lagos). For upper Guinea, they commissioned "Jacobo" Faber, an American and the brother of a major Rio Pongo slaver. Although Faber's venture failed (as we shall see), it introduced Cuban traders to the Gallinas region, south of Sierra Leone, and paved the way for the complex run later by Pedro Blanco. Joint ventures in this period also introduced Cuban merchants to the trading community on the Rio Pongo, to the north of Sierra Leone, which, as we will see, quickly became a steady source of captives for the Ever Faithful Isle (as Cuba was called).[28]

By 1820, their time served and with African installations of their own, the Cuban apprentices had progressed to journeymen, even masters of the trade, and the Americans suffered a demotion of sorts. The case of Adolph Lacoste, captain of the schooner *Science,* illustrates the Americans' changed position. Lacoste worked for the Spaniard Eugene Malibran, a New York–based merchant who specialized in coffee and molasses, in conjunction with his brother in Cuba. In 1820, Malibran hired Lacoste to take the *Science* from New York to Puerto Rico, where he was to reflag it as a Spanish vessel and sail it to Africa. Malibran was interested primarily in Lacoste's American citizenship and navigational abilities, not his commercial acumen. For that, Lacoste was to rely on detailed written instructions that were "given by a very experienced person, and it is important to follow them as much as will be possible for you." Meanwhile, some Americans in the Cuban trade were now getting out. Edward Spalding, for example, continued to do business in Trinidad de Cuba, but there is little suggestion that he directly involved himself in the slave trade. The increased punishment under American law may have driven out a few, mostly sailors, but the maturation of the Cuban slave trade was probably much more decisive.[29]

Cuban traders still needed American vessels, however. As Cubans organized more voyages, and as American and British direct participation declined, the problem grew. Local shipbuilding was not up to the task, as sugar making consumed the necessary timber. Enter the Americans, with their numerous shipyards, especially those on Chesapeake

Bay, which rose in significance with the deforestation of southern New England. Chesapeake shipwrights specialized in sharp-built vessels that traded cargo capacity for speed, which made them popular during the embargo and War of 1812 eras. In peacetime, however, the speed-over-capacity formula made them less popular, so with each shipyard turning out an average of two to three vessels per year, builders needed customers. Any vessel that did not sell locally could be loaded with cargo and sent to another port for sale, and if no sale resulted, the vessel could simply try another port. With Britain barring its own merchants from purchasing U.S.-built vessels after 1812, Latin America and the Caribbean became vital markets for American shipbuilders. Starting in the 1820s, then, American participation in the slave trade increasingly centered on supplying ships. As a Freetown resident wrote in 1822, "There is scarcely a slave vessel of any description on the coast that may not be traced, at one time or other, to original American proprietorship."[30]

In addition to selling vessels directly to Cuban merchants, Americans began acting as ship brokers. The ship broker was a relatively new occupation, a consequence of a major restructuring in the global shipping business. From medieval times, merchants usually owned the vessels that carried their cargoes, though ownership was often divided by shares. The emergence of a regularly scheduled New York–Liverpool packet service in 1817 changed the economics of American shipping. Keeping to a schedule meant that the packets could not wait to fill their holds. At the same time, vessels grew in size, leaving them with ever larger holds to fill. Commerce and shipowning, which had long been connected, increasingly became separate, specialized pursuits. The transformation took time, but by 1830 most American shipping probably operated on the new, specialized model. Other maritime powers underwent a similar restructuring, albeit with variations in timing and circumstance. It was a global phenomenon.[31]

Ship brokers brought merchants and shipowners together. Brokering was Charles Tyng's main business in the 1840s, but the previous generation of American merchants pioneered this mode of involvement in the Cuban slave trade. In 1830–1831, for example, the Havana firm of Murdock, Storey & Co. handled the slaving brig *Almirante*. That made the owners of that firm slave traders, without a doubt, but that was hardly their main line. Advertisements in a Havana newspaper show them selling the occasional vessel, probably on commission, but mostly brokering cargo space on vessels bound for ports as diverse as Boston, Gibraltar, and the Netherlands. James J. Wright of Santiago de Cuba was another broker who, in tandem with a Cuban partner named Sole, procured vessels on several occasions over the years. The ship brokering activities of Murdock, Storey & Co. and Wright typified American slave trading in the 1820s and early 1830s.[32]

Most of the vessels procured by these brokers were constructed in the United States, so the percentage of U.S.-built ships should offer some evidence of their level of involvement. Unfortunately, information on the place of construction for slave ships during 1821–1834 exists for only 14 out of 370 vessels departing from Cuba. Of these, 6 vessels (43 percent) were built in the United States, which seems low but is probably not too far from the true figure. Records for the years after 1835 are much more complete and suggest that American shipyards supplied about 63 percent of the vessels in the slave trade at large, but this was partly because of the "equipment clause" that was added to the Anglo-Spanish treaty of 1835, which resulted in increased American participation, more captures, and more information. Still, there is little doubt that U.S.-built ships were becoming very important to the slave trade.[33]

As Cubans took the lead in the slave trade, and as Americans increasingly gravitated toward brokerage, the heyday of the American supercargo ended. The story of one of the few "American" supercargoes of the post-1820 period illustrates the shift. Isidro Powell was born in Havana to American parents and spoke English and Spanish fluently. He began his career as a clerk in a Havana merchant house and later moved to the American enclave in Matanzas, where he specialized—almost certainly with some level of American involvement—in the Rio Pongo and Gallinas trades. His extensive contacts on the upper Guinea coast and reputation for "considerable" skill in the slave trade were surely what induced a Cacheu-based Portuguese slaver named Rosa Carvalho Alvarenza to hire him as supercargo in 1831. On her behalf, Powell first went to Cabo Verde, where he chartered the schooner *Rosa* (thereby procuring Portuguese colors), sailed to Cacheu, and took on one hundred captives on Carvalho's account. Under their agreement,

Powell would transport the captives to Matanzas, where he would pay Carvalho a fixed price for each one. The *Rosa* never reached Matanzas, because the vessel was captured, but the voyage, featuring an American supercargo who was actually Cuban but was caught while working for a Portuguese trader, illustrates the changed nature of the U.S. slave trade.[34]

With slave trading illegal in the United States as of 1808 and in the Spanish Empire as of mid-1820, collaborations between Americans and Cubans were by definition criminal networks. These networks were similar in many ways to criminal organizations in other times and places, particularly in their reliance on brokers to transact business across national boundaries. And because sailing a slave ship directly into Havana would have attracted unwanted British attention, clandestine disembarkations in remote areas became the rule. This practice forced slavers to construct networks of boatmen and safe houses in rural areas. By contrast, in the counting houses of Havana, slavers operated almost as legitimate businessmen. Official corruption and toleration were the principal enabling factors. Broad sections of Cuban-Spanish society, right up to the policy makers in Madrid, believed the slave trade was necessary to the island's prosperity, which meant that treaty obligations could be ignored. One captain general reportedly received a half ounce of gold for every captive landed. Voyage organizers sold shares openly. The Bank of San Fernando, founded in 1832, reportedly lent to slavers. Shipowners used the Tribunal de Comercio, Havana's merchants' court, to enforce contracts (though they were probably careful not to admit to gross violations of the law). And, crucially, slavers were able to insure their voyages through two separate companies, in violation of the basic principal that policies on illegal voyages were unenforceable. Illegality would eventually undermine all of these institutions, but for the time being it was possible to act almost openly.[35]

Back in the United States, a series of court decisions made it increasingly difficult for slavers to conduct business as usual by undermining the enforceability of insurance policies and other contracts. In the earliest case, *Murden v. Insurance Company,* a Massachusetts court voided the policy on a vessel that had sailed for Africa in June 1807 but arrived in Havana after January 1, 1808. The policy had stipulated that the vessel could not stay in Africa for longer than four months and that the company would not be liable for any losses incurred after December 1, 1807. Similarly, in *Touro v. Cassin*, a Massachusetts court cited the old 1788 state law against slave trading in holding that promissory notes used to pay the premium on an illegal slaving voyage were void. But the most important case was *Fales v. Mayberry* (1815), in which a federal court in Rhode Island ruled that any and all contracts pertaining to illegal voyages were unenforceable, even those entered into in good faith. Decisions like these confirmed to slavers that the vast majority of business would have to be conducted in Cuba's friendlier legal environment.[36]

Later decisions did carve out exceptions, particularly in cases when the plaintiffs convinced a jury that the voyage was not originally intended as a slaving voyage. In one case involving a life-insurance contract, the sister of the dead captain managed to collect by arguing that her brother had not planned to go to Africa but that the nature of the voyage changed after embarkation. By 1845, the notion that "a subsequent illegality, not contemplated or intended by the assured when the policy was effected, can never wholly defeat the insurance" was an established principle of insurance-related case law.[37] In fact, a few slavers actually won suits in U.S. courts. Several of these involved traders from the Rio Pongo, who brought cases in the United States on the rationalization that no competent courts existed in Africa. In *Greenwood v. Curtis* (1810), for example, a Massachusetts court upheld an 1802 contract made on the African coast on the grounds that the slave trade was not illegal in Africa or in South Carolina, the vessel's destination, at the time of signing. By the legal principle of comity, in which one state must recognize the validity of another's laws, the contract was legal. Additional actions followed, as when the executors for the estate of a supercargo who died on a voyage in 1817 sued Daniel Botifeur, a slaver who split his time between Cuba and the Pongo, for his "privilege" of eight captives. The captain's executors lost the case, although on grounds other than the illegality of the contract. And in 1823, relatives of the Pongo trader John Fraser successfully contested his will in a Charleston court, with another Pongo slaver, Stiles Lightbourn, given power of attorney to make decisions on their behalf.[38]

The near total absence of American naval patrols contributed to an environment in which slavers could operate quasi-openly. Congress had appropriated funds for naval patrols in the act of 1819, but most of those went to support the Liberian colony. Between 1823 and 1841, only twenty-two U.S. naval vessels visited Africa, again focusing more on Liberia than on interdiction. These constituted the whole of the American naval suppression effort. Six of those years saw no patrols at all. Poor naval enforcement emboldened slavers by minimizing the chances that they would be caught. It became clear in later years that a large percentage of criminal trials for slave trading originated in naval captures (the others stemmed from denunciations in port). Indeed, naval interdiction produced the only execution of an American citizen for slave trading.[39]

One frequently overlooked arena of American participation in the illegal slave trade was on the African coast. U.S. citizens established permanent factories in the Rio Pongo estuary in the late eighteenth century. Although some of the Pongo traders, such as Thomas Gaffery and Benjamin and Thomas Curtis, came from New England, the strongest links were to Charleston, South Carolina, and its economic hinterland, including Georgia and Florida. Other Pongo traders, such as John Irving, John Fraser, and Stiles Lightbourn, were not American-born but had strong personal and business ties there. The Rio Pongo constitutes a unique chapter in the annals of the American slave trade. For the first and only time, American slavers owned and ran factories on the African coast. In the 1810s and 1820s, there were no fewer than thirteen American installations in the Pongo, where they handled a mostly American but also a growing Cuban clientele. Next to the building of vessels, the procurement of captives on the Rio Pongo many have constituted the most significant mode of American participation in the post-1808 slave trade.[40]

The Rio Pongo was an ideal source of captives for the illegal era. In addition to enjoying good links with interior trade routes, the Pongo's location in a labyrinth of mangroves, streams, and islands made it difficult for naval patrols to approach with any stealth. Multiple channels connected the Pongo with the Atlantic, which made it almost impossible to blockade. The installations themselves were a combination of fortress and prison, surrounded by high mud palisades to defend against attacks from without and rebellion from within. The most elaborate had towers atop the battlements and mounted dozens of artillery pieces. Factories also included comfortable residences for the trader and his clerks, housing for the numerous factory slaves and *grumetes* (laborers), and warehouses for trade goods. Lightbourn's factory stood on a rise overlooking the river, enclosed by a square mud wall with musket holes for defense. Paul Faber's double ramparts enclosed a compound that was laid out in the manner of a Cuban plantation, with a large *batey,* or courtyard, that was filled with fruit trees.[41]

The Americans established themselves on the Rio Pongo by marrying into the kinship system that governed politics and trade. The Baga were the area's "firstcomers," who chose political leadership through a council of elders that was linked to the Simo secret society. During the eighteenth century, Susu traders arrived in the region and intermarried with the Baga firstcomers. The new arrangement benefited both, since the Susu were a Mande people who enjoyed strong trade connections with the interior. By the start of the nineteenth century, a dual system had emerged, consisting of "land kings," legitimated most often through Baga lineage, and political chiefs, usually of Susu descent. The leading trader of the era was the legendary "Mongo John" Ormond, the son of a British sailor and an elite Susu woman. Educated in Liverpool, Ormond returned to the Pongo in about 1805, after a long maritime career, and laid claim to political chiefhood (and the title "Mongo") through his mother's Susu lineage and with her kin group's support. The Americans in the region, such as Benjamin Curtis, Stiles Lightbourn, and the brothers Paul and Jacob Faber, married into local Baga and Susu families, which gave them standing, but they were never able to claim political power comparable to Ormond's. Their position was governed by the landlord-stranger convention, by which the former offered protection in exchange for a tax on trade, a ground rent, and general deference. By the 1820s, a second generation was coming of age, men like Benjamin Curtis Jr. and his brother Thomas, fluent in both European and African ways. In other cases, the traders' widows took over their operations and became known as *nharas,* or "big women."[42]

British attacks during the 1810s tested the stability of these relationships. Successive governors at Freetown viewed the Pongo as a problem.
Not only was it a slave-trading enclave, it was full of Americans with
contraband trade goods, who, between 1812 and 1814, were officially enemies of Britain. From Freetown, the British mounted a series of raids
against the Pongo traders, destroying factories and capturing ships and
crew. Following the war, Britain claimed possession of the nearby Isles
de Los, which shut down a bulking center for the slave trade, as it tried
to establish a commercial monopoly based on "legitimate" goods. British raids continued into 1820, as officials in Freetown feared that the
ACS might use the area to resettle former slaves. British pressure both
disrupted the slave trade and fractured the Pongo's trading alliances.
Some traders, such as Benjamin Curtis, declared their allegiance to
Britain and promised (falsely) to abandon the slave trade for legitimate
trade. The move strained Curtis's relationship with his landlords, who
unequivocally wanted the slave trade to continue.[43]

The situation in the 1810s was further complicated by the intervention of the Futa Jallon state, which was directly connected to the area
via the trading paths that ran from the coast into the highlands. Futa
Jallon had continued as a source of captives, despite strictures on the
sale of captives to non-Muslims. The extensive warfare of the late eighteenth century was over, and Futa Jallon now acquired captives through
smaller raids on the neighboring Koranko and Limba peoples. Theophilus Conneau, who visited Futa Jallon in the late 1820s, reported that
some Fulbe dealers also resorted to the use of an "African press-gang,"
meaning abduction, against the residents of one of its own slave villages.
This was a clear violation of the strictures that governed slavery and
points to an ongoing crisis in Futa Jallon brought on by abolition. The
decline of the slave trade in some areas, such as the Gambia, had presented Futa Jallon with a problem, and the leadership oscillated between
emphasizing new "legitimate trade" ties with Sierra Leone and continuing the slave trade. Those clerics who were uncomfortable selling captives to non-Muslims favored legitimate trade, but coastal groups often
blocked the roads to Freetown, the main outlet. So although Futa Jallon
did engage in legitimate trade, the difficulties associated with it, along
with the economic strength of the Pongo slavers, kept the slave trade

alive. Fulbe agents increasingly appeared in the region to ensure loyalty and to collect taxes. Among local slavers, Ormond enjoyed the closest ties with Futa Jallon, and was even able to call upon it for military support. His factory on the Bangalan basin became a major stopping point for the caravans that arrived during every dry season. Americans like the Fabers and Lightbourn also enjoyed close ties with Futa Jallon.[44]

The Rio Pongo traders were, in essence, commission merchants. Their strong connections to both South Carolina and Cuba brought numerous vessels with consignments for specific traders. The standard practice since 1809 was to share the commission with the other traders. This was both practical, since it was often impossible for a single merchant to fill an entire hold with captives, and advantageous, since it eliminated competition among traders. Once the price was set and the trade goods delivered to the appropriate merchants, the landlord took his percentage and the vessels departed for Cabo Verde to wait for the captives to be delivered, in a desperate attempt to avoid the river's notorious fevers. The tactic rarely worked, and there are reports of vessels losing all or nearly all of their crews to disease. Meanwhile, the Pongo traders sent the goods inland via their own networks. In this way, American and European credit was extended into the interior of Africa, with the nominal term being thirty days but in practice much longer. During the dry season, Fulbe caravans carried the goods directly to the Futa Jallon, but when the rainy season made travel impossible, factory employees went on "trading expeditions" by boat to neighboring coastal areas.[45]

Given the amount of time needed to procure captives, which could run to several months, the goods carried aboard a given ship were not the same ones used to pay for the captives who were embarked on that ship. Pongo traders maintained a continuous trade with their counterparts in the interior, warehousing and advancing credit in the form of goods and collecting in the form of captives and other commodities. The continuous circulation of credit and commodities sped the delivery of captives to the factories, which in turn pleased the factors' New World customers and kept the business coming. One veteran slaver argued that the Pongo traders functioned as the region's bank. Captives, he said, were both currency and "walking" commodities that could be "transform[ed] into a draft on sight, with the advantage that it carries itself." Slave dealers along the various routes, he said, "collect and pay debts, and in emergency they take the place of the Bailiff and kidnap in the shape of sequestration."[46]

Gradually over the 1810s and 1820s, the Rio Pongo became more tightly connected with Cuba. With so many Cuban-American collaborations of the 1810s focused on upper Guinea, and especially the Pongo, it was almost inevitable that Cuban traders would take over those networks once they came of age. Spanish became one of the languages spoken on the Pongo, and the traders began to use Havana's Tribunal de Comercio as a legal forum. Cuban-American traders like Isidro Powell, mentioned earlier, and Esteban Tillinghast, the Matanzas-based son of a Rhode Islander who was probably involved in the Carolina trade, led the way, but they were soon followed by others with no American ties. The resemblance of Faber's compound to a sugar plantation was probably not accidental: it was likely the work of Cuban artisans.[47]

Despite the profitability of the slave trade, the Rio Pongo of the nineteenth century was riven by factionalism and conflict. When the Americans arrived, the region was under the nominal political control of Cumba Bali and his clan, who were clients of Futa Jallon. Around 1800, Uli Kati displaced Cumba Bali as the nominal political chief, though his actual power was limited to the river's right bank. Most of the Americans resided on the right bank, so they naturally allied with Uli Kati, who quarreled sporadically with Futa Jallon. When the War of 1812 began and the British began raiding the Americans' compounds, they relied on Kati for support. When Kati died in 1816, Americans like Benjamin and Thomas Curtis, Stiles Lightbourn, and David Lawrence reaffirmed their allegiance to Kati's heir, Yati Yende. This set up a confrontation with Ormond, whose fortunes were more closely tied to the Futa Jallon. In 1824, when Ormond attempted to block the paths connecting Futa Jallon with rival traders, Yende's strangers, including the Curtises, Lawrence, and Lightbourn, attacked Ormond's establishment. Ormond then called upon his Futa Jallon allies to retaliate, which resulted in the destruction of Lawrence's factory.[48]

Ormond won the Pongo civil war, propped up by Futa Jallon. Ormond's rivals continued to trade, but after his death in about 1832, the Pongo was directly subject to the vicissitudes of Futa Jallon politics. There, the ongoing rivalry between the Alfaya and Soria factions, which dated to the mid-eighteenth century, came to the Pongo. When Yende Yati, the Americans' landlord, died in 1842, it pitted Uli Kati's old strangers and clients against those of his predecessor, Cumba Bali. By then, the Lightbourns and Fabers were aligned with the pro–Futa Jallon faction, but the Curtises were still tied by blood and marriage to the Kati clan. The Futa Jallon faction, backed by a slave army that had been raised by the Lightbourns and Fabers, won the day but agreed to consult with their rivals. The Curtises' position on the Pongo was preserved, and the region continued to be a major source of captives until the final decline of the slave trade in the 1850s.[49]

Americans were also active on the Gallinas River, less as principals and more in support of their Spanish-Cuban employers. The Kerefe, which is the Vai name for the Gallinas, is a small stream about three miles northwest of the much larger Moa River. The Kerefe consists of a maze of small mangrove-choked creeks that are covered, as one visitor said, in a "gloomy canopy" of vines. The river does not stretch far into the interior, and only small boats can navigate any distance upstream. Low islands form a lagoon at the mouth, and much of the coast to the north and south is essentially swamp. With multiple channels and inland water connections to Sherbro, the Gallinas was difficult to patrol, an ideal site for an illegal installation. In that sense, the Gallinas bore a passing resemblance to the Rio Pongo.[50]

The resemblance ends there. While the Pongo had been an important source of captives since at least 1750 (and likely earlier), the Gallinas only emerged as one during the 1790s. The main reason was that the Gallinas did not enjoy the same strong inland trade connections as the Rio Pongo did with Futa Jallon. The Juula and other networks, while not entirely absent at Gallinas, were nonetheless much weaker than on the Pongo. The main inland trade route from the Gallinas had two branches, one leading straight toward Falaba in the Mende country, the other leading westward closer to the coast, to the Krim-speaking areas. Recent analysis of the names of liberated Africans embarked at and nearby the Gallinas confirms that the almost seven in ten captives came from within one hundred miles of the coast, with 56 percent consisting of Mende and Sherbro names. The *Amistad* captives, who had originally embarked from Gallinas, were typical in that respect, with fifteen of thirty-six telling interviewers that they came from the "Mendi country," along with Temne, Koranko, and Bandi speakers from surrounding areas.[51]

The Gallinas traders also differed from their Pongo counterparts in that they never married into the local elite. King Siaka, the ruler of the Gallinas kingdom, kept a tight control over the trade. He consolidated power over the region sometime after 1808, likely with the help of arms and powder bought with captives. Initially, Siaka traded directly with slavers and enjoyed a reputation for prompt delivery of captives, but after a rebellion in the barracoons in 1825, he decided to let strangers run the factories and charged a duty on those shipped. All of this suggests that Siaka may have seen intermarriage and the resulting Eurafrican lineages as a potential threat to his own power. After all, he had long experience with existing lineages, such as the Corker, Rogers, and Gomez families, groups with their own trade links, who could become enemies just as easily as allies. Whatever the reason, Siaka never let the white traders of the Gallinas acquire the same rootedness or political power as their counterparts on the Pongo.[52]

In the first decade of the nineteenth century, when the earliest known factories operated, most dealers appear to have been of British origin. The arrival of "Jacobo" Faber, an American and brother of the Pongo's Paul Faber, in 1816, marked the beginnings of the Spanish-Cuban era in the region's history. Faber's backer was José Ricardo O'Farrill y Herrera, principal of one of Cuba's major slave-trading firms. O'Farrill advanced Faber 12,514 pesos to set up the factory, with more promised for the actual purchase of captives. In exchange for setting up the factory, Faber would earn a 5 percent commission on all captives sold in Havana. To get started, Faber chartered four vessels, including the Boston schooner *Iris,* and hired William L. Reaney, a Boston merchant specializing in West India goods, to work as his chief factor. Faber had bought out an old Liverpool dealer at Gallinas, which became his base. Using the *Iris* as a floating factory and the American crew as his ferrymen, he dispatched goods to Vai slavers up the Gallinas and to smaller out-factories to the south at Mano, Sugare, Cape Mount, Cape Mesurado, and Bassa. Meanwhile, Spanish-crewed vessels arrived from Havana to transport the captives across the Atlantic.[53]

The O'Farrills' venture failed. Faber's knowledge of the Pongo apparently did not transfer to Gallinas, since he foolishly began his activities during a war between King Siaka and Amara Lalu, the two most powerful political figures in the region. In December 1816, Faber received a letter from Siaka, rejecting Faber's profession of neutrality and demanding that he cease supplying his enemies. When Faber did not comply, Siaka and his allies attacked Faber's factory. As Faber's chief factor, Reaney, fled to safety aboard one of the ships, local forces, aided by two American slave ships, plundered the installation. Faber and his men had to flee thirty miles overland to safety. Faber returned to Cuba in 1819 having dispatched a total of 691 captives, fewer than the company had hoped, although with good prices, the partners turned a reasonable profit.[54]

The demise of the O'Farrills' Gallinas venture did not discourage Cuban traders. In the wake of Faber's escapade, more Cuba-based traders set up shop. One of these was the notorious Pedro Blanco, a licensed pilot from Málaga, who skippered slavers for Santiago Cuesta y Manzanal. In 1828, he established himself as a slave dealer on the Gallinas, and over the next dozen or so years became a major force in the Cuban slave trade. Blanco's network, and indeed those of all of the Gallinas traders, was essentially Spanish-Cuban. Merchant Lino Carballo handled business in Havana, and a circle of trusted correspondents, including one in Baltimore and one in New York, furnished occasional goods and services. Blanco's New York connection was the Cádiz-born Peter Harmony, who advertised himself as a merchant specializing in the Cuban molasses and sugar trade. Harmony had been connected with Eugene Malibran's slaver *Science* and later worked with the Zuluetas, Cuba's premier slave-trading family. Some of his slave-trading profits almost certainly helped to fund his Harmony Manufacturing Co. of Cohoes, New York. Robert Barry, Blanco's Baltimore contact, was a merchant specializing in trade with Latin America. Though members of the Pedro Blanco network, both men played a distinctly auxiliary role.[55]

American citizens also played a supporting role at Gallinas factories. According to a French seaman who left a detailed description of the
Gallinas in the early 1820s, American and British employees there made
frequent trips to inland bulking stations, which probably included King
Siaka's town of Kindama and possibly the centers that dotted the main
road from the coast. To evade criminal prosecution, the Americans on
the Gallinas hid their nationalities by using only first names and conducting their business in Vai and other local languages. For a time, at
least, the Gallinas even featured a school for the children of the local
elite (and presumably those of the factors), where lessons were given
in English.[56]

The Gallinas was a miserable place, even by the standards of the
slave trade. François Hataulx, the French seaman who visited in the early
1820s, compared it unfavorably with the Rio Pongo, noting that the traditional African restriction on selling "family slaves," or those born into
the community, did not operate on the Gallinas, a charge corroborated
by John Frazer, a liberated African. Captives, Hataulx noted, were kept
strictly separate from free residents, and those who did become familiar
with a free resident could find themselves suddenly subject to "insult-
ing taunts upon their abject condition, to which cuffs and kicks, and
other acts of the most degrading violence are generally added." Chronic
food shortages added to the misery. The Gallinas soils were not fertile,
and the region relied on rice imports from outlying areas. George Howland, Faber's employee, described "several hundreds or thousands" of
captives, subject to beatings and brandings, and kept during the rainy
season in a "large pen" with no roof, with only a small piece of bark
cloth to wear. Rations were a few palm nuts per day, which left the captives "emaciated." Captives aboard a departing Spanish schooner were
so hungry that when the vessel foundered in the surf off Gallinas, before
abandoning ship they made sure to eat the rice that had been cooking
on the stove.[57]

With Blanco and other Cuba-based traders running the factories,
the Americans played their usual auxiliary role. No doubt, some Americans worked at the factories through the end of the transatlantic slave
trade, which in the Gallinas came in the 1850s. And as the shipping news

column of the Freetown newspaper reveals, American legitimate traders frequently stopped in the Gallinas. One of these was Jacob Faber's former boatman, George Howland, who returned to the Gallinas in 1822 as a mate aboard a vessel in the ivory and dyewood trade. The slave trade had by this time completely displaced the trade in other commodities, so Howland's supercargo decided to sell some of their goods to the seven French and Dutch slavers riding at anchor just beyond the surf. These goods, Howland later said, "they no doubt exchanged for slaves," a perfect illustration of the symbiosis between the American legitimate and slave trades.[58]

In the years after 1808, the American slave trade had transformed. The slaving dynasties that dominated Rhode Island for generations were almost all out of the business by 1815. Even the D'Wolfs were largely finished with slave trading (though not with plantation slavery) by 1820. Newport and Bristol, where slave trading had once been deeply embedded in civic life, were now ordinary, provincial ports. Indeed, no American city of the era can be said to have been a true "slaving port." Baltimore provided ships, and Charleston furnished supplies and occasional legal services, but these activities were of minimal importance to the economic lives of those cities; the axis of the American slave trade now ran between Havana and the Rio Pongo. American slavers, who in 1807 were central figures in the global slave trade, were, within a dozen or so years, providing auxiliary services to Cuba-based merchants.

Illegality and escalating penalties for slave trading drove these changes. The acts of 1807–1820 were not sufficient to end slave trading altogether. As long as American politicians and diplomats refused to permit Royal Navy searches, or until Congress committed to a consistent, robust system of U.S. Navy patrols (neither of which was politically feasible), the trade would continue. But the acts of 1807–1820 were still significant, even transformative. They made it impossible to be both respectable and a slave trader, and they forced those wanting to pursue the trade to move offshore. The shift to Cuba had the unintended consequence of reversing the polarity of the Cuban-American mercantile relationship. Whereas Americans initially used Cuba as a staging ground and the Spanish flag as a cover, Havana-based merchants were soon using them to procure vessels and goods. Although events after 1835 revived American involvement in the transatlantic slave trade, the fundamental, structural changes of the 1810s and 1820s were never to be reversed.

T • E • N

Shills, Hirelings, and True Believers, 1835–1865

By 1835, American participation in the transatlantic slave trade consisted almost entirely in providing ships. American merchants rarely organized voyages of their own, and even American seamen were a rare sight aboard vessels. This diminished presence reversed in the later 1830s, as Americans began turning up everywhere. The cause was the adoption of equipment clauses in the treaties between Britain and the major slave-trading powers. With the clauses, Courts of Mixed Commission could condemn vessels even when there were no captives aboard. The simple presence of chains and shackles, excess provisions, large water casks, extra planking (for a slave deck), grates rather than hatches (for ventilation of the hold), and large boilers (for cooking), was now sufficient. Because the United States still refused to allow Britain the right of search, slavers everywhere responded to the equipment clauses by employing U.S.-registered vessels. The use of the Stars and Stripes as a flag of convenience brought more Americans into the transatlantic slave trade, though it did not alter their subordinate position; Spaniards, Cubans, Portuguese, and Brazilians continued as the principal orchestrators. Americans did become even more important as suppliers of vessels, however, and many discovered that their citizenship made them valuable as straw owners and "flag captains." Ship brokers, commission merchants, seamen, even bystand-

ers with no maritime skills fronted for a geographically scattered, poly-
glot collection of merchants. This was the American slave trade in its
final iteration.

Illegality continued to shape the trade, for Americans more than
most. U.S. law had grown progressively more restrictive during the
1810s, culminating in the designation of slave trading as a capital of-
fense in 1820, and American slavers became role players in Cuban networks, which were comparatively resistant to legal pressure. After 1835,
however, it became increasingly difficult to use the normal institutions
of business to enforce contracts, to insure vessels, and to send remittances from slaving ventures. Slavers met these challenges by construct-
ing ever more sophisticated networks of brokers, shills, bagmen, agents,
and corrupt officials. These networks were designed not only to evade
the law, but to create mechanisms of trust and regularity outside of the
legal system. As Americans became full-fledged (if junior) members of
international criminal networks, New York emerged as the slaving capital of the Atlantic, with the number of vessels leaving from U.S. ports
reaching heights not seen since the Carolina slave rush of 1804–1807. As
this occurred, a small number of southerners, true believers in the righ-
teousness of slavery, began to agitate for a repeal of federal slave-trade
legislation. Although they generated a great deal of sound and fury and
have entered the popular imagination as the embodiment of the illegal
American slave trade, these amateurish slaver-ideologues were more interested in politics than trade and ultimately organized only a handful
of voyages. In reality, most American slavers were maritime professionals serving the Brazil and Cuba trades.

In 1835, after nearly a decade of diplomatic pressure, Britain prevailed
on Spain to agree that vessels carrying slave-trading equipment but no
captives could be condemned before the Courts of Mixed Commission.
The previous treaty, the Anglo-Spanish convention of 1817, lacked such
a clause, and as a result only those vessels that were caught with captives
aboard could be condemned. Spanish officials, arguing that the colony
needed a steady supply of enslaved labor to prosper, were prepared to
defer action indefinitely. In 1835, the Spanish Liberal government finally
agreed to a new treaty that included an equipment clause as the price for

British support in the Carlist Wars. Condemnations soared, as British cruisers could intercept vessels before they even made landfall in Africa. Britain also began destroying condemned slavers to prevent their repurchase and reuse.[1]

The equipment clause came into effect just as the Cuban sugar economy was reaching maturity. Fueled by the demand for sugar in the United States and Europe, Cuban planters had spent the 1820s expanding into new regions. Taking advantage of the latest technology, they soon commanded the world's most advanced plantation society. Steam-powered mills first appeared early in the century and spread slowly but steadily. The first railroad, linking Havana and Güines, was completed in 1838. This and later railroads opened new regions to sugar planting, driving growth to even higher levels. An emergent merchant-banker class, fluent in the ways of modern finance and linked to the commercial houses of London and New York, backed the transformation. Of course, plantation expansion required ever increasing numbers of laborers. The 1830s saw more than two hundred thousand enslaved Africans landed in Cuba, more than in any other decade. A majority of the captives arrived aboard Spanish/Cuban-owned vessels, but Portuguese/Brazilian merchants were responsible for a significant share. As near as can be determined, only about 4 percent of the captives landed in Cuba during the 1830s arrived aboard bona fide American vessels, virtually all of which appear to have sailed from Havana.[2]

The equipment clause in the Anglo-Spanish treaty of 1835 ushered in a brief period in which nearly half of all Cuban vessels were captured by the Royal Navy. Slavers fled the Spanish flag for those without equipment-clause treaties. Portugal was the leading choice by far. From 1831 to 1835, Portuguese-flagged vessels accounted for less than 10 percent of the vessels carrying captives to Cuba; the Spanish flag covered almost nine in ten. In the five years following the new treaty, the poles were almost reversed, with Portuguese-flagged vessels accounting for 70 percent and Spanish vessels accounting for less than a quarter.[3]

A dozen slavers flew the U.S. flag during those same years, a distant second to Portugal as a flag of convenience. That figure, however, applies only to vessels that actually carried captives. American participation looks quite a bit larger when taking into account an innovation in the trade, the use of vessels known as "auxiliaries" to carry slaving equipment and trade goods to Africa. Auxiliaries constituted a simple and perhaps predictable response to an equipment clause that rendered Spanish vessels vulnerable to seizure for carrying shackles and food. American vessels were not subject to seizure for carrying these items, but American citizens were potentially subject to the death penalty for participating in the slave trade. It became common, then, for American vessels to carry the equipment to Africa, leaving Spanish- (or Portuguese-) flagged vessels to carry the captives back to Cuba. The U.S. crew would return either as passengers aboard the slaver or on another vessel. In 1836, British and American authorities suspected that five U.S.-flagged vessels had been involved in the slave trade. The following year it was eleven, rising to nineteen in 1838, and twenty-two in 1839. Few of these actually carried captives; most were auxiliaries.[4]

Variations on the theme were many, but the case of the brig *Mary*, from 1839, exemplifies the typical elements. The original owner, Joseph S. Snowden of Philadelphia, sent the *Mary* to Havana along with a power of attorney empowering merchant Pedro Manegat to sell the brig. Eight days after the *Mary* arrived in Havana, Manegat sold it to Pedro Sabate, a naturalized U.S. citizen, for $4,500, which allowed the vessel to retain its American registry. Although on paper Manegat was the seller of the *Mary*, he was in reality the buyer and had been involved in at least four previous slaving ventures. To retain U.S. registry, it was necessary to hire a U.S. citizen as the captain, who in this case was a man who called himself David Tomlinson but who had been working as a carpenter in Havana under the name of Pilo B. Tomlimerzt and who appeared in other documents as "Thomason." The crew consisted of four Americans, two Portuguese, and one Italian, but there were also five Spanish "passengers" who would man the vessel once in Africa, and one of them even kept a log. The *Mary* cleared Havana with a cargo consigned to Pedro Blanco, Lino Carvallo, and Pedro Martínez in the Gallinas, with additional goods consigned to Manegat and Tomás Echevarria, the vessel's actual skipper. A British cruiser captured the *Mary* off Cape Mount on suspicion that the U.S. flag was a cover for Spanish ownership. The Court of Mixed Commission at Freetown, however, dismissed the case on the grounds that the American flag protected the vessel from visitation by the Royal Navy in the first place. Because the *Mary* had not taken on captives, the voyage was never completed, but the flag had protected vessel and cargo from seizure and no doubt forced future captors to think twice.[5]

Americans were even more important as suppliers of vessels to Cuban (and later, Brazilian) slavers, responsible for 63 percent of those used in the 1830s, 51 percent in the 1840s, and a stunning 91 percent of those employed in the 1850s. The trend had begun in the 1810s but accelerated after 1835, especially once condemned ships began to be broken up, which forced slavers to acquire new vessels. The practice was a fillip to the American shipbuilding industry, but probably not to the extent that some historians have claimed. The United States launched 8,989 ships during the 1830s. Slavers employed an estimated 1,070 U.S.-built vessels during the same period, a figure equal to almost 12 percent of total national output. However, because many of the vessels employed by slavers were built in previous decades, as well as the fact that many individual vessels made multiple voyages, the 12 percent figure significantly overstates the importance of the slave trade to American shipbuilders. The true figure was probably much lower, probably below 5 percent. It does not appear that shipyards frequently built new slave vessels to order, although there are a few examples, particularly from Baltimore. Still, the vast majority of slave ships were certainly purchased "second hand."[6]

Moreover, the notion that the slave trade furnished a significant outlet for distressed American shipbuilders after the Panic of 1837 does not accord with the historic cycle of the industry. The leading historian of the U.S. shipping industry has characterized the years 1835–1838 as a "moderate recession" for shipbuilders, followed by a "moderate revival" from 1839 to 1846, with a "boom" beginning in 1847. That boom, however, was fueled by demand in other sectors, such as passenger service to California and the cotton trade. The ratio of American-built slave ships to overall U.S. production was only 2.5 percent in the 1840s and 1.8 percent in the 1850s, with the same caveat that many of these were older and "second hand" vessels applying. In sum, even though shipbuilders in the 1830s probably sold a few extra vessels to slavers, the actual number was likely insignificant, and the slave-ship market was even less significant in the 1840s and 1850s. That does not, however, mean that U.S.-built vessels were insignificant to the slave trade. American ships provided the backbone for the global slaving fleet from 1835 until the final ships sailed in the 1860s.[7]

No figure better exemplified the American role as purveyor of vessels than Nicholas P. Trist. Famous later as James K. Polk's wayward negotiator at Guadalupe-Hidalgo, Trist first came to the public's attention as the U.S. consul in Havana, an office he held from 1833 to 1841. Although he saw slavery as a curse on the American republic, he nonetheless viewed abolitionists, especially British ones, with contempt; and although he did not participate directly in the slave trade, Trist did more for slavers than any other American of his time. One of his duties as consul was to register all U.S. vessel transfers. The standard practice for a Cuban or Portuguese slave trader was to buy an American vessel at Havana but post-date the actual transfer until the ship arrived on the African coast. Although it was obvious that Cuban slavers were buying U.S. vessels and hiring American citizens as flag captains to evade the new equipment clause, Trist routinely signed off with no questions asked. Acting simultaneously as the Portuguese consul, he provided the same service for slavers of that nation.[8]

British authorities in Havana protested Trist's actions to the State Department. President Martin Van Buren was no abolitionist (he opposed the freedom of the *Amistad* captives, and his run as a Free Soil Party presidential candidate was still a decade away) but he regarded slave trading as a crime and publically deplored the "prostitution" of the flag as a cover for slavers. Van Buren appointed Alexander Everett of Massachusetts, a veteran diplomat, man of letters, and Democratic political operative, to investigate Trist's activities. Everett's report was scathing. Although he never interviewed Trist (who was conveniently absent during his visit to Havana), his review of the consul's correspondence and conversations with British officials led him to conclude that Trist had violated U.S. slave-trading laws, as well as more general directives against facilitating illegal activity by American citizens. Anticipating that Trist might plead ignorance regarding the purpose of the transfers, Everett argued that he must have known what he was doing and even believed that Trist felt a "decided gratification" in certifying the transfers of slavers, mostly out of contempt for the British. Trist responded with a barrage of petulant missives to the secretary of state, arguing that consuls had no right to question the motives behind a vessel transfer. If an American shipowner wanted to sell or charter a vessel, then it was not in the consul's power to prevent it. In making this case, Trist had put his finger on the most important deficiency in American slave-trade policy: with the provision of ships constituting the most important mode of American participation, there was realistically very little that could be done to prevent U.S.-built vessels from falling into the hands of slavers.[9]

As it happened, the numbers of American slavers flying the American flag soon fell, although they would remain a mainstay of the trade to the end. Changes in British policy partially diminished the appeal of the U.S. flag. When officials in Westminster learned that some Courts of Mixed Commission were refusing to try obvious misuses of the U.S. flag, they urged commissioners to rethink the question, which resulted in the quick condemnation of seven U.S.-flagged vessels. The number of slavers flying the American flag quickly dropped to just two in 1842, although this does not include auxiliaries. The policies of Gerónimo Valdés, installed as captain general of Cuba in 1842, also reduced the use of the U.S. flag. Valdés was the first governor to take slave-trade suppression seriously, instituting a ban on the purchase and reflagging of foreign vessels, among other measures. Vessels remaining in American hands, including those that were merely chartered rather than sold, could continue to fly the flag, of course, but the order foreclosed a favorite ruse. Also in 1842, the United States and Britain agreed to joint naval patrols off the African coast (as will be seen). Finally, a series of slave rebellions and conspiracies on the island in 1843 and 1844 prompted a backlash against the slave trade in many quarters of Cuban society. As planters explored alternatives, such as Chinese indentured labor, the volume of the Cuban slave trade fell sharply and did not recover for nearly ten years.[10]

The prosecution of several Baltimore shipbuilders and merchants in 1839 furnished an additional deterrent. Two were convicted but three were acquitted, and two others skipped bail. Mixed results notwithstanding, the Baltimore prosecutions set important legal precedents. The first concerned John F. Strohm, a commission merchant and con-

sul for Venezuela who dealt in everything from cigars to cheese. As agent
for a Brazil-based concern, Strohm had commissioned the building and
outfitting of two slavers and registered himself as the owner of one.
When the customs collector at Baltimore seized the vessel, Strohm argued that he had simply acted on his clients' instructions and did not
know how they intended to use the vessel. The case reached the Supreme Court, where Chief Justice Roger B. Taney's majority opinion
held that a factor's knowledge of a vessel's purpose was immaterial. Factors were agents of the owner's intent, which was clearly to engage in the
slave trade, so the conviction stood. The Taney Court issued another
important ruling in *United States v. Morris* (1840). Isaac Morris had
commanded the *Butterfly*, a Baltimore-built, Spanish-flagged schooner
that was registered at New Orleans but began its voyage in Havana. British cruisers captured the *Butterfly* off Luanda, finding no captives but
all of the usual equipment for a slaver. Morris appealed his conviction,
arguing that the act of 1800 only applied if captives were actually aboard.
The Supreme Court disagreed and upheld the conviction, establishing
a de facto equipment clause in U.S. law. American vessels continued to
figure prominently in the trade, but the legal risks were mounting.[11]

As Cuba-based traders moved away from the American flag, Brazil-
based slavers were discovering its advantages. Brazilian plantations were
in the middle of a coffee-driven expansion that depended on the slave
trade. Americans had been occasional participants in the Brazilian slave
trade since about 1800, often as part of the Río de la Plata trade. After
Britain forced open the Brazilian market in 1808, Americans became a
major source of manufactured goods and credit, trailing only the British. American merchants in Rio de Janeiro handled the exchanges and
developed strong relationships with their Brazilian counterparts. This,
along with the fact that the United States was the single largest market for Brazilian coffee, meant that Americans played a major role in
the growth of Brazilian slavery during the nineteenth century, making
it almost inevitable that they would become involved in the Brazilian
slave trade.[12]

As with Spain in 1835, a sudden vulnerability to seizure for carrying
slave-trading equipment prompted Brazilians to seek the cover of the

American flag. Neither the initial Anglo-Portuguese Treaty of 1815 nor the Anglo-Brazilian Treaty of 1826 contained an equipment clause, so slavers evaded patrols with relative ease. Britain pushed both powers to accept an equipment clause but met with the usual delays. In 1839, Lord Palmerston, then the foreign minister, unilaterally imposed an equipment clause on Portugal. The Portuguese government protested, to no avail, as slavers rallied to other banners. American firms in Rio suddenly became key nodes in Brazilian criminal networks, supplying trade goods and procuring vessels to transport those goods to Africa under the protection of the U.S. flag. Two firms stand out as particularly active in the slave trade—Maxwell, Wright & Co. and James "Diogo" Birckhead & Co. The former was a partnership between the British (Gibraltar) native Joseph Maxwell, who came to Brazil in 1809, and William Henry DeCourcy Wright, son of a former senator and governor of Maryland. Birckhead was a Maryland native who had been living in Brazil since at least the 1820s. The core business of both firms involved exchanging American wheat and flour for Brazilian coffee. Both men were close associates of Manoel Pinto da Fonseca, one of Rio's leading slave factors, furnishing him with ships and goods. Fonseca, in turn, dispensed these goods to smaller slavers in Rio. The relationship between the American firms and Fonseca therefore paralleled the Cuban configuration: Fonseca was the main organizer and financier of the voyages, and Maxwell, Wright & Co. and Birckhead, along with others, procured U.S.-flagged vessels and crews. There can be no doubt that Wright and Birckhead knew exactly what they were doing. Both men were far too experienced to be deceived.[13]

With Rio emerging as a major market for shady American shipowners, successive U.S. consuls tried to stop the transfers but were repeatedly defeated by legal loopholes. Slavers who could not find a loophole got by on naked fraud and perjury. On a few occasions, senior U.S. diplomats thwarted efforts to prevent vessel transfers. George W. Slacum was the first consul to take action against the sales. In one instance, he halted a false vessel transfer to a ship captain who was acting on behalf of James Birckhead, who in turn acted for a local slaving concern. The slavers countered by simply chartering the vessel. The U.S. chargé d'affaires even brokered the charter and told Slacum that withholding the vessel's papers "would not be justified." Consuls in Bahia and else-where reported similar activity, though on a lower scale.[14]

The situation in Rio attracted national attention after President John Tyler appointed Henry A. Wise, a Virginia congressman, as U.S. minister to Brazil in 1844. Often described as "rash," Wise had beaten an erratic path through national politics, affiliating at various times with both the Democrats and the Whigs and somehow managing to ally and then fall out with every major political figure of the era, including Andrew Jackson, Henry Clay, John Tyler, and John C. Calhoun. At a time when nuanced positions on slavery were increasingly untenable, Wise clung to the classic Virginia vision of bondage as a drag on political and economic development, but he was equally suspicious of abolitionism. He was best known as an ardent defender of the congressional "gag rule," which barred the reception of anti-slavery petitions, but later promoted the annexation of Texas in order to "mitigate [slavery's] severity." If any one theme can reconcile these contradictions, it was a strong opposition to what he termed "fanaticism." For Wise, this involved both denouncing British and American abolitionists *and* reining in the slave trade. When the scale of American involvement in the Brazilian slave trade became apparent to him, he threw himself into ending it. To those who might question his fealty to southern principles, he responded, "The fact of my being a slaveholder, is itself a pledge & guarantee that I am no *fanatic,* foolishly & wickedly bent on running amuck against any lawful property or trade." Wise's position was still typical of most southerners' at the time: support for slavery as an institution demanded opposition to the transatlantic slave trade.[15]

Wise began his campaign in late 1844 by confronting William Wright of Maxwell, Wright & Co. about his ship brokerage (as a British subject, Maxwell was beyond his influence). The two men knew each other before Wise's turn as minister to Brazil and had been on friendly terms, but Wise did not let that stop him from confronting his old acquaintance. Taken aback, the firm protested that chartering and selling vessels "has been heretofore considered a perfectly legal trade," to which Wise responded that it might indeed be legal "if done in good faith" but that a lawful act becomes unlawful "by its intentional connexion with crime." Wright then sought advice from the State Department, which responded noncommittally, saying only that it was U.S. policy to encourage commerce while deterring the slave trade and that it would be up to the courts to interpret the law. The response was apparently too equivocal for Wright, so the firm began refusing future charters and sales to obvious slavers. Wise investigated other suspected slavers, ultimately totaling between twenty and thirty cases. In the process, he alienated the Brazilian government and temporarily killed all chances for a trade deal. In addition to sending several vessels and a dozen American citizens home for trial, Wise revoked the appointments of several U.S. consuls whom he suspected of signing false ownership papers.[16]

Wise's zeal for protecting the honor of the American flag eventually precipitated a major diplomatic incident. The focus was the brig *Porpoise*, owned by G. F. Richardson and skippered by Cyrus Libby, both of Maine. The *Porpoise* was an auxiliary that had cleared Rio for Africa three times between 1843 and 1845, twice returning in ballast and once with ten slavers as passengers. When the *Porpoise* arrived for the third time, in January 1845, Wise dispatched the usual boat to pick up letters. A crew member dropped a note to one of the boatmen saying that among the Brazilian passengers were two boys who were being held as slaves. Wise called on a U.S. naval vessel to send a marine guard aboard the *Porpoise* in order to prevent the escape of passengers and crew, pending an investigation. When the Brazilian authorities learned that U.S. Marines had boarded a vessel and detained Brazilian citizens in Brazilian waters, they surrounded the *Porpoise* with soldiers and gunboats and demanded that Wise release all passengers. Wise countered by offering to release the Brazilian passengers for trial (since the slave trade was illegal under Brazilian law) and requesting the extradition of the U.S. citizens to the United States. Brazil refused, viewing such a move as a violation of its sovereignty. Left with little choice, Wise released everyone. He had erred, and the incident almost led to open conflict. Wise's diplomatic effectiveness had become null, and he left with U.S.-Brazilian relations at an ebb.[17]

Gorham Parks, the new consul, picked up where Wise left off. Because the U.S. government never took up Slacum's suggestion for a ban on all American trade to Africa from foreign countries, he was left to try half measures. Parks's main tactic was to require American captains who claimed ownership of a vessel to explain under oath how they managed to finance the purchase of the ship, as a precondition to receiving clearance to sail. The tactic failed to stop outbound traffic to Africa. Secretary of State James Buchanan had issued instructions proscribing the denial of sea letters, or permission to sail, but Parks did manage to elicit some tall stories from some of the captains. One of them, Joshua Clapp, became infamous for "owning" a fleet of nine vessels. He claimed, as most false captains did, to have raised the money by receiving advance payments on charters. John A. Forsyth's explanation was more colorful. He claimed to have bought the brig *Joseph* at auction using two years' wages and money borrowed from clerks at two mercantile houses, including Birckhead's. To this he added forty ounces in gold, earned from previous voyages, the proceeds from the sale of some horses, a stray $1,000 from an unspecified "venture," and a winning lottery ticket. Undercut by Buchanan's directive, Parks issued ten sea letters and denied only one.[18]

Shipping records kept by Consuls George W. Gordon and Gorham Parks reveal the vast scale of U.S. involvement in the Brazilian slave trade during the 1840s. By their accounts, 137 American vessels cleared Rio for Africa between 1841 and 1849, and 87 entered the port of Rio during those same years. The overwhelming majority of these—it is tempting to say nearly all of them—were involved in the slave trade. Thirty (22 percent) are on record as having embarked captives in Africa, which suggests that most of the remaining 107 (78 percent) were auxiliaries. This is not surprising given what we know about Brazilian practice, which called for flying the U.S. flag on the outbound but not the inbound passage. The vessels hailed from virtually every American port, from such major hubs as Baltimore and New York to smaller towns like Key West, Florida, and Wiscasset, Maine. Twenty vessels made at least two trips to Africa, eight made three, and one, the schooner *Morris* of Baltimore, made four round trips for a total of seven Atlantic crossings in the space of one year.[19]

The business came to an end around 1850, though not as a result of any action taken in the United States. After decades of diplomatic futility, Britain mounted naval attacks on slave-trading facilities in both Africa and Brazil. The Brazilian government responded by passing and

actually enforcing a much stronger slave-trade law. Although it was controversial and resented, the new law effectively ended the Brazilian slave
trade by 1852. That is not the end of the story, however. As the Brazilian government cracked down on slave-trading networks, many of the
slavers fled the country. When they failed to receive a warm welcome in
Cuba (a logical first choice since it was the hemisphere's last surviving
market for African captives), they tried their luck in the busiest port in
the Americas: New York.

One consequence of the ongoing Cuban trade, along with the Brazilian
episode, was the conclusion of the Webster-Ashburton Treaty in 1842.
The treaty was an effort to settle several outstanding Anglo-American
conflicts, with the issue of vessel searches by the Royal Navy being just
one of them. With the coming of the equipment clauses after 1835, Britain began stopping U.S.-flagged vessels to determine whether they were
legitimately American or just flying flags of convenience. To justify the
policy, Britain asserted a distinction between a "right to visit" for the
sole purpose of determining the "true nature" of a vessel, and a full-
scale right to search. Hypersensitive to British searches on the high
seas, the vast majority of American politicians regarded the policy as an
outrage. The conclusion of a Quintuple Treaty in 1841 between Britain,
Austria, Prussia, and Russia (France signed but did not ratify) declaring the trade to be piracy further alarmed American officials. Britain
invited the United States to sign but noted that should it refuse, the
signatories would assume the right to board American-flagged vessels.
For the Americans, the Quintuple Treaty lent urgency to the question
of searches.[20]

The Webster-Ashburton Treaty, which primarily concerned the
U.S.-Canada border, addressed naval searches in Article VIII, which
obligated the United States to maintain a permanent naval squadron
of no fewer than eighty guns off the coast of Africa. In theory, the U.S.
squadron would act "in concert and cooperation" with the Royal Navy,
with a special responsibility to stop and search suspicious U.S.-flagged
vessels. The treaty, however, barely dented the slave trade. This was due
more to a lack of interest on the part of American officials than to a
deliberate campaign of sabotage. As ever in American policy, the slave

trade was a low-priority issue, especially as the captives were not entering the United States. Few politicians of any stripe were willing to buck
the era's nationalist sentiment just to stop captives from entering Cuba.
From the start, Navy Secretary Abel Upshur, a Virginian, ignored the
recommendations of experienced naval officers and deployed a thirty-
six-gun frigate for the inaugural cruise. The choice of such a large vessel,
which alone accounted for almost half of the required guns, instantly
limited the squadron's effectiveness. The remainder of the eighty-gun
requirement would be met by three smaller vessels. A much better strategy, one that had been recommended by naval officers, would have been
to deploy many smaller vessels. That would have allowed the squadron
to cover more coastline and better patrol rivers and estuaries. Unfortunately, the single large frigate with a few smaller vessels set the tone for
much of the squadron's history.[21]

Many additional factors undermined the squadron's effectiveness.
The choice of Praia, Cabo Verde, as the base of operations meant that
vessels needed to sail more than three thousand miles to reach the principal slaving area near the Congo River. Squadrons therefore spent an
inordinate amount of time in transit rather than on patrol. They also
spent a great deal of time in temperate ports like Funchal, Madeira, to
allow crews to recover from malaria and other diseases. In addition, the
standing instructions that commanders received could be interpreted as
placing the protection of commerce above anti-slave-trade duties, which
ran counter to the treaty's stated purpose. The instructions furnished a
ready-made excuse for those commanders who lacked enthusiasm for
the task of interdiction, as several palpably did. Finally, two lawsuits by
shipowners against the naval commanders who had seized their vessels
led some to act very cautiously, although the eventual dismissal of these
cases removed the threat.[22]

There were a few bright spots. Some commanders were zealous
in their efforts. Interestingly, as a group, those officers who came from
slave states actually captured more slavers than those hailing from free
states. The single most successful was a Marylander who would later
serve in the Confederate Navy. From 1845–1859, the navy also operated
a Brazil Squadron, which was more successful than the Africa Squadron, with the *Porpoise* as its most famous capture. After 1858, under

President James Buchanan, the navy also patrolled the Cuban coast, netting a number of very well-publicized captures. The following year, the navy moved its main base from Cabo Verde to Luanda, which was much closer to the principal trading zone on the Congo River. Also in 1859, the navy finally deployed five steamboats, which had long been recognized as more effective than sailing vessels. As a result of these changes, captures rose significantly. Between 1844 and 1857, the navy seized 18 slavers, or 1.4 per year; from 1858 to 1861, it seized 17, for an average of more than 4 per year. Because vessel seizures resulted in arrests, criminal prosecutions rose. Even so, it is impossible to portray the Africa Squadron and similar efforts in Brazil and Cuba as a success. The Africa Squadron was created primarily to forestall British attempts to search American vessels. With the possible exception of the post-1858 period, it constituted only a minor obstacle to the trade.[23]

In the 1850s, the American slave trade suddenly became a major issue in national politics. Before that date, the transatlantic trade had not been a major political issue. To be certain, in previous decades there had been debate over specific legislation. Divisions were often sectional, but never could they be characterized as polarizing. Many southern legislators had supported strengthening the laws, but northern Republicans had sometimes opposed them. After 1850, two related developments combined to create, for the first time, a pro-slave-trade political movement. The first of these was the emergence of a highly elaborated pro-slavery argument, with strong connections to an increasingly scientistic discourse of race. The second was the emergence after 1853 of a political faction devoted to repealing existing slave-trade legislation. The aim was not so much to legalize the current business of American slavers, who, after all, served the Cuban market, but to repeal legislation barring the introduction of enslaved Africans into the United States.

Mid-nineteenth-century southern views on slavery saw a noticeable shift from the "necessary evil" stance of Thomas Jefferson toward the "positive good" position of John C. Calhoun in response to the Missouri Crisis, the Nullification Crisis, Garrisonian abolitionism, and the Nat Turner Rebellion. A growing insistence of African biological and cognitive inferiority abetted the shift, backed by new "scientific" studies by such figures as Samuel G. Morton, Samuel A. Cartwright, and Josiah Nott. The new biological discourse underlay the developing notion that white equality, and hence democracy itself, was only possible because people of African descent (and other non-"Caucasian" peoples) constituted the "mud-sill" of southern society. The pro-slavery implications are obvious, but as historian Sharla M. Fett has found, these ideas also influenced how white Americans viewed the transatlantic slave trade. During the late 1850s, several thousand Africans were taken from American slave ships and held in camps, pending deportation to Liberia. The popular press covered their stories, adopting a quasi-ethnographic stance that "othered" its subjects as it catered to readers' curiosity. One of the more famous images was an engraving of naked, emaciated liberated Africans aboard the New York bark *Wildfire,* which appeared in *Harpers Weekly.* This and other voyeuristic, mass-circulated images shifted American views of Africans, in Fett's words, from an Enlightenment-inspired "'noble savage' to the 'savage,'" of the Gothic imagination. The images were anti-slave-trade in their intent and did not offer direct support for pro-slavery policies. But in portraying slave-holding and enslavement in Africa as "ethnographic fact" and Africans as people without history, they reinforced an existing sense of racial difference. Needless to say, pro-slavery partisans had little trouble mobilizing discourses of African savagery to support their cause.[24]

Yet although a large majority of white Americans believed Africans and their descendants to be cognitively and culturally inferior, the link between racism and pro-slave-trade politics was never as direct as might be supposed. Simply put, white racism did not lead inexorably to pro-slavery politics, and pro-slavery ideas did not lead inevitably to pro-slave-trade advocacy. Millions of northern whites subscribed to some version of scientific racism, yet very few of them believed that slavery was a good thing, and almost all would have condemned the slave trade. Virtually all white southerners subscribed to some version of scientific racism, and most supported slavery as a positive good, yet for only a minority did these arguments add up to the need to reopen the slave trade. Pro-slavery politics and scientific racism both had strong influences on the American slave trade, but in complex ways. The impact of pro-slavery ideology on the politics of the transatlantic slave trade is best understood as a spectrum of influence, with some political developments growing directly out of pro-slavery thought, and others being influenced only indirectly.

The movement to reopen the transatlantic slave trade was the most direct outgrowth of the new pro-slavery ideology. Its logic was internally sound: if slavery was a positive good, then the process that created it must also be good. This was essentially the same reasoning that John Randolph had applied in the congressional debates of 1807–1820, although he argued the obverse, that criticism of the slave trade implied criticism of slavery. Yet it was one thing to make that point in the pre-1850 period, when pro-slavery ideology was poorly developed and sectional polarization was less pronounced. To the pro-slavery absolutists of the 1850s, on the other hand, the slightest intimation of criticism or assertion of a federal right to regulate the institution was an outrage or even an existential threat.

The movement to re-legalize the transatlantic slave trade originated in South Carolina, the hotbed of southern radicalism. It started in 1853 with the purchase of the *Southern Standard*, a Charleston newspaper, by Leonidas W. Spratt. Spratt was not a major slaveholder, but his campaign immediately attracted the attention of the state's wealthiest, secessionist, Lowcountry planters. Fueled by the intense debate over the Kansas-Nebraska Act the following year, the movement caught on among like-minded radicals. Indeed, the list of advocates is a Who's Who of pro-slavery ideologues, including the Virginia propagandist George Fitzhugh, the New Orleans editor J. D. B. De Bow, and the Alabama fire-eater William Lowndes Yancey. The movement was strongest in South Carolina, where it may even have attracted the sympathies of a majority of voters and enjoyed a minority following throughout the Lower South. However, it never enjoyed the support of a majority of white southerners, certainly when considering the Upper South. The movement's major victories came when the Southern Methodist Church rescinded its proscription of the trade and when a few southern commercial conventions passed resolutions in favor of reopening. These successes were offset by the failure of pro-slave-trade resolutions in virtually every legislative forum, including South Carolina's, where they never passed the committee stage. The most important rejection came in 1856, when the House of Representatives approved a resolution declaring the repeal of the federal slave-trading statutes "inexpedient, unwise, and contrary to the settled policy of the United States" by a margin of 183 – 8 (although it must be said, southern representatives had opposed an earlier resolution condemning the slave trade outright).[25]

The apostles of re-legalization offered a grab bag of supporting arguments. Some of these were practical in nature. Inspired by the "popular sovereignty" clauses of the Kansas-Nebraska Act, which implied that the future of slavery would depend on population growth, they argued that importing captives was necessary to allow the South to match the immigration-driven North in the battle for congressional control. Worried that rising slave prices and a corresponding decline in the percentage of white southerners owning slaves would sap political support for the institution, they argued that a reopened trade would give yeoman farmers a stake in the system. Other arguments were purely ideological. Yancey, for example, explained that he favored repealing the slave trade laws as part of a larger effort "to strip the Southern ship of State for battle" but did not favor resuming the actual trade. Only a few southerners seriously contemplated organizing voyages, and even these were largely for political purposes. Finally, many proponents fused the practical with the ideological by arguing that nullifying slave-trade laws would both grow slavery and precipitate a constitutional crisis that would force the more moderate slave states to join in secession.[26]

The most action-oriented of these ideologues was Charles Augustus Lafayette Lamar of Savannah. The son of a commission merchant who dabbled in the shipping business, Lamar had failed at a number of pursuits, including shipping, plank roads, gold mining, and the domestic interregional slave trade. After hearing Spratt speak at a commercial convention, he became a keen follower of the movement, believing that if slavery was a positive good, the slave trade must be as well. Lamar was so "crazy on that Negro question" that family members predicted he would end up either in the penitentiary or the lunatic asylum. Lamar's idea was to test the constitutionality of the slave-trade laws by presenting the courts with a fait accompli. Accordingly, he organized a voyage for his bark, the *E. A. Rawlins,* in 1857. The first voyage got no farther than Madeira and failed to procure any captives, despite the expenditure of

$1,800 in gold. Lamar's captain, a slave-trade neophyte, was scared off by rumors of British patrols in the area. Lamar decided to try again, this time with a new captain and a supercargo, though, again, neither had slave-trade experience. The pair navigated the *E. A. Rawlins* to São Tomé for provisions en route to the Congo River. When Portuguese authorities refused to clear the vessel for departure, the mate sailed away with the ship, leaving his captain and supercargo to languish in jail. The *E. A. Rawlins* returned to Savannah, having failed again.[27]

Undaunted, Lamar continued his efforts. At one point, he tried to procure and import African "apprentices," a practice pursued by the British and French in the wake of the slave trade and the topic of much discussion in the Lower South, but was foiled by the refusal of his cousin by marriage, Treasury Secretary Howell Cobb, to permit his vessel to sail. In 1857, Lamar purchased a sleek, New York–built racing yacht called the *Wanderer*. His partners in the venture were a veritable ship of fools with no fewer than three "captains," including a former salesman-lobbyist and an ex-filibuster. The *Wanderer*'s preparations were the worst-kept secret in and around New York Harbor that summer, and authorities ordered its detention as it tried to depart. After an inspection, authorities allowed the vessel to clear for Trinidad, but it sailed to the Congo River, where it took on some 487 captives. The *Wanderer* landed at Jekyll Island, Georgia, after a six-week voyage on which 80 captives perished.[28]

The rest of the story would be comical if it were not so tragic. The captives were quickly lightered to shore, marched overland, and sold. Hearing rumors of the landing and of a trio of rough-looking characters splashing gold coins around Savannah, the U.S. attorney launched an investigation. He eventually indicted several participants, including one of the captains and several sailors. Lamar himself evaded indictment by claiming before a sympathetic magistrate that he already owned the people in question, not the last perversion of justice in this case. He then bought back the *Wanderer* at an auction, managing in the process to assault a rival bidder. Feeling immune from prosecution, Lamar began driving around Savannah in a carriage with an illegally enslaved African boy. The stunt eventually brought an indictment, with additional charges for holding thirty-eight others in illegal bondage and for orchestrating the jailbreak of one of his accomplices (who surrendered the next day). Juries acquitted four participants on piracy charges; the proceeding against of one of the "captains" ended in mistrial, and yet another was acquitted of "holding" illegal captives. Prosecutors dropped the charges against Lamar when they decided they could not prove that the African-born boy had been illegally imported. Lamar then outfitted the *Wanderer* for a second voyage, which ended in fiasco when one of his partners hijacked the vessel and used it to rob other ships. Authorities seized the *Wanderer* when it entered Boston Harbor in 1859. Lamar, who in addition to his political agenda apparently hoped to profit from the voyage, claimed that almost all of the returns were eaten up by the high captive death rate and by fraud on the part of his partners.[29]

Timothy Meaher was another slave-trading ideologue, and a much more competent one than Lamar. The son of an Irish Catholic immigrant, Meaher was a native of Maine who moved to Alabama in 1835 and was eventually joined by several of his brothers. He found success, first as a steamboat captain and later as a shipowner in the lumber trade to the Caribbean, which allowed him and his brothers to branch into other businesses, including plantation ownership. Meaher's business success indicates a practical mind, but his support for filibusters like William Walker suggests that he, like Lamar, was at home in the more extreme corners of pro-slavery politics. According to later reports, Meaher first conceived the idea of organizing an African voyage in conversation with several other men aboard one of his steamers. Discussing the latest slave-trade news, one of the men opined that hanging one slaver would "scare the rest off." Meaher reportedly replied, "They'll hang nobody— they'll scare nobody," and wagered "a large sum," variously reported at either $100 or $1,000, that he could bring a slave ship into Mobile "under the officers' noses." Meaher and his partners bought the fast-sailing schooner *Clotilda* for $35,000, and loaded it with $3,500 in aguardiente, textiles, and manufactures, along with $9,000 in gold.[30]

Meaher and his captain and partner, William Foster, chose to send the *Clotilda* to Ouidah, on the Bight of Benin. They may have done so based on reports in the local press that gave the price of captives there at fifty to sixty dollars each. After a difficult outbound passage, the *Clotilda* put in at Cabo Verde, where the U.S. consul obligingly offered advice on where to trade. On arrival at Ouidah, Foster dealt directly with representatives of the Dahomey kingdom. For a new skipper like Foster, this was a risky strategy that could easily end badly, but offering one hundred dollars in specie per captive, approximately twice the usual price, brought success. Even so, Foster was forced to abandon between fifteen and twenty captives during embarkation when a suspected British cruiser was spotted on the horizon. Fearing arrest and trial on capital charges, Foster's men threatened to mutiny and only stayed with the vessel because they realized the surf was too treacherous for them row to shore.[31]

The *Clotilda* arrived off Mobile with 110 captives after a passage of forty-five days. A tug towed it up the Alabama River, the captives were disembarked, and the vessel was burned to the waterline. Word had leaked out, however, and authorities arrested Meaher on information from the tug captain. The judge in the case, however, was a pro-slave-trade friend of Meaher's, who two years previously had dismissed the case against the *Wanderer* purchasers. He performed the same favor for Meaher and his associates, asserting that the absence of any Africans meant that the evidence for prosecution was insufficient. Although some of the *Clotilda* captives were sold off to dealers and scattered, most wound up living in the area on properties owned by Meaher, his family, and his associates. This meant that when emancipation came in 1865, the *Clotilda* shipmates were able eventually to find each other and purchase land, which became known as "Africa Town." The lives of these former captives can be traced through census, court, and other types of records, along with interviews with some of the survivors done in the 1930s by Zora Neale Hurston.[32]

Although the *Wanderer* and *Clotilda* are among the best-known American slave ships, they were far from typical. The movement to reopen the transatlantic slave trade generated a great deal of political heat but resulted in very few voyages. Proponents were more interested in using the issue to bring about secession than in importing laborers from Africa. Moreover, in contrast with the professionals who worked in the Cuba and Brazil trades, the slaver-ideologues of the 1850s were neophytes. In five attempts (possibly six—there were rumors that the *E. A. Rawlins* undertook a third voyage), Lamar managed to land only one captive cargo. Meaher's success rate was better, but he seems to have overpaid, and his skipper left almost 20 percent of his captives on the beach. This was hardly a recipe for a sustainable slave trade, but these incidents have managed to convince both historians and the general public that direct importation into the United States was the predominant mode of the post-1808 American slave trade. In reality, the transatlantic captive trade to the United States accounted for a tiny number of cases. By far, the bulk of the activity was in the Cuba and Brazil trades.

"Pro-slavery internationalism" was another outgrowth of the politics of the 1850s, offering support, albeit indirect, for the transatlantic slave trade. There were multiple expressions of this ideology, but at its heart was the belief that the survival of slavery required the annexation of various circum-Caribbean lands, with Cuba as the most important. Not all annexationists supported a reopened slave trade, but the movement did enable the American slave trade by forcing politicians to take an aggressive stance against British interdiction efforts in Cuban waters. Anglo-American tension over Cuba was continuous through the decade but reached a crisis point in 1858, when Britain began patrolling the Cuban coast in addition to the African coast. As of May, the Royal Navy reported boarding 116 vessels, of which 61 were American. For President Buchanan, an annexationist and northern doughface who supported southern political causes, the British blockade of Cuba was unacceptable. After much American pressure, Britain ceased the patrols, which of course was good news for slavers. The strong opposition to British patrols off Cuba contrasts with the attitude toward the even more aggressive British action against Brazil just a few years earlier. The difference was that Brazil was far enough away not to be a target for U.S. annexationists; pro-slavery politics, by contrast, and the Monroe Doctrine more generally, made similar action by Britain in Cuba diplomatically intolerable. Any British effort to increase patrols in the Caribbean would draw automatic warnings from the United States. Pro-slavery politics thus combined with nationalism to keep the Cuban slave trade open.[33]

The pro-slavery politics of the 1850s also influenced the application of the slave-trade laws in the United States. The effect is difficult to measure because each case was unique. Complicating matters is the fact that under U.S. law, slave-trade cases were of two distinct types. One involved libels against vessels, in which the federal courts functioned as courts of admiralty, where the rules of evidence were loose and verdicts were rendered by a judge. This contrasted with criminal prosecutions against owners and crew that were tried in common-law courts, where the rules of evidence were strict and verdicts were rendered by juries. Even before the 1850s, this dualism often produced split decisions in which a vessel was condemned but the captain and crew were acquitted. Judges, moreover, varied in their interpretations of both law and evidence. Presiding over the trial of Cyrus Libby in 1846, Justice Charles L. Woodbury ruled (in seeming contradiction to *United States v. Morris*) that the shipment of goods to Africa and even selling them to slave traders was not prime facie evidence of a crime; for that, a trader needed to have a personal interest in the venture. Although this decision essentially provided a shield for auxiliaries (and parallels to some extent the infamous trial of Pedro Zulueta three years earlier in Britain), Woodbury, a New Englander, was not a pro-slavery ideologue. A Democrat who had read law in Alabama, he simply did not view the slave trade as enough of a concern to let it influence his thinking about due process. His indifference to the larger implications of his ruling was common, but he was not trying to protect the slave trade.[34]

As the 1850s progressed, pro-slavery ideological bias grew more decisive. An analysis of cases from the 1830s to the 1850s suggests a growing unwillingness to indict and convict. Still, the tendency was not as pronounced as might be expected, given the heated rhetoric surrounding the slave trade. Vessel condemnation rates did not change much over time, remaining just above 50 percent for a quarter of a century. In proceedings against vessels that commenced before 1850, the condemnation percentage was actually higher in slave-state courts than in free-state courts. Condemnation rates fell in the slave states after 1850 but were still higher than in free-state courts (table 8). Criminal prosecutions were a very different matter. Juries nationwide hesitated to convict fellow citizens on any slaving charge and were especially reluctant to impose the death penalty. Conviction rates declined from 19.4 percent before 1850 to less than 14.3 percent after 1850. A large percentage of cases never even went to trial, whether as a result of a decision to drop the charges, a

Table 8. Vessel Condemnations by Region and Era, 1837–1861

Region	Number Condemned, 1837–1849	Percentage Condemned, 1837–1849	Number Condemned, 1850–1861	Percentage Condemned, 1850–1861	Total
Free States	8	47.1	23	51.1	31
Upper South	2	100.0	8	72.7	10
Lower South	6	66.7	11	52.4	17
Total	16	57.1	42	54.5	58

Source: Warren S. Howard, *American Slavers and the Federal Law, 1837–1862* (Berkeley and Los Angeles: University of California Press, 1963), appendix A, 214–223.

Table 9. Convictions in Criminal Prosecutions by Region and Era, 1839–1863

Region	Number Convicted, 1839–1849	Percentage Convicted, 1839–1849	Number Convicted, 1850–1863	Percentage Convicted, 1850–1863	Total
Free States	3	13.6	13	17.8	16
Upper South	2	25.0	0	0.0	2
Lower South	2	33.3	0	0.0	2
Total	7	19.4	13	14.3	20

Source: Warren S. Howard, *American Slavers and the Federal Law, 1837–1862* (Berkeley and Los Angeles: University of California Press, 1963), appendix B, 224–235. Note: This table counts trial verdicts, not defendants. In several cases, multiple defendants were tried together. For these cases, only one verdict has been entered into the table.

refusal by the grand jury to indict, or because the defendant skipped bail or escaped, which happened in four cases. Still, even though the number of cases is admittedly very small, it is nevertheless true that before 1850 slave-trade prosecutions stood a better chance in a southern court than in a northern one (table 9).

After 1850, the national total conviction percentage fell from about 19 percent to 14 percent. This was entirely due to the failure—or refusal—of southern judges and juries to convict. The record in northern cases was not stellar, but convictions actually rose over the decade. This was undercut by the fact that at least twelve defendants skipped bail or escaped, which speaks more to corruption in the police force than to ideologically motivated juries (and about one-quarter of those who were convicted eventually managed to secure presidential pardons). But even considering the dismal record of the northern justice system, especially in the Southern District of New York, it is hard not to conclude that southern juries systematically discounted the evidence and engaged in "jury nullification." There are important caveats, of course: each case is different, and we can never know what a jury was thinking, but the pattern is clear.

The case of the *Echo* is the clearest example of ideologically motivated legal obstruction in southern courts. In 1858, the U.S.-built *Echo,* owned by Portuguese slavers, sailed with an American crew from New Orleans to Havana and then to Cabinda, where it embarked 450 captives. A U.S. navy cruiser captured the *Echo* as it returned to Havana and brought it to Charleston for adjudication, with some 137 captives having died. Aware that winning a conviction in South Carolina would be difficult, the prosecutor nevertheless charged the captain and crew with piracy under the 1820 act. His initial skepticism was correct: a grand jury refused to indict. Federal prosecutors refiled charges in 1859, this time securing indictments. In the ensuing trials, Leonidas Spratt participated in the defense and advanced the explicitly ideological thesis that the federal government did not have a right to regulate the slave trade, which implied that the piracy act of 1820 was unconstitutional. Presiding over the trial was Judge Andrew McGrath, a moderate secessionist who would later become governor of South Carolina, and an opponent of federal slave trade laws. McGrath's rulings throughout the trial—his finding, for example, that the presence of Africans aboard a ship was not evidence of slave trading—pleased Spratt and the other defense attorneys. The jury acquitted the captain and crew in short order, with the former going on to command another slave ship. Two juries and a judge had effectively nullified federal law.[35]

The *Wanderer* spawned several trials, and these too were marred by ideologically motivated subversion on the part of none other than Judge McGrath. As with the *Echo* case, McGrath offered disingenuous interpretations of the law, ruling, for example, that the piracy act of 1820 did not apply to the slave trade because it required the violent physical seizure or capture of a free person and excluded the simple purchase or transfer of a person who had already been enslaved. The fix was in, and none of the defendants faced serious consequences for their involvement in the voyage. The *Echo* and *Wanderer* trials demonstrate that federal slave-trading statutes were null and void in South Carolina and Georgia, and had they been tested elsewhere in the Lower South, the outcome would probably have been the same. Secession, of course, put an end to southern slave-trade prosecutions, so the issue never came up. In any event, the vast majority of prosecutions took place in the northern jurisdictions that dispatched the most vessels. Justice was rarely administered perfectly in northern courts, but at least the judges and juries did not baldly nullify the law.[36]

The final phase of the American slave trade saw a shift of scene to New York City. New York had been a home port for slavers in the seventeenth and eighteenth centuries, but always on a small scale. That changed suddenly in the 1850s, so that by the end of the decade, New York was a major slave-trading center. Contemporaries and historians alike have argued that New York was the "capital" of the trade in the latter part of the 1850s, and by some measures it was, although in many respects it was merely a satellite of Havana. Dubious honors aside, there is no questioning New York's significance. Between 1850 and 1861, at least fifty-eight slavers sailed from New York, but that does not tell the entire story. New York-based slavers dispersed their activities to other ports, such as Boston, where they bought old cargo vessels, and New Bedford, where they purchased old whalers. And most of all, regardless of where a vessel ultimately embarked for Africa, New York was the source for a very high percentage of the vessels used in the trade.[37]

As with most of the post-1808 U.S. slave trade, the New York trade of the 1850s focused almost entirely on Cuba. The volume of the New York trade in the 1850s was the second highest in American history after the 1804–1807 period, although because the vessels were on average about three times larger, the number of voyages was much lower. Several factors explain the sudden rise of the New York slave trade. The first was simply the size and vitality of the port itself. New York was home to thousands of seamen, the largest port in the fast-developing United States. With a surfeit of cheap vessels left over from the California Gold

Rush, it was an excellent place to procure a ship without attracting undue attention. New York also had a sizable "legitimate" African trade, which gave slavers plausible deniability for their clearances.[38]

Of course, those things were true before the 1850s, so they cannot by themselves explain the sudden explosion of slave trading that occurred during the decade. The missing ingredient, then, or the sufficient condition to produce a major slave trade, was the existence of a sprawling, sophisticated criminal network of slave traders. The network—really several networks—arrived in New York in the mid-1850s, after Brazil expelled its active slavers. These men, mostly of Portuguese background but including some Spaniards and Cubans, established themselves in New York after a brief but harried sojourn in Havana. With them came the necessary capital, extensive African experience, and well-honed networks, all of which would soon distinguish New York from other U.S. ports.[39]

The most important of these transplants were the associates who made up what was sometimes called the "Portuguese Company," though formally speaking, no such entity existed. In reality, the Portuguese Company was a loose collection of merchants who sometimes collaborated and often overlapped in their activities. Several figures associated with the Portuguese Company had worked with the Rio factor Manoel Pinto da Fonseca, who bought or chartered many American vessels during the 1840s, which almost certainly influenced their decision to move to New York. Key figures included Manoel Basílio da Cunha Reis, João José Lima Vianna (Viana), and John Albert Machado. All had extensive slave trading experience, and Vianna had actually managed the Congo River barracoons of Guilherme José da Silva Correia, better known as "Guilherme of Zaire." Other associates of the Portuguese Company included Albranches, Almeida & Co., Guilherme de la Figanière, who also served as the Portuguese consul, and the Botelho brothers, Antonio and Manuel.[40]

The arrival of the Portuguese Company obviated the slow but necessary process of establishing contacts, building trust, and cultivating networks that most slaving ports went through. Because virtually all of the associates had extensive contacts in Africa, specifically in the area around the Congo River, New York suddenly enjoyed strong ties to the world's most important captive-exporting region. Crucially, however, the Portuguese Company's Cuban network was not as strong. The reason for this was simple: Cuban slavers dominated the island and were not about to allow the Portuguese, with their excellent African connections, to take over the local captive trade. The Cuban trade was by this time well developed, and it was even rumored that the market was dominated by a single, large joint-stock company. There is reason to question whether these rumors were completely true (illegal enterprises are seldom that large or integrated), but there can be no doubting the dominance of Cuban merchants on the island. The Cuban traders needed the Portuguese/Brazilians for their African connections, but wanted to protect their position in the Cuban market. For that reason, it makes perfect sense that Cuba-based traders would use their political influence to deny the Portuguese/Brazilians a foothold on the island. In New York, on the other hand, the Portuguese Company could do business with the Cuba-based traders without threatening to take over the island's market. For the slavers, it was a workable arrangement.[41]

What emerged in New York was not just another merchant network, but a classic criminal network. Criminal networks resemble legitimate enterprises in their economic rationality, but the simple fact of illegality poses special risks and forecloses certain practices. The major risks are the unenforceability of contracts, the vulnerability of assets to confiscation, and the danger of arrest and imprisonment. The implications of these risks for criminal networks are several. First, criminal networks must minimize exposure to law enforcement and establish trust within the group by limiting themselves to a small core of participants. This runs counter to popular stereotypes based on the American Mafia, with Godfather-like dons, capos, and consiglieri, and armies of "button men." In reality, having too many permanent "employees" is risky for an illegal enterprise, as they may use their knowledge either to inform or to compete. This same principle makes vertical integration rare, especially over large distances. Instead, groups specializing in one activity usually liaise with groups specializing in another, resulting in loose but overlapping partnerships of short duration.[42]

Second, the need to connect discretely with different groups, which might include legitimate businesses, elevates the broker or middleman to special prominence in criminal networks. Brokers had been a fixture

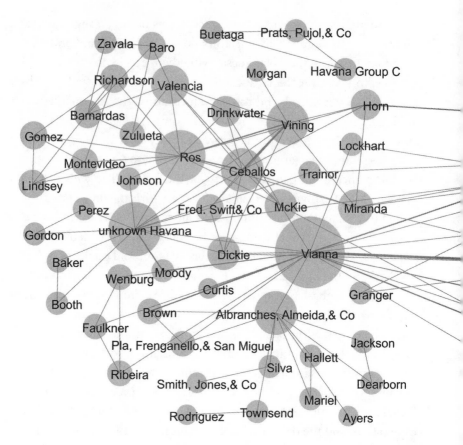

Chart 7. New York slave-trading networks, 1859–1861. (British National Archives FO 84/1086, FO 84/1111, FO 84/1138, FO 84/1139; *Slave Voyages,* www.slave voyages.org; Warren S. Howard, *American Slavers and the Federal Law, 1837–1862* [Berkeley and Los Angeles: University of California Press, 1963], appendix I, 249–252. Drawn by Kartikay Chadha, WalkWithWeb.)

in the American slave trade since the 1810s but became still more significant in the 1850s as the trade moved to New York. Third, recruitment into an illegal enterprise usually comes either via kinship or from related legitimate industries, what criminologists call "opportunistic structures," with the maritime trades being the most relevant to slaving. Put differently, many illegal enterprise participants are not criminals by nature but, rather, decide to participate when presented with the chance

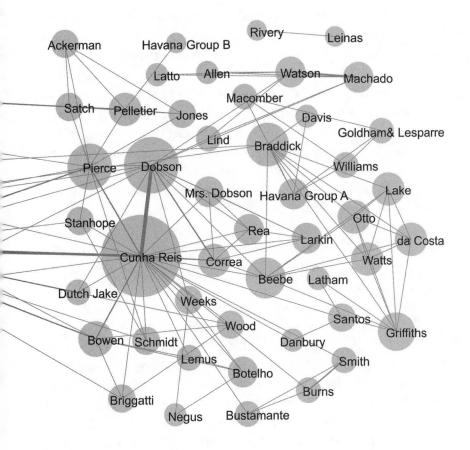

to turn a quick profit. The net result is not a static, top-down syndicate or even a cartel, but rather a core of small, independent, interconnected nodes of specialized activity and a continuously shifting, ad hoc cast of peripheral actors who are not privy to critical information and whose involvement may be fleeting.[43]

New York's slaver networks are best grasped visually, rather than via verbal description, through a graphic representation showing the networks that ran the New York–based slave trade at its height, from approximately 1859 to 1861 (chart 7). It is based on the detailed reports of Emilio Sánchez, a Cuban former slave trader who worked as a paid informant for the British consul in New York and covers forty-six voyages.

Each person involved is rendered as a dot, or "node," and each relationship, regardless of its nature, is rendered as a line or "edge." The largest nodes represent those actors with the most connections to the others in the network, though not necessarily the most voyages (Cunha Reis and Vianna were two of the biggest slavers in New York, however, so it works out rather well in that regard). The diagram includes voyages that were organized by New York–based slavers, for example involving the purchase of vessels in Massachusetts, but it does not include voyages organized in other ports, such as New Orleans. The graphic does not distinguish among the roles played by the actors, either: owners, captains, ship brokers, and front men are all treated equally. Finally, it is important to understand that the information is not complete. Sánchez named more participants for some voyages than for others. The diagram is therefore imperfect, more an impressionistic sketch than a precise measurement.[44]

With those caveats in mind, the first conclusion to draw from the graphic is that the network it portrays conforms quite closely to the theoretical model of an illegal enterprise. The Portuguese Company dominates, but rather than acting as a single, centrally run enterprise, it appears as a series of overlapping ventures by Cunha Reis, Vianna, and Albranches, Almeida & Co. Cunha Reis collaborated at times with Vianna, and Vianna with Albranches, but Cunha Reis and Albranches never worked together during this period, according to these sources. Vianna had links to various unknown Havana slavers, and he surely procured vessels for them and used his African contacts to supply them with captives, but neither Cunha Reis nor Albranches had direct ties to Cuba, at least here. Cunha Reis, however, had ties to two major Portuguese/Brazilian traders, Botelho and Correa. Botelho had been more active in New York a few years earlier, but by this time was pulling out, so his node is small. Correa (Correia), as "Guilherme of Zaire," was a major African dealer but was only passing through, hence his relatively small presence in the diagram.

Cuban interests in New York come off, by contrast, as dispersed and relatively weak. This seems surprising and may be a function of Sánchez's intelligence gathering. Still, it probably gets at a real difference with the Portuguese Company, which actually based itself in New York.

Cuban merchants, by contrast, were based in Havana and used New York only for certain purposes. The "unknown Havana" group appears to be the largest, but it probably was not a single group. Havana Groups A, B, and C were, to the extent it can be deduced from the sources, three distinct partnerships. None of them were directly connected with the Portuguese Company (though if any are part of unknown Havana, then they would be linked with Vianna). Havana interests used New York mostly as a source of ships and captains. Havana Group A, for example, was connected with a captain and several shipping agents. Havana Group C is entirely cut off from the rest, indicating that it operated mostly within the Spanish mercantile community. The same can be said for Julián Zulueta, Cuba's biggest slaver by far, who in this diagram is connected mostly with other Spanish/Cuban merchants (although he may have been behind the other Cuban groups).

The agents, or people who acted on behalf of voyage organizers to buy, charter, register, or clear vessels, to procure trade goods, or to hire captains and crew, are well represented in the network map. Indeed, if the vast majority of voyage organizers were Portuguese/Brazilian or Spanish/Cuban, most agents were U.S. citizens. This made perfect sense, since federal law required that to qualify for U.S. registration, a vessel had to be owned by citizens. Local ship brokers, agents, and chandlers, therefore, earned extra income by fronting for foreign slavers. Because the law also required that U.S.-registered vessels be captained by a citizen, skippers often did double duty by serving (on paper) as the owner or agent. As the diagram illustrates, many agents had a relatively low number of connections. This would suggest that, for many, fronting for slavers was a one-time chance, a "structural opportunity," in the language of criminology. But several others, such as Harrison S. Vining, made a business out of it. Vining, listed in the 1860 census as a shipping and commission merchant with $5,000 in personal property, fronted for Spanish merchant John M. Ceballos on at least three voyages. But the most intriguing of all agents was Jesse Braddick, a sailmaker by trade. Braddick was connected with at least five voyages, and on two occasions he stood bail for incarcerated slavers. Not all agents were American, however. Spanish-born Ceballos was involved in at least five voyages on behalf of Cuban interests. He often employed his clerk,

Antonio M. Ros, a native of Cuba but a naturalized U.S. citizen since at least 1859, as a front man. But Ceballos apparently preferred not to rely solely on Ros, since he hired additional U.S. citizens to front for him, such as William Richardson.[45]

Most of the names in the diagram are actually those of the American ship captains who were hired by voyage organizers, often through the agents. A majority were involved in just a single voyage. This contrasts with previous generations of slavers, who relied on veteran skippers. In this era, however, it was figures like Cunha Reis and Vianna who possessed the knowledge and networks on the African coast, not the captains. What slavers needed from their skippers was their U.S. citizenship, a sense of discretion, and nautical skills—in that order. As mere "flag captains," some never commanded the vessel at all. For voyage organizers, hiring different captains and keeping them at arm's length was a good way to prevent them from learning too much about their illegal enterprise, though there were exceptions. The most notable of these was Jonathan Dobson, who was listed as the captain of three suspicious vessels and unquestionably commanded one slaver. But Dobson was unusual in that he apparently partnered with Cunha Reis and Vianna, among others, and owned shares (along with his wife) in at least two voyages. Few American captains of the era matched Dobson's deep enmeshment in the slave trade. Most voyage organizers recognized the need to hold detailed information about the enterprise as close as possible.[46]

Finally, the illegal networks of the 1850s operated with the participation of corrupt federal officials, though whether these should be considered as members of the enterprise or merely as contacts is a matter of debate. Surprisingly, given its reputation for corruption and its pro-southern leanings, Tammany Hall played no discernible role in the operation of the New York–based slave trade. Jurisdiction over the slave trade lay entirely with the federal government, so slavers targeted those officials, particularly federal marshals, who were responsible for the apprehension and incarceration of suspects. Two marshals lost their jobs for deliberately fumbling an assignment to prevent a slaver from sailing, but the resulting charges were eventually dropped. Quite a few slavers escaped from jail, not just in New York but in cities such as Boston, which points to widespread bribery. Violence appears to have been rare within slaving organizations, though there were occasional threats. A federal marshal who had been involved in several cases received an anonymous letter warning him that the man he had arrested "has rich and power friends [and] will use [a] desperate cure for desparate cases." The senders threatened him with death, making reference to a recent murder case that had nothing to do with the slave trade. This tendency to ground the network in mechanisms other than violence is actually more common in criminal organizations than generally realized, and slavers were no different. There was, however, one major exception, as we will soon see.[47]

Sophisticated though they may have been, the slavers' networks could not circumvent all of the problems of illegality. The more people who knew about an enterprise, the less secure it was. For illegal slave-trading networks, the weakest links were those with the least stake in the venture—the mariners. To be certain, American seamen had a strong incentive to keep quiet about any involvement in slaving voyages. Juries were reluctant to convict under the piracy act of 1820, but the law did exist. Still, time and again, seamen denounced slavers to the authorities. Denunciations of merchants and captains by sailors was a common-place of maritime life, but the piracy act raised the stakes considerably, as mundane disputes over pay or rations might result in arrest and trial on capital charges. Sailors invariably said that they were deceived into signing on to a slaver, and in those instances when it was true, it led to great resentment and risk for the organizers. Merchants and captains recognized the danger posed by loose-lipped seamen and on at least some occasions sought to kill them. The problem seems to have been most acute in Cuba during the 1850s, when slavers, behaving like the criminals they were, tried to silence potential witnesses.

    Mundane disputes of the kind that existed on all voyages resulted in denunciations. Richard J. Hill, a cook and steward aboard the brig *Casket*, was motivated by a disagreement over money and rations. He tried to leave the ship when it arrived in Brazil, but Captain Henry Woodbury refused him permission, threatened him with pistols, put him in irons, and embarked for Cabinda. When a U.S. patrol boarded the *Casket*, Hill gave a full accounting of the voyage, including the names of the vessel's American owners, which he had overheard. Naval commanders sent the vessel to Boston on the strength of Hill's statement, but the judge dismissed the charges. In a more successful case, Cyrus Libby of *Porpoise* fame was convicted on evidence provided by Peter Johnson after Johnson was refused his discharge and forced to sail to Mozambique. The fact that Johnson was a free Black sailor introduces the possibility of an additional political motive. Divergent legal outcomes aside, both cases illustrate how vulnerable slavers could be to alienated laborers.[48]

The crew of the bark *Isla de Cuba* handed their vessel over to authorities because they feared being implicated in an illegal voyage. The *Isla de Cuba* had cleared New York for Loango in 1858 under the command of Jonathan Dobson and with several Portuguese-speaking passengers, one of whom turned out to be Guilherme of Zaire. Mate Levi W. Turner became suspicious when he discovered casks, boards, and beans, all classic slaver items, during a stop in the Azores. With the captain ashore and with the backing of the entire crew, Turner put the passengers in a boat 120 miles off Flores Island and surrendered the vessel to authorities in Boston. In 1848, when the crew of the *Mary Ann* discovered the true purpose of its voyage, they put the captain ashore at Gallinas and returned with the vessel to New York. In court, the men claimed that they acted when they became suspicious about the voyage, but testimony suggests they may have become angry when told they were sailing to Bahia rather than to New York, in violation of the ship's articles. Neither case resulted in forfeiture or conviction, but in both, the crews caused the voyage to fail and cost the slavers a great deal of money.[49]

The obvious question, given the illegal nature of slaver networks, is whether those in charge ever emulated other criminal organizations in killing members who knew too much. The answer is that they did, at least occasionally. The practice of using American seamen for the outbound but not the homebound voyage created an ideal opportunity to silence possible informants by stranding them in Africa. The three sailors from the Baltimore brig *Solon* told the consul in Rio that they suspected a plot to abandon them at Cabinda. They made it home and never explained the reason for their suspicions or why the plot was not carried out, but the crew of the brig *Sophia* was not as fortunate. The

Sophia sailed for Angola with a mixed crew that included several Americans. Once there, the captain sold the vessel, paid off the crew, put them ashore, and took passage aboard a different vessel. The sole survivor from the *Sophia*'s crew gave a detailed deposition, but as with the *Solon,* no legal action resulted.[50]

The danger for American seamen increased during the 1850s, a function of the rising number of voyages originating in U.S. ports and the raised stakes, since participants now ran a greater risk of prosecution in both U.S. and Cuban courts. Most of the reports concerned the land-based networks that handled disembarkations in Cuba. By this time, the Cuban captains general were taking slave-trade enforcement more seriously, and reports of landings would at least trigger an official inquiry. Slavers, often with very powerful patrons, succeeded in frustrating most of these investigations, but some deemed the risk of conviction to be serious enough to assassinate witnesses. The most notable case was that of the New York bark *Jasper,* which landed captives in Cuba in 1854. The crew was an international one that included Americans. When the slavers set the vessel on fire (a common practice designed to destroy evidence), three American sailors, perhaps anticipating trouble, stole a boat and tried to escape but were arrested and jailed. At that point (if not earlier), the Cuban organization decided to kill the remaining crew and began shuttling them to various cays and plantations, and they were eventually merged with the crew of the *Nueva Empresa,* another slaver. At one point, the gang reportedly secured the services of a local man to kill the seamen, but because the two crews resolved not to separate, the opportunity never came. Eventually, the gang set the crews adrift in a small boat, hoping they would be lost at sea. Instead, Cuban patrollers picked them up and jailed them.[51]

It is difficult to say how common the killing of seamen was. Reviewing the case of the *Jasper,* the Havana correspondent for the *New York Times* alleged that many of those who sailed aboard slavers "have walked the plank or received the knife," and that murder had been the fate of "some sixty crews" who had sailed to Africa "and never since been heard of." These claims were obviously exaggerated: it seems very unlikely that sixty entire crews vanished, and there are many explanations for why individual sailors would disappear without a word. The

danger may have been real, but voyages almost never ended in the massacre of the crew. More often, Cuban gangs temporarily imprisoned
slaver crews in warehouses, plantation cellars, or lonely cays to prevent
them from attracting attention. Some sailors escaped, some were bribed
for their silence, some were released when the heat was off, and some
probably died. Others found themselves charged with crimes. Such was
the fate of the crew of the *Esperanza*, which sailed from New York in
1854, having signed on for a voyage to the Cape of Good Hope. When
the crew discovered the true nature of the voyage, the captain threatened to abandon them in Africa if they would not sail the vessel to Cuba.
On arrival in Cuba, with the captives safely ashore and the vessel burned
to the waterline, local operatives ushered the crew and captives into a
nearby forest, where they subsisted on plants and snails for twenty days.
Eventually, the gang put the seamen aboard a schooner. Cuban authorities later arrested the men when they came ashore for some water. Needless to say, they never received wages for the voyage. At last report, they
were in "miserable condition" in a Cuban jail.[52]

For slavers, the inability to use the legal system to enforce contracts
or procure justice was at least as big a problem as sailor-informants. In
a few instances, front men or partners outright stole vessels. As we have
seen, Charles Lamar lost the *Wanderer* that way. His lack of networks
and experience made him an easy mark. But even the well-networked
New Yorkers were vulnerable. When Antonio Botelho and some Cuban merchants gave $18,000 to John P. Weeks—a heretofore reliable
front man—to buy the *William H. Stewart*, Weeks sent the vessel to
Ireland and later resold it to New Orleans slavers. The poor interface
between the Portuguese Company and the major Cuban traders was
a recurrent problem, with payments often made slowly or not at all.
When the *Pierre Soulé* arrived in Cuba, local operators forced the captain to sell at below-market rates, for a total loss of $48,000. Similarly,
in 1858, Cunha Reis lacked a Cuban contact for his slaver *Ellen,* so the
captain was forced to sell at low prices. When the bark *Emily* landed
in Cuba, the local official reportedly kept 150 out of 900 captives for
himself. The official was surely on the payroll of the Cuban traders but
owed no allegiance to New York. In another case from 1861, Cuban slavers cheated their captain out of his salary. His information led to three

convictions, although whether the slavers served their entire sentences is another question. And when the Portuguese owners of the *Haidee* refused to pay Emilio Sánchez his 2 percent commission for acting as a straw purchaser, he responded by becoming a paid informant for the British consul in New York. Sánchez ultimately gave the British actionable intelligence on scores of slavers, all because he was cheated.[53]

Operating beyond the law, slavers lacked access to many of the normal sources of credit and financing. The options varied depending on their relationship with political authorities. In Cuba, where much of the political establishment viewed the slave trade as a necessity and abolition as an unwanted intrusion, slavers could operate quasi-openly. The same was true in Brazil until the crackdown of the 1850s. After that, investors refused to lend to slavers and even denounced them to the police. As hirelings in the Cuban and Brazilian trades, American slavers did not need to raise capital; Havana, Rio, and even Luanda supplied that. But foreign traders based in the United States did face significant risks in making remittances. Reports of slavers hand-delivering gold and other assets offer a glimpse of the problem. When the *Porpoise* returned to Rio, it reportedly carried between $70,000 and $80,000 in gold, and the *Flying Eagle* reportedly carried 432 gold dubloons. As far as we know, nobody ever stole the entire proceeds from a voyage, but the possibility must have weighed on the slavers' minds. Without insurance or the ability to enforce contracts in court, there were few remedies available to them.[54]

Faced with the risk of fraud and robbery, slavers converted their profits into other forms whenever possible. Plantation produce was a natural option, since slavers usually dealt in it. Cunha Reis once instructed Vianna to convert his voyage profits into coffee. In fact, before it was turned over to the authorities by its crew, the *Isla de Cuba* had been principally employed in transporting its owners' slave-trading profits around the Atlantic rim in the form of plantation goods. But this method entailed its own risk, since commodities are not a good store of value, and prices can easily drop during the time it takes to transport them. Moreover, some mercantile firms flatly refused to handle slavers' commodities, as happened when Cunha Reis sent the *Isla de Cuba* to Carvalho & Rocha of Rio de Janeiro.[55]

Bills of exchange were another option and probably accounted for the bulk of the remittances in the illegal slave trade. But bills entailed risks even for legitimate businessmen (hence the constant admonishment to accept only "good bills"), and for criminals they created additional costly headaches. To start, slavers needed to find merchant houses or banks that would accept their bills. Cuba's Banco de Fernando VII reportedly served slavers during the 1840s, and the Banco Español probably did the same during the 1850s, but strong Cuban connections were presumably needed to access both of these, which would have excluded the Portuguese Company. Empirical evidence is lacking, but illegality almost surely limited the pool of merchants willing to accept the bills. And like modern-day money launderers, we would have to suppose, those who did accept them would charge a premium for assuming the risks. Presumably, the New York merchant Henry Coit did exactly that when he endorsed $12,000 in bills from Vianna. Alternately, a slaver might be able to deal with a reputable merchant-banker through an intermediary, but the intermediary would surely charge a commission and extract the same premium for his services. Bills were, moreover, negotiable by their very nature, so we can assume that bill brokers dealing with suspected criminals took full advantage.[56]

The risk of robbery was also present on the Cuban side, but it was the human contraband rather than the cash that was the target. Like a modern-day drug dealer who gets robbed, slavers could not turn to the justice system for help. Criminal gangs with no apparent connection to the slaver networks preyed on the captives during the dangerous interval between disembarkation and final distribution. Slavers usually took captives to safe houses on nearby farms and plantations, but sometimes had to leave them in makeshift shelters in the forest or another remote location, shuttling them from one place to another to avoid discovery. Because so many captives were weak or ill from the voyage, they might spend weeks regaining their strength in these hideouts. Local bandits sometimes raided these outposts and groups in transit, knowing that slavers could not report them. One gang, pretending to be officials investigating an illegal landing, surprised some slavers who had hidden captives in a canefield. The robbers demanded ten ounces of gold per head to leave the party alone. The slavers, who never believed the bandits' cover story, negotiated them down to five ounces.[57]

Finally, as we have already seen, illegality made it impossible to insure vessels, at least in the United States. Case law opened a few loopholes, especially when the illegal nature of the voyage was unknown, but slavers wisely did not rush to test them. Cuban slavers insured vessels into the 1840s, but insurers soon discovered that illegal policies were not enforceable in court, thus sinking the business. It appears, then, that the slaving voyages that left New York in the 1850s sailed without insurance. Instead, to manage risk, slavers reverted to pre-Lloyds methods, which relied solely on the sale of voyage shares.[58]

Despite the unique problems and costs posed by illegality, there can be no denying that slave trading was very profitable in this era. In the end, the criminal networks achieved their purpose. Networks not only enabled the trade itself, they helped to compensate for the problems of denunciation, contract enforcement, and the payment of remittances. These networks were far from infallible, but they did mitigate the problems of illegality. It helped greatly that the price of slaves in Cuba reached historic highs during the 1850s, just as the Portuguese Company was moving to New York, with real prices doubling between 1850 and 1859. Thanks to the extraordinary demand for captives, slavers could afford to lose one vessel in six to condemnation (and burn the rest to destroy evidence), to bribe officials, to lose money to fraudsters and thieves, and to pay a premium for the handling of their remittances. Crime entailed extra costs, but it paid.[59]

Most of the captives who traveled on American slave ships in this era embarked in West Central Africa, a break with nearly two hundred years of precedent. The only time when the region had played a major role in the American slave trade was during the rush of 1804–1807, but even then, most of the vessels sailing that route were British-owned or employed British supercargoes. From 1835 to 1865, there was a sudden shift, with more than 85 percent of vessels sailing from American ports going to West Central Africa. The Congo River was the most frequent destination by far, followed by Ambriz and Cabinda. The same region also accounted for a large proportion of those U.S. vessels that began their voyages in Brazil in the 1840s and Cuba in the 1850s.[60]

This sudden, historic change can be traced directly to the partnership between Portuguese/Brazilian slavers and American merchants that began in the Brazil trade during the 1840s and continued into the 1850s with the activities of the Portuguese Company. In essence, the Lusophone traders absorbed the Americans into their networks, which had historically centered on the Angola–Brazil route. These networks were strong but had undergone much modification as a result of abolition. The Anglo-Portuguese Treaty of 1815 had committed Portugal to abolition north of the equator but allowed slave trading to continue south of the line until 1830. Brazil, after independence in 1822, did not view itself as bound by Portuguese agreements. However, in 1826, after much negotiation, it agreed to end all slave trading within three years of ratification, which worked out to be 1830. Illegality brought great change to the Brazilian trade, as most of the pre-1830 slavers abandoned the business, but as illicit trading continued under new management, West Central Africa retained its historical preeminence as a source for captive labor.[61]

Developments in the early nineteenth century shifted the focus of the regional slave trade from the city of Luanda to the Congo River, two hundred miles to the north. The process began in the 1810s, when Brazil-based traders discovered that captive prices were lower at Ambriz than in Luanda. The northward shift accelerated after 1825, when Portugal instituted a tax on foreign goods entering Luanda, to the disadvantage of the Brazilians. Finally, after 1830, when the slave trade south of the equator became illegal, British naval vessels began to frequent the region. As the only European-style port in Atlantic Africa, Luanda's compactness and exposed position made it easy to patrol. The Congo estuary, by contrast, offered much more cover. Even Ambriz and Cabinda were preferable to Luanda because the barracoons were located several miles inland from the town, safe from naval raids. Eventually, in the 1850s, members of the Portuguese Company expanded their operations to the Congo River estuary, which soon eclipsed Ambriz and Cabinda as a source for captives. The New York–based slavers of the 1850s sent most of their vessels to the Congo River and surrounding area.[62]

Ambriz, Cabinda, and the Congo estuary were all part of the same trading system. For a long time, historians believed that by the nineteenth century the Central African "slaving frontier," or the expanding zone of warfare that generated captives, extended several hundred miles inland. Journeys to the coast, it was thought, were extremely long, and captives came from cultural and linguistic groups that were very different from those on the coast. Such journeys certainly took place, but recent work based on narratives and the names of "Liberated Africans" has complicated this picture, demonstrating that in the mid-nineteenth century at least, more than half of the captives who embarked from West Central African ports came from less than three hundred miles inland. The implications are not so much that the slave trade was any less brutal (journeys still took months, and marching any distance in a coffle is torturous) but that the cultural-linguistic backgrounds of captor and captive were not as different as supposed. Most spoke dialects of Kikongo and related languages, with some Kimbundu speakers from southern areas. Outsiderness, and hence enslaveability, were reckoned not in cultural terms or even in political terms, although the region encompassed many polities with potential conflicts. Rather, as biographical information reveals, judicial enslavement, kidnapping, and sale by lineage heads— what Roquinaldo Ferreira has termed "everyday enslavement"—were the more common avenues. Everyday enslavement was symptomatic of a society in which slave trading had become fundamental to the economy. People were enslaved not as a by-product of war or politics, but because the long-standing existence of an external market had transformed society's institutions into a supply mechanism for captives.[63]

The Central African enslavement zone was enormous, with captives arriving on the coast via multiple routes. One of these ran along the Congo River and connected the massive central basin above the Malebo Pool with the entrepôts near the mouth, such as Boma and Ponta da Lenha. Roughly one captive in six arrived via this route. Those captives traveling the entire route to the coast would have been transported by two to three separate trading networks. At the far end were Bobangi traders, former fishermen who became middlemen in the riverine canoe trade and prospered by connecting the region's different ecological zones. Captives were just one of the goods they traded, along with manioc and ivory, and were usually purchased at the fairs that were established at various points. A system of paired villages established trust and linked Bobangi merchants along the river. The Bobangi network linked up with several others at the village of Tchumbiri, just above the Pool. Most Bobangi traders transferred their captives to residents there or to the Tio merchants, who sold them to the Vili traders, who then marched them on paths the rest of the way, to Boma, Punto da Lenha, Cabinda, or Ambriz.[64]

The Vili traders who controlled the trade below the Pool, as well as the important routes to the Kongo Kingdom and points south, were members of the Lemba society. Like the Bobangi, Juula, and similar networks, Lemba served a commercial function by creating the trust needed for long-distance trade. It also exercised some of the functions of a state, administering justice and settling conflicts. Members were initiated into the society through a series of rituals, which framed these relations as sacred and spiritual. This gave Lemba a therapeutic or healing function, which was necessary as a result of the brutality inherent in slave trading. As members understood it, enslavement and the trade in captives entailed a great deal of conflict and evil. Lemba ritual provided a way for communities to absorb the social antagonisms introduced by slave trading. Lemba networks were extensive, connecting the Kongo Kingdom south of the river with the estuary and the ports to the north, including Ambriz and Cabinda.[65]

The mid-nineteenth-century Central African slave trade was historically unusual for its pronounced demographic imbalance: roughly 80 percent of all captives were male, against about 63 percent for the transatlantic slave trade as a whole. Part of the reason had to do with Cuban sugar planters' preference for male laborers, which was communicated to African merchants through the networks, but African decisions were probably more significant. Women were always preferred as slaves in African societies, both for their labor and for their ability to bear children. The shift toward "legitimate" trade created a demand for labor in Africa that was increasingly met via enslavement, even as the Atlantic slave trade continued. Central African societies, then, retained increasing numbers of women and sold the men to Europeans.

In addition to being overwhelmingly male, captives embarking for the Americas in these final years of the trade were extraordinarily young. Analyzing two French "free" migrant vessels that called in the Congo estuary in 1857, which drew on the very same sources as the slavers, Jelmer Vos found that more than a third were under twenty years old and four-fifths were younger than twenty-four. This preponderance of young people, including many children, was typical of everyday enslavement and the illegal slave trade. In fact, historians have proposed that illegality drove the shift. Children were less able to resist slavers, which became important in an era when captives needed to be loaded onto ships as quickly as possible to avoid capture by patrollers.[66]

The New York–based vessels of the 1850s purchased more than 22,000-people—roughly half of all they embarked—on the Congo River estuary. Affiliates of the Portuguese Company maintained an extensive system of barracoons in and around the estuary, so they naturally directed their ships there. The estuary had emerged as a destination for slave ships at the end of the eighteenth century, but it surged to prominence during the final years of the slave trade, especially in the later 1850s, as Luanda-based merchants established their factories at Boma and Punta da Lenha. These ports grew even more important during the later 1850s when the French established stations for the procurement of "free" migrants to replace enslaved laborers in their Caribbean colonies. They did this most often by purchasing and "liberating" captives, so the free migrant trade relied on and stimulated the very same processes that fed the slave trade. Finally, the emergence of a "legitimate" trade in commodities strengthened the region's Atlantic connection while providing a cover story for slavers, who could always claim to be trading for ivory and palm oil.[67]

Foremost among estuary traders was Guilherme Correia—Guilherme of Zaire—who owned several installations, including one at Punta da Lenha and one slightly to the south with the colorful name of "Snake's Head," and who almost certainly maintained a factory at Boma, the region's main caravan terminus. Before coming to New York, João José Lima Vianna had managed Correia's barracoons, so he knew the area well. Correia and Vianna were not the only members of the Portuguese Company with connections to the estuary. João Carlos de

Avallar, the consul for Hamburg in New York, was a cousin of one of the major estuary slavers and procured vessels for him. Guilherme José da Motta and João (aka John) Alberto Machado also served as agents for Avallar.[68]

Instability and conflict threatened the Congo estuary installations. As elsewhere, slavers did their business with the permission of the polities that hosted them. Even when relations between traders and their hosts were good, conflicts between the landlords and neighboring polities could create problems. Boma, the main entrepôt, was governed by a consortium of nine rulers who were at least nominally subordinate to the Kongo Kingdom. In addition to receiving customs from factors and vessels, the rulers benefited from direct access to trade goods, which they could sell or dispense to enhance their own power. A group up-river, known as the Mussurongos in European sources, was excluded from this arrangement, so they plundered any vessel that came within reach. In 1852, Mussurongo forces attacked an American ship captained by the mercurial filibuster and sometime slaver Appleton Oaksmith. Oblivious to the estuary's politics, Oaksmith had apparently attempted to circumvent the middlemen at Punta da Lenha. His blunder provoked an attack by a large force, which he estimated generously at three thousand, and necessitated a rescue by the Royal Navy. Conflict between the Kongolese landlords and the Mussurongos became so dangerous that in 1857 Correia was forced to abandon his Snake's Head factory, deeming it at risk.[69]

Cabinda, a collection of towns situated on a rise on the Atlantic coast north of the Congo River, was the second most frequent destination for New York slavers during the 1850s. It had strong historical ties to Brazil, primarily as a result of the mafouk Francisco "Chico" Franque, who had been sent there in the 1780s for his education and returned to dominate the local slave trade. Ambriz was another destination for the Americans, similarly dominated by Portuguese/Brazilian traders, with Correia and Fonseca both owning installations, and was served by the same networks as elsewhere. Unlike the other two regions, Ambriz hosted American factories, at times as many as three. However, these appear to have been engaged in "legitimate" trade; at least, no accusations were leveled against them for slave trading. The factories did, however, sell trade goods to slavers, and the bearers who brought the ivory, wax, and other commodities to the factories were usually sold off to slavers, illustrating yet again the symbiosis that existed between the two trades. Still, the absence of accusations of direct American participation in the captive trade, particularly by the British, confirms that the slave trade in this region was very much in Portuguese/Brazilian hands.[70]

The Portuguese installations linked the interior and Atlantic trading systems. In contrast to previous eras, when much of the credit that financed the slave trade originated in Europe or the Americas, in the waning years of the trade it sometimes originated in Africa. Traders like Correia were based in Africa and spent much time in Luanda, and hired people like Vianna to manage their Congo River facilities. Correia and others advanced credit to Lemba caravan leaders and took payment in captives, making sure to pay rent and customs to their landlords. They then "freighted" the captives to the Americas, which is to say they bought "places" aboard ships for them and retained ownership of them through the Atlantic passage up to the point of sale in Cuba. This, of course, is why the safe transport of remittances from Cuba was such a crucial issue for them: they often needed to pay freight. Although freighting was well-suited to the illegal period because it reduced the risk of capture that came with a drawn-out bartering process, it had been a fixture of the Angolan slave trade since the seventeenth century. This system was the reason why Africa-based slavers like Correia had to seek out their own vessels and ultimately why they chose New York as a base of operations. Without freighting, it is difficult to imagine New York becoming a major source of voyages.[71]

The American slave trade had two endings, one provisional and one permanent. The provisional ending came in 1861, with the inauguration of a Republican president, Abraham Lincoln. Initially, the new administration had little effect on the trade. Lincoln's first slave-trade-related action as president was, ironically, to call home most of the Africa Squadron, leaving just one vessel, which was insufficient for any serious interdiction effort. Slavers seem to have judged that the federal government would be too distracted to pay them much attention, and at least five vessels sailed from U.S. ports in the months following the election. As of mid-1861, it appeared that the slave trade would continue as before.[72]

Behind the scenes, however, things were changing. One month before the new administration took office, the British consul in New York was pleased to report "a diminution of outfits," which he attributed to a "consciousness on the part of the Traders, that their movements are closely watched," particularly by his own spies. After Inauguration Day, the new Republican federal prosecutors and marshals, mostly but not exclusively in New York, produced a series of high-profile arrests. The most significant involved Captain Nathaniel Gordon, of the *Erie*. Gordon had likely skippered at least one other slaver in the Brazil trade a dozen years earlier. A New York grand jury had indicted Gordon and his officers under the act of 1800 and the piracy law of 1820, but little happened under the lame-duck administration. When things resumed in April 1861, the new Republican prosecutor, an ally of Lincoln's secretary of state, William Henry Seward, was intent on a conviction. At trial, Gordon's lawyers employed an array of time-tested arguments to create reasonable doubt, maintaining that the vessel was not American and that Gordon was just a passenger. The tactic worked, and the trial ended in a hung jury. Prosecutors, however, believed they could secure a conviction, so they gathered additional evidence and refiled charges. To make it easier for the jury to impose a capital sentence, prosecutors allowed Gordon's officers to plead to a lesser slave-trading charge, leaving only one person to face the death penalty. This time, the jury found Gordon guilty of piracy. Lincoln issued a temporary stay of execution but eventually signed the death warrant. On February 21, 1862, Gordon became the first and only American to hang for slave trading.[73]

Gordon's execution did not trigger a wave of convictions under the act of 1820, however. Several others were indicted after him, but the cases collapsed for procedural reasons. Still, as far as the fight against the slave trade was concerned, it hardly mattered. Gordon's execution caught the slavers' attention, and those who remained in town fled to Cuba or other locales to continue their activities. As this happened, Secretary of State Seward entered into talks with Britain on the long-standing question of the right of search. Tensions between the two countries were high as a result of the Trent Affair, British trade with the Confederacy, and

Westminster's neutrality declaration. From Lincoln's perspective, coming to an accord on the searches could ease general tensions between the two nations while putting an end to the slave trade. In April 1862, the two powers signed the Lyons-Seward Treaty, in which the United States agreed to allow Royal Navy seizures of suspected slavers and to set up a Court of Mixed Commission in New York. That court never heard a case and was disbanded several years later. The last slave ship known to sail from an American port was Vianna's *Mariquita,* which left New York in late 1862 for London (to which Vianna had fled) and took on captives in the Congo River. Thanks to the new treaty, the British captured and eventually condemned the vessel at a vice-admiralty court on the island of Saint Helena.[74]

These measures brought a provisional end to the American slave trade, but its final extinction hinged on events in Cuba. Had the Cuban slave trade survived, it is almost certain that American ship brokers and mariners would have re-entered it after the war. Criminals, by definition, do not respect the law, and illicit profits are always a temptation. Yet although the Cuban slave trade survived the loss of New York as a base of operations—many of the same personalities continued their operations from Spain— it did not live out the decade.

The Cuban slave trade ended as a result of political change in both Spain and Cuba. Coming into the 1860s, metropolitan and colonial officials agreed on several points: that continued Spanish control depended on a productive plantation economy; that the slave system was essential to maintaining the plantations; and that the transatlantic slave trade was essential to maintaining slavery. Two developments shattered that consensus. The first, of course, was U.S. emancipation in 1865, which left Cuba, and on a much smaller scale, Puerto Rico, as the Northern Hemisphere's only remaining slave societies. The Lyons-Seward Treaty contributed not just by shutting down the American slave trade, but by allowing Britain to increase its patrols off the Cuban coast. These developments combined with a growing liberal movement in Spain, which had the support of many Cuban Creoles, who increasingly viewed slavery as a barrier to imperial reform. Even those who were committed to the maintenance of slavery came to view the abolition of the slave trade as essential, since continuing the trade in violation of international agreements opened the door to foreign intervention that might destabilize the institution.[75]

As a result of these changes, Cuban captains general began to enforce existing laws. In one instance officials sought and secured the extradition of a Spanish slaver from the United States, an occurrence that would have been unimaginable before 1861. The extradited party responded by exposing widespread corruption, creating much embarrassment for Cuban officials and revealing just how entrenched the slave trade was. In Madrid, these revelations combined with a renewed push for colonial reform, which resulted in the passage of a wide-ranging slave trade bill in 1866. By that time, the Cuban slave trade had slowed greatly, so the new law was never seriously tested, but its existence deterred new voyages. Although there were occasional rumors of voyages and landings into the early 1870s, the last confirmed landing of captives in Cuba took place in March 1866, and the last slaver was condemned in September of that year. The Cuban slave trade was truly over, but all remaining doubt was extinguished in 1868, when pro-independence Creoles rebelled and set in motion the long process that would result in the end of Cuban slavery. Even had they been inclined, slavers would have had to think twice about organizing voyages in such an unstable environment. Although no U.S. citizens are known to have been involved after 1863, it was only with the end of the Cuban trade that the extinction of the American slave trade could be guaranteed.[76]

Conclusion
A Reckoning of Accounts

Robert, whose story began this book, understood the American slave trade better than we ever will. His journey from upper Guinea to Georgia took him to the heart of the American slave system. By 1802, he was serving as an enslaved body servant to Jabez Bowen of Savannah, where extreme mistreatment was a commonplace. Still, nothing compared to what he saw happen to a young woman named Delia when she spilled gravy on her mistress while waiting at table. Another diner dragged Delia outside and slit her throat, almost decapitating her, then casually returned to finish his meal. Delia's murder went unpunished, and the memory would haunt Robert for the rest of his life. Though the killing took place on land, it was a direct outgrowth of an American slave trade that caused the deaths of at least 52,000 people and devastated the lives of six times as many. When we consider that each person transported was a member of a family and community, the removal of 305,000 people needs to be multiplied by several times to begin to appreciate the full impact of the trade. Though it is difficult for us to comprehend destruction on such a scale, that truth must be the starting point for any summation of the American slave trade.[1]

Moving beyond moral truths toward a more specific historical assessment is complicated, however, by the fact that the American slave trade lasted so long and passed through so many different iterations. It began in the seventeenth century as a series of occasional ventures by Puritan settlers and Anglo-Dutch traders. By the mid-eighteenth century, it was dominated by Rhode Islanders, who discovered that they could peddle rum for captives on the Gold Coast and thus built the trade into a regional economic institution. The American Revolution disrupted the trade for eight years, and when it resumed, a new anti-slavery political ethos had taken hold. For the next three decades, sla-vers, mostly from Rhode Island, skirted the restrictions, although that was not necessary for the climactic years 1804–1807, when, for the only time in its history, the trade focused primarily on the United States. Af-ter the trade was outlawed in 1808, Americans evaded the law by mov-ing offshore to Cuba and, over time, became absorbed into Cuban net-works. In its final phase after 1835, the trade was carried out mostly by Americans working on behalf of Cuban and Brazilian traders, with pro-slavery ideologues organizing a handful of additional ventures. Lincoln's election and the Civil War ended virtually all activity by 1863, but only with Cuban abolition in 1866 could the epitaph of the American slave trade finally be written.

With such a long and varied history, many contradictory state-ments are true of the American slave trade: it was a rum trade except when it was not; it had little impact on the ports that engaged in the trade, but with notable exceptions; the ships going out were not the same as the ships coming in, except when they were; it focused pri-marily on Africa's Gold Coast, but not always; it was orchestrated by American citizens in American ports, until that changed. The three questions that are essential to making sense of this history are "When?" "Where?" and "What is an American?" Start with the estimated 305,000 people embarked aboard American slave ships. That figure represents about 2.4 percent of all of the Africans embarked from 1500 to 1867. It places the Americans squarely in the bottom tier of participating na-tions, above only Denmark and the Baltic states. An apologist for the American slave trade (when not so confused as to deny its existence, as my high school teacher was) might point to that figure to minimize its importance.

But that 2.4 percent aggregate figure interferes with our ability to assess the American slave trade. The problem is that it compares an American trade that was concentrated in an eighty-year span with metropolitan slave trades that lasted twice as long, or more. A more meaningful approach would be to focus on the main period of American involvement, roughly 1730–1807, a time when the colonies/states had developed the financial strength needed to sustain a regular trade. During those years, the Americans topped the second tier of slave-trading powers, below Portugal, Britain, and France, but above the Netherlands, Denmark, and Spain. At the trade's apex, from 1804 to 1807, the United States edged into the top tier, behind only Portugal and Britain. So although it is certainly true that the Americans were minor contributors to the transatlantic slave trade in the aggregate, it is also true that for nearly eighty years they were substantial participants, and that for a few years the United States was a major slave-trading nation.

The aggregate figure of 2.4 percent is even less illuminating for the post-1808 slave trade. For that period, much depends on the definition of the term "American," keeping in mind that national designations are problematic for an era when the slave trade was largely conducted by transnational criminal organizations. If the term refers only to voyages organized by American citizens and embarking from American ports—a definition that applies well to the pre-1808 trade—then the post-1808 transatlantic trade was almost nonexistent. If "American" refers to voyages embarking from U.S. ports but not necessarily organized by Americans, then the United States becomes a larger, though not a truly significant, force until the 1850s. If the term refers to voyages that were undertaken with any kind of American involvement, including the use of American-built ships, regardless of the port of departure or the citizenship of the organizers, then the United States was an increasingly important player, especially after 1835. When considering as well the role of American foreign policy in preventing Britain from suppressing the slave trade in Cuba as aggressively as it had in Brazil, the United States was very influential, indeed. Had Britain been allowed to do in Cuba what it had in Brazil, is not unreasonable to conclude that the transatlantic slave trade would have ended in the 1850s, forestalling the transportation of some 150,000 people. In that sense, the United States was the great enabler of the Cuban slave trade.[2]

The effect of the American slave trade on Africa is another important question. Apart from the human dimensions of enslavement and transportation, the slave trade had a major economic impact, subtracting productive workers and exporting skills, as well as a political impact, fostering the growth of predatory states in some places and spreading insecurity everywhere else. In the aggregate, the impact of the American slave trade on Africa was minimal, at least when compared with other powers—that same 2.4 percent figure. But in addition to addressing the question of "When?" any meaningful assessment of the American role must also pose the question "Where?" In contrast to such major powers as Britain and France, for most of their involvement in the slave trade, the Americans had neither an Asian empire to supply them with textiles nor a manufacturing sector capable of producing trade goods on a large scale; nor could they profitably re-export manufactured goods, at least before the neutral trade boom of the 1790s. So whereas Britain, with its Asian empire and manufacturing sector, operated in virtually all of the major captive markets in Africa (and France in most of them), the Americans before 1807 were limited to the Gold Coast and upper Guinea. In the nineteenth century, of course, the Americans did develop a manufacturing sector capable of supporting trade anywhere in Africa, but by that time relatively few voyages were being organized from U.S. ports. American manufactures did find their way on to Cuban and Brazilian slave ships, though the exact quantities are elusive.[3]

As before, rather than focus on the impact of the American slave trade on Africa as a whole and across all time periods, it is more useful to ask what the impact was on those regions and in those time periods in which it was most active. On the Gold Coast, the leading source of captives for American slavers, the Americans played a moderate role, accounting for more than 10 percent across all time periods. During the years 1730–1807, the Americans had a greater impact, removing more than 15 percent of all captives. That actually makes the Americans the second leading participants in the Gold Coast slave trade, after Britain. The same point applies to upper Guinea (chiefly Senegambia and Sierra Leone, by the coastal designations), where the Americans carried off

17 percent of all captives over the 1730–1807 period, trailing only Britain and slightly edging France and Portugal.

It is the Rio Pongo, however, where the United States had its greatest impact, not only as a destination for ships, but as the site of the only American slave-trading enclave in Africa. It is difficult to measure the impact of the American slave trade on the Rio Pongo, but it was undoubtedly considerable. According to the *Voyages* database, U.S.-flagged vessels outnumbered all others at the Rio Pongo, carrying off nearly seven thousand people, with Spanish (Cuban) vessels accounting for slightly more than five thousand (many of these with some American involvement). But here as elsewhere, much depends on how "American" is defined. If "American" is taken to encompass factories that are owned and run by American citizens and their children (and keeping in mind that for many years the Pongo factors shared all commissions), then American dealers were involved in the sale or transportation, or both, of a majority of the captives embarked there. Far from being marginal actors, Americans were central players on the Rio Pongo, both as dealers and as carriers.[4]

Similarly, any assessment of the impact of the American slave trade on New World plantation societies must look beyond the 2.4 percent aggregate figure. American slave traders sold more than half of their captives in the Caribbean, led by Cuba (17 percent) and Barbados (12 percent). Yet although a majority of American captives went to the Caribbean, in percentage terms the trade had its largest impact on the United States, where it was responsible for 28 percent of the 389,000 captives who arrived directly from Africa. Britain, however, disembarked more than twice as many captives in North America as the Americans did, accounting for 68 percent. The American share would have been even lower if not for the Carolina slave rush of 1804–1807, which by itself accounted for 17 percent of all captives arriving in North America directly from Africa. Had that never happened, the impact of the American slave trade on the United States would have been much less than it was.

Outside of the United States, the American slave trade had its greatest impact on three colonies, although in all three it can be described as marginal. The first of these, at 14 percent, is the Río de la

Plata. This comes as a surprise since at no time was the region a leading destination for American slavers. The total number of captives carried is comparatively small, so its top ranking is a statistical anomaly. More substantively, the American slave trade was a moderately significant supplier to Barbados and Cuba, responsible for about 6 percent in each case. The Cuban total, however, would be much higher if we were to count American-built ships, regardless of who organized the voyages. American-built vessels, as Leonardo Marques has shown, carried about six out of ten captives between 1831 and 1860, a major, even indispensable contribution to the transatlantic slave trade as a whole. American ships, in the nineteenth century at least, were anything but marginal to the trade.[5]

Assessing the role of the American slave trade in the economic development of the United States is another important task, especially given the decades-long debate over the significance of slave-trading and sugar profits to British industrialization. For the most part, the consensus among historians has been that although slavery and plantation agriculture may have been important to American economic development, transatlantic slave trading was not. A recent collection of essays on the relationship between slavery and capitalism in the United States makes virtually no mention of American involvement in the transatlantic slave trade.[6] This focus on the slave system in the economic development of the United States, rather than on the transatlantic slave trade per se, is essentially correct, at least on a national scale. In 1807, the single most prolific year of the American slave trade, the value of the captives landed by U.S. vessels was equal to about 0.3 percent of gross domestic product. In most years, however, the number of captives carried was about one-sixth of the 1807 peak. In sum, whereas the trade certainly enriched those who participated in it, the actual business of transporting captives did not contribute significantly to the national economy.

   That is not the same as saying the American slave trade was economically unimportant. The real economic significance of the slave trade lay not in the profits it generated for slave traders, but in the labor power of the captives it supplied to U.S. tobacco, rice, sugar, and especially cotton plantations (still keeping in mind that most went to the Caribbean). In other words, in national economic terms, plantation slavery mattered much more than the slave trade. From this perspective, the 1804–1807 period was tremendously important, not just to South Carolina but to all of the cotton-producing states. In just four years, more than sixty-six thousand people landed in Charleston. With American ships delivering forty-seven thousand of them, equivalent to one-third of South Carolina's enslaved population in 1800, the impact of the 1804–1807 slave rush cannot be overstated. It is no exaggeration to say that American slavers furnished, in just these years, a large proportion of the labor force for the early Cotton Kingdom. In the end, however, it was the wealth that the captives and their children produced that mattered the most. In fact, as far as the maritime contribution to American slavery goes, U.S. vessels sailing the "cotton triangle" of the mid-nineteenth century, which linked the North, the South, and Europe, employed forty thousand seamen annually, absorbed 47 percent of national shipping capacity, and generated far more profit and capital than slave trading ever did.[7]

Yet again, focusing solely on the aggregate impact of the slave trade on the national economy misses its regional importance. The slave trade was significant to the New England economy in the late colonial period, with the value of the captives that were sold ranking below only fish and lumber on the list of exports (and well below the carrying trade in general). For Rhode Island during the peak years of 1730–1807, the slave trade played a very significant economic role, far larger than in Massachusetts, New York, or any other state. Before 1776, the profits paid for between one-quarter and one-third of Rhode Island's imported luxury goods and helped to finance many public buildings, such as the Old Colony House, the Redwood Library, most of the churches and houses of worship, and many of the wharves. With no banks, insurance companies, or industry during the colonial era, there were few other places to put the money.

After the American Revolution, slavers did diversify by investing in banks, insurance companies, and textile mills. There is no question that slave-trade profits found their way into these businesses and from there into other things, such as university endowments, with virtually every branch of early national finance tainted. The real question is not whether slave trading contributed to these enterprises, but what proportion of the capital originated in the trade. Unfortunately, that question is likely unanswerable. Given the nature of the documentary record, it is impossible to determine just how much slavers earned from the trade in people versus their other pursuits. Moreover, slave trading always constituted just a fraction of overall economic activity. Even in Newport, Africa never accounted for more than 4 percent of clearances, although the high value of the slavers' human cargoes gave those voyages more weight than shipping figures would indicate. For a dozen or so years in the 1790s and 1800s, the trade was likely more central to Bristol's economy than to Newport's, but other trades were still more valuable. For Rhode Island, it is safe to say that slave-trading profits were considerable and that they found their way into almost every corner of the financial system, but that the profits from transporting plantation produce and other goods played an even greater role in financing its banking and manufacturing enterprises.

Outside of Rhode Island, the economic impact of the slave trade would have been proportionately very small. Boston and New York each dispatched nearly two hundred slave ships, but those represented a tiny fraction of their overall shipping. In the late colonial period, only 0.6 percent of Boston's clearances were for Africa; New York was comparable. And there does not appear to be any significant link between Boston's slave-trading merchants and industrialization in the early national period. Of seventy-eight merchants who were part of the Boston Associates—the group that financed the industrial complex in Lowell, Massachusetts—only two can be directly connected to a slave-trading voyage, with one more involved indirectly as an insurance underwriter. Slave-trading profits were, of course, quite significant to the Charleston economy, but those were generated mostly by commissions on British ships coming in rather than by local ships going out. As always, the 1804–1807 period constitutes an exception, but even then most voyages were organized by traders from elsewhere, with most of the profit accruing to merchants in Rhode Island and Britain. The American slave trade did have a major impact on South Carolina, but more as a supplier of labor for the cotton plantations than as a source of profit in itself.[8]

In 1808, Jabez Bowen manumitted Robert. By this time, Bowen was suffering from mental illness, and he died in 1815 after several failed efforts at treatment. From this time on, Robert's life can be read as an effort to reverse the effects of his enslavement and to ensure that nobody else suffered as he had. At some point, probably early on, he took a surname, Johnson. Surnames speak to family and lineage, which is why they are denied to the enslaved. By taking the name—and significantly, not the name of his former master—he was leaving behind the kinlessness of slavery. Sometime after 1810, he left Rhode Island for Massachusetts, moving first to Worcester County, later to Boston, and finally to Roxbury. At some point, he married Vianna, a Black woman from New Hampshire. The couple raised four children, Susan (b. 1825), Vianna (b. 1834), Robert (b. 1835), and Hercules (b. 1840). The fact that both Robert and Vianna passed on their names to their children suggests once more an emphasis on kinship, lineage, and belonging.

Three aspects of Robert Johnson's later life speak to his lifelong quest to battle racism and slavery. The first of these was his work as a doctor. He first appeared in documents as a physician or doctor starting in 1835 and continued to be identified as such for the rest of his life. Little is known about the nature of his work in that area. He certainly would not have attended medical school, and given the attitudes of the era, he was probably limited to practicing within the Black community. Johnson's second area of activity was as a member of Boston's African Baptist Church. The choice to identify as "African" was common in the early republic, reflecting both pride and unity. It was a new, inclusive identity, much broader than Kissi, his original ethnolinguistic group, so Johnson's membership, along with the fact that he consistently gave his birthplace as "Africa," suggests that he embraced it wholeheartedly. Johnson's third area of activity was in anti-slavery politics. We know his life story mostly because he told it at a meeting of the Massachusetts Anti-Slavery Society in 1837 and again in an interview with a member of that organization. A Garrisonian, Johnson appears to have maintained a lasting engagement with the anti-slavery movement. Much of his life, then, was dedicated to reclaiming what the transatlantic network of Vai traders, Captain Edward Boss, the slave dealers Jennings and Watt, and the Bowens stole from him back in 1797.[9]

Robert Johnson died of pleurisy in 1861 on Tremont Street, Roxbury, at the reported age of eighty-nine. He had seen the American slave trade up close and came within just a few years of witnessing its end.

Chronology

1644	The first "American" transatlantic slave ship, the *Rainbow*, sails from Boston to Senegambia.
1672	The Royal African Company, successor to several previous companies, is incorporated with monopoly privileges barring colonists from trading in Africa.
1673	Nasir al-Din, a Muslim cleric, leads an uprising in Senegambia against the military ceddo states, the first of several jihads that would affect the slave trade well into the nineteenth century.
1696	Parliament passes a new Navigation Act, heralding a crackdown on smuggling and piracy and threatening the New York–Madagascar slave trade.
1698	Parliament reorganizes the East India Company, effectively barring colonists from trading east of the Cape of Good Hope.
1698	Parliament partially rescinds the Royal African Company monopoly. Colonists can legally trade in Africa on payment of a 10 percent duty on exported goods.
1712	Parliament completely rescinds the Royal African Company's monopoly, leaving no restrictions on the slave trade.
1726	Jihad begins in the Futa Jallon, upper Guinea, resulting in the establishment of a theocratic state.
1730	The Board of Trade in London bars colonies from extending the redemption period for paper money. Rhode Island claims to be exempt and continues printing currency, helping to finance a surge in slave trading.
1730	Akyem, a state on the Gold Coast, defeats neighboring Akwamu, sending thousands of captives into the slave trade.
1739	The War of Jenkins' Ear ushers in a decade of naval conflict. The American slave trade declines as merchants shift to privateering and other pursuits.

1742	Asante defeats Akyem, consolidating its power in the interior of the Gold Coast.
1750s	Britain builds a fort at Anomabu, on the Gold Coast, establishing a focal point for American slavers.
1751	Karamoko Alfa, Muslim cleric and leader of Futa Jallon, dies and is succeeded by Ibrahima Sori, a military leader who wages war against neighboring states. In the ensuing decades, the number of people sold into slavery in upper Guinea rises sharply.
1764	The main road from Asante to Anomabu reopens for the first time since 1748, easing the movement of captives to the coast.
1774	Article 2 of the Continental Association bars colonists from slave trading as of December 1.
1776	Futa Toro, a revolutionary Islamic state in Senegambia, is established, disrupting the slave trade.
1783	The American slave trade revives as the Revolutionary War ends.
1787	Rhode Island bans all slave trading, but the law is ineffective.
1787	The U.S. Constitution mandates that the importation of captives remain legal until at least January 1, 1808.
1787	South Carolina, the nation's largest slave market, outlaws the importation of captives from Africa.
1788	Massachusetts and Connecticut outlaw slave trading.
1789	Spain liberalizes its colonial trade laws, allowing foreigners to carry captives to Cuba.
1780s	First American traders establish slave factories on the Rio Pongo.
1793	Whitney's gin sets off a boom in upland cotton, increasing the demand for enslaved labor in the United States.
1794	Congress outlaws the transportation of captives to foreign destinations. The importation of captives into the United States remains legal under federal law, but individual states may bar their entry.
1795	The Jay Treaty allows Americans to trade with the British Caribbean, but its terms effectively exclude the slave trade and force the Americans to find other captive markets.
1796	In Senegambia, Futa Toro invades Kayor for refusing to stop selling Muslims into slavery.
1800	Congress strengthens the ban on the foreign slave trade.
1803	Congress bars the importation of captives into those states where it is prohibited by law.
1803	South Carolina re-legalizes the importation of captives, setting off a rush to land captives from Africa.
1804	Congress bars newly acquired Louisiana from importing captives from overseas, making Charleston into a major transshipment point for the New Orleans slave market.
1807	U.S. slaver *Amedie* is captured by Britain. In the ensuing litigation, Britain asserts the right to enforce the slave-trading laws of other nations.

1807	Thomas Jefferson's embargo becomes effective on December 22, damaging all foreign trade.
1808	The importation of captives into the United States becomes illegal as of January 1. Slave trading from U.S. ports plummets as slavers move to Cuba and dispatch voyages under the Spanish flag.
1812	War with Britain increases pressure on U.S.-based merchants and U.S.-flagged vessels.
1814	British forces at Sierra Leone raid the American slaving installations on the Rio Pongo.
1817	A British court repudiates the *Amedie* decision. Britain's anti-slavery policy now centers on negotiating suppression treaties with individual nations.
1818	Congress revises the 1807 federal slave-trade statute.
1819	Congress closes a major loophole in earlier legislation by decreeing that all captives removed from illegal vessels should be resettled in Africa and appropriates funds for naval enforcement.
1820	Congress defines slave trading as a form of piracy, punishable by death.
1820	All slave trading becomes illegal in Spain's colonial empire, although the trade continues.
1824	A proposed Anglo-American convention allowing Britain to search suspected U.S. slave ships fails. For the next several decades, the United States refuses to allow its vessels to be searched by the Royal Navy.
1824	After a civil war among the Rio Pongo traders, Futa Jallon extends its influence to the coast, ensuring the continuation of the slave trade on the upper Guinea coast into the 1850s.
1830	The Brazilian slave trade becomes illegal but continues, as slave traders move operations from Luanda to Ambriz and Cabinda, and later to the Congo River estuary.
1835	Britain and Spain agree to a new treaty that includes an equipment clause, prompting Cuban slavers to fly the U.S. flag (among others) as a cover.
1840	Brazil-based merchants begin using U.S. ships as both auxiliaries and slavers.
1842	Article VIII of the Webster-Ashburton Treaty obligates the United States to maintain a naval force of at least eighty guns off the African coast to stop and search vessels flying the U.S. flag.
1850	Brazil passes and enforces a new slave-trade law. American and Portuguese slavers abandon Brazil, with some eventually moving to New York.
1853	Leonidas Spratt inaugurates a movement to re-legalize the transatlantic slave trade to the United States.
1858	Britain begins to patrol the Cuban coast but abandons the policy under pressure from the Buchanan administration.
1858	The U.S. Navy begins patrols off the Cuban coast, resulting in more slave-ship seizures.
1860	The last vessel to disembark captives in North America, the *Clotilda*, transports 110 people to Alabama.

1862   Nathaniel Gordon becomes the first and only American slaver to be executed under the piracy act of 1820.

1862   After decades of resistance, the United States signs a treaty allowing Britain to seize American slave ships.

1863   The last known American slave ship, the *Mariquita,* is captured by the Royal Navy.

1866   Spain passes a strengthened slave-trade act, effectively ending the Cuban slave trade.

Abbreviations

ANR	*Aspinwall Notarial Records from 1644–1651* (Boston: Municipal Printing Office, 1903)
BHPS	Bristol (R.I.) Historical and Preservation Society
BNA	British National Archives
BPP	British Parliamentary Papers
BPR	Bristol (R.I.) Probate Record (accessed via ancestry.com)
CDCE	Charleston (S.C.) District Court of Equity
CMTA	Company of Merchants Trading to Africa
CSP	Kevin Davies, ed., *Calendar of State Papers, Colonial Series, America and West Indies*, 45 vols. (London: Stationery Office, 1994)
HCA	Records of the High Court of Admiralty and Colonial Vice-Admiralty Courts, British National Archives
HIA	*History in Africa*
HU	Baker Library, Harvard University, Boston, Mass.
IJAHS	*The International Journal of African Historical Studies*
JAH	*The Journal of African History*
JCB	Brown Family Papers, John Carter Brown Library, Providence, R.I.
JEH	*Journal of Economic History*
JER	*Journal of the Early Republic*
LOC	Library of Congress
MAC	Massachusetts Archives Collection, Massachusetts State Archives
MDHS	Maryland Historical Society, Baltimore, Md.
MHS	Massachusetts Historical Society, Boston, Mass.
MSTL	Medford Slave Trade Letters, Medford (Mass.) Historical Society, online at www.medfordhistorical.org/collections/slave-trade-letters/

NARA   National Archives and Records Administration
NDAR   William Clark et al., eds., *Naval Documents of the American Revolution*,
            13 vols. (Washington, D.C.: GPO, 1964)
NHS   Newport (R.I.) Historical Society
NPR   Newport (R.I.) Probate Record (accessed via ancestry.com)
NTCR   Newport (R.I.) Town Council Record (accessed via ancestry.com)
NYHS   Slavery Collection, New-York Historical Society
NYPL   New York Public Library
PAST   Jay Coughtry, ed., *Papers of the American Slave Trade*, microfilm ed.
            (Bethesda, Md.: University Publications of America, 1998).
PEI   Peabody Essex Institute, Salem, Mass.
RAC   Royal African Company
RCRI   John Russell Bartlett, ed., *Records of the Colony of Rhode Island and
            Providence Plantations in New England*, 10 vols. (Providence, R.I.:
            Knowles, Anthony, 1860).
RISCJRC   Rhode Island State Supreme Court of Judicature Research Center
SA   *Slavery & Abolition*
SCDAH   South Carolina Department of Archives and History
SDNY   Records of the District Courts of the United States, Southern District of
            New York
UM   Cuban Heritage Collection, University of Miami, Fla.
WMQ   *The William and Mary Quarterly*, 3rd ser.

Notes

Introduction: Ships Coming In, Ships Going Out

1. Randy J. Sparks, *Africans in the Old South: Mapping Exceptional Lives Across the Atlantic World* (Cambridge: Harvard University Press, 2016), 81–85. For the original narratives, see *Fifth Annual Report of the Board of Managers of the Massachusetts Anti-Slavery Society* (Boston: Isaac Kemp, 1837), 72, xxvi–xxviii. The basic details of the narratives can be corroborated, but there are some inconsistencies. In one, the narrator says that he was sold to a Dr. Jennings at Cape Mount and then to Captain Edward Boss, "by whom I was brought to Savannah in the ship Hunter, commanded by Capt. Robert Watt or Watts." According to the *Slave Voyages* database (hereafter in these notes, simply *Voyages*, www.slavevoyages.org), in 1795–1797, Edward Boss skippered two slavers that carried captives from Cape Mount to Savannah. See *Voyages*, nos. 36622, 36661. There is no record of a Jennings operating near Cape Mount, but a Daniel Jennings did operate as a Guinea factor in Charleston during the 1780s. See James A. McMillin, *Final Victims: Foreign Slave Trade to North America, 1783–1810* (Columbia: University of South Carolina Press, 2004), 126–127, CD-ROM insert. There is no *Voyages* record for "Capt. Watt/ Watts" or a ship called the *Hunter* fitting the description in the narrative. However, there was a Guinea factor named Robert Watts operating in Savannah during the period that Mr. Johnson landed, so that may be the source of the name in Johnson's narrative. See McMillin, *Final Victims*, CD-ROM insert. The most probable scenario is the simplest: Boss transported the boy to Savannah, where Jennings or Watts sold him to Bowen.

2. Information on the early life of Edward Boss is scarce, but he was almost certainly the son of one of two Newport freemen by that name who lived in the 1740s and 1750s. See Bruce C. MacGunnigle, comp., *Rhode Island Freemen: A Census of Registered Voters, 1747–1755* (Baltimore: Genealogical Publishing, 1977), 15. The career of Edward Boss can be traced in the following sources: *Voyages*, nos. 36522, 36601, 36611, 36622,

36661; Crew List of the *Susanna*, NARA RG 36, French Spoliation Claims, District of Providence, Outward Manifests and Crew Lists; U.S. Census of 1800, Newport, Rhode Island; *Pennsylvania Packet*, December 16, 1788, 1; *The Diary, or Loudoun's Register*, August 1, 1793, 3; *Independent Gazetteer*, June 21, 1794, 3; *City Gazette*, June 25, 1796, 3; *Columbian Centinel*, February 5, 1800, 1; *Commercial Advertiser*, June 16, 1800, 3; *Newport Mercury*, August 12, 1800, 3; *City Gazette*, July 9, 1808, 2; *Rhode Island American*, December 9, 1814, 3.

3. *Voyages*, Estimates, online at www.slavevoyages.org/estimates/7XfKpzvH. Unless otherwise noted, all slave trade statistics are taken from the *Voyages* database. In addition to these definitions, David Eltis points out that the term can also describe the use of the American flag by slave-carrying vessels of various national origins, which was most common during the nineteenth century. See David Eltis, "The U.S. Transatlantic Slave Trade, 1644–1867: An Assessment," *Civil War History* 54 (December 2008): 348. It should not be forgotten that "American slave trade" can also denote the buying and selling of enslaved people inside the United States. Finally, it is worth noting a related term, "foreign slave trade," which was used in the nineteenth century, to describe the transportation of people to North America from the Caribbean as well as from Africa.

4. Thomas Jefferson, "'Original Rough Draft' of the Declaration of Independence," Founders Online, founders.archives.gov/documents/Jefferson/01-01-02-0176 -0004; *Voyages*, Estimates, www.slavevoyages.org/estimates/0SB70vDV.

5. Benjamin Franklin, "A Conversation on Slavery," *Public Advertiser*, January 30, 1770, reproduced in Founders Online, founders.archives.gov/documents/Franklin/01 -17-02-0019. For Livingston's father, see Philip Misevich, "In Pursuit of Human Cargo: Philip Livingston and the Voyage of the Sloop *Rhode Island*," *New York History* 86, no. 3 (2005): 185–204. For Ellery's father, see Cynthia Mestad Johnson, *James DeWolf and the Rhode Island Slave Trade* (Charleston, S.C.: History Press, 2014), 68–69; Ronald Bailey, "The Slave(ry) Trade and the Development of Capitalism in the United States: The Textile Industry in New England," *Social Science History* 14 (Autumn 1990): 373–414.

6. See *Voyages*, no. 25371.

7. Elizabeth Donnan, ed., *Documents Illustrative of the History of the Slave Trade to America*, 4 vols. (Washington, D.C.: Carnegie Institution, 1931; repr. Octagon, 1965); Elizabeth Donnan, "The Slave Trade into South Carolina Before the American Revolution," *American Historical Review* 33, no. 4 (July 1928): 804–828; Elizabeth Donnan, "The New England Slave Trade After the Revolution," *New England Quarterly* 3, no. 2 (April 1930): 251–278. W. E. B. Du Bois made this error in his influential *Suppression of the Slave Trade to the United States of America, 1638–1870* (New York: Longmans, Green, 1894). For other examples, see Charles M. Andrews, "Colonial Commerce," *American Historical Review* 20, no. 1 (October 1914): 60–61; Curtis P. Nettels, *Roots of American Civilization: A History of Colonial Life*, 2nd ed. (New York: Appleton, Century, Crofts, 1963), 435–436; Arthur Cecil Bining and Thomas C. Cochran, *The Rise of American Economic Life*, 4th ed. (New York: Scribner's, 1964), 65, 106–107; James F. Shepherd and Gary M. Walton, *Shipping, Maritime Trade, and the Economic Development of Colonial North America* (Cambridge: Cambridge University Press, 1972), 96–97, 107, 141–144. For a more recent

example, see Ernest Obadele-Starks, *Freebooters and Smugglers: The Foreign Slave Trade in the United States After 1808* (Fayetteville: University of Arkansas Press, 2008).

8. Gilman M. Ostrander, "The Colonial Molasses Trade," *Agricultural History* 30, no. 2 (April 1956): 77–84; Gilman M. Ostrander, "The Making of the Triangular Trade Myth," *WMQ* 30, no. 4 (October 1973): 635. See also John J. McCusker, *Rum and the American Revolution: The Rum Trade and the Balance of Payments of the Thirteen Continental Colonies, 1650–1775* (New York: Garland, 1989), 493; Virginia B. Platt, "'And Don't Forget the Guinea Voyage': The Slave Trade of Aaron Lopez of Newport," *WMQ* 32, no. 4 (1975): 1–22; Sarah Deutsch, "The Elusive Guineaman: Newport Slavers, 1735–1774," *New England Quarterly* 55, no. 2 (1982): 229–253.

9. Jay Coughtry, *The Notorious Triangle: Rhode Island and the African Slave Trade, 1700–1807* (Philadelphia: Temple University Press, 1981). It should be noted that while Coughtry's work was by far the most consequential and influential, other historians were producing high-quality work, mostly in article form; for example, Darold D. Wax, "A Philadelphia Surgeon on a Slaving Voyage to Africa, 1749–1751," *Pennsylvania Magazine of History & Biography* 92, no. 4 (1968); Darold D. Wax, "The Browns of Providence and the Slaving Voyage of the Brig 'Sally,' 1764–1765," *American Neptune* 32, no. 3 (1972); Darold D. Wax, "Thomas Rogers and the Rhode Island Slave Trade," *American Neptune* 35 (October 1975); Elaine F. Crane, "The First Wheel of Commerce: Newport, Rhode Island, and the Slave Trade, 1760–1776," *SA* 1 (March 1980); David Richardson, "West African Consumption Patterns and Their Influence on the Eighteenth-Century English Slave Trade," in *The Uncommon Market: Essays in the Economic History of the Atlantic Slave Trade*, ed. Henry A. Gemery and Jan S. Hogendorn (New York: Academic Press, 1979); David Richardson, "Slavery, Trade, and Economic Growth in Eighteenth-Century New England," in *Slavery and the Rise of the Atlantic System*, ed. B. L. Solow (Cambridge: Cambridge University Press, 1991); Alison Jones, "The Rhode Island Slave Trade: A Trading Advantage in Africa," *SA* 2, no. 3 (1981).

10. *Voyages*, www.slavevoyages.org; Leonardo Marques, *The United States and the Transatlantic Slave Trade to the Americas, 1776–1867* (New Haven: Yale University Press, 2016); Sharla Fett, *Recaptured Africans: Surviving Slave Ships, Detention, and Dislocation in the Final Years of the Slave Trade* (Chapel Hill: University of North Carolina Press, 2017); John Harris, *The Last Slave Ships: New York and the End of the Middle Passage* (New Haven: Yale University Press, 2011). See also T. R. Fehrenbacher, *The Slaveholding Republic: An Account of the United States Government's Relations to Slavery* (New York: Oxford University Press, 2001).

11. Wendy Warren, *New England Bound: Slavery and Colonization in Early America* (New York: Liveright, 2017), 36–47; Mark Peterson, *The City-State of Boston: The Rise and Fall of an Atlantic Power, 1630–1865* (Princeton: Princeton University Press, 2019), 61–62.

12. Robert C. Ritchie, *Captain Kidd and the War Against the Pirates* (Cambridge: Harvard University Press, 1989); Kevin P. MacDonald, *Pirates, Merchants, Slaves: Colonial America and the Indo-Atlantic World* (Berkeley: University of California Press, 2015); Mark G. Hanna, *Pirate Nests and the Origins of the British Empire, 1570–1740*

(Williamsburg, Va., and Chapel Hill: Omohundro Institute of Early American History and Culture and University of North Carolina Press, 2015).

13. Here, I am defining "American" slaving voyages as those departing from American ports. See *Voyages*, www.slavevoyages.org/voyages/DLMCUKqc.

14. Anne Farrow, Joel Lang, and Jennifer Frank, *Complicity: How the North Promoted, Prolonged, and Profited from Slavery* (New York: Ballantine, 2006), 95–119; Anne Farrow, *The Logbooks: Connecticut's Slave Ships and Human Memory* (Middletown, Conn.: Wesleyan University Press, 2014); Thomas Norman DeWolf, *Inheriting the Trade: A Northern Family Confronts Its Legacy as the Largest Slave-Trading Dynasty in the United States* (Boston: Beacon, 2009). See also the film *Traces of the Trade: A Story from the Deep North*, directed by Katrina Browne (2009).

15. The total was approximately one hundred thousand people. Jennie K. Williams, "Oceans of Kinfolk: The Coastwise Traffic of Enslaved People to New Orleans, 1820–1860" (Ph.D. diss., Johns Hopkins University, 2020); Jennie K. Williams, personal communication, January 10, 2022. I would like to thank Dr. Williams for supplying this estimate.

16. Anne C. Bailey, *The Weeping Time: Memory and the Largest Slave Auction in American History* (Cambridge: Cambridge University Press, 2017). For the *Memphis*, see *Voyages*, no. 4315. Determining the biggest American slave cargo with any certainty is a complicated matter. It depends in part on the definition of an "American" slave ship, as discussed in chapters 9 and 10.

17. Helen Tunnicliff Catterall, ed., *Judicial Cases Concerning American Slavery and the Negro*, 5 vols. (Washington, D.C.: Carnegie Institution, 1926; repr., Octagon, 1968), 2:300. On the rate of insurrection aboard slave ships, see Stephen D. Behrendt, David Eltis, and David Richardson, "The Costs of Coercion: African Agency in the Pre-Modern Atlantic World," *Economic History Review* 54, no. 3 (2001): 467–468. For Aptheker's estimate, see Herbert Aptheker, *American Negro Slave Revolts*, 5th ed. (New York: International Publishers, 1987), 162.

18. Jack P. Greene and J. R. Pole, "Reconstructing British-American Colonial History: An Introduction," in *Colonial British America: Essays in the New History of the Early Modern Era*, ed. Jack P. Greene and J. R. Pole (Baltimore: Johns Hopkins University Press, 1984), 14–15.

19. *Voyages*, www.slavevoyages.org/estimates/qL6d4FNz.

20. For recent examples, see Edward Baptist, *The Half Has Never Been Told: Slavery and the Making of American Capitalism* (New York: Basic, 2014), xix, 82–95; Calvin Schermerhorn, *The Business of Slavery and the Rise of American Capitalism, 1815–1860* (New Haven: Yale University Press, 2015), 1–3, 243; Sven Beckert and Seth Rockman, "Introduction," in *Slavery's Capitalism: A New History of American Economic Development*, ed. Sven Beckert and Seth Rockman (Philadelphia: University of Pennsylvania Press, 2016), 1–2; Caitlin Rosenthal, *Accounting for Slavery: Masters and Management* (Cambridge: Harvard University Press, 2018), 3.

21. On outsiderness as a central characteristic of slavery, see Paul E. Lovejoy, *Transformations in Slavery: A History of Slavery in Africa*, 3rd ed. (Cambridge: Cam-

bridge University Press, 2012), 2–3; Sean Stilwell, *Slavery and Slaving in African History* (Cambridge: Cambridge University Press, 2014), 5–12. For a different perspective, see John K. Thornton, *A Cultural History of the Atlantic World, 1250–1820* (Cambridge: Cambridge University Press, 2012), 60–82.

22. France Nkokomane Ntoledibe, "Revisiting Modes of Enslavement: The Role of Raiding, Kidnapping, and Wars in the European Slave Trade," *African Identities* 16, no. 3 (2018): 349–364.

23. Walter Rodney, "African Slavery and Other Forms of Social Oppression on the Upper Guinea Coast in the Context of the Atlantic Slave-Trade," *JAH* 7, no. 3 (1966): 431–443. For a recent discussion of slavery in Africa before the fifteenth century, see Michael A. Gomez, *African Dominion: A New History of Empire in Early and Medieval West Africa* (Princeton: Princeton University Press, 2018), 43–57.

24. Stanley B. Alpern, "What Africans Got for Their Slaves: A Master List of European Trade Goods," *HIA* 22 (1995): 5–43; Emmanuel Kwaku Akyeampong, *Drink, Power, and Cultural Change: A Social History of Alcohol in Ghana, c. 1800 to Recent Times* (Portsmouth, N.H.: James Currey, 1996); José C. Curto, *Enslaving Spirits: The Portuguese-Brazilian Alcohol Trade at Luanda and Its Hinterland, 1550–1830* (Leiden, Netherlands, and Boston: Brill, 2004); Colleen Kriger, *Cloth in West African History* (Lanham, Md.: AltaMira, 2006); Anne Elizabeth Ruderman, "Supplying the Slave Trade: How Europeans Met African Demand for European Manufactured Products, Commodities and Re-exports, 1670–1790" (Ph.D. diss., Yale University, 2016); Kazuo Kobayashi, *Indian Cotton Textiles in West Africa: African Agency, Consumer Demand, and the Making of the Global Economy, 1750–1850* (Cham, Switzerland: Palgrave, 2019).

25. Stephen D. Behrendt, "Human Capital in the British Slave Trade," in *Liverpool and Transatlantic Slavery,* ed. David Richardson, Suzanne Schwarz, and Anthony Tibbles (Liverpool: Liverpool University Press, 2007), 66–97; Philip D. Curtin, *Cross-Cultural Trade in World History* (Cambridge: Cambridge University Press, 1984); Toby Green, *The Rise of the Trans-Atlantic Slave Trade in Western Africa, 1300–1589* (Cambridge: Cambridge University Press, 2012); Roquinaldo Ferreira, *Cross-Cultural Exchange in the Atlantic World: Angola and Brazil During the Era of the Slave Trade* (Cambridge: Cambridge University Press, 2014); David Richardson and Filipa Ribeiro da Silva, *Networks and Trans-Cultural Exchange: Slave Trading in the South Atlantic, 1590–1867* (Leiden, Netherlands: Brill, 2015).

26. On regions of Africa, see Henry B. Lovejoy et al., "Redefining African Regions for Linking Open-Source Data," *HIA* 46 (2019): 5–36.

27. Endangered Archives Programme, British Library, eap.bl.uk/.

28. Farrow, Lang, and Frank, *Complicity.*

Part 1. Slavers as Settlers, 1644–1700

1. This narrative is based on the documents from the trials of Miles Cawson and Robert Shapton before England's High Court of Admiralty. See BNA HCA 24/8; HCA 24/108; HCA 13/60. For a complete discussion, see Sean M. Kelley, "Massacre

at Portudal?: Reexamining the Rainbow, Boston's First Transatlantic Slaving Voyage, 1644–1645," *Historical Journal of Massachusetts* 49, no. 1 (Winter 2021): 113–137.

2. MAC, 60:290. The agreement is reproduced in Donnan, *Documents*, 3:4.

3. There has been some confusion over whether the *Rainbow* was the first North American vessel to engage in the transatlantic slave trade. Bernard Bailyn, citing John Winthrop's journal, points to a 1643 voyage to Cabo Verde as the first, and the anecdote has been cited in several subsequent works. However, the reference appears in the 1645 section of Winthrop's diary, and there is nothing in the entry to suggest that the voyage took place two years before. The reference is almost certainly to the voyage of the *Rainbow,* and there is little doubt that the *Rainbow*'s voyage took place in 1644–1645. See Bernard Bailyn, *The New England Merchants in the Seventeenth Century* (Cambridge: Harvard University Press, 1955), 84, 213 n. 25; K. G. Davies, *The North Atlantic World in the Seventeenth Century* (Minneapolis: University of Minnesota Press, 1974), 114–115.

Chapter 1. Puritan Slavers, 1644–1700

1. Michael Guasco, *Slaves and Englishmen: Human Bondage in the Early Modern Atlantic World* (Philadelphia: University of Pennsylvania Press, 2014), 73, 208–209, 228; P. E. H. Hair, "The Experiences of the Sixteenth-Century English Voyages to Guinea," *Mariner's Mirror* 83, no. 1 (1997): 3–13. Hawkins, of course, attempted to sell several hundred captives at Vera Cruz in 1568 in violation of Spanish trade restrictions. Most of his fleet was destroyed as it attempted to escape the harbor. See Harry Kelsey, *Sir John Hawkins: Queen Elizabeth's Slave Trader* (New Haven: Yale University Press, 2003), 88–90.

2. Bailyn, *New England Merchants,* 32–44; John J. McCusker and Russell R. Menard, *The Economy of British America, 1607–1789* (Chapel Hill: University of North Carolina Press, 1985), 94–95; Margaret Ellen Newell, *From Dependency to Independence: Economic Revolution in New England* (Ithaca, N.Y.: Cornell University Press, 1998), 51–55.

3. Bailyn, *New England Merchants,* 49–74; McCusker and Menard, *Economy of British America,* 95–97; Newell, *From Dependency to Independence,* 52–58; Peterson, *City-State of Boston,* 32–66.

4. Daniel Vickers, *Farmers and Fishermen: Two Centuries of Work in Essex County, Massachusetts, 1630–1850* (Williamsburg, Va., and Chapel Hill: Omohundro Institute of Early American History and Culture and University of North Carolina Press, 1994), 86–100; Mark Kurlansky, *Cod: A Biography of the Fish That Changed the World* (New York: Walker Publishing, 1997; repr., Vintage, 1999), 32–34.

5. McCusker and Menard, *Economy of British America,* 97–100; Daniel Vickers and Vince Walsh, *Young Men and the Sea: Yankee Seafarers in the Age of Sail* (New Haven: Yale University Press, 2005), 25–60; Alex Roland, W. Jeffrey Bolster, and Alexander Keyssar, *The Way of the Ship: America's Maritime History Reenvisioned* (Hoboken, N.J.: John Wiley & Sons, 2008), 31–36; Shepherd and Walton, *Shipping,* 116–136.

6. David Cressy, *Coming Over: Migration and Communication Between England and New England in the Seventeenth Century* (Cambridge: Cambridge University Press,

1987), 156; John Josselyn, *An Account of Two Voyages to New England, Made During the Years 1638, 1663* (Boston: William Veazie, 1865), 32.

7. David Hancock, *Oceans of Wine: Madeira and the Emergence of American Trade and Taste* (New Haven: Yale University Press, 2009), 108–110; T. Bentley Duncan, *Atlantic Islands: Madeira, the Azores and the Cape Verdes in Seventeenth-Century Commerce and Navigation* (Chicago: University of Chicago Press, 1972), 137–157.

8. Hancock, *Oceans of Wine,* 109–110. On connections with the Azores, Canaries, and Cabo Verde, see the many documents in the *ANR.* On Cabo Verde as a slave-trading center, see Duncan, *Atlantic Islands,* 195–238; Toby Green, *The Rise of the Trans-Atlantic Slave Trade in Western Africa, 1300–1589* (Cambridge: Cambridge University Press, 2012); David Wheat, *Atlantic Africa and the Spanish Caribbean, 1570–1640* (Williamsburg, Va., and Chapel Hill: Omohundro Institute of Early American History and Culture and University of North Carolina Press, 2016), 20–67. For Smith's previous visit to Cabo Verde, see BNA HCA 23/14, p. 90.

9. Karen Ordahl Kupperman, *Providence Island, 1630–1641: The Other Puritan Colony* (Cambridge: Cambridge University Press, 1993), 170, 338–339.

10. Richard S. Dunn, *Sugar and Slaves: The Rise of the Planter Class in the English West Indies, 1624–1713,* Norton Library ed., 1973 (Chapel Hill: University of North Carolina Press, 1972), 75–76, 87; John J. McCusker and Russell R. Menard, "The Sugar Industry in the Seventeenth Century: A New Perspective on the Barbadian 'Sugar Revolution,'" in *Tropical Babylons: Sugar and the Making of the Atlantic World, 1450–1680,* ed. Stuart B. Schwartz (Chapel Hill: University of North Carolina Press, 2004), table 9.2; Simon P. Newman, *A New World of Labor: The Development of Plantation Slavery in the British Atlantic* (Philadelphia: University of Pennsylvania Press, 2013), 193.

11. Guasco, *Slaves and Englishmen,* 11–79.

12. Orlando Patterson, *Slavery and Social Death: A Comparative Study* (Cambridge: Harvard University Press, 1982); Claude Meillassoux, *The Anthropology of Slavery: The Womb of Iron and Gold,* trans. Alide Dasnois (Chicago: University of Chicago Press, 1991). For a discussion of the place of slavery in Islam, especially as applied to Africa, see John Hunwick, "Islamic Law and Polemics over Black Slavery in Morocco and West Africa," in *Slavery in the Islamic Middle East,* ed. Shaun E. Marmon (Princeton: Princeton University Press, 1999), 43–68; Paul E. Lovejoy, ed., *Slavery on the Frontiers of Islam* (Princeton: Markus Wiener, 2004). On English constructions of African difference, see James H. Sweet, "The Iberian Roots of American Racist Thought," *WMQ* 14 (January 1997): 143–166; Jennifer L. Morgan, *Laboring Women: Reproduction and Gender in New World Slavery* (Philadelphia: University of Pennsylvania Press, 2004), 12–49.

13. A. Leon Higginbotham, *In the Matter of Color: Race and the American Legal Process: The Colonial Period* (New York: Oxford University Press, 1978), 35, 39. For a discussion focused on New England, see Richard A. Bailey, *Race and Redemption in Puritan New England* (New York: Oxford University Press, 2011).

14. Warren, *New England Bound,* 38–42; Kelley, "Massacre at Portudal?" 126–129.

15. Kelley, "Massacre at Portudal?" 126–129.

16. Donnan, *Documents,* 3:15–16.

17. For a good summary and analysis of the episode, see Warren, *New England Bound*, 221–245.

18. Albert J. von Frank, "John Saffin: Slavery and Racism in Colonial Massachusetts," *Early American Literature* 29, no. 3 (1994): 254–258.

19. Mark A. Peterson has argued that Sewall was part of a broader Atlantic antislavery "Protestant International." See Mark A. Peterson, "The Selling of Joseph: Bostonians, Antislavery, and the Protestant International, 1689–1733," *Massachusetts Historical Review* 4, no. 1 (2002): 1–22. "The Negroes Character," from Von Frank, "John Saffin," 254. For more on early anti-slavery activism, see Manisha Sinha, *The Slave's Cause: A History of Abolition* (New Haven: Yale University Press, 2016), 9–33.

20. Von Frank, "John Saffin," 254–258.

21. Warren, *New England Bound*, 45; Larry D. Gragg, "'To Procure Negroes: The English Slave Trade to Barbados, 1627–1660,'" *SA* 16, no. 1 (1995): 73. The Board of Trade in London investigated numerous complaints about New England's commercial practices, but slave trading was notably absent; for example, George Carr to Arlington, December 14, 1665, in *CSP*, 5:346; Report of the Lords of Trade, July 19, 1677, *CSP*, 10:123; Robert Holden to Commissioner of the Customs, June 10, 1679, *CSP*, 10:372–373; Governor Dudley to the Council of Trade and Plantations, October 1, 1708, *CSP*, 24:110–111.

22. George Frederick Zook, *The Company of Royal Adventurers Trading into Africa* (Lancaster, Pa.: New Era Press, 1919), 5–7; J. W. Blake, "The English Guinea Company, 1618–1660," *Belfast Natural History and Philosophical Society*, ser. 3 (1945–1946): 14–27; K. G. Davies, *The Royal African Company* (London: Longman, 1957; repr., Atheneum, 1970), 38–46.

23. Davies, *Royal African Company*, 122–151; William A. Pettigrew, *Freedom's Debt: The RAC and the Politics of the Atlantic Slave Trade, 1672–1752* (Williamsburg, Va., and Chapel Hill: Omohundro Institute of Early American History and Culture and University of North Carolina Press, 2013), 17–19. On colonial governors' instructions to prevent slave trading, see the Lords of Trade Proclamation of November 25, 1674, in *CSP*, 7:626.

24. BNA CO 155/1, 26–30.

25. BNA CO 155/1, 26–30.

26. Ralph Davis, *The Rise of the English Shipping Industry in the Seventeenth and Eighteenth Centuries* (London: St. Martin's Press, 1962), 81–109. For the quotation, see p. 181. The RAC, which chartered most of its vessels, is a major exception to the rule. See Davies, *Royal African Company*, 194–197; David Eltis, Frank D. Lewis, and Kimberly McIntyre, "Accounting for the Traffic in Africans: Transport Costs on Slaving Voyages," *JEH* 70, no. 4 (2010): 940–963.

27. Bernard Bailyn and Lotte Bailyn, *Massachusetts Shipping, 1697–1714* (Cambridge: Harvard University Press, 1959), 27–40, 56–73, 93, 127–133.

28. Paulette Clark Kaufman, "David Selleck of Somerset, England, and of Massachusetts and Virginia: Soap Maker and Merchant Trader," *The Genealogist* 19, no. 1 (2005): 3–40. On Grosse, see Samuel Adams Drake, *Old Boston Taverns and Tavern Clubs* (Boston: W. A. Butterfield, 1917), 122; Samuel Peck Bradshaw, "Gross Geneal-

ogy: The Descendants of Ezra Carter Gross and His Line of Descent from Isaac Gross," (1921), 3, online at archive.org/details/grossgenealogydeoobrad.

29. On charter parties, see Douglas L. Stein, *American Maritime Documents, 1776–1860* (Mystic, Conn.: Mystic Seaport Museum, 1992), 33–35; John Irving Maxwell, *The Spirit of Marine Law; or, a Compendium of the Statutes Relating to the Admiralty* (London: Chapman, 1800), 214.

30. *ANR,* 220, 291–292, 300–301, 411.

31. *ANR,* 285–287. Williams appears to have been based in England. See *CSP,* 18:477.

32. *ANR,* 220, 291–292, 300–301. For Windsor's nativity, see *Boston, MA: Births, Baptisms, Marriages, and Deaths, 1630–1699* (online database, AmericanAncestors.org, New England Historic Genealogical Society, 2015), originally published as *A Report of the Record Commissioners of the City of Boston Containing Boston Births, Baptisms, Marriages, and Deaths, 1630–1699* (Boston: Rockwell and Churchill, City Printers, 1883).

33. *ANR,* 300. There was relatively little slave trading at Cape Lopez. See Phyllis Martin, *The External Trade of the Loango Coast: The Effects of Changing Commercial Relations on the Vili Kingdom of Loango, 1576–1870* (New York: Oxford University Press), 124. In this case, "Cape Lopez" likely refers to a different location or is an error.

34. Philip D. Curtin, *Economic Change in Precolonial Africa: Senegambia in the Era of the Slave Trade* (Madison: University of Wisconsin Press, 1975), 309–311; on tobacco, see David Northup, *Africa's Discovery of Europe, 1450–1850* (New York: Oxford University Press, 2009), 92.

35. Frederick H. Smith, *Caribbean Rum: A Social and Economic History* (Gainesville: University Press of Florida, 2005), 12–15.

36. Duncan, *Atlantic Islands;* Green, *Rise of the Trans-Atlantic Slave Trade;* Kriger, *Cloth in West African History.*

37. Larry D. Gragg, "The Barbados Connection: John Parris and the Early New England Trade with the West Indies," *New England Historical & Genealogical Register* 140 (April 1986): 106–111.

38. Data on outbound voyages is difficult to come by, especially for the seventeenth century, but probably averaged more than two months when winds were not favorable. On the Senegambia-Caribbean passage, see www.slavevoyages.org/voyages/cGS1nR55. The average journey from all regions of Africa to the Americas took sixty days. On winds, see Daniel B. Domingues da Silva, "Winds and Sea Currents of the Atlantic Slave Trade," in *The Rise and Demise of Slavery and the Slave Trade in the Atlantic World,* ed. Kristen Mann and Philip Misevich (Rochester, N.Y.: University of Rochester Press, 2016), 152–167. For the New England vessels on the Gold Coast, see Robin Law, ed., *The English in West Africa* (Oxford: British Academy, 1997–2006), 1:157, 159, 3:47, 63, 149.

39. George E. Brooks, *Landlords and Strangers: Ecology, Society, and Trade in Western Africa, 1000–1630* (Boulder, Colo.: Westview Press, 1993), 188–196.

40. Charlotte A. Quinn, *Mandingo Kingdoms of the Senegambia: Traditionalism, Islam, and European Expansion* (London: Longman, 1972), 5–17; Donald R. Wright, *The*

World and a Very Small Place in Africa: A History of Globalization in Niumi, the Gambia, 3rd ed. (New York: Routledge, 2010), 88–89.

41. Wright, *World and a Very Small Place in Africa,* 45–50, 69–72; Mamadou Manê, "Contribution à l'histoire du Kaabu, des origines au XIXᵉ siècle," *Bulletin de l'Institut Fondamental d'Afrique Noire* 40 (1978): 87–159; Carolos Lopes, *Kaabunké: Espaço, território, e poder na Guiné-Bissau, Gâmbia e Casamance Pré-Colonais,* trans. Maria Agusta Júdice and Lurdes Júdice (Lisbon: Comissão Nacional para as Comemorações dos Descobrimentos Portugueses, 1999); Al Haji Bakari Sidibé, *A Brief History of Kaabu and Fuladu (1300–1930): A Narrative Based on Some Oral Traditions of the Senegambia (West Africa)* (Paris: L'Harmattan, 2005), 13–33.

42. On defensive measures, see Walter Hawthorne, *Planting Rice, Harvesting Slaves: Transformations Along the Guinea-Bissau Coast, 1400–1900* (Portsmouth, N.H.: Heinemann, 2003), 121–123. Hawthorne's focus is on defense against raids by African "predatory states," but his insights can be generalized to other instances of slave raiding.

43. *ANR,* 220. On purchasing horses in Cabo Verde for export to Africa, see the *Boston Gazette,* December 13, 1736, 2.

44. Wheat, *Atlantic Africa,* 20–67.

45. Bubacar Barry, *Senegambia and the Atlantic Slave Trade* (Cambridge: Cambridge University Press, 1998), 15–17; Paul E. Lovejoy, *Jihad in West Africa During the Age of Revolutions* (Athens: Ohio University Press, 2016); Rudolph T. Ware III, *The Walking Qur'an: Islamic Education, Embodied Knowledge, and History in West Africa* (Chapel Hill: University of North Carolina Press, 2014), 103–105.

Chapter 2. The Madagascar Moment, 1680–1700

1. BNA HCA 1/98, pp. 24–25; Kevin P. McDonald, *Pirates, Merchants, Settlers, and Slaves: Colonial America and the Indo-Atlantic World* (Berkeley: University of California Press, 2015), 31–36, 107–109; Jacob Judd, "Frederick Philipse and the Madagascar Trade," *New-York Historical Society Quarterly* 55, no. 4 (1971): 354–374.

2. BNA HCA 1/98, pp. 138–150; Judd, "Frederick Philipse," 367–368; *Voyages,* no. 70201.

3. Charles T. Gehring, ed., *Correspondence, 1647–1653,* 13 vols., New Netherlands Documents (Syracuse, N.Y.: Syracuse University Press, 2000), 11:55, 134–135, 145, 214; Johannes Postma, *The Dutch in the Atlantic Slave Trade, 1600–1815* (Cambridge: Cambridge University Press, 1999), 13, 25; P. C. Emmer, *The Dutch Slave Trade, 1500–1850* (New York: Bergahn, 2006), 27; Jaap Jacobs, *The Colony of New Netherland: A Dutch Settlement in Seventeenth-Century America* (Ithaca, N.Y.: Cornell University Press, 2009), 202.

4. *Voyages,* www.slavevoyages.org/voyages/ZKVQZJ5I. Several vessels were missing from the *Voyages* database when this search was conducted; for example, the New England vessel *Swift,* Captain Knott in 1696, in *CSP,* 16:374. Four additional New York vessels, the *New York,* which sailed ca. 1689–1690; the *Pembroke,* belonging to Frederick Philipse, which sailed ca. 1701; and two unnamed vessels belonging to Philipse that sailed

ca. 1703–1705 are mentioned in Alfred Grandidier et al., *Collection des ouvrages anciens concernant Madagascar*, 9 vols. (Paris: Comité de Madagascar, 1903–1907), 3:456–458, 562, 617–619.

5. James C. Armstrong, "Madagascar and the Slave Trade in the Seventeenth Century," *Omaly sy Anio* 17–20 (1983–1984): 217, 222–231; McDonald, *Pirates, Merchants, Settlers, and Slaves*, 67–77.

6. Virginia Bever Platt, "The East India Company and the Madagascar Slave Trade," *WMQ* 26, no. 4 (1969): 548–549; Peter R. Christoph, ed., *The Dongan Papers, 1683–1688, Part 1: Admiralty Court and Other Records of the Administration of New York Governor Thomas Dongan* (Syracuse, N.Y.: Syracuse University Press, 1993), 246–247, 250.

7. Platt, "East India Company," 548–549; Hanna, *Pirate Nests*, 185–187, 201–203.

8. *CSP*, 16:480–482; Ritchie, *Captain Kidd*, 38–39; Hanna, *Pirate Nests*, 183–221; McDonald, *Pirates, Merchants, Settlers, and Slaves*, 37–47.

9. Ritchie, *Captain Kidd*, 50; Hanna, *Pirate Nests*, 232–233.

10. *CSP*, 16:221–222, 507, 587; Ritchie, *Captain Kidd*, 168–171.

11. Platt, "East India Company," 552–553. For the post-1700 voyages, Grandidier et al., *Collection*, 3:617–619.

12. Cathy Matson, *Merchants and Empire: Trading in Colonial New York* (Baltimore: Johns Hopkins University Press, 1998), 50, 54–58; Jacobs, *Colony of New Netherland*, 140–143.

13. Matson, *Merchants and Empire*, 56–60.

14. Hanna, *Pirate Nests*, 195–204.

15. Matson, *Merchants and Empire*, 63; McDonald, *Pirates, Merchants, Settlers, and Slaves*, 51; Dumas Malone, ed., *Dictionary of American Biography* (New York: Scribner's, 1928–1934), 14:538.

16. Christoph, *Dongan Papers*, 268–272. On Dutch domination of the trade at Loango in the late seventeenth century, see *Voyages*, www.slavevoyages.org/voyages/OBSdFWF6; Martin, *External Trade of the Loango Coast*, 73–78.

17. BNA HCA 1/98, pp. 138–150, 162–166.

18. "Deposition of Adam Baldridge," May 5, 1699, in *Privateering and Piracy in the Colonial Period: Illustrative Documents*, ed. John Franklin Jameson (New York: Macmillan, 1923), 180–187; *CSP*, 16:106–108, 17:289, 404; Jane Hooper, "Pirates and Kings: Power on the Shores of Early Modern Madagascar and the Indian Ocean," *Journal of World History* 22, no. 2 (2011): 227–228.

19. BNA HCA 1/98, pp. 200–201, 203; "Deposition of Adam Baldridge," 182–183.

20. For example, Baldridge's letters to Philipse, BNA HCA 1/98, pp. 200–201, 203.

21. On the destruction of Baldridge's fort, see "Deposition of Adam Baldridge," 186–187. For Welch's wounding, see BNA HCA 1/98, p. 197. On Welch's dealings with other slave traders, see BNA HCA 1/98, pp. 145–150, 162–166; *CSP*, 17:289. On Welch's death, see Hooper, "Pirates and Kings," 229.

22. For the tonnages of several Madagascar-bound vessels, see "Deposition of Adam Baldridge," 180–187. For the *Margaret*, see BNA HCA 1/98, p. 19, and for the

Peter, see BNA HCA 1/98, p. 159. American vessels of thirty tons were able to take on an average of about 111 captives. See *Voyages,* www.slavevoyages.org/voyages/WnjNwf6n.

23. Christoph, *Dongan Papers,* 268–272.

24. See *Voyages,* www.slavevoyages.org/voyages/1wst5wFL; BNA HCA 1/98, p. 245.

25. On instructions in general, see Davis, *Rise of the English Shipping Industry,* 168–174.

26. BNA HCA 1/98, pp. 140–144.

27. BNA HCA 1/98, pp. 162–166.

28. BNA HCA 1/98, pp. 140–150, 162–166.

29. BNA CO 323/2, p. 383; BNA HCA 1/98, p. 122, 133–155. "Deposition of Adam Baldridge," 182–183. See also BNA HCA 1/98, p. 159.

30. BNA HCA 1/98, p. 254.

31. BNA HCA 1/98, pp. 245–247. On wage labor, see Davis, *Rise of the English Shipping Industry,* 133–136; Marcus Rediker, *Between the Devil and the Deep Blue Sea: Merchant Seamen, Pirates, and the Anglo-American Maritime World, 1700–1750* (Cambridge: Cambridge University Press, 1989), 118–119.

32. Hooper, "Pirates and Kings," 230–235; McDonald, *Pirates, Merchants, Settlers, and Slaves.*

33. BNA HCA 1/98, p. 247; McDonald, *Pirates, Merchants, Settlers, and Slaves,* 99–116; Jacobs, *Colony of New Netherland,* 55.

34. Jane Hooper, "An Empire in the Indian Ocean: The Sakalava Empire of Madagascar" (Ph.D. diss., Emory University, 2010), 78–98.

35. R. K. Kent, "Madagascar and Africa: II. The Sakalava, Maroserana, Dady, and Tromba before 1700," *Journal of African History* 9, no. 4 (1968), 540–546; Arne Bialuschewski, "Pirates, Slavers, and the Indigenous Population of Madagascar, c. 1690–1715," *IJAHS* 38, no. 3 (2005): 415–416; Armstrong, "Madagascar and the Slave Trade in the Seventeenth Century," 214–216.

36. John K. Thornton, *Warfare in Atlantic Africa, 1500–1800* (London: Routledge, 1999), 150–151; David Northrup, *Africa's Discovery of Europe, 1450–1850,* 3rd ed. (New York: Oxford University Press, 2014), 96–105.

37. Hooper, "Empire in the Indian Ocean," 86–87, 99; Armstrong, "Madagascar and the Slave Trade in the Seventeenth Century," 220–222; Kent, "Madagascar and Africa," 542, 544; Bialuschewski, "Pirates, Slavers, and the Indigenous Population of Madagascar," 415–417.

38. BNA HCA 1/98, pp. 135–138.

39. BNA HCA 1/98, pp. 197, 200–201. On the demand for silver on Madagascar, see R. K. Kent, *Early Kingdoms in Madagascar, 1500–1700* (New York: Holt, Rinehart and Winston, 1970), 194. On Abraham Samuel, see Bialuschewski, "Pirates, Slavers, and the Indigenous Population of Madagascar," 413–414. For an argument that ties between pirates and the Malagasy were strong, see McDonald, *Pirates, Merchants, Settlers, and Slaves,* 92–98. McDonald's focus, however, is less on the economic connections of the slave trade than on Betsimisaraka ethnogenesis.

40. On the demand for personal items, see Bialuschewski, "Pirates, Slavers, and the Indigenous Population of Madagascar."

41. BNA HCA 1/98, pp. 140. "Deposition of Adam Baldridge,"183–184. For other mentions of North Americans at locations other than Saint Mary's, see BNA HCA 1/98, p. 197; *CSP*, 18:278; Grandidier et al., *Collection*, 3:456–458. See also J. T. Hardyman, "Outline of the Maritime History of St. Augustine's Bay (Madagascar)," *Studia* 11 (1963): 324–325.

42. Judd, "Frederick Philipse," 367–374. For the later voyages, see Grandidier et al., *Collection*, 3:617–619.

Part 2. Slavers as Britons, 1700–1775

1. "Marine Society Fellowship Club," ed. Marine Society (Newport, R.I.: Henry Barber, 1799); "Laws of the Marine Society: Instituted at Newport, Dec. 5, 1752, Under the Title of Fellowship-Club; and Incorporated by Government, Anno. 1754 Under Said Title, and a New Charter Granted, Anno, 1785, Altering Said Title and Entitling Them the Marine Society," ed. Marine Society (Newport, R.I.: Southwick & Barber, 1785). Voyage totals for each captain are from *Voyages*, www.slavevoyages.org.

2. "Laws of the Marine Society." See also Fellowship Club Minutes, 1755–1771, Marine Society Records, Box 2, NHS.

Chapter 3. Newport and the Rise of the Rum Men, 1700–1750

1. *Voyages*, www.slavevoyages.org/voyages/lYS5FSlM. On the intra-American trade, see Gregory E. O'Malley, *Final Passages: The Intra-American Slave Trade of British America, 1619–1807* (Williamsburg, Va., and Chapel Hill: Omohundro Institute of Early American History and Culture and University of North Carolina Press, 2014), 95–99.

2. BNA CO 389/17, pp. 1–6, 38–43, 48–50, 173; Donnan, *Documents*, 4:14; Marion Tinling, ed., *The Correspondence of the Three William Byrds of Westover, Virginia, 1684–1776*, 2 vols. (Charlottesville: University Press of Virginia, 1977), 1:183–184; *CSP*, 18:449; Louis B. Wright, "William Byrd I and the Slave Trade," *Huntington Library Quarterly* 8, no. 4 (1945): 379–387; Hugh Thomas, *The Slave Trade: The Story of the Atlantic Slave Trade, 1440–1870* (New York: Simon & Schuster, 1999), 330; Jacob Price, "Micaiah Perry," *Oxford Dictionary of National Biography*, doi.org/10.1093/ref:odnb/49953.

3. For the Carolina trade, see BNA T 70/355, pp. 1–3. On piracy in Carolina, see Hanna, *Pirate Nests*, 150–155.

4. Nicholas Radburn, "Keeping 'the Wheel in Motion': Trans-Atlantic Credit Terms, Slave Prices, and the Geography of Slavery in the British Americas, 1755–1807," *JEH* 75, no. 3 (2015): 660–689; Nicholas Radburn, "Guinea Factors, Slave Sales, and the Profits of the Transatlantic Slave Trade in Late Eighteenth-Century Jamaica: The Case of John Tailyour," *WMQ* 72, no. 2 (2015): 243–286. On bilateral trading, see Sean M. Kelley, "New World Slave Traders and the Problem of Trade Goods: Brazil, Barbados, Cuba,

and North America in Comparative Perspective," *English Historical Review* 134, no. 567 (April 2019): 302–333.

5. O'Malley, *Final Passages,* 174–187.

6. For the bilateral trades of New York and New England, see *Voyages,* www .slavevoyages.org/voyages/zubgsjSg and www.slavevoyages.org/voyages/kiAoMjim. On the significance of the carrying trade and invisible earnings, see Shepherd and Walton, *Shipping,* 130–136; McCusker and Menard, *Economy of British America,* 109–110. On the slave trade as a carrying trade, see Bailey, "Slave(ry) Trade," 373–414.

7. *Historical Statistics of the United States, Colonial Times to 1970,* 2 vols. (Washington, D.C.: General Printing Office, 1975), 2:1168; Bailyn and Bailyn, *Massachusetts Shipping,* table X, table XXVI; Davis, *Rise of the English Shipping Industry,* 35; *RCRI,* 4:60.

8. Thomas Richardson to Thomas Bond, May 3, 1712, Thomas Richardson Account Book, vol. 71, NHS; Sydney V. James, *Colonial Rhode Island: A History* (New York: Scribner's, 1975), 169–170.

9. For a useful summary of the literature on agglomerations and clusters, see Edward L. Glaeser and Joshua D. Gottlieb, "The Wealth of Cities: Agglomeration Economies and Spatial Equilibrium in the United States," *Journal of Economic Literature* 47, no. 4 (2009): 983–1028. On the significance for the slave trade, see Behrendt, "Human Capital in the British Slave Trade," 66–97.

10. John Gunthorp to Abraham Redwood, July 22, 1740, Donnan, *Documents,* 3:134–135.

11. John J. McCusker, *Money and Exchange in Europe and America, 1600–1775* (Chapel Hill: Institute for Early American History and Culture by the University of North Carolina Press, 1978), 125–131; Newell, *From Dependency to Independence,* 181–213.

12. McCusker, *Money and Exchange,* 126–131; Newell, *From Dependency to Independence,* 186–188, 196–202; James, *Colonial Rhode Island,* 172–185.

13. Quoted in Newell, *From Dependency to Independence,* 186–187; James, *Colonial Rhode Island,* 178–180.

14. On the Brazilian tobacco trade, see Robin Law, *The Slave Coast of West Africa, 1550–1750* (Oxford, U.K.: Clarendon, 1991), 123, 134–136.

15. Smith, *Caribbean Rum,* 15–16, 28.

16. Bailyn, *New England Merchants,* 129; McCusker, *Rum and the American Revolution,* 434–437, 469–470; McCusker and Menard, *Economy of British America,* 290–291.

17. Kelley, "New World Slave Traders." For the *Mary,* see BNA CO 33/13; MAC 7:158–159.

18. BNA CO 33/14; BNA T 70/355, p. 9; MAC 7:374; *Voyages,* no. 24078. For Captain Thomas's employment by the Belchers, see MAC 7:385, 478.

19. Coughtry, *Notorious Triangle,* 90, 108; McCusker, "Rum and the American Revolution," 770–773, 821. Testimony of Dennis Driscoll, in Donnan, *Documents,* 3:49; Robert Elliott to Samuel and William Vernon, December 5, 1771, NYHS. See also Dorothy S. Towle, *Records of the Vice-Admiralty Court of Rhode Island, 1716–1752* (Washington, D.C.: American Historical Association, 1936), 119.

20. Abraham Redwood to James Woodcock, April 4, 1740, in Donnan, *Documents,* 3:134–135. Gerard Beekman to Peleg Thurston, December 7, 1748, in Philip L. White, ed., *The Beekman Mercantile Papers, 1746–1799,* 3 vols. (New York: New York Historical Society, 1956), 1:70; Chief Agents at James Fort to the CMTA, May 30, 1751, BNA CO 388/45, p. 95 (third set of p. nos.).

21. John Barnes to CMTA, May 31, 1765, in BNA CO 388/52, p. 311.

22. Robert Heatley to Samuel and William Vernon, October 19, 1774, NYHS.

23. *Boston Gazette,* December 13, 1736, 2; Francis Moore, *Travels into the Inland Parts of Africa Containing a Description of the Several Nations for the Space of Six Hundred Miles up the River Gambia* (London: E. Cave, 1738), 111, 116.

24. Smith, *Caribbean Rum,* 10–33; Curto, *Enslaving Spirits,* 19–89.

25. Law, *Slave Coast,* 202; Curto, *Enslaving Spirits,* 19–89; David Northrup, *Trade Without Rulers: Pre-Colonial Economic Development in South-Eastern Nigeria* (Oxford, U.K.: Clarendon, 1978), 166; David Eltis, *The Rise of African Slavery in the Americas* (Cambridge: Cambridge University Press, 2000), 168. On the difficulty of answering this question, see Sidney W. Mintz, *Tasting Food, Tasting Freedom: Excursions into Eating, Culture, and the Past* (Boston: Beacon, 1996), 18–19. For explorations in the dynamics of taste, see Pierre Bourdieu, *Distinction: A Social Critique of the Judgment of Taste,* trans. Richard Nice (London: Routledge, 1984); Carolyn Korsmeyer, ed., *The Taste Culture Reader: Experiencing Food and Drink* (Oxford, U.K.: Berg, 2005); Alan Warde, *Consumption, Food and Taste* (London: Sage, 1997). On alcohol in general, see Gina Hames, *Alcohol in World History,* Themes in World History (London: Routledge, 2012); Mack P. Holt, ed., *Alcohol: A Social and Cultural History* (Oxford, U.K.: Berg, 2006).

26. Mungo Park, *Travels in the Interior of Africa* (Ware, Hertfordshire: Wordsworth, 2002), 29; Barry, *Senegambia,* 35–36, 185–186; Wright, *World and a Very Small Place in Africa,* 67–72, 81, 109–110.

27. Barry, *Senegambia,* 22–23; Al Haji Bakary Sidibé, *A Brief History of Kaabu and Fuladu (1300–1930): A Narrative Based on Some Oral Traditions of the Senegambia (West Africa)* (Paris: L'Harmattan, 2004), 26–27. Confusingly, the term "Soninke" was also applied to these regimes. See Park, *Travels,* 29.

28. Moore, *Travels,* 77; BNA T 70/22, p. 15.

29. Moore, *Travels,* 46, 58–60, 77; BNA CO 388/45, p. 101.

30. BNA CO 388/45, p. 101 (third set of p. nos.); Thomas Thompson, *An Account of Two Missionary Voyages, by the Appointment of the Society for the Propagation of the Gospel in Foreign Parts* (London: Benjamin Dodd, 1763; repr., Society for Promoting Christian Knowledge, 1937), 31–32; J. Montefiore, *An Authentic Account of the Late Expedition to Bulam on the Coast of Africa* (London: J. Johnson, 1794), 40–41.

31. Brooks, *Landlords and Strangers,* 51–52, 59–77; Moore, *Travels,* 31–32. For arrangoes, see Alpern, "What Africans Got for Their Slaves," 23.

32. Moore, *Travels,* 28, 60; Barry, *Senegambia,* 81–106; Ware, *Walking Qur'an,* 100–109; Joseph Earl Harris, "The Kingdom of Fouta-Diallon" (Ph.D. diss., University of Illinois, 1965); Walter Rodney, "Jihad and Social Revolution in Fuuta DJallon in the

Eighteenth Century," *Journal of the Historical Society of Nigeria* 4 (June 1968): 269–284; Barry, *Senegambia*, 94–106; Lovejoy, *Jihad in West Africa*, 36–51, 141–147.

33. *Boston Gazette*, December 13, 1736, p. 2; Moore, *Travels*, 148.

34. Moore, *Travels*, 63, 72, 79. On the term *silatigi*, see Curtin, *Economic Change*, 271.

35. Moore, *Travels*, 79–80; Bruce Mouser, "Walking Caravans of Nineteenth-Century Fuuta Jaloo, Western Africa," *Mande Studies* 12 (2010): 32.

36. Moore, *Travels*, 111, 116.

37. *Voyages*, online at www.slavevoyages.org/voyages/ih7y30Pb. I have omitted those voyages labeled "other Africa" from the total. The overwhelming majority represent voyages for which the African region is unknown, rather than vessels that actually visited other parts of Africa.

38. Kwame Yeboa Daaku, *Trade and Politics on the Gold Coast, 1600–1720: A Study of the African Reaction to European Trade* (Oxford, U.K.: Clarendon, 1970), 21–47; Ray A. Kea, *Settlements, Trade, and Polities in the Seventeenth-Century Gold Coast* (Baltimore: Johns Hopkins University Press, 1982), 176–186, 197–201.

39. For regional overviews, see J. K. Fynn, *Asante and Its Neighbours, 1700–1807* (Evanston, Ill.: Longman, 1971); Ivor Wilks, *Forests of Gold: Essays on the Akan and the Kingdom of Asante* (Athens: Ohio University Press, 1993); Kwasi Konadu and Campbell C. Clifton, eds., *The Ghana Reader: History, Culture, Politics* (Durham, N.C.: Duke University Press, 2016).

40. T. C. McCaskie, "Denkyira in the Making of Asante, c. 1660–1720," *JAH* 48, no. 1 (2007): 1–25.

41. Ivor Wilks, Nehemia Levtzion, and Bruce Haight, eds., *Chronicles from Gonja: A Tradition of West African Muslim Historiography* (Cambridge: Cambridge University Press, 1986), 98, 99, 104, 126–127, 134; Ivor Wilks, *Asante in the Nineteenth Century: The Structure and Evolution of a Political Order* (Cambridge: Cambridge University Press, 1975), 19–23; Fynn, *Asante and Its Neighbours*, 77–78.

42. Ivor Wilks, "The Rise of the Akwamu Empire, 1650–1710," *Transactions of the Historical Society of Ghana* 3, no. 2 (1957): 25–62; Fynn, *Asante and Its Neighbours*, 68–71. Robin Law has argued that the relationship between Akwamu and Ouidah during these years was an alliance rather than a tributary one. See Law, *Slave Coast*, 251.

43. Fynn, *Asante and Its Neighbours*, 72–76. Theoretically, Asante also had an outlet through the Dutch fort of Elmina, but the road to it was easily and frequently blocked by the Fante. See Rebecca Shumway, *The Fante and the Transatlantic Slave Trade* (Rochester, N.Y.: University of Rochester Press, 2011), 106.

44. There has been some debate over the timing of Fante emergence, as well as its nature and strength. See A. Adu Boahen, "Asante and Fante A.D. 1000–1800," in *A Thousand Years of West African History*, ed. J. F. A. Ajayi and I. Epsie (Ibadan, Nigeria: Ibadan University Press, 1965), 175–182; Daaku, *Trade and Politics on the Gold Coast*, 166–170; Robin Law, "Fante Expansion Reconsidered: Seventeenth-Century Origins," *Transactions of the Historical Society of Ghana* 14, no. 1 (2012): 41–78; James Sanders, "The Expansion of the Fante and the Emergence of Asante in the Eighteenth Century,"

JAH 20, no. 3 (1979): 349–364; Shumway, *Fante and the Transatlantic Slave Trade,* 96–108; Randy J. Sparks, *Where the Negroes Are Masters: An African Port in the Era of the Slave Trade* (Cambridge: Harvard University Press, 2014), 18.

45. *Voyages,* online at www.slavevoyages.org/voyages/dPjWQBEF.

46. "Wilhelm Johann Müller's Description of the Fetu Country, 1662–1669," in *German Sources for West African History, 1599–1669,* ed. Adam Jones (Wiesbaden, Germany: Franz Steiner Verlag, 1983), 211–212.

47. "Samuel Brun's Voyages of 1611–1620," in Jones, *German Sources,* 67.

48. Jones, *German Sources,* 213; Sean M. Kelley, "American Rum, African Consumers, and the Transatlantic Slave Trade," *African Economic History* 46, no. 2 (2018): 7. There are many references to rum in RAC correspondence. For examples, see RAC to Robert Plunkett, May 16, 1721, and RAC to Walter Charles, July 18, 1728, BNA T 70/60.

49. Ole Justesen, ed., *Danish Sources for the History of Ghana, 1657–1754,* 2 vols. (Copenhagen: Royal Danish Academy of Sciences and Letters, 2005), 1:296, 292, 608; BNA T 70/5, 1705–1715, p. 6; BNA CO 388/45, p. 3.

50. BNA CO 388/45, p. 3.

51. Eltis, *Rise of African Slavery,* 300; George Metcalf, "A Microcosm of Why Africans Sold Slaves: Akan Consumption Patterns in the 1770s," *JAH* 28, no. 3 (1987): 380, 382, 385–386; *Voyages,* www.slavevoyages.org/estimates/WZkozQNX.

52. C. G. A. Oldendorp, *Historie der Caribischen Inseln Sanct Thomas, Sanct Crux, und Sanct Jan,* ed. G. Meier, S. Palmié, P. Stein, and H. Ulbricht (Berlin: Verlag für Wissenschaft und Bildung, 2000), 1:399; Bryan Edwards, *The History, Civil and Commercial, of the British Colonies in the West Indies* (Dublin: Luke White, 1793), 2:63–64.

Chapter 4. Knowledge and Networks, 1751–1775

1. *Voyages,* www.slavevoyages.org/voyages/NJ5bcTw5.

2. E. Phillip LeVeen, "The African Slave Supply Response," *African Studies Review* 18, no. 1 (1975): 18–19. See also Lovejoy, *Transformations,* 51–52; Patrick Manning, *Slavery and African Life: Occidental, Oriental, and African Slave Trades* (Cambridge: Cambridge University Press, 1990), 96–104.

3. Sean M. Kelley, *The Voyage of the Slave Ship Hare: A Journey into Captivity from Sierra Leone to South Carolina* (Chapel Hill: University of North Carolina Press, 2016), 23–27.

4. The Vernons' slaving voyages can be found at *Voyages,* www.slavevoyages.org/voyages/F8xk8sHV. For the Vernons' non-slaving voyages, see Account of Duties Received Under Acts of Parliament, 1768–1776, NARA RG 36, Records of the U.S. Customs Service, Records of the Customhouses.

5. Coughtry, *Notorious Triangle,* 19–20. Studies of profitability in the British and French slave trades have all suggested average rates of return of approximately 10 percent, possibly lower. If the American rate of return were significantly higher than the European rate, it is likely that British merchants would have taken advantage by partnering with colonial merchants, but that rarely happened. On British and French

profits, see David Richardson, "Profits in the Liverpool Slave Trade: The Accounts of William Davenport, 1757–1784," in *Liverpool, the African Slave Trade, and Abolition,* ed. Roger Anstey (Liverpool: Liverpool University Press, 1976), 60–90; Guillaume Daudin, "Profitability of Slave and Long-Distance Trading in Context: The Case of Eighteenth-Century France," *JEH* 64, no. 1 (2004): 144–171.

6. *Voyages,* www.slavevoyages.org/voyages/3HgHbRle.

7. Timothy Fitch to William Ellery, January 14, 1759, and Timothy Fitch to Peter Gwinn, January 12, 1760, MSTL; William Vernon and Abraham Redwood to Thomas Rogers, June 18, 1756, NYHS; Aaron Lopez and Jacob Rivera to William English, May 29, 1770, *PAST,* ser. B, pt. 2, reel 17. See also Philip Misevich, "In Pursuit of Human Cargo: Philip Livingston and the Voyage of the Sloop *Rhode Island,*" *New York History* 86, no. 3 (2005): 185–204; Darold D. Wax, "A Philadelphia Surgeon on a Slaving Voyage to Africa, 1749–1751," *Pennsylvania Magazine of History & Biography* 92, no. 4 (1968): 465–467.

8. *Voyages,* www.slavevoyages.org/voyages/3HgHbRle. On the Vernons, see Kelley, *Voyage of the Slave Ship Hare,* 23–27. On Lopez and Rivera, see Platt, "'And Don't Forget the Guinea Voyage.'"

9. Joseph A. Goldenberg, *Shipbuilding in Colonial America* (Newport News and Charlottesville, Va.: Mariner's Museum and University Press of Virginia, 1976).

10. *Voyages,* www.slavevoyages.org/voyages/3HgHbRle; Tax List for Newport, R.I., 1772, NHS.

11. *Voyages,* www.slavevoyages.org/voyages/Urp6Lsxk. See also Eltis, "U.S. Transatlantic Slave Trade," 365–366. The figure given assumes that all or nearly all of the voyages listed as originating in "Rhode Island, port unspecified" actually belonged to Newport. This is based on the fact that Newport was a much more important town in the colonial era, with a much larger and wealthier merchant community, as well as the fact that virtually all of the merchants and captains listed for these voyages were associated with Newport. Moreover, by contemporary usage, "Rhode Island" was frequently used interchangeably with "Newport," a practice that dated to the early settlement of the colony. The original Separatist settlement founded by Roger Williams was known as "Providence" and was not located on an island, while a second antinomian settlement was located on Aquidneck Island, which became known as "Rhode Island." The original distinction between the two survives in the official state name, "Rhode Island and Providence Plantations." See James, *Colonial Rhode Island,* 15–28.

12. Peleg Clarke to John Fletcher, May 19, 1772, in *PAST,* ser. B, pt. 1: Selections from the Newport Historical Society, reel 16.

13. William W. Fowler, Jr., "Marine Insurance in Boston: The Early Years of the Boston Marine Insurance Company, 1799–1807," in *Entrepreneurs: The Boston Business Community, 1799–1850,* ed. Conrad Edick Wright and Katheryn P. Viens (Boston: MHS, 1997), 156–159; Christopher Kingston, "Marine Insurance in Britain and America, 1720–1844: A Comparative Institutional Analysis," *JEH* 67 (June 2007): 381. For examples from Rhode Island, see Roffe v. Vernon, November 8, 1759, and Earl v. Vernon, November 6, 1760, RISCJRC.

14. Robin Pearson and David Richardson, "Insuring the Slave Trade," *JEH* 79, no. 2 (2019): 24–25; Gerard Beekman to Thomas Cranston, February 28, 1763, in White, *Beekman Mercantile Papers,* 1:432. The issue of insurance in the slave trade has received much attention in connection with the famous case of the ship *Zong.* See Jeremy Krikler, "The *Zong* and the Lord Chief Justice," *History Workshop Journal* 64 (2007): 29–47.

15. The Vernons' instructions can be found in their papers at NYHS. Fitch's instructions are online at www.medfordhistorical.org/collections/slave-trade-letters/.

16. Albert van Dantzig, *Forts and Castles of Ghana* (Accra, Ghana: Sedco, 1980), 59; Sparks, *Where the Negroes Are Masters,* 35–38, 53–64.

17. For example, John Duncan to Samuel and William Vernon, June 28, 1770, NYHS; Samuel Snell to Christopher Champlin, June 16, 1772, in Charles Francis Adams et al., eds., *Commerce of Rhode Island, 1726–1774* (Boston: MHS, 1914), 1:401–402.

18. Aaron Lopez and Jacob Rivera, instructions to William English, November 1772, in *PAST,* ser. B, pt. 1. The instructions and other documents relating to the voyage have been published in Roderick Terry, "Some Old Papers Relating to the Newport Slave Trade," *Newport Historical Society Bulletin* 62, no. 1 (1927): 13–28. See also Platt, "'And Don't Forget the Guinea Voyage'" 608, 612–614.

19. *A Treatise upon the Trade from Great-Britain to Africa* (London: n.p., 1772), appendix H, 86. See also Peter Dordin to Samuel and William Vernon, July 13, 1763, NYHS. For ship repairs, see John Roberts to "George," November 7, 1754, BNA T 70/1478. Merchants in Britain were another market for American ships, but most of those vessels would have arrived directly, not via Africa. Approximately 30 percent of all British slave-trading voyages between 1750 and 1775 were undertaken in American-built ships.

20. Margaret Priestley, *West African Trade and Coast Society: A Family Study* (Oxford: Oxford University Press, 1969), chaps. 1–3.

21. Fynn, *Asante and Its Neighbours,* 104–108; Sparks, *Where the Negroes Are Masters,* 68–121.

22. Protest of Joseph Gidion [*sic*] Wanton, August 2, 1758, in BNA CO 388/48, pp. 83–84; *Pennsylvania Gazette,* October 26, 1758, 2. See also Anne Farrow, *The Logbooks: Connecticut's Slave Ships and Human Memory* (Middletown, Conn.: Wesleyan University Press, 2014), 105–108.

23. Brew's dealings can be traced in the following trade books: for the schooner *Active,* the snow *Venus,* the brig *Marigold,* and an unidentified vessel, probably the *Royal Charlotte,* NYHS. See also Peleg Clarke Letterbook, NHS. Brew is also referenced in numerous letters.

24. Peleg Clarke to Richard Miles and Jeremy Bernard Weaver, September 4, 1776, Peleg Clarke Letterbook, vol. 76, NHS; Land and Notarial Records, vol. 6, p. 503, Rhode Island State Archives.

25. *South Carolina Gazette,* October 31, 1766, 2; *Pennsylvania Gazette,* October 16, 1766, 2; Peter Dordin to Samuel and William Vernon, July 13, 1763, NYHS.

26. Petition, n.d., 1769, BNA CO 388/57, p. 124. It is difficult not to read the word "Convenant" as a blend of "convenient" and "covenant," which points to the specific influence of the New Englanders.

27. John Grossle to the Committee of the CMTA, September 8, 1769, BNA CO 388/57, p. 119; extract of a letter from John Grossle to the Committee of the CMTA, October 26, 1769, BNA CO 388/57, p. 159. On Dunn's partnership with Grossle, see *A Treatise upon the Trade*, 85–86.

28. Richard Brew to the Committee of the CMTA, July 23, 1759, BNA CO 388/48, pp. 211–212; Donnan, *Documents*, 3:271.

29. Priestley, *West African Trade*, 71 n. 71; Sparks, *Where the Negroes Are Masters*, 145–154; Schooner *Active* Trade Book, NYHS; Snow *Venus* Trade Book, 1756. Additional mention of gold-takers can be found in the trade books of the *Othello* and *Royal Charlotte*, NYHS, and Verner W. Crane, ed., *A Rhode Island Slaver: Trade Book of the Sloop Adventure, 1773–1774* (Providence: Shepley Library, 1922), 7.

30. Peleg Clarke to John Fletcher, January 8, 1777, in *PAST*, ser. B, pt. 1, reel 15. For pawnship on the Gold Coast, see Randy J. Sparks, "Gold Coast Merchant Families, Pawning, and the Eighteenth-Century British Slave Trade," *WMQ* 70, no. 3 (2013): 317–342; Judith Spicksley, "Pawns on the Gold Coast: The Rise of Asante and Shifts in Security for Debt, 1680–1750," *JAH* 54, no. 1 (2013): 147–175.

31. Thomas Melvil to the CMTA, n.d., ca. 1753, in BNA CO 388/46, p. 52; William Chancellor Diary, MDHS, p. 31; John Grossle to the CMTA, September 8, 1769, in BNA CO 388/57, p. 119. Chancellor seems also have written that gold-takers who defraud their clients were enslaved, but the handwriting is ambiguous in the original.

32. Peleg Clarke to John Fletcher, July 25, 1772, Peleg Clarke Letterbook, vol. 75, NHS. See also William Chancellor Diary, entry for August 10, 1750, MDHS.

33. Fynn, *Asante and Its Neighbours*, 84–98 (quotation on p. 85). *Voyages*, www.slavevoyages.org/voyages/eTuHxEel.

34. Fynn, *Asante and its Neighbours*, 93–97.

35. Fynn, *Asante and its Neighbours*, 99–115; Wilks, *Asante in the Nineteenth Century*, 26–28; *Voyages*, www.slavevoyages.org/voyages/6QZo4orM; www.slavevoyages.org/voyages/eTuHxEel.

36. *Voyages*, www.slavevoyages.org/voyages/b9PNner4; www.slavevoyages.org/voyages/XsoCFS9E.

37. For example, Aaron Lopez to William English, May 29, 1770, *PAST*, ser. B, pt. 1. Lopez, however, did this anticipating that the upper Guinea trade would be poor. See also the voyages of the *Rhode Island*, no. 24944; the *Stork*, no. 27218, and the *Wolf*, no. 25340, William Chancellor Diary, MDHS.

38. For example, Charles Bell to CMTA, June 20, 1770, BNA CO 388/58, p. 83.

39. Aaron Lopez and Jacob Rivera, instructions to William English, November 1772, in *PAST*, ser. B, pt. 1.

40. Robert Heatley to Samuel and William Vernon, October 19, 1774, NYHS; Kelley, "American Rum," 1–29.

41. Rodney, "Jihad and Social Revolution," 270; Barry, *Senegambia*, 7, 95–97; Lovejoy, *Jihad in West Africa*, 41–42; Ware, *Walking Qur'an*, 128–129.

42. Christopher Fyfe, *Sierra Leone Inheritance* (London: Oxford University Press, 1964), 78–80; Harris, "Kingdom of Fouta-Diallon," chap. 2; Rodney, "Jihad and So-

cial Revolution," 269–284; Roger Botte, "Les Rapports nord-sud, la traite négrière et le Fuuta Jaloo a fin du 18ᵉ siecle," *Annales: Histoire, Sciences Sociales* 46, no. 6 (1991): 1411–1435; Barry, *Senegambia*, 95–102.

43. Figures come from the "Estimates" section of *Voyages* and include Senegambia, Sierra Leone, and the Windward Coast. Historians emphasizing the Futa Jallon jihad as a stimulus for the slave trade include Rodney, "Jihad and Social Revolution"; Botte, "Les Rapports nord-sud"; Barry, *Senegambia*. For a discussion of Muslim attitudes toward the slave trade in these years, see Lovejoy, *Jihad in West Africa*, 133–146, 159–166; Ware, *Walking Qur'an*, 105–122.

44. Barry, *Senegambia*, 98–99; A. G. Laing, *Travels in the Timannee, Kooranko, and Soolima Countries* (London: John Murray, 1825), 403–410.

45. Timothy Fitch to Peter Gwinn, November 8, 1760, Fitch to Gwinn, October 1762, MSTL; Samuel and William Vernon to John Duncan, August 22, 1772, NYHS.

46. Curtin, *Economic Change*, 68–91; Brooks, *Landlords and Strangers*, 59–77.

47. Curtin, *Economic Change*, 59–91, 271–278; Mouser, "Walking Caravans," 19–104; Park, *Travels*, 324, 330.

48. Robert Elliott to Samuel and William Vernon, December 5, 1771; Brig *Sally* Account Book, Brown University, online at library.brown.edu/cds/catalog/catalog.php ?verb=render&colid=17&id=1161038386638650; See also the unidentified trade book, NYHS, which is for the *Othello*, George Sweet, *Voyages*, no. 36495.

49. Governor and Council at James Fort to CMTA, August 1, 1759, BNA CO 388/48, pp. 222, 225–226; Debat to CMTA, August 20, 1761, BNA CO 388/48, pp. 176–177; Paul E. Lovejoy, "Forgotten Colony in Africa: The British Province of Senegambia, 1765–1783," in *Slavery, Abolition, and the Transition to Colonialism in Sierra Leone*, ed. Paul E. Lovejoy and Suzanne Schwarz (Trenton, N.J.: Africa World Press, 2015), 109–125.

50. On the importance of Niani Maru, see Governor and Council to CMTA, August 1, 1759, BNA CO 388/48; Robert Elliott to Samuel and William Vernon, December 5, 1771, NYHS; Samuel and William Vernon to George Sweet, December 26, 1774, NYHS. See also the earlier accounts in Moore, *Travels*, 63, 72, 111, 116, 148. On the Isles de Los, Bance Island, and Sierra Leone in general, see Melissa Elder, *The Slave Trade and the Economic Development of Eighteenth-Century Lancaster* (Keele, U.K.: Keele University Press, 1992), 147–150; David Hancock, *Citizens of the World: London Merchants and the Integration of the British Atlantic Community, 1735–1785* (Cambridge: Cambridge University Press, 1995), 172–220; Bruce L. Mouser, "Iles de Los as Bulking Center in the Slave Trade 1750–1800," *Revue Française d'Histoire d'Outre-Mer* 83, no. 4 (1996): 45–64; Kelley, *Voyage*, 78–92.

51. Testimony of Thomas Eldrid, in Sheila Lambert, ed., *House of Commons Sessional Papers of the Eighteenth Century*, 145 vols. (Wilmington, Del.: Scholarly Resources, 1975), 69:11.

52. Brig *Sally* Account Book, Brown University, online at library.brown.edu/cds/catalog/catalog.php?verb=render&colid=17&id=1161038386638650. On palaver, see Sean Kelley, "The Dirty Business of Panyarring and Palaver: Slave Trading on the Upper Guinea Coast in the Eighteenth Century," in *Slavery, Abolition, and the Transition to*

Colonialism in Sierra Leone, ed. Lovejoy and Schwarz, 89–107; Quinn, *Mandingo Kingdoms,* 15.

53. Thomas Winterbottom, *An Account of the Native Africans in the Neighbourhood of Sierra Leone, to Which Is Added an Account of the Present State of Medicine Among Them,* 2 vols. (London: C. Whittingham, 1803), 1:170–171, 176. See also Kelley, "Dirty Business of Panyarring and Palaver," 94–102.

54. Debat to CMTA, July 4, 1764, BNA CO 388/52, p. 44. For additional examples, see Debat to CMTA, August 20, 1761, BNA CO 388/48, p. 174; BNA CO 388/46, pp. 90, 120–121, 131–133, 151; *South Carolina Gazette,* July 4, 1754, 2; *New York Mercury,* August 12, 1754, 2.

55. Caleb Godfrey to Samuel and William Vernon, October 16, 1754, NYHS.

56. *Treatise upon the Trade,* appendix H, 86; *Voyages,* nos. 25251, 25376.

57. Correspondence can be found in the Peleg Clarke Letterbooks, NHS. They are also on microfilm with *PAST,* ser. B, pt. 1, reels 15 and 16. Excerpts have been published in Donnan, *Documents,* 3:251–254, 255–257, 259–260, 261–263, 286–289, 291–292, 295–300, 302–307, 308–309, 311–332.

58. The voyage can be followed in Peleg Clarke to John Fletcher, February 24, 1772; July 25, 1772; October 3, 1772; and November 24, 1772, in Peleg Clarke Letterbook NHS. For the second voyage, see *Voyages,* no. 36470.

59. John Fletcher to Peleg Clarke, June 19, 1773; John Fletcher to Peleg Clarke, September 1, 1773, *PAST,* ser. B., pt. 1, reel 16.

60. *RCRI,* 6:378–383.

61. The estimate is based on the average for the years 1761–1763, with 3,359 captives sold at an average price of twenty-seven pounds and with an average profit of 10 percent. See *Voyages,* www.slavevoyages.org/voyages/KEUwPwCn.

Part 3. Slavers as Americans, 1775–1807

1. New England Shipmasters to the Rhode Island Assembly, September 19, 1775, in *NDAR,* 2:156–158; *Voyages,* no. 36511.

Chapter 5. Revolution and Reorientation, 1775–1803

1. Elaine Forman Crane, *A Dependent People: Newport, Rhode Island, in the Revolutionary Era* (New York: Fordham University Press, 1985), 111–116; James, *Colonial Rhode Island,* 329–330.

2. Crane, *A Dependent People,* 119–123.

3. *Voyages,* www.slavevoyages.org/voyages/XsoCFS9E; *NDAR,* 2:156–158. For the text of the Association, see Founders Online, founders.archives.gov/documents/Jefferson/01-01-02-0094.

4. The essential documents can be found in the Peleg Clarke Letterbook, vol. 76, NHS. See entries of October 19, 1775; July, n.d., 1776; September 4, 1776; October 1, 1776; December 1, 1776; December 15, 1776; January 1, 1777; May 8, 1777; March 9, 1778.

5. Gilbert Petrie to the CMTA, October 21, 1768, BNA CO 388, p. 101. On British fears, see CMTA to the Governor of Cape Coast, August 21, 1778, BNA T 70/69, p. 129; *NDAR*, 3:364. For the captures, see *NDAR*, 5:1120–1121.

6. *NDAR*, 10:998; John Bondfield to the Commissioners, May 8, 1778, Papers of John Adams, 6:99–101, Founders Online, founders.archives.gov/documents/Adams/06 -06-02-0071. On the Graftons, see *Voyages*, www.slavevoyages.org/voyages/XsoCFS9E. On Waters, see John Sinclair to Joseph Waters, April 16, 1791, and Insurance policy for the *Abeona*, April 13, 1790, Joseph Waters Papers, MSS 92, box 1, folder 2, PEI. On the destruction of James Fort, see John M. Gray, *A History of the Gambia* (London: Cass, 1940; repr., 1966), 268–269.

7. Sinha, *Slave's Cause*, 10–24.

8. Du Bois, *Suppression*, 5–25, 141–142, 147–154; Paul Finkleman, "Regulating the African Slave Trade," *Civil War History* 54 (December 2008): 380–383.

9. "A Conversation on Slavery," *Public Advertiser*, January 30, 1770.

10. Douglas R. Egerton, *Death or Liberty: African Americans and Revolutionary America* (New York: Oxford University Press, 2011), 62. Complaint of Charles Sorisco, July 7, 1773, in John W. Francis, *Old New York: or, Reminiscences of the Past Sixty Years; with a Memoir of the Author by Henry T. Tuckerman*, bound-volume manuscript edition, NYHS, 9:34.

11. Egerton, *Death or Liberty*, 44–61, 103–121. For a detailed critique of gradual emancipation in New England, see Joanne Pope Melish, *Disowning Slavery: Gradual Emancipation and "Race" in New England, 1780–1860* (Ithaca, N.Y.: Cornell University Press, 1998).

12. Moses Brown to Samuel Hopkins, October 24, 1788, in *PAST*, ser. A, pt. 1, reel 18; Sinha, *Slave's Cause*, 75–76; Charles Rappleye, *Sons of Providence: The Brown Brothers, the Slave Trade, and the American Revolution* (New York: Simon & Schuster, 2006), 226–231, 246–248.

13. *RCRI*, 10:262; *The Laws of the Commonwealth of Massachusetts, Passed from the Year 1780, to the End of the Year 1800*, 2 vols. (Boston: General Court, 1801), 1:407–409; *Acts and Laws of the State of Connecticut, in America* (Hartford: Hudson & Goodwin, 1805), 399–401.

14. Coughtry, *Notorious Triangle*, 207–210. *Columbian Centinel*, October 26, 1791, 50. Coughtry and most accounts give the plaintiff as William Rotch of New Bedford, but the plaintiff was recorded in the press as William Gordon. It may be that the suit was financed by William Rotch of New Bedford but brought by Gordon.

15. Cleveland v. Waters and Sinclair, Essex County Court of Common Pleas, vol. 14, 1792–1794, reel no. 877225, pp. 45–50, PEI.

16. Coughtry, *Notorious Triangle*, 211–212; Leonardo Marques, "Slave Trading in a New World: The Strategies of North American Slave Traders in the Age of Abolition," *JER* 32, no. 2 (2012): 240–241. Perhaps because the state laws are viewed as ineffective, most scholars have had little to say about them, focusing instead on the federal laws; for example, Du Bois, *Suppression*, 23–25; Fehrenbacher, *Slaveholding Republic*, 139–141; Finkleman, "Regulating the African Slave Trade," 383.

17. Samuel Brown to Samuel and William Vernon, June 8, 1789, NYHS.

18. *Columbian Centinel,* October 26, 1791, 50; Groves v. Sinclair, Essex County Court of Common Pleas, vol. 14, 1792–1794, reel no. 877225, PEI; William Bentley, *The Diary of William Bentley, D.D., Pastor of the East Church of Salem, Massachusetts,* 4 vols. (Gloucester, Mass.: Peter Smith, 1962), 1:104–105, 384–386; 2:77, 80, 439, 442.

19. Du Bois, *Suppression,* 38–47; Fehrenbacher, *Slaveholding Republic,* 34–35; Finkleman, "Regulating the African Slave Trade," 384–393; Joseph Grafton to Nathaniel Russell, April 8, 1787, February 8, 1788, PEI; *Massachusetts Centinel,* June 14, 1788, 103.

20. Du Bois, *Suppression,* 55; William C. diGiacomantonio, "'For the Gratification of a Volunteering Society': Antislavery Pressure Group Politics in the First Federal Congress," *JER* 15 (1995): 169–197; Rappleye, *Sons of Providence,* 295–299; Sinha, *Slave's Cause,* 105–106.

21. Navy Secretary to Captain William Bainbridge, July 31, 1800, in *Naval Documents Related to the Quasi-War Between the United States and France,* ed. Dudley W. Knox (Washington, D.C.: GPO, 1936), 6:209; Navy Secretary to Lt. John Smith, February 4, 1801, in *NDAR,* 7:116. U.S. law did not actually prescribe freedom for illegally imported captives until 1819. For the text of the statutes, see "An Act to Prohibit the Carrying on [*sic*] the Slave Trade from the United States to any Foreign Place or Country," Act of March 22, 1794, chap. 11, 1 Stat. 347; "An Act in Addition to the Act Intitled 'An Act to Prohibit the Carrying on the Slave Trade,'" Act of May 10, 1800, chap. 51, 2 Stat. 70; and "An Act to Prevent the Importation of Certain Persons into Certain States," Act of February 28, 1803, chap. 10, 2 Stat. 205. For discussion, see Finkleman, "Regulating the Slave Trade," 399, 401–403; Fett, *Recaptured Africans,* 23–24. For the earliest known (1798) capture of a slave ship by the U.S. Navy, see Fabio Cascadura, "The *Ganges* Affair: An Early Case of Liberated Africans in the Atlantic World," unpublished paper presented at the conference African Ethnonyms in the Era of the Transatlantic Slave Trade, University of Essex, September 8, 2022.

22. Du Bois, *Suppression,* 51; Coughtry, *Notorious Triangle,* 212–220.

23. Coughtry, *Notorious Triangle,* 213–215; Finkleman, "Regulating the Slave Trade," 404.

24. All statistics are from *Voyages.* It is impossible to measure the relative importance of the Providence and Newport slave trades in the post-revolutionary era with precision, because records usually list the port of embarkation as "Rhode Island." It was also common for Providence-based vessels to at least stop in Newport to take on rum and other supplies. This is less of a problem for the colonial era because Providence simply was not a major port. It is therefore safe to assume that nearly all colonial-era slaving voyages leaving from "Rhode Island" were organized in Newport, but that does not apply to the post-war period. For discussion, see Lynne Withey, *Urban Growth in Colonial Rhode Island: Newport and Providence in the Eighteenth Century* (Albany: State University of New York Press, 1984). For the South Carolina merchants, see Petitions of John Holman, January 23, 1791; Christopher Fitzsimmons and William Stephens, December 7, 1792; Daniel O'Hara and John Conarly [Connelly?], December 7, 1792, in *Petitions to Southern Legislatures, 1777–1867,* microfilm ed. (Bethesda, Md.: University Publications

of America, 1998), Race, Slavery and Free Blacks, ser. 1, microfilm ed., reel 8, Accession no. 11379102.

25. Joseph Grafton to Harrison and Matthews, January 6, 1787; Joseph Grafton to James Crowdson, January 6, 1787; Joseph Grafton to James Morque, January 6, 1787; Joseph Grafton to Hunter and Blanchard, January 7, 1787, Joseph Grafton Journal and Letters, 1781–1788, PEI. On Salem in general, see Robert Booth, "Salem as Enterprise Zone, 1783–1786," in *Salem: Place, Myth, History,* ed. Dane Anthony Morrison and Nancy Lusignan Schultz (Boston: Northeastern University Press, 2015), 68–69, 72–73.

26. Edward Oliver Fitch, ed., *The Diary of William Pynchon of Salem: A Picture of Salem Life, Social and Political, a Century Ago* (Boston and New York: Houghton Mifflin, 1890), 236; Bentley, *Diary of William Bentley,* 1:216, 385; Roland, Bolster, and Keyssar, *Way of the Ship,* 102; James R. Fichter, *So Great a Proffit: How the East Indies Trade Transformed Anglo-American Capitalism* (Cambridge: Harvard University Press, 2010).

27. Mark Anthony DeWolfe Howe, *Bristol, Rhode Island: A Town Biography* (Cambridge: Harvard University Press, 1930), 31–57; Johnson, *James DeWolf,* 15–22, 59–67. The family name is spelled in various ways. I have adopted "D'Wolf," on the advice of the staff at the Bristol Historical and Preservation Society, where the D'Wolf Family Papers are held.

28. Bristol Insurance Company Records, in *PAST,* ser. 2, pt. A, reel 12; Mount Hope Insurance Company Records, BHPS; James Madison to Jonathan Russell, December 6, 1816, Papers of James Madison, Founders Online, founders.archives.gov/documents/Madison/03-11-02-0566; Johnson, *James DeWolf,* 51–55; Peter J. Coleman, *The Transformation of Rhode Island, 1790–1860* (Providence: Brown University Press, 1961), 211–212.

29. Coughtry, *Notorious Triangle.* For Collins's relationship to D'Wolf, see Johnson, *James DeWolf,* 42, 85.

30. The full story of the D'Wolfs' integrated enterprise remains to be written. For the basic outline, see George Howe, *Mount Hope: A New England Chronicle* (New York: Viking, 1959), 97–133; Coughtry, *Notorious Triangle,* 47–49, 222–229; James A. Rawley, *The Transatlantic Slave Trade: A History* (New York: W.W. Norton, 1981), 381–384; Johnson, *James DeWolf,* 51–55, 115–126; Marques, "Slave Trading in a New World," 233–260.

31. Joseph Grafton to Moses M. Hays, March 27, 1787, Joseph Grafton Journal and Letters, 1781–1788, log 1, PEI; Policies on the Schooner *Aboena,* April 13, 1790, March 8, 1791, and September 14, 1791, Joseph Waters Papers, MSS 92, box 1, folder 2, PEI.

32. Mary Elizabeth Ruwell, *Eighteenth-Century Capitalism: The Formation of American Marine Insurance Companies* (New York: Garland, 1993), 60, 75–76, 111–112; William W. Fowler, Jr., "Marine Insurance in Boston: The Early Years of the Boston Marine Insurance Company, 1799–1807," in *Entrepreneurs: The Boston Business Community, 1799–1850,* ed. Conrad Edick Wright and Katheryn P. Viens (Boston: MHS, 1997), 160–176; Christopher Kingston, "Marine Insurance in Britain and America, 1720–1844: A Comparative Institutional Analysis," *JEH* 67, no. 3 (2007): 379–409.

33. Bristol Insurance Company Records, in *PAST,* ser. 2, pt. A, reel 12; Mount Hope Insurance Company Records, BHPS; James Madison to Jonathan Russell, December 6,

1816, Papers of James Madison, Founders Online, founders.archives.gov/documents/
Madison/03-11-02-0566; Johnson, *James DeWolf*, 51–55; Coleman, *Transformation of
Rhode Island*, 211–212. For Peter Chardon Brooks, see the policies dated March 9, 1796,
D'Wolf Collection, Ships' Documents, box 1, and October 21, 1801, D'Wolf Collection,
Ships' Documents, box 2, BHPS; Coleman, *Transformation of Rhode Island*, 211–212;
Marques, *United States and the Transatlantic Slave Trade*, 31.

34. Martin Benson to Brown, Benson, and Ives, August 12, 1795, Martin Benson, box 44, folder 12, JCB; Brown and Ives to Martin Benson, August 30, 1799, box 44, folder 13, JCB; Kelley, "American Rum," 20.

35. *Voyages*, www.slavevoyages.org/assessment/estimates; Frances Armytage, *The Free Port System in the British West Indies: A Study in Commercial Policy, 1766–1822* (London: Longmans, Green, 1953), 53–54, 65. Many of the U.S. ships that landed captives in the British Caribbean after 1776 did so because they had been captured and condemned in the prize courts. See *Voyages*, www.slavevoyages.org/voyages/UO6lL5Nw.

36. *Voyages*, www.slavevoyages.org/assessment/estimates. On French regulations, see Joseph Grafton to Harrison and Matthews, January 6, 1785, Joseph Grafton Journal and Letters, 1781–1788, log 13, PEI. On Suriname, see Cornelis Ch. Goslinga, *The Dutch in the Caribbean and Suriname, 1791/5–1942* (Assen/Maastricht, Netherlands: Van Gorcum, 1990), 165–174, 183–193.

37. *Voyages*, www.slavevoyages.org/assessment/estimates. Sylvia R. Frey, *Water from the Rock: Black Resistance in a Revolutionary Age* (Princeton: Princeton University Press, 1991), 142, 174–181; Lacy K. Ford, *Deliver Us from Evil: The Slavery Question in the Old South* (New York: Oxford University Press, 2009), 81–84, 94–104.

38. *City Gazette*, March 17, 1800, 4.

39. José Luciano Franco, *Comercio clandestino de esclavos* (Havana, Cuba: Editorial de Ciencas Sociales, 1980), 93–101; David R. Murray, *Odious Commerce: Britain, Spain and the Abolition of the Cuban Slave Trade* (Cambridge: Cambridge University Press, 1980), 8–17; Ada Ferrer, *Freedom's Mirror: Cuba and Haiti in the Age of Revolution* (Cambridge: Cambridge University Press, 2014), 17–43.

40. Luis A. Pérez, *Cuba and the United States: Ties of Singular Intimacy* (Athens and London: University of Georgia Press, 1997), 7, 18. For the D'Wolfs, see at BHPS: unknown to John Sabens, November 16, 1803, D'Wolf Collection, Ships' Documents, box 4, and James D'Wolf to John D'Wolf, December 20, 1805, D'Wolf Collection, Ships' Documents, box 6; Invoice, February 12, 1800, box 4; Account, April 21, 1791, box 3; Account, April 27, 1805, box 2; Account, April 27, 1804, box 1. For Tunno and Cox, see Richard Stone Blayney to Adam Johnson, September 22, 1805, BNA HCA 42/409, pp. 35–41; George Cushing to Nathaniel Jones, March 11, 1800, George A. Cushing Letter Book, 1799–1802, MSS: 766 799-1802 C984, HU.

41. Stephen Chambers, *No God but Gain: The Untold Story of Cuban Slavery, the Monroe Doctrine and the Making of the United States* (London: Verso, 2015), 25, 33–42. For the D'Wolfs, see, for example, the account of the bark *Polly* with James D'Wolf, April 21, 1791, D'Wolf Collection, Ships' Documents, box 3, BHPS. For William Vernon, see David Nagle to William Vernon, March 16, 1793, NYHS. For Fales and Ahearn, see

Instructions to George Shearman, January 3, 1798, HCA 42/299/486; on Santa Maria y Cuesta, see George Cushing to John Parker, January 3, 1801; George Cushing to John Luis de la Cuesta, February 22, 1801; and George Cushing to John Luis de la Cuesta, September 12, 1801, Cushing Letter Book, HU.

42. Chambers, *No God but Gain,* 39; George Cushing to Father, April 18, 1799, Cushing Letter Book, HU.

43. See *Voyages.* The proportion varies depending on whether and how one queries the database or the Estimates, www.slavevoyages.org/assessment/estimates.

44. Sparks, *Where the Negroes Are Masters,* 211–215; Ty M. Reese, "Liberty, Insolence and Rum: Cape Coast and the American Revolution," *Itinerario* 28, no. 3 (2004): 25–26.

45. Coughtry, *Notorious Triangle,* 115–117; Reese, "Liberty, Insolence and Rum," 26–27.

46. Priestley, *West African Trade,* 80; *Journal of the Commissioners for Trade and Plantations,* 14 vols. (London: Stationery Office, 1933), 14:129–132, 134–137, 141–146.

47. Samuel Brown to William Vernon, March 11, 1792, NYHS; John Sabens to John D'Wolf[?], n.d., D'Wolf Collection, Ships' Documents, box 6, BHPS; Wilfred Howard Munro, *History of Bristol, R.I.: The Story of the Mount Hope Lands* (Providence: J. A. & R. A. Reid, 1880), 350–351. For American vessels stopping at Cape Apollonia, see John Fletcher to Peleg Clarke, October 19, 1775, Peleg Clarke Letterbooks, 1774–1782, item 76, NHS; *Journal of the Commissioners for Trade and Plantations,* 14:129–131; Navigation Logs and Accounts for the Ship *Charlotte,* also for the Schooners *Dolphin* and *Punch,* 1803–1806, BHPS. Entry for January 23, 1806, Deposition of James Gardner Butler, BNA HCA 42/331/1226, pp. 6–8.

48. Walter Rodney, "Gold and Slaves on the Gold Coast," *Transactions of the Historical Society of Ghana* 10, no. 1 (1969): 23; Marion Johnson, "The Ounce in Eighteenth-Century West African Trade," *JAH* 7, no. 2 (1966): 204; George Metcalf, "Gold, Assortments and the Trade Ounce: Fante Merchants and the Problem of Supply and Demand in the 1770s," *JAH* 28, no. 1 (1987): 34–36; Spicksley, "Pawns on the Gold Coast," 147–175; T. C. McCaskie, *State and Society in Pre-Colonial Asante* (Cambridge: Cambridge University Press, 1995), 38–41.

49. Fynn, *Asante and Its Neighbours,* 124–126.

50. *Voyages,* www.slavevoyages.org/assessment/estimates; Fynn, *Asante and its Neighbours,* 137–140.

51. Samuel Brown to Samuel and William Vernon, October 30, 1785; Samuel Brown to Samuel and William Vernon, July 3, 1792; William Vernon to Samuel Vernon, January 20, 1793, NYHS; *Voyages,* www.slavevoyages.org/voyages/XsoCFS9E; Alex Borucki, "The U.S. Slave Ship Ascension in the Río de la Plata: Slave Routes and Circuits of Silver in the Late Eighteenth-Century Atlantic and Beyond," *Colonial Latin American Review* 29, no. 4 (2020): 630–657.

52. Deposition of Caleb Green, n.d., 1802, box 15, NARA Boston, RG 21, Records of the U.S. District Court for Massachusetts; Deposition of George Shearman, BNA HCA 42/299/486.

53. David Robinson, "The Islamic Revolution of Fuuta Toro," *IJAHS* 8, no. 2 (1975): 185–221; Martin A. Klein, "Servitude Among the Wolof and Sereer of Senegambia," in *Slavery in Africa: Historical and Anthropological Perspectives,* ed. Suzanne Miers and Igor Kopytoff (Madison: University of Wisconsin Press, 1977), 342–343; Barry, *Senegambia,* 102–105; Lovejoy, *Jihad in West Africa,* 42–45.

54. James F. Searing, *West African Slavery and Atlantic Commerce: The Senegal River Valley, 1700–1860* (Cambridge: Cambridge University Press, 1993), 157–162; Barry, *Senegambia,* 104–106; Ware, *Walking Qur'an,* 125–140; Lovejoy, *Jihad in West Africa,* 44–45.

55. Searing, *West African Slavery,* 130–131; Richard Roberts, *Warriors, Merchants, and Slaves: The State and the Economy in the Middle Niger Valley, 1700–1914* (Stanford, Calif.: Stanford University Press, 1987), 47.

56. Christopher Fyfe, *A History of Sierra Leone* (London: Oxford University Press, 1962); John Peterson, *Province of Freedom: A History of Sierra Leone, 1787–1870* (Evanston, Ill.: Northwestern University Press, 1969); Lovejoy and Schwarz, eds., *Slavery, Abolition, and the Transition to Colonialism in Sierra Leone.*

57. *Substance of the Report Delivered by the Court of Directors of the Sierra Leone Company* (London: James Phillips and George Yard, 1794), 90, 95–96, 102–103.

58. *Substance of the Report,* 121–122. The Sierra Leone Council reported at least four Massachusetts vessels to state authorities between 1793 and 1795. See "Extract from the Letters of the Governor and Council at Sierra Leone to the Court of Directors of the Sierra Leone Company" and letter from Henry Thornton in London, dated March 12, 1795, Black History Collection, Sierra Leone Company, box 3, LOC.

59. Bruce L. Mouser, "Trade, Coasters, and Conflict in the Rio Pongo from 1790 to 1808," *JAH* 14, no. 1 (1973): 45–64; Bruce L. Mouser, *American Colony on the Rio Pongo: The War of 1812, the Slave Trade, and the Proposed Settlement of African Americans, 1810–1830* (Trenton, N.J.: Africa World Press, 2013), 19–30, 44–45.

60. Bill of Complaint by Daniel McNeill, 1810, CDCE, reel 180, SCDAH; Greenwood v. Curtis, Massachusetts Supreme Judicial Court, 6 Mass. 358.

61. Harris, "Kingdom of Fouta-Diallon," chap. 2; Barry, *Senegambia,* 99; Bruce L. Mouser, ed., *Journal of James Watt: Expedition to Timbo Capital of the Fulbe Empire in 1794* (Madison: African Studies Program, University of Wisconsin, 1994), 44, 62.

62. *Herald of Freedom,* May 18, 1790, 74; Bruce L. Mouser, "Rebellion, Marronage, and *Jihad:* Strategies of Resistance to Slavery on the Sierra Leone Coast, c. 1783–1796," *JAH* 48, no. 1 (2007): 38–40; Lovejoy, *Jihad in West Africa,* 42, 45.

Chapter 6. Crescendo, 1804–1807

1. *Voyages,* www.slavevoyages.org/voyages/nTwqKbPl. Eltis, "U.S. Transatlantic Slave Trade," 363, 369; Marques, *United States and the Transatlantic Slave Trade;* Donnan, *Documents,* 4:526–527.

2. Rachel N. Klein, *Unification of a Slave State: The Rise of the Planter Class in the South Carolina Backcountry* (Chapel Hill: University of North Carolina Press,

1990), 246–257; Michael Tadman, *Speculators and Slaves: Masters, Traders, and Slaves in the Old South* (Madison: University of Wisconsin Press, 1989), 12, 226. The 28 percent figure represents Tadman's estimate of twenty-nine thousand captives retained in South Carolina and Georgia as a percentage of the enslaved population growth from 1800 to 1810.

3. Gwendolyn Midlo Hall, *Africans in Colonial Louisiana: The Development of Afro-Creole Culture in the Eighteenth Century* (Baton Rouge: Louisiana State University Press, 1992), 34–35, 120–122; Adam Rothman, *Slave Country: American Expansion and the Origins of the Deep South* (Cambridge: Harvard University Press, 2005), 73–78.

4. Hall, *Africans in Colonial Louisiana*, 57–58, 278; Rothman, *Slave Country*, 85–88. Gwendolyn Midlo Hall, *Afro-Louisiana History and Genealogy, 1719–1820* (database), online at www.ibiblio.org/laslave/calcs/slaveOrDec.jpg; Kevin David Roberts, "Slaves and Slavery in Louisiana: The Evolution of Atlantic World Identities, 1791–1831" (Ph.D. diss., University of Texas, 2003), 103–121.

5. Tadman, *Speculators and Slaves*, 12, 226.

6. Manuel Moreno Fraginals, *El Ingenio: Complejo económico-social cubano del azúcar* (Barcelona: Crítica, 2001; 1974), 81; *Voyages*, www.slavevoyages.org/estimates/O2ThL8Lk. For price data, see Laird W. Bergad, Fe Iglesias García, and María del Carmen Barcia, *The Cuban Slave Market, 1790–1880* (Cambridge: Cambridge University Press), 162–163.

7. Georgia permitted the landing of enslaved Africans before 1798, and North Carolina allowed it from 1790 to 1794. See Fehrenbacher, *Slaveholding Republic*, 139.

8. Ford, *Deliver Us from Evil*, 82–85. The trajectory of these laws can be traced in Thomas Cooper and James McCord, eds., *The Statutes at Large of South Carolina*, 10 vols. (Columbia, S.C.: A. S. Johnston, 1837), 7:430–449.

9. Ford, *Deliver Us from Evil*, 94–101; Donnan, *Documents*, 4:503.

10. Ford, *Deliver Us from Evil*, 107–111; Rothman, *Slave Country*, 23–25; *Annals of Congress*, 8th Cong., 1st Sess., January 26, 1804, 240–241.

11. *Carolina Gazette*, December 7, 1804, 3; December 11, 1805, 3; December 13, 1805, 3.

12. Smith's list can be found in *Annals of Congress*, 16th Cong., 2d Sess., December 8, 1820, 73–76. Similarly, James A. McMillin has compiled a list of "Slave Merchants," without distinguishing between the commission merchants who handled sales and those who organized voyages. Materials in McMillin's appendix B (on CD-ROM) suggest that the vast majority of these merchants handled incoming vessels and did not organize voyages. The list also includes merchants who were involved in the local and intra-American trades. See McMillin, *Final Victims*, 120–152 and CD-ROM.

13. *City Gazette*, January 4, 1804, 3; McMillin, *Final Victims*, 128; Thomas, *Slave Trade*, 545–546. For biographical details on Phillips, see *Newport Mercury*, November 21, 1818, 3; for Gardner, see Rhode Island: Historical Cemeteries, 1647–2000, online database: AmericanAncestors.org, New England Historic Genealogical Society, 2018.

14. Johnson, *James DeWolf*, 94; Bill No. 60, CDCE, reel 177, 1807 SCDAH; McMillin, *Final Victims*, 130.

15. C. Clark and W. Finnelly, *Reports of Cases Decided in the House of Lords . . . During the Sessions 1839 & 1840,* vol. 7 (London: V. and R. Stevens and G. S. Norton, 1842), 707; *City Gazette,* August 14, 1801, 1; *City Gazette,* October 29, 1805, 3; *City Gazette,* February 12, 1807, 1; Will of William Broadfoot, May 13, 1827, Charleston Wills, SCDAH.

16. *The Times* (London), December 12, 1805, 3; Bill No. 24, 1809, CDCE, reel 179, SCDAH; *Voyages,* slavevoyages.org/voyages/ixcBmBRX; Will of William Boyd, May 20, 1814, Charleston Wills, SCDAH. For another very complex Boyd-owned slaving voyage, see BNA HCA 42/327/1185.

17. Campbell's activities can be traced in Bill No. 24, 1808, CDCE, reel 178, and Bill No. 33, 1809, CDCE, reel 179, SCDAH. According to one of his partners, Campbell intended to send a sixth vessel to Africa but died before it could sail.

18. Examination of Duncan Stewart, BNA HCA 42/521/1283; Clark and Finnelly, *Reports of Cases,* 707–710.

19. Statement of James Taylor, BNA HCA 45/61/4. For another example of a local merchant hiring a British supercargo, see Michael E. Stevens, "To Get as Many Slaves as You Can: An 1807 Slaving Voyage," *South Carolina Historical Magazine* 87 (July 1986): 188. In this instance, the vessel sailed to upper Guinea.

20. Catterall, *Judicial Cases,* 2:295; Donnan, *Documents,* 4:573, 579.

21. *City Gazette,* December 11, 1805, 1; September 4, 1806, 1; October 13, 1806, 1; January 23, 1807, 1; January 31, 1807, 1.

22. *City Gazette,* September 7, 1804, 3; March 3, 1806, 3.

23. Petition of Christopher Fitzsimons, December 7, 1792, *Petitions to Southern Legislatures, 1777–1867* (Bethesda, Md.: University Publications of America, 1998), Race, Slavery and Free Blacks, ser. 1, microfilm ed., reel 8, Accession no. 11379207; *City Gazette,* November 27, 1801, 1. Fitzsimons also handled captive sales as a commission merchant. See *City Gazette,* November 6, 1804, 2; January 3, 1808, 3.

24. For example, ship *Charlotte* Account Book, D'Wolf Collection, Ships' Documents, box 2, BHPS; undated letter, ca. 1804–1807, D'Wolf Collection, Ships' Documents, box 2, folder 23, BHPS. The highest total observed for an American vessel at Goreé in these years was fifty-seven captives. See the deposition of Capt. William Milbery, BNA HCA 42/456/766.

25. W. Munro to John Sabens, December 11, 1804; John Sabens to John D'Wolf, January 1, 1805; Ship *Charlotte* Account Book, D'Wolf Collection, Ships' Documents, box 2, BHPS. American vessels had begun visiting the Gallinas as part of the southward shift from the Gambia to Sierra Leone. For three other American vessels at the Gallinas in 1800, see Walter Dalton to James D'Wolf, June 19, 1800, BNA HCA 45/44/20. On Futa Toro, see Robinson, "Islamic Revolution," 210–211. On the slave trade at the Gallinas, see Adam Jones, *From Slaves to Palm Kernels: A History of the Galinhas Country (West Africa), 1730–1890* (Wiesbaden, Germany: Franz Steiner Verlag, 1983), 37–38.

26. Crew examinations and ships' papers for the *Tartar,* BNA HCA 45/61/4; Donnan, *Documents,* 4:530. One of the traders who consigned captives to the *Tartar* was Samuel Samo, who would later be the subject of a major slave-trading prosecution. One

examination in the *Tartar* case says Samo was a U.S. citizen, but this is contradicted at his own trial by prosecutors, who claimed he was British. Still other documents suggest he was Dutch. See Mouser, *American Colony*, 26.

27. *Voyages,* www.slavevoyages.org/voyages/CQyBHOVV; Donnan, *Documents,* 4:556–558.

28. Phyllis M. Martin, "Power, Cloth, and Currency on the Loango Coast," *African Economic History* 15, no. 1 (1986): 1–9.

29. BNA HCA 42/521/1283; HCA 42/455/757; HCA 42/409/408.

30. Martin, *External Trade of the Loango Coast,* 107–108; Stacey Jean Muriel Sommerdyk, "Trade and the Merchant Community of the Loango Coast in the Eighteenth Century" (Ph.D. diss., University of Hull, 2012), 104–105, 190, 194–195.

31. Holmes to Charles Christie, December 12, 1806, Bill No. 27, 1807, CDCE, reel 176, SCDAH.

32. *City Gazette,* April 23, 1807, 2; Omar Ibn Said, *A Muslim American Slave: The Life of Omar Ibn Said,* ed. Ala Alryyes (Madison: University of Wisconsin Press, 2011); Sitiki, *Odyssey of an African Slave,* ed. Patricia Griffin (Gainesville: University of Florida Press, 2009).

33. Ships' Documents, box 4, D'Wolf Collection, BHPS; Benjamin Joy Papers, MHS; BNA HCA 42/321/1149; HCA 42/455/757; George W. Erving to James Madison, October 25, 1804, Founders Online, founders.archives.gov/documents/Madison/02-08-02-0220.

34. Alex Borucki, "The Slave Trade to the Río de la Plata, 1777–1812: Trans-Imperial Networks and Atlantic Warfare," *Colonial Latin American Review* 20, no. 1 (2011): 85–86, 89; Fabrício Prado, "Conexões Atlânticas: Redes c omerciais entre o Rio da Prata e os Estados Unidos (1790–1822)," *Anos 90* 24 (July 2017): 139–143. For the D'Wolfs, see John Sabens to James D'Wolf, December 21, 1800, D'Wolf Collection, Ships' Documents, box 4, BHPS; Marques, *United States and the Transatlantic Slave Trade,* 30. For Holmes and the *Hindustan,* see Instructions from Holmes & Co. to Charles Christie, December 12, 1806, Bill No. 27, 1807, CDCE, reel 176, SCDAH.

35. John Sabens to James D'Wolf, December 21, 1800; Manuel de Sarratea to John Sabens, January 2, 1801, Ships' Documents, box 4, D'Wolf Collection, BHPS.

36. Joseph Russell to Benjamin Joy, July 24, 1802, December 21, 1802, March 15, 1803, April 12, 1803, June 10, 1803, August, 30, 1803; Memorial of Joseph Russell, February 22, 1819, Benjamin Joy Papers, MHS.

37. Instructions to Captain Milbery, n.d. 1805, BNA HCA 42/456/766; Bill of Lading, May 18, 1801, box 4, Ships' Documents, D'Wolf Collection, BHPS. On tasajo, see Andrew Sluyter, "The Hispanic Atlantic's Tasajo Trail," *Latin American Research Review* 45, no. 1 (2010): 98–120.

38. Agreement with Captain John Sabens, May 17, 1801; Bill of Lading, May 18, 1801, box 4, D'Wolf Collection, Ships' Documents, BHPS; Bill No. 33, 1809, CDCE, reel 179, SCDAH; Instructions to Captain Milbery, n.d. 1805, BNA HCA 42/456/766.

39. Mason, "Slavery Overshadowed: Congress Debates Prohibiting the Atlantic Slave Trade to the United States, 1806–1807," *JER* 20, no. 1 (2000): 62–63.

40. Mason, "Slavery Overshadowed," 63–71; Thomas Jefferson, Sixth Annual Message to Congress, December 2, 1806, online at the Avalon Project, avalon.law.yale.edu/19th_century/jeffmes6.asp; *Annals of Congress,* 9th Cong., 2d Sess., December 29, 1806, 220–221, 477–478, 483–484, 486–487, 626, 636–638.

41. Mason, "Slavery Overshadowed," 70–73; *Annals of Congress,* 9th Cong., 2d Sess., 636–637; for the full text, see "An Act to Prohibit the Importation of Slaves," Act of March 2, 1807, chap. 22, 2 Stat. 426.

42. *Voyages,* slavevoyages.org/voyages/ixcBmBRX. For a vessel carrying "cash," see Examination of Joshua Viall, BNA HCA 42/472/864.

43. Charles Clarke to "Mamma," January 17, 1808, Ships' Documents, box 3, D'Wolf Collection, BHPS.

44. U.S. v. The *Kitty,* 26 Fed. Cas., 791; Phillips and Gardner to Joshua Viall, June 5, 1807, BNA HCA 42/472/864; Archibald M. Cock to James Madison, May 31, 1808, Founders Online, founders.archives.gov/documents/Madison/99-01-02-3136; John Frazer to James Madison, May 4, 1809, Founders Online, founders.archives.gov/documents/Madison/03-01-02-0191. Frazer claimed that he sold most of his captives at Saint Kitts, a British colony. Additional details of the voyage are not known. However, if Frazer's claim is true, this would have been a violation of Britain's Slave Trade Abolition Act, which decreed that any captives landed after May 1, 1807, would be confiscated by the Crown, "liberated," and entered into apprenticeships or enlisted into the military. It is also possible that Frazer was not telling the whole truth in his petition.

45. Sean M. Kelley, "Precedents: The 'Captured Negroes' of Tortola, 1807–1822," in *Liberated Africans and the Abolition of the Slave Trade, 1807–1896,* ed. Richard Anderson and Henry B. Lovejoy (Rochester, N.Y.: University of Rochester Press, 2020), 31.

46. Kelley, "Precedents," 29–33.

47. Kelley, "Precedents," 33–38; Jenny S. Martinez, *The Slave Trade and the Origins of International Human Rights Law* (New York: Oxford University Press, 2012), 25.

48. Kelley, "Precedents," 34–35.

Part 4. Life and Death in the Slave Trade, 1700–1807

1. Information about these and other markers can be found by searching the "Comments" for "Africa" at rihistoriccemeteries.org/searchgravesComments.aspx.

2. This estimate is based on the following assumptions: 945 Rhode Island voyages, average crew of ten, 60 percent of crew members from Rhode Island, and 20 percent mortality.

3. See God's Little Acre, at rhodetour.org/items/show/40?tour=5&index=3.

Chapter 7. Captivity

1. On enslavement as production and/or reproduction, see Meillassoux, *Anthropology of Slavery,* 23–40; Richard Roberts, "Production and Reproduction of War-

rior States: Segu Bambara and Segu Tokolor, c. 1712–1890," *IJAHS* 13, no. 3 (1980): 389, 399–400.

2. For examples of abduction by American slavers, see "Deposition of Adam Baldridge"; *Boston Gazette,* December 13, 1736, 2; Bernard Martin and Mark Spurrell, eds., *Journal of a Slave Trader (John Newton) 1750–1754* (London: Epworth Press, 1962), 38–39; Memorial of Private Traders, July 4, 1764, BNA CO 388/52, p. 44; Peleg Clarke to John Fletcher, January 8, 1777, Peleg Clarke Letterbook, *PAST,* ser. B, pt. 1, reel 15; Alexander Peter Kup, ed., *Adam Afzelius Sierra Leone Journal, 1795–1796* (Uppsala, Sweden: Almqvist & Wiksells, 1967), 128–129; Catterall, *Judicial Cases,* 2:300.

3. Igor Kopytoff and Suzanne Miers, "Introduction: African Slavery as an Institution of Marginality," in *Slavery in Africa: Historical and Anthropological Perspectives,* ed. Suzanne Miers and Igor Kopytoff (Madison: University of Wisconsin Press, 1977), 3–11, 12.

4. Emma Christopher, *Slave Ship Sailors and Their Captive Cargoes, 1730–1807* (Cambridge: Cambridge University Press, 2006), 163–194; Stephanie Smallwood, *Saltwater Slavery: A Middle Passage from Africa to American Diaspora* (Cambridge: Harvard University Press, 2007), 36; Marcus Rediker, *The Slave Ship: A Human History* (New York: Viking, 2007), 45; Sowande' Mustakeem, *Slavery at Sea: Terror, Sex, and Sickness in the Middle Passage* (Urbana: University of Illinois Press, 2016), 14, 80, 131–132. It is, of course, entirely correct to say that the commodification process continued aboard slave ships.

5. Meillassoux, *Anthropology of Slavery,* 33–40; Lovejoy, *Transformations,* 3; Stilwell, *Slavery and Slaving in African History,* 5–12. See also M. I. Finley, *Ancient Slavery and Modern Ideology* (New York: Viking, 1980), 75; Orlando Patterson, *Slavery and Social Death: A Comparative Study* (Cambridge: Harvard University Press), 7–8.

6. On narratives by Africans from the era of the slave trade, see Sean M. Kelley, "Enslavement in Upper Guinea During the Era of the Transatlantic Slave Trade," *African Economic History* 48, no. 1 (2020): 50–51. All of the narratives used here will eventually be available online at *Freedom Narratives* (freedomnarratives.org/). Until they are, see the individual citations in these notes.

7. Lovejoy, *Transformations,* 8–11; Stilwell, *Slavery and Slaving in Africa,* 48–50, 132–142; Meillassoux, *Anthropology of Slavery,* 24–26, 85–95.

8. Barry, *Senegambia,* 27–46; Rodney, "Jihad and Social Revolution," 269–284. *Voyages,* Estimates section for Senegambia, Sierra Leone, and the Windward Coast, www.slavevoyages.org/estimates/cC8BNlHn.

9. Barry, *Senegambia,* 121–122; Wright, *World and a Very Small Place in Africa,* 82, 99–100; Mouser, "Rebellion, Marronage, and *Jihad,*" 27–44.

10. Martin Klein, "The Slave Trade and Decentralized Societies," *JAH* 42, no. 1 (2001): 49–65; Hawthorne, *Planting Rice,* 93; Walter Hawthorne, "Strategies of the Decentralized: Defending Communities from Slave Raiders in Coastal Guinea-Bissau, 1450–1815," in *Fighting the Slave Trade: West African Strategies,* ed. Sylviane Diouf (Athens: Ohio University Press, 2003), 156–160.

11. Paul E. Lovejoy, "Slavery, the Bilād al-Sūdān, and the Frontiers of the African Diaspora," in Lovejoy, *Slavery on the Frontiers of Islam,* 14–15; Peter Caron, "'Of a Nation Which the Others Do Not Understand': Bambara Slaves and African Ethnicity in Colonial Louisiana," *SA* 18, no. 1 (1997): 101, 102, 105; Klein, "Servitude Among the Wolof and Sereer," 343–344; Roberts, "Production and Reproduction," 407–409.

12. Kup, ed., *Adam Afzelius Sierra Leone Journal,* 128–129.

13. Britain abolished its trade in 1807, and the United States did so as of 1808. The Netherlands abolished slave trading in 1814, and France outlawed its trade in 1815, although illegal slaving continued at a high level until 1830. Of much more consequence for this discussion was the abolition of the trade by Spain, which became official in 1820. Slave trading continued, but illegality forced changes in organization. For discussion, see David Eltis, *Economic Growth and the Ending of the Transatlantic Slave Trade* (New York: Oxford University Press, 1987), 145–184.

14. Lovejoy, *Jihad in West Africa,* 133–141.

15. Adam Jones, Robin Law, and P. E. H. Hair, eds., *Barbot on Guinea* (Farnham, U.K.: Ashgate, 1991), 1:132–133; Park, *Travels,* 237. On the enslavement and distribution of prisoners of war in Segu, see Roberts, "Production and Reproduction," 407–408.

16. Park, *Travels,* 335.

17. Jon F. Sensbach, *A Separate Canaan: The Making of an Afro-American World in North Carolina, 1763–1840* (Williamsburg, Va., and Chapel Hill: Omohundro Institute of Early American History and Culture and University of North Carolina Press, 1998), 309–311.

18. Allan D Austin, *African Muslims in Antebellum America: A Sourcebook* (New York: Garland, 1984), 121–189; Terry Alford, *Prince Among Slaves: The True Story of an African Prince Sold into Slavery in the American South,* 30th Anniversary Edition (New York: Oxford University Press, 1977; repr. 2007).

19. "Some Account of Mohammedu-Siseï, a Mandingo, of Nyáni-Marú on the Gambia," *Journal of the Royal Geographical Society of London* 8 (1838): 448–454.

20. Sitiki, *Odyssey of an African Slave,* 14–15. On warfare in Segu, see Roberts, "Production and Reproduction," 407.

21. Philip D. Curtin, ed., *Africa Remembered: Narratives by West Africans from the Era of the Slave Trade* (Madison: University of Wisconsin Press, 1967), 151.

22. Austin, *African Muslims in Antebellum America,* 542. For more on Muhammad Kaba Sagahanugu, see Yacine Dadi Addoun and Paul E. Lovejoy, "Muhammad Kaba Sagahanugu and the Muslim Community of Jamaica," in Lovejoy, *Slavery on the Frontiers of Islam,* 199–218.

23. S. W. Koelle, *Polyglotta Africana; or a Comparative Vocabulary of Nearly Three Hundred Words and Phrases, in More than one Hundred Distinct African Languages* (London: Church Missionary Society, 1854), 16. Benjamin N. Lawrence, *Amistad's Orphans: An Atlantic Story of Children, Slavery, and Smuggling* (New Haven: Yale University Press, 2014), 35–39.

24. Kelley, "Enslavement," 55–58.

25. Brooks, *Landlords and Strangers,* 4; Searing, *West African Slavery,* 3–5, 31–32; Thornton, *Warfare,* 21–28.

26. Oldendorp, *Historie,* 1:480.

27. *Voyages,* slavevoyages.org/voyages/ixcBmBRX; Oldendorp, *Historie,* 381. On gender and enslavement, see the various essays in Gwyn Campbell, Suzanne Miers, and Joseph C. Miller, eds., *Women and Slavery,* 2 vols. (Athens: Ohio University Press, 2007). See also Claire C. Robertson and Martin A. Klein, eds., *Women and Slavery in Africa* (Madison: University of Wisconsin Press, 1983); David Eltis and S. L. Engerman, "Was the Slave Trade Dominated by Men?" *Journal of Interdisciplinary History* 23, no. 2 (1992): 237–257; G. Ugo Nwokeji, "African Conceptions of Gender and the Slave Traffic," *WMQ* 58, no. 1 (2001): 47–68.

28. Lovejoy, *Transformations,* 122.

29. D. J. E. Maier, "Military Acquisition of Slaves in Asante," in *West African Economic and Social History,* ed. David P. Henige and T. C. McCaskie (Madison: University of Wisconsin African Studies Program, 1990), 124.

30. Maier, "Military Acquisition," 127–128; Benedict G. Der, *The Slave Trade in Northern Ghana* (Accra, Ghana: Woeli Publishing, 1998), 10–12, 27.

31. The number of captives embarking on the Gold Coast plummeted from approximately ten thousand in 1807 to two thousand in 1808. Smaller numbers embarked intermittently until the 1840s, when the Atlantic trade essentially fell to negligible levels. See *Voyages,* Estimates, slavevoyages.org/estimates/CbFiBOD7.

32. The narratives are fragmented into two sections in Oldendorp, *Historie,* 1:373–449, 480–490. For more on Oldendorp and the complex history of his publication, see G. Meier, "Preliminary Remarks on the Oldendorp Manuscripts and Their History," in *Slave Cultures and Cultures of Slavery,* ed. S. Palmié (Knoxville: University of Tennessee Press, 1995), 67–71.

33. Oldendorp, *Historie,* 1:482, 485. This discussion assumes that Oldendorp's "Amina" were from Asante. For more discussion, see Sean M. Kelley and Paul E. Lovejoy, "Oldendorp's 'Amina': Ethnonyms, History, and Identity in the African Disapora," forthcoming.

34. Oldendorp, *Historie,* 1:484, 485; Edwards, *History, Civil and Commercial,* 2:105.

35. Walter C. Rucker, *Gold Coast Diasporas: Identity, Culture, and Power* (Urbana: University of Illinois Press, 2015), 99; Der, *Slave Trade in Northern Ghana,* 15. On the background of Venture Smith, see Paul E. Lovejoy, "The African Background of Venture Smith," in *Venture Smith and the Business of Slavery and Freedom,* ed. James Brewer Stewart (Amherst: University of Massachusetts Press, 2010), 43, 51.

36. Oldendorp, *Historie,* 1:483–484, 485, 486.

37. Oldendorp, *Historie,* 1:482, 486.

38. Oldendorp, *Historie,* 1:485; Quobna Ottobah Cugoano, "Thoughts and Sentiments on the Evil and Wicked Traffic of the Slavery and Commerce of the Human Species," in *Unchained Voices: An Anthology of Black Authors in the English-Speaking World of the 18th Century,* expanded edition, ed. Vincent Caretta (Lexington: University Press of Kentucky, 2004), 147–150.

39. Edwards, *History, Civil and Commercial,* 2:80–81, 126; Oldendorp, *Historie,* 1:484.

40. Jennifer Lofkranz, "Introduction: Ransoming Practices in Africa: Past and Present," *African Economic History* 42 (2014): 1–10.

41. Park, *Travels,* 280, 282; Oldendorp, *Historie,* 1:481; *Report of the Committee of the African Institution,* vol. 6 (1812): 144–145.

42. Oldendorp, *Historie,* 1:482, 483–484.

43. Hawthorne, *Planting Rice,* 69–82; Wheat, *Atlantic Africa,* 24; Daniel B. Domingues da Silva, *The Atlantic Slave Trade from West Central Africa, 1780–1867* (Cambridge: Cambridge University Press, 2017), 73–86.

44. Curtin, *Africa Remembered,* 151.

45. Wilks, *Asante in the Nineteenth Century,* 8–9, 16–17; Edwards, *History, Civil and Commercial,* 2:63, 107–108; Lovejoy, *Transformations,* 97.

46. Oldendorp, *Historie,* 1:407 n. 84, and 399 n. 79; Curtin, *Africa Remembered,* 162, 168–169.

47. Park, *Travels,* 295–330.

48. Mouser, "Walking Caravans," 70, 72; Koelle, *Polyglotta,* 22.

49. Descriptions of the forts are many. For a good sense of the variety, see Van Dantzig, *Forts and Castles.* For Castle Brew, see Priestley, *West African Trade,* 56–58. For the picture of the Sherbro facility, see Nicholas Owen, *Journal of a Slave Dealer,* ed. Evaline Martin (Boston: Houghton Mifflin, 1930), 60. The Gallinas barracoon image was published in the *Illustrated London News,* April 14, 1849, 237, and can be seen at www.slaveryimages.org/s/slaveryimages/item/1937.

50. Kup, *Adam Afzelius Sierra Leone Journal,* 103, 106; Winterbottom, *Account of the Native Africans,* 170–171, 176.

51. Lovejoy, *Transformations,* 1–2.

52. Olaudah Equiano, *The Interesting Narrative and Other Writings,* ed. Vincent Carretta (New York: Penguin, 2003), 55; Sitiki, *Odyssey of an African Slave,* 166; Daniel B. Thorp, "Chattel with A Soul: The Autobiography of a Moravian Slave," *Pennsylvania Magazine of History and Biography* 112, no. 3 (1988): 448; Alryyes, *A Muslim American Slave,* 63; Curtin, *Africa Remembered,* 162.

53. *Scots Magazine,* June 1772, 302; "History of George Dale, a Native of Africa," National Archive of Scotland, online at www.nrscotland.gov.uk/files//images/features/Transcript%20-%20The%20History%20of%20George%20Dale.pdf; Kelley, *Voyage,* 109; Jeffrey Brace, *The Blind African Slave, or Memoirs of Boyrereau Brinch, Nicknamed Jeffrey Brace,* ed. Kari J. Winter (Madison: University of Wisconsin Press, 2004), 126; Donnan, *Documents,* 3:374.

54. *Voyages,* slavevoyages.org/voyages/ixcBmBRX; Trade Book of the Sloop *Rhode Island,* NYHS; Jerome S. Handler, "Life Stories of Enslaved Africans in Barbados," *SA* 19, no. 1 (April 1998): 103.

55. Lydia Huntley Sigourney, *Sketch of Connecticut, Forty Years Since* (Hartford, Conn.: Oliver D. Cooke & Sons, 1824), 81–90; Margaret Schutt to William Milbery, November 25, 1805, BNA HCA 42/456/766. The most complete description of an American

slave ship is in George Pinckard, *Notes on the West Indies* (London: Longman Hurst, Reese, and Orme, 1806), 1:229–237.

56. Margaret Schutt to William Milbery, November 25, 1805, BNA HCA 42/476/456.

57. *Voyages,* slavevoyages.org/voyages/ixcBmBRX.

58. The number of captives per ton has been computed from data in *Voyages;* Pinckard, *Notes,* 1:234; William Chancellor Diary, MDHS, pp. 23, 58, 60; Caleb Godfrey to William Vernon, January 29, 1755, and February 5, 1755, NYHS.

59. Park, *Travels,* 335; Pinckard, *Notes,* 1:236.

60. Although there was no correlation between tonnage and mortality for the transatlantic slave trade as a whole, there was a moderate statistical correlation of .69 for American vessels. See *Voyages,* www.slavevoyages.org/voyages/2nXeHbyO.

61. Marques, "Slave Trading in a New World," 233. D'Wolf was actually indicted for murder in Rhode Island but avoided the consequences by fleeing to Sint Eustatius. Authorities there filed charges against him, but he fought back and they were eventually dropped.

62. John Duncan to Samuel and William Vernon, February 14, 1769, NYHS.

63. William Chancellor Diary, MDHS, pp. 44, 86.

64. Sigourney, *Sketch of Connecticut,* 81–90.

65. BNA HCA 42/409/408, doc. no. 74; *Pennsylvania Gazette,* November 7, 1765, 2; Captain Fletcher to John Fletcher, December 15, 1776, Peleg Clarke Letterbook, *PAST,* ser. B, pt. 1, reel 15.

66. *Voyages,* slavevoyages.org/voyages/ixcBmBRX; David Richardson, "Shipboard Revolts, African Authority, and the Atlantic Slave Trade," *WMQ* 58, no. 1 (January 2001): 73–74; David Eltis, "Iberian Dominance and the Intrusion of Northern Europeans into the Atlantic World: Slave Trading as a Result of Economic Growth," *Almanack* 22 (May–August 2019), online at doi.org/10.1590/2236-463320192210.

67. Detailed accounts of revolts aboard American vessels include *Newport Mercury,* June 6, 1763, 3; BNA HCA 42/472/864, pp. 8, 15–21; William Fairfield to Rebecca Fairfield, April 23, 1789, *Essex Institute Historical Collections* 25: 311–312; William Chancellor Diary, entries for August 30, 1750, and ca. October 10, 1750, MDHS; Captain Fletcher to John Fletcher, December 15, 1776, Peleg Clarke Letterbook; *Pennsylvania Gazette,* June 16, 1763, 2; Donnan, *Documents,* 3:374.

68. Donnan, ed., *Documents,* 1:118–121; Protest of Thomas Rogers, October 4, 1765, in Jane Fletcher Fiske, ed., *Gleanings from Newport Court Files, 1659–1783* (Boxford, Mass.: n.p., 1998), entry no. 1070.

69. "Extract from the Letters of the Governor and Council at Sierra Leone to the Chairman of Directors of the Sierra Leone Company," Black History Collection, box 3, LOC.

70. Catterall, *Judicial Cases,* 2:292, 300; BNA HCA 42/371/70.

71. *Voyages,* slavevoyages.org/estimates/mvY2IDqp.

72. Kelley, *Voyage,* 81–91, 131–132.

73. Kelley, *Voyage,* 159–180.

74. Kevin Tulimieri, "Venture Smith's Gravestone: Its Maker and Its Message," in Stewart, *Venture Smith and the Business of Slavery and Freedom*, 252.

75. Kelley, "Precedents," 27, 36–42.

76. BPP, Reports by Coms. of Inquiry into State of Africans apprenticed in W. Indies: II. Further Papers relating to Captured Negroes; Correspondence with Governors of Sierra Leone, Mauritius and Cape of Good Hope, 1825 (115), 21.

77. Kelley, "Precedents," 36–41.

78. BNA CO 318/2; BPP, Reports by Coms. of Inquiry (114), 28–29.

79. BNA CO 318/2; BPP, Reports by Coms. of Inquiry (114), 30–31.

80. BPP, Reports by Coms. of Inquiry (114), 31–33.

81. BPP, Reports by Coms. of Inquiry (114), 40.

82. BPP, Reports by Coms. of Inquiry (114), 224, 240.

Chapter 8. Slave-Trading Communities

1. "Cost & Outset of Sloop *Prudent Abigail*," July 1739, *PAST*, ser. B, pt. 1, reel 28; George G. Channing, *Early Recollections of Newport, from the Year 1793 to 1811* (Newport, R.I.: A. J. Ward and Charles E. Hammett, 1868), 142.

2. Richardson, "Slavery, Trade, and Economic Growth," table 3, p. 254; *Voyages*, slavevoyages.org/voyages/ixcBmBRX. Few crew lists for Charleston-based vessels survive; for example, the *Margaret*, BNA HCA 42/456/766; the *Tartar*, BNA HCA 45/614, 65, 68; the *Washington*, HCA 42/521/283 (lacks birthplaces).

3. Richardson, "Slavery, Trade, and Economic Growth," table 3, p. 254; Marques, *United States and the Transatlantic Slave Trade*, table 2.5, p. 31. Because vessels bound for Africa and Asia carried much more valuable cargo than Caribbean-bound and coastwise vessels, the actual number of clearances for Africa and Asia was likely much smaller than their proportion of insured cargoes.

4. This figure is based on a rough average of ten voyages per year with an average crew of ten. For the percentage of female-headed households, see Crane, *A Dependent People*, 70.

5. Rediker, *Between the Devil and the Deep Blue Sea*, and Gary B. Nash, *The Urban Crucible: Social Change, Political Consciousness, and the Origins of the American Revolution* (Cambridge: Cambridge University Press, 1979): both focus on larger ports and emphasize class as the major factor in sailors' lives. Vickers and Walsh, in *Young Men and the Sea*, look at Salem, a small port, and emphasize kinship and community.

6. Evarts B. Greene and Virginia D. Harrington, *American Population Before the Federal Census of 1790* (New York: Columbia University Press, 1932), 67; *Heads of Families at the First Census of the United States Taken in the Year 1790: Rhode Island* (Washington, D.C.: GPO, 1908), 8–9; *Return of the Whole Number of Persons Within the Several Districts of the United States* (Washington, D.C.: n.p., 1801), 8, 26; *Aggregate Amount of Each Description of Persons Within the United States of America* (Washington, D.C.: n.p., 1811), 3:10, 23.

7. Crane, *A Dependent People*, 25–29. On Aaron Lopez, see Stanley F. Chyet, *Lopez of Newport: Colonial American Merchant Prince* (Detroit: Wayne State University Press, 1970), 16–25. On Gardner, see Ezra Stiles, *Extracts from the Itineraries and Other Miscellanies of Ezra Stiles, D.D., L.L.D., 1755–1794*, ed. Franklin Bowditch Dexter (New Haven: Yale University Press, 1916), 56–57. The Pearson correlation coefficient for the number of slaving voyages and the amount of tax owed was r=0.79 for the top 1 percent, r=0.62 for the top decile, and r=0.24 for all taxpayers. Unless otherwise indicated, the definition of slave-ship owner refers to individuals who are recorded as owners for at least two voyages in the *Voyages* database. A number of people invested in a single voyage, but these were almost always merchants whose main line was something else, so including them as slave-ship owners would tend to distort the analysis.

8. Newport Tax List, 1772, NHS. The names of slavers are taken from *Slave Voyages*, www.slavevoyages.org.

9. For the slavers' wealth, see NPR, vols. 2–16; BPR, vols. 1–4. For the bank board, see *Newport Mercury*, January 7, 1800, 3, and May 25, 1805, 3; for Mount Hope Insurance Company, see the *Mount Hope Eagle*, July 11, 1807, 4; for the Bristol Insurance Company, see the *Rhode Island Republican*, February 6, 1802, 3.

10. NPR, vols. 2–16; BPR, vols. 1–4.

11. Crane, *A Dependent People*, 61.

12. James Birket, *Some Cursory Remarks Made by James Birket in his Voyage to North America, 1750–1751* (New Haven: Yale University Press, 1916), 27; Rhode Island Historical Preservation Commission, *The Southern Thames Street Neighborhood in Newport, Rhode Island* (Providence: Rhode Island Historical Preservation Commission, 1980), 6, 40. Several slavers' houses are listed in the Historic American Buildings Survey for Newport; see www.loc.gov/collections/historic-american-buildings-landscapes-and-engineering-records/?q=newport&sp=1.

13. *Historic and Architectural Resources of Bristol, Rhode Island* (Providence: Rhode Island Historical Commission, 1990), 16–17.

14. Rachel Chernos Lin, "The Rhode Island Slave-Traders: Butchers, Bakers, and Candlestick-Makers," *SA* 23, no. 3 (December 2002): 21–38.

15. For the captains' experiences, see the individual entries in *Voyages*. The backgrounds of Liverpool's slave traders present an interesting comparison. Like those of Rhode Island, most were of middling origin, though less often from the maritime trades. Slave trading also offered them a chance at upward social mobility, though this was hardly guaranteed. See David Pope, "The Wealth and Social Aspirations of Liverpool's Slave Merchants of the Second Half of the Eighteenth Century," in *Liverpool and Transatlantic Slavery*, ed. David Richardson, Suzanne Schwarz, and Anthony Tibbles (Liverpool: Liverpool University Press, 2007), 164–193.

16. For representative examples, see the portledge bills for the *Hannah* and the *Africa, PAST*, ser. B, pt. 1, reel 28; portledge bills for the *Hare, Marigold, Royal Charlotte, Othello*, NYHS; portledge bill for the *Adventure* in Crane, *A Rhode Island Slaver;* and the portledge bill for the *Neptune*, BNA HCA 42/303/1013. On British captains, see Stephen

D. Behrendt, "The Captains in the British Slave Trade from 1785 to 1807," *Transactions of the Historical Society of Lancashire and Cheshire* 140 (1991): 81–140.

17. For representative examples, see Samuel and William Vernon to Caleb Godfrey, November 8, 1755, NYHS; Isaac Elizer and Samuel Moses to John Peck, October 29, 1762, in Adams, *Commerce of Rhode Island,* 1:96–97; Agreement Between Malcolm & Nevinson and Peleg Clarke, Peleg Clarke Letterbook, vol. 76, NHS; Account of John Sabens with David Nagle, April 27, 1805, BHPS.

18. This discussion is based on a voyage for the *Hannah.* For wages, see *PAST,* ser. B, pt. 2, reel 28; for the number of captives and the sale price at Jamaica, see *Voyages,* www.slavevoyages.org/voyages/kzhIzfeQ; coast commission and mortality of 15 percent has been assumed. Currency conversions are Old Tenor to sterling at 35.6:1 and sterling to dollars at 1:4.44. See McCusker, *Money and Exchange,* 136; John J. McCusker, *How Much Is That in Real Money?: A Historical Commodity Price Index for Use as a Deflator of Money Values in the Economy of the United States* (Worcester, Mass.: American Antiquarian Society, 2001), 33.

19. *Voyages,* www.slavevoyages.org/voyages/3HgHbRle.

20. For Lindsay, see NTCR, 16:117; for Elliott, see NPR, 1:39; for Moore, see NPR, 2:223. Guinea factors in the Americas customarily paid the captain's coast commission in order to attract the sale. For an example of a factor refusing to pay, see Kelley, *Voyage,* 183–184. All estate values have been adjusted to 1800 dollars.

21. Ship accounts, 1754–1764, *PAST,* ser. B, vol. 1, reel 28; Kelley, *Voyage,* 37–38; Deposition of Jonathan Fitch, August 20, 1807, BNA HCA 42/455/757. The *Mendon* changed its destination to Havana but was captured by the British and taken to Dominica. The case was heard in Barbados.

22. Probate inventories were taken from NPR, NTCR, BPR, and Providence Wills. A t-test was run on a sample of thirty-nine slavers and fifty-two non-slavers. It should be noted that the non-slavers were mostly described as "mariners," the standard term for ship captains, but it is possible that some of them never rose that high. As men of property, however, we can at least be fairly sure that there were no ordinary seamen among them.

23. Representative examples include the inventories of Daniel Gardner (1789), NPR, 2:124; Elijah Briggs (1797), Providence Wills, 7:949–952; 8:120; Jabez Gibbs (1806), Bristol Inventories, 3:106–108; Benjamin Weaver (1808), NPR, 4:522; and Samuel Taggart (1809), NPR, 4:628.

24. Will of Thomas Rogers, January 12, 1774, NTCR, 16:261; Inventory of Francis Malbone (1785), NPR, 1:248; Inventory of Abraham All (1789), NPR, 2:106–107; Inventory of James Carpenter (1790), NPR, 2:146.

25. *Charter of the Marine Society of the Town of Newport* (Newport, R.I.: Newport Mercury, 1806), 17–23; Godfrey v. Vernon, no. 14,159, RISCJRC; Depositions and Memoranda Re: Vernons v. Rogers, NYHS; Fiske, *Gleanings,* case no. 1070; Wax, "Thomas Rogers," 295–297.

26. For the crew lists of the *Dove* (1793) and the *Fair Eliza* (1793), see NARA RG 36, Bureau of Customs, French Spoliation Cases, Dist. of Newport, Outward Foreign Mani-

fests & Crew Lists; for the *New Adventure* (1798), see BNA HCA 42/299/486. Additional crew lists survive but not all list birthplaces and residences.

27. This calculation is based on a hypothetical voyage for the *Hannah.* For wages, see *PAST,* ser. B, pt. 2, reel 28; for the number of captives and the sale price at Jamaica, see *Voyages,* www.slavevoyages.org/voyages/kzhIzfeQ; coast commission and mortality of 15 percent has been assumed.; Fiske, *Gleanings,* case no. 1068.

28. Crew lists were taken from *PAST,* ser. B, pts. 1 and 2; Slavery Collection, NYHS; Brown Family Papers, BFBR Vessels, Schooner *Wheel of Fortune,* 1758, January 10, 1759, box 654, folder 2, JCB; Crane, *A Rhode Island Slaver;* NARA RG 36, French Spoliation Claims, District of Providence, Outward Manifests and Crew Lists; NARA RG 36, French Spoliation Claims, District of Newport Outward Foreign Manifests, Entry 718; BNA HCA 42/299/486; BNA HCA 42 303 1013; Articles for the Brig *Sally,* online at library.brown.edu/cds/sally/browse.php?browsetype=type&show_subtype=contracts%20(legal%20documents).

29. Several John Stantons, perhaps up to three, appear to have captained slave ships in Newport between 1761 and 1800. They may represent multiple generations in the slave trade. See the portledge bills for the *Marigold* and the *Othello* (no. 36345) and *Voyages,* slavevoyages.org/voyages/ixcBmBRX. For D'Wolf, see NARA RG 36, French Spoliation Claims, District of Providence, Outward Manifests and Crew Lists.

30. Richard H. Rudolph, "Eighteenth Century Newport and Its Merchants, Part II," *Newport History* 51, no. 3 (1978): 50.

31. Nicholas Owen, *Journal of a Slave-Dealer,* ed. Evaline Martin (Boston and New York: Houghton Mifflin, 1930), 23–29, 32, 36–37. Crew lists were checked against Ancestry.com, FamilySearch.com, and AmericanAncestors.org. Results were often ambiguous, with multiple possible matches. Many of the names did match with Rhode Islanders and New Englanders, though often more than one, which made it impossible to identify the individual in question.

32. Coughtry, *Notorious Triangle,* 59.

33. NARA RG 36, French Spoliation Claims, District of Providence, Outward Manifests and Crew Lists; NARA RG 36, French Spoliation Claims, District of Newport Outward Foreign Manifests, entry 718; BNA HCA 42/303/1013.

34. *RCRI,* 4:60, 6:381.

35. E. Jennifer Monaghan, "Literacy Instruction and Gender in Colonial New England," *American Quarterly* 40, no. 1 (March 1988): 18.

36. Ruth Wallis Herndon, *Unwelcome Americans: Living on the Margins in Early New England* (Philadelphia: University of Pennsylvania Press, 2001), 18, 20, 81–84, 132–134, 159.

37. Fiske, *Gleanings,* case nos. 226, 739, 985, 1037. See also case nos. 198, 492, 857, 875, 970, and 1007.

38. Fiske, *Gleanings,* case nos. 588, 757, 876, 974, 1125. For insurance on ventures, see Bristol Insurance Company Letterbook, *PAST,* ser. A, pt. 2.

39. Fiske, *Gleanings,* case nos. 766, 1040; Towle, *Records of the Vice-Admiralty Court of Rhode Island,* 118–119, 123–124, 243–245, 337–338, 383–385; Rediker, *Slave Ship,*

239; Christopher, *Slave Ship Sailors*, 97–102; Peter Earle, *Sailors: English Merchant Seamen, 1650–1775* (London: Methuen, 2007), 145–163; Vickers and Walsh, *Young Men and the Sea*, 2–6, 62, 78–80, 94–95.

40. For examples of brutality, see the Deposition of Dayne[?] Martin, August 12, 1806, folder 31, box 2, D'Wolf Collection, Ships' Documents, BHPS; William Chancellor Diary, MDHS, p. 89; Kelley, *Voyage*, 104–105, 116–118; Fitch, *Diary of William Pynchon*, 236; Groves v. Sinclair, PEI; Francis, *Old New York*, NYHS, 9:34; Samuel Patterson, *Narrative of the Adventures and Sufferings of Samuel Patterson* (Palmer, Mass.: From the Press in Palmer, 1817), 45–47. For desertion, see Earle, *Sailors*, 168; Crane, *A Rhode Island Slaver*, 9; the *Hannah*, PAST, ser. B, pt. 1, reel 28; and the *Othello* (no. 36495), NYHS.

41. Portledge bill for the *Hannah*, Aaron Lopez Collection, NHS, in *PAST*, ser. B, pt. 2, reel 28; portledge bill for the *Othello* (1774), NYHS; portledge bill for the brig *Ann*, NHS, in *PAST*, ser. B, pt. 1, Selected Collections, reel 17; portledge bill for the *Sally*, online at repository.library.brown.edu/studio/item/bdr:303415/.

42. Portledge bill for the *Hannah*, PAST, ser. B, pt. 1, reel 28.

43. George Scott to unknown, June 13, 1740, in Donnan, *Documents*, 3:135.

44. Fiske, *Gleanings*, case no. 744; see also 704, 1077. Note, however, that Scott's ship was not a slave ship.

45. Portledge bill and ship accounts for the *Ann*, PAST, ser. B, pt. 1, reel 17; portledge bill for the *Hannah*, PAST, ser. B, pt. 1, reel 28.

46. Martin, *Journal of a Slave-Dealer*, 32, 36–37; John Hoxse, *The Yankee Tar: An Authentic Narrative of the Voyages of John Hoxse* (Northampton, Mass.: John Metcalf, 1840), 9; Patterson, *Narrative*, 40–41.

47. Deposition of Thomas Cook, January 10, 1801; Deposition of William Williams, ca. 1802/1803, Isaac Shearman v. Charles D'Wolf, NARA Boston, RG 21, Records of the U.S. District Court for Rhode Island.

48. Patterson, *Narrative*, 45–47; Hoxse, *Yankee Tar*, 12–14. On serial voyages by officers, see Coughtry, *Notorious Triangle*, 57. Coughtry found that during the peak years of 1803–1807, seamen did make serial voyages, and many gained promotions. I have not been able to verify the finding, but it is certainly plausible given the unique circumstances. For earlier periods, however, this does not appear to be the case.

49. Joseph Wardwell, *The Way of the World: Or, a Short Sketch of the Manners and Customs of Mankind* (n.p., 1813), 13–16.

50. Barbara Laslett and Johanna Brenner, "Gender and Social Reproduction: Historical Perspectives," *Annual Review of Sociology* 15 (1989): 383; Evelyn Nakano Glenn, "From Servitude to Service Work: Historical Continuities in the Racial Division of Paid Reproductive Labor," *Signs* 18, no. 1 (Autumn 1992): 1–43. On Rhode Island in particular, see Ruth Wallis Herndon, "The Domestic Cost of Seafaring," in *Iron Men, Wooden Women: Gender and Seafaring in the Atlantic World*, ed. Lisa Norling and Margaret Creighton (Baltimore: Johns Hopkins University Press, 1996), 55–69; Ellen Hartigan-O'Connor, *Ties That Buy: Women and Commerce in Revolutionary America* (Philadelphia: University of Pennsylvania Press, 2009), 39–68. On women in New England whaling communities, which were similar to slave-trading ports in the sense that

the voyages were long, see Lisa Norling, *Ahab Had a Wife: New England Women and the Whalefishery, 1720–1870* (Chapel Hill: University of North Carolina Press, 2000). For slavers owning spinning wheels, see the probate inventories of Ebenezer Shearman, NPR, 4:622; Cromwell Child, BPR, 2:337; and Caleb Gardner, NPR, 3:364.

51. Howe, *Bristol,* 52–57. The figures are based on 102 D'Wolf-owned (or part-owned) ships transporting an average of 111 captives each. See *Voyages,* slavevoyages.org/voyages/ixcBmBRX.

52. John R. Bartlett, ed., *Inhabitants of the Colony of Rhode Island and Providence Plantations, Taken by Order of the General Assembly in 1774* (Providence: Knowles, Anthony, 1858), 180. For an example of a sailor's parents warning him away from the slave trade, see Patterson, *Narrative,* 40.

53. John D'Wolf to John Sabens, October 24, 1804, December 7, 1804, D'Wolf Collection, Ships' Documents, box 2, BHPS.

54. Norling, *Captain Ahab Had a Wife,* 33.

55. Vickers and Walsh, *Young Men and the Sea,* 32.

56. Hartigan-O'Connor, *Ties That Buy,* 56–57.

57. Sara T. Damiano, "Agents at Home: Wives, Lawyers, and Financial Competence in Eighteenth-Century New England Port Cities," *Eighteenth-Century Studies* 13, no. 4 (Fall 2015): 808–835.

58. Benjamin Goodwin Daybook, vol. 2, entries for March 11 and March 13, 1769, MHS; Jonathan Ward, Jr., to Philana Ward, May 1, 1800, BNA HCA 42/303/1013; Elizabeth Paeko[?] to Elias Rouse, March 23, 1698, BNA HCA 98/1, p. 110.

59. Will of Leonard Bradford, July 22, 1812, BPR, 4:29–30; Will of Edward Wanton, September 17, 1773, NPR, 3:36; Will of George Gibbs, October 4, 1803, NPR, 4:106–108; U.S. v. the *Betsy* (1799), NARA Boston, RG 21, Records of the District Court of Rhode Island.

60. BNA HCA 42/456/766. In addition to Mrs. Johnson, only one other woman is listed as an owner of a vessel in the pre-1808 American slave trade, apparently in partnership with several men. Though the vessel sailed from Virginia, it appears to have been British-owned. See *Voyages,* no. 25799. A handful of women also owned shares in American slave ships in the nineteenth century.

61. Depositions of Lewis Fillis, July 11, 1803, and Phineas Dean, July 14, 1803, in Isaac Shearman v. *Charming Sally* (1803), RG 21, Records of the U.S. District Court for Massachusetts, NARA Boston.

62. Hartigan-O'Connor, *Ties That Buy,* 42; Herndon, "Domestic Costs of Seafaring," 55–69; Herndon, *Unwelcome Americans,* 1–22. On "maritime paternalism," see Norling, *Captain Ahab Had a Wife,* 28–33.

63. Sarah Horne to Jacob Horne, June 5, p. 169; Ede Wilday to Richard Wilday, June 5, 1698, p. 116; Henry Crosley to Robert Crosley, June 10, 1698, pp. 154–155—all in BNA HCA 98/1.

64. Wardwell, *Way of the World,* 11.

65. Crane, *A Dependent People,* 58, 65; Ira Berlin, *Many Thousands Gone: The First Two Centuries of Slavery in North America* (Cambridge: Belknap Press of Harvard

University Press, 1998), 372–373; Christy Clark-Pujara, *Dark Work: The Business of Slavery in Rhode Island* (New York: NYU Press, 2016), 24–29.

66. For additional examples, see "Copy of the Outsett of the Brigg. Little George," *PAST*, ser. B, pt. 1, reel 28; Brig *Renard* Day Book, LOC Black History Collection, box 3; Accounts of the *Renard*, gen. MSS file 409, Beinecke Library, Yale University.

67. God's Little Acre Stone Inventory, online at ripnewport.com/God's%20Little%20Acre%20stone%20inventory%20a-z%20online.pdf.

68. God's Little Acre Stone Inventory; Berlin, *Many Thousands Gone*, 177; Akeia Benard, "The Free African American Cultural Landscape: Newport, RI, 1774–1826," (Ph.D. diss., University of Connecticut, 2008), 115.

69. *Voyages*, slavevoyages.org/voyages/ixcBmBRX; Wilks, "Rise of the Akwamu Empire," 50–51; Robin Law, "Ethnicities of Enslaved Africans in the Diaspora: On the Meanings of 'Mina' (Again)," *History in Africa* 32 (2005): 251–255; Rucker, *Gold Coast Diasporas*, 82–93.

70. A third person interred in God's Little Acre, Charles Quamine Gardner, may also have been Duchess Quamino's child, because she apparently did have a son named Charles. If so, the use of the name may represent an effort to mark his membership in the Quamino family while he was still legally a member of the Gardner household (through his enslavement). Charles died in 1798, probably as a free man, which, if the assumption is correct, raises the unanswerable question of why he kept the Gardner name. For genealogies, see Benard, "Free African American Cultural Landscape," 108–109, 188, 212.

71. *Papers of the New Haven Colony Historical Society* (New Haven, Conn.: New Haven Colony Historical Society, 1900): 6:323–324. For another description, see Edward Peterson, *History of Rhode Island* (New York: John Taylor, 1853), 104. On Election Day in general, see Berlin, *Many Thousands Gone*, 191–193. On Rhode Island and Newport, see Crane, *A Dependent People*, 78–79; Benard, "Free African American Cultural Landscape," 122–126; Clark-Pujara, *Dark Work*, 57–59.

72. Rucker, *Gold Coast Diasporas*, 152–164 (quotation on p. 153).

73. Clark-Pujara, *Dark Work*, 75–76. For captains holding people in slavery after 1784, see the probate inventories of Abraham All, NPR, 2:106–107 (1789); James Carpenter, NPR, 2:145–146 (1790). On the illegal landing of privilege slaves in Bristol, see Howe, *Mount Hope*, 126–128.

74. William H. Robinson, ed., *The Proceedings of the Free African Union Society and the African Benevolent Society, Newport, Rhode Island, 1780–1824* (Providence: Urban League of Rhode Island, 1976), 31, 43. On the idea of Africa in this period, see James Sidbury, *Becoming African in America: Race and Nation in the Early Black Atlantic* (New York: Oxford University Press, 2007), 6–7.

75. Robinson, *Proceedings*, 86–87.

76. Greene and Harrington, *American Population*, 67; *Heads of Families*, 8–9; *Return of the Whole Number of Persons*, 8, 26; *Aggregate Amount*, 3:10, 23.

77. Clark-Pujara, *Dark Work*, 94–109; Herndon, *Unwelcome Americans*, 11–12, 16–20, 205–206.

78. Herndon, *Unwelcome Americans*, 20; Newport Town Council Meeting (Tiverton, R.I.), May 7, July 2, September 3, and November 5, 1804, and November 4, 1805.

79. W. Jeffrey Bolster, *Black Jacks: African American Seamen in the Age of Sail* (Cambridge: Harvard University Press, 1997), 158–162, 74–78; Christopher, *Slave Ship Sailors*, 83, 236–238; Clark-Pujara, *Dark Work*, 97–98.

80. Rappleye, *Sons of Providence*, 228–230, 240; excerpt from Matthias Christian Sprengel, "The Origins of the Negroe Slave Trade," NYHS. On Sprengel, see Heike Raphael-Hernandez and Pia Wiegmink, "German Entanglements in Transatlantic Slavery: An Introduction," *Atlantic Studies* 14, no. 4 (2017): 424.

81. On the notion of a "slave society," see Finley, *Ancient Slavery and Modern Ideology*, 79–80; Berlin, *Many Thousands Gone*, 8–9.

82. Howe, *Mount Hope*, 127, 129; Howe, *Bristol*, 43, 67.

83. Fiske, *Gleanings*, case nos. 974, 976; Crane, *Dependent People*, 64–65.

84. Clark-Pujara, *Dark Work*, 29–38; Benard, "Free African American Cultural Landscape," 106.

85. Lambert, *House of Commons Sessional Papers*, 69:11; Samuel and William Vernon Accounts, NYHS; Receipt dated November 15, 1804, D'Wolf Collection, Ships' Documents, box 2, BHPS. For another example of Arabic writing in the papers of an American slaver, see Mallaurey[?] to Paul Cross, October 30, 1781, Paul Cross Papers, South Caroliniana Library.

86. William Chancellor Diary, entries for May 18–21, June 23, July 2, July 30, August 4, September 14, September 20, 1750, MDHS.

87. William Chancellor Diary, entries for June 20, June 25–26, July 17, August 18, August 23, 1750, MDHS; *Mt. Hope Eagle*, June 18, 1808, p. 4; Bentley, *Diary of William Bentley*, 2:439.

Part 5. Slavers as Outlaws, 1808–1865

1. Charles Tyng, *Before the Wind: The Memoir of an American Sea Captain, 1808–1833* (New York: Penguin, 1999), 2, 188, 252–253; *Newburyport Herald*, October 17, 1837, 8.

2. Tyng can be connected with the following vessels in the *Voyages* database: *Catherine*, no. 2627; *Asp*, no. 2663; *Lark*, no. 2664; *Eliza Davidson*, no. 2675; *Uncas*, no. 3484; *Hudson*, no. 2025; *Plant*, no. 2646. Several other voyages are not in the database either because they were seized before they could sail or because they were auxiliaries, that is, vessels that carried trade goods but not captives. These include the *Julius and Edward* (1842), *Douglas* (1839), *Echo* (1840), *Lone* (1840), *Seminole* (1840), *Kite* (1840), *Boston* (1845), and *Spitfire* (1845). See HCP 1843 (484), pp. 256–276; HCP 1841, Sess. 1 (333), p. 832; HCP 1842 (551-551-II), p. 398; Serial Set, 26th Congress, 2d Sess., H. Doc. No. 115, p. 215; *Diario de la Marina* (Havana newspaper), February 4, 1845, 1. For the guano contract, see *New York Herald*, March 23, 1857, 1. For the shipping dispute, see H. L. Janes, "The Black Warrior Affair," *American Historical Review* 12 (January 1907): 280–298. And for a recent overview of Tyng and his career, see Paul Joseph Michaels,

"New England Slave Trader: The Case of Charles Tyng" (M.A. thesis, California Polytechnic State University, 2019).

3. Tyng, *Before the Wind*, 58–59, 148, 170, 172, 178, 180, 202, 228.

4. "An Act to Continue in Force 'An Act to Protect the Commerce of the United States,'" Act of May 15, 1820, chap. 113, 3 Stat. 600; Murray, *Odious Commerce*, 70. The Anglo-Spanish Treaty was signed in 1817, but a complete ban did not take effect until October 1820.

Chapter 9. Evasion, 1808–1835

1. *Voyages*, www.slavevoyages.org/voyages/CbABg9Wb, www.slavevoyages.org/voyages/CQyBHOVV.

2. Marshall Smelser, *The Democratic Republic, 1801–1815* (New York: Harper Torchbooks, 1968), 163–169, 192–199; Donald R. Hickey, *The War of 1812: A Forgotten Conflict*, Bicentennial Edition (Urbana: University of Illinois Press, 2012), 18–21; William Jeffrey Bolster, "The Impact of Jefferson's Embargo on Coastal Commerce," *Log of Mystic Seaport* 37 (Winter 1986): 111–123. For D'Wolf's privateering, see Gordon S. Wood, *Empire of Liberty: A History of the Early Republic, 1789–1815* (New York: Oxford University Press, 2009), 682. See also Marques, *United States and the Transatlantic Slave Trade*, 68–69. For privateers seizing captives, see 16th Cong., 2d Sess., H.R. Doc. No. 59, 40.

3. Marques, *United States and the Transatlantic Slave Trade*, 72–85.

4. BNA HCA 40/101.

5. Catterall, *Judicial Cases*, 2:297–298.

6. 16th Cong., 2d Sess., H.R. Doc. No. 59, 30, 40; BNA HCA 40/101. Several vessels condemned at Sierra Leone are not yet in the *Voyages* database: *Rapid* (1809), *Pepe* (1812), *Nueva Constitucion* (1812), *Doña Luizia* (1813), *Juan* (1813), *Phoenix/Fenix* (1813), *San Joaquin* (1815), and *Rebecca* (1816). For additional examples, see González, "Foundation and Growth," 107–108.

7. Howard v. Wales, 1812, box 21, NARA Boston, RG 21, Records of the Massachusetts Circuit Court. See also *Voyages*, no. 14497.

8. Javier Moreno Rico, "Hombres y barcos del comercio negrero en España, 1789–1870," *Drassana: Revista del Museu Marítim de Barcelona* 25 (2017): 76–78; Pablo E. Pérez-Mallaína, *Spain's Men of the Sea: Daily Life in the Indies Fleets of the Sixteenth Century*, trans. Carla Rahn Phillips (Baltimore: Johns Hopkins University Press, 1998), 35–36, 39–41.

9. BPP, Select Committee on Papers Presented from the Committee on the African Company, 1816 (506) vol. 7.B.1:122; Report of the Commissioners for Investigating the State of Settlements on the Coast of Africa, 1812 (101), 10:277–278; BNA HCA 32/1838 pt. 1; BNA FO 84/3, pp. 57–58; FO 84/11, pp. 27; FO 84/13, pp. 20. See also D. J. M'Cord, *Chancery Cases Argued and Determined in the Court of Appeals of South Carolina, from January 1825 to May 1826* (Philadelphia: Carey, Lea & Carney, 1827), 1:156; *Rhode Island*

American, October 2, 1821, 2. For an American supercargo aboard a Portuguese-flagged vessel, see *The Royal Gazette and Sierra Leone Advertiser,* February 14, 1818, 47.

10. Marques, *United States and the Transatlantic Slave Trade,* 80–84; BNA HCA 267/34; HCA 40/101; "Factura de Cargamento," 1819–1820, Financial Records of Edward Spalding, 1816–1821, Spalding Papers, UM; J. Bush to Charles D'Wolf, December 6, 1818; José García Álvarez to Edward Spalding, February 29, 1820 and February 15, 1820; P. C. Greene to T. W. Payton, August 21, 1820; James Dooley to Jacob Bobbitt, September 10, 1820, Spalding Papers, UM; Bruce Mouser, *American Colony on the Rio Pongo: The War of 1812, The Slave Trade, and the Proposed Settlement of African Americans, 1810–1830* (Trenton, N.J.: African World Press, 2013), 64. See also "Copy of a Communication Allowing the Entrance of 80 African Slaves That Arrived on *El Dorado,* an American Slaver," Endangered Archives Programme, EAP060/1/1/8, British Library, eap.bl.uk/archive-file/EAP060-1-1-8, Archivo Historico Provincial de Matanzas. There were at least three slave traders named Madan operating in Cuba during the early nineteenth century, and records do not always list given names, but it is likely that some of the activity attributed to "Madan" was undertaken by Joaquín. See González, "Foundation and Growth," 119, 167, 276, 179, 283, 186. On Baker's Pongo ties, see Bruce L. Mouser, "Lightbourn Family of Farenya, Rio Pongo," *Mande Studies* 13, no. 1 (2011), 30.

11. David Head, "Slave Smuggling by Foreign Privateers: The Illegal Slave Trade and the Geopolitics of the Early Republic," *JER* 33 (Fall 2013): 440–442, 455–456. In the early 1810s Galveston Island was another entrepôt for captured slave vessels, with captives smuggled into Louisiana. See also Sarah A. Batterson, "An Ill-Judged Piece of Business: The Failure of Slave Trade Suppression in a Slaveholding Republic" (Ph.D. diss., University of New Hampshire, 2013), 80–99.

12. Donald L. Canney, *Africa Squadron: The U.S. Navy and the Slave Trade, 1842–1861* (Washington, D.C.: Potomac, 2006), 8–9; *Franklin Gazette,* May 27, 1820, 2; *New Hampshire Sentinel,* July 15, 1820, 2; *Boston Daily Advertiser,* November 7, 1820, 2; *Kentucky Reporter,* July 26, 1820, 3.

13. *Annals of Congress,* 15th Cong., 1st Sess., Senate, pp. 73–78, 93–108, 1740–1741; "An Act in Addition to 'An Act to Prohibit the Introduction (Importation) of Slaves,'" Act of April 20, 1818, chap. 91, 3 Stat. 450; Du Bois, *Suppression,* 80–81; Finkleman, "Regulating the Slave Trade," 402–403.

14. Du Bois, *Suppression,* 81, 90 n. 116; Finkleman, "Regulating the Slave Trade," 403; *Annals of Congress,* 15th Cong., 2d Sess., House, pp. 1430–1431, Senate, pp. 442–443; "An Act in Addition to the Acts Prohibiting the Slave Trade," Act of March 3, 1819, chap. 101, 3 Stat. 532.

15. *Annals of Congress,* 16th Cong., 1st Sess., House, pp. 925–926, 2207–2210, 2236–2237; "An Act to Continue in Force," 3 Stat. 600.

16. Eltis, *Economic Growth,* 81–83.

17. Eltis, *Economic Growth,* 84–87; Martinez, *Slave Trade,* 25–37.

18. James Monroe to John Quincy Adams, May 20, 1824, Gilder Lehrman Collection, Item 969, Gilder Lehrman Institute.

19. Fehrenbacher, *Slaveholding Republic*, 159–161; Harry Ammon, *James Monroe and the Quest for National Identity* (New York: McGraw-Hill, 1971), 520–527; Mary W. M. Hargreaves, *The Presidency of John Quincy Adams* (Lawrence: University of Kansas Press, 1985), 33.

20. *Rhode Island American*, June 18, 1824, 2; Fehrenbacher, *Slaveholding Republic*, 159–161; *American State Papers: Foreign Relations* (Washington, D.C.: Gales and Seaton, 1832–1861), 5:360–362. George Howe mistakenly credits D'Wolf with offering an amendment to an Anglo-American treaty that barred the mutual right of search. See Howe, *Mount Hope*, 191. Peter J. Coleman, *Transformation of Rhode Island*, 57, asserts that D'Wolf was responsible for amending an 1819 "treaty" with Britain that exempted U.S. vessels from search, but no such treaty existed. See Charles I. Bevans, ed., *Treaties and Other International Agreements of the United States of America, 1776–1949* (Washington, D.C.: Department of State, 1974), 12:iii. Coleman surely meant the Slave Trade Act of 1819, but D'Wolf was not in the Senate in 1819. For further examples, see Thomas, *Slave Trade*, 618; Johnson, *James DeWolf*, 121.

21. Mercer's post-1824 efforts have received very little attention but can be followed in 1 Cong. Deb. appendix, 73 (1825); 1 Cong. Deb. 626, 736, 739 (1825); 2 Cong. Deb. 2753 (1826); 7 Cong. Deb. 850–851 (1831).

22. "Famous Presidential Speeches," online at the Miller Center, University of Virginia, millercenter.org/the-presidency/presidential-speeches.

23. Du Bois, *Suppression*, 97–98, 107–108; Hugh B. Soulsby, *The Right of Search and the Slave Trade in Anglo-American Relations, 1814–1862* (Baltimore: Johns Hopkins University Press, 1933), 9–11, 17–38; Fehrenbacher, *Slaveholding Republic*, 158–161.

24. Philip D. Curtin estimated that approximately 1,000 Africans entered the United States each year after 1808. See Philip D. Curtin, *The Atlantic Slave Trade: A Census* (Madison: University of Wisconsin Press, 1969), 74–75. More recent estimates suggest a figure of just more than 6,000 for the entire 1808–1865 period. See Eltis, "U.S. Transatlantic Slave Trade," 351–353. In contrast, recent estimates for the U.S. interregional trade are around 875,000. See Steven Deyle, *Carry Me Back: The Domestic Slave Trade in American Life* (New York: Oxford University Press, 2005), 289.

25. William W. Freehling, *Prelude to Civil War: The Nullification Controversy in South Carolina, 1816–1836* (New York: Harper & Row, 1965) provides an excellent overview of this issue.

26. *Niles' Weekly Register*, June 5, 1824, 1.

27. Joseph de Larraury[?] to Santa Maria & Cuesta, June 5, 1798, BNA HCA 42/299/486; José Guadalupe Ortega, "Cuban Merchants, Slave Trade Knowledge, and the Atlantic World, 1790s–1820s," *Colonial Latin American Historical Review* 15, no. 3 (2006): 235–237; María del Carmen Barcia Zequeira, *Pedro Blanco, El Negrero: Mito, realidad, y espacios* (Havana: Ediciones Boloña, Publicaciones de la Oficina del Historiador de la Ciudad de la Havana, 2018), 92–93; González, "Foundation and Growth," 78–83.

28. Barcia Zequeira, *Pedro Blanco*, 72, 94–95.

29. Eugene Malibran to Adolphe Lacoste, January 1, 1820 in U.S. v. Malibran, RG 21, SDNY. For an English translation, see E. Malibran to Adolph Lacoste, January 1, 1820, in the *Boston Daily Advertiser,* November 7, 1820, 2. Although Malibran wrote to Lacoste in French, the latter does appear to have been a native of South Carolina and thus a U.S. citizen. On the decline in activity by U.S. merchants in Cuba, see Edward Spalding Financial Records, 1816–1820, 1821, 1822, Special Collections, Miami University, online at digitalcollections.library.miami.edu/digital/collection/chco184.

30. González, "Foundation and Growth," 128; John G. B. Hutchins, *The American Maritime Industries and Public Policy, 1789–1914* (Cambridge: Harvard University Press, 1941), 127–128, 178, 218, 238; Roland, Bolster, and Keyssar, *Way of the Ship,* 174; *Royal Gazette and Sierra Leone Advertiser,* March 23, 1822, 47.

31. Roland, Bolster, and Keyssar, *Way of the Ship,* 158–171. On specialization, see Simon Ville, "The Growth of Specialization in English Shipowning, 1750–1850," *Economic History Review* 44, no. 4 (1993): 716–717; Jesús Ma Valdaliso, "The Rise of Specialist Firms in Spanish Shipping and their Strategies of Growth, 1860 to 1930," *Business History Review* 74 (Summer 2000): 273–274.

32. BPP, "Correspondence with the British Commissioners," 1831–1832 (010) vol. 47:95; *Noticio Mercantil,* January 17, 1825, 1; July 12, 1825, 3; September 5, 1825, 1; September 24, 1825, 1; August 26, 1828, 1; BNA FO 84/11, p. 26; FO 84/78, p. 97; FO 84/192, p. 73; BPP, Slave Trade, 1836 (001), Class A, 85; On Wright, see Clyde Norman Wilson, Robert Lee Meriwether, and William Edward Hemphill, eds., *The Papers of John C. Calhoun* (Columbia: South Carolina Department of Archives and History and the South Carolina Society, 1959), 20:200; Louis A. Pérez Jr., *On Becoming Cuban: Identity, Nationality, and Culture* (Chapel Hill: University of North Carolina Press, 2012), 507. "Sole" was probably José Soler, who was involved in multiple voyages during 1815–1820, with a special focus on the Rio Pongo. See González, "Foundation and Growth," 221, 279, 280, 286, 287.

33. *Voyages,* www.slavevoyages.org/voyages/1SlLMH2z; Marques, *United States and the Transatlantic Slave Trade,* 109, 129–130.

34. BPP, Correspondence with the British Commissioners, 1831–1832 (10), 101–109.

35. On rural networks, see María del Carmen Barcia Zequeira, ed., *Una sociedad distinta: espacios del comercio negrero en el occidente de Cuba (1836–1866)* (Havana, Cuba: UH Editorial, 2017). On insurance and banking, see David Turnbull, *Travels in the West: Cuba, with Notices of Porto Rico, and the Slave Trade* (London: Longman, 1840), 365–366; R. R. Madden, *The Island of Cuba: Its Resources, Progress, and Prospects* (London: Charles Gilpin, 1849), 33; Justo Reyes, *Apuntaciones de un empleado de Real Hacienda* (Key West, Fla.: G. F. Hopkins & Son, 1838), 31; González, "Foundation and Growth," 142–143.

36. Catterall, *Judicial Cases,* 2:302–303, 306–307, 4:450.

37. Theophilus Parsons, *A Treatise on Maritime Law* (Boston: Little, Brown, 1859), 2:88–89; John Duer, *The Law and Practice of Marine Insurance* (New York: John S.

Voorhies, 1845), 1:344–345. On Rhode Island, see Paul Finkleman, *An Imperfect Union: Slavery, Federalism, and Comity* (Chapel Hill: University of North Carolina Press, 1981), 80. These were all Massachusetts cases. While similar cases were probably filed in Rhode Island, these are obscure due to the difficulty of archival access and the fact that there was no Supreme Court reporter until 1845.

38. Catterall, *Judicial Cases*, 4:484, 489–490; D. J. M'Cord, *Chancery Cases Argued and Determined in the Court of Appeals of South Carolina, from January 1825 to May 1826* (Philadelphia: Carey, Lea & Carney, 1827), 1:156–166; Mouser, "Lightbourn Family of Farenya," 57–58. For more analysis of Greenwood v. Curtis, see Finkleman, *An Imperfect Union*, 80–81. One of the judges who upheld Greenwood's contract with Curtis was Theophilus Parsons, author of *A Treatise on Maritime Law.*

39. Canney, *Africa Squadron*, 15–18; David F. Ericson, "The United States Navy, Slave-Trade Suppression, and State Development," *Journal of Policy History* 33, no. 3 (2021): 231–255; Thomas Blake Earle, "'A Sufficient and Adequate Squadron:' The Navy, the Transatlantic Slave Trade, and the American Commercial Empire," *International Journal of Maritime History* 33, no. 3 (2021): 509–524.

40. Mouser, *American Colony*, 22, 26, 42, 47; Mouser, "Lightbourn Family," 26. For this discussion, I have chosen not to rely on John Hawkins, *A History of a Voyage to the Coast of Africa* (Troy, N.Y.: Luther Pratt, 1797) due to questions regarding accuracy and authenticity.

41. "Notes on the Rio Pongas," BNA FO 84/15; Mouser, *American Colony*, 5–6; R. B. Estrada, "Geografía. Relación de un viaje á las Yslas de Cabo Verde, y algunos puntos del Río Pongo," in Barcia Zequiera, *Pedro Blanco*, 163–164.

42. Mouser, *American Colony*, 4–8; Bruce L. Mouser, "Traders, Coasters, and Conflict in the Rio Pongo from 1790 to 1808," *JAH* 14, no. 1 (1973): 50–54, 63–64; Bruce L. Mouser, "Landlords-Strangers: A Process of Accommodation and Assimilation," *IJAHS* 8, no. 1 (1975): 425–440; Mouser, "Lightbourn Family," 27–30.

43. Mouser, *American Colony*, 63–88.

44. Barry, *Senegambia*, 133–136, 148–150, 158–160, 165–169; Laing, *Travels*, 416–417; Theophilus Conneau, *A Slaver's Log Book* (Englewood Cliffs, N.J.: Prentice-Hall, 1976), 142.

45. Conneau, *A Slaver's Log Book*, 64–70, 76–79, 90, 173, 196; Estrada, "Geografía," 162–169.

46. Conneau, *A Slaver's Log Book*, 106; Estrada, "Geografía," 162.

47. Mouser, *American Colony*, 48; González, "Foundation and Growth," 126.

48. Mouser, *American Colony*, 66–69, 73–76, 84–88, 93–101, 105–106; Barry, *Senegambia*, 165–166.

49. Barry, *Senegambia*, 165–166.

50. Jones, *From Slaves to Palm Kernels*, 1–5; Norman R. Bennett and George E. Brooks, eds., *New England Merchants in Africa: A History Through Documents, 1802–1865* (Boston: Boston University Press, 1965), 82.

51. Jones, *From Slaves to Palm Kernels*, 45–50, 73; Philip R. Misevich, "On the Frontier of 'Freedom': Abolition and the Transformation of Atlantic Commerce in

Southern Sierra Leone, 1790s to 1860s" (Ph.D. diss., Emory University, 2009), 81, 86–88; Philip R. Misevich, "The Origins of Slaves Leaving the Upper Guinea Coast in the Nineteenth Century," in *Extending the Frontiers: Essays on the New Transatlantic Slave Trade Database*, ed. David Eltis and David Richardson (New Haven: Yale University Press, 2008), 164–172; John W. Barber, *History of the Amistad Captives* (New Haven: E. L. and J. W. Barber, 1840), 9–15. It is perhaps worth noting that the *Amistad* was not a transatlantic slave ship, so it has not received detailed coverage here.

52. Jones, *From Slaves to Palm Kernels*, 56–63.

53. Barcia Zequeira, *Pedro Blanco*, 72; Julio D. Rojas Rodríguez, "La Conquista del espacio Atlántico sobre hombros negros: la familia O'Farrill y el comercio de esclavos (1716–1866)," *Irish Migration Studies in Latin America* 9, no. 2 (2019): 19–20; Bennett and Brooks, *New England Merchants*, 82–91; *New England Palladium*, July 12, 1816, 1. Reaney appears in the Spanish documents as "Guillermo L. Renney." On Reaney, see *Boston Commercial Gazette*, November 5, 1804, 3.

54. Bennett and Brooks, *New England Merchants*, 82; Barcia Zequeira, *Pedro Blanco*, 72–74; Ortega, "Cuban Merchants," 244; Rojas Rodriguez, "Conquista del espacio," 19–20. It is possible that the war was between Siaka and another leader. Barcia Zequeira mentions a "local chief, Amarat," but his position in the conflict is not clear. Jones, *From Slaves to Palm Kernels*, 56–61, makes no mention of a war between Siaka and Amara Lalu ca. 1817 but says that one began "about 1818." It seems very likely that this is the same conflict described by Barcia Zequeira.

55. Barcia Zequeira, *Pedro Blanco*, 21–31; BPP, "Correspondence with the British Commissioners, Relating to the Slave Trade," 1836, vol. 50 (005), 72–75; *Mercantile Advertiser*, December 11, 1809, 1; Randy S. Koniowka, *Legendary Locals of Cohoes* (Mt. Pleasant, S.C.: Arcadia Publishing, 2013), 28; *African Repository and Colonial Journal*, 21, no. 6 (June 1845): 80–81; *Baltimore Patriot*, February 4, 1824, 3.

56. BPP, Correspondence with British Coms. at Sierra Leone, Havana, Rio de Janeiro, and Suriname on Slave Trade: 1823–1824, 1824 (002), Class B, 18–19.

57. BPP, Correspondence with British Coms. at Sierra Leone, Havana, Rio de Janeiro, and Suriname on Slave Trade: 1823–1824, 1824 (002), Class B, 18–19; BPP, Select Committee on the Slave Trade, First Report, Minutes of Evidence, appendix, 1847–1848 (272), 82; Bennett and Brooks, *New England Merchants*, 84, 86–87.

58. For example, see *Royal Gazette and Sierra Leone Advertiser*, March 1808, 11; January 10, 1818, 28; October 2, 1824, 364; July 9, 1825, 524; May 20, 1826, 704; July 21, 1826, 846; March 3, 1827, 840. On Howland, see Bennett and Brooks, *New England Merchants*, 107.

Chapter 10. Shills, Hirelings, and True Believers, 1835–1865

1. Murray, *Odious Commerce*, 99.

2. Moreno Fraginals, *El Ingenio*, 120–124, Franklin W. Knight, *Slave Society in Cuba During the Nineteenth Century* (Madison: University of Wisconsin Press, 1970), 30–32; Laird W. Bergad, *Cuban Rural Society in the Nineteenth Century: The Social and*

Economic History of Monoculture in Matanzas (Princeton: Princeton University Press, 1990), 54–55, 109–114. For the slave trade, see *Voyages,* www.slavevoyages.org/voyages/YAP1NanY and http://www.slavevoyages.org/estimates/dv5AsQ4Y.

3. *Voyages,* www.slavevoyages.org/voyages/YAP1NanY.

4. 26th Cong., 2d. Sess., H.R. Exec. Doc. No. 115 (1841), 133, 190–192, 215, 220–221.

5. BPP, Slave Trade, 1840 (330), Class A, 93–95.

6. Figures on total production are from Roland, Bolster, and Keyssar, *Way of the Ship,* appendix D, 439–440. Estimates for the number of U.S.-built slavers are from Leonardo Marques, "U.S. Shipbuilding, Atlantic Markets, and the Structures of the Contraband Slave Trade," in *The Rise and Demise of Slavery and the Slave Trade in the Atlantic World,* ed. Philip Misevich and Kristin Mann (Rochester, N.Y.: University of Rochester Press, 2016), 205. For the prosecutions, see Warren S. Howard, *American Slavers and the Federal Law, 1837–1862* (Berkeley and Los Angeles: University of California Press, 1963), 38–39.

7. Hutchins, *American Maritime Industries,* 274. For the argument that a slave-ship construction "boom" rescued Baltimore shipbuilders after 1837, see Murray, *Odious Commerce,* 185.

8. A good summary of the practice can be found in A. H. Everett to John Forsythe, July 21, 1840, in 26th Cong., 2d. Sess., H.R. Exec. Doc. No. 115 (1841), 473. There were many variations, of course.

9. Martin Van Buren, Fourth Annual Message to Congress, December 5, 1840, online at millercenter.org/the-presidency/presidential-speeches/december-5-1840-fourth-annual-message-congress; A. H. Everett to John Forsyth, July 21, 1840, 26th Cong., 2d. Sess., H.R. Doc. No. 115, 475. A good sampling of Trist's correspondence can be found throughout 26th Cong., 2d. Sess., H.R. Doc. No. 115.

10. Murray, *Odious Commerce,* 185; Bergad, Iglesias García, and Barcia, *Cuban Slave Market,* 65; Warren, *American Slavers and the Federal Law,* 39–40; Robert L. Paquette, *Sugar Is Made with Blood: The Conspiracy of la Escalera and the Conflict Between Empires over Slavery in Cuba* (Middletown, Conn.: Wesleyan University Press, 1988), 264–265; Dale T. Graden, *Disease, Resistance, and Lies: The Demise of the Transatlantic Slave Trade to Brazil and Cuba* (Baton Rouge: Louisiana State University Press, 2014), 101–115; *Voyages,* www.slavevoyages.org/voyages/5MneKAdv.

11. Warren, *American Slavers and the Federal Law,* 38–39; Marques, *United States and the Transatlantic Slave Trade,* 133–134; BPP, Slave Trade, 1840 (330), vol. 30, Class A, 99–100; U.S. v. Morris, 39 U.S. 464; Strohm v. U.S., 23 Fed. Cas. 240, online at cite.case.law/f-cas/23/240/. On Strohm as commission merchant, see *Baltimore Sun,* July 27, 1839, 2; *Baltimore Wholesale Business Directory and Business Calendar* (Baltimore: John Murphy, 1845), 123. Lower courts had condemned vessels without captives aboard on several previous occasions; for example, the *Alexander* (1823), 1 Fed. Cas, 362; the *Emily* and the *Caroline* (1824), 9 Wheaton 381; U.S. v. Gooding (1827), 12 Wheaton 460.

12. Leslie Bethell and José Murilo de Carvalho, "1822–1850," in *Brazil: Empire and Republic, 1822–1930,* ed. Leslie Bethell (Cambridge: Cambridge University Press, 1989), 47, 89. U.S. involvement in the Brazilian slave trade has received much attention. See

Robert Edgar Conrad, *World of Sorrow: The African Slave Trade to Brazil* (Baton Rouge: Louisiana University Press, 1986), 133–153; Gerald Horne, *The Deepest South: The United States, Brazil, and the African Slave-Trade* (New York: NYU Press, 2007), 53–84; Graden, *Disease, Resistance, and Lies;* Marques, *United States and the Transatlantic Slave Trade,* 139–184; Matthew Karp, *This Vast Southern Empire: Slaveholders at the Helm of American Foreign Policy* (Cambridge: Harvard University Press, 2016), 73–81.

13. On Maxwell, Wright & Co., see Laura Jarnagin, *A Confluence of Transatlantic Networks: Elites, Capitalism, and Confederate Migration to Brazil* (Tuscaloosa: University of Alabama Press, 2008), 111–130; João Marcos Mesquita, "O comércio ilegal de escravos no Atlântico: a trajetória de Manoel Pinto da Fonseca, c. 1831–c. 1850" (M.A. thesis, Universidade Federal do Estado do Rio de Janeiro, 2019), 20–49. On Birckhead, see *Jornal do Commercio,* October 1, 1827, 3; November 22, 1827, 4.

14. George W. Slacum to Daniel Webster, September 14, 1841, in 29th Cong., 1st Sess., H.R. Doc. No. 43, 10–11; George W. Slacum to Daniel Webster, July 1, 1843, in 29th Cong., 1st Sess., H.R. Doc. No. 43, 18. On Gordon's activities, see folder 16, George W. Gordon Papers, NYPL.

15. Craig M. Simpson, *A Good Southerner: The Life of Henry A. Wise of Virginia* (Chapel Hill: University of North Carolina Press, 1985), 10–59, quotation on p. 65. See also Karp, *This Vast Southern Empire,* 75.

16. Henry A. Wise to Maxwell, Wright & Co., December 9, 1844, in 28th Cong., 2d Sess., H.R. Doc. No. 148, 63–69; Jarnagin, *A Confluence of Transatlantic Networks,* 126–128; Simpson, *A Good Southerner,* 64–67; Marques, *United States and the Transatlantic Slave Trade,* 160–166.

17. Wise's narrative is in Wise to John C. Calhoun, February 18, 1845, 30th Cong., 2d Sess., H.R. Exec. Doc. No. 61, 70–86. Additional documents are contained in the same volume.

18. 30th Cong., 2d Sess., H.R. Exec. Doc. No. 61, 22–35. For Clapp's purchases, see 31st Cong., 2d Sess., S. Exec. Doc. No. 6, 41.

19. Based on folder 16, George W. Gordon Papers, NYPL, and 31st Cong., 2d Sess., S. Exec. Doc. No. 6, 37–40.

20. Howard Jones, *To the Webster-Ashburton Treaty: A Study in Anglo-American Relations, 1783–1843* (Chapel Hill: University of North Carolina Press, 1977), 72–78, 142–144; Eltis, *Economic Growth,* 87.

21. Jones, *To the Webster-Ashburton Treaty,* 143, 186; Canney, *Africa Squadron,* 45–51.

22. Canney, *Africa Squadron,* 39, 57, 164–165, 222–227.

23. Canney, *Africa Squadron,* 111–120, 201–206, 220–222, 233–234.

24. The literature on pro-slavery is extensive, but for the basic contours, see William Sumner Jenkins, *The Pro-Slavery Argument in the Old South* (Chapel Hill: University of North Carolina Press, 1935); Eugene D. Genovese, *The World the Slaveholders Made: Two Essays in Interpretation* (New York: Random House, 1969); Drew Gilpin Faust, *The Ideology of Slavery* (Baton Rouge: Louisiana State University, 1981); Larry Tise, *Proslavery: A History of the Defense of Slavery in America* (Athens: University of Georgia

Press, 1987); Ford, *Deliver Us from Evil*. On pro-slavery and Liberated Africans as spectacle, see Fett, *Recaptured Africans*, 34, 36.

25. Ronald T. Takaki, *A Pro-Slavery Crusade: The Agitation to Reopen the African Slave Trade* (New York: Macmillan, 1971), 1–22, 32, 136–137; Manisha Sinha, *The Counterrevolution of Slavery: Politics and Ideology in Antebellum South Carolina* (Chapel Hill: University of North Carolina Press, 2000), 125–142; Fehrenbacher, *Slaveholding Republic*, 180–181.

26. Takaki, *A Pro-Slavery Crusade*, 23–85; Sinha, *Counterrevolution of Slavery*, 125–142.

27. Tom Henderson Wells, *The Slave Ship* Wanderer (Athens: University of Georgia Press, 1967), 3–6; Jim Jordan, "Charles Augustus Lafayette Lamar and the Movement to Reopen the Slave Trade," *Georgia Historical Quarterly* 93, no. 3 (2009): 247–290; "A Slave-Trader's Letter-Book," *North American Review* 143, no. 5 (1886): 455. Erik Calonius, *The Wanderer: The Last American Slave Ship and the Conspiracy That Set Its Sails* (New York: St. Martin's, 2006), unfortunately, is unreliable, containing numerous errors and outright fabrications.

28. Jordan, "Charles Augustus Lafayette Lamar," 265–276.

29. Jordan, "Charles Augustus Lafayette Lamar," 278–287.

30. Sylviane A. Diouf, *Dreams of Africa in Alabama: The Slave Ship Clotilda and the Story of the Last Africans Brought to America* (New York: Oxford University Press, 2007), 7–25.

31. Diouf, *Dreams of Africa*, 55–62.

32. Diouf, *Dreams of Africa*, 74–181; Zora Neale Hurston, *Barracoon: The Story of the Last "Black Cargo"* (New York: Harper Collins, 2018).

33. Karp, *This Vast Southern Empire*, 191–198; Murray, *Odious Commerce*, 239–240, 263–265. Gerald Horne points out that some annexationists did target Brazil; see Horne, *Deepest South*, 107–127. Even so, most annexationist attention was focused on the Caribbean.

34. On courts and evidence, see Fehrenbacher, *Slaveholding Republic*, 191–192, 195–198.

35. Sinha, *Counterrevolution of Slavery*, 154–161; John Harris, "The Voyage of the *Echo*: Trials of an Illegal Trans-Atlantic Slave Ship," Low-Country Digital History Initiative, online at ldhi.library.cofc.edu/exhibits/show/voyage-of-the-echo-the-trials. See also *Argument Before the United States Circuit Court by Isaac W. Hayne, Esq., on the Motion to Discharge the Crew of the* Echo, *delivered in Columbia, S.C., December, 1858* (Albany, N.Y.: Weed, Parsons, 1859).

36. Wells, *Slave Ship* Wanderer, 53–62; Sinha, *Counterrevolution of Slavery*, 162–171.

37. *Voyages*, www.slavevoyages.org/voyages/TJZaTAPZ. It is very likely that a majority of the vessels in the global slaving fleet were owned, purchased, or chartered in New York, although this is very difficult to measure. We do know that almost 90 percent of the slavers used between 1851 and 1866 were built in the United States. See Marques, *United States and the Transatlantic Slave Trade*, 202.

38. Hutchins, *American Maritime Industry*, 316–319.

39. Marques, *United States and the Transatlantic Slave Trade*, 188–200; Harris, *Last Slave Ships*, 6–7.

40. Howard, *American Slavers and the Federal Law*, 49–51; Marques, *United States and the Transatlantic Slave Trade*, 193–194. On the experience of the Portuguese Company associates, see Roquinaldo Amaral Ferreira, "Dos sertões ao Atlântico: tráfico ilegal de escravos e comércio lícito em Angola, 1830–1860" (M.A. thesis, Universidade Federal do Rio de Janeiro, 1996), chaps. 4–5.

41. Marques, *United States and the Transatlantic Slave Trade*, 194.

42. This discussion is based on Peter Reuter, *Disorganized Crime: The Economics of the Visible Hand* (Cambridge, Mass.: MIT Press, 1986), 109–131; Mark H. Haller, "Illegal Enterprise: A Theoretical and Historical Interpretation," *Criminology* 28, no. 2 (1990): 207–235; Edward R. Kleemans and Henk G. van de Bunt, "The Social Embeddedness of Organized Crime," *Transnational Organized Crime* 5, no.1 (1999): 19–36; Martin Bouchard and Carlo Morselli, "Opportunistic Structures of Organized Crime," in *The Oxford Handbook of Organized Crime*, ed. Letizia Paoli (Oxford: Oxford University Press, 2014), 288–302; Edward R. Kleemans, "Theoretical Perspectives on Organized Crime," in *The Oxford Handbook of Organized Crime*, 32–52.

43. Reuter, *Disorganized Crime*, 109–131; Haller, "Illegal Enterprise," 207–235; Kleemans and van de Bunt, "Social Embeddedness," 19–36; Bouchard and Morselli, "Opportunistic Structures," 288–302; Kleemans, "Theoretical Perspectives," 32–52.

44. Besides BNA, additional sources, including *Voyages*, were consulted to fill in gaps. With the exception of Vianna, names are as given in the sources.

45. On Vining, see BNA FO 84/1086, pp. 41, 42, 98; on Braddick, see BNA FO 84/1086, pp. 45, 58, 108, and FO 84/1111, pp. 165, 171, 196, 198, 225, 240, 247, 248, 250, 272; on Ceballos, see BNA FO 84/1086, pp. 41, 42, 98, 296, and Civil War Draft Registrations for New York City, 1863–1865; on Ros, see BNA FO 84/1086, pp. 41, 42, 159, and FO 84/1111, pp. 196, 235, 237, 240, 272; and U.S. passport application, n.d. 1876, on Ancestry.com.

46. Dobson appears in the *Voyages* database as the owner of two vessels, but his name crops up more frequently in Sánchez's reports. See BNA FO 84/1086, pp. 45, 53, 58, 60, 172, and FO 84/1138, pp. 72, 78; and U.S. v. the *Island of Cuba*, RG 21, SDNY.

47. On corruption and the prosecution of the marshals, see Howard, *American Slavers and the Federal Law*, 128–130. For the death threats, see the undated newspaper clipping in BNA FO 84/1138, p. 181.

48. Deposition of Richard J. Hill, n.d., in Woodbury v. Lewis E. Simonds, NARA Boston, RG 21, Records of the Federal District Court for Massachusetts; Testimony of Peter Johnson, January 30, 1845, 30th Cong., 2d Sess., H.R. Exec. Doc. No. 61, 137–147. For additional examples, see Harris, *Last Slave Ships*, 135, 164.

49. Deposition of Levi W. Turner, November 11, 1858, U.S. v. the *Island of Cuba*, NARA RG 21, SDNY; The *Mary Ann*, 16 Fed. Cas. 949 (Abb. Adm. 270), April 1848, online at law.resource.org/pub/us/case/reporter/F.Cas/0016.f.cas/0016.f.cas.0949.7.html.

50. 29th Cong., 1st Sess., H.R. Exec. Doc. No. 43, 6–7, 9–10, 14–15.

51. BPP, Slave Trade, 1854–1855 (4), Class B, 468–488; *New York Times,* January 23, 1854, 2; *New York Times,* April 21, 1854, 3; María del Carmen Barcia Zequeira, "Un entorno propicio: la trata negrera en el occidente de Cuba," in *Una sociedad distinta: espacios del comercio negrero en el occidente de Cuba (1836–1866),* ed. María del Carmen Barcia Zequeira (Havana: Editorial Universidad de la Havana, 2017), 112–113.

52. *New York Times,* April 5, 1854, 2; *New York Times,* September 18, 1854, 1; Barcia Zequeira, "Un entorno propicio," 114–121, 143.

53. For the *William H. Stewart,* see BNA FO 84/1086, p. 58. On the *Ellen,* see BNA FO 84/1086, p. 58, and FO 84/1111, p. 272. For the *Emily,* see the clipping from the *Evening Post,* August 22, 1860, in BNA FO 84/1111, p. 310, and Howard, *American Slavers and the Federal Law,* 250. For the 1861 case, see BNA FO 84/1111, p. 58. On the *Pierre Soulé* and the *Haidee,* see BNA FO 84/1066, pp. 76–77, and Harris, *Last Slave Ships,* 78–80, 153–154. For another example of fraud against a Brazil-based slaver by Cuban buyers, see the example of Francisco Ruviroza y Urzelas in Ferreira, "Dos sertões ao Atlântico," chap. 5. Ruviroza (Rovirosa) had dealt with American slavers in Rio during the 1840s.

54. Madden, *Island of Cuba,* 33; José Guadalupe Ortega, "Cuban Merchants, Slave Trade Knowledge, and the Atlantic World, 1790s–1820s," *Colonial Latin American Research Review* 15, no. 3 (2006): 248–249; Ferreira, "Dos sertões ao Atlântico," chap. 5; John Harris, "Financing the Illegal Slave Trade, 1850–1860," *Journal of Global History* 11, no. 1 (2016): 425–427; Henry A. Wise to John C. Calhoun, February 18, 1845, in 30th Cong., 2d. Sess., H.R. Exec. Doc. No. 61, 73.

55. John A. E. Harris, "Circuits of Wealth, Circuits of Sorrow: Financing the Illegal Transatlantic Slave Trade in the Age of Suppression, 1850–1866," *Journal of Global History* 11, no. 3 (November 2016): 426–427; Ferreira, "Dos sertões ao Atlântico," chap. 5.

56. Harris, "Circuits of Wealth," 416.

57. Miriam Herrera Jerez, "Fondeados en Sagua: el paisaje del tráfico ilegal de esclavos (1852–1858), in Barcia Zequeira, *Una sociedad distinta,* 198, 200–201.

58. Madden, *Island of Cuba,* 33; Turnbull, *Travels in the West,* 365–366.

59. Bergad, Iglesias García, and Barcia, *Cuban Slave Market,* 159.

60. *Voyages,* slavevoyages.org/voyages/s84XYE3C.

61. Leslie Bethell, *The Abolition of the Brazilian Slave Trade: Britain, Brazil, and the Slave Trade Question, 1807–1869* (Cambridge: Cambridge University Press, 1970), 27–61.

62. Joseph C. Miller, *Way of Death: Merchant Capitalism and the Angola Slave Trade, 1780–1830* (Madison: University of Wisconsin Press, 1988), 140–152; Ferreira, "Dos sertões ao Atlântico," chap. 4; Maria Cristina Cortez Wissenbach, "Dinâmicas históricas de um porto centro-africano: Ambriz e o Baixo Congo nos finais do tráfico Atlântico de escravos (1840–1870)," *Revista História* 34, no. 2 (2015): 165–178; Domingues da Silva, *Atlantic Slave Trade,* 29–36.

63. Ferreira, *Cross-Cultural Exchange,* 15–16; Domingues, *Atlantic Slave Trade,* 86, 145–146; Robert W. Harms, *River of Wealth, River of Sorrow: The Central Zaire Basin in the Era of the Slave and Ivory Trade, 1500–1891* (New Haven: Yale University Press, 1981), 32–39.

64. There were several variations on this system. See Harms, *River of Wealth*, 30–39, 79–85.

65. John M. Janzen, *Lemba: A Drum Affliction in Africa and the New World* (New York: Garland, 1982), 3–7.

66. Jelmer Vos, "Without the Slave Trade, No Recruitment: From Slave Trading to 'Migrant Recruitment' in the Lower Congo, 1830–1890," in *Trafficking in Slavery's Wake: Law and the Experience of Women and Children in Africa*, ed. Benjamin N. Lawrance and Richard L. Roberts (Athens: Ohio University Press, 2012), table 2.3; Domingues, *Atlantic Slave Trade*, 103–120.

67. *Voyages*, www.slavevoyages.org/voyages/6wFqUWcP; Vos, "Without the Slave Trade," 45–65.

68. Ferreira, "Dos sertões ao Atlântico," chap. 4.

69. Joachim John Monteiro, *Angola and the River Congo* (London: Macmillan, 1875), 1:83, 91–93; Ferreira, "Dos sertões ao Atlântico," chap. 5. In 1861, a Massachusetts court convicted Oaksmith of organizing another voyage. He escaped from jail in Boston and was later pardoned. He retired in North Carolina. See U.S. v. Oaksmith, Records of the U.S. District Court for the District of Massachusetts, RG 21; Appleton Oaksmith file, David M. Rubenstein Rare Book and Manuscript Library, Duke University.

70. Phyllis Martin, "Family Strategies in Nineteenth-Century Cabinda," *JAH* 28, no. 1 (1987): 65–76. For Fonseca's dealings at Cabinda with a U.S. vessel, see Mesquita, "Comercio ilegal," 54–93. On the powers of the mafouk, see Martin, *External Trade of the Loango Coast*, 97–99; Cortez Wissenbach, "Dinâmicas históricas," 181; G. Tams, *Visit to the Portuguese Possessions in South-Western Africa* (London: T. C. Newby, 1845), 2:158–161; Monteiro, *Angola and the River Congo*, 1:152–153; Brooks, *Yankee Traders*, 106. For an account of an American legitimate trader at Ambriz, see Bennett and Brooks, *New England Merchants*, 174–176.

71. On freighting in the nineteenth-century slave trade, see Harris, *Last Slave Ships*, 75–78. On its earlier use in Angola, see Joseph C. Miller, "Capitalism and Slaving: The Financial and Commercial Accounts of the Angolan Slave Trade According to the Accounts of Antonio Coelho Guerreiro (1684–1692)," *IJAHS* 17, no. 1 (1984): 1–56; and Miller, *Way of Death*, 314–318, 324–335.

72. Ted Maris-Wolf, "'Of Blood and Treasure': Recaptive Africans and the Politics of Slave Trade Suppression," *Journal of the Civil War Era* 4, no. 1 (2014): 53–83; *Voyages*, www.slavevoyages.org/voyages/9hi8kUyR.

73. Archibald to the Foreign Office, February 1, 1861, BNA FO 84/1138, p. 44; Howard, *American Slavers and the Federal Law*, 199–202.

74. Marques, *United States and the Transatlantic Slave Trade*, 249–255; Soulsby, *Right of Search*, 170–176; BPP, Slave Trade, 1863 (3339-I), Class B, 190–195. The text of the treaty, subsequent annexes, and the 1870 accord that superseded it can be found in Bevans, *Treaties*, 12:136–153, 161–166.

75. Murray, *Odious Commerce*, 306–310.

76. Murray, *Odious Commerce*, 310–325.

Conclusion: A Reckoning of Accounts

1. Unless otherwise indicated, all statistics are derived from *Voyages*, including the "Estimates" section. The figure fifty-two thousand is the approximate number of people who died aboard U.S.-flagged vessels, so it obviously represents the lowest possible estimate.

2. Several of these questions are explored in Eltis, "U.S. Transatlantic Slave Trade."

3. There has been much debate on this point. Representative statements include Walter Rodney, *How Europe Underdeveloped Africa* (Washington, D.C.: Howard University Press, 1972), 95–146; J. E. Inikori, ed., *Forced Migration: The Impact of the Export Slave Trade on African Societies* (London: Hutchinson University Library, 1982); Eltis, *Economic Growth*, 64–77; Manning, *Slavery and African Life*; John K. Thornton, *Africa and Africans in the Making of the Atlantic World, 1400–1680* (Cambridge: Cambridge University Press, 1992), 72–97; Lovejoy, *Transformations*, 61–69.

4. *Voyages*, www.slavevoyages.org/voyages/PGvXxNvw.

5. These figures are adapted from Marques, "U.S. Shipbuilding," table 7.2, p. 205.

6. Eric Williams, *Capitalism and Slavery* (Chapel Hill: University of North Carolina Press, 1944); Seymour Drescher, *Econocide: British Slavery in the Era of Abolition* (Pittsburgh: University of Pittsburgh Press, 1977); J. E. Inikori, *Africans and the Industrial Revolution in England: A Study in International Trade and Development* (Cambridge: Cambridge University Press, 2001); Sven Beckert and Seth Rockman, eds., *Slavery's Capitalism: A New History of American Development* (Philadelphia: University of Pennsylvania Press, 2016). For a contrary view, see Bailey, "Slave(ry) Trade," 374–375, 377–380.

7. On the much-overlooked "cotton triangle," see Hutchins, *American Maritime Industries*, 236–237, 264–265.

8. Richardson, "Slavery, Trade, and Economic Growth," table 3, p. 254. For the Boston Associates, see the appendix in Robert F. Dalzell, Jr., *Enterprising Elite: The Story Behind the Men Who Made America's First Industrial Revolution* (Cambridge: Harvard University Press, 1987; New York: Norton, 1993), 233–238; and *Voyages*. T. H. and J. Perkins were involved in Voyage no. 25300, and Peter Chardon Brooks was the insurance underwriter.

9. Sparks, *Africans in the Old South*, 93–98.

Acknowledgments

Once more, I find myself reflecting on the number of people who offered their time, expertise, and resources to help me bring this project to fruition. I am especially grateful to David Eltis, Paul Lovejoy, and Suzanne Schwarz, all of whom read the entire manuscript and offered extensive feedback, and all of whom gave support and encouragement throughout the project. Leonardo Marques read the entire manuscript and generously shared numerous Brazilian and Portuguese sources with me. Jorge Felipe-González read the manuscript on extremely short notice and offered valuable feedback. My friend and colleague Jeremy Krikler, who commented extensively on several chapters over long walks during lockdown, deserves special thanks. Those discussions shaped this book in many ways. My old friends Eric Altice and Roark Atkinson brought their Americanist perspective to several of the early chapters. Other friends and colleagues, including Richard Anderson, Robin Blackburn, Henry Lovejoy, and Matthias Röhrig Assunção, read and commented either on chapters or on related publications, as did anonymous readers on several related journal articles. I would also like to thank the many archivists who shared their knowledge and materials with me, with special appreciation to Derry Riding and the staff at the Bristol Historical and Preservation Society, who not only offered their time and expertise, but found local accommodations for me during an unexpected ice storm. Thanks also to JoAnne and Bill Norton for opening their home to me on numerous trips to the Boston area, and to Erin Kelley and David Klempner for putting me up (and putting up with me) on multiple visits to New York.

I am also fortunate to have had institutional support for this project. Faculty Trustee Grants from Hartwick College in 2013 and 2014 allowed me to visit archives in New England and South Carolina. A Trans-Atlantic Partnership NWO/ESRC grant (ES/T015314/1) helped to pay for the collection of African narratives. I am particularly thankful to the University of Essex for granting me research leave in 2017 and 2021 and to the Department of History's Research Support Fund, which paid for numerous trips to the National Archives at Kew. And a fellowship at the Gilder Lehrman Center for the Study of Slavery, Resistance, and Abolition allowed me to access the many excellent resources at Yale, as well as to visit additional archives in the region. Thanks are also due to my editors, Adina Popescu Berk, Kate Davis, Phillip King, and the staff at Yale University Press for their professionalism and patience, to Bill Nelson for preparing the maps, and to Kartikay Chadha and the team at WalkWithWeb for making the network diagram.

Finally, I would like to thank Vicki and Kathleen for tolerating my absences and absentmindedness over the years. This book would not exist without their support.

Index

Page numbers in italics refer to illustrations

Abbie, Edward, 276
abolitionist movement, 154, 195, 221
Abolition Society, 158, 161, 163
ACS. *See* American Colonization Society
Adams, David, 195
Adams, John Quincy, 318, 319
Africa: American networks in, 125–26; American privateering in, 153–54; American slave trade impact in, 390–91; British slave trade in, 23–24; enslaved people in, 216–17; exchanging goods for captives, 13–14; settlements, 185–87. *See also* Central African slave trade; Gold Coast; Guinea, upper
Africa (ship), 208–9
Africa Squadron, 351–52, 383, 385
agglomeration concept, 84–85
Akan people, 102, 103, 104, 226, 230–31, 234, 235; and gold production, 100, 101, 227, 231; Islam and, 227; language and culture of, in Newport and Rhode Island, 212, 213, 231, 245, 289–92, 300; and slave trade, 101

Akan (Twi) language, 99, 245
Akwamu state, 102–3, 132, 290
Akyem state, 102–3, 132–34
Albranches, Almeida & Co., 364, 368
Alfa, Karamoko, 136, 137–38
Almirante (ship), 323–24
Ambriz, 377, 378, 382
Amedie (ship), 207, 209, 250, 253, 317
Amelia (ship), 247
Amelia Island, 314, 315
American Colonization Society (ACS), 314–16, 320, 329
American Revolution, 110, 112, 153, 156, 174, 292
Angela (ship), 202
Anglo-American convention (1824), 318–21
Anglo-Dutch Wars, 33–35, 50
Anglo-Portuguese Treaty (1815), 346, 378
Anglo-Spanish treaty (1817), 306, 317, 339, 399, 448n4
Anglo-Spanish treaty (1835), 307, 338, 339–40

463

Ann (*Anne,* ship), 208, 281
Annamaboo (ship), 127
Anomabu, 126, 131, 132–33, 174, 176, 243, 277, 299; American slave trading at, 103–4, 124, 152, 249; prices for captives at, 110, 111–12; slave-trading departures from, 124, 133, 235, 240, 243; slave-trading installations at, 101, 103, 105, 124, 234, 237
anti-slavery movement, 154–56, 159, 184, 189, 204, 293, 395–96; British laws, 195, 198, 207, 250, 434n44; laws enacted by states, 155, 156–59, 162, 163, 166, 262, 268, 292; slave trade, laws restricting, 191, 309–10, 316–18, 343–44
apprenticeship, 250, 251, 294
Aptheker, Herbert, 7
Arabella (ship), 24
asantehene, 101, 102, 107, 127, 131, 132, 177, 229
Asante state, 101–3, 107, 127, 132–34, 175, 176, 177, 227–28, 229–30, 231, 233, 234, 235, 290, 418n43
Assin Manso, 176–77, 235
auxiliaries, 341, 344, 349, 360
Avallar, João Carlos de, 381–82
Aylwin, George, 194, 195, 201
Ayrault, Steven, 284

Bacchus (ship), 117
Bailey, Ronald, 4
Bailyn, Bernard, 37, 408n3
Bailyn, Lotte, 37
Baker, John, 313
Balanta people, 219–20
Baldridge, Adam, 58–60, 64, 68
Bali, Cumba, 331, 332
Baltimore prosecutions, 344–45
Baltimore Society of Friends, 315
"Bambara" (ethnonym), 220
Bank of North America, 168
Bank of Rhode Island, 261
banks, 376

Bank of San Fernando, 325
Bank of the United States, 166, 168, 260
Baol state, 43, 46
Barbados, 28, 30, 31, 38, 39, 40–41, 42, 51, 57, 143–44, 242, 248, 268, 391, 392; rum distilling, 41, 45, 63, 79, 88–89, 104
Barnes, John, 91
barricado (wooden barrier), 241
Barry, Robert, 334
Bayard, Nicholas, 56
Bayliss, George, 312
Beggar's Benison (ship), 144
Beginning (ship), 38–39, 40–41, 45
Belcher, Jonathan, 89
Belisario, John. *See* Sano, John
Bellamont, Richard Coot, Earl of, 54, 70
Benezet, Anthony, 154
Benson, Martin, 169
Bentley, William, 159, 165
Biafra, Bight of, 78, 93
Bidwell, Barnabas, 203
Bilali, Salih, 224, 235, 249
Birckhead, James, 346
Black Dick's Nursery, 212–13
Blanco, Pedro, 334, 341
Blossom (ship), 19–20, 30
Board of Trade in London, 86
Bobangi people, 379–80
Bobbitt, Jacob, 313
Boma entrepôt, 379, 381, 382
Bonsu, Osei, 177
Borbor Fante, 103
Boss, Edward, 1, 2, 270, 396, 403nn1–2
Boss, Edward, Jr., 2
Boston, Mass., 55, 196, 324; Black population in, 287, 395; Madeira trading axis, 26, 27, 39; Newport slave trade and, 81, 83, 84, 85, 86, 87, 106, 257, 273; post-revolutionary slave trading, 164; role in American slave trade, 77, 80, 81, 87, 119–20, 151, 164, 256, 394; shipowning in, 37, 89, 168, 199, 205, 312; slave ships from, 6, 10, 18, 19, 45, 51, 59, 142, 143,

144, 152, 158, 164, 201, 202, 247, 256, 321, 394; slave ships landing in, 30, 357, 372; slave traders and merchants connected to, 37, 38, 39, 145, 168, 175, 177, 182, 283, 285, 305, 306, 333, 363, 394; waterfront, 17, 18

"Boston" factory (in Africa), 182

Boston Marine Insurance Company, 168

Botelho, Antonio and Manuel, 364, 368, 374

Botifeur, Daniel, 326

Bourne, Benjamin, 166

Bowen, Jabez, 387, 395

Bowen, Oliver, 1–2, 396, 403n1

Boyd, William, 193–94, 198, 209

Bradbury, Francis, 201

Braddick, Jesse, 369

Bradford, Sally and Leonard, 283

Bradford, William, 166

Bradley, Stephen Row, 203

Brazilian slave trade, 79, 201, 307, 339, 345, 347, 375, 378, 382, 389–90; American vessel supply, 342; Anglo-Brazilian Treaty, 346; ending of, 349–50; *Porpoise* (ship) case, 348; shipping records, 349

Brazil Squadron, 351

Brew, Richard, 126–30, 132, 144, 152, 174, 175, 182

Briggs, Nathaniel, 125, 263–65, 276

Brinah, Konta, 138

Brinch, Boyrereau, 239–40

Bristol, Mass., 89, 165

Bristol, R.I.: Black population in, 293–94, 296, 300–301; insurance companies in, 166, 168–69, 261; maritime life in, 258, 269; slave-ship crews in, 269, 271, 272, 273, 275, 276, 278, 279; slave trade in, 11–12, 165, 166–68, 173, 205, 214, 256–57, 258, 259, 292, 300, 311, 336, 394; slave traders from, 148, 165–67, 172, 173, 258, 259–60, 261, 262, 263, 312, 313; slave traders' political domination in, 166–67, 262, 280, 300; social structure and

race in, 280, 281, 296, 298, 300–301; women in, 258–59, 282, 283, 286

British-American ventures, 144–45

British Royal Navy, 153, 207, 208, 238, 250, 284, 307, 311, 317–19, 340, 342, 350, 359, 382, 385

British slave trade, 94, 118, 195, 419n5; abolition of, 436n13; on Gold Coast, 134; slave merchants, awakening of, 143–44; voyage organizers in, 37; voyages to Africa, 23–24

Broadfoot, James, 193, 195, 199

Broadfoot, William, 193

Brooks, Peter Chardon, 168

Brown, John, 151, 157, 163, 164, 295, 309

Brown, Moses, 157–59, 161

Brown, Samuel, 158–59, 177

Brun, Samuel, 104

Buchanan, James, 349, 352, 359

Buffum, Walter, 127

bulking centers, 124, 140, 182, 329

Bull, Nathan, 277

Burch, Benjamin, 275

Burgess, Samuel, 49, 58, 59, 61–63, 65, 68–70

Bush, Elizabeth, 212

Bush, John, 212

Butler, Thomas, 316

Butterfly (ship), 345

Byrd, William, I, 78

Cabinda, 362, 371, 377, 378, 379, 380, 382

Cabo Verde, 23, 27, 35, 36, 41, 42, 45, 57, 92, 97, 98, 324, 330

Cahoone, James, 74

Calhoun, John C., 347, 352

California Gold Rush, 363–64

Campbell, John, 194, 432n17

Canary Islands, 26, 42

Cape Coast Castle, 73, 74, 125, 126, 213

Cape of Good Hope, 34, 48, 52, 54, 64, 70, 374

captivity of African people, 238–39; by abduction, 215–17, 224, 239–42; deaths of captives, 242–45; enslavement for debt, 229, 231–34; environment issues, 225–26; imprisonment of captives, 237–38; long journeys and, 235–37; narratives from enslaved people, 217, 221–23, 229–30; possibility of redemption, 234–35; post-voyage survival, 248–54; shipboard rebellions, 245–48; in upper Guinea, 217–20, 224–25, 236; Voltaic slavery, 226–29; warfare and, 221, 223–24, 230–31

Carballo (Carvallo), Lino, 334, 341

Carolina slave rush (1804–1807), 186–87, 339, 391; battle between Lowcountry planters and Upcountry slaveholders, 190–91; British and Irish merchants, voyages of, 193–97; Georgia Upcountry labor market and, 187; issue of captive importations, 190; and labor demand in cotton fields, 188–89; Loango Coast trade, textile-based, 198–200; Yankee merchants, voyages of, 192–93

Caroline (ship), 311

Carr, Isaac, 238

Cartwright, Samuel A., 353

Carvalho Alvarenza, Rosa, 324–25

Casada Garden (ship), 118

Casket (ship), 371–72

Cawson, Miles, 19, 407n1

Ceballos, John M., 369–70

ceddo ("soldier") states, 46, 94, 95, 96–97, 135, 136, 179, 183, 221–22

cemeteries, names in, 212–14, 288–90

Central African slave trade, 379–83

Champlin, Christopher, 118, 127, 163, 259, 261

Champlin, George, 118, 127, 163, 261

Champlin, Sarah, 284

Chancellor, William, 131, 244, 299, 300, 422n31

Channing, Walter, 261

Charles (ship), 57–59, 61

Charleston, S.C., 78–80, 159, 162, 209–10; post-revolutionary slave trading, 164; re-legalization of transatlantic slave trade, 186; slave-trade impact, 256

"Charleston" factory (in Africa), 182

Charming Sally (ship), 285

"charter party" documents, 38, 40, 41

chattel slavery, 29, 215

Chesapeake colonies, 77–78

Christian, Charles, 192

Christianity, 29, 30, 32

Christie, Charles, 199–200

Christopher, Emma, 295

Clapp, Joshua, 349

Clark, John, 275

Clarke, Charles, 206

Clarke, Peleg, 121, 128, 131, 132, 144–45, 152–53, 163, 261, 263

Clarkson, Thomas, 293

Clay, Henry, 347

Clotilda (ship), 357–58

CMTA. *See* Company of Merchants Trading to Africa

Cobb, Howell, 356

Cochrane, Alexander, 250, 253

cod fishing, 25–26

Coggeshall, Boston, 276–77, 279

Coit, Henry, 376

Collins, Charles, 167

commercial cluster concept, 84

commission merchants, 192–94, 197, 198, 205, 209, 338

Company of Merchants Trading to Africa (CMTA), 90, 91, 126–29, 130, 131, 140, 144, 153

Congdon, Charles, 212

Congo River–based slave trade, 50, 57, 177, 194–95, 199, 351, 356, 364, 377–79, 381–83, 385

Conneau, Theophilus, 329

Connecticut, 127, 157, 158, 166, 250, 287
Constitutional Convention, Philadelphia, 160–61
Continental Association, 148–49, 152
Continental Congress, 149, 156–57
Corrantee, John. *See* Kurentsi, Eno Baisee
Correia, Guilherme José da Silva, 364, 368, 381, 383
Cortlandt, Jacobus van, 48, 56
Cortlandt, Stephanus van, 56
Côte d'Ivoire, 15, 226
"cotton boom," in United States, 186–87, 189–90, 209
Coughtry, Jay, 6–7, 8, 89, 115, 272–73, 405n9, 425n14, 444n48
Courteen, William, 51
Courts of Mixed Commission, 338, 339, 341, 344, 385
coverture, 282–83
Crawford, William, 318
Creole (ship), 304
Crooke, Robert, 119
Crosley, Robert, 286
Cross, Paul, 182
Crowninshield merchant family, 165
Cruger, John, 56
Cuban-American collaborations, 309–10, 312–14, 321–23; criminal networks, 325; and Rio Pongo, 327–31, 336–37; ship brokers, role of, 323–25
Cuban slave trade, 340, 365, 368, 389; with American merchants, 172–73; ending of, 386; "First Dance of the Millions," 188–89; to Spanish America, 171–72; United States contributions in, 389–90
Cugoano, Ottobah, 228, 232
Cunha Reis, Manoel Basílio da, 364, 368, 370, 374, 375
currency: bills of exchange, 80, 83–84, 85, 106, 121, 126, 128, 145, 146, 164–65, 171, 173, 267, 376; captives as, 83, 330–31; cloth as, 198; colonial paper money

emissions, 85–87, 106; gold and silver, 85, 146, 173, 176; Iroquois, 57; "Old Tenor," 86, 255, 264, 442n18; rum as, 106; ship captain earnings, 264
Currency Act (1751), 87
Curtin, Philip D., 15, 40, 450n24
Curtis, Benjamin, 183, 328, 329, 331
Curtis, Thomas, 328, 331
Cushing, George, 172, 201
Cyane (ship), 314–15, 316

Dagomba Drum History, 228
Dale, George, 239
Davis, Amasa, 201
Davis, Ralph, 37
De Bow, J. D. B., 354
Declaration of Independence, U.S., 3–4, 155
De Lancey, Stephen, 56
Denkyira state, 101, 102, 132
DePau, Francis, 247
Derby merchant family, 165
Dha, Dhiagola, 239
Diallo, Ayuba Suleiman, 249
Dimans (merchant family), 166
Din, Nasir al-, 46, 97
Dobson, Jonathan, 370, 372, 457n46
Dole, Ann, 283
Domingo, Francisco, 48–49, 65
Donnan, Elizabeth, 5
Dooley, James, 314
Dordin, Peter, 74
Dowers, John, 35–36
Drake, Francis, 53
Du Bois, W. E. B., 8, 319–20, 404n7
Dunbar, James, 277
Duncan, John, 74, 243, 271
Dunn, David, 144, 175
Dutch West India Company (WIC), 50–51, 55, 56
D'Wolf, Abigail, 165
D'Wolf, Charles, 166, 312

D'Wolf, Henry, 192
D'Wolf, James, *147*, 172, 176; non-slave-trading activity, 167; political career and influence, 148, 166–67, 263, 318–19, 450n20; privateering by, 311; slave-trading career, 148, 263, 278; woman captive murdered by, 148, 243
D'Wolf, John, 166, 282
D'Wolf, Levi, 166
D'Wolf, Mark Anthony, 165–66, 281
D'Wolf, Samuel, 271
D'Wolf, William, 166
D'Wolf family, 166, 167, 168, 172, 173, 189, 192, 195, 199, 263, 309, 311, 313–14, 315, 336; Bristol, R.I., controlled by, 258, 262, 280; insurance companies, 168–69, 261; recruitment of seamen, 278–79, 280; vessel ownership, 201, 203, 206; women of, 282

E. A. Rawlins (ship), 355–56, 358
Early, Peter, 204
East India Company of England (EIC), 51, 52, 54–55, 69–71
Easton, John, 53, 74, 154
Echevarria, Tomás, 341
Echo (ship) case, 362–63
Edes, Daniel, 201
Edney, William, 252
Edwards, Bryan, 107, 235
EIC. *See* East India Company of England
Eight Sons (ship), 304
Eldrid, Thomas, 141, 298
Eliza (ship), 202, 281
Elizabeth (ship), 31
Ellen (ship), 374
Ellery, James, 191
Ellery, William, 4, 117, 167
Elliott, Robert, 266
Eltis, David, 317, 404n4
Embargo Act (1807), 310, 311
Emerson, Ralph Waldo, 304

Emily (ship), 374
Endangered Archives Programme, 15
English, William, 125, 135
English Civil War (1642–1651), 24, 25, 35
equipment clauses, 338, 339–40, 341–42, 346
Erie (ship), 384
Esperanza (ship), 374
Everett, Alexander, 343

Faber, Jacob ("Jacobo") and Paul, 322, 328, 330, 331, 332, 333, 334, 336
factories, in Africa, 182, 327–28, 330, 333, 335, 382–83, 391
Fales, Phebe, 286–87
Fales v. Mayberry (1815), 326
Fame (ship), 199, 245
Fanny (ship), 171, 283
Fante states, 101, 103, 105, 125, 127, 128, 129, 130, 132, 133, 134, 174, 176–77, 231, 232, 235, 243, 299–300; Anomabu port, 103–4
Fellowship Club, 74–75, 107, 268
Ferreira, Roquinaldo, 379
Fett, Sharla M., 6, 8
Figanière, Guilherme de la, 364
financial innovations after American Revolution, 167–69; emergence of marine insurance companies, 168–69
Fitch, Jonathan, 266–67
Fitch, Timothy, 117, 138, 163
Fitzhugh, George, 354
Fitzsimons, Christopher, 196, 432n23
Fletcher, Benjamin, 53, 54, 57
Fletcher, John, 144, 145, 152
Fletcher (ship), 145
Flying Eagle (ship), 375
Flypsen, Frederick. *See* Philipse, Frederick
Fonseca, Manoel Pinto da, 346, 364, 382
Foreign Slave Trade Act (1806), 195, 198
Forsyth, John A., 349

fort trade, 124–25; American networks in Africa, 125–26; rum men's dealing with, 130; in upper Guinea, 139–40, 141
Fortune (ship), 38, 39, 58
Foster, William, 357, 358
Fox (ship), 127
Foye, William, 89
France: French Revolution, 10, 178, 196; slave trade in, 419n5; slave trade abolished, 436n13
Francisco (ship), 313
Franklin, Benjamin, 4, 155, 161
Franque, Francisco "Chico," 382
Frazer, James, 206–7
Frazer, John, 326, 327, 434n44
Free African Union Society, 292–93, 295
Fulbe people, 136
Fuller, Gilbert, 270
Futa Jallon state, 136–38; and slave trade, 97, 137, 138, 140, 178–79, 183, 218–19, 223, 236–37, 329–30, 331–32
Futa Toro state, 178–79, 197

Gallinas state and river, 332–36, 438n49
Galveston Island, 449n11
Gambia River, 43–44; American slave trade on, 92, 96, 98–99, 135, 139–41, 153–54; British slave trade on, 94; Loango Coast trade on, 199
Gambia (ship), 98
gambling debts, 231–32
García Álvarez, José, 314
Gardner, Caleb, 128, 129, 144, 158, 159, 163, 167, 259, 261, 263
Gardner, Charles Quamine, 446n70
Gardner, John, 192, 206
Gariba, 228
Gaspee (ship), 151
Gay, Henry, 39
George III (king of England), 3
Georgia, 119, 162, 170–71, 187, 431n7
Georgia Upcountry, 187
Gibbs, Cuffe, 213

Gibbs, George, 261, 284
Gibbs, Pompe (Zingo), 213
Gibson, William, 193
Gift of God (ship), 38, 39–41
Glorious Revolution (1688), 35, 52
Godfrey, Caleb, 74, 85, 123, 142–43, 239, 266, 268
Godfrey, John, 85
God's Little Acre Cemetery, 213, 288–90
gold, 107; California Gold Rush, 363–64; as currency, 146, 173, 176; production of, 100, 101, 227, 231; in trade with Africa, 23–24, 35, 39, 44–45, 50, 100–101, 102, 130–31, 139, 146, 175–76, 231, 356, 357, 375; in wealth of ship captains, 267, 325, 349
Gold Coast, 15, 42, 74, 81, 99–100, 103–4, 108, 145, 245, 388; American networks on, 123–26; American tobacco market, 91; British slave trade on, 134; economic factors in slave trade, 110, 112, 174–75; fall in captive embarkations, 437n31; geopolitics, 101–2; gold trading on, 130–31, 175–76; liquor market, 99, 104–5; New England slave trade on, 196–97; Opoku Ware's death impact in slave trade, 131–34; political developments, 176–77; relationship with Rhode Island, 81; Richard Brew's connection with, 126. *See also* Guinea, upper
"gold-takers" (brokers), 129–31
Gordon, George W., 349
Gordon, Nathaniel, 384
Gordon, William, 158, 425n14
Gorges, Ferdinando, 34–35
Grafton, Joseph, 154, 160, 164–65, 172
Grafton, Joshua, 154, 165, 172
Great Migration (1630–1642), 24, 55
Greene, Jack P., 8, 10
Greene, P. C., 313–14
Greenwood v. Curtis (1810), 326
Grigg, James, 252

Grosse, Isaac, 37, 38, 39

Grossle, John, 129, 131, 144, 175

Groves, Thomas, 159

Guilherme of Zaire. *See* Correia, Guilherme José da Silva

Guinea, upper, 15, 94, 108, 134–36, 143, 307; American post-war trade, 178–84; American ship trade in, 139–40; costs for captives in, 113; economic factors in slave trade, 112, 114; expansion of slavery in, 217–20, 224–25; Futa Jallon jihad in, 136–38; gender issues in, 226; market for American rum, 94, 96–97; military regimes in, 136; narratives from enslaved people, 221–23; New England slave trade on, 196–97. *See also* Africa; Gold Coast

Guinea Company, 35

Guinea factors, 160, 192, 193, 266, 442n20

Gunthorp, John, 85

Gwinn, Peter, 117

Haidee (ship), 375

Hakluyt, Richard, 28

Hammond, Pollipus, 85

Hammond, Violet, 213

Hannah (ship), 278

Hare (ship), 142–43, 239, 248–49

Harmony, Peter, 334

Harris, John, 6, 8

Harrison, Peter, 262

Hataulx, François, 335

Hawke (ship), 89

Hawkins, John, 24, 53, 408n1

Hawthorne, Walter, 412n42

Hazard, Stanton, 148–49, 152

Heatley, Robert, 91, 135

Herndon, Ruth Wallis, 274

Herring, Benjamin, 65

Hicks, Benjamin, 74

Hicks, Whitehead, 154, 156

Hill, Richard J., 78, 371–72

Hillhouse, James, 191

Hindustan (ship), 199, 201

Holman, John, Jr., 182, 197, 238

Holman, John, Sr., 182

Hooper, Jane, 67

Hope (ship) case, 78, 158, 159

Hopkins, Esek, 270

Horne, Sarah, 286

Howard, Azel, 312

Howe, George, 450n20

Howland, George, 335, 336

Hoxse, John, 278, 279–80

Hunter (ship), 403n1

Hurston, Zora Neale, 358

Imperial Crisis, 110, 114, 151

Independence (ship), 7, 247

Ingraham, Nathaniel, 171

Ingraham family, 166

insurance, for slave-ship voyages, 121–23, 166, 168–69, 246, 275, 284, 306–7, 309, 325, 326, 394; illegality of, 157–58, 168, 325–26, 375, 377

insurance companies, investment in, 260–61, 393

interloper trades, 77

Iris (ship), 333

Irving, John, 327

Isla de Cuba (ship), 372, 375

Islam/Islamic reform, 29, 96, 97, 178–79, 183; rules on enslavement, 136; in Senegambia, 197; and Sharia, 177; in upper Guinea, 96–97

Isles de Los, 139, 140, 141, 165, 329

Jackson, Andrew, 319, 347

Jacobs, Cornelius, 61

James II (king of England), 35

James "Diogo" Birckhead & Co., 346

Jamineau, Daniel, 78

Jasper (ship), 373

Jay Treaty (1795), 169

Jefferson, Thomas, 3–4, 12, 155, 166, 167, 190, 191, 203–4, 206, 310, 352

Jennings, Daniel, 396, 403n1
Johnson, James, 207
Johnson, Peter, 372
Johnson, Robert, 1–2, 128, 233, 387, 395–96, 403n1
Johnston, Lawrence, 58
Jones, Evan, 64
Jones, Josiah, 278
Jordan, Barthelmy, 63–64
Joseph (ship), 349
Joy, George and Benjamin, 201, 202
Juula networks, 139, 220, 236, 239, 332, 380

Kaabu state, 44, 46, 94, 218, 219, 220, 222, 223
Kader, Abdul, 197
Kansas-Nebraska Act (1854), 354, 355
Karimou, 184
Kati, Uli, 331–32
Kayor (Kajor) state, 43, 46, 179, 180, 222
Kebe, Lamen, 224
Kerefe River, 332. *See also* Gallinas state and river
Keyssar, John, 30, 40
Kidd, William, 54
King of Prussia (ship), 127
Kitty (ship), 206
Kizzell, John, 234
Knight, George, 306
Koi, Mansa, 223
Kopytoff, Igor, 216, 220
Kurentsi, Eno Baisee (John Corrantee), 124, 299
Kwadwo, Osei, 133–34
Kwame, Osei, 177

Lacoste, Adolph, 322, 451n29
Lalu, Amara, 333
Lamar, Charles Augustus Lafayette, 355–57, 358, 374
Lawrell (ship), 36
Lawrence, David, 331
Lawton, John, 74

Lazinbey, Weybrand, 65
Leander (ship), 247
Leisler, Jacob, 52–53
Lemba society, 380
Lewis, James, 269–70
Lewis, Sarah, 270
Libby, Cyrus, 348, 360, 372
Lightbourn, Stiles, 326, 327, 328, 330, 331, 332
Lincoln, Abraham, 383, 385, 388
Lindsay, David, 266, 299
Little George (ship), 246, 247
Livingston, Philip, 4
Livingston, Robert, 54
Lloyds of London, 121–22, 284
Loango Coast, 50, 57, 209; textile-based trade, 198–200
Lopez, Aaron, 118, 119, 125, 128, 135, 163, 259
Louisiana: Central African settlement in, 194; market for enslaved labor, 187–88; U.S. acquisition of, 190, 191
Lovell, John, 156
Lowell, Mass., 394
Lyons-Seward Treaty (1862), 385

Machado, John Albert (João Alberto), 364, 382
Mackey, John, 199, 201
Macon, Nathaniel, 319
Macon's Bill Number 2 (1810), 311
Madagascar trade. *See* New York—Madagascar trade network
Madan (Madden), Joaquín, 313–14, 449n10
Madeira trade axis, 26, 27, 39
Madison, James, 161, 311
mafouks, 199
Major, John, 98
Malbone, Francis, 152
Malbone, Godfrey, 262
Malibran, Eugene, 322, 334, 451n29
Manegat, Pedro, 341

Mansa, Salam, 223

marabout (religious teacher), 46, 136

Margaret (ship), 48–49, 58, 61, 63–65, 67, 70, 284

Marigold (ship), 271

Mariquita (ship), 385

Marques, Leonardo, 6, 8, 392

Martin, Simeon, 261

Martindale, Sion, 130

Martinez, Jenny S., 280

Martínez, Pedro, 341

Mary (ship) case, 89, 240, 341–42

Mary Ann (ship), 372

Mason, Benjamin, 163, 259

Massachusetts, 19, 54, 155; Body of Liberties, 29; insurance on slaving vessels illegal, 157, 166, 168, 325–26; merchant fleet, 37, 81–83; monetary policy, 86–87; rum distilling in, 88; slavery in, 29, 287; slavery and slave-trade abolition, 156, 157, 158–59; slave-trade voyages from, 81, *82*, 159. *See also* Boston, Mass.

Massachusetts Anti-Slavery Society, 395

Massachusetts Bay Colony, 24, 25, 81

Massachusetts Bay Company, 24

Massachusetts Centinel, 160

mates, 74, 238, 263, 269–71

matrilineal societies, 227, 290

Matson, Cathy, 61

Mattatanna, 68

Maxwell, Joseph, 346, 347

Maxwell, Wright & Co., 346

Mayberry, Freeman, 263

McCusker, John, 90

McGrath, Andrew, 362

McMillin, James A., 431n12

McNeal, Hector, 129

McNeill, Daniel, 182

Meaher, Timothy, 357–58, 359

Meillasoux, Claude, 216, 218, 220

Memphis (ship), 7

Menabe kingdom, 66

Mendon (ship), 199, 267, 442n21

Mercer, Charles F., 316, 319, 450n21

Miers, Suzanne, 216, 220

Miles, Richard, 106

Mill, David, 125, 126, 128, 132, 182

monetary policy, 81, 85, 86–87, 106. *See also* currency

Monroe, James, 314, 318

Moore, Charles, 266, 267

Moore, Francis, 95, 96–97

Moore, Samuel, 92

Morgan, Henry, 53

Moria state, 183, 219

Morris, Isaac, 345

Morris (ship), 349

Morton, Samuel G., 353

Mostyn, Thomas, 61

Motta, Guilherme José da, 382

Mount Hope Insurance Company, 169, 261

Muhammad, Bilali, 249

Murden v. Insurance Company, 325–26

Murdock, Storey & Co., 324

Muslim enslavement, Futa Jallon jihad against, 136–38

Mussurongo people, 382

Nagle, David, 173

Nancy (ship), 206, 250–53

Napoleon I (emperor of France), 311

Napoleonic Wars, 317

Natchez District of Mississippi, 188

Nat Turner Rebellion, 7, 352

Navigation Acts, 21, 27, 53, 55, 56, 69, 273

New Adventure (ship), 173, 178, 321

New Bedford, Mass., 258, 363

New England, 119–20, 159; paper money exchange in colonies, 85

—slave trade of, 6, 24–28, 43, 80, 196; captives purchased in Senegambia, 42–43, 46; cod fishing and, 25–26; crews from maritime communities, 39–40; experimental voyage organization, 36–37, 41–42; on Gambia

River, 43–44; on Gold Coast, 196; justifications for slavery and, 29–30; metropolitan shipowning, 37–38; New England–Barbados–Africa trade, 89; obstacles of, 40–41; role of John Parris, 38–39; rum-for-captives trade, 195–96; Saffin's case, 31–33; seventeenth-century voyages, 33–36, 45–47; state prohibitions of, 160; strategies of economic recalibration, 25, 44–45; trade networks of, 40, 61

New London, Conn., 119, 256

Newport, R.I., 2, 5–6, 11–12, 85, 106–7, 108, 256–58, 300–301, 336, 394; American Revolution and, 292; bills of exchange in, 83–84, 85; Black communities in, 287–88, 292–94; cemeteries in, 212–14, 288–90; colonial currency emissions, 86–87; commercial cluster and agglomeration, 84–85; Continental Association and, 152; contribution in slave trade voyages, 119–20; enslaved population, origin of, 288–92; Fellowship Club, 74–75, 268; in Imperial Crisis, 151; maritime laborers in, 257–58, 273, 276–79; Massachusetts and, 81, 83; ordinary seamen in, 271, 272, 274; post-revolutionary slave trading, 163–64; prohibitions on slave trading, 156–57; racialization in, 296–300; Rhode Island law and, 157, 158; rum-for-captives trade, 88–90, 92–97, 99, 104–7; slave trade in, 81, 82, 83, 100, 115–16, 213, 257, 259, 260, 420n11, 426n24; slave-trade law (1787), 166; slave traders and merchants of, 260–63; slave-trading Quakers, 154; trade goods, 87–88, 91–92; women in slave trade, 257

Newport Insurance Company, 168

New York, 55, 164, 394; Liverpool packet service, 323

—Madagascar trade network, 6, 48–51, 67–68, 80; ending of, 70–71; illegality of, 69–70; ownership and manning of vessels, 61, 65–66; Philipse-Baldridge relationship in, 58–60; piracy and, 49–50, 53–54, 56, 66, 68–69; political factors, 52–53; reorganization of EIC and, 54–55; ships, trade goods, and networks, 60–64, 68–69; transatlantic merchants, role of, 56–57

—slave trade of, 55–56, 363–64; agents as voyage organizers, 369–70; Angola–Brazil route for, 377–79; association with Portuguese Company, 364–65, 368; bills of exchange, 376; corruption and criminality in, 364, 365–68, 366–367, 370–74; Cuban merchants and, 365, 368–69; illegality and, 374–75, 377; opportunistic structures, 366, 369; risk of robbery, 376–77; voyages organized in, 81, 82, 119–20

New York Stock Exchange, 168

Nichols, Jonathan, 274

Niumi state, 43–44, 140, 153, 219

Non-Intercourse Act (1809), 310–11

Nott, Josiah, 353

Nueva Empresa (ship), 373

Numancia (ship), 312

Nyaanco military aristocracy, 44, 94

Oaksmith, Appleton, 382, 459n68

Obodum, Kusi, 132, 133

O'Farrill y Herrera, José Ricardo, 333, 334

Oldendorp, C. G. A., 107, 228, 229, 230, 231–33, 235

Ormond, "Mongo John," 328, 330, 331–32

Othello (ship), 245, 246, 268, 270, 271

Otis, James, 156

outsiders, enslavement and, 29, 215, 217, 218, 220–21, 231, 379

Owen, Nicholas, 271, 278

Packard, Isaac, 312

Paeko, Elizabeth, 283

palavers, 19, 105, 141–42, 298

Palmerston, Lord (Henry John Temple, 3rd viscount), 346
Park, Mungo, 222, 233, 236, 242, 300
Parkes, Henry, 39
Parks, Gorham, 348–49
Parris, John, 38, 40, 42, 89, 117
Parsons, Clement, 304
patriarchal social organization, 281, 282–83
Patterson, Samuel, 278, 279
Pease, Simon, 259, 262
Pedro Martínez & Co., 306
Peggy (ship), 117
Perry, Micaiah, 78
Perth Amboy, N.J., 6, 119, 256
Peter (ship), 61, 62, 64, 69
Peters, John, 39
Peterson, Mark A., 410n19
Petite Côte, 43, 44
Philadelphia, Pa., 6, 88, 119, 122, 128, 162, 172, 199, 245; Constitutional Convention in, 160
Philipse, Adolph, 70
Philipse, Frederick, 50–51, 55, 56; death of, 70; involvement in Madagascar slave trade, 57–58, 68–69, 89; loss of *Margaret* ship, 64–65, 67; relationship with Baldridge, 58–60, 68; slave trade networks, 61–64
Phillips, John, 192, 206
Pierre Soulé (ship), 374
Pinckard, George, 241, 242
Pinnegar, William, 243
piracy, 49–50, 53–54, 56, 69; British law on (1824), 318; United States law on (1820), 317, 362, 384
Plymouth Colony, 24, 25
Poëy y Hernandez family, 173, 312
Pole, J. R., 8, 10
Polk, James K., 343
Polly (ship), 281
Pompey (ship), 117
"popular sovereignty," 355

Porpoise (ship) case, 348, 372, 375
portledge bills, 274, 276, 279
Port Mary (ship), 194
Portsmouth, N.H., 6, 30–31, 119
Portuguese Company, 364–65, 368, 381
Potter, Abigail, 281, 282
Potter, Simeon, 165–66, 281
Powell, Isidro, 324–25, 331
privilege slaves, 40, 212, 213, 263–65, 269, 287, 292, 296
Prohibitory Act (1775), 145, 153
Providence, R.I., 88, 119, 151, 163, 164, 166, 172, 262, 272, 278, 279, 420n11, 426n24
Providence Island colony, 27, 28
Providence Society for the Abolition of the Slave Trade, 157, 163, 293
Providence Washington Insurance Company, 168
Prudent Abigail (ship), 255–56, 257
Punch (ship), 203
Purchas, Samuel, 28
Puritans, 28–31, 33, 88, 388
Pynchon, William, 165

Quakers, slave traders and abolitionists, 145, 154, 157, 171
Quamino, Duchess, 213, 290, 446n70
Quintuple Treaty (1841), 350

RAC. *See* Royal African Company
racism, 154, 294, 296–300; scientific, 353
Rahman, Abdul, 223–24
Rainbow (ship): ownership of, 37–38, 39; transatlantic slaving voyage, 19–20, 23, 24, 26, 27, 28, 30, 31, 33, 40, 43, 45, 92, 97, 233, 408n3
Randolph, John, 203, 204, 205, 317
Rapid (ship), 311
Reaney, William L., 333, 334
Redwood, Abraham, 85
Redwood, William, Jr., 119, 154
Renard (ship), 128
Rensselaer, Jonathan, 62–63

Rhett, William, 78, 89

Rhode Island: Black community in, 157, 212, 213, 287, 292, 293–95; Boston and, 86, 87; and British revenue acts, 151; cemeteries in, 212; maritime insurance in, 122, 157–58, 166, 168; merchants and trade of, 81–83, 84, 87, 106, 115–16, 394; monetary policy, 81, 85, 86–87, 106; and piracy, 54; political power of slave traders, 262, 295, 309, 318–19; poor relief in, 294, 298; prohibitions on slave-trading and slavery, 155, 156–57, 158, 159, 163, 166, 262, 268, 292; Remonstrance to Parliament (1764), 146, 149, 151, 273; role in American slave trade, 5, 6, 81, 146, 184, 212, 388, 393, 394; rum distilling in, 88, 145; seamen and slave-ship crews from, 212, 270, 271, 272, 273, 278, 279, 295, 297; slave-ship owners, 119; slave traders from, 4, 130, 141, 142, 154, 158, 167, 192, 263, 331, 336, 388; slave-trading communities of, 11–12, 256–57; slave-trading ships from, 38–39, 82, 126, 148, 239, 240, 276, 289, 420n11, 426n24; and U.S. Constitution, 160; women in, 213, 257, 280, 285. See also Bristol, R.I.; Newport, R.I.; Providence, R.I.

Rhode Island (ship), 113, 240

Richardson, G. F., 348

Richardson, William, 370

Rio de Janeiro, 186, 202, 284, 317, 345

Río de la Plata slave trade, 194, 200–203, 267, 391–92

Rio Pongo, 181–83, 197, 219; American slave trade on, 391; Cuban-American collaborations, 327–31, 336–37; political transition, 331–32

Rising Sun (ship), 202

Rivera, Jacob, 115, 118, 125, 128

Robin, Martin, 207

Rogers, Thomas, 268–70

Ropes, George, 300

Ros, Antonio M., 370

Rose (ship), 35–36, 43, 45, 324–25

Rotch, William, 425n14

Rouse, Edward, 274

Roux, Francis, 195

Royal Adventurers, 35

Royal African Company (RAC), 9, 35, 52, 94–95, 99, 104, 143; Carolina plantation colony, 78; New York–Madagascar slave trade, 70–71; violation of monopoly of, 31, 36, 47, 70, 77–78, 80

Royal Navy. *See* British Royal Navy

Rucker, Walter, 292

rum-for-captives trade, 88–90, 92–95, 108, 130, 169, 388–89; in Gold Coast, 99, 104–7; Islam and, 96–97; in upper Guinea, 97

Russell, Joseph, 202

Sabate, Pedro, 341

Sabens, John, 176, 196–97, 203, 282, 299

Sabens, Sally, 282

Saffin, John, 31–33

Sagahanugu, Muhammad Kaba, 224

Said, Omar Ibn, 200, 239, 249

Saint Augustine, 68–69

Saint Mary's island, 48, 59–60, 62, 64, 65, 68, 69

Sakalava Empire, 66–68

Salem, Mass., 119, 164–65, 258

Sally (ship), 141, 281

Saloum state ("Barsally"), 44, 95; king of, 95, 97

Saltonstall, Samuel, 30, 174–75

Salvador de Bahia, 186

Samo, Samuel, 432–33n26

Samuel, Abraham, 68

Sánchez, Emilio, 367, 374

San Joaquín (ship), 313

Sankaran region, 138

Sano, John, 251–52, 253

Schutt, Casper, 284

Schutt, Margaret, 201, 203, 284–85

Schuyler, Brant, 56, 58, 62, 69

Schuyler, Peter, 56

Science (ship), 322

scientific racism, 353

Scofield, John, 278

Scott, George, 85, 277

Scott, Joseph, 277

Seaflower (ship), 19–20, 30

seamen, ordinary, 258, 271, 272, 274, 279, 338; racial privilege for whites, 297; wives and families of, 285–87

Searing, Benjamin, 212

Searing, James, 212, 270

Segu state, 138, 180, 218, 219, 222, 224, 235

Selleck, David, 37, 39

Selling of Joseph, The (1700), 31–32

Senegal Adventurers, 34

Senegambia, 15, 18, 78, 91, 92, 94, 99, 106, 222; enslaved people from, 41, 81, 244; Muslims and alcohol in, 96, 97, 104, 197; Nasir al-Din rebellion, 46, 97; slave rebellions and, 245; slave trade in, 42–43, 46, 114, 137, 178, 179, 180, 181, 183, 390

Seven Years' War, 109, 114, 127

Sewall, Samuel, 31–33

Seward, William Henry, 384

Shapton, Robert, 19, 407n1

ship captains, role of, 263–68

Siaka (ruler), 333, 334, 335

Siddiq, Abu Bakr al-, 235, 239

Sierra Leone, 1; American rum market, 94; anti-slavery settlement, 181; British colony settlement at, 180; economic factors in slave trade, 114; Muslim revolts impact, 136, 137, 138; shipboard rebellion, 245, 246–47; trading with American slavers, 114, 142, 174, 180–81, 196

Sierra Leone Council, 430n58

Sierra Leone River, 140

Silk, Thomas, 92

Silveira, Andrés Pinto de, 322

silver, 58, 65, 68, 85, 87, 92, 96, 97, 99, 173, 202, 203, 267

Sinclair, William, 159

Sisei, Mohammedu, 223

Sisson, Robert, Jr., 275

Sitiki ("Uncle Jack"), 200, 224, 239

Slacum, George W., 346, 348

slave trade, 7–9, 21, 23, 77, 115, 185–86, 404n4; American privateering in Africa, 153–54, 390–91; average annual departures, 108–10; causes of palavers, 141; connections with American captive markets in Caribbean, 14–15; with Cuban merchants, 172–73, 309–10; economic development of United States, 9–10, 110, 112, 392–93; endings of, 191–92, 203–9, 383–85; enslaveability and, 29, 220, 231, 379; exclusion with British Caribbean, 169–70; Fellowship Club, 74–75, 107, 268; Gold Coast, post-war, 174–77; historical assessment of, 387–88; intra-American (intercolonial), 15, 34, 56, 77, 80, 187, 188, 249; involvement of seaports, 119–20; issues in national politics, 352–53; legislative battles, 155; marine insurance and, 121–23; Mozambique, voyages to, 177–78; networks of North American slave traders, 123–24; New World destinations, 120–21; and New World plantation societies, 391; partnership strategy for purchasing captives, 117–18; political and economic importance in North America, 145–46; post-revolutionary traders, 163; prices for captives, 111–12; profitability of, 115–16; on Río de la Plata trade, 200–203; rum trade, 124, 388–89; "ships coming in" and "ships going out," 2–8, 155, 185, 248; South Carolina, impact in, 394–95; supercargoes, role of, 312–14; tax system in, 119; on upper Guinea, 139–40, 141,

178–84; vessel ownership, 118–19; voyages, data on, 116–17

—illegality of, 166, 313–15, 327–31, 339; Anglo-American convention and, 318–21; anti-slave-trade legislation and, 309–10, 316–18, 343–44; Baltimore prosecutions, 344–45; and shift to Brazil, 342, 345–47; and shift to Cuba, 311–13, 325–26, 342

—laws restricting, 315–17, 320–21; Act to Prohibit the Importation of Slaves (1807), 309–10, 311; Embargo Act (1807), 310, 311; Foreign Slave Trade Act (Britain, 1806), 195, 198; Prohibitory Act (Britain, 1775), 145, 153; Slave Trade Abolition Act (Britain, 1807), 195, 207, 250, 434n44; Slave Trade Act (1794), 161–63; by states, 155, 156–59, 162, 163, 166, 262, 268, 292; and volume of slave trade, 310

—pro-slave-trade political movement, 352–54, 360; and convictions in criminal prosecutions, 360–62, 361; *Echo* (ship) case, 362–63; Lamar's efforts for, 355–57, 358; Meaher's efforts for, 357–58, 359; vessel condemnation, 360, 361

Slave Trade Abolition Act (Britain, 1807), 195, 207, 250, 434n44

Slave Trade Act (Britain, 1794), 161–63

Slave Voyages database, 6, 15, 310, 391, 403n1, 404n3, 426n24, 441n7

Smith, Benjamin, 212

Smith, Frederick H., 88

Smith, Horatio, 174

Smith, James, 19, 20, 27, 30–31, 37, 39, 40, 45

Smith, John, 426n21

Smith, Venture, 228, 231

Smith, William Loughton, 5, 191–92, 316

Snowden, Joseph S., 341

Soler, José, 324, 451n32

Solon (ship), 372, 373

Sophia (ship), 372–73

Sori, Ibrahima, 183, 218

Sori Mawdo ("Sori the Great"), 138

Sorisco, Charles, 156

South Carolina: market for captives in, 170–71; pro-slave-trade political movement in, 354–55; trade in, 78–80. *See also* Carolina slave rush (1804–1807)

"South Carolina" factory (in Africa), 182

Southern Standard, 354

South Kingstown, R.I., 212

Spalding, Edward, 313, 322

Spanswick, Richard, 39

Spratt, Leonidas W., 354, 355, 362

Sprengel, Matthias Christian, 295

Stamp Act (1765), 114

Stanton, John, 158, 271, 443n29

Sterry, Cyprian, 163, 164

Sterry, Nathan, 240

Stewart, Duncan, 195

Stono Rebellion (1739), 155

Strohm, John F., 344–45

Strother, George, 316

Sugar Act (1764), 146, 151

Sulimana state, 138

supercargoes, 58, 356; American, 312–13, 321, 324, 325; British, 194–95, 199, 207, 377; Charles Christie, 199; Isidro Powell, 324; John Campbell, 194; Jonathan Rensselaer, 62; Joseph Russell, 202

Suriname, 170, 277

Swift (ship), 59, 412n4

Tadman, Michael, 187, 188

Tammany Hall political machine, 370

Taney, Roger B., 345

Tartar (ship), 195, 197, 432–33n26

"Tasajo Trail," 202–3

Tavel, Frederick, 195, 197

taxation, 86, 87, 119, 139, 155, 259–60, 317, 328, 330, 378, 441n7

Taylor, Thomas Teakle, 85, 265

Taylor, William, 127

Thames (ship), 145, 245
Thomas, Richard, 89
Thompson, John, 39, 40
Thornton, Henry, 430n58
Three Mariners (ship), 38
Thurber, John, 61
Thurston, Jonathan, 119, 154
Thurston, Joseph, 255
Tillinghast, Esteban, 331
Tillinghast, Joseph, 119
Titt Bitt (ship), 118
Tiverton, R.I., 294
tobacco, 28, 38, 56, 57, 78, 87, 91, 141, 164, 187, 280, 312
Tomlinson, David (Pilo B. Tomlimerzt), 341
Touro v. Cassin, 326
Townshend Duties (1767), 109, 114
Transatlantic Slave Trade Database. See *Slave Voyages* database
Treaty of Amity and Commerce (1778), 170
Trist, Nicholas P., 343–44
Turnbull, Eliza, 252, 253
Turnbull, Kate, 251
Turner, Levi W., 372
Tutu, Osei, 101–2
Twifo state, 101, 132, 134
Tyler, John, 347
Tyng, Charles, 304–7, 323, 447n2

United States v. Morris (1840), 345
Upshur, Abel, 351
Usher, John, 296–97

Valdés, Gerónimo, 344
Van Buren, Martin, 343
Van Dam, Rip, 56, 62, 69
Vassa, Gustavaus, 239, 249
Venus (ship), 243, 244
Vernon, Samuel and William: ships owned by, 118, 128, 271; slave-trading career of, 115, 116, 117–18, 119, 122,
127, 135, 139, 158–59, 163, 167, 173, 176, 177–78, 200, 259, 266, 268–69, 295–96
Vianna (Viana), João José Lima, 364, 368, 370, 375, 381, 383, 385
Vili people, 198, 200, 380
Vining, Harrison S., 369
Virginia, 77–78; labor enslavement in, 27–28; RAC shipments, 77–78; slave trade in, 27, 31; statute (1660), 30; tobacco trade, 38, 56, 57
Voltaic slavery, 226–29
Vos, Jelmer, 381
Voss, Antonio, 98
Voyages database. See *Slave Voyages* database
Vries, Margaret Hardenbroeck de, 57

Waalo state, 43, 46, 179, 180
Walker, William, 357
Wanderer (ship), 356–57, 358, 363, 374
Wanton, Edward, 283
Wanton, Joseph, Jr., 119
Wanton, Joseph G., Sr., 118, 119, 127, 167, 259, 263
Wanton, William, 118, 119, 167, 259
Ward, Philana and Jonathan, 283
Wardwell, Joseph, 166, 280
Wardwell, William, 166, 286
Ware, Opoku, 102, 103, 104, 107, 131–32, 228
warfare, captives procured from, 221, 223–24, 230–31
War of Spanish Succession, 55, 69, 85
Washington, George, 161
Washington (ship), 195, 199
Wassa state, 101, 133–34
Waters, Joseph, 154, 158
Watt, James, 183, 396
Watts, Robert, 403n1
Webster-Ashburton Treaty (1842), 350–52
Weeks, John P., 374
Welch, Edward, 60, 61, 62, 64, 68, 69, 313
Wenham, Thomas, 56, 58, 62, 69

WIC. *See* Dutch West India Company

Wilday, Ede, 286

Wildfire (ship), liberated Africans aboard, *303, 304*

William III (king of England), 53

William and Jane (ship), 78

William H. Stewart (ship), 374

Williams, Aaron, 39

Williams, Roger, 420n11

Willoughby, John, 35–36

Willoughby, Thomas, 38

Windsor, Thomas, 38, 39, 42

Winthrop, John, 23, 24, 32, 408n3

Wise, Henry A., 347–48

Withington, William, 38, 39, 40, 45

Wolf (ship), 241

women, 213; in Africa, 227; in American colonial economy, 255, 257, 282, 285; and American slave trade, 257, 258–59, 280–87; enslaved people, 218, 221, 226, 232–33, 238, 239–40, 245, 246, 250

Woodbury, Charles L., 360

Woodbury, Henry, 371

Woodman, Elizabeth, 284

Woolman, John, 154

Wooma, Ofodobendo, 239

Wright, James J., 324

Wright, William Henry DeCourcy, 346, 347, 348

Yancey, William Lowndes, 354, 355

Yende, Yati, 331, 332

York (ship), 156

Zulueta, Julián, 369

Zulueta, Pedro, 360